AESTHETICISM & MODERNISM

Edited by Richard Danson Brown & Suman Gupta

Debating Twentieth-Century Literature 1900–1960

Routledge in association with

The Open University

This publication forms part of an Open University course A300, *Twentieth-Century Literature: Texts and Debates*. The complete list of texts which make up this course can be found in the Preface. Details of this and other Open University courses can be obtained from the Customer Contact Centre, The Open University, Milton Keynes MK7 6AA, United Kingdom: tel. +44 (0)1908 653231; e-mail general-enquiries@open.ac.uk

Alternatively, you may visit the Open University website at http://www.open.ac.uk where you can learn more about the wide range of courses and packs offered at all levels by The Open University.

To purchase a selection of Open University course materials visit the webshop at www.ouw.co.uk, or contact Open University Worldwide, Michael Young Building, Walton Hall, Milton Keynes MK7 6AA, United Kingdom for a brochure: tel. +44 (0)1908 858785; fax +44 (0)1908 858787; e-mail ouwenq@open.ac.uk

Published by Routledge; written and produced by The Open University

Routledge
2 Park Square
Milton Park
Abingdon
Oxfordshire
OX14 4RN

The Open University
Walton Hall
Milton Keynes
MK7 6AA

First published 2005.

Edited, designed and typeset by The Open University.

Printed in the United Kingdom by TJ International Ltd, Padstow.

British Library Cataloguing in Publication Data: applied for

Library of Congress Cataloging in Publication Data: applied for

ISBN 0 415 35168 5

1.1

The paper used in this publication contains pulp sourced from forests independently certified to the Forest Stewardship Council (FSC) principles and criteria. Chain of custody certification allows the pulp from these forests to be tracked to the end use (see www.fsc-uk.org).

CONTENTS

PREFACE

Aestheticism and Modernism: Debating Twentieth-Century Literature 1900–1960 is the first book in a three-volume series designed for the third-level Open University course A300 *Twentieth-Century Literature: Texts and Debates*. The other books in the series are *The Popular and the Canonical: Debating Twentieth-Century Literature 1940–2000* (edited by David Johnson) and *A Twentieth-Century Literature Reader: Texts and Debates* (edited by Suman Gupta and David Johnson).

Ideally, these books should be read as a series of linked studies and debates; on its own, *Aestheticism and Modernism* offers an exciting and innovative way of reading the literature of the first half of the twentieth century. Unlike standard literary histories, we present an eclectic mix of texts and authors to convey a broader sense of twentieth-century literary writing. The book considers an international cast of twentieth-century writers, chosen to reflect a wide variety of literary cultures and milieux. Each chapter discusses the set texts in the light of the vital critical and intellectual debates either to which they responded or which they prompted. This is the first survey of twentieth-century literature that foregrounds the concept of debate. The sense of debate is also conveyed through the dialogic style of the chapters, which, through in-text exercises, engage the reader with the issues discussed. It is ideally suited to undergraduates studying twentieth-century literature and to general readers interested in developing their sense of the richness of the writing of the period.

This book is divided into two parts. The first, 'What is literature for?', explores debates about the meaning and purpose of literature in the early part of the twentieth century. We begin with the ideas of the Aesthetic movement, which retained critical and intellectual authority long after their heyday in the 1890s. We juxtapose aestheticism (or the thinking connoted by the more familiar slogan 'art for art's sake') with the equally influential notion that literary texts should have purposes and agendas beyond the purely literary sphere. Throughout the four main chapters, the impulse towards artistic perfection can be seen to be counterbalanced by instrumental theories, which argue that literature should teach, persuade, convince and even propagandize. These debates are grounded in studies of key early twentieth-century texts and writers: Anton Chekhov's play *The Cherry Orchard*, Katherine Mansfield's short stories, Lewis Grassic Gibbon's novel *Sunset Song* and the poetry of the 1930s, in particular works by W.H. Auden, Louis MacNeice, Stephen Spender and David Gascoyne. The Introduction to Part 1 situates the debate between aestheticists and instrumentalists by exploring the critical ideas of Oscar Wilde and George Orwell, and by providing a comparison of two important twentieth-century poems.

The second part, entitled 'Contending modernisms', addresses early twentieth-century debates about what is understood by literary modernism and what it means to be a literary modernist. Some of the debates discussed in the first part are naturally picked up again here, since attempts at understanding the modernism of literary texts and authors are inevitably informed by the aesthetic and extra-literary agendas involved. There is some discussion in Part 2 of what may be regarded as a 'mainstream' literary modernism – that is, a view of modernism that is associated with the critical formulations and formally innovative writings of T.S. Eliot and others, and with artistic/literary groupings such as Symbolists, Imagists and Vorticists. However, as the Introduction to Part 2 explains, this mainstream view is only one among many influential views of modernism, pertaining to other political ideologies and cultural identities. It is, therefore, more appropriate to think of several contending forms of modernism in twentieth-century literature, which give rise to numerous debates. This Introduction also gives a brief overview of the manner in which ideas of modernism in the twentieth century derived from debates prior to that. The debates examined here are presented through discussions of the following texts and writers: T.S. Eliot's poems in *Prufrock and Other Observations*, Virginia Woolf's novel *Orlando*, Bertolt Brecht's play *Life of Galileo* and the poetry of Christopher Okigbo.

Open University courses are collaborative ventures that involve the labours of a range of different people. We would like to thank the members of the A300 course team who did not write for this volume but who participated in the discussions that helped to shape and develop it: Sue Asbee, Katie Gramich, Lynda Morgan, Susheila Nasta, W.R. Owens, Steve Padley, Lynda Prescott and Clare Spencer; the course manager, Martyn Field; the course editors, Julie Bennett, Hazel Coleman and Alan Finch; and the external assessor, Susan Bassnett.

R.D.B. and S.G.

PART 1

What is literature for?

Introduction to Part 1

RICHARD DANSON BROWN

The first part of this book addresses a fundamental question: 'What is literature for?' Focusing on a range of texts comprising drama, novel, short story and poetry from about 1900 to 1940, we introduce you to significant features of early twentieth-century writing and the debates that such writing has responded to and prompted. You will acquire the critical skills both to analyse these texts and to participate in these often tense and fascinating discussions.

Sara Haslam's study of Anton Chekhov's *The Cherry Orchard* (1904) articulates our concern with the purpose of literature. Since Chekhov's work is especially prized for its openness to a variety of interpretations, Haslam pays particular attention to the ways in which *The Cherry Orchard* has been performed. Though Chekhov avoided political or moral agendas, his work bears witness to the rapid social and economic changes that were taking place in Russia at the beginning of the twentieth century. For this reason, Haslam considers the relationship between literature and context. The second chapter focuses on Katherine Mansfield's *Selected Short Stories* (written between 1910 and 1922), which Delia da Sousa Correa presents as a distinctively modern and self-consciously aesthetic kind of fiction. She pays particular attention to Mansfield's treatment of gender, alongside her social and literary contexts. In the third chapter, David Johnson examines Lewis Grassic Gibbon's *Sunset Song* (1932) as a novel that attempts to marry artistic excellence with a firm political agenda. Gibbon was a committed socialist and *Sunset Song* shows his evocation of a community in north east Scotland just before the outbreak of the First World War. Finally, through Robin Skelton's *Poetry of the Thirties* anthology (first published 1964), I explore the work of W.H. Auden, Louis MacNeice, David Gascoyne and others. You will read their work alongside debates about the social and political function of literature, through which you will assess the competing claims of poetry as an independent art form and poetry written in the service of political ideology.

Integral to each of these chapters are the ways in which the writer or texts under consideration respond to our central question. The idea that literature needs justifying is a very old one. The fourth-century BCE Greek philosopher Plato notoriously banished poets from his ideal republic because of his sense that poems as fictional imitations of reality were fundamentally delusive. For Plato, poets create 'images far removed from the truth', which can strengthen 'the lower elements in the mind to the detriment of reason' (1974, p.435). He was particularly concerned by passages from the ancient Greek epic poet Homer where Gods commit adultery, which he considered 'hardly suitable to encourage the young to self-control' (*ibid.*, p.145).

Though these may seem like wild claims, Plato's arguments still reverberate in academic and public debates about the arts and censorship. Consider this example: on 1 January 2003, two black teenagers were shot dead in Birmingham as they were caught in the crossfire between gangs. In the aftermath of this horrific event, the culture minister Kim Howells drew a link between gun crime and the lyrics to rap songs:

> For years I have been very worried about these hateful lyrics that these boasting macho idiot rappers come out with. It is a big cultural problem. Lyrics don't kill people but they don't half enhance the fare we get from videos and films. It has created a culture where killing is almost a fashion accessory.
>
> (quoted in Gibbons, 2003, p.3)

Howells unconsciously mirrors Plato's objection to poetry: 'It has a terrible power to corrupt even the best characters' (Plato, 1974, p.436). For both philosopher and politician, unfettered artistic expression is dangerous because the state cannot control the ways in which it is consumed. According to this view, reading poetry and listening to rap can have similar effects: a corruption of the mental sinews and an erosion of the ability to perceive the difference between fantasy and reality. The danger of art is that its consumers are so affected by it that it warps their beliefs and behaviours.

Underlying these positions is the perception that art should be different. To the question 'What is literature for?', Plato responds: 'To provide moral guidance.' Because of Plato's enormous importance to western philosophy and literary studies, this view recurs in many different forms in different places. Plato suggests that literature is not an end in itself; it has a broader social responsibility which imposes a duty on poets to make sure that their works are not immoral or untrue. Poetry and art in general have fundamental responsibilities to the society that produces them. If poets are unwilling to tether their imitations of life to the demands of that society, Plato argues, then they should be kicked out of the republic. He provides an instrumental view of art, which claims that it should be an instrument for the assertion of moral and political values. We use the term in this way in Part 1 of this book: instrumental writing is writing that is used for a specific, extra-literary purpose.

But how do these arguments relate to twentieth-century literature? As *The Republic* suggests, there has always been a tension between instrumental and anti-instrumental theories of literature. These tensions were particularly apparent at the end of the nineteenth century in Britain and France, as writers such as Oscar Wilde and Joris-Karl Huysmans advocated a view of art which denied that it should have any moral, political or social function. This movement is usually known as aestheticism, and its adherents as aesthetes, meaning people who have a special appreciation of beauty. (The term 'aesthetic', however, has a broader application, relating to theories of and judgements about literature: a writer can have an aesthetic without being an aesthete.) According to aestheticism, art should be primarily beautiful: it should not seek to proselytize, persuade or in any way influence its audience. Art should be an end in itself, leading to the famous slogan 'art for art's sake', which seems to have been first used, in the eighteenth century, by the German writer Gotthold Ephraim Lessing (Cuddon, 1982, p.59). You may be familiar with the formulation of the English poet John Keats in the last two lines of his 'Ode on a Grecian Urn' (1820): ' "Beauty is truth, truth beauty" – that is all / Ye know on earth, and all ye need to know' (1972, p.537). In Keats's vision, truth and beauty – as exemplified by works of art like the Grecian urn – are identical and mutually sustaining. Though aestheticism lost much of its critical authority during the course of the twentieth century, it remains an important influence, especially on the writers we consider in Part 1 of this book. In this context Wilde's Preface to his novel *The Picture of Dorian Gray* (1891) is illuminating. He issues a series of aphoristic assertions rather than a sequential argument, but for all its brevity the Preface amounts to a radical assertion of the autonomy of art.

Read through Wilde's Preface to *The Picture of Dorian Gray* (Reader, Item 1). List as many adjectives as you can find. Why do you think Wilde selected these words?

Though the Preface is very short, it is studded with striking adjectives: my list would include *beautiful, highest, lowest, ugly, corrupt, charming, cultivated, moral, immoral, perfect, imperfect, true, ethical, unpardonable, morbid, new, complex, vital, useful, useless.* Wilde's adjectives are full of discriminations and judgements, such as '*Those who find ugly meanings in beautiful things are corrupt without being charming.*' As this example demonstrates, the Preface is full of antithetical pairings, such as *beautiful / ugly*, which powerfully convey Wilde's point of view: the appreciation of beauty is an end in itself; if you try to find '*ugly meanings in beautiful things*', you '*corrupt*' your own judgement. Wilde thus uses adjectives in a way that is at once challenging and idiosyncratic. This is clearest in the final two paragraphs: '*We can forgive a man for making a useful thing as long as he does not admire it. The only excuse for making a useless thing is that one admires it intensely. All art is quite useless.*' Conventionally, 'useless' is a negative term, but here it takes on a radical, positive inflection. Art is useless but intensely admirable; in contrast, useful things are not admirable at all. Wilde was a master of paradoxes: the assertion that '*art is quite useless*' appears to collude with criticisms of the social function of art, but here it is a declaration of faith rather than an admission of incompetence. The '*useless*' is infinitely more valuable than the '*useful*', or than the '*moral*' or the '*ethical*'. Wilde is reacting against the teachings of Utilitarianism, a highly influential nineteenth-century philosophy which argued that art had to be socially useful.

To answer the second part of my earlier question, I would say that Wilde uses these highly coloured adjectives as a way of provoking the reader. A statement such as '*Those who find beautiful meanings in beautiful things are the cultivated. For these there is hope*' invites us to become '*cultivated*' by agreeing with Wilde. We should also note that Wilde's conception of art in the Preface is in itself highly stylized. Rather than paying any attention to the content of books, he repeatedly implies that writing is predominantly a matter of style: '*Books are well written or badly written. That is all ... No artist has ethical sympathies. An ethical sympathy in an artist is an unpardonable mannerism of style.*' The object of the writer, in Wilde's view, is to create something that is at once stylish and beautiful: content is less important than the way in which a text is written. In a very real sense, Wilde's artist is a self-conscious poseur who revels in the artificiality of his or her '*useless*' work.

To see what objections were raised against this aesthetic during the twentieth century, I would like to turn to a review by George Orwell from 1936. Like much of Orwell's journalism, it is a characteristically pugnacious piece of writing – he has very little patience with Marxist literary criticism, though he was a socialist and fought in support of the government during the Spanish Civil War.

Read Orwell's review of *The Novel Today* by Philip Henderson (Reader, Item 2). Paying particular attention to the second and third paragraphs, try to summarize Orwell's attitude to 'art for art's sake' in a couple of sentences.

Orwell's attitude towards 'art for art's sake' is one of withering contempt. Moving from the comic description of a cartoon about 'an intolerable youth' who wants to 'just *write*', he attacks the 'literary cant' of the view that ' "art has nothing to do with morality" '. He focuses his disdain on the vagueness of the aesthetic 'pursuit of something called "Beauty" ', and on the posturing implicit in the idea that critics should respond to books only on the basis of 'abstract aesthetic standards'. In Orwell's view, though aestheticism is dated (note that he says that 'art for art's sake' has 'been discarded as ninety-ish' – in other words, the slogan derives from the 1890s), its pernicious influence remains. Even Communists and Catholics, whom Orwell backhandedly praises for their resistance to aestheticism, employ 'a double set of values and dodg[e] from one to the other according as it suits them'. For Orwell, the confusion in critical standards would be cleared if more people were prepared to say – as he does –that 'art and propaganda are the same thing'.

Where Wilde presents art as the disinterested pursuit of 'beautiful things' by a cultural elite of artists and critics, Orwell responds with a conflation of art and propaganda. The recourse to 'abstract aesthetic standards' mendaciously disguises the fact that we like or dislike books inasmuch as we agree or disagree with the opinions which they express. Like Wilde,

Orwell gives a deliberately provocative statement of his views. As the rest of the review makes clear, Orwell is attacking not only aestheticism, but Marxism.

Irrespective of the virtues of Orwell's position (and it is important that we recognize that he is engaged in a form of critical name-calling), what is important is the view that 'art and propaganda are the same thing'. What does he mean by this? Despite his focus on Marxism, this does not mean simply that 'art and *political* propaganda are the same thing'. By citing Catholics as well as Communists, Orwell's 'propaganda' embraces a broader conspectus of activities. As he puts it, 'Both the Communist and the Catholic usually believe ... that abstract aesthetic standards are all bunkum and that a book is only a "good" book if it preaches the right sermon.' 'Propaganda', in his view, comprises religious as much as political persuasion; using Orwell's position, we might suggest that Wilde was propagandizing on behalf of art. Most importantly, Orwell's view exactly reverses Wilde's: where Wilde suggests that the search for formal perfection is '*the morality of art*', Orwell responds that it is content which chiefly conditions our responses to literary texts.

Such a comparison might lead us to believe that aestheticism and instrumentalism are critical opposites and that the two positions never overlap. Yet literary texts seldom fit such neat categories. *The Picture of Dorian Gray*, despite the fighting talk of the Preface, can be read as a profoundly moral tale about its protagonist's culpable self-absorption. Similarly, though Orwell claims in this review that content is always more important than style, elsewhere he concedes that part of his motivation as a writer came from some form of 'abstract aesthetic standards': 'I could not do the work of writing a book ... if it were not also an aesthetic experience' (1970, p.28). The point you need to bear in mind is that answers to the question 'What is literature for?' typically oscillate between the opposing poles of aestheticism ('writing should aim only at being beautiful') and instrumentalism ('writing should teach appropriate moral, political or religious ideology'). In practice, most writers and critics find it difficult to sustain either of these absolute positions. Yet the poles themselves continue to be relevant to the study of literature: in the following chapters we are therefore particularly concerned with the ways in which our selected writers position themselves and their work in terms of these debates.

To give a sense of how instrumental and aesthetic theories contrast in practice, I am going to look at two twentieth-century poems: Wilfred Owen's 'Dulce et Decorum Est' (1917) and Elizabeth Bishop's 'The Fish' (1940). Though this section centres on poetry – which after all was Plato's chief example – you should remember that these issues are also germane to the study of plays and prose fiction. Since his death in November 1918 at the age of twenty-five, during one of the final battles of the First World War, Owen has become the most celebrated English poet connected with this, and arguably any other, war. His reputation rests on the fierce realism and innovative poetic diction characteristic of poems like 'Dulce et Decorum Est'. **Before turning to the poem, read the 'Preface' by Owen (Reader, Item 3). What position does Owen take here – does he seem closer to an aestheticist or an instrumental view of poetry?**

Owen stresses that he is 'not concerned with Poetry', and that 'All a poet can do today is warn.' His focus is on 'War, and the pity of War'. There is no recourse to 'abstract aesthetic standards' and a firm underlining of the crucial importance of his subject matter: his poems are 'elegies ... to this generation'. Though the Preface makes no pretensions to being a substantive critical essay (it was, in fact, a fragment found among his papers after his death), it outlines an anti-aestheticist view of poetry. For Owen, poetry was a way of memorializing the dead and warning the living. But even here, it is worth sounding a note of caution: as Dominic Hibberd has pointed out, Owen was pivotally influenced by his reading of French aestheticist and decadent poets (1989, pp.29–33).

With this in mind, now read 'Dulce et Decorum Est'. Where in the poem do you think the impulses to memorialize and to warn are most evident?

Dulce et Decorum Est

Bent double, like old beggars under sacks,
Knock-kneed, coughing like hags, we cursed through sludge,
Till on the haunting flares we turned our backs
And towards our distant rest began to trudge.
Men marched asleep. Many had lost their boots
But limped on, blood-shod. All went lame; all blind;
Drunk with fatigue; deaf even to the hoots
Of tired, outstripped Five-Nines that dropped behind.

Gas! Gas! Quick, boys! – An ecstasy of fumbling,
Fitting the clumsy helmets just in time;
But someone still was yelling out and stumbling
And flound'ring like a man in fire or lime ...
Dim, through the misty panes and thick green light,
As under a green sea, I saw him drowning.

In all my dreams, before my helpless sight,
He plunges at me, guttering, choking, drowning.

If in some smothering dreams you too could pace
Behind the wagon that we flung him in,
And watch the white eyes writhing in his face,
His hanging face, like a devil's sick of sin;
If you could hear, at every jolt, the blood
Come gargling from the froth-corrupted lungs,
Obscene as cancer, bitter as the cud
Of vile, incurable sores on innocent tongues, –
My friend, you would not tell with such high zest
To children ardent for some desperate glory,
The old Lie: Dulce et decorum est
Pro patria mori.

(Owen, 1963, p.55)

I hope that in doing this exercise you felt some sense of shock. The word 'memorialize' suggests something calm, or at least controlled, like a war memorial, in which a sculptor creates a public work that embodies a sense of communal loss. Owen's poem has none of this calmness or monumentality. Instead, its work of memorialization takes the form of a literally disgusting description of someone being gassed. The poem does not record this incident out of any sense of a bond between the speaker and the dead man. Rather, Owen suggests the compulsive quality of a memory that his speaker cannot rid himself of: 'In all my dreams, before my helpless sight, / He plunges at me, guttering, choking, drowning.' I would say that the impulse to memorialize – which is in fact a compulsion – occurs in the third verse paragraph. After the description of the soldiers marching 'Drunk with fatigue' and the subsequent gas attack, these lines insist that the sight of the dying man is literally unforgettable.

The warning follows directly on from this couplet, as Owen simultaneously elaborates the description of the process of dying from gas and rebukes the reader with a bitter invective against casual patriotism. Again, though, I would say that 'warning' is too weak a word to convey the power of Owen's admonishment in this verse paragraph. The poem juxtaposes an unvarnished evocation of what happens to the victim of a gas attack – 'the blood ... gargling from the froth-corrupted lungs' – with one of the clichés of patriotic sentiment, 'Dulce et decorum est pro patria mori'.

Owen explained in a letter to his mother that 'The famous Latin tag means of course *It is sweet and meet to die for one's country*'; he added in exasperation, '*Sweet*! And *decorous*!' (quoted in Hibberd, 2002, p.276). As he would have known, the phrase comes from a poem in the third book of *Odes* by the first-century BCE Roman poet Horace. Horace's work was a staple part of school and university curricula across Europe, which informed the cultural and ideological background of young, middle-class officers like Owen. As the historian John Keegan observes of this period, 'Europe's educated classes held much of its culture in common ... the study of the classics remained universal' (1999, p.15). This poem, which is one of the so-called 'Roman Odes' written in praise of the Emperor Augustus, affirms the value of dying for one's country:

> Sweet it is and honourable to die for one's native land.
> Death hunts down even the man who runs away
>   and does not spare the back
>   or the hamstrings of young cowards.
>
> (Horace, 2002, p.23)

By incorporating this phrase into his poem, Owen undermines unthinking patriotism. Note the way in which he deforms the Latin as well as the shape of his verse paragraph by rhyming 'est' ('is') with 'zest' and 'mori' ('to die') with 'glory', so that the poem ends with a deliberate half line. As David West's very literal translation shows, classical Latin poetry does not rhyme. By forcing Horace's idealized text to rhyme with his undeceived, realistic English, Owen graphically undermines its authority. The twisted, truncated form of these lines mirrors both the effects of gas on the soldier and the morally twisting impact of Horace's patriotism; for Owen it is quite simply 'The old Lie'.

But Horace was not Owen's only target in this passage. Early drafts of the poem dedicated it to Jessie Pope, 'a certain Poetess' (Owen, 1963, p.55). Pope wrote popular war poems, which were published both in the *Daily Mail* (then, as now, a bastion of conservative values) and in book form as *Jessie Pope's War Poems* (1915). Jon Stallworthy (1974, p.227) has linked 'Dulce et Decorum Est' to Pope's 'The Call', which jocosely invites young men to join up and fight in France:

> Who'll earn the Empire's thanks –
> Will you, my laddie?
> Who'll swell the victors' ranks –
> Will you, my laddie?
>
> (Pope, 1915, p.38)

The full impact of Pope's cloying blend of rabble-rousing, sentimentality and what now seems a ludicrously idealized conception of warfare can be gauged by a stanza from 'Play the Game', a poem that invites Englishmen to abandon football for the trenches:

> Football's a sport, and rare sport too,
>   Don't make it a source of shame.
> To-day there are worthier things to do.
>   Englishman, play the game!

A truce to the League, a truce to the Cup,
     Get to work with a *gun*.
When our country's at war we must all buck up –
     It's the only thing to be done!

(Pope, 1915, p.11)

It is easy to see what would have horrified Owen about Pope's versified homilies. As in this example, she shows no understanding of the realities of trench warfare, while complacently appropriating the language of sport: 'play the game'; 'we must all buck up'. 'Dulce et Decorum Est' precisely rebukes this kind of disengaged patriotism by suggesting that if Pope had any experience of what was actually happening in France, she would find it impossible to 'tell with such high zest ... The old Lie'.

My reading of Owen's poem has emphasized the ways in which it works as an instrumental text. It is worth stressing, however, that 'Dulce et Decorum Est' is not simply an anti-war slogan. It attacks the rehearsal of patriotic clichés 'To children ardent for some desperate glory' rather than war itself. Though the poem has a palpable design on its readers, that design is not part of a broader programme of action: Owen is not advocating pacifism but is instead insisting that warfare must be spoken and written about realistically. This might suggest that the poem approximates to a sort of journalism in verse – a transcript of real life in the trenches. Such an approach would, however, underestimate the aesthetic qualities of the poem. Again, 'aesthetic' may seem a strange word to describe a text that is so harrowing in its evocation of the effects of gas on soldiers. Yet it is largely on account of the brilliance of Owen's use of language that the poem has survived. We have already looked at the dextrous way in which the poem uses Horace's Latin in the final paragraph; consider the second verse paragraph, which modulates from the urgency of the gas attack to the speaker's isolated contemplation of the dying man. Owen's choice of words repays careful study. 'An ecstasy of fumbling' couples the awkwardness of soldiers 'Fitting the clumsy helmets just in time' with a sense of the almost orgasmic compulsiveness of their actions. 'Ecstasy' is a deliberately provocative word to use in this context: by depicting soldiers in such unheroic terms, Owen again challenges his readers' preconceptions of what soldiers 'ought' to look like. The last two lines of the paragraph – 'Dim, through the misty panes of thick green light, / As under a green sea, I saw him drowning' – are puzzling in a different way. On a first reading, it looks as though Owen is indulging in a species of conventional poetic description: the dying soldier disappears from view 'As under a green sea'. But though the idiom of these lines is heightened, Owen was in fact describing what could be seen of a mustard gas attack from behind 'the misty panes' of a gas mask. It seems to me that although 'Dulce' is a poem with a definite moral agenda, we should not restrict our reading to its moralizing features alone. You could argue that the poem preaches an effective sermon because it gives its readers an aesthetic experience that is painfully memorable. Equally, you may feel that the language of aesthetics remains inappropriate for such a text.

We turn now to 'The Fish' by Elizabeth Bishop. Bishop certainly was no Wildean aesthete; as Jamie McKendrick has argued, her work depends on 'an aesthetic of what really happened', which is nevertheless 'at a considerable remove from reportage and from straight description' (2002, p.142). Bishop's poems offer meticulously observed descriptions of places and things, which in turn have a striking metaphorical power. Her interest in the poetic description of external reality means that it is hard to extrapolate any clear-cut 'message' from her work. In the words of her mentor, the poet Marianne Moore, Bishop was 'someone who knows, who is not didactic' (quoted in Page, 2002, p.16); as Barbara Page explains, 'one who is didactic does have a fixed perspective, and from this angle is the enemy of the artist, or at any rate a poet of Bishop's disposition' (2002, p.16). 'Didactic' means 'teacherly' or 'instructive'; didacticism is another form of instrumentalism – we might reasonably describe 'Dulce et Decorum Est' as a didactic poem because it teaches its readers a lesson in the realities of war. Bishop's work largely eschews such strategies.

Bishop was not prone to making grandiose statements of poetic intent. Yet her letters exhibit her concern with the complex liaisons between art and life. Writing in 1957 to Robert Lowell, Bishop praises manuscript versions of autobiographical poems Lowell would later publish in the *Life Studies* volume of 1959:

> [Your poems] have that sure feeling, as if you'd been in a stretch (I've felt that way for very short stretches once in a long while) when everything and anything suddenly seemed material for poetry – or not material, seemed to *be* poetry, and all the past was illuminated in long shafts here and there, like a long-waited for sunrise. If only one could see everything that way all the time! It seems to me *it's* the whole purpose of art, to the artist (not the audience) – that rare feeling of control, illumination – life *is* all right, for the time being.

> (Bishop, 1996, p.350)

This letter is highly suggestive of Bishop's poetics: note her emphasis on the writing of poetry as a process of illumination. Since this is a letter to a colleague, it is unsurprising that Bishop does not consider what 'the whole purpose of art' might be for the reader. Nevertheless, the suggestion that 'stretches' of inspiration can transform 'everything and anything' into a poetry which controls and illuminates life is indicative of Bishop's artistic orientation. Poetry appears to be an art of almost spiritual revelation.

Now read 'The Fish'. Looking particularly at the use of language and subject matter, try to pick out two or three points of contrast between Bishop's poem and 'Dulce et Decorum Est'. What would you say are the major differences between the two poems?

The Fish

I caught a tremendous fish
and held him beside the boat
half out of water, with my hook
fast in a corner of his mouth.
He didn't fight.
He hadn't fought at all.
He hung a grunting weight,
battered and venerable
and homely. Here and there
his brown skin hung in strips
like ancient wallpaper,
and its pattern of darker brown
was like wallpaper:
shapes like full-blown roses
stained and lost through age.
He was speckled with barnacles,
fine rosettes of lime,
and infested
with tiny white sea-lice,
and underneath two or three
rags of green weed hung down.
While his gills were breathing in
the terrible oxygen
– the frightening gills,
fresh and crisp with blood,
that can cut so badly –
I thought of the coarse white flesh
packed in like feathers,
the big bones and the little bones,
the dramatic reds and blacks
of his shiny entrails,
and the pink swim-bladder
like a big peony.
I looked into his eyes
which were far larger than mine
but shallower, and yellowed,
the irises backed and packed

with tarnished tinfoil
seen through the lenses
of old scratched isinglass.
They shifted a little, but not
to return my stare.
– It was more like the tipping
of an object toward the light.
I admired his sullen face,
the mechanism of his jaw,
and then I saw
that from his lower lip
– if you could call it a lip –
grim, wet, and weaponlike,
hung five old pieces of fish-line,
or four and a wire leader
with the swivel still attached,
with all their five big hooks
grown firmly in his mouth.
A green line, frayed at the end
where he broke it, two heavier lines,
and a fine black thread
still crimped from the strain and snap
when it broke and he got away.
Like medals with their ribbons
frayed and wavering,
a five-haired beard of wisdom
trailing from his aching jaw.
I stared and stared
and victory filled up
the little rented boat,
from the pool of bilge
where oil had spread a rainbow
around the rusted engine
to the bailer rusted orange,
the sun-cracked thwarts,
the oarlocks on their strings,
the gunnels – until everything
was rainbow, rainbow, rainbow!
And I let the fish go.

(Bishop, 1983, pp.42–4)

Here are three points that occurred to me.

Line length and rhyme

Where Owen uses predominantly a pentameter, or five-beat line (for example, 'In **all** my **dreams**, be**fore** my **help**less **sight**', a line with five major stresses; marked in bold), Bishop veers between different sorts of shorter line – the three-beat ('I **caught** a tre**mend**ous **fish**'), the two-beat ('like a **big pe**ony') and even, possibly, a one-beat ('and in**fest**ed'). As these examples demonstrate, Bishop's metre is less stable than Owen's. Where Owen's basic model is the iambic rhythm (in which a stressed syllable follows an unstressed), Bishop opts for a looser metrical pattern. This makes 'The Fish' sound conversational, as though the speaker were talking directly to the reader. Note also the impact of Bishop's repetitions; I have marked the stresses here to show you how the poem avoids iambic regularity: 'While his **gills** were **breath**ing **in** / the **terr**ible **ox**ygen / – the **fright**ening **gills**'. The conversational quality is also evident in Bishop's sparing use of rhyme. Where Owen rhymes every line, Bishop only does so sporadically, as in the last two lines, where sound clinches the climax: 'everything / was rainbow, rainbow, rainbow! / And I let the fish go.' But the rhyme falls on unstressed syllables, as though deflecting attention from the poem's artifice and maintaining a plausibly conversational tone.

Description of the body

Where 'Dulce et Decorum Est' focuses on the horrific evocation of the soldier's body, 'The Fish' centres on a colourfully imagined itemization of the fish's insides: 'the dramatic reds and blacks / of his shiny entrails'. Though 'Dulce' is challenging because of the realism of its description, set beside 'The Fish' it lacks a forensic interest in anatomy. Bishop effectively conducts a poetic autopsy on the fish as it dangles from the hook. It is also intriguing that though the poem is far removed from the battlefield, metaphorically she invests the fish with military dignity: the lines caught in his jaw become 'Like medals with their ribbons / frayed and wavering'.

Poetic structure

As we have seen, 'Dulce et Decorum Est' is organized around the lesson that Owen preaches. It is carefully designed to convey both the horror of the gas attack and the glibness of patriotic sentiment. Its structure is clearly visible in the four verse paragraphs, in which Owen moves from narrative, via nightmare, to expostulation. In contrast, the structure of 'The Fish' is much less clearly delineated by its typographical layout. I would say that the poem has two major sections: the first sixty-four lines and the final twelve. The first section offers a detailed, fascinated description of 'a tremendous fish', while the final section unexpectedly resolves the poem not with the angler bringing the fish home but with its enigmatic release. Unlike 'Dulce', 'The Fish' does not explain itself or its purpose through its poetic structure. Rather, it invites the reader to contemplate the fish with the angler through the medium of words.

It seems to me that the major difference between the poems is connected with their poetic structures: where 'Dulce et Decorum Est' announces its agenda, 'The Fish' does not. Indeed, part of what makes Bishop's poem so compelling is that she does not disclose why she has written it, or indeed what it might be 'for'. In this sense, it can be aligned (at least temporarily) with Wilde's conception of art as something that is fundamentally *'useless'*. 'The Fish' is not a work of persuasion or instruction.

But we might want to say a little more about its metaphorical power – the ways in which, as a poetic narrative, it implies other resonances and possibilities. As we have seen, the poem centres on the process of describing the fish; we might elaborate on this to say that it is concerned with how the angler's perception of her catch changes the more she looks at it. You might have noticed the nimble way in which the poem reverses our expectations: it begins, almost boastfully, 'I caught a tremendous fish'. Yet this is complicated by the fish's age and decrepitude ('his brown skin hung in strips / like ancient wallpaper') and by the angler's growing attentiveness to the physical evidence of the fish's extraordinary life. The poem enacts the process through which the angler's act of watching – 'I stared and stared' – develops into a realization of something deeper than the simple fact of catching the fish. The 'victory' is not the angler's triumph over the fish but the implied empathetic relationship between the two protagonists. In her essay on the poem, which contextualizes it in terms of typically male narratives about fishing as a metaphor for machismo, Vicki Feaver argues that 'Bishop transforms a narrative about possession and domination and death into one about sympathy and survival and the triumph of love' (2002, p.93). Using the terms Bishop employs in her letter to Lowell, we might modify this to say that the poem conveys an 'illuminated' incident from the past: it sheds 'long shafts here and there' onto an apparently mundane incident 'until everything / was rainbow, rainbow, rainbow!' Although 'The Fish' is not an instrumental text, close reading reveals that it is more than simply what Wilde called a *'beautiful thing'*. To be sure, it would be hard to deduce any *'useful'* lesson from the poem (though it does contain solid facts about the anatomy of fish); rather, in aiming to illuminate this particular narrative, Bishop encapsulates a moment of secular vision. Such a vision is of course less immediately didactic than Owen's invective, but if the reader's perceptions shift along with the angler's, then Bishop's enigmatic poem may change our ways of thinking, or at least of seeing.

In this Introduction we have looked at aestheticist and instrumental answers to the question 'What is literature for?' through critical debates and close reading of poems. In the following chapters, you will need to make up your own mind about what the most compelling answers to this question are. I have stressed that the tension between aestheticist and instrumental theories is both rich and complicated; you will see that the prestige of these theories also changes in the light of different historical circumstances. The need to justify literature – to find compelling arguments to defend it and to clarify what it ought to be – remains central to the activity of literary criticism.

Works cited

Bishop, E. (1983) *Complete Poems*, London: Chatto & Windus.

Bishop, E. (1996) *One Art: The Selected Letters of Elizabeth Bishop*, ed. by R. Giroux, London: Pimlico.

Cuddon, J.A. (ed.) (1982) *A Dictionary of Literary Terms*, Harmondsworth: Penguin.

Feaver, V. (2002) 'Elizabeth Bishop: The Reclamation of Female Space', in L. Anderson and J. Shapcott (eds), *Elizabeth Bishop: Poet of the Periphery*, Newcastle upon Tyne: University of Newcastle and Bloodaxe, pp.87–102.

Gibbons, F. (2003) 'Minister Labelled Racist after Attack on Rap "Idiots" ', *Guardian*, 6 January, p.3.

Hibberd, D. (1989) *Owen the Poet*, Basingstoke: Macmillian.

Hibberd, D. (2002) *Wilfred Owen: A New Biography*, London: Weidenfeld & Nicolson.

Horace (2002) *Odes III: Dulce Periculum*, ed. and trans. by D. West, Oxford: Oxford University Press.

Keats, J. (1972) *The Poems of John Keats*, ed. by M. Allott, London: Longman.

Keegan, J. (1999) *The First World War*, London: Pimlico.

McKendrick, J. (2002) 'Bishop's Birds', in L. Anderson and J. Shapcott (eds), *Elizabeth Bishop: Poet of the Periphery*, Newcastle upon Tyne: University of Newcastle and Bloodaxe, pp.123–42.

Orwell, G. (1970) *The Collected Essays, Journalism and Letters of George Orwell*, vol.1: *An Age Like This 1920–1940*, ed. by S. Orwell and I. Angus, Harmondsworth: Penguin.

Owen, W. (1963) *The Collected Poems of Wilfred Owen*, ed. by C. Day Lewis, London: Chatto & Windus.

Page, B. (2002) 'Elizabeth Bishop: Stops, Starts and Dreamy Divagations', in L. Anderson and J. Shapcott (eds), *Elizabeth Bishop: Poet of the Periphery*, Newcastle upon Tyne: University of Newcastle and Bloodaxe, pp.12–30.

Plato (1974) *The Republic*, trans. and intro. by D. Lee, Penguin Classics, Harmondsworth: Penguin.

Pope, J. (1915) *Jessie Pope's War Poems*, London: Grant Richards.

Stallworthy, J. (1974) *Wilfred Owen*, London: Oxford University Press.

CHAPTER 1

Anton Chekhov, *The Cherry Orchard*

SARA HASLAM

Overview

Following a brief introduction to Chekhov and to the themes of his play, the first section of this chapter investigates the dramatic impact of *The Cherry Orchard* as performed on a selection of British, American and Russian stages since 1904. Shifting the focus from performance, the second section is called 'Reading plays'; here I consider some conventions that inform the ways in which readers engage with dramatic texts. In the third section, *The Cherry Orchard* is studied as a literary text, first by developing an overview of the play and then through close reading of a key passage. The following section extends this detailed thinking into contextual issues; I examine Chekhov and his play in historical, cultural and biographical terms. Returning to performance of the play, the fifth section addresses two crucial questions: is *The Cherry Orchard* a tragedy or a comedy? Does the play demonstrate that literature has a purpose? Progress through this section includes analysis of the themes of the play, and exploration of how its aspects can be made to resonate more or less tragically, more or less comically, and more or less purposefully, according to the focus and emphasis of a director. The concluding section draws together ideas raised by the questions treated in the previous section and offers some final thoughts on what *The Cherry Orchard* might suggest literature is for.

Introduction

Anton Pavlovich Chekhov was a Russian dramatist and short-story writer; he was born in 1860 and died in 1904. He is arguably the most popular Russian author outside his own country and has been described as 'one of the greatest influences on contemporary theatre' (Andrew, 1982, p.ix). He studied medicine at Moscow University, and qualified as a doctor in 1884; his second career, as a writer, began with short stories and humorous sketches while he was a student. *The Steppe*, one of his best-known short stories, was published in 1888, and he wrote another fifty or so that together explain his prominence in this genre. The plays that made him famous did not start to appear until the closing years of the nineteenth century; *Ivanov* was first performed in Moscow in 1887, *The Seagull* in St Petersburg in 1896, *Uncle*

Vanya in Moscow in 1899, *Three Sisters* in Moscow in 1901 and *The Cherry Orchard* also in Moscow in 1904. It is on the basis of these five plays that 'Chekhov's worldwide reputation rests' (Chekhov, 1998, back cover). The number of screen adaptations of his plays is one indication of his popularity – there have been far more than of the plays of his contemporaries Oscar Wilde, Henrik Ibsen and August Strindberg. Chekhov's plays are also performed regularly on stage, all over the world, testifying to their continuing though changing relevance. Trevor Nunn, one-time artistic head of the Royal Shakespeare Company, has written of Chekhov's 'extraordinary durability, the sheer toughness of the material and how well made his plays are' (2000, p.101). Nunn also terms him 'the other great writer' – Shakespeare's companion – because of the provocative nature, the variety and the richness of his material (*ibid.*, p.108). Despite these assessments, it is important to recognize that critical opinion of Chekhov has been more divided than they suggest. His dramatic work, particularly, has been heavily criticized by some as irrelevant and overly pessimistic. One early reviewer – Leo Weiner, writing in 1903 – suggested that his characters were fit subjects for the psychiatrist not for the stage (in Emeljanow, 1981, p.68).

Chekhov has a reputation for generating a wealth and variety of responses. 'When I write I rely fully on the reader', Chekhov said, 'presuming that he will add the subjective elements missing in my story' (quoted in Connolly, 1989, p.363). In keeping with this reliance, he is often seen as a stimulating, rather than a dogmatic, author – one who resists telling people what to think. Some of the issues that are raised in this open style by *The Cherry Orchard* include:

- marital dissolution;

- sexual frustration;

- political idealism;

- patrician love of land and property;

- the rights of the masses to what the few had enjoyed in Russia;

- social loneliness for those who cross class divides;

- the role of servants as society 'progresses'.

Finally, before we start to explore Chekhov's play, I would like to raise one more crucial introductory issue, which will help further to explain his reputation – and his place in this book. The Russian novelist Leo Tolstoy stated in 1911 that 'Chekhov created new forms of writing, completely new, in my opinion, to the entire world, the like of which I have encountered nowhere' (in Jackson, 1967, p.27). In some ways this novelty was related to modernism (a term used to describe broad and radical shifts in the arts around the turn of the twentieth century); it is also important to relate it to other literary, and political, contexts in Russia. Chekhov was part of a developing tradition in Russia. Humorous writers already figured in the St Petersburg comic weekly in which he was first published, and literary figures, such as Tolstoy, influenced his work. But, as Tolstoy says, Chekhov also stood out from the crowd. It was, in part, his open, or diagnostic, stance (one that recognized a problem, but offered no solution for it) that was seen to constitute what was new – and different – about Chekhov.

The Cherry Orchard on stage

Now watch a production or a video/DVD of the play, or read the text. Your aim should be an overview rather than detailed thinking at this point, so try to enjoy this first encounter. Is the play funny? Is it dramatic and/or exciting? Which characters stand out?

In general, there is no better introduction to a play than to investigate, at first hand, something of its impact. Many early critics of the play found that it was not terribly exciting or dramatic, and that the things Chekhov concentrated on were, by contrast, 'ordinary, constant, recurring and habitual' (in Jackson, 1967, p.75). It is possible that you found much 'everyday' matter as you watched or read (and it may also be that, as we proceed, we discover that the everyday can be treated in exciting or dramatic ways). Victor Emeljanow, editor of *Chekhov: The Critical Heritage*, found, however, in his study of reviews of the play, that Firs's character seemed to transcend the everyday:

> It is curious that the character of the old retainer, Firs, remained extra-ordinarily memorable in all English productions. It seemed as if Madame Ranevskys could come and go, but Firs could go on for ever, and especially when played by actors like O.B. Clarence, who would appeal to English sentimentality.
>
> (Emeljanow, 1981, p.23)

The Cherry Orchard in the West

Extracts from four reviews are reproduced below. These reviews point towards many of the contentious issues – to do with content, reception and performance – that will occupy us throughout this chapter. Each reviewer adopts a different tone and emphasizes different issues; **try to describe the tone and identify some of these issues as you read each review**. At times, you might find it difficult to believe that they are talking about the same play; crucially, they are referring to different productions of it.

Daily Telegraph review of the first production in England in 1911

There were signs of revolt in the usually docile audience attending the performance of the Stage Society at the Aldwych Theatre. For once a certain amount of impatience was shown, as though the dramatic fare provided was a little too difficult to swallow ... Neither an English audience nor a French audience is very quick in assimilating new ideas, especially when presented in a thoroughly unfamiliar form ... When we have to add to this the fact that this particular play of Chekhov, like most of his others, is quite formless, and wanting in dramatic movement, it is hardly surprising that it did not receive anything but a very chilly welcome from the members of the Stage Society.

(in Emeljanow, 1981, p.93)

Observer review of a British performance in 1920

I declare that this play, by a dead Russian, is a masterpiece which, to our shame, has only been performed in England by obscure societies ... And what a play 'The Cherry Orchard' is! How imperceptibly all that irrelevant small talk by garrulous and puerile people is gathered up into a profound illumination ... Out of that apparently meaningless movement comes unity, comes purpose, comes, above all, great illumination. If only we could induce our Labour M.P.s to be quit of politics in order that they might take to the consideration of literature, how much more hopeful some of us would feel about the future of England!

(in Emeljanow, 1981, pp.193–5)

Dial review of a New York performance in Russian in 1923

[The Moscow Art Theatre] represents the higher reaches of the realistic movement ... It is this extremely difficult formula which the Russians have brought to perfection in the theatre ... They present a surface so perfectly convincing as realism that we can scarcely believe when we leave the theatre that we have not been actual visitors in a Russian household.

(in Emeljanow, 1981, p.236)

New York *Herald-Tribune* review of a performance in English in 1933

Without drawing from 'The Cherry Orchard' the social and economic morals which latter-day supporters of the new Russian political order most cherish, this piece is such a poignant allegory of futility ... that the observer has no difficulty in imagining at least some of the reasons for the decline of the old Russian scheme of things on a far more comprehensive scale than that embraced by the childlike and footlessly gentle family with which the play is concerned.

Its progress toward catastrophe from threat to impending reality and from reality to the accomplishment of doom last evening was so moving as to provoke many a latent gesture toward pocket handkerchiefs as the final curtain descended simultaneously with the outrageous ax upon the trees themselves.

(in Emeljanow, 1981, p.377)

The inauspicious performance described in the *Daily Telegraph* review, received in 'very chilly' fashion, was at the Aldwych Theatre. According to the reviewer, the audience was in revolt because of the 'newness' of the dramatic structure in general, and of the plot in particular. (Russian commentators were not alone in ascribing novelty to Chekhov.) The audience was probably looking for a particular kind of climax and a particular kind of resolution to the play. It received neither. In the second, very positive extract, published in the *Observer*, the reviewer is so struck by the 'illumination' of the play that the word is repeated. The review in *Dial* describes, also in glowing terms, a performance in Russian by the company from Moscow for which the play had been written. This performance is praised for the way it represents Russian life on an American stage (evidence that treatment of the everyday can provide a satisfying dramatic experience). The New York *Herald-Tribune* review also refers to a performance given on an American stage, but this time in English translation. Here, a nostalgic and political tone is present: the reviewer judges the axe that destroys the cherry orchard to be 'outrageous'. It is the symbol of the destruction of an age and a way of life of which the reviewer seems to approve.

These extracts chart something of the changes in the ways in which the play has been responded to through time – something of its reception history. Reviewers' key points include:

- the revolt of an audience as its expectations were foiled;

- the sense of purpose that is manifested by the play;

- the realism of its presentation and message (in other words, its interest in representing aspects of human life and experience);

- the identification of the play's tragic qualities (and perhaps a consequential lack of humour).

These varied critical responses tell us something about time and space (or context). When and where, as well as how, the play was performed will have helped to determine each of the stances adopted by the reviewers. More importantly for our immediate purpose, these reviews also tell us something about the play, and the challenges it offers.

Having explored some aspects of *The Cherry Orchard*'s reception history, I want to continue by introducing another way of thinking about Chekhov's work. Focusing on author intentionality – on the design and purpose of the author – has much to offer in terms of raising issues and recognizing the challenges of this play (though it is important not to be limited to this approach). We will see that although Chekhov may not have sought explicitly to tell society how to mend itself in his work, he did have opinions about how his ideas should be realized on stage.

The Cherry Orchard in Russia

The play might be expected to have had a less complicated (or varied) reception in Chekhov's homeland than it did elsewhere. It was written specially for the Moscow Art Theatre (MKhAT) and received its premier there on 17 January 1904 (five months before Chekhov's death). A special relationship already existed between Chekhov and the MKhAT: in 1898, a revival of *The Seagull* was staged there and in 1901 Chekhov wrote *The Three Sisters* specially for the theatre.

The MKhAT was a recent and exciting development in Russian drama. It was founded in 1898 by playwright and critic Vladimir Nemirovich-Danchenko and the already established actor-director Konstantin Stanislavski. Stanislavski is most famous now because the 'Method' style of acting is derived from his teaching. The Method is characterized by improvization, spontaneity and psychological realism. According to David Allen, both Nemirovich-Danchenko and Stanislavski 'deplored the current state of the professional Russian theatre, and were determined to wage war against the clichés and routine "lies" of the stage' (2000, p.11). In the following extract, Stanislavski provides what might be called a manifesto for the MKhAT:

> We rebelled against the old manner of acting, against theatricality, against false pathos, declamation and artificiality, against bad conventions of staging and décor ... against the whole system of production, and the contemptible repertoire, in theatres at that time.
>
> (quoted in Allen, 2000, p.11)

Chekhov's 'new forms of writing', to use Tolstoy's phrase, were to find expression on a new kind of stage. The two were united, in the opinion of Stanislavski, by the desire 'to achieve artistic simplicity and truthfulness' on that stage (quoted in Allen, 2000, p.11). The relationship between the

MKhAT and Chekhov's plays continued long after Chekhov's death (in 1985, the Soviet leader Mikhail Gorbachev was in the audience at a production there of *Uncle Vanya*), and in the early years of productions, this relationship led to what became widely known in Russia as the Chekhovian 'theatre of mood'. The phrase referred to the ways in which directors, particularly Stanislavski, used sound and lighting effects to reflect what they saw as the inner feelings of Chekhov's characters. Atmosphere was crucial, as was making a strong impression on the audience; despite what Stanislavski says in the quotation above about 'simplicity and truthfulness', many critics felt that the most notable aspect of these early productions was the emotional atmosphere he sought to create.

This close association was productive for both parties, but the relationship between Chekhov and Stanislavski was not always harmonious, and they fell out over the first production of *The Cherry Orchard*. This is, perhaps, surprising, because the performance was a huge success, punctuated by riotous applause, speeches and plaudits for its creator. Nonetheless, Stanislavski had not done with the play what Chekhov had intended that he, or the theatre company, should. 'Stanislavski has ruined my play', Chekhov famously complained in a letter to his wife in March 1904, referring in the main to the production's emphasis on tragedy as opposed to the comedy dear to Chekhov's heart (quoted in Allen, 2000, p.43). He had identified the same problem, a problem caused by differences between his own assessment of the nature of the play and that of Stanislavski, in the MKhAT's 1901 production of *Three Sisters*.

To summarize, if one takes into account the different perceptions and intentions of director and author, as well as the responses of an audience, the play had just as complicated a reception in Russia as elsewhere. There are multiple and opposed focus points in its Russian reception history with which to engage. When Stanislavski emphasized the tragic qualities of *The Cherry Orchard*, he provoked the hostility of its author, but secured the nostalgic response of a satisfied audience. This tension, established at the time of the first performance of the play, has never been resolved; much later, other Moscow theatres, such as the Maly, staged productions of Chekhov that emphasized comedy. *The Cherry Orchard*'s uncertain status – as a comedy or as a tragedy – has proved to be the subject of lasting debate about genre, and offers important ways of addressing the question 'What is literature for?' Interpretation of a play – by a director, an audience or a critic – is closely bound to its perceived genre. A farce, for example, is likely to be experienced as less instructive or instrumental than a tragedy or, perhaps, than a satire.

Examine Figure 1.1, a photograph of the 1904 Moscow Art Theatre production of *The Cherry Orchard*. Are any elements of the play that have been discussed so far manifested in this image?

Figure 1.1 *The Cherry Orchard*, Act 2, Moscow Art Theatre (1904), directed by Konstantin Stanislavski. (Moscow Art Theatre Museum.)

The realistic nature of the stage is of particular note here. The trees do look like trees, though it is hard to tell whether the stage examples are actually made of wood and leaves. The costumes are realistic too, and contemporary. The lighting of the characters appears to be stark and dramatic, effecting an impression on the audience, or creating a stirring atmosphere, in keeping with what we have learned of Stanislavski's preferred techniques. It might not be possible to discern anything about whether the play is more or less funny – the subject of the debate between Chekhov and Stanislavski – from this still image.

Reading plays

I will return to the performance of Chekhov's play later in the chapter. Now I would like to consider other ways of getting to know and understand *The Cherry Orchard*. **Turn to Act 2 and read from Yasha's speech that starts 'Go back to the house ...' (Chekhov, 1998, p.260; unless otherwise stated, all subsequent references are to this edition) as far as Mrs Ranevsky's 'Off with you' (*ibid.*, p.261). As you read, reflect on the differences between reading a play and reading a novel.**

Reading a play *is* different from reading a novel or poetry. When you read a play, you are reading a text that is intended for performance. The words on the page will not only be heard, which is why there are instructions to indicate how something is to be said (such as 'imploringly' in the extract you have just read), but they will also be given some kind of visual life, which is why there are instructions for how something is to be done (Dunyasha embraces Yasha 'impulsively'). Together, these characteristics of a dramatic text mean that the experience of reading it is one in which the flow is interrupted, and during which it might be difficult to be 'carried away'.

Drama possesses other characteristics specific to the genre. A narrator, such as the one we encounter at the start of Jane Austen's novel *Emma* (1816), say, is a rare phenomenon in a play. Austen's novel begins:

> Emma Woodhouse, handsome, clever, and rich, with a
> comfortable home and happy disposition, seemed to unite some
> of the best blessings of existence; and had lived nearly twenty-one
> years in the world with very little to distress or vex her.
>
> (Austen, [1816] 2003, p.7)

Austen's narrator can be described as one who serves to suggest what we might think or how we might react to occurrences. Use of the word 'seemed', coupled with the build-up of all the perfect aspects of Emma's life, communicates to the reader that we are to understand that everything is about to change, and that she is going to receive her comeuppance. Right from the start of the text, the reader knows that the narrator's estimation of Emma is different from her estimation of herself: play scripts cannot ironize in this way.

Although there is usually no narrator in a play, no-one to tell us what message to take away or what to think, there *are* other ways in which the writer can signify his or her intentions for performance (and this is related to the discussion in the last section). Using stage directions, Chekhov tries unusually hard to determine how his plays are performed and the ways in which the actors move and speak. From what we already know about Chekhov's thoughts on this play, we might guess that his stage directions are to do with emphasizing comedy. There are about 175 directions on how the lines are to be spoken in *The Cherry Orchard*, and this gives a very detailed picture of how Chekhov imagined his words would be realized. However, such directions are in most cases (depending on the dramatist) less fundamentally important to the reader of a play than the narrator is to the reader of a novel. And though we might pay them careful attention when we read a play, in performance we are inevitably less conscious of stage directions; more significantly, as we have seen, they can be ignored by a director and the actors in any production of the play.

In short, the interpretative act is one that Chekhov cannot control. The text can, and will, be read – and interpreted – by you. It has also been read – and interpreted – by me. (In both cases, time and increasing knowledge and experience of the play will develop and change those interpretations.) As preparation for performances, Chekhov's text will have been read – and interpreted – by many directors, actors, designers and producers. All these interpretations are, in part, contextually determined and may therefore differ, sometimes substantially. Although this sense of plurality can be confusing, it also helps to generate what can be a liberating discovery: a play, perhaps more obviously than a novel or a poem, can be shown to mean, and illuminate, many things according to time, place and perspective.

As I hope I have made clear in this section, it is vitally important to recognize the heard and visible aspects of dramatic words, as well as to read them. To this end, as you engage with the text through the first half of this chapter, it might be a good idea occasionally to read some sections aloud. I will return to analysis of performance in the second half of the chapter, but remember, if you watch a production, you are viewing just one representation of the setting and action that help to give life to Chekhov's words. I will discuss various performance choices as we proceed.

Working with the text

Paying particular attention to the language and subject matter of the play, read the opening of Act 1, as far as Anya's 'Good night, Uncle' (p.247). What, if anything, draws your attention to the fact that this text was not written in English? Chekhov has been called the 'historian of the age of small deeds' (as opposed to heroic ones, for example) (Connolly, 1989, p.334). **Think about any 'small deeds' you encounter as you read (if you have seen a performance, cast your mind back to this too). Try to focus on a particular detail of this passage that is interesting or perplexing to you. Discussion of these issues will recur throughout this section.**

The first thing to note here, perhaps, is that Russian names are likely to appear strange, particularly in their spelling. However, Ronald Hingley's edition for the Oxford World's Classics does anglicize names, whereas, for example, in the current Penguin Classics edition, Mrs Ranevsky is known as Ranyevskaia. The spelling of her name in the Penguin version indicates her marriage in its 'a' ending, as it does in Russian. (In July 2002, there was a debate about the dramatization of *Anna Karenina* on BBC Radio 4. Some listeners were incensed at the decision to call it *Anna Karenin* to make it less alien to its British audience.) I was also struck by the complexity of the social strata to which we are introduced in the first pages: for example, the intricate hierarchy of the servants, which is compounded by the arrival of the family. Conversely, some themes or occurrences are familiar – the representation of a nursery, the sense of excited anticipation, the human tendency to reminisce. These issues share a common thread: they are to do with a representation of reality that may vary little depending on culture and/or language.

I have said little so far about one central concern when encountering Chekhov (or any writer in a different language from that in which he or she wrote): the fact of translation. Raised as a peripheral issue by one or two of the reviews reproduced in the first section of this chapter, it is important that we think about translation in more detail. In some instances, Chekhov was first read and played in the West via Stanislavski and the Moscow Art Theatre, in Russian (the 1923 New York *Herald-Tribune* review relates to just such an occasion). More usually, of course, Chekhov was first read and played in the West via the interpretative art of translation.

Working with translations

'Few playwrights of the last two or three hundred years have had a greater impact than Anton Chekhov', Hingley proclaims at the start of his edition (1998, p.vii). Despite the warmth of his assessment, this impact, in its positive sense, was delayed, particularly outside Russia. Why? Partly because of issues to do with form and content that we shall be exploring later in relation to *The Cherry Orchard*. But that is not all. The *Daily Telegraph* review exposes a sense of difficulty to do with cultural perspectives, and makes issues of nationality a significant factor in the response to the performance. Different and later audiences, watching different productions, evidently surmounted the barriers that are perceived and experienced by this reviewer. Nonetheless, these barriers may have meant that Chekhov's play failed in its first UK performance.

Read the unsigned notice from *The Times* relating to a performance of *The Cherry Orchard* in English in 1911 (Reader, Item 4). Give special attention to the ideas raised about the issue of translation. What are the main problems with translation as experienced by this reviewer?

The opinion set out here is a striking one, and I have suggested that you read it because it is provocative, and can be contested. Its author is affirming the belief that literature which is translated from language to language and from culture to culture becomes unrecognizable as the medium for communication that was envisaged by its creator. This is not the only loss, or the most serious: out of context, moved between cultures, it also ceases to make sense. From the perspective of the audience, the argument goes, works of literature cannot be understood or appreciated, and therefore should not be presented, in a different language and a different country from those in which they were produced. 'If you do not speak Russian, and know Russia, then you will find yourself bewildered by this play', might be one paraphrase of this point of view. **Are you persuaded by it?**

There is something to be said for this argument, and the Chekhov that we will read in translation has been interpreted and then scripted by translators, each of whom produces their text in a very different context from

ДЕЙСТВИЕ ТРЕТЬЕ

Гостиная, отделенная аркой от залы. Горит люстра. Слышно, как в передней играет еврейский оркестр, тот самый, о котором упоминается во II акте. Вечер. В зале танцуют grand rond. Голос Симеонова-Пищика: — «Promenade à une paire!» Выходят в гостиную: в первой паре Пищик и Шарлотта Ивановна, во второй — Трофимов и Любовь Андреевна, в третьей — Аня с почтовым чиновником, в четвертой — Варя с начальником станции и т. д. Варя тихо плачет и, танцуя, утирает слезы. В последней паре Дуняша. Идут по гостиной, Пищик кричит: — «Grand rond, balancez!» и «Les cavaliers à genoux et remerciez vos dames!».[1]

Фирс во фраке проносит на подносе сельтерскую воду. Входят в гостиную Пищик и Трофимов

Пищик. Я полнокровный, со мной уже два раза удар был, танцовать трудно, но, как говорится, попал в стаю, лай не лай, а хвостом виляй. Здоровье-то у меня лошадиное. Мой покойный родитель, шутник, царство небесное, насчет нашего происхождения говорил так, будто древний род наш Симеоновых-Пищиков происходит будто бы от той самой лошади, которую Калигула[2] посадил в сенате... (Садится.) Но вот беда: денег нет! Голодная собака верует только в мясо... (Храпит и тотчас же просыпается.) Так и я... могу только про деньги...

Трофимов. А у вас в фигуре в самом деле есть что-то лошадиное.

Пищик. Что ж... лошадь хороший зверь... лошадь продать можно...

(Слышно, как в соседней комнате играют на бильярде. В зале под аркой показывается Варя.)

Трофимов (дразнит). Мадам Лопахина! Мадам Лопахина!..

Варя (сердито). Облезлый барин!

Трофимов. Да, я облезлый барин и горжусь этим!

Варя (в горьком раздумьи). Вот наняли музыкантов, а чем платить? (Уходит.)

---

[1] Все эти французские выражения — названия танцовальных фигур и обращения при танцах.
[2] Калигула — римский император.

Figure 1.2   Russian text of *The Cherry Orchard*, opening of Act 3.

the writer in early twentieth-century Russia. Because interpretation is, in part, a transformative activity, a translator's *Cherry Orchard* is not the same text as that which would be read in Russian. One might therefore claim, with justification, that the text does not make the sense it was intended to make. One might even claim that it makes no sense at all, as the reviewer does, because the link between it and its historical and geographical contexts, on which one relies (or so the reviewer believes), has been severed. Looking at the Russian text of the play (if one cannot speak Russian or read the Cyrillic alphabet) may be one way of experiencing the sense of alienation from a text in another language that is described by the reviewer (Figure 1.2).

Despite these strong claims in support of this argument, there are also significant ways of countering it. The unsigned notice assumes a lack of empathetic imagination on the part of those viewing the play, an ability that may, on the contrary, be highly developed. The argument fails to take account of possible connections between people based on, say, class and gender – connections that might be said to transcend national borders. These connections would challenge the vocabulary of 'aliens' and 'grotesques' adopted by the reviewer, and undermine the unpleasant assumption that identifiable 'types', and the ability to make dramatic sense of them, emerge from specific nationalities.

In addition, and in keeping with the dependence on interpretation characteristic of the dramatic genre, an examination of the strengths and weaknesses of different translations (as well as productions) of the same work may reveal a variety of ways of making it a success on the stage. *The Cherry Orchard* is capable of meaning many things to many people, instead of one thing to Russians alone. Finally, and at a more general level, context applies to more than language: it applies to time and history too. The logical extension of the 'translation–transvaluation' argument is that art cannot be appreciated by anybody other than a local contemporary of its production. To support this notion, authorial intention would have to be realized to produce a definitive version that, absurdly, could be prevented from altering in production and reception terms through time. From what we have learned so far, such an artefact would be impossible to sustain – Chekhov could not even impose his will on productions while he was alive.

Consideration of translation also necessitates thinking about the relative virtues of different translated versions of the same text. Over time, there is rarely just one translation, especially of a famous text. Even in the short section of the play you have read, significant differences can be detected on comparing translations. **Look at the middle of Lopakhin's speech at the beginning of Act 1, from 'Little peasant' (p.241) to 'I'm just another country bumpkin' (*ibid.*), and compare it with the following translation by Elizaveta Fen from the Penguin Classics edition. How do the differences affect your reading of the play?**

> 'Little peasant'.... She was right enough, my father was a peasant.
> Yet here I am – all dressed up in a white waistcoat and brown
> shoes.... But you can't make a silk purse out of a sow's ear. I am
> rich, I've got a lot of money, but anyone can see I'm just a
> peasant, anyone who takes the trouble to think about me and look
> under my skin.
>
> (Chekhov, 1951, p.334)

In Fen's translation for Penguin we see different use of pauses, different
vocabulary and, as a result of both, a slightly different articulation of
Lopakhin's character. I found him to be more plaintive in Fen's translation,
and more defensive in Hingley's Oxford World's Classics version. Pauses
make a difference, both to an audience, and also in terms of a particular
development of a character that they help to promote. In a silence, the
audience will consider the words that have just been spoken, allowing them
to resonate, and perhaps to become more meaningful. In this instance, a
pause might help to indicate a sense of hesitancy in Lopakhin's character, a
feeling of his not being quite at home in the world he now perceives about
him. A pause, in more theoretical terms, can also help to associate the play
with a realist tradition (speech, after all, is almost never fluent). However,
this is not always the case; pauses in dialogue or action can also prove to be
deeply unsettling and alienating, and can help to rupture the sense of realism
depending on how they are used (they function in this way in Samuel
Beckett's *Waiting for Godot*; 1955). A company producing the play would
have to make decisions about issues such as these when choosing a text to
work from for performance.

In *The Real Chekhov*, David Magarshack bemoans the fact that when
Chekhov was first being performed in the UK, the only 'widely recognized
translator from the Russian was Constance Garnett, whose admirable zeal
and indefatigable perseverance was only equalled by her inadequate
knowledge of Russian which never rose above the dictionary level' (1972,
p.13). (Magarshack's perspective is, no doubt, determined partly by the fact
that he is also a translator.) His view – which is not shared by all
commentators – is that Garnett's limited knowledge of Russian hampered
her ability to render Chekhov's sense in English. Adopting an extreme
position, he states that 'the mistranslation of a single word may sometimes be
enough to ruin a Chekhov play by reducing one of its chief characters to a
state of utter idiocy' (*ibid.*, p.15). He illustrates his point with a translation,
used in a production, that renders Trofimov's advice to Lopakhin not to wave
his arms about as 'Don't flap your hands' (p.285). 'Lopakhin in this
production', Magarshack goes on, 'kept flapping his hands all through this
play. He would do so even in the middle of a speech' (1972, p.16). This does
make Lopakhin sound idiotic, and is despite the fact that Chekhov's
conception of Lopakhin is entirely different. 'His behaviour', thought

Chekhov, 'must be entirely proper, cultivated and free of pettiness or clowning' (quoted in Brahms, 1976, p.115). We know that Chekhov's imperative can be ignored, along with other aspects of authorial intention. The point here is that translations can affect fundamentally performance choices and, ultimately, the meaning that is made by those performances. In addition, it is likely that the reception of Chekhov's play on the stage outside Russia in its early life was to an unfair degree determined by the low number of contemporary translators interested in his work.

The greatest difficulty for a translator can reside in the use of idiom, or colloquialism, especially when significant interpretation is at stake. In her translation of the play, Fen (who is Russian) translates Lopakhin's Act 1 interruption of Anya and Varya as a 'Me-e-e' (Chekhov, 1951, p.338), the bleat of a sheep; Hingley makes it the 'Moo-oo-oo' of a cow (Chekhov, 1998, p.245). Fen's 'Me-e-e' makes more sense (although is not necessarily how one would transcribe the bleat of a sheep in English in the twenty-first century), and is thus the better translation in this instance, *if* one accepts a particular interpretation of this scene: Lopakhin wanting to show the girls how foolish and narrow-minded they are being when he can solve all their problems. Despite this apparently negative comparison, I have chosen to use Hingley's translation in this chapter because of the subtleties of his language, and for his analysis, and replication, of Chekhov's comic 'lightness of touch' (see Hingley, 1998, p.xxi).

If you have watched a production of the play, consider how it dealt with this scene. Which translation did it opt for, and how did this affect its dramatic sense?

Richard Eyre's production of the play for BBC television (1981) introduces a third option: here, Lopakhin bursts in imitating a chicken. Anya and Varya's foolishness is being emphasized (as is Lopakhin's playfulness), and there are similarities, therefore, between Eyre's rendition and those of Fen and Hingley. However, Eyre stops short of Fen's implication that the girls are following the crowd in their refusal to accept the future. There is something unique, then, about Fen's choice.

In this section, we have seen that translation issues must be borne in mind as an integral part of the appreciation and understanding of a text written in a language different from that in which it is being read or performed. In one sense, in *The Cherry Orchard* we are reading Chekhov's words filtered and adapted by other creative imaginations (including those of directors and actors once they are involved in the process). The potential for confusion, and for illumination, is thus multiplied. One translator describes his endeavour as an 'impossible art' as a way of communicating its difficulty and its simultaneous rewards (Don Taylor, in Sophocles, 1986, p.189); one director of *The Cherry Orchard* revels in the choice between the cool, rigorous translation of the end of Act 2 by Michael Frayn, and the dramatic, and what he calls 'orgasmic', version by David Mamet (Dromgoole, 2003). From Chekhov's perspective, however, remember that such multiplication occurred even without translation interfering; Stanislavski's 1904 performance was, of course, in Russian. In drama, someone else must almost always interpret the author's words for performance (unless you are considering an actor writing a self-directed one-person play).

To supplement your knowledge of translation issues, read Beverley Hahn's 'A Note on Translations' (Reader, Item 5). In this essay, Hahn gives cause for optimism in working with Chekhov in translation. What are the main points of her argument?

Central to Hahn's argument are what she calls 'special factors' in Chekhov's dramatic art. These include: its formal properties (the structured patterns that survive translation); his use of images derived from nature, which might be said to transcend national and linguistic borders; and the emergence of a distinctive 'Chekhovian sensibility' in English translations of his work – which means they are largely true to the '*kind* of writer' Chekhov is. While Hahn suggests that there is a common Chekhovian idiom which readily translates into English, Mamet's radical version implies that this may not be the case.

An overview of the text

Now read the play through once from the beginning, this time making notes on its main events and whether you find it funny or not. Do you agree that in general we are treated to 'fragmentary … glimpses into characters' in this play, as John Reid (2002) claims?

In a play, events based on conflicts of various kinds usually determine progress. One interest clashes with another, providing dramatic tension, and the conflict is either resolved or re-emerges in other ways in the text. Conflict can be evoked using love, and associated relationships, as in Shakespeare's *Romeo and Juliet* (c.1595–6), or using war, as in his *Henry V* (c.1599). Gender debates can be stimulating in this respect, as in Henrik Ibsen's *A Doll's House* (1879), and the ideological shortcomings of the American Dream function similarly for some writers, as in Arthur Miller's *Death of a Salesman* (1949). In comparison, it might be possible to think that not a great deal actually happens in *The Cherry Orchard*, and that it does not offer much by way of dramatic conflict. A cherry orchard is sold, and there is much, usually genial, discussion about it along the way. When Trofimov gets overexcited about the process in Act 2, Chekhov might be seen as encouraging us to laugh at him rather than grant him dramatic force. If the discussion about the orchard is not genial, it is often based on denial instead, which is equally undramatic (Mrs Ranevsky somehow always manages to change the subject from the pressing need to sell; see, for example, pp.250, 260, 261). A Russian essay published in 1948 describes the way in which contemporary reviewers accused Chekhov of ' "insufficient action" and "weakness of plot" ' (in Jackson, 1967, p.69) – and is reminiscent of the *Daily Telegraph* review in this respect.

Regarding character, the identity of the hero, or the villain – the central figures through which one often approaches drama – is one obvious place to start. We all tend to look for an Othello, or an Iago, as we watch a play. But in *The Cherry Orchard* we are presented with a wide variety of characters, each of them with some strengths and some weaknesses. Even the neurotic Mrs Ranevsky can tell Trofimov entirely reasonably that he has not grown up until he has taken a lover (p.276). None of the characters seems to stand absolutely condemned, or absolutely supported, by Chekhov. (This may well have helped to contribute to a sense of fragmentary glimpses into character.) By extension, therefore, Trofimov's dignified sense of belief in human progress prevents Mrs Ranevsky's observation about his sex life from cutting too deep.

Finally, a particularly striking characteristic of this play is the way in which the potential for comedy and the potential for tragedy do not ever seem fully to be realized. (Though in productions different directors may work hard to emphasize one or the other.) Does Firs die, or is he merely forgotten, to be rediscovered soon in a pathetic way? When Charlotte ruminates on the very basis of her identity at the outset of Act 2, why does she simultaneously eat a cucumber?

My points in the paragraphs above represent some initial reactions to a first read through of the play, but it is profitable to analyse further the subjects they introduce. One way of doing this is by beginning to explore Chekhov's own views on art and here I am offering some initial ways of thinking about what Chekhov may have suggested literature was for. To Chekhov, literature was not about imposing a pattern on life in order to make sense of it, but was about reflecting life as it seems to be. To him, the aim of literature was to present 'the truth, unconditional and honest', as he wrote in 1887 (quoted in Andrew, 1982, p.160). First, this meant that the temptation to render life in terms of dramatic conflicts and dénouements had to be resisted; truth, after all, is a relative, and invariably complex, concept that is dependent on perspective. As I have suggested, dramatic conflict is conspicuously absent in *The Cherry Orchard*: this goes towards explaining why.

Second, such views also affect the representation of character. If truth is a relative concept, then it can reside in the perception of more than one character, and can be shown to do so without contradiction. Thus, each of Chekhov's characters in this play is in possession of his or her bit of truth, which could be described as an individual perspective on the main theme of the play: social change. This is how the sense of Chekhov as a 'historian of small deeds' can be squared with the concept of a writer who also deals in the big ideas, such as social change. We do not see one experience of that change, or one view of it, but several. Some of these perspectives will be explored in the subsection entitled 'Working in detail with the text' below. Characters are rarely (if ever) wholly good or wholly evil in Chekhov, as this would be akin to imposing a directed plot or pattern on life that rarely exists in reality. When Lopakhin is made to be unremittingly foolish, this is more to do with the director's view of the rather simplistic needs of the audience (or perhaps his or her own needs and resultant (mis)reading of Lopakhin) than with Chekhov's view of life. Lopakhin may be a self-made man, the harbinger of death to an old regime, but what use is a cherry orchard that no longer produces cherries, or a political system that privileges those who have a thoroughly childish attitude to money?

Finally, Chekhov's ideas on art and truth can also be related to the status of comedy versus tragedy in the play (to be investigated in detail later in this chapter). In *The Cherry Orchard* both tragedy and comedy are present, often simultaneously; the one is constantly subverted by the other, suggesting that Chekhov believed that they both had a part to play in representing life (the matter of emphasis is perhaps the only contentious issue). The interplay between tragedy and comedy is described by one reviewer from the 1930s as 'the key of the play'. It is 'a comedy and a farce and a tragedy in the sense in which life is all these things, being made up of change and loss, and a certain sparkling recovery, and a grimly ludicrous, ironic, riotous play of unknown forces over it all' (in Emeljanow, 1981, p.96). In this curiously non-hierarchical sentence, the play is shown to be concerned with several seemingly contradictory aspects of life at once, without much sense of which is more important. As a further illustration of this point, turn to Act 3 of the play: while Mrs Ranevsky learns her fate and weeps, the band plays and her guests dance around her (pp.281–2).

I hope you feel that your initial responses to the play have been developed or challenged by what you have learned about Chekhov's views on art, or that you can, at least, see them in a new critical light. We must remember, though, that Chekhov's views do not provide the only relevant context for interpretation of his play.

Working in detail with the text

Read Act 1 from Mrs Ranevsky's line 'Cut it down?' (p.249), to Pishchik's 'Extraordinary thing' (p.250). In order to practise your skills in close reading, try to ascertain how many different views of the cherry orchard are contained in this short section.

The heart of the play is in this extract. It is the first time that Lopakhin mentions his modern solution to an ancient problem: the decline in the fortunes of the aristocracy. The various perspectives of the protagonists are stressed here – Lopakhin has recently said 'I feel I want to tell you something nice and cheerful' in the run up to his big idea. To those hearing his proposal, it can hardly be expected to be that.

The faith in what is 'interesting' about the cherry orchard possessed by Mrs Ranevsky and Gayev may be touching (unless you consider Mrs Ranevsky too patronizing and overbearing in her remark 'My dear man ... you don't know what you're talking about'). However, it is also bewildering to Lopakhin, who cannot register Gayev's concern for the mention of the orchard in 'the Encyclopaedia' – a symbol, perhaps, of educated intellectualism and privilege over the common good and practicality. (Chekhov may well range himself with Lopakhin here: in a letter of 1888 to a friend and mentor, Dmitry Grigorovich, he jokes, 'who knows, maybe even an encyclopedia can have its uses'; Chekhov, 1973, p.92.) Lopakhin ignores Gayev's grand statement, his interest caught by his own watch. In this glance at his watch, he demonstrates that his viewpoint is dominated instead by immediate time and the need to use it to make money. Countering Gayev, Lopakhin's position is, in its turn, also balanced by the distance of Firs's perspective. Firs is attuned to the far-away past, almost beyond memory, which is the last time the cherries produced anything financially worthwhile or edible. The past indicated by Gayev and Mrs Ranevsky is a less practical and less knowledgeable one, based on an idiosyncratic assessment of the orchard's interest. Lopakhin is calling them to the inexorable nature of the present, and to the fact of the auction.

Pishchik, however, represents an alternative, and more attractive, perspective on the present to Mrs Ranevsky, who chooses to answer his question regarding Paris rather than to respond to Lopakhin. She does so with one of those nonsensical and comic remarks that punctuates this play: 'I ate crocodiles.' (The first such remark belongs to Charlotte: 'My dog eats nuts too'; p.243.) These utterances partly serve to emphasize the distinctive and separate (and occasionally bizarre) relationship with the world that each character possesses. The reasons why Mrs Ranevsky favours talk of Paris over the future of the cherry orchard are threefold. Most obviously, it allows her to dodge the issue at hand. Paris also represents the sophisticated 'other' to the backwardness of Russia in this play (educated Russians still spoke French at this time, a sign of contemporary Francophilia) and coincides with Mrs Ranevsky's view of herself. Finally, Mrs Ranevsky's lover lives in Paris and he is the prime cause of their current financial distress.

In this scene, the modern energy of Lopakhin's idea is ultimately matched and resisted in ingenious ways by the varying aristocratic and traditionalist responses to it. The plot, therefore, does not progress in obvious ways (in ways related to a narrow conception of 'action', for example). No character is remotely persuaded to quit the narrow sphere of interest and concern that they inhabit; everyone is perfectly able to rebuff appeals made by those with different experience and perspectives. At this point, we might seem to have reached an impasse. Typically, though, Chekhov does not create this sense at all; we are merely moved on, our heads buzzing with the opposing energies and the different views on a common problem that are animated by this scene.

Having developed both an overview of the play and a more focused response to its themes and structure, we are now going to broaden our approach. In the following section, I will consider the historical and cultural contexts of the play. Addressing contexts will help us to think more about the play's reception history, and, looking forward, will help to equip us for tackling the 'key questions' addressed later in the chapter.

Chekhov and *The Cherry Orchard* in context

In most examples of its practice, literary criticism recognizes history, to a greater or lesser extent, as a significant aspect of the study of a text. 'History' can mean the political and cultural contexts that helped to generate the text, and can extend to the biography of its author. One edition of Elizabeth Gaskell's *Wives and Daughters* (1864–6), for example, claims that 'set in a provincial English town in the early nineteenth century, the novel is a subtle representation of historical change explored in human terms' (Gaskell, 1987, back cover). Though this assessment omits mention of Gaskell's biography, it suggests that the novel can most profitably be read as an illustration of the characters' experience of real social and political events in nineteenth-century England.

In the last section, I introduced the idea of Chekhov's main theme in *The Cherry Orchard* being social change. It is therefore important to know something of the political and historical context in Russia at the time he was writing, even as we retain our understanding that history – even recent history – alters according to perspective, as do the characters' perceptions in this play. Mrs Ranevsky can be expected to think differently about the emancipation of the serfs from the way Lopakhin does, just as the French Revolution looks different if you view it from the position of Marie Antoinette, or from that of a French revolutionary hero of 1789. Directors' perspectives vary in similar ways. There is more than one history; consequently, there is more than one way of defining a text's relationship to it. This issue is particularly well illustrated by *The Cherry Orchard*. The play was produced in a society that did not suffer from just one form of overt censorship, or control of literary production, but two different and powerful forms: by the state, and by the often radical literary editorial elite in charge of the 'thick journals'. However, *The Cherry Orchard* 'was almost untouched by the censor' (Andrew, 1982, p.174). I consider the reasons for this later in the chapter.

Russian contexts

Historical contexts

Even after the break-up of the Soviet Union, Russia remains the largest country in the world, spanning eleven time zones and 160 degrees of longitude (nearly halfway round the earth). It is a vast country. Size is an issue in *The Cherry Orchard*, and numerous directors of the play have recorded their attempts to ascertain the exact extent of the orchard in preparation for their productions. The orchard covers an area of about 10 square kilometres, obviously not immense in itself, but this *is* enormous for an orchard. There is a reason for this: Chekhov is indicating right from the start that the aristocracy is becoming increasingly unsustainable, like an orchard of this size (Brown, 2000, p.115).

In the still-feudal period before the setting of *The Cherry Orchard*, huge tracts of land, or estates, were owned by aristocrats like the Ranevskys. These estates were worked by serfs; a man's wealth was judged in part according to the number of 'souls' he owned. (Denied freedom of movement and other rights, a serf was a peasant under the control of the lord whose lands he or she worked.) However, in one of the most important recent historical events in Russia, serfdom was abolished in 1861 – and if Chekhov's grandfather had not bought his freedom from serfdom, Chekhov would have been born a serf a year before emancipation. From this point in time, the control of the aristocracy began to decline, although even after the emancipation, as is made clear by the play, wealthy families still owned servants. Somewhat curiously, the emancipation of the serfs is referred to by Firs as 'the troubles' (p.267), because of the way it put everything at 'sixes and sevens' (p.265). He seems to feel nostalgic about this oppressive past.

Now read 'Peasant Benefactor and Chronicler', an extract from Hingley's biography of Chekhov, *A New Life of Anton Chekhov* (Reader, Item 6). What light does Hingley's account shed on the social strata illustrated in *The Cherry Orchard*? In what ways is the situation, as represented in Chekhov's play, more complex?

The variety of characters in Chekhov's play means that we do not get the same sense of the sheer overwhelming proportion of peasants in Russian society as is depicted in the Hingley biography. (Leon Trotsky's phrase for this (as translated by Anya Bostock) is 'the colossal numerical preponderance of the peasantry'; Trotsky, [1922] 1972, p.296.) It is important to Chekhov that he illustrates all possible perspectives in his play, therefore peasants do not outnumber other characters (the one place where they might is at the end of the play, when large numbers are implied as Mrs Ranevsky and Gayev say goodbye to the workers they have employed; p.284). The situation in Chekhov's play is more complex than that represented in the extract in two ways. First, Firs does not express the unequivocal hatred of the land-owning class that we might expect – as I pointed out above, he calls emancipation 'the troubles', implying it had a negative impact on him and his position.

Second, Firs feels baffled by the ways in which he is supposed to relate to those who used to own him and for whom he still works – hence his feeling that all is at 'sixes and sevens'. The past was simple, according to Firs and his way of interpreting his place in the world; the present is complicated. This confusion spreads to the other workers from the estate. The question of the landowners' responsibility for the serfs they used to own still remains. Now, with the estate in ruins, the Ranevskys are effectively abandoning those for whom they should care. The emancipation seems to make this abandonment easier.

The theme of social change is represented in Chekhov's play in ways such as these. Firs represents the way things used to be, as do Mrs Ranevsky and, in particular, Gayev. Now, in the present, the cherry orchard is defunct; the estate is to be sold; Gayev needs to take a job in a bank to supplement his exhausted reserves.

Finally, in terms of historical contexts, as Chekhov was writing, Russia was an autocracy, led by a Christian emperor who was supported by a court of grandees (including one branch of the Tolstoys). Reform was slow. When serfdom was abolished, simultaneous attempts were made to reform the judicial system, education and local government. A far more radical attempt occurred in the form of a revolution in 1905, the year after Chekhov's death. At this point a parliament (the Duma) was established. The second, major, Russian Revolution occurred in 1917, partly because of the hardship suffered by the people in the First World War. The Romanov dynasty, headed at this time by Tsar Nicholas II, was overthrown. This revolution led to the establishment of the communist Bolshevik Soviet Union.

Cultural contexts

Considering the cultural contexts that contributed to the production of *The Cherry Orchard*, the critic Joe Andrew (1982) makes some important observations about Russian society. His comments emanate from one central point: the intensity of Russian writers' literary relationship with their contemporary society. The poet Alexander Pushkin provides an early example of what was at stake in this relationship: he was expelled from St Petersburg in 1820 for writing revolutionary epigrams, and then dismissed from the civil service in 1824 for atheistic writings. Despite the evident dangers, from the 1840s onwards, Russian intellectual thought was increasingly engaged with social issues. The debate about what literature was for – about its relationship to reality, or its status as visionary – was key. (In one extreme illustration of this continuing debate, the twentieth-century Russian composer Dmitri Shostakovich relates a slogan popular in the nineteenth century: 'A pair of boots is worth more than Shakespeare'; Volkov, 1979, preface.) Other significant writers in this debate include Tolstoy, Fyodor Dostoevsky, Ivan Turgenev and, later, Chekhov.

A contemporary political situation that stifled debate contributed to the way in which literature and the criticism of it developed into an important means of focusing dissenting energies and ideas in Russia. Turgenev's novel *Fathers and Sons*, published in 1862, caused a tumult because of its criticism of the 'Fathers' (the aristocracy) in favour of the 'Sons' (the non-aristocratic intelligentsia). Discussing the role that literature came to have, Andrew observes that 'both opposition and government' in nineteenth-century Russia 'viewed literature as a kind of "alternative government", a second voice which was able, if only indirectly, to offer some kind of challenge to established ideas and behaviour' (1982, p.x). This concept of an 'alternative government' is a powerful one – and writers such as Pushkin and Mikhail Lermontov (a writer arrested for a poem on the death of Pushkin in 1837) helped to ensure that it was current at the time.

Think about the ways in which the idea of an 'alternative government' of literature seems to apply to Chekhov's play. Bear in mind that a government does not just legislate: it also debates issues of policy and principle.

Chekhov's play can clearly be seen to raise serious social and political issues for discussion and debate. Some of these have provided the focus for this chapter. But Chekhov, as we know, seemed to resist an instrumental approach to the role of literature; he may have chosen not to contribute to the imagined alternative government in a legislative fashion. From the beginning of this chapter I have highlighted ways in which this resistance is manifested in aspects of his play: in his diagnostic stance; in the privileging of the sense of multiple perspectives; in showing the struggle with difficult questions; and in sidestepping climaxes. Andrew's description of the role of literature as an 'alternative government' therefore helps to explain why, at the end of a century in which Dostoevsky and Tolstoy wrote novels critiquing contemporary society, Chekhov's decision not to do so in his plays provoked both outrage and confusion in Russian audiences. It also goes some way towards explaining directors' choices (like those of Stanislavski) that do emphasize one aspect of *The Cherry Orchard*. As we learned at the outset of this chapter (in the review from the *Herald-Tribune*), such simplification of the play met with approval from audiences. Despite Chekhov's views, some *productions* of his play might be said to contribute to the 'alternative government' of the day. It is important to note here, however, that productions that emphasized the play's tragic qualities might be described as backward- rather than forward-looking, and would by no means have appealed to all Russian commentators.

Finally, Chekhov proved culturally provocative in another fashion too. In Russia, the nineteenth century was the time of the great realist novels, as exemplified largely by Tolstoy's *War and Peace* (1869) and *Anna Karenina* (1877), and by Dostoevsky's *Crime and Punishment* (1866) and *The Brothers Karamazov* (1880). (*Anna Karenina* would form a useful comparison to Chekhov's play.) In contrast, Chekhov wrote mainly humorous sketches and, when pushed, short stories, followed by plays. He was also a talented travel writer. His one novel, *The Shooting Party*, a detective story, was published in 1884 and has not enjoyed a central place in his oeuvre (although there have been film versions of it). Attention to genre can provide ways of answering the question 'What is literature for?' Novels, especially nineteenth-century novels, were more likely to suggest answers to the problems they described, or at least to indicate a view on the rights and wrongs of the matter. (In nineteenth-century England, writers such as Gaskell produced what became known as 'condition of England' novels for this reason.) Short stories are more open-ended, and in general less didactic. Some critics consider the short story to be a genre more suited to the modern age (this issue will be addressed in Chapter 2 in relation to Katherine Mansfield). Such can also be the case with plays.

Biographical contexts

Hingley provides a biographical account of Chekhov in the introduction to his edition of the plays. Or, at least, major biographical events are discussed as part of the analysis of contemporary works. There are, however, a few crucial points that I would like to investigate further in order to help in the approach to *The Cherry Orchard*.

Read Hingley's Introduction to Chekhov's plays, as far as '... southern Germany' (p.xxiii), then try to identify some key aspects of Chekhov's life as Hingley has presented them. Which elements were interesting or unusual to you? Which elements made you think differently about the text we are studying?

Chekhov's birth in a backwater, Taganrog, is significant, partly because of the provincial, rather than urban, perspective that this would have initially given him as an artist. It is a provincial perspective, in the main, that we are treated to in *The Cherry Orchard*. However, the town does make its presence felt in Act 2 (even though it is the most intensely rural section of the play), as does industry; Paris represents a different perspective throughout the play, one based on sophistication and, supposedly, opportunity. Tied to this aspect of his birth is Chekhov's descendance from serfs: his grandfather bought freedom for his family in 1860. Broadening this perspective were Chekhov's moves to Moscow and, later, Yalta, along with his travel to the prison island of Sakhalin, to Europe and elsewhere.

Figure 1.3 Chekhov at Melikhovo, April 1897. (© Bettmann/CORBIS.)

Chekhov's first career as a doctor is also worthy of note. Literary commentators often make much of the crossover between his two careers: as a writer he focused on detail, adopting a scientific method in the way in which he described people and places. (Boris Eichenbaum, for example, describes medicine as 'precious to him, both as a true method for obtaining knowledge of man and society, and as a scientific support for artistic observation and analysis of material'; in Jackson, 1967, p.25.) Chekhov displays this kind of detailed observation, especially perhaps in the contradictions of Mrs Ranevsky's character – look at its complex delineation in Act 1, and at the way in which her hysteria comes and goes. Both careers were necessary to Chekhov financially, at least at the beginning (see Chekhov, 1973, pp.97, 98). His writing was initially driven by the desperate need to make money, so he was market-led into humour, rather than into the serious realist and educative tomes more usually produced by his Russian literary forebears (many of whom – though not Dostoevsky – were independently wealthy, and therefore able to work with less regard for the market). These factors may have combined to produce a writer who strove for objectivity but was irreverent towards people's feelings and expectations, while still aiming to make them laugh. As we discovered at the start of this chapter, Chekhov left his readers to add 'the subjective elements' to his writing.

A further striking element to this introduction is Chekhov's transition from medicine, to short-story writing, to drama. Eventually, the first wife was replaced by the mistress, who in turn became challenged by a second mistress. (Chekhov constantly employs this metaphoric language in talking about his careers in his letters and elsewhere; see Chekhov, 1973, p.107.) This shifty approach to the question of genre, described by him in terms analogous to pleasure and disloyalty, can also be witnessed in his experimental attitude: 'I began [*The Seagull*] *forte* and finished *pianissimo*, contrary to all the laws of the theatre', he exults (Hingley, 1976, p.220). Also of note in this quotation is the musical metaphor: these abound in Chekhov. Later, Shostakovich was to describe Chekhov's plays as symphonies, written in movements (quoted in Volkov, 1979, p.172).

Overall, of course, a text is produced as a result of a hugely complex set of circumstances. It would be impossible to disentangle all these different influences, one from the other, and to identify them as distinct and visible threads in the play. Nonetheless, this section has provided you with some of the tools necessary to engage with Chekhov's play as an artefact of its time. Think back to your first encounter with the play, and see if this information has helped you to engage with it at different levels; Chekhov's multiple perspectives, and the play's mutable, and not easily definable, relationship with Russian society, should have been further explained. **As a conclusion to this section, read the extract from Smeliansky's short essay 'Chekhov at the Moscow Art Theatre' (Reader, Item 7).** This essay provides further examples of the ways in which political and cultural contexts affect works of art. Note Nemirovich-Danchenko's letter to Stanislavski, written after the 1917 Revolution, and after the Civil War, in which he says that 'they won't allow a play [*The Cherry Orchard*] which is seen to lament the lost estates of the gentry'. '*Ivanov*', he goes on to say, 'is completely out of tune with this positive, "cheerful" epoch.' It seems it was hard to perform Chekhov in Russia in 1922.

In the following section I think in more detail about the play as performance. I start by looking at the key questions that it poses, and whether there are answers to them. From this point forward the focus is on the question 'What is literature for?', as illustrated by this play.

Key questions

If you have not yet managed to see a production of the play, please try to do so before beginning this section. If this is not possible, read the play once more, trying to imagine how the play might look on the stage. As you watch, or read, think about the balance between tragedy and comedy in the play.

Tragedy or comedy?

As highlighted in the Introduction to this chapter, and by Smeliansky's essay, the issue of whether *The Cherry Orchard* is to be considered as a tragedy or as a comedy has attracted much of the critical debate surrounding the play. On 21 October 1903, after rehearsals had begun at the Moscow Art Theatre, Stanislavski sent Chekhov a telegram in Yalta. In it he wrote, 'the reading of your play to the cast has taken place. Exceptional, brilliant success. Listeners enthralled from the first act. Every subtlety praised. All wept after the last act' (quoted in Magarshack, 1972, p.191). The actors' response seems to form the logical precedent for the tears implied in the *Herald-Tribune* review (which talked of 'gesture[s] toward pocket handkerchiefs'). It was not the response for which Chekhov said he was looking: 'The last act will be very gay', he wrote to his wife, the actress Olga Knipper, in September, 'and the whole play is gay and lighthearted' (quoted in *ibid.*, pp.189–90). I now want to consider these apparently opposed readings of the play independently of each other, to see what they have to offer as ways of engaging with Chekhov's text and determining whether it is instrumental in character.

The tragic reading

Read the definition of tragedy given below. How far does this concept of tragedy match your feelings about the play?

> **Tragedy**. The term is broadly applied to literary, and especially to dramatic, representations of serious and important actions which eventuate in a disastrous conclusion for the protagonist, or chief character ... Aristotle defined tragedy [in his *Poetics*] as 'the imitation of an action that is serious and also, as having magnitude, complete in itself', in the medium of poetic language and in the manner of dramatic rather than of narrative presentation, which incorporates 'incidents arousing pity and fear, wherewith to accomplish the catharsis [or therapeutic purging] of such emotions'.
>
> (Abrams, 1957, p.212)

Two immediate issues struck me as I thought about this definition of tragedy and its relationship to the play. The first was the lack of an unambiguous central protagonist in *The Cherry Orchard*. As the play lacks this formal device, which would allow an audience closely to follow, and identify with, one character's fortunes, one might imagine that it cannot aim at tragic status. In addition, an audience cannot expect to witness the climactic 'disastrous conclusion' devoted to one character, and thus experience the resultant catharsis, normal in tragedy. And yet in some productions of the play, tragedy *was* emphasized; people wept, so directors must have found ways around this. I will consider what these might be in what follows.

The second issue that occurred to me concerns the notion of 'completeness' in a tragic drama. Aristotle's definition – still influential despite dating from the fourth century BCE – relates the level of seriousness of the subject matter to its ability to be represented as a finished product, a completed cycle of events, again allowing for the audience's experience of catharsis. In Sophocles' *Oedipus the King* (*c.*427 BCE), the text analysed by Aristotle in the *Poetics*, the climax comes as the protagonist realizes that the horrific prophesy controlling his life has come true: he has murdered his father and married his mother. He puts out his own eyes in his expression of the grief to which this has brought him. In turn, his audience must process the extraordinary and powerful emotion that has been roused, and brought to a conclusion, as the play closes. In contrast, in some ways Chekhov's play leaves us at a beginning, rather than at an ending: with Trofimov's and Anya's optimism; with Lopakhin's success; with Mrs Ranevsky's excitement at the next stage of her life. But in accordance with a tragic focus, it also offers a powerful sense of endings, from Firs's perspective, from that of Varya and, more generally, from that of the dominant aristocratic classes.

In his examination of tragedy, Abrams draws further on Aristotle's definition from the *Poetics*. The aim of arousing pity and fear in the audience is central to this concept of the genre. Though *The Cherry Orchard* presents us with more than one protagonist, and more than one perspective on the changing nature of Russia, pity at least may well be forthcoming. Viewing it through a tragic lens, we can see that each character is, in fact, accorded his or her experience of (sometimes meagre) tragedy. Such experience demands a response. The tragic potential is realized by focusing on its aspects that do reach a conclusion, as discussed above. The end of Varya's hopes for married life (where 'she sits on the floor ... quietly sobbing'; p.292) and Firs's forgotten and dedicated service represent possibilities in this respect. Finally, the arrival of characters such as Lopakhin can be seen to represent the end of a particular experience of Russia (in the *Herald-Tribune* review the point of the play was seen to be grief for the past). This experience of Russia is one that was based on aristocratic power, feudalism and serfdom.

Following on from this analysis, it makes sense to focus on the conclusion of the play for this examination of tragedy. **Reread Act 4 now.**

In Stanislavski's 'tragic' production, this act lasted for a staggering 40 minutes; Chekhov wanted it to be no longer than 12 (Chekhov quoted in Margarshack, 1972, p.192): this suggests that comedy is to be associated, in part, with a brisk tempo, and tragedy with a much slower pace. Magarshack states that in the final act Stanislavski was 'piling on the non-existent agony' (1972, p.192, footnote), acting as midwife to a grief Chekhov did not feel.

Finding the tragedy in Act 4

If you have a version of the play on video or DVD, watch Act 4 again and time it. In Richard Eyre's production for BBC television it is about 25 minutes; in a production by the Oxford Stage Company in 2003 it was more like 22 minutes. Imagine that you are a director who wants to produce the play as a tragedy. How might you find 40 minutes of action? How might you go about articulating the 'agony'? It cannot be true that it is entirely 'non-existent' as Magarshack writes, so the exercise concerns emphasizing what tragic material is there.

There is great potential for agonized time in drawing out the speeches and leave-takings. The tortuous exchange between Varya and Lopakhin on the subject of their never-to-be-realized marriage is a strong candidate for tragic treatment of this kind. Silences could be elongated, heightening the impending doom affecting the estate and the house. Tragedy, as suggested above, is more suited than other genres to lengthy broodings and attenuated soliloquies (a soliloquy is a speech delivered by a character who is alone on stage). The relative absence of soliloquies might have given you pause in this instance, but some leeway is provided by Firs's final speech. All this said, 40 minutes still seems like an inordinate time to spend on this few pages of dialogue. Elements that do not involve speech can also be investigated: action, for example, or scenery. Attention might be given to what was going on in the orchard, or to those items of furniture that, according to the stage directions, are still left. Some of these may be objects crucial to the Ranevsky outlook: the bookcase, the side table, a nursery accoutrement. The windows looking out from the nursery over the orchard have also figured strongly and evocatively in much of the play. This is the case because they symbolize the boundary between inside and outside, but being transparent they serve to draw the orchard, and thus the past, into both the domestic space and the present. Perhaps these could be brought prominently back into the action somehow, by echoing or developing Mrs Ranevsky's vision of her mother from Act 1 (p.253) (a difficult task, maybe, without speech).

Attention to the stage directions can provide more material to work with. Directors of some productions, including Eyre, choose not to realize the sounds of the peasant voices as they say their goodbyes to the family.

Remember that this event almost undoubtedly means an uncertain future for some, and an end to employment: Lopakhin has only 'taken on' Yepikhodov along with the estate (p.291).

Above all, there is the sound of the axes striking the cherry trees with which to conjure. In addition, the destruction of Russia's 'great' period of empire could be signified with the use of video footage or tableaux. Sounds were important to Chekhov; he thought the sound effects in Acts 2 and 4 should be 'shorter, much shorter' than in the version staged by Stanislavski (quoted in Magarshack, 1972, p.192). Despite his view (and after all in this exercise you are asked to be a different kind of director from Chekhov's ideal), there are possibilities here for developing the tragedy.

The focus on tragedy does not just relate to the experience of the audience in terms of the potential for catharsis, as raised by Aristotle's definition, though this is an important part of what tragic literature is for. Nor is it restricted to analysis of Act 4. There is no doubt that this focus also helps to articulate some of the most powerful themes of the play. Analysing the tragedy discretely as viewers or readers can only assist us in coming to the fullest understanding possible of Chekhov's text. Such discrete focus will allow one kind of understanding fully to emerge; this can then be complemented and challenged by a different understanding, one rooted in comedy instead. To begin this process, we will now spend some time working with the themes of the play that are most powerfully experienced through a tragic lens. These are:

- time and change;

- age;

- childhood;

- individuality.

In what ways does the play represent these themes, thus contributing to its tragic potential? For the first of them I would suggest concentrating your thoughts on the opening of the play, and on the end of Act 3; Act 1 may give you most ideas in relation to childhood. The other two themes receive treatment throughout the play.

Time and change

It is in respect of this theme that the sense of endings is, perhaps, strongest. The play opens with a forceful evocation of the process of looking back. Lopakhin uses time to indicate the ways in which he has progressed materially from his peasant status, but he remembers Mrs Ranevsky's ministrations to his child-self fondly and gracefully, and as though from a comparatively lonely and confusing adulthood. If money were everything, he should feel in control of his situation, but he does not. He has essentially retained the same character, and status, in the eyes of the disapproving societal observer that he seems to be imagining. Time is shown to be many-layered, with the changes that have come to Lopakhin doing little, in the end, to counter (at least yet) the legacy of the social system that has obtained in Russia. But time, being at this point generally held as universal, is not in favour of the Ranevskys either. (It was not until later in the modernist period that writers experimented with the notion of individual relationships with time.) 'You can't put the clock back now' (p.282), Lopakhin points out, in a key phrase, to a weeping Mrs Ranevsky after the orchard sale. He is also weeping, out of pity for her, but perhaps for himself too – indicating that in some ways their perspectives and political positions have begun to converge. It is now too late for Mrs Ranevsky to grasp the rescue that Lopakhin offered before he embarked on the next stage in his social progression (i.e. owning an estate). She was too foolish to understand the narrowness of her window of self-preservation, and the sense of danger could not penetrate a naive self-delusion (in)bred by generations of privilege. In the same scene, Lopakhin utters the heartfelt wish that 'this could all be over quickly, if our miserable, mixed-up lives could somehow hurry up and change' (p.282). Time will not accommodate him either. The tortuous nature of this period of transition is the hardest thing to bear; no character knows his or her role or future, and anxiety is a dominant emotion for those who do not seem drunk on their own restricted definition of opportunity, such as Yasha, and, differently, Trofimov and Anya.

This is another reason why the tragedy of this play is more complex than in some examples. In plays, the tragedy usually builds to a climax at the end of the play or near it (for example, when Oedipus puts out his eyes in *Oedipus the King*). In *The Cherry Orchard* that climax is attenuated, and built primarily of diffuse uncertainty. As the play closes, Charlotte, Varya and Firs are left with the necessity of finding employment (if, in fact, Firs is not left to die); the opportunities awaiting them are not presented as desirable in any way. Though Mrs Ranevsky, in her neurotic fashion, has recovered her spirits as she leaves for Paris, one wonders how long the money from the aunt will last, and one suspects that it represents merely a temporary halt to the Ranevsky decline. Even Lopakhin must last out this period of transition, and who knows whether his position will look as comfortable, and as assured, on the other side?

Age

Gayev's infirmity, and that of his sister, may well, of course, be amusing at times. It is also distressing when one considers the difficulties of the future that they face as they exit the play. Wisdom emphatically does not come with their increased years. Still naive, enfeebled, talking to bookcases and of billiards, their hold on their place in the world is tenuous – perhaps deservedly so. As this is the case, one might expect to look to the young for a sense of hope, but part of the tragedy of the play rests on a lack of implied fulfilment in key respects here. Varya loses her potential husband. The implication that this leaves her 'on the shelf', especially when this is combined with the declared intention of Anya and Trofimov that sexual love (and thus children) should not form part of their future, produces a sterile, barren atmosphere. It also has worrying implications for the future of Russia, both in a traditionalist sense that old names may die out (remember that Mrs Ranevsky's son has drowned), and in the more modern, degenerative sense that the classes are not mixing, and are not producing the offspring suited to this new age.

With this in mind, examine the photograph of the 1993 performance of *The Cherry Orchard* at the Romanian National Theatre (Figure 1.4). How would you describe the atmosphere created by the set, designed by Santa Loquasto?

Its plain whiteness could indicate purity and peace; scenography expert Arnold Aronson has suggested that this purity is more like barrenness, or sterility, because of its stark nature (2000, p.142). The white-on-white colour scheme, for him, emphasized the isolation of the characters, from one another and from their surroundings.

And so Chekhov's focus seems to be on progress to an unenlightened death ('We shall all die anyway', states Gayev; p.266), rather than on youthful and productive vitality. Indeed, it is difficult to reach another conclusion

Figure 1.4 *The Cherry Orchard*, Act 1, Romanian National Theatre (1993), directed by Andrei Serban, designed by Santo Loquasto. (Photo: Alexandra Plettenberg-Serban.)

about the play. Lopakhin, in his newly strange and transitory social position, may find it hard to attract another woman. Yasha, too, leaves Dunyasha behind without a backward glance, his mind focused on the (very short-term) material gain of remaining with Mrs Ranevsky. Charlotte is a different kind of misfit from Lopakhin. Oddly classless, she is not presented as desirable marriage material; in any case, her take on life is too original and quirky for this to appear to be a realistic future for her character. The way in which she ventriloquizes her own baby boy (p.289) – brilliantly enacted in Richard Eyre's production – and then drops the baby-shaped bundle to the floor, suddenly, to enquire about her working future is a good example of this. The tragedy in all this is that the transitional phase identified by Lopakhin needs a progressive population to push it forward. As we have seen, that population is not forthcoming; it is certainly not being produced by the characters of the play.

Childhood

Some of the most moving aspects of Chekhov's play are to do with the sense of a lost childhood. In Act 1, Mrs Ranevsky's belief that she catches sight of her mother in the orchard as she looks out of the window suggests symbolically that things would not have come to this were her mother still alive. In the exclamation of desire both for her mother and for her 'innocent childhood!' (p.253) lies the unconscious understanding that this, her vision, represents the only way of resisting the corrosive power of time. She yearns for continued protection and nourishment, showing her reluctance to grow up and take a responsible place in a difficult world. The strength of the nursery set supports this theme, and Mrs Ranevsky's obsessive relationship with some of the objects she associates with her youth further develops it. One of these objects is her brother, who, as far as we know, is unmarried. Mrs Ranevsky has outlived her husband; she can do without Varya; she has to do without her son. Gayev, however, accompanies her everywhere, a permanent reminder of her mother, of her childhood and of how things used to be. He is complicit in this arrangement: 'And now I'm fifty-one', he muses, 'unlikely as it may sound' (p.247). Attuned to their childhood, and resistant to the idea of progress, as is his sister, he is unable to recognize Lopakhin's explanation of his attainment of late middle age (as it was then): that 'time marches on' (p.247). The tragedy of this is that childhood, and innocence, cannot be rediscovered; time does indeed 'march on'. The resultant sense of loss is palpable, especially as we gradually identify the ways in which these ageing and irresponsible characters are not fitted for existence in a modern world (their relationship with money is, of course, crucial here).

Individuality

This is a brief note on a broad theme: attention to the fate of the individual characters of this play, rather than to the meaning that is made from the interaction between them, encourages a tragic focus. When Stanislavski dragged out the final act, it would have been by devoting energy to Firs's abandonment, to Mrs Ranevsky's grief at leaving the house or to Varya's rejection by Lopakhin. This is what slows down the tempo of the piece, a tempo that Chekhov affirmed should, instead, be upbeat (note again the musical analogies); he wanted the focus not on individuality, but on the sharp interactions between different types of human subject as they are thrown by a changing world.

A sound effect crucial to this play is that of the breaking string (pp.267, 294). Hahn claims that 'as soon as the sound is heard ... a whole series of changes occurs' (1977, p.28). In this tragic scheme of things, the breaking string might be said to represent a death-knell, or chaos. Often, in more tragic productions, this noise reduces all the characters to frightened or mystified silence, granting it fatal import. An audience may well respond similarly to a stage version of this kind.

Chekhov's text, in this way of seeing it, is about tragic identification, catharsis, and expressing grief for political and individual pasts that cannot be revisited, however comforting they seem from a distance. As we have seen, tragedy not only can be discerned in *The Cherry Orchard*, but can be seen to be working instrumentally too. And yet analysis of the play must also take into account its comic nature, aptly illustrated by Yepikhodov on page 2 of the text.

The comic reading

Read the definition of the comic genre given below. How far does it describe the play as you have come to understand it?

> **Comedy.** In the most common literary application, a comedy is a work in which the materials are selected and managed primarily in order to interest, involve, and amuse us: the characters and their discomfitures engage our pleasurable attention rather than our profound concern, we are made to feel confident that no great disaster will occur, and usually the action turns out happily for the chief characters.
>
> (Abrams, 1957, pp.28–9)

The immediate problem with applying this definition to Chekhov's play has in essence already been exposed by the investigation of the play's tragic potential in the previous subsection. Yet the comic angle is one that the play's author would have supported (and is illustrated in a performance in Figure 1.5). I hope that you have found some comic elements in the play as

Figure 1.5 *The Cherry Orchard*, Act 3, Vivian Beaumont Theatre (1977), directed by Andrei Serban, designed by Santo Loquasto. (Photo: George E. Joseph. © George E. Joseph.)

you have read and watched it; you will have the chance to do some detailed work on these elements shortly. First, however, we are going to think about Act 4 again.

Finding the comedy in Act 4

Now imagine you are a director who believes the play is a comedy. Try to envisage shrinking Act 4 to the 12 minutes cited by Chekhov as his comic ideal.

One way of achieving this time limit would be by presenting a farcical, Marx brothers-inspired mêlée. Rather than dwelling on speeches and leave-takings, you could push these forward with unseemly haste. No-one would be allowed to linger over their hurt feelings, Dunyasha's and Varya's chances of marriage would disappear painlessly, and a sense of animated chaos would reign, as all of the characters disperse at the end of the play without ceremony. It makes for an almost unrecognizable prospect, when compared with the tragic version of this act.

Think in more detail now. What are some of the different kinds of comedy found in this play (for example: farce – causing laughter; satire – exposing abuses or evils; wit – revealing a quick and amusing intellect; parody – using imitation humorously)?

Each of the elements of comedy mentioned in parenthesis above features in Chekhov's play. As we shall see as this discussion proceeds, investigation of these elements allows the amplification of certain themes in the play. Sometimes these are the same themes that were highlighted in the tragedy subsection, but from an alternative perspective; sometimes they will be new to our analysis.

Farce

Perhaps this is the most obvious comedic element; it is certainly the one that figures earliest in the play, with Yepikhodov's first entrance (p.242). It affects Trofimov too, as he falls down the stairs in Act 3 (p.277). Lopakhin also becomes a victim of farce in the same act, when Varya hits him over the head with a stick, mistaking him as he comes through the door for an unrepentant Yepikhodov (p.280). I am sure that you found other examples of farce, but the key question is what purpose it serves in the play. Earlier, I described farce as generically resistant to instrumentalist intent. The entrance just mentioned heralds the scene that could be the tragic climax of the play. But it seems to set an entirely different tone: the farcical element serves to diffuse any tragic tension that may have been building up. Such an introduction to Lopakhin's announcement might prevent us from seeing the sale of the estate, and his buying of it, as a tragedy. A more general possibility is that farce allows Chekhov to revel in the tendency of human nature to take itself too seriously. In the case of Trofimov, vanity will be punished when he is brought down to size by a comic fate. Varya, too, is punished in a different way for not letting Lopakhin know how she feels, and for her romantic resistance to pragmatic reality; she is reduced to violence as the only way of expressing her emotions. Yepikhodov is not vain; he, it might be argued, provides light relief instead.

Satire

Satire can be witnessed in the cruelty with which the naivety of Gayev and Mrs Ranevsky concerning money is exposed. This is the case primarily amid the pastoral 'bliss' of Act 2, but occurs throughout the play whenever Lopakhin tries to inform them of the precariousness of their position. Chekhov's anger towards the childishness and irresponsibility of the aristocracy can be felt in the ferocity with which this satire operates. (Satire is, generically, more instrumental than farce. By building up this comic aspect of his play Chekhov could have ensured it operated more rather than less instrumentally.) This anger is closely related to the theme of time and change; the refusal of Gayev and his sister to exercise some mental agility and rigour in this respect helps to mark their class in some evolutionary sense for the destruction the play indicates is coming. A more gentle function of satire is, perhaps, evident in Trofimov's Act 2 political speeches. While there is some admiration for his passion and his commitment (after all, Chekhov grants him by far the longest and most persuasive – and the only polemical – speech in the play), the satire may be present in his incompleteness. It is also present in his missed opportunity to make love to Anya in the dusk when they are alone. Obsessed at this moment with the long perspective, he does not see the beauty or desirability of the woman who is in front of his eyes. Trofimov wears glasses in most productions; one wonders whether he is thought to be long- or short-sighted. With this use of a symbolic device Chekhov is shown to satirize the overly intellectual young man.

Wit

Both Lopakhin and Trofimov can be sharp with their differently presented intellects. Their wit is apparent in quick exchanges: when Lopakhin remarks on Firs's longing for the past in Act 2, for example, or when Trofimov analyses Lopakhin's place in evolutionary progress and causes a general laugh. The wit could be there to signify what these young men might offer to the new Russia. These ideas, however, are not fully developed in the play.

Parody

Parody is perhaps one of the more interesting of the comedic offerings of this play, primarily because it encourages analysis of the wonderful Charlotte (and by extension consideration of Chekhov's portrayal and construction of gender). To Chekhov, Charlotte was one of the strongest characters in *The Cherry Orchard*. He wrote to his wife on 29 September 1903 exclaiming 'Oh, if only you'd play the governess in my play! It is the best part' (quoted in Magarshack, 1972, p.190). In terms of parody, her power is revealed in her rejection of motherhood, as she imitates it by dropping the 'baby' in Act 4. She does not fit, sociologically speaking, anywhere else either, certainly not as a governess; her energy seems to be too dangerous and otherworldly for that role. As Cynthia Marsh points out, the inability to find a 'sociological niche' is common when trying to describe Chekhov's women, particularly those who work for a living (2000, p.218). Charlotte is of indeterminate age, so cannot be fixed in this way either, and her sexuality is unclear. In short, she promotes uncertainty – and challenges reality with her magic skills and puppetry. Her existence on the edge of the world of the play serves as a challenge to tragedy and to farce, and as such she functions as an ideal Chekhovian character in this play.

Overall, in this comic scheme of things, the sound of the breaking string symbolizes mainly the brightness of change, an alteration in the energy of the time and the play that should encourage the characters to realign. The focus, rather than being on individuals and their fate (which tends to belong more to tragedy), becomes humanity's inclination to take itself too seriously, and its reluctance to adapt to changing circumstance. In keeping with this focus, the humour of *The Cherry Orchard* is, actually, rarely of a farcical kind: it tends to provoke wry smiles instead of belly laughs; it does not preclude seriousness. Most importantly, the comedy works in conjunction with the play's tragic aspects: as we have seen, it is the *balance* of this mixture that is the crucial thing. Balance means that an audience may be affected by the comedy (and be interested and amused), as well as by the tragedy (and undergo a cathartic experience). This is a difficult task for a playwright – and a director – to achieve.

In contrast to my assessment of the significance of the tragic–comic balance, one theoretical approach to the play rejects completely its tragic characteristics. The critic S.D. Balukhaty denies all those aspects of the play that might be said to figure in a tragic reading. In his close analysis of the play – first published, in Russian, in 1927 – he suggests that its structure prevents these aspects from resonating with the audience:

> The play has no dramatic plot, that is, the play has no such correlation of 'events' as would make it possible to develop or bring out the characters, or disclose the phases of their 'movement.' Therefore, there are no dramatic moments in the play. The fate of characters, their actions and behavior, are entirely motivated by common everyday situations and 'events.' The basic everyday 'event' – the sale of the estate – is predetermined from the start of the play and ... is the motive force which organises the characters and the plot structure of the play, that is, the background against which the characters unfold. There are no love themes and relationships in the play: the relationship of Trofimov to Anya is qualified as one which is not a love relationship; the relations of Lopakhin and Varya are not revealed; the love theme of Ranevskaya – of which there are clear hints – also is not spelled out in the play; the love themes of Dunyasha and Yepikhodov or of Dunyasha and Yasha come across as plain comedy, almost on the plane of parody.
>
> (in Jackson, 1967, p.140)

Finally, before I conclude this subsection, and as a way of introducing the next, it is, perhaps, in considering the end of the play that its particular comedy, as well as its tragedy, can become most evident. There are as many conclusions as there are characters, a state of affairs that can be exploited to produce a comic climax. Though there is death, or the implication of it (a common end for a tragedy), focus on this might be challenged by a series of other endings (two non-marriages, Lopakhin's travel, Pishchik's success) and loose ends (Anya and Trofimov, Mrs Ranevsky). These endings, some of which seem more like beginnings, contain comic aspects that may serve to diffuse the tragic import.

An instrumental play?

Despite the instrumentalist intent discernible through a tragic (and, more mutedly and occasionally, a comic) lens, Chekhov did not consider himself an instrumentalist writer, nor was he considered to be so by his contemporaries. This is, perhaps, because Chekhov 'undermined any belief in inevitable progress' (Bristol, 1989, p.390). His plays may have exposed societal weaknesses, and encouraged audiences to laugh at them, but the diagnosis stopped there – conspicuously short of a cure. Even more obviously tragic productions of his work, like those by Stanislavski, for example, were not seen as offering moral and political ways forward for Russia. A critic from 1949 captures the wearied tone of this kind of production in the title of his essay '*The Cherry Orchard*: A Theater-Poem of the Suffering of Change' (in Jackson, 1967, p.147). In a similar way to the work of Oscar Wilde in 1890s' Britain, Chekhov's art could be said to form a 'rejection of the purposive' (Pykett, 1995, p.19). As mentioned in the Introduction to Part 1, Wilde put it more starkly still in his Preface to *Dorian Gray*: '*All art is quite useless*' (see Reader, Item 1), so was Chekhov's art, like Wilde's, more aesthetically minded instead? No, Chekhov would not have held with the aesthetic principle of art for art's sake. He had more of a stake in realism, as Connolly suggests:

> the new approach in these years [1880–95] was that of Anton Chekhov, the 'voice of twilight Russia', as he has been called, the chronicler of the land-owning class which was becoming ever less economically viable after the liberation of the serfs in 1861, the observer of the intelligentsia which had somehow lost its spiritual moorings, a physician who could diagnose his society's ailments brilliantly, but who ... had no prescription for a cure. He chronicled the cultural and spiritual malaise of his day, but ... he lacked any 'guiding idea' in his life, unlike Tolstoy.
>
> (Connolly, 1989, pp.333–4)

Rather than thinking of Chekhov as aesthetically minded, many of his contemporaries might well have agreed with this critical assessment instead. 'Chekhov is so objective, so objective!' complained the radical A.V. Lunacharsky about *The Three Sisters* (in Jackson, 1967, p.12). The common critical position, manifested by both Connolly and Lunacharsky, holds that Tolstoy and Dostoevsky presented a cure, a 'guiding idea', whereas the pessimistic Chekhov had none to offer in a time of social instability. However, as we shall see in the remainder of this subsection, there may be ways of reading Chekhov instrumentally, ways that have nothing to do with the issues of genre as we have discussed them so far.

To see how this might be possible, consider the following questions.

- **How crucial is the role of money to the action? Who has it? Who loses it? How far does it determine the relationships between the characters, and between which characters in particular?**

- **How far are the play's outcomes determined by the sex of the characters and the ways in which they are restricted because of this?**

The play can in some ways be seen as illustrating, and advocating, major societal transformations that occur as a result of certain changes in economic structures. Money is mentioned on the first page of the text, as Lopakhin bemoans the fact that though he has money, he lacks 'class' and thus real impact in his society. As the play progresses, however, his understanding of the power that money brings is made to change. Lopakhin achieves influence, to the extent that he will not deign to marry Mrs Ranevsky's adopted daughter. In this reading, there is a kind of revolution as the climax to the play: Lopakhin gets money; Mrs Ranevsky loses it; Lopakhin moves into the 'big house'; Mrs Ranevsky emigrates. You may have decided that individual characters' relationships with money are rendered of secondary importance: it is the societal change itself that is significant. As the play closes, there has been a redistribution of wealth (remember, too, that although Pishchik is also an impoverished landowner, his ultimate wealth comes from rich England).

The play can also be interpreted as illustrating, and condemning, Mrs Ranevsky's inevitable decline in the face of patriarchy. Abused by her husband and her lover, let down by an ineffectual brother and ousted by a former male employee who benefits from the end of feudalism, this matriarch is eventually beaten by the system. Her daughters offer alternative, or corrective, models of behaviour by rejecting marriage (with greater or lesser degrees of autonomy) and childbearing. In this reading, biological sex, and cultural attitudes to it, would be taken as determining factors in the development of character and plot.

The play might be read instrumentally in other ways too. I have said that Trofimov is shown by the play to take himself too seriously, that he is sometimes blinkered and that he is mocked for these failings. But it is a gentle mockery. Although the extent of Trofimov's faith in human progress is seen to be extreme (the corrective 'Life's slipped by just as if I'd never lived at all' is almost the last line of the play; p.294), as is his belief in political solutions, we are asked to admire his characterful contributions to the debate by the way in which they are presented. Compare Trofimov's series of speeches in Act 2 (in which he does become overly romantic and starry-eyed), with that of Mrs Ranevsky that precedes them (pp.262–3). In her speech, which is inward-looking instead of outward-looking, there is real melodrama and emptiness as she narrates what seems to be someone else's story, instead of events that intricately involve her heart. By comparison, Trofimov seems inspired and forthright. It seems that Trofimov, the political idealist, offers more than we thought to an instrumentalist analysis of the play.

In his belief in revolution, and his belief in work, it is possible to interpret Trofimov as an agent of Marxist analysis in the play, thus rendering it an allegory of class struggle. Louis Althusser provides a useful description of Karl Marx's conception of the structure of society. **As you read the extract that follows, think about the ways in which it could be said to apply to** *The Cherry Orchard*.

> [Marx's] representation of the structure of every society as an edifice containing a base on which are erected the two 'floors' of the superstructure, is ... a spatial metaphor ... [T]he upper floors could not 'stay up' (in the air) alone, if they did not rest precisely on their base.
>
> ... The effect of this spatial metaphor is to endow the base with an index of effectivity ... the determination in the last instance of what happens in the upper 'floors' (of the superstructure) by what happens in the economic base.
>
> (in Tallack, 1995, pp.298–9)

This description of a metaphor is useful for providing us with a way of reading *The Cherry Orchard* instrumentally, from a Marxist perspective, as supporting and advocating change. The base of the structure is representative of the productive forces in society (the peasant classes in Russia and in the play); the upper floors house the law, the state and ideology. It helps to explain the seriousness of the anxiety produced by events in *The Cherry Orchard* (in audiences as well as in characters) when the base is imagined to be an entire class that is becoming mobile (as evidenced in Lopakhin) and destabilizing the comfortable existence of the aristocracy, or other manifestations of the state. It also helps to explain why the older generation in the play might be so completely baffled by the changes that confront it: no act, no individual human agency, could hope to arrest this full-scale shift. Trotsky, a contemporary of Chekhov, summarizes this model in comparative, yet more stark, terms: 'The historical life of every society is founded on production; that production gives rise to classes and to groupings of classes ... the state is formed on the foundations of class struggle' (Trotsky, 1972, p.332).

Lopakhin, the profiteer, is a candidate for a different kind of instrumental reading of the play, although his eloquence lags behind Trofimov's. Here, the focus is on the triumph of nascent capitalism, and the new possibility in

Russia of what might be termed a functioning meritocracy (where success is available to all who work hard). Even Mrs Ranevsky has an offering in this respect: outdone, and not meritorious, she abandons Russia and takes her remaining cash elsewhere to spend – to an environment less close to revolution, as we can say with hindsight.

The impersonality of nature and the supremacy of fate are two themes that could be said to function instrumentally. There is no 'God' in this play to show the characters how they must act or how things will proceed (just as there is no equivalent of the Tolstoyan authorial voice, no character who could be said to represent Chekhov). The lack of external authoritative influence can itself be said to be instrumental. It indicates a belief, on the part of Chekhov, in an element of passivity in human existence that he wants to show at work in his play. Mrs Ranevsky and Gayev are shown to be helpless in the face of their fate: they are unable or unwilling to adapt in order to survive social change. Varya feels she can do nothing to assert herself when it comes to her marriage, and even Yasha seems powerless when his mother comes to call in Act 4. Lesser characters, too, are helpless: Dunyasha, Yepikhodov, Firs. Anya is shown to be in thrall to Trofimov, as well as in love with him. There is an indiscriminate sense about this, especially as Lopakhin, who is the closest the play gets to a hero, cannot escape the anxiety his new status brings. His personality is not strong enough to stamp itself on his surroundings with complete credibility. Chekhov's men and women, in this reading, are locked into a series of actions and behaviours that prove a determinacy that is complex, internalized and psychological, rather than dogmatically religious or moral. It can also be read as social/biological too: the older generation is simply worn out, too enervated to fight for its continuing dominance.

In all these examples of instrumentalist potential, the *plurality* rather than the singularity of Chekhov's approach is emphasized again: this is an important reason why Chekhov's play received a 'light touch' at the hands of the censors. If it is impossible to distinguish one argument for change, or one critical stance (based on politics, or economics, or gender, for example), how would it be possible adequately to censor or to interrupt communication of it? The very structure of the play, in this respect, resists the censor's interference, and the viewing public's interpretation of what *exactly* Chekhov meant by it. It is difficult to see only one instrumental point to *The Cherry Orchard*, if indeed one sees any at all. This is very different from the kind of debate you are going to encounter in the final chapter of Part 1: some of the poets of the 1930s were more clearly instrumental in their attitudes to their art.

I have indicated in this section that there are elements of this play (including the tendency towards a comic or a tragic reading in a production) which can be interpreted as instrumentalist. These elements might suggest that Chekhov is offering a role for literature as 'purposive' after all, even if in a complex and plural fashion. In short, literature might be said to be for different things, at different times, in different productions of Chekhov's play. In *The Free State* (1999), the South African writer Janet Suzman scripted a contemporary take on Chekhov's play, illustrating its purposive potential (the title was chosen partly because the Free State is the only area of South Africa where cherries will grow). In her introduction to the play, Suzman writes of seeing *The Cherry Orchard* 'through the prism of politics' as part of celebrating the 'enticing possibility' of a post-apartheid, new South Africa (2000, p.xxii). It is important to her reading of the play that Chekhov's pre-revolutionary Russians are 'dreaming of better times' (*ibid.*, p.xxvii). In my conclusion to this chapter, I offer some final suggestions as to why Suzman's answer to the question 'What is literature for?', when reading *The Cherry Orchard*, may yet differ from Chekhov's.

What is literature for?

In Russia, as elsewhere, modernism helped to change the parameters of the debate as to what literature is for (in Russia the period 1895–1925 can be called the 'era of modernism'; Bristol, 1989, p.387). You will be investigating aspects of modernism in more detail in the next chapter of this book and throughout Part 2, but as we come to the end of this chapter on Chekhov, a basic understanding of the concept of modernism will help us to make some final observations regarding Chekhov's play, and the reasons he wrote it in the way that he did.

The dates 1895–1925, proposed by Bristol as marking the beginning and end of modernism in Russia, obviously relate to the period at the end of Chekhov's writing life. But dates used in this fashion tend to suggest that ideas spring out of nowhere, and must be treated with caution. Questions to do with genre, structure, subject and whether art was for its own sake or for something else – questions that were associated with modernist movements – are broached by Chekhov and acknowledged in his drama and his prose. In addition, many writers associated with modernism took a stand on the role of literature that Chekhov would have recognized and often endorsed. Literature, to modernist writers such as Joseph Conrad, Ford Madox Ford and Virginia Woolf, was for representing life in all its turbulent, confusing, contradictory plurality. It was also for focusing on the individual's often alienating experience of life.

As a related but separate addition to the debate in Russia, six years before the first performance of *The Cherry Orchard* Tolstoy published 'What is Art?', a treatise dedicated to a moral and religious vision of art. (Tolstoy's religious vision was a development late in his life and career: it repudiated the novels for which he is famous.) In it, he sounds like the Plato discussed in the Introduction to Part 1 of this book. 'What is Art?' argued that permissible themes for art were 'the eternal ones, those that elevated man to a higher awareness of life and taught him the underlying moral truths of human existence' (quoted in Andrew, 1982, p.113). It categorized works of art according to the feelings that they evoked. 'In the highest category', according to Julian Connolly's summary of Tolstoy's view, was ' "Christian" art – art transmitting feelings flowing from a religious perception of our filial relationship to God and our fraternal relationship to our fellow humans' (1989, p.341). This treatise has been described as the 'most notorious example of Russian antiaesthetics' (Morson, 1986, p.24) – as far as it is possible to travel from the aesthetic view that art is for art's sake alone. Chekhov would always have had difficulty with Tolstoy's perspective. In 1888, he wrote of himself as having 'no political, religious and philosophical views' (quoted in Hingley, 1976, p.119; see also Chekhov, 1973, p.109). His opinion of Tolstoy's treatise is given below:

> Judging from the excerpt printed in *New Times*, Lev Nikolayevich [Tolstoy]'s article on art is of no particular interest. It's all so old hat. Saying that art has grown decrepit and entered a blind alley, that it isn't what it ought to be, and so on and so forth is like saying that the desire to eat and drink has gone out of date, outlived its usefulness, and is no longer necessary. Of course hunger is old hat and the desire to eat has led us into a blind alley, but eating is necessary all the same, and we will go on eating no matter what fortunes our philosophers and angry old men dream up for us in their clouded crystal balls.
>
> (Chekhov, 1973, p.312)

Chekhov did not think much of Tolstoy's moral fervour, or of his vision for art's purpose – as far back as 1888 he anticipated with horror literature 'falling prey to a thousand score false doctrines' (Chekhov, 1973, p.97). In return, it is hard to imagine a production of *The Cherry Orchard* – even a tragic production – that would have rated highly in Tolstoy's system. In fact, Tolstoy wrote to Chekhov, notifying him that 'I cannot abide Shakespeare, but your plays are even worse' (quoted in Morson, 1986, p.24). Chekhov would not have intended *The Cherry Orchard* to rate in Tolstoy's system. 'Truth', for Chekhov, depended on experience and perspective, it was not an underlying given that he felt charged to communicate. As we have approached Chekhov and his writing, he has been seen to make his stance outside Tolstoy's view of the role of literature in three main ways: by writing plays (and short stories) not novels; by writing the kind of play that he did in *The Cherry Orchard*; by directing his attention to ideas associated with modernism.

Drama can be described as a democratic genre: it can allow for, and positively encourage, the manifestation of multiple points of view and debate. Drama thrives on conflict, not on religious certainty nor, for that matter, on fraternity. Used in a particular way, and because of these characteristics, it can serve to heighten a sense of insecurity about what the viewer of the work of art is supposed to think. Drama is also a performance genre. This means that, unlike in the novel or the short story, numerous mediating influences become involved in its reception: directors, designers, producers and actors, as well as the audience (the pluralistic and sometimes unpredictable equivalent of the reader of a novel). The question of what the work of art is for can therefore be answered in one way, or in a variety of ways, by the playwright, and then later on by others in different ways. Hence, in drama that answer is often complex, and with certain famous exceptions (such as the plays of George Bernard Shaw) almost never doctrinal.

Other plays that Chekhov wrote were not quite like *The Cherry Orchard*, and, perhaps more importantly, they did not end in the same way. Although audiences were unhappy at the first productions of *Ivanov*, because Chekhov 'came nowhere near to condemning Ivanov outright' (Hingley, 1976, p.91), they at least had the comparative certainty of a tragic ending. (It is with *Uncle Vanya* that Chekhov's *penchant* for what has been nicely termed ' "zero" endings' began; Connolly, 1989, p.363.) At the climax of *Ivanov* the protagonist – and in contrast to *The Cherry Orchard* there *is* a clear protagonist here – '*Runs to one side and shoots himself*' (Chekhov, 1998, p.63). In *The Cherry Orchard*, there seem to be as many endings as there have been characters on stage. Chekhov's design in this later play perhaps privileges the experience of political, social and historical diversity. Not only do Trofimov's understanding of the past and vision of the future differ radically from those of Mrs Ranevsky, and of Lopakhin, but they all only mean something in

Figure 1.6   *The Cherry Orchard*, Act 4, Moscow Art Theatre (1904), directed by Konstantin Stanislavski. (Moscow Art Theatre Museum.)

relation to one another. As these characters are forced to encounter one another in Chekhov's play, the differences between them provide a lesson into the way that the world works according to perspective. Chekhov's position, and the reasons for it, seem to render absurd the belief in a simplistic moral vision of the kind projected by Tolstoy. For Chekhov, art is not for showing God, but for knowing earth and those who inhabit it. He chooses a genre that will help him in his pursuit of this knowledge, in all its complexity.

In the same way, Chekhov displays his affiliation to modernist ways of conceptualizing the world in art. Modernism, in its development from the late nineteenth century, placed emphasis on the plural rather than the singular, on impression rather than dogma, on fragmentation rather than wholeness. 'Everything in this world is changing,' Chekhov wrote in 1886, 'everything in this world is mutable, approximate, and relative' (quoted in Hahn, 1977, p.311). For Chekhov, the role of literature was not to disguise this mutability and relativity, but to revel in it instead.

Works cited

Abrams, M.H. (1957) *A Glossary of Literary Terms*, Orlando, FL: Harcourt Brace.

Allen, D. (2000) *Performing Chekhov*, London: Routledge.

Andrew, J. (1982) *Russian Writers and Society in the Second Half of the Nineteenth Century*, London: Macmillan.

Aronson, A. (2000) 'The Scenography of Chekhov', in V. Gottlieb and P. Allain (eds), *The Cambridge Companion to Chekhov*, Cambridge: Cambridge University Press, pp.134–8.

Austen, J. ([1816] 2003) *Emma*, ed. and intro. by F. Stafford, Penguin Classics, London: Penguin.

Brahms, C. (1976) *Reflections in a Lake: A Study of Chekhov's Four Greatest Plays*, London: Weidenfeld & Nicolson.

Bristol, E. (1989) 'Turn of a Century: Modernism, 1895–1925', in C.A. Moser (ed.), *The Cambridge History of Russian Literature*, Cambridge: Cambridge University Press, pp.387–457.

Brown, E. (2000) '*The Cherry Orchard*', in V. Gottlieb and P. Allain (eds), *The Cambridge Companion to Chekhov*, Cambridge: Cambridge University Press, pp.111–20.

Chekhov, A. (1951) *Plays*, ed. and trans. by E. Fen, Penguin Classics, London: Penguin.

Chekhov, A. (1973) *The Letters of Anton Chekhov*, ed. by S. Karlinsky, London: The Bodley Head.

Chekhov, A. (1998) *Five Plays*, ed. and trans. by R. Hingley, Oxford World's Classics, Oxford: Oxford University Press.

Connolly, J. (1989) 'The Nineteenth Century: Between Realism and Modernism, 1880–95', in C.A. Moser (ed.), *The Cambridge History of Russian Literature*, Cambridge: Cambridge University Press, pp.333–86.

Dromgoole, D. (2003) 'Translations', The Oxford Stage Company's programme for *The Cherry Orchard* at the Oxford Playhouse.

Emeljanow, V. (ed.) (1981) *Chekhov: The Critical Heritage*, London: Routledge & Kegan Paul.

Gaskell, E. ([1864–6] 1987) *Wives and Daughters*, ed. and intro. by A. Easson, The World's Classics, Oxford: Oxford University Press.

Hahn, B. (1977) *Chekhov: A Study of the Major Stories and Plays*, Cambridge: Cambridge University Press.

Hingley, R. (1976) *A New Life of Anton Chekhov*, Oxford: Oxford University Press.

Hingley, R. (1998) 'Introduction', A. Chekhov, *Five Plays*, Oxford World's Classics, Oxford: Oxford University Press.

Jackson, R.L. (ed.) (1967) *Chekhov: A Collection of Critical Essays*, Englewood Cliffs, NJ: Prentice Hall.

Lang, B. and Williams, F. (eds) (1972) *Marxism and Art: Writings in Aesthetics and Criticism*, New York: Longman.

Magarshack, D. (1972) *The Real Chekhov: An Introduction to Chekhov's Last Plays*, London: George Allen & Unwin.

Marsh, C. (2000) 'The Stage Representation of Chekhov's Women', in V. Gottlieb and P. Allain (eds), *The Cambridge Companion to Chekhov*, Cambridge: Cambridge University Press, pp.216–27.

Morson, G.S. (ed.) (1986) *Literature and History: Theoretical Problems and Russian Case Studies*, Stanford, CA: Stanford University Press.

Nunn, T. (2000) 'Notes from a Director: *Three Sisters*', in V. Gottlieb and P. Allain (eds), *The Cambridge Companion to Chekhov*, Cambridge: Cambridge University Press, pp.101–10.

Pykett, L. (1995) *Engendering Fiction*, London: Edward Arnold.

Reid, J. (2002) 'The Cherry Orchard', in R. Clark, E. Eliot and J. Todd (eds), *The Literary Encyclopedia and Literary Dictionary* [online], The Literary Dictionary Company Limited. Available from: http://www.literarydictionary.com [accessed 26 August 2004] (to reach this essay select 'One work' from the home page, then search for *The Cherry Orchard*).

Sophocles (1986) *The Theban Plays*, trans. and intro. by D. Taylor, Methuen's World Dramatists, London: Methuen.

Suzman, J. (2000) *The Free State: A South African Response to Chekhov's 'The Cherry Orchard'*, London: Methuen.

Tallack, D. (ed.) (1995) *Critical Theory: A Reader*, London: Harvester Wheatsheaf.

Trotsky, L. ([1922] 1972) *1905*, trans. by A. Bostock, Harmondsworth: Penguin.

Volkov, S. (ed.) (1979) *Testimony: The Memoirs of Dmitri Shostakovich*, trans. by A. Bouis, London: Hamish Hamilton.

Wilde, O. ([1890] 1998) *The Picture of Dorian Gray*, ed. by I. Murray, Oxford World's Classics, Oxford: Oxford University Press.

Further reading

Benedetti, J. (1990) *Stanislavski: A Biography*, London: Methuen. This title provides much useful information about the theatrical contexts for Chekhov's dramatic art.

Chekhov, A. (1923) *The Cherry Orchard, and Other Plays*, ed. and trans. by C. Garnett, London: Chatto & Windus.

Chekhov, A. (1985) *The Cherry Orchard*, adapted by D. Mamet, New York: Grove. Both these titles may be of interest to those who would like to investigate and to compare other versions of the play.

Chekhov, A. (1991) *The Steppe and Other Stories*, ed. by R. Hingley, Oxford: Oxford University Press. A good collection of Chekhov's short stories, providing an opportunity to compare his dramatic and prose works.

Figes, O. (1997) *A People's Tragedy: The Russian Revolution 1891–1924*, London: Pimlico. A valuable study for those who would like to know more about the political and social contexts for Chekhov's work.

Styan, J.L. (1971) *Chekhov in Performance: A Commentary on the Major Plays*, Cambridge: Cambridge University Press. A useful text for those who want to continue to investigate performance choices in Chekhov.

Wilson, E. ([1943] 1973) *A Window on Russia*, London: Macmillan.
    A short, accessible and conversational introduction to Russian
    language and culture; it includes a section on Chekhov.

CHAPTER 2

The stories of Katherine Mansfield

DELIA DA SOUSA CORREA

Overview

In this chapter, a selection of Mansfield's stories is discussed in detail, while others are referred to more briefly. The main works that feature here are, first, three early stories, 'Frau Brechenmacher Attends a Wedding', 'How Pearl Button Was Kidnapped' (both 1910) and 'The Woman at the Store' (1912). In these we can see Mansfield developing the fusion of realist and Symbolist techniques that structures her later work; her pervasive interest in the effects of gender difference is also evident. The readings of these stories introduce the question of how we read Mansfield in relation to the debates over aesthetic and instrumental views of literature, framed by the question 'What is literature for?' 'Prelude' (1918), the next story considered, marks an important point in a move by Mansfield away from conventional plot structures. 'Bliss' (1918) provides a focus for discussion of the pleasures of reading. There is discussion, too, of Mansfield's use of irony and her typically modernist emphasis on moments of revelation, or 'epiphany'. Two late works, 'The Daughters of the Late Colonel' and 'At the Bay' (both 1921), show Mansfield refining techniques developed in her earlier stories. Further stories alluded to in the course of the chapter are 'Je ne parle pas français' (1919), 'Sun and Moon' (1920), 'Miss Brill' (1920), 'Marriage à la Mode' (1921), 'The Garden Party', 'The Fly' and 'The Doll's House' (all 1922). It will of course be an advantage to read other Mansfield short stories to enrich your study of her work.

Introduction

> Over there on the weed-hung rocks that looked at low tide like shaggy beasts come down to the water to drink, the sunlight seemed to spin like a silver coin dropped into each of the small rock pools. They danced, they quivered, and minute ripples laved the porous shores. Looking down, bending over, each pool was like a lake with pink and blue houses clustered on the shores; and oh! the vast mountainous country behind those houses – the ravines, the passes, the dangerous creeks and fearful tracks that led to the water's edge. Underneath waved the sea-forest – pink thread-like trees, velvet anemones, and orange berry-spotted

weeds. Now a stone on the bottom moved, rocked and there was a glimpse of a black feeler; now a thread-like creature wavered by and was lost. Something was happening to the pink waving trees; they were changing to a cold moonlight blue. And now there sounded the faintest 'plop'. Who made that sound? What was going on down there? And how strong, how damp the seaweed smelt in the hot sun. ...

(Mansfield, 2002, p.297; unless otherwise stated, all subsequent page references are to this edition)

This is a passage from Katherine Mansfield's late story 'At the Bay'). 'Late' and 'mature' are adjectives applied to the stories that Mansfield wrote in the last years of her life, before her death from tuberculosis in 1923 at the age of thirty-four. By this date, she had transformed the short story in English. 'She had the same kind of directive influence on the art of the short story as Joyce had on the novel', declared Ian Gordon in his 1954 contribution to the British Council's 'Writers and their Work' series. 'After Joyce and Katherine Mansfield neither the novel nor the short story can ever be quite the same again' (1954, p.17). In 1957, the novelist and short-story writer Elizabeth Bowen reflected that Mansfield would, had she lived, have been a woman of sixty-nine. Her literary experimentation, as much as her premature death, meant that 'a fellow writer cannot but look on Katherine Mansfield's work as interrupted ... Page after page gives off the feeling of being still warm from the touch, fresh from the pen. Where is she – our missing contemporary?' (Bowen, 1957, p.10). Assessing her still-crucial development of a particular strand of the short story, Bowen wrote:

> We owe to her the prosperity of the 'free' story: she untrammelled it from conventions and, still more, gained for it a prestige till then unthought of. How much ground Katherine Mansfield broke for her successors may not be realized. Her imagination kindled unlikely matter; she was to alter for good and all our idea of what goes to make a story ... The effort she was involved in involves us – how can we feel her other than a contemporary?
>
> (Bowen, 1957, pp.15, 26)

The passage from 'At the Bay' quoted above displays many of the features noticed by critics of Mansfield's work from the time of her stories' first publication: the creation of mood and atmosphere through a concentrated, rhythmic use of language; an emphasis on colour and sensory perception; an unnerving skill in representing situations and landscapes as if through the minds of her fictional characters. The vantage point here is implicitly that of the child Kezia, who – along with other members of the Burnell family – features in several of Mansfield's New Zealand stories. Mansfield's anthropomorphic animation of an underwater world of houses and ravines,

Figure 2.1   Anne Estelle Rice, *Portrait of Katherine Mansfield*, 1918, oil on canvas, 66 × 52 cm. (Museum of New Zealand/Te Papa Tongarewa. © Estate of Anne Estelle Rice.)

where 'black feelers' and 'thread-like creatures' are glimpsed moving about, lends her account a slightly uncanny quality and enhances the sense of a child's perception: 'Who made that sound?' The ellipsis at the end of the paragraph is Mansfield's own, suggesting the incomplete thought patterns of her character. Mansfield's interiorized style of writing, often labelled 'free indirect discourse', has parallels in the techniques used in some of the famous landmarks of modernist fiction, including Virginia Woolf's *Mrs Dalloway* and James Joyce's *Ulysses*, where the perceptions of the characters, rather than the sequential events of plot, move the narrative along. In the next chapter, David Johnson uses the related term 'internal focalization' to describe the similar technique of Lewis Grassic Gibbon in *Sunset Song*. However, *Ulysses* (together with T.S. Eliot's *The Waste Land*) was published in 1922, when Mansfield had only months to live, and *Mrs Dalloway* was not published until 1925. Mansfield had been experimenting with stories that dispensed with conventional plots since her teens; her technical innovations in her published works frequently preceded those of other modernist writers.

Mansfield is not a forgotten, nor a particularly neglected, writer. Her stories have remained popular and in print, and her biography has proved a source of constant fascination. Angela Smith provides a useful account of Mansfield's life in her introduction to the *Selected Stories* (2002), in which she emphasizes the importance of the experience of colonial life for Mansfield's writing. During the decades following her death, Mansfield's reputation was shaped by her husband, John Middleton Murry, who edited and published her letters and other writings. Subsequent critics have felt the need to 'rescue' Mansfield from reductively biographical readings of her work and especially from the legend created by Murry. More recent biographies and authoritative editions of her letters and notebooks have made possible a more complete and independent picture of her life and work. Meanwhile, criticism has increasingly tried to move beyond reading her stories for their biographical interest, or for their purely formal qualities, to consider their wider literary and historical context, although the extent and nature of this engagement remains open to debate.

The originality of Mansfield's writing is not generally disputed, but many critics feel that the full extent of her innovation, its influence on other writers and thus of her contribution to literary modernism has been insufficiently acknowledged. 'Mansfield's contributions to the development of modern fiction have been largely taken for granted', comments Sydney Janet Kaplan: 'Her innovations in the short-fiction genre ... have been absorbed and assimilated – often unconsciously – by writers and readers of the short story' (1991, pp.2–3). Mansfield's most significant innovations in Kaplan's view are 'the "plotless" story, the incorporation of the "stream of consciousness" into the content of fiction, and the emphasis on the psychological "moment" ' (*ibid.*, p.3), aspects of her writing that I will consider in my discussion of her stories.

Although there are numerous individual studies of her work, Mansfield tends not to feature in major accounts of the development of modernism. However, she has become particularly important to feminist critics, who see her non-appearance in accounts of the evolution of modernism in relation to a wider neglect of the full contribution to modernism made by women. Their reassessments are designed to show that 'women are at the center rather than the margins of British modernism, and this is no less the case with Katherine Mansfield than it is with Virginia Woolf' (Kaplan, 1991, p.6).

While the beauty of her language and her use of complex symbolism have always been appreciated by critics, the extent to which Mansfield's stories may also be read as providing a critique of her society has been emphasized in more recent analysis of her work. Feminist critics have turned with increasing interest to Mansfield's earliest published stories, written in a more overtly satirical vein than her later, lyrical works, to suggest that the more political concerns apparent in these stories continue to underpin Mansfield's later writing. Other recent accounts of Mansfield's work have also been keen to refute the once-prevailing view of her as 'indifferent to political and social controversy' (Garver, 2001, p.225).

In this chapter I consider a selection of Mansfield's stories in roughly chronological order. This will give us the opportunity to look closely at the techniques that Mansfield developed to revolutionize the short-story form. I also consider the question of how much political engagement can be discerned in Mansfield's work and how this relates to the categories of 'aesthetic' and 'instrumental' art that are explored in the Introduction to Part 1 of this book.

Gender and satire: 'Frau Brechenmacher Attends a Wedding'

I begin with 'Frau Brechenmacher Attends a Wedding', a story from Mansfield's first published collection, *In a German Pension* (1911). The stories collected as *In a German Pension* first appeared during 1910 in the radical journal *New Age*, edited by the philosopher A.R. Orage. By this stage, Mansfield had already put herself through a considerable apprenticeship as a writer. Her previous publications included stories for journals in New Zealand, Australia and Britain; her unpublished work included poetry, fictional vignettes and an unfinished novel. The South African writer Beatrice Hastings, Orage's collaborator and lover, encouraged Mansfield to develop the gift for satire that is particularly evident in the stories of this collection. The title *In a German Pension* echoes that of the highly successful *Elizabeth and her German Garden* (1898) by Mansfield's cousin Elizabeth von Arnim, who had married into the German aristocracy. Mansfield had moved to London three years previously in order to establish herself as a writer and may have intended her title to signal her own arrival as an author worthy of notice. Von Arnim's treatment of German family life is rather more gently satirical than Mansfield's, although *The Caravaners* (1909) is merciless in its ridicule of a humourless German baron, relishing his discomfort when his dutiful wife becomes less blindly deferential as the result of her contact with a lively group of English people on a camping holiday. Published before the First World War, the balance of satire in Mansfield's 'German Pension' stories also seems weighted as much against relations between men and women as against German national characteristics. **Read 'Frau Brechenmacher Attends a Wedding' now. To what extent is it a satirical story? (You may find it useful here to look back over the discussions of satire in Chapter 1.)**

Through its openly satirical portrayal of Herr Brechenmacher, and the wedding that the couple attend, the story mocks conventions of domestic bliss. You may also reflect that satire here does not rule out sympathy – for the oppressed Frau, for the daughter whom she is training to follow in her footsteps and for the unhappy bride who already has an illegitimate daughter and has been coerced into the marriage. (Arguably the Herr, who returns home late from his work as a postman, is himself the brutalized product of an oppressive society, although his representation in the story makes it difficult to feel much sympathy for him.) The story follows the couple as they prepare to attend a wedding. On her first trip outside the house for several weeks, presumably since the birth of her fifth child, Frau Brechenmacher struggles to keep up with her husband as they set out along the icy road to the function room of the local inn. The Frau's initial expectation of enjoyment diminishes as she looks across at the bride who is 'in a white dress trimmed with stripes and bows of coloured ribbon, giving her the appearance of an iced cake all ready to be cut and served in neat little pieces to the bridegroom beside her' (p.5). From this point, the irony with which the reader has been invited to view the diligent 'little Frau' increasingly modulates into sympathy for her situation. Wedged between two other women, who have added to her discomfort by pointing out that, having dressed in the dark passage to allow her husband more space, she has left her petticoat strings showing at the back of her dress, the Frau briefly forgets her domestic trials as the dance music plays. She is rudely jolted into a sense of reality and alienation by her husband's crass wedding-speech and the practical joke with which he insults the bride, offering her a coffee-pot that contains a baby's bottle and two toy cradles. On the bleak walk home the Frau utters the first direct protest against her role: 'Na, what is it all for?' (p.8). The sense of menace implicit in the wedding scene emerges in disturbing memories of her own wedding night.

Perhaps you sensed a level of violence and anger that runs throughout this story, culminating in the violence associated with its closing image. 'Frau Brechenmacher Attends a Wedding' is the story from *In a German Pension* most often reprinted in selections of Mansfield's work. Its satire is darker than that of the rest of the collection and it is easy to see why feminist studies have focused on stories such as this. Indignation at the stupidity of conventional gender roles is foregrounded in Mansfield's early fiction, which is 'both more overtly aggressive and more obviously politically embattled than the later work' (Fullbrook, 1986, p.35). Unlike Virginia Woolf, Mansfield did not leave a body of theoretical and critical writing specifically concerned with questions of gender. However, it is impossible to miss the thematic importance of such issues in 'Frau Brechenmacher', and similar concerns arguably underpin much of Mansfield's later work. In thinking about the tone of the story, you may have begun to think about *how* Mansfield's story achieves its impact. **From whose point of view is the story told? How are its satirical effects and sense of menace achieved?**

The story is told in the third person, and is not without some of the ironic distance that this narrative voice permits, yet readers experience the story through Frau Brechenmacher's eyes. Mansfield manages to achieve sophisticated effects while conveying the perceptions of an unsophisticated character. Reflecting on the wedding scene, Smith comments that 'The narrative perspective modulates in and out of Frau Brechenmacher's vision, but the overall impression is that the text sees as she sees, and what she perceives here is violent' (2000, p.62).

Given the force of satire in the story, it is perhaps surprising to realize how little of this is the product of direct narrative statement. There is some overt satire levelled against Herr Brechenmacher by the narrator: for example, in the phrase '[he] so far forgot his rights as a husband as to beg his wife's pardon for jostling her against the banisters' (p.4). However, the main perspective throughout is that of the Frau, who questions her role only at the end of the story. Before this, her chief comment is the meek affirmation that 'Girls have a lot to learn' (p.7). Yet the sense of outrage denied to this character is alive in the text. It emerges indirectly, as an effect of Mansfield's method of writing, rather than from direct comment by the narrator or characters.

This sense of anger and indignation that emanates from the text is built up through the emphasis on particular details. The bride is like a cake waiting to be cut into pieces. Images of this bride, her illegitimate daughter, the grim mother who has forced her into the marriage (and whose masculine beer-spitting is echoed in the picture of Herr Brechenmacher 'gesticulating wildly, the saliva spluttering out of his mouth as he talked') are juxtaposed with snatches of dialogue to produce a vividly patterned and dramatic account of the scene (pp.6, 7). Mansfield's stories are meticulous in their observation of detail, uniting what Bowen described as 'factual firmness' with symbolic depth (1957, p.20).

Mansfield's expressive use of objects and gestures shows her employing techniques learned from the study of Symbolist writers: Oscar Wilde was an important early influence and, as T.S. Eliot was later to do, Mansfield read Arthur Symons's work on the French Symbolists, *The Symbolist Movement in Literature* (discussed in relation to Eliot in Chapter 5). Many of Mansfield's first published works were 'vignettes' – prose poems characterized by conspicuously symbolic descriptions of flowers and other natural detail, the Symbolist patterning of the prose extending to a syntax characterized by the use of phrases that balance and echo each other. The techniques that she practised in these vignettes and in many of her notebook writings are incorporated in less explicit ways into her story-writing. This is perhaps most apparent in more 'poetic' passages, such as the paragraph from 'At the Bay' with which I began, with its overt patterning of phrase and imagery. However, even within the 'realist' mode of *In a German Pension*, Mansfield

makes use of Symbolist patterning to structure her story: Herr Brechenmacher's prank with the baby's rattle and toys in the coffee-pot is echoed by the
later surfacing of his wife's suppressed anger about her own wedding night
and the life of domestic servitude that has followed. Objects and actions
become emblematic, their meaning emerging indirectly, but so powerfully
that, in the reader's mind, the text explodes with the anger that is muffled in
its docile protagonist.

Mansfield concludes her story by selecting one overwhelmingly
expressive gesture as the Frau 'lay down on the bed and put her arm across
her face like a child who expected to be hurt as Herr Brechenmacher lurched
in' (p.9). 'It is the *manner* of writing that posits an alternative response to the
familiar situation of the woman in the story', suggests Kate Fullbrook:
'Mansfield is testing a kind of writing that is suited to suggesting complex
responses to the reader while the narrative surface remains simple ... It
neither denies the sordidness of women's history nor accepts it as the only
paradigm for the future; it initiates a new register in women's satire' (1986,
p.57). For Fullbrook, Mansfield's analysis of gender in this story has an effect
akin to the ethical and political provocation traditionally at the heart of satire
(a serious moral purpose has formed the conventional defence of satire from
its beginnings in ancient Greece and Rome and, in English, by John Dryden,
Alexander Pope, Jonathan Swift and others). The critic Ian Jack comments
that 'Satire is born of the instinct to protest; it is protest become art' (quoted
in Cuddon, 1992, p.828). Satire continues to modulate the lyricism of
Mansfield's later stories. How far her writing offers a protest that might allow
us to think of her stories as having instrumental qualities is something I will
pause to consider after discussing three further examples of her early work.

Mansfield has often been described as a disciple of Chekhov, whose
stories she knew and loved. Indeed, one of Mansfield's 'German Pension'
stories, 'The Child who Was Tired' (1910), is a close reworking of Chekhov's
'Sleepy' (1888). The correspondences between these two stories has
provoked debate over whether Mansfield was guilty of plagiarism, but has
also led critics to focus on the differences that distinguish the two writers'
styles, even when working with the same material. Both wrote open-ended
stories that assert the profound importance of the apparently ordinary. Both
made use of highly expressive imagery, rather than plot, to portray individual
psychology and complex relationships. However, the highly wrought
symbolic structures of Mansfield's writing set it apart from Chekhov's less
systematic use of imagery in his stories. In her pioneering 1952 study of
Mansfield, Sylvia Berkman stressed the differences as well as similarities
between the two writers, finding in Mansfield a particular intensity generated
by her use of more poetic imagery, strong colour and such modernist
techniques as flashback and interior monologue (1952, pp.155–8). More

recent critics have also tended to emphasize contrasts between Mansfield's modernist style and the more dominant realism of Chekhov's fiction (see Hanson and Gurr, 1981, pp.19, 33–4).

Mansfield's innovative marriage of symbolism and realism allows her to develop a prose style that is both concentrated and uncluttered. Every word or phrase of the surface narrative of her stories also has symbolic resonance. The effect on the reader is powerful and immediate, if less than easy to analyse. Like 'Frau Brechenmacher Attends a Wedding', the next story which we are going to consider demonstrates that it is a mode of writing well suited to the sophisticated representation of unsophisticated perceptions. As the passage from 'At the Bay' with which I began also illustrates, this skill in generating stories as if through the eyes of her characters is a feature of Mansfield's writing that she continued to refine in subsequent stories. Her letters and journals frequently describe an intense empathy with the people and objects that she writes about, an empathy that passes beyond simple identification to 'the moment when you are *more* duck, *more* apple or *more* Natasha than any of these objects could ever possibly be, and so you *create* them anew' (Mansfield, 1984–96, vol.1, p.330).

Points of view and questions of race: 'How Pearl Button Was Kidnapped'

In 'How Pearl Button Was Kidnapped', another story written in 1910, Mansfield begins by choosing vocabulary which indicates that the story is told from the viewpoint of a very young child, banished from her 'House of Boxes' by a mother who is 'ironing-because-its-Tuesday' (p.20). **Read this story now. How does Mansfield convey a child's vision and what do the child's perceptions reveal to the adult reader of the story?**

Mansfield's most obvious technique here is the specific, perhaps dangerously near-sentimental, childlike phraseology that she uses to describe the 'sunshiny day' on which Pearl Button amuses herself singing a 'small song' and reflecting that the clouds of dust disturbed by the wind 'are like when mother peppered her fish and the top of the pepper came off' (p.21). Frequently, the structure of sentences underpins this effect: Mansfield uses short, simple sentences to convey Pearl's observations of her journey – 'Then the country came.' (*ibid.*) – and her first experience of paddling in the sea – 'She paddled in the shallow water. It was warm. She made a cup of her hands and caught some of it' (p.23). Throughout the story, a child's view of events predominates. The setting is Mansfield's native New Zealand. At some point in the narrative, the adult reader realizes that the two barefoot women who approach Pearl as she swings on the gate are Maori. Pearl herself is aware that they are 'dark' and different in various ways, but is not consciously aware of their race (p.20). Taking her with them to their communal meeting-place, her 'kidnappers' treat her with kindness, helping her to overcome her fear of disapproval as she dribbles peach-juice down her dress, and then her initial terror at her first sight of the sea. Pearl wonders at the freedom of their life: ' "Haven't you got any Houses of Boxes?" ... "Don't you live in a row?" ' (p.22). Arriving at their village, the two women release Pearl from her restrictive clothing and she joins them digging for shellfish on the beach.

Through the child's perception, Mansfield represents an archetypal conflict between nature and 'civilization' that, as confirmed by Pearl Button's screams as the soldiers descend to 'rescue' her, emphasizes the horrors of restrictive social codes and presents an alternative, utopian vision. The story has been described as 'almost pure allegory' (Fullbrook, 1986, p.41). Mansfield is also drawing on her wide reading of nineteenth-century fiction. Her story echoes Maggie Tulliver's attempt to join the gypsies in George Eliot's *The Mill on the Floss* (1860), for example, and is reminiscent of the way in which Charles Dickens pits the world of his circus characters against Victorian materialism in *Hard Times* (1854). Feminist accounts of modernism emphasize that the legacy of nineteenth-century literature remained a particularly vital inheritance for women writers of the modernist period. Nineteenth-century women novelists such as Jane Austen and Eliot were significant influences on Mansfield's work, as were the 'plotless' stories of late nineteenth-century contributors to the aestheticist periodical *The Yellow Book*. With its echoes of the earlier novelists, this story provides an interesting example of Mansfield making use of features encountered in more expansive literary forms within her highly condensed treatment of the short story.

'How Pearl Button Was Kidnapped' allows us to appreciate very clearly that Mansfield's formal experimentation in this story is integral to the representation of a child's perceptions. Indeed, much of the story's allegorical force arises because Pearl Button does not define the world according to adult categories of meaning: 'The expectations raised by the title are not fulfilled; there is no tension in the story' (Smith, 2000, p.41). Instead of a taut plot involving kidnap and possible rescue as intimated by the story's title, we are free to contemplate the deeper meanings beneath Pearl Button's ingenuous understanding of her adventure. Thinking about the form and language of this story, we might agree that, as in 'Frau Brechenmacher Attends a Wedding', Mansfield evokes complex responses in her reader through a clear and simple mode of narrative. Bowen compared her technique with Jane Austen's:

> She uses no literary shock tactics. The singular beauty of her language consists, partly, in its hardly seeming to be language at all, so glass-transparent is it to her meaning. Words had but one appeal for her, that of speakingness ... She was to evolve from noun, verb, adjective, a marvellous sensory notation hitherto

undreamed of outside poetry; nonetheless, she stayed subject to prose discipline. And her style, when the story-context requires, can be curt, decisive, factual. It is a style generated by subject and tuned to mood – so flexible as to be hardly a style at all.

(Bowen, 1957, p.15)

Despite – or rather *through* – its simple, almost fairytale quality, 'How Pearl Button Was Kidnapped' is a precursor of Mansfield's complex portrayals of child psychology in later stories such as 'Prelude'. Just before the soldiers arrive, Mansfield describes Pearl's delighted discovery that the blue water of the sea no longer remains blue once she scoops it into her hands. This revelation prompts her to rush up to one of the two Maori women and hug her passionately (p.23). Similar moments of revelation – often closely followed, as here, by disillusion – occur frequently in Mansfield's stories. They have an affinity with the moments of 'epiphany' that were to be crucial in other modernist works, including Joyce's short-story cycle *Dubliners* (1914). Literary epiphanies provide moments of transcendent or disillusioning insight for fictional protagonists and/or for readers. Here, the movement from Pearl's moment of joy to its reversal is underpinned by Mansfield's symbolist use of colour, as the blue of the sea finds a sinister reflection in the wave of 'little blue men' that come running towards her.

Although many of the details of the story are authentically New Zealand, Mansfield was writing predominantly for a European audience and does not assume knowledge of New Zealand race relations on the part of her reader (the draft of 'The Aloe', a later story, contains a reference to 'the Maori war', which Mansfield edited out of the version that was subsequently published as 'Prelude'). New Zealand readers will probably recognize that the Maori women take Pearl Button to their 'marae', or communal meeting-place, and the story will have important resonances for them in terms of its national context – as evidenced in the response by Witi Ihimaera mentioned below. But Mansfield uses no specifically Maori terminology and her story operates as a highly generalized account of race relations for readers unaware of the specific context, especially as it turns so conspicuously to European tradition for its literary frame of reference. Nevertheless, this early story has provoked recent critical interest because Mansfield uses a child's apprehensions of the world to convey a concern with questions of race as well as with gender. **Can you identify parts of the story where issues of race and gender are intertwined?**

The story suggests an identity between the interests of the Maori characters and their girl 'captive'. Fullbrook reads 'How Pearl Button Was Kidnapped' as a utopian dream of female escape that makes use of the 'romantic tradition that glorifies the "naturalness" and "freedom" of the savage over the inhibitions and pleasure-denying aspects of mechanical civilisation' (1986, p.9). (Part of this Romantic tradition is, of course, the valorization of the child's imagination as corresponding to the unspoiled state of 'primitive' humanity.) 'The story is clear', Fullbrook observes, 'in uniting the non-white and the as yet unsubdued girl-child as natural allies against the authority of patriarchy represented by the police' (*ibid.*, p.43). In a fictional tribute to this reading of the story entitled 'The Affectionate Kidnappers', the Maori writer Witi Ihimaera follows the two Maori women of Mansfield's story to the police cells, where their chief visits them and hears their account of events (1989, pp.110–14). Though few of Mansfield's other works deal as directly with questions of race, recent critics of her work, such as Vincent O'Sullivan and Angela Smith, see her writing as permeated by awareness of her country's colonial inheritance, an awareness that feeds into a more widely diffused indignation against injustice. The next story I am going to discuss could certainly support this view. Like 'Frau Brechenmacher Attends a Wedding', 'The Woman at the Store' conveys a sense of fury at the biological entrapment of women. However, as in 'How Pearl Button Was Kidnapped' the setting is Mansfield's native New Zealand and issues of gender are complicated by the colonial context in which they arise.

Rhythm and suspense: 'The Woman at the Store'

Written in 1910, 'How Pearl Button Was Kidnapped' was first published in 1912 in *Rhythm*, an avant-garde journal edited by John Middleton Murry. Mansfield became Murry's lover and the co-editor of *Rhythm*. 'The Woman at the Store', her first story for the journal, appeared in spring 1912. Murry wanted writing of 'guts' and 'bloodiness' for the journal and 'The Woman at the Store' fitted the bill (Smith, 2000, p.81).

Rhythm was founded by Murry in conjunction with the Scottish colourist J.D. Fergusson and other painters and writers who wanted to convey their excitement at the latest developments in art and philosophy, particularly those that they had encountered in Paris, where Fergusson and his associates were pursuing the Fauvist principles established by the painters Henri Matisse, André Derain and Maurice de Vlaminck (see Figure 2.2). In 1910, Serge Diaghilev's Ballets Russes appeared in Paris for the first time. With scores by Claude Debussy and Igor Stravinsky, the Ballets Russes offered an art that, like Fauvist painting, exploited the expressive power of colour, be it in pigment or tone, and of 'barbaric' rhythmic vigour in movement and line. At the same time, the philosopher Henri Bergson was lecturing on the importance of intuitive rather than intellectual modes of knowledge.

For Murry and Fergusson, rhythm was the all-important quality in art – hence the title of their magazine. Through her association with the journal, Mansfield came to know a number of contemporary artists, including Fergusson and the American painter Anne Estelle Rice (whose portrait of Mansfield is reproduced in Figure 2.1). There are many correspondences between Post-Impressionist painting and Mansfield's writing, some of which

Figure 2.2   John Duncan Fergusson, *St Jacques Studio*, 1909, oil on board, 37 × 36 cm. (Private Collection/Fine Art Society, London, UK/ www.bridgeman.co.uk. © The Fergusson Gallery, Perth & Kinross Council, Scotland.)

are apparent in this first story for *Rhythm*. Her encounters with art that strove not for realist depiction, but to portray a deeper reality about its subject by using symbol and colour to capture a particular mood or atmosphere, added impetus to Mansfield's established practice of using symbolic detail in place of description or analysis to convey the themes of her writing. Mansfield later recalled how Vincent van Gogh's painting of 'Yellow flowers – brimming with sun in a pot', seen in Roger Fry's 1910 Post-Impressionist Exhibition in London, 'taught me something about writing ... a kind of freedom – or rather, a shaking free' (Mansfield, 1984–96, vol.4, p.333).

Much of the material for 'The Woman at the Store' is drawn from a lengthy camping trip that Mansfield undertook shortly before leaving New Zealand in 1907 (see Figures 2.3 and 2.4). The story is one of a group of three similar stories set in the remote rural 'backblocks' that includes 'Millie' and 'Ole Underwood' (both 1913). Its opening conveys the merciless heat and dust through which a group of travellers make their way in search of the store run by the woman of the story's title. The story has sometimes been termed a 'thriller' and critics note that it has more by way of a conventional plot than other stories by Mansfield. **Now read the story. How appropriate is it to think of 'The Woman at the Store' as a 'thriller' in your view? How important is its plot in generating the interest and structure of her story?**

The story certainly contains enough drama and suspense to justify the title of 'thriller', although this does not really seem an adequate description of its effect on the reader. Though it offers us a fairly simple linear narrative, not a great deal actually happens. As Clare Hanson and Andrew Gurr point out, 'The story begins abruptly ("All that day the heat was terrible") and ends casually ("A bend in the road, and the whole place disappeared")' (1981, p.39). Most of the action happens in the past (or potentially in the future). The central ' "drama" is conveyed wordlessly, diagrammatically, by means of a child's drawing', a device 'which seems itself emblematic of the oblique narrative technique' employed by Mansfield, which is 'concerned primarily with mood and atmosphere' (*ibid.*, p.38). Right from the story's opening, the landscape conveys an atmosphere of desolation and impoverishment. Mansfield can be seen as conducting another experiment with the

Figure 2.3   Katherine Mansfield (standing on left, wearing white blouse and dark skirt) and local Maori on her North Island camping trip, at Te Whaiti, Whakatane, 1907. (Alexander Turnbull Library, Wellington, NZ. Ref: F-2584-1/2.)

Figure 2.4   The Rangitaiki Hotel, on the Napier–Taupo road, where Katherine Mansfield stayed during her 1907 trip. (Post and Telegraph Collection, Alexander Turnbull Library, Wellington, NZ. Ref: F-19611-1/4.)

Romantic tropes (rhetorical and figurative devices) that she employs in 'How Pearl Button Was Kidnapped'. Here, however, Romantic views of nature as a benign and nourishing force are sharply reversed. Nature is harsh and hostile and the settlers who despoil it are made savage by its savagery. In place of the 'profuse strains of unpremeditated art' valorized in Percy Bysshe Shelley's famous ode 'To a Skylark' (1820), 'larks shrilled – the sky was slate colour, and the sound of the larks reminded me of slate pencils scraping over its surface' (p.10).

As with nature, so gender stereotypes are shown to be particularly inappropriate in this harsh setting. The reader's own assumptions about gender are unsettled by uncertainty over the sex of the story's narrator. Unusually for Mansfield, the text has a first-person narrator, who might be assumed to share the male gender of the two other travellers until after the narrator has bathed in the river and the child confesses to having 'looked at her where she wouldn't see me from' (p.15). And how would any woman travel through that country, except on horseback and as much covered by pumice dust as her male companions and the horses they ride? The woman at the store has obviously been cruelly affected by her environment. Described in stereotypical terms by Hin (a name that sounds Maori, although it is one of the story's many narrative omissions that his race is never defined) as having 'blue eyes and yellow hair', she has become a mockery of the doll-like image his description suggests, a grotesque puppet with 'nothing but sticks and wires' under her clothes. She was once ' "as pretty as a wax doll" ', Hin protests (p.14) – but we can imagine what becomes of wax in the New Zealand sun. The colonial context provides the sharp realist detail that, fused with Symbolist technique, distinguishes the embryonic modernism that Mansfield brought with her to Europe (see Williams, 2000). It also intensifies the ironic gap between stereotype and reality. Inside the house, the pictures of Queen Victoria's Jubilee from English periodicals, so comically at odds with the room they decorate, highlight the gulf between the idealized images of femininity to which the characters in the story have access and the realities of their existence. Social stereotypes are sharply satirized in this instance of what O'Sullivan terms the 'exchange of perspectives between the heart of Empire, and Empire's furthest reaches' in her stories (1997, p.5). O'Sullivan sees this exchange as fundamental to Mansfield's view of gender and class relations both in Europe and in colonial New Zealand. In 'The Woman at the Store', the violence that is sublimated within these relationships in most of Mansfield's writing is made explicit. The hostile natural environment exacerbates the inherent destructiveness of the woman's domestic situation. Her experience of repeated pregnancy suggests a biological entrapment, and although given her missing teeth and mutterings about 'child-murder' it is unclear whether the miscarriages resulted from the privations of her life or from physical violence on the part of her husband (p.16).

Such gaps (clues that are never explained), rather than a conventional thriller-like plot, contribute to tension in the story. Further suspense is generated by the way Mansfield builds an oppressive and threatening atmosphere. Bereft of a long poetic twilight, the New Zealand dusk is 'a curious half-hour when everything appears grotesque – it frightens – as though the savage spirit of the country walked abroad and sneered at what it saw' (p.13). (Here, Mansfield's rejection of a Romantic twilight nonetheless inspires a sense of uncanny presences in nature that might be thought of as quintessentially Romantic – the 'spirit of the country' mocks the beleaguered settlers scraping a living from its territory in a savage version of the severe but sublimely ministering spirits that haunt William Wordsworth's nature.) This inimical landscape was not long since the site of land-wars and shows the recent signs of the colonial clearances that still scar much of the country today. On her Urewera camping trip, Mansfield recorded the 'charred logs' and uncanny 'skeleton army' of the still upright trunks of native hardwood trees that peopled the areas through which she rode (Mansfield, 1997, vol.1, p.136). Europeans are unwelcome intruders. Mansfield's sensitivity to this, and perhaps her disquiet at her own status as a colonial of European descent, emerges elsewhere in her writing. In the early vignette 'In the Botanical

Gardens' (1907), the bush casts a sudden and reproachful shadow over a description of orderly and sunlit beds of non-native flowers. In 'The Woman at the Store', the disquieting atmosphere conjured by the arrival of dusk is extended as the characters get grotesquely drunk to the accompaniment of a thunder storm that lights up the night 'as though a bush fire was raging' (p.18). The inebriated humour of Hin and the narrator tips swiftly into an acute sense of the macabre once the child's drawing has shown them what became of the woman's husband.

In a sense, this moment supplies a basic 'whodunit' element in the story. However, the murder happens outside the narrative timeframe and the mystery of what has become of the woman's husband is never central to the narrative, which concentrates on the effect on his wife of the husband's repeated absences rather than on the reason for his current disappearance. There is no particular resolution to the plot either – the two characters in possession of knowledge of the murder do nothing with it other than to ride away, leaving Jo to an uncertain fate.

One might reflect that the girl's drawing is an example of 'instrumental' art: a straightforward communication that provokes a particular course of action in its audience. The distance between this drawing and Mansfield's mode of writing about it might suggest how far removed Mansfield's own practice and implied aesthetic is from instrumentality. Mansfield's handling of the picture, as with other details, is anything but simple. Much of the story's structure is the result not of plot but of a patterning of images which produces a 'rhythmical structure' that might be seen, not as comparable to the girl's rough sketch, but as 'analogous to ... a Post-Impressionist painting' (Hanson and Gurr, 1981, p.39). One such pattern is produced by repeated reference to the colour red (pre-eminent in the Fauvist palette). The red spots of the hanky Jo is wearing at the beginning of the story are echoed later by the 'two red spots' that burn on the woman's cheeks and the colour of Jo's drunken face (pp.10, 16, 18). This repetition of colour works alongside other symbolic patterns. The physical deterioration of the woman and her sickly child correspond to the state of their immediate surroundings and the wider landscape. The woman has 'red pulpy hands' and her garden is planted with cabbages that 'smelled like stale dishwater' (p.12). Her child's 'whitish hair, and weak eyes' (p.15) are a reminder of the choking white dust that covers the travellers in the opening paragraph. On a second reading one can appreciate how many of the images in 'The Woman at the Store' form part of a pattern that foreshadows the future. The woman's first appearance carrying a gun foreshadows what the child's drawing will uncover. The story's account of this drawing, like the blood-like spots on Jo's handkerchief, suggests what may happen to him if he abandons the woman to her life of isolation once more.

Symbolist techniques and aestheticism: 'Prelude'

As stories like 'How Pearl Button Was Kidnapped' and 'The Woman at the Store' show, Mansfield's memories of New Zealand were an important source for her fiction from early in her career. After the death of her younger brother in the First World War, this connection acquired a new intensity. In 1915, Mansfield had begun work on a story set in New Zealand. Originally entitled 'The Aloe', the text was extensively revised by Mansfield into the form finally published as *Prelude* by Virginia and Leonard Woolf's Hogarth Press in 1918. Writing in her notebook in January 1916, Mansfield charted a change in her preoccupations as a writer:

> the form that I would choose has changed utterly. I feel no longer concerned with the same appearances of things. The people who lived or who I wished to bring into my stories don't interest me any more. The plots of my stories leave me perfectly cold.
>
> (Mansfield, 1997, vol.2, p.32)

A change of creative direction that coincided with a wish to memorialize her brother encouraged her to turn to her storehouse of New Zealand memories:

> I want for one moment to make our undiscovered country leap into the eyes of the old world. It must be mysterious, as though floating – it must take the breath. It must be 'one of those islands' ... I shall tell everything, even of how the laundry basket squeaked at '75' – but all must be told with a sense of mystery, a radiance, an after glow.
>
> (Mansfield, 1997, vol.2, p.32)

Mansfield's notebook entry contains the same combination of realism and symbolism – mystery and the squeaking of the laundry basket – that animates her stories. In the continuation of this passage, Mansfield describes herself as constantly possessed by a wish to write poetry – and yet, she decides, what she most needs for her new mode of writing is 'a kind of special prose' (Mansfield, 1997, vol.2, p.33). This was her own term for what Bowen was to call 'a marvellous sensory notation hitherto undreamed of outside poetry' yet 'nonetheless ... subject to prose discipline' (1957, p.15). 'One of Katherine Mansfield's greatest achievements', according to Gordon, was 'the creation of a prose style which could borrow from poetry, but which nevertheless remains prose, firmly based on a simple and even colloquial movement' (1954, p.26).

At the beginning of her work on 'The Aloe', Mansfield referred to the piece interchangeably as her 'book', 'work' and 'story'. She seems to have envisaged it as the starting point of a New Zealand novel. The change of title to 'Prelude' (at Murry's suggestion) may have partly been with this in mind – 'Prelude' is the title of the opening section of George Eliot's *Middlemarch* (1872) in which the nineteenth-century writer introduces some of the ideas about gender and vocation that are elaborated in the novel. Mansfield's title also echoes *The Prelude*, Wordsworth's intense poem of childhood and the growth of poetic imagination (which like Mansfield's story was always intended to form part of a larger work). Whether or not these literary parallels were deliberately invoked, *Prelude* is certainly a companion name to *Rhythm*, the by-then-defunct journal that she had helped Murry to edit. The musical associations of the title must have appealed to Mansfield. Like many modernist writers, she frequently used musical analogy to describe the sort of prose that she wanted to achieve, and her own early training as a cellist lent a specific relevance to such comparisons. Describing the writing of her story 'Miss Brill' (1920), she wrote that 'I chose not only the length of every sentence, but even the sound of every sentence ... I read it aloud ... just as one would *play over* a musical composition' (Mansfield, 1984–96, vol.4, p.165). The analogy is one that also applies to Mansfield's method in the rest of her stories. Here, the title 'Prelude' is also appropriate for the new beginning symbolized by the house move portrayed in the story, and the new direction in which Mansfield was developing her writing.

The full-length New Zealand novel was never written, but composition of 'The Aloe' and its revision as 'Prelude' marked a turning-point in Mansfield's career. New Zealand, as refracted through memory and exile, became a powerful land of the imagination, a rich store for the innovative writing methods explored in this and subsequent stories to make a radical departure from the traditional short-story form. When she had at last finished 'Prelude' and sent it to the Woolfs in October 1917, she gave an account of the process of writing the story to her friend, the painter Dorothy Brett:

> I threw my darling to the wolves and they ate it up and served me up so much praise in such a golden bowl that I couldn't help feeling gratified ... What form is it? You ask. Ah Brett, its so difficult to say. As far as I know its more or less my own invention. And how have I shaped it? This is about as much as I can say about it. You know, if the truth were known I have a perfect passion for the island where I was born ... Well, in the early morning there I always remember feeling that this little island has dipped back into the dark blue sea during the night only to rise again at beam of day, all hung with bright spangles and glittering drops – (When you ran over the dewy grass you positively felt that your feet tasted salt.) I tried to catch that moment – with something of its sparkle and its flavour. And just as on those mornings white milky mists rise and uncover some beauty, then smother it again and then again disclose it. I tried to lift that mist from my people and let them be seen and then to hide them again ...

> (Mansfield, 1984–96, vol.1, pp.330–1)

'Prelude' moves through a series of twelve episodes, each one centred on the mind of a single individual or moving between the thoughts of a small group of characters. The story begins on the evening of the Burnell family's move to their new house. It follows them through the next day, then returns to the same characters and setting some days later. The sections are not arranged so as to provide a complete and continuous narrative. As she recounts in the letter just quoted, Mansfield selects key moments at which to reveal and then hide her characters and their surroundings. Memory for Mansfield is a selective and creative faculty, rather than a passive process of recollection. She was highly critical of writers who failed to exert memory's power to shape and select, attacking the novelist Dorothy Richardson for producing 'bits, fragments, flashing glimpses, half scenes and whole scenes, all of them quite distinct and separate, and all of them of equal importance' (Mansfield, 1987, pp.49–50). **Read through 'Prelude' now, taking note of how the different sections shift between individuals and groups of characters. How does Mansfield use the house move portrayed in the story to illuminate the psychology of her characters?**

The sections of 'Prelude' produce an almost cyclical effect as the narrative moves slowly back and forth between different characters rather than progressing to a narrative climax. You can see this if you look over Sections V and VI, for example. Section V concentrates on Linda, with a brief interlude of dialogue with Stanley before his departure. Section VI begins with Mrs Fairfield alone. She is joined by Beryl, then Linda. Beryl's departure leaves Linda and her mother together until a reference to Kezia moves the narrative back to her as she explores the magical new garden. The section comes to a close as Kezia and her mother converge on the mysterious aloe. Most of the sections are more loosely linked than this, the next two begin abruptly with Stanley on his return from work and the children playing with their cousins some days later, yet Mansfield's concentration on the perceptions, memories and thoughts of the members of a single household, and the symbolic structures that underpin this, create the sense of a closely unified whole.

'Prelude' ends – as Kezia tiptoes guiltily away from her aunt's dressing table – with an ellipsis rather than a conclusion, gesturing towards continuity (the narrative is in fact taken up again in Mansfield's later story 'At the Bay') and leaving us with a sense of the deep significance of ordinary events. At the beginning of her story, Mansfield uses 'the simple event of house-moving to illuminate the different ways we think of the future' (Caffin, 1982, p.45). For all the characters, the move arouses expectations: of another child for Linda (a son, her husband hopes), possible romance for Beryl, an unknown future for Kezia. Seen through Kezia's eyes, the departure for the new house is a scene of high drama. She is left to explore the empty house, which takes on a life of its own as sunlight and shadows move across its empty spaces and the remnants of its previous occupants. This looks forward to Virginia Woolf's more extended treatment of the house in the 'Time Passes' section of *To the Lighthouse* (1927), an elegiac, memory-drenched novel that may in part have been inspired by Mansfield's story. The relationships between Mansfield's and Woolf's writing have received increasing critical attention in recent years. The two writers had an intense, if sometimes barbed, friendship; both were aware of a peculiar affinity between their aspirations as writers. Woolf described Mansfield's as 'the only writing I have ever been jealous of' (1977a, vol.2, p.227). She frequently felt haunted by Mansfield after her death and her diary records the emotional aftermath of a night of dreaming about her during the time that she was writing *Orlando* (*ibid.*, vol.3, p.187).

The scene in 'Prelude' is a distinctively New Zealand one. As in 'The Woman at the Store', the onset of darkness is sudden and uncanny. An accompanying wind rises, and Kezia's intensely portrayed visual perceptions are abruptly replaced by the auditory: the creaking of wooden walls and floors and the forlorn banging of a loose piece of corrugated iron on the roof, sounds that fill the house with terrifying presences (p.83). A sense of disorientation is continued on the journey to the new house by the unfamiliar aspect of places usually seen by day. The new house is also alive: 'A strange beautiful excitement seemed to stream from the house in quivering ripples' as they arrive (p.85). Later, as the narrative slows its pace and moves from the family group around the supper table to follow individual members of the household as they go to bed, Kezia listens as 'The house itself creaked and popped' in accompaniment to the adult voices downstairs (p.99). The section concluding the Burnell's house move ends with the soft call of a native owl from the garden, while the harsh 'clatter' of an opossum in the bush beyond is a remote and mocking reminder, amid the prevailing tranquillity, of a world and a future beyond the sleeping household – a reminder to us also of the satirical bite of even Mansfield's most tender and nostalgic writing.

This household, its human occupants and the house and garden themselves seem an enclosed yet endangered circle, threatened by the contradictory affections and hostilities at work within it and by the fragility of life. Mansfield's prose moves within and between the minds of her characters and their surroundings with remarkably little by way of narrative explanation. The reader interprets according to what he or she is shown, rather than what he or she is told. The story is presided over by the mysterious symbol of the aloe, the tall spiked plant growing in the midst of the 'island' in the Burnell's front garden. **Pause now and reread the account of the aloe at the end of Section VI (p.98). What is the significance of this image?**

The aloe's 'curving leaves seemed to be hiding something'. Kezia is at a loss to know what to make of it and asks her mother for an explanation – the only direct encounter between these two characters in the story. The 'fat

Figure 2.5   Chesney Wold, Karori Road, *c.*1880s, the house outside Wellington to which Katherine Mansfield's family moved in 1893 and which formed the model for the new house in 'Prelude'. (Lady Smedley Collection, Alexander Turnbull Library, Wellington, NZ. Ref: F-84690-1/2.)

swelling plant with its cruel leaves and fleshy stem' may suggest a phallus and echoes the terrifying swelling creatures that populate the imaginations of both Kezia and her mother. Mansfield, however, was impatient with what she saw as an excessive preoccupation with sexualized imagery in writers such as D.H. Lawrence, whom she otherwise admired. The aloe remains an enigmatic symbol that means different things to different characters and to different readers. The plant appears strong and invincible, 'the blind stem cut into the air as if no wind could ever shake it'. However, set to flower once in a hundred years and then die, it also prompts associations with cycles of life and death. (Its imminent flowering might also be seen as having a symbolic relationship with the story itself and with Mansfield's method of writing it: she later alluded to what she called 'the *Prelude* method – it just unfolds and opens'; Mansfield, 1984–96, vol.4, p.156.)

The aloe works as an equivocal embodiment of future promise and future threat. Linda subsequently identifies with its hardness, so that its sharp thorns represent not male violence, but a protecting power that could guard her longed-for escape from childbearing. Thus, the aloe is also ambiguously gendered. In his cover drawing for the first edition of *Prelude*, J.D. Fergusson produced a design in which the spiky leaves of the plant enfolded a female face (Figure 2.6). This design appeared on only a few copies of the story as the Woolfs disliked it. (Their friend, the art critic Roger Fry, did not admire Fergusson's work and had excluded him from his 1910 Post-Impressionist exhibition.) It is true that the illustration gives a more restricted sense of the aloe's symbolic significance than that offered in the story. Smith (1999, p.96) suggests that Mansfield and Woolf share a sense of the way symbolism should function. Woolf was later to describe the lighthouse in her own novel as a 'central line', which functioned 'to hold the design together' (Woolf, 1977b, p.385). The aloe forms a similar reference point, around which different associations cluster for different people – both characters and readers – rather than as a symbol whose exact meaning can be decoded.

In 'Prelude', Mansfield extends the expressive and rhythmic use of imagery, especially of colour, evident in her earlier stories: 'Dawn came sharp and chill with red clouds on a faint green sky' (p.90). As in her later story 'At the Bay' and the notebook entry quoted above, her account of early morning in 'Prelude' – 'drops of water on every leaf and blade' – exemplifies in both form and content the New Zealand writer C.K. Stead's observation of 'an indefinable all-pervasive freshness in her writing, as if every sentence had been struck off first thing on a brilliant morning' (1977, p.19). The reader

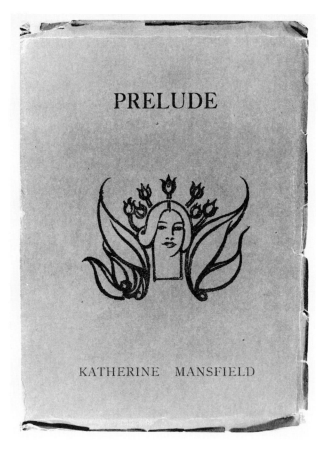

Figure 2.6 J.D. Fergusson, cover drawing for *Prelude*. (Alexander Turnbull Library, Wellington, NZ. Ref: F-113400-1/2. © The Fergusson Gallery, Perth and Kinross council, Scotland.)

shares the sense of anticipation that infuses the story, following Kezia's enchantment as she explores the mysterious garden. Most New Zealand readers would recognize the account of the striped camellias that grow to magical tree-like proportions around colonial houses; Mansfield transports all her readers to a 'New Zealand' of the mind, the mysterious island evoked in her notebook entry.

Dawn signals the new beginning promised by the title of 'Prelude'. The new house and garden explored by the children on their first day have edenic qualities. Mansfield intended the story as an elegy for her brother and a 'debt of love' to the places and people of the childhood that she longed to 'renew … in writing' (Mansfield, 1997, vol.2, p.32). Yet despite the 'after glow' of memory that infuses the story, childhood in 'Prelude' is no protected paradise. Anticipations of the future hold excitement but also fear, as dramatized by Kezia's sudden confrontation with the aloe and, through the beheading of the duck, with death. Like many of her contemporaries, Mansfield was interested in the psychological theories of Sigmund Freud. For all the charm of her portrayal of child characters and their surroundings, her story shows a very modern understanding of a connection between adult experience and the fears of childhood. This is most apparent in the way in which Kezia's fear of the 'IT' that stalks her in the empty house is echoed by Linda's waking nightmares that 'THEY' were in the room and watching her (pp.82, 93). Kezia's dislike of 'rushing animals like dogs and parrots' is echoed very closely by Linda's wish that her 'Newfoundland dog' of a husband 'wouldn't jump at her so', for 'she had always hated things that rush at her, from a child' (pp.84, 115). These parallels, which form part of the symbolic structure of 'Prelude', suggest that Kezia, for all her present vitality, is the potential inheritor of her mother's sexual fears and her confused and debilitating dissatisfaction with her life. The connection is even more explicitly made in the original version of the story through descriptions, subsequently cut by Mansfield, of Linda as a lively and adventurous child.

Mansfield made substantial changes to 'The Aloe', pruning away words and phrases throughout the text and cutting completely several major sections of the narrative before it reached its final form as 'Prelude'. The New Zealand writer Vincent O'Sullivan has produced a parallel edition of 'The Aloe' and 'Prelude' that allows us to see something of the way that Mansfield worked to achieve her new kind of prose. Seeing some of these developments 'in action' provides a helpful way of considering Mansfield's writing technique more generally. **Read the opening of 'The Aloe' and brief extracts from two other sections that Mansfield altered or cut entirely from 'Prelude' (Appendix). What difference does the removal of the cancelled passages make to the story? What are the main changes that Mansfield has made to the story's opening, and to what effect?**

The cancelled passages elaborate the character of Linda in ways that are carefully suppressed in 'Prelude'. The Linda of 'The Aloe' is more active and constantly makes fun at the expense of her mother and sisters. Her third sister, Mrs Trout, who habitually dreams up catastrophic 'novels' featuring members of her family, is cut completely from the revised version of the story, as is an outburst from Beryl against Linda's habitual flippancy. Beryl sees this as arising from Linda's loss of her special relationship with their father, a relationship to which 'Prelude' makes only the most passing reference. In 'The Aloe', reminiscences of her father provide some context for Linda's dream. An account of the time when she plotted to explore the world with her father as 'a couple of boys together' highlights the contrast between her adventurous spirit then and the confused passivity in her role as wife and mother, suggesting some of the reasons why she is dissatisfied with her present state. In 'Prelude', all this explanatory framework is stripped away.

After starting 'The Aloe', Mansfield wrote to Murry that 'It will be a funny book' (Mansfield, 1984–96, vol.1, p.186). 'Prelude' frequently is funny, but Linda is no longer a major vehicle of this humour. Long sections of verbal repartee are cut and we are left with the internalized hysteria of her wish to ask her children to stand on their heads on the lawn alongside the chairs and table awaiting collection by the storeman (p.79). In the later story, the passive, inward aspects of Linda's character have come to dominate. Changes that Mansfield made to the opening of the story initiate this. In 'Prelude', it is the grandmother, not their mother, who agrees to Mrs Samuel Joseph's offer to look after the children. 'Prelude' leaves most of Linda's feelings about her marriage to be inferred rather than communicating them directly. Mansfield omits Linda's satirical descriptions of a conquering Stanley rowing to the office from a flooded house and measuring the consequent increase in his chest muscle, and dispenses with her habitual teasing loss of her wedding ring. In 'The Aloe' this shows vulnerabilities in Stanley that are more obliquely suggested in 'Prelude', while Linda's longing for escape is communicated in the later story by a brief sentence where she imagines 'driving away from everybody and not even waving' (p.91).

Other sections of 'The Aloe' which Mansfield cut include several that draw attention outwards from her main narrative, such as a more detailed account of the 'swarm' of Samuel Joseph's children, an incident where Kezia retaliates to their teasing by tricking them into eating the burning centres of arum lilies, a comic account of the social function at which Linda and Stanley first meet, and a passage where Beryl remembers both enjoying and warding off the devoted attentions of her friend Nan.

Even the minimal interest that Linda takes in her children in 'The Aloe' is absent from the later story. In the earlier version, Mansfield had used Kezia's exploration of the empty house as an opportunity to specify some of

Linda's feelings about motherhood: 'Kezia had been born in that room', the narrator of 'The Aloe' explains, 'She had come forth squealing out of a reluctant mother in the teeth of a "Southerly Buster"'' (the harshest winds come from the south in the Antipodes) (Mansfield, 1983, p.35). The omission of much of the material relating to Stanley from 'Prelude' means that the full extent of Linda's equivocal feelings for her husband are saved for the passage towards the end of the story where she contemplates the aloe and confronts the strong measure of hate that co-exists with her love for him. Its delayed appearance gives this clear realization of hatred something of the shock value for the reader that Linda delightedly imagines it giving Stanley himself, should she reveal it to him. The emotional force of the story seems to have been enhanced rather than diminished by Mansfield's rigorous pruning of narrative context; we apprehend Linda's equivocal feelings about marriage and motherhood no less strongly for knowing less of their causes.

Mansfield herself clearly felt that the gaps in her story were of greater value than narrative continuity. The reader is free to focus, both consciously and unconsciously, on resonances between and within characters. Stripped of analysis, Mansfield's story is conveyed through an extraordinarily supple style that links individuals and landscapes into a rhythmic and unified whole, even at the level of the individual sentence. **Reread the opening sentences of 'Prelude'. Whose perceptions are represented here?**

The first two sentences already modulate into Linda's thought patterns. This is not the technique of interior monologue, so famously to be used by Joyce in the Molly Bloom sequence of *Ulysses*, in which thought patterns are constructed as first-person internalized speech:

> her tongue is a bit too long for my taste your blouse is open too low she says to me the pan calling the kettle blackbottom and I had to tell her not to cock her legs up like that on show on the windowsill before all the people passing they all look at her like me when I was her age

> (Joyce, [1922] 1993, p.717)

In 'The Aloe' manuscript, there is a passage where, writing of Mrs Trout's imagined novels, Mansfield perhaps indicates some of her reasons for preferring third-person to first-person narration: 'she always thought of herself in the third person: it was more "touching" somehow)' (see Appendix). **What is the effect of Mansfield's choice of third-person narration?**

As with Linda's musings on her 'hatred', the opening sentence of 'Prelude' is in a form of free indirect discourse through which a third-person narrative incorporates images and symbols – here the children become as items of luggage in Linda's mind – to represent the non-verbal unconscious experiences of characters as well as their conscious thoughts. The style of writing enacts the blending of conscious and unconscious perceptions that makes up experience. This view of experience cohered with the theories of Henri Bergson, whose ideas were influential on Mansfield and her contemporaries who worked on the journals *New Age* and *Rhythm*. Bergson maintained that time existed on two levels, a surface level and a deeper level of 'duration', at which our experience is of a non-linear overlapping and merging of different psychological states. (See Chapter 5 and Reader, Item 18.2.) Mansfield's use of symbol (which leaves the reader to intuit the themes of her stories rather than offering direct intellectual analysis), and her movement away from the surface level of plot in an effort to portray a deeper level of experience (that on which Linda can both love and hate her husband), could be viewed as literary parallels to Bergson's theories. Mansfield gave an account of her intention to portray the complexity of experience in a letter to the novelist William Gerhardi about her late New Zealand story 'The Garden Party' (1922). Laura, the heroine of the story, tries to reconcile the conflicting and overlapping experiences of a single day: empathy with those outside her social class, frivolous enjoyment of a party and a new hat, and an epiphanic encounter with death. As Mansfield comments in her letter, 'Laura says "But all these things must not happen at once". And Life answers "Why not? How are they divided from each other"' (1928, vol.2, p.196).

Mansfield's deployment of free indirect discourse to portray the multiplicity of experience is a radical development in the treatment of literary character. When the individual is shown as a synchronous series of overlapping and divergent thoughts and feelings, identity becomes fluid, multiple. Free indirect discourse is also a mode of writing that allows movement between the minds of several characters; in Mansfield, as in the 'stream-of-consciousness' writing made famous by Woolf, it erases the distinction between character and setting. Conscious and unconscious thoughts and emotions are caught up together with external objects in a single syntax.

Mansfield's prose is not difficult to read. Its translucent clarity and the psychological power of her stories made them popular from their first publication. (Mansfield even expressed ironic concern that 'Prelude' would be considered childishly simple: 'won't the "Intellectuals" just hate it. They'll think its a New Primer for Infant Readers'; 1984–96, vol.2, p.169.) Nonetheless, while Mansfield sought and achieved this powerful and direct effect upon her readers' intuitive understanding, she achieved much of it through methods – such as symbolism and her highly developed form of free indirect discourse – that are inherently indirect. As soon as we try to look more closely at how her stories are made, we find ourselves needing to call on critical resources more frequently required for the reading of poetry than of prose.

C.K. Stead compares Mansfield's task of self-editorship to the role that Ezra Pound was later to play on behalf of T.S. Eliot's *The Waste Land* (1922). What Pound showed Eliot, as Mansfield discovered for herself in her quest for a special kind of prose, is that 'the structural elements are almost always non-poetic, and are better dispensed with' (in Pilditch, 1996, p.169). Looking at the two versions of the story in parallel can make us aware of how Mansfield's careful paring away of explanation makes her text not simply more poetic and more mysterious, but more open to reconstruction by the reader: 'Mansfield removes narrative explanation of the characters' psychological states; the disruption ... leaves ... the reader's imagination to fill the gaps' (Smith, 2000, p.116). The removal of the narrative 'background' which would help to explain the psychology of her characters means that the reader concentrates on the symbolic patterns of her writing and may find in them a greater psychological resonance than if they were attached to more explicit character histories. Linda's dread of her husband's sexual attentions, no longer 'explained' by information about her relationship with her father, comes to signify women's anxieties about marriage and childbearing in a more generalized and universal, but no less potent, manner.

Discursive explanation, it seems, is scarcely a requirement for the powerful representation of characters and their interaction. The mode of writing that Mansfield developed in 'Prelude', moving by implication rather than narrative statement, proved to be a method through which the dynamics of gender and family relations were powerfully suggested. Writing of 'Prelude' in 1936, the American novelist Willa Cather commented:

> I doubt that any contemporary writer has made one feel more keenly the many kinds of personal relations which exist in an everyday 'happy family' who are merely going on living their daily lives, with no crises or shocks or bewildering complications to try them. Yet every individual in that household (even the children) is clinging passionately to his individual soul, is in terror of losing it in the general family flavour. As in most families, the mere struggle to have anything of one's own, to be one's self at all, creates an element of strain which keeps everybody almost at breaking point ... Katherine Mansfield's peculiar gift lay in her interpretation of those secret accords and antipathies which lie hidden under our everyday behaviour, and which more than any outward events make our lives happy or unhappy.

(Cather, 1936, pp.152–4)

Feminist critics have found it illuminating to return to 'The Aloe' to highlight the more explicit concern with gender in which 'Prelude' had its roots. They occasionally look to 'The Aloe' for 'lost' clues to the gender dynamics of 'Prelude' and lament the lack of explicit focus on gender issues in the later story. However, in *Katherine Mansfield and the Origins of Modernist Fiction*, Sydney Janet Kaplan sees Mansfield's revision of her narrative as intensifying rather than detracting from the concern with gender evident in the earlier text. Kaplan sees Mansfield as having achieved 'something new: a mixed genre, a multi-levelled, spatially ordered narrative' (1991, p.103). **Read the extract from Kaplan's analysis of Mansfield's transformation of 'The Aloe' into 'Prelude' (Reader, Item 8). How does Kaplan see Mansfield's revision of the story as making it a more effective exploration of gender?**

For Kaplan, 'the overriding theme of the story is female sexual identity'. She sees the story as focused on the 'engendering' of Kezia and her 'realisation of male dominance'. The way in which Mansfield's narrative moves between different female consciousnesses generates a sense of a spatial arrangement through which the reader can encounter multiple points of view. Kaplan extends her sense of 'Prelude' as spatially organized to suggest that it is itself 'structured like a female organism'. She points out that this 'spatial rendering' of the inner lives of several characters anticipates Woolf's technique in *Mrs Dalloway*.

The different modes of female perception represented offer models for Kezia's future womanhood. The link with her mother is the most obvious, but there is also Beryl and her grandmother. (Kezia is allowed to carry the lamp for her grandmother: a symbolic suggestion that she may one day inherit her role.) Certain explicit narrative contrasts that are significant to the theme of female identity in 'The Aloe' are lost in revision. Kaplan chooses the example of the passage about the swarm of Samuel Joseph's children that Mansfield cut from 'Prelude' and which underpins Linda's evident horror of motherhood at the start of 'The Aloe'. The omission of Beryl's reminiscing about her friend's lesbian advances makes this dimension of female sexuality merely implicit in the later story. (Mansfield also deleted all reference to Linda's sister Mrs Trout, a character whose morbid imaginings, described in the story as 'novels', represent a multiplicity of alternative futures for the characters of 'The Aloe'.) However, Kaplan reads Mansfield's poetic use of language as in itself highly sexualized, suggesting that the rays of sunlight that penetrate the empty house are symbolic of Kezia's embryonic perceptions of sexual difference. Thus, '*The Aloe* becomes, through its evolution into "Prelude," an awakening into female sexuality.'

Kaplan's chapter ends with a gendered interpretation of Kezia's distress at the handyman Pat's beheading of the duck and her subsequent distraction from her grief by the discovery of his golden earrings. Kezia is surprised – 'She never knew that men wore ear-rings' (p.109) – but also reassured. Kaplan quotes Kate Fullbrook, who suggests that 'Kezia is only recalled from her terror through the evidence of Pat's likeness to women' (1986, pp.74–5). Kaplan sees the moment as expressive of Kezia's wish not to be gendered as female, but to 'go back and forth in the costumes of gender' as the children do in their games, a wish no more realistic, Kaplan implies, than the wish to avoid death itself.

The different potential modes of female sexual identity highlighted by Kaplan's account might suggest that Kezia does not inevitably share the future of the mother whom she resembles, that she may be more effective in finding the escape of which her mother dreams. However, in Kaplan's reading the spatial organization of 'Prelude' ultimately has a thematic significance which reasserts 'the typical linear pattern of individual development' that belongs to the *Bildungsroman* (a novel concerned with the education of a young person in the world). Kaplan sees the different women as embodying the different stages of the single female life-cycle – childhood, adolescence, motherhood and old age – thus implying the 'inevitability of the continuation of conventional female roles'. As with the very different story 'Frau Brechenmacher Attends a Wedding', we have to look to the manner of Mansfield's writing for any protest against conventional gender roles, rather than to the actions, or potential actions, of her characters.

'A cry against corruption'

The unified symbolic structures of Mansfield's writing and its lack of a direct social or political mission have tended to mean that she was long treated predominantly as an 'aesthetic' writer. These qualities made her especially attractive to adherents of the mid-twentieth-century school of 'New Criticism', which advocated detailed textual analysis independent of any intellectual or historical context. Clearly it would take a reader uniquely insensitive to language to regard Mansfield's writing as primarily polemical. However, many critics have seen her stories as pervaded by feminist sympathies and sensitivity to individual and social injustice, at the same time as they stress the non-realist qualities of her writing. Mansfield identified '*a cry against corruption*' as a primary motivation for her writing, adding, 'Not a protest – a *cry*, and I mean corruption in the widest sense of the word, of course' (1984–6, vol.2, p.54). In Bowen's view, 'Indignation at injustice, from time to time, makes her no less inflammatory a writer than Charles Dickens':

> she concerns herself with bad cases rather than bad systems: political awareness or social criticism do not directly express themselves in the stories ... Unimaginativeness, with regard to others, seemed to her one of the grosser sins. The denial of love, the stunting of sorrow, or the cheating of joy was to her not short of an enormity.
>
> (Bowen, 1957, pp.23–4)

Feminist critics, with a sharpened sense that 'the personal is political', have felt that Mansfield's work demands to be read more explicitly in the light of its social and political contexts; the extract from Kaplan's analysis that you have just read views Mansfield's technical innovations and a concern with gender as inseparable, implying that it is inadequate to read her stories for their formal qualities alone. A number of stories, such as 'Life of Ma Parker' (1921), 'The Garden Party' (1922) and 'The Doll's House' (1922), also expose the harshness of class differences, even when they are not overtly political. In the Introduction to Part 1 of this book we asked you think about the question 'What is literature for?' and to ponder the opposing categories of 'aesthetic' and 'instrumental' literature. Perhaps no work of literature fits neatly into either of these classifications: oppositions between them become constantly undermined. **Do you find it possible to place Mansfield in relation to these categories?**

The legacy of aestheticism was clearly important for Mansfield. I have paid some attention to her use of Symbolist techniques. However, the way in which Mansfield's work concerns itself with issues of injustice and displays the pervasive preoccupation with gender that can sustain feminist readings would seem to make it inappropriate to describe her writing as purely 'aesthetic'. These concerns, and her blending of realist and Symbolist techniques, imply that she saw art as engaged with and nourished by reality – as we have seen, she was eager for her writing to convey the simultaneous and contradictory experiences of life.

Mansfield detested literature that was lacking in emotion. She criticized Eliot's poetry on these grounds and was extremely disappointed by the failure of Woolf's novel *Night and Day* (1919) to convey what, in a letter of 1919, she calls the 'tragic knowledge' brought by the First World War (Mansfield, 1984–96, vol.3, p.97). Only one of Mansfield's own stories, 'The Fly' (1922), refers directly to the war. She is not critical of the subject matter of Woolf's novel – 'I dont want G. forbid mobilisation and the violation of Belgium' (*ibid.*, p.82) – so much as of some less direct failure in aesthetic sensibility in that novel. (In contrast, Mansfield's 1919 review of Woolf's story 'Kew Gardens' praised it for the 'vivid and disturbing beauty' of its vision; Mansfield, 1987, p.53.) Mansfield saw the war as something that must transform writers' responses to the world, making them see the common things of life with a new intensity and illumination. Artists who failed to take this into account she described, in strong terms, as 'traitors'; 'We have to face our war', she asserted (1984–96, vol.3, p.82). However, for Mansfield, this transformation had to be communicated indirectly. Quoting the seventeenth-century poet Andrew Marvell's poem 'To his Coy Mistress', she explained that she felt a new consciousness of 'deserts of vast eternity'. But, in a paragraph that illuminates her use of symbolism to give oblique expression to this consciousness, she explains: 'I couldn't tell anybody *bang out* about those deserts. They are my secret. I might write about a boy eating strawberries or a woman combing her hair on a windy morning & that is the only way I can ever mention them. But they *must* be there. Nothing less will do' (Mansfield, 1984–96, vol.3, pp.97–8).

Read 'The Fly' now. What role does the war play in this story? The war has killed the only son of the story's protagonist, 'the boss'. 'The Fly' is not explicitly an anti-war story, although the way in which personal loss and a lifetime of bullying others seem to have damaged the boss's own capacity to feel may be read as implicit criticism of the values that underpin war. The boss's torment of the fly that has fallen into his ink well has even been seen as an allegorical account of how old men like him sent the younger generation into battle (Tate, 1995, p.3).

Among Mansfield's work, this story has inspired some of the most intense critical discussion. In 1962, there was extensive debate in the journal *Essays in Criticism* about the methods of criticism and interpretations appropriate to reading 'The Fly'. Contributors argued about whether the story's sharply observed details carried an allegorical anti-war message or whether they provoked less specific moral reactions in the reader.

Several later critics have noticed that the story contains disturbing ambiguities. Con Coroneos draws attention to the way in which the boss's torment of the fly 'involves a curious affection and sensuousness; he breathes on the fly tenderly to bring it back to life, and the tactile pleasure of struggling legs – which links with old Woodfield's pleasure in the whisky, and numerous other closely registered details of touch and taste – produces further cruelty' (1997, p.213). Many readers do identify an indirect, if confused, protest against the war as the implicit message of the story, but the status of the war in Mansfield's writing is never clear or straightforward.

Mansfield's indirect response to the cataclysmic events of her time complicates the question of whether her writing should be thought of as primarily aesthetic: 'what constitutes a *response* to the war ... how should we read what is not said?' (Tate and Raitt, 1997, p.13). To the extent that Mansfield's stories offer, or imply, a social critique, they could arguably also have an instrumental effect, whether or not this was her intention. Mansfield's own view of art, however, is certainly not 'instrumental' in the sense that she does not advocate that art should try to transform the world: 'it is not the business of the artist to grind an axe, to try to impose his vision of Life upon the existing world' (1997, vol.2, p.267). Her vocabulary here implies that she regards a strictly instrumental view of art as a coercive attempt by the artist to shape reality, when the artist's job is, rather, to shape a distinctive vision – one that draws on and co-exists with reality rather than tries to appropriate reality to itself: 'Art is not an attempt to reconcile existence with [the artist's] vision; it is an attempt to create his own world *in* this world ... we single out, we bring into the light, we put up higher' (*ibid.*).

This is a view that both emphasizes the creative role of the artist and seems to recoil from the imperiousness of assuming that the artist should exercise command over existence. The exact relationship of the world of the artist and 'this world' remains a vague and shifting one, yet it seems only appropriate that a writer who so subtly blends realist and Symbolist modes of writing should assert that art itself exists in a complex and oblique relation to reality.

'Bliss', epiphany and the pleasures of the text

The publication of 'Prelude' marked a turning point in Mansfield's writing. Further stories with both New Zealand and European settings followed and were collected together for publication as *Bliss and Other Stories* in 1920. The title story, first published in *The English Review* in 1918, is one of Mansfield's best known, and has provoked strong and mixed reactions in readers since it first appeared. The story extends some of the techniques developed during the long gestation and revision of 'Prelude', this time in a London setting with the focus on a single character and narrative line. As in 'Prelude', Mansfield blends a third-person narrative voice with the thoughts and perceptions of her character. You can see this in the first sentence, which vocalizes Bertha Young's thoughts, and throughout the story, where phrases suggestive of Bertha's own speech are frequently used. **Read 'Bliss' now. How did you respond to the narrative voice?**

Although the reader is brought into an intimate relationship with Bertha, we are unlikely simply to identify with her. The text sets up an ironic distance between character and reader. We suspect from the start that Bertha's feeling of bliss is likely to be shattered, at the same time as we share some of her enjoyment of the sensuous beauty of the fruit she arranges in a luminous blue bowl, the excitement of the 'shower of sparks' that seem to crackle in 'every particle' of her being, and the beauty of the 'tall, slender pear tree in fullest, richest bloom' that 'stood perfect, as though becalmed against the jade green sky' (pp.174–5, 177). Mansfield draws us in by using the second person to describe Bertha's feelings. We are implicated in 'What can you do if you are over thirty ...' (p.174). At the same time, we stand back, looking askance at some of the borrowed phrases – 'at nothing simply' – through which Bertha tries to dramatize her experience (*ibid.*). Bertha's enthusiasm for her 'modern, thrilling friends' seems naive if not contrived (p.178). Through Bertha, Mansfield satirizes a conventionally 'feminine' style of emotional rapture. Look, for example, at the paragraph beginning 'Really – really – she had everything ...' (*ibid.*). As Kaplan points out, 'the sentence structure itself provides us with clues to Mansfield's attitude towards Bertha's mental style. Simply by using the conjunction "and" so many times she coordinates all the details of Bertha's "bliss" on the same level; "adorable baby," "books" and "dressmaker" come to mean the same thing' (to Kaplan's list we could add the new cook's 'superb omelettes') (1991, p.160; 'Bliss', p.178). Bertha is guilty of the lack of selectivity that Mansfield criticized in the writing of Dorothy Richardson (Mansfield, 1987, p.50).

Nevertheless, the degree of ridicule directed at Bertha is relatively gentle compared with the sharp satire aimed at her guests, the Norman Knights, a bourgeois couple with modern pretensions and a desire to patronize the arts, and at the poet Eddie, with his ludicrous diction and exaggerated aestheticized accounts of his journey by taxi and of his moonlit socks. Similar 'artistic' characters are satirized in other stories that Mansfield wrote at this time, including 'Marriage à la Mode' (1921). Bertha imagines that the superficially decorative grouping of her guests around the table suggests a scene in Chekhov. The very presence of Chekhov's name here intensifies the satire arising from the discussion of plays with titles such as 'Love in False Teeth' (p.181). A similar series of vacuous titles highlights the empty literary pretensions of the despicable narrator of 'Je ne parle pas français' (1919). Mansfield's satire in both stories has a potentially instrumental effect as a protest against bad writing and aesthetic affectations. 'Bliss' raises serious issues about art and the dubious exploitative relationship between artists and the middle classes. We can also sense Mansfield's enjoyment of the scope given here for her comic gifts.

In common with previous stories, 'Bliss' achieves its impact through tautly organized patterns of imagery. Bertha finds that her white and green costume echoes the colours of the pear tree outside the window. She comes downstairs rustling her 'petals' to greet Mrs Norman Knight, whose coat, decorated with a frieze of monkeys, provokes a comparison with her own monkey-like appearance. **What do you make of Mansfield's use of imagery in this story?** These trivial comparisons in Bertha's mind contribute to the story's satirical and comic elements. At the same time, they do provoke a sense of potentially significant correspondences, which, like the story's play on the pear tree and Pear(l) Fulton's name, add to the suspense arising from Bertha's ecstatic sense that 'something divine' is about to happen (p.174). Other recurrent images include the moon, associated especially with the silvery Pearl Fulton and her 'moonbeam fingers', which, in Bertha's mind, confirms her identity with the pear tree that stands bathed in moonlight outside the room (pp.180, 182, 185). It is disquieting to recall that the original rationale for the moon's introduction into the story was that it served to illuminate Eddie's extremely white socks (p.179). Bertha's transcendent bliss is enmeshed in a pattern of hyper-aestheticized trivia that counterpoints her delusion and eventual disillusion. At the very moment of her disenchantment, Eddie is enthusing about the beauty of a poem that begins 'Why Must it Always be Tomato Soup?'; 'It is so *deeply* true, don't you feel?' he asks, just as Bertha has seen Harry and Pearl embracing in the hallway, 'Tomato soup is so *dreadfully* eternal' (p.185). This is both artistic satire and a rather horrible mockery of Bertha's illusory sense of communion with Pearl, for the absurd image echoes one from earlier in the story when 'Bertha knew ... that Pearl Fulton, stirring the beautiful red soup in the grey plate, was feeling just what she was feeling' (p.181). This passage is a prelude to the apparently crucial moment that the two women later share in front of the pear tree. In a fashion that is typical of Mansfield's rhythmic disposition of imagery, the reappearance of the tomato soup heralds the way in which the culmination of Bertha's misconceived bliss is derided by Pearl Fulton's departing words 'your lovely pear tree!' (p.185).

Many of the story's readers have found 'Bliss' cruel or shallow. Bowen was to describe it, in the preface to her 1957 selection of Mansfield's stories, as 'flawless ... yet ... for all its accomplishment ... to me one of her few disagreeable stories' (1957, p.17). In her diary for 1918, Virginia Woolf complained that 'Bliss' achieved 'superficial smartness', not depth, and was 'not the vision of an interesting mind' (1977a, vol.1, p.179). **Do you agree with these criticisms?** Others have seen the story differently. Taking up Woolf's criticism, Clare Hanson and Andrew Gurr, to whose account of symbolism in Mansfield's work my own mode of reading her work is indebted, suggest that 'The appeal of "Bliss" is precisely not to or from "the mind"'; they see it as 'a Symbolist story in which meaning cannot be apprehended or summarised discursively' (1981, p.59). They propose that 'the charge of cruelty or disagreeableness stems from the resultant lack of a clearly defined authorial presence in the story':

> Mansfield effaces the narrator-figure as nearly as possible, leaving the text and its controlling network of images to 'speak for itself'. The absence of a controlling 'metalanguage' to direct our responses may consequently create a sense of moral or ethical vacuum. Again, close reading is necessary for appreciation of the technique of muted direction which gives the story its very definite moral edge.
>
> (Hanson and Gurr, 1981, p.59)

For these critics, the story is a near tragic portrayal of a character just self-conscious enough to know her limitations. They point out that Mansfield described to Murry the intended effect of the borrowed phrases that she gave Bertha, who, 'not being an artist, was yet artist manqué enough to realise that these words and expressions were not and couldn't be hers' (quoted in Hanson and Gurr, 1981, p.60). Nevertheless, it is understandable that both the lack of a declared authorial viewpoint and the intricate ambiguity of the patterns of imagery in 'Bliss' that we have already discussed should provoke conflicting critical responses. The impact of the story depends after all on a degree of the same intense aestheticization that it simultaneously criticizes, demonstrating the 'fine line in Mansfield's work ... between the art she attacks and the art in which that art is attacked' (Coroneos, 1997, p.210).

Among the enthusiastic contemporary readers of the story was the poet T.S. Eliot. In *After Strange Gods*, in which he explored the experimental qualities of contemporary fiction, he described 'Bliss' as 'brief, poignant and in the best sense, slight', admiring the 'skill with which the author has handled perfectly the *minimum* material' (1934, pp.35, 36). Eliot regarded the minimalism and lack of overt morality in Mansfield's story as 'feminine' (*ibid.*, p.36). The moral implications of Mansfield's story were to him 'negligible: the centre of interest is the wife's feeling, first of ecstatic happiness, and then at the moment of revelation' (*ibid.*, pp.35–6). As far as Eliot was concerned, 'We are given neither comment nor suggestion of any moral issue of good and evil ... The story is limited to this sudden change of feeling, and the moral and social ramifications are outside the terms of reference' (*ibid.*, p.36). Feminist critics have not surprisingly taken issue with Eliot's use of the term 'feminine' here. Many readers have felt that while Mansfield offers no direct moral comment and undoubtedly does concentrate on Bertha's feelings of bliss and their reversal, strong moral implications nevertheless emerge from this and other stories she wrote at the time. Moreover, it could be argued that Mansfield's use of irony has certain 'moral' effects on her readers, encouraging them to see Bertha as naive and deluded (see Meisel, 1994).

Although it was not universally liked, 'Bliss' 'established Katherine Mansfield as one of the moderns' (Hanson and Gurr, 1981, p.58). Mansfield's description of T.S. Eliot's ' The Love Song of J. Alfred Prufrock' (1917) in a letter to Virginia Woolf as 'after all a short story' suggests a sense of affinity with his methods (quoted in *ibid.*, p.59). It also suggests that she saw her chosen genre as central to the modernist enterprise. The short-story form is sometimes described as a quintessentially modernist form, especially suited to such sensibilities, preoccupations and writing methods. The same critics who make this point often lament that the form is under-represented in histories of modernism – that Joyce's *Ulysses* is more confidently placed as a milestone in literary history than is *Dubliners*, for example. In that case, Mansfield shares something of the fate of the form in which she wrote: as I mentioned previously, histories of modernism have frequently neglected to assess her contribution.

The short story was certainly an ideal medium in which to explore the modernist preoccupation with epiphany – or 'the moment of revelation' as Eliot termed it in his comments on 'Bliss' (1934, p.36) – and it was used in this way by other modernist writers, including Joyce and Lawrence. **Read Hanson and Gurr's brief summary of the development of the short-**

story form and the importance of what Mansfield herself described as the 'one blazing moment' (Reader, Item 9). What sort of epiphany do we encounter in 'Bliss' and in other stories by Mansfield?

I have already talked about the epiphany in 'How Pearl Button Was Kidnapped', which centres on a vivid moment of childhood perception. In 'The Woman at the Store' there is the shocking instant of realization when Hin and the narrator see the child's drawing of her father's murder. Frau Brechenmacher's 'Na, what is it all for?' is a more muted moment of realization. In 'Prelude', Kezia's encounter with death is an epiphany, as is her mother's clear acknowledgement of the hatred that accompanies her love for her husband. All these might be seen as examples of the 'internal crises' identified by Hanson and Gurr as having replaced the 'external crises of plot' in modern fiction.

'Bliss' builds to a moment of epiphany for Bertha. Her feelings of happiness crystallize in an erotic fascination with the mysterious Pearl Fulton. This culminates in the apparently shared moment when Bertha shows Pearl her prized pear tree. As the guests leave, the erotic attraction embodied in Pearl is suddenly transferred to Bertha's husband, for whom Bertha feels genuine desire for the first time. All the potential hingeing on her false epiphany – the shared moment of bliss – is shattered when she realizes that Pearl and Harry are themselves engaged in an affair that excludes her. The ugliness of the revelation is mirrored by similar moments of disillusionment in other stories that Mansfield wrote at this time.

In 'Sun and Moon' (1920), it is a child's view of a magical world that is shattered as he views a scene of drunken despoliation at his parents' evening party. (The parallel with Bertha is made closer by the fact that she is portrayed as something of a child-woman.) 'Miss Brill' (1920), one of Mansfield's most devastating depictions of loneliness, shows the main character delighted by the sense that she and all the other visitors to the park where she goes each Sunday are united by playing roles in a shared play. This sense of communion is callously broken when she overhears the young couple who share her bench joking about her. Mansfield also wrote stories that sustain a positive epiphany rather than disillusion. Her late New Zealand story 'The Doll's House' (1922) finishes with a moment where the individual imagination briefly transcends the class divisions that form a menacing context for the story. Kezia, defying her parents' orders not to play with the daughters of a washerwoman, shows the two sisters the Burnell's new doll's house. Afterwards, the generally silent Else's 'I seen the little lamp' grants her possession of the same vision that has entranced Kezia (p.356).

In 'Bliss', the moment when Bertha shows Pearl the blossoming pear tree seems an instant of profound communion, of which Pearl's later '"Your lovely pear tree"' (p.185) is a bitter mockery. Both in her focus on epiphanic moments and in her portrayals of the difficulty of attaining the genuine communication that such moments appear to offer, Mansfield is dramatizing points made by Walter Pater in his famous and much quoted 'Conclusion' to *The Renaissance* (1873). It is a text of fundamental importance for the study of modernism in general, and you may want to return to it at various points in the chapters ahead. **Read Pater's 'Conclusion' (Reader, Item 10) and think about how his work might illuminate your understanding of Mansfield's writing.** (You may also find it helpful to refer to Wilde's Preface to *The Picture of Dorian Gray* (Reader, Item 1), which is discussed in the Introduction to Part 1 of this book.)

Pater describes genuine communication between people as hopelessly elusive. We are each of us surrounded by a 'thick wall of personality through which no real voice has ever pierced, on its way to us, or from us'. Much of the modernist emphasis on the elusive importance of the epiphanic moment arises from Pater's formulation that 'the narrow chamber of the individual mind' is penetrated only by 'impressions' that are 'unstable, flickering, inconsistent' and that it is art that can transform these passing impressions into something of worth. It was on these grounds that he infamously advocated 'the love of art for art's sake ... for art comes to you proposing frankly to give nothing but the highest quality to your moments as they pass, and simply for those moments' sake'.

Clearly, Bertha's ultimate 'moment' in 'Bliss' is one of disillusion rather than of positive illumination. In 'Prelude', the presiding symbol of the aloe means different things to the different characters who encounter it. In 'Bliss', the pear tree becomes a more sharply defined focus for the disjunction of individual consciousnesses. Mansfield in this story paints a bleak picture of communication between individuals. However, the 'bliss' of her title is both ironized and affirmed in the serene closing vision of the pear tree that 'was as lovely as ever and as full of flower and as still' (p.185).

Andrew Bennett and Nicholas Royle provide a valuable account of 'Bliss' in a chapter on 'Pleasure' in their book *An Introduction to Literature, Criticism and Theory* (1995). **Read the extract from 'Pleasure' now (Reader, Item 11). What are some of the broader literary concerns that 'Bliss' allows Bennett and Royle to explore?**

Essentially, Bennett and Royle take Eliot's observation that the story's 'centre of interest is the wife's feeling ... of ecstatic happiness' as their starting point (Eliot, 1934, p.36). 'Bliss' provides a text that both describes moments of bliss and enacts them. Bennett and Royle discuss the story's portrayal of Bertha's feelings of bliss and list some of the pleasures that it offers to its readers: 'identification, irony, suspense and social satire' and most importantly, 'a pleasure in words'. Their discussion of Mansfield's story includes a helpful account of its narrative voice, and the way in which irony and suspense are generated. They consider the story's treatment of 'the curious temporality of pleasure' within the specific historical context of the

Paterian 'moment', as well as its wider relevance. Reflecting on the experience of reading Mansfield's text leads them to suggest some more general ideas about the relation of pleasure to literature: first, the notion that literature itself, because it has to seduce the reader, is always 'erotic', always 'about the possibility of pleasure'. The Freudian concept of 'disavowal', or the reader's 'willing suspension of disbelief' in the face of ironic knowledge, plays an important part in this process of seduction. Bennett and Royle find that Mansfield's story 'dramatizes the way in which pleasure is concerned with strangeness (the nothingness of laughter), paradox (the inarticulable) and contradiction (disavowal)'.

Reading Mansfield's 'Bliss' facilitates a transition from the discussion of pleasure as a topic to the issue of 'pleasure' as a distinctively literary concept. Bennett and Royle define the story as a distinctively modernist text and one that provides fruitful material for the illumination of more recent theories of reading. Chief among these is the French structuralist critic Roland Barthes's investigation of pleasure in relation to practices of reading, an account of which is provided in the extract. Far from being merely a question of hedonism or aesthetic enjoyment, pleasure is crucially tied up with issues of identity and its dissolution. **What do you think of Bennett and Royle's elaboration of this idea of pleasure in relation to 'Bliss'?** We are reminded that Bertha is in danger of scattering into a 'shower of sparks' and Bennett and Royle suggest that as readers, our own identity is subject to the contradictions inherent in the pleasures of reading. We might reflect that this metaphor of showering sparks looks forward to Mansfield's dramatization of the 'one blazing moment' as one of disintegration as much as of revelation. Critics of 'Bliss' have frequently described Bertha as 'hysterical'; Bennett and Royle's account implicates us too, as readers of the story. All readers, male and female, might experience hysteria: we can see the theme of hysteria in the story as a non-gendered analogue for the loss of identity contingent on the pleasures of reading itself. Mansfield's story provides ideal material to illuminate these theoretical and critical concerns. It offers fertile ground for exploring some of the things that happen when we read – in particular, the role of the reader in the creation of literary meaning.

Free indirect discourse: 'The Daughters of the Late Colonel'

While 'Bliss' concentrates on a single character, the next story that I want to consider is, like 'Prelude', remarkable for the way in which it moves between the minds of different characters. **Read 'The Daughters of the Late Colonel' (1921) now. What are some of the ways in which it elaborates the techniques established in 'Prelude'?**

'The Daughters of the Late Colonel' was the story that Mansfield specifically described as 'the outcome of the *Prelude* method – it just unfolds and opens' (1984–96, vol.4, p.156). Like 'Prelude', the story is organized into twelve sections. The twelve sections fall into two mirroring groups of six. Each of the story's sections unfurls into the next, frequently opening with an echo of the sisters' haphazard thoughts – 'Another thing', 'But, after all', 'Well, at any rate' – and going on to follow their woolly conversations, imprecise dreams and mental 'tangents' (pp.232, 233, 235, 240).

We might regard the disparity between the sisters' vagueness and the clear narrative structure as contributing to the story's ironic effects. It helps the reader to recognize the deterministic structures that trap the two sisters, organizing their lives for them before they have time to take action. From another perspective, we might also agree with Smith that the way in which Mansfield allows her characters' illogical mental lives to flow over the boundaries of the different sections of the stories might be seen as making a mockery of attempts to organize experience into tidy categories (Smith, 1999, p.196).

Mansfield characterizes the two sisters Constantia and Josephine in prose that reflects their indeterminate thoughts. The opening paragraph's list of participles and its incomplete concluding sentence exemplify this: the sisters are introduced to us as they lie 'thinking things out, talking things over, wondering, deciding, trying to remember where ….' (p.230). The story makes palpable the extent of paternal tyranny under which they still live: it has left them both incapable of deciding anything and Constantia so timid that she winces at the cracking of a meringue shell (p.241). They are overcome by fear that father will be angry with them for burying him and for the expense of his funeral (p.236). Convinced that he is still somewhere in the flat, they are unable to face opening the drawers or wardrobe in his room, which, shrouded in white, becomes a comical gothic chamber of horrors, a recognizable if oblique echo of the red room with its luminous white death-bed in which Jane Eyre is incarcerated in Charlotte Brontë's 1848 novel (pp.237, 238). Brontë's novel is a powerful comment on the condition of nineteenth-century womanhood; a strong underlying concern with gender issues can be identified in Mansfield's story, illustrating the way in which the legacy of nineteenth-century fiction was arguably of greater importance for female modernists than for their male contemporaries. Mansfield's biographer Antony Alpers notes that the 'Edwardian victims' in her '*dame seule* stories have more of history in them than has been acknowledged' (1980, p.328). Literary history too, perhaps. Smith sees the story as commenting on the conventions that govern the heroines of fiction, the sisters' passivity and vagueness of speech draws attention to the fact that literature has generally had no more idea than has society of how to script the parts of two elderly and dependent women (1999, p.216).

'The Daughters of the Late Colonel' begins with both sisters caught up in the mental turmoil that follows their father's death. **How does Mansfield's narrative voice link together the different characters in the story?**

The narrative weaves in and out between the thoughts of the two sisters, at times including other characters too – as at the moment when Kate enters, and the perceptions of the sisters overlap with her own assessment of herself as 'the enchanted princess' (p.233). This image moves between the thought patterns of several characters without any explanatory context, within a single matter-of-fact sentence of third-person narrative. The narrative twists so subtly between the sisters that we tend to lose track of whose thoughts we are following; at times they seem pretty much to share the same thought – as in their initially indistinguishable visions of an Indian messenger running to deliver their father's watch (p.239). Although they are ultimately unable to communicate their most important feelings, the sisters live in a vague mental intimacy which blurs their individual identities, so that, for example, the thought processes that lead to Josephine's decision about their father's watch are conjoined, or at any rate are accepted, as unamenable to explanation (p.244). In their study of Mansfield, Hanson and Gurr describe her technique in this story as giving the effect of 'interior monologue externalized by the use of the third person' (1981, p.88). The term 'monologue' does perhaps express the way in which the two sisters seem barely to enjoy separate identities and conveys the strange, blurred doubling that the story conjures. Other critics have also described Mansfield's technique as an extension of interior monologue (Gordon, 1954, p.24). However, 'free indirect discourse' possibly remains a more appropriate term with which to describe the way that Mansfield pulls together thoughts and images as much as the speech patterns of different characters. As I mentioned previously, her narrative technique is closer to the free indirect discourse of Woolf's stream-of-consciousness writing than to the interior monologue proper of Joyce's *Ulysses*.

Now reread the second half of 'The Daughters of the Late Colonel' (from Section VI; p.236) and think about how these sections mirror the first part of the story and work towards its conclusion.

As with Section I, Section VII shows the two sisters alone and more incapable of action than ever. They ponder what they should do with their father's watch. Pamela Dunbar suggests that Josephine's idea that they should send it hidden inside a corset box figures female oppression – the watch a ticking heart imprisoned within (1997, p.154). For Smith, this is a rebellious joke on Josephine's part, a subversive counterpart to Constantia's more heroic vision of their brother as a colonial administrator in a pith helmet; the corset box would provoke gratifying embarrassment and show that, despite being treated as a girl, the dependent daughter of the late Colonel has the body of a mature woman (1999, pp.220–1).

In Section VIII, the sisters look forward to a visit from their nephew Cyril. Here Mansfield introduces a subtle indeterminacy of tense until we realize that rather than moving forward, the narrative has slid into the past. This retrospective account of their nephew's previous visit unfolds into Section IX, a recollection, mirroring that in Section III in the first half of the story, of the father, whose lingering presence still so tangibly dominates their thoughts and thus the text. Their hopeless indecision about Kate, the inheritor of some of their father's tyrannous power, brings the story back to the sisters' present experience and leads into the story's final section.

Here, the sound of a barrel-organ provides a rhythmic accompaniment to the sisters' tentative realization that they will never again need to answer to the thumping summons of their father's stick (although even now, their father's voice is woven into the narrative with his 'make that monkey take his noise somewhere else'; p.246). A wavering, then steady, glow of sunlight enters the room with 'a fountain of bubbling notes' from the barrel-organ, hinting at a possible liberation: ' "The sun's out," said Josephine, as though it really mattered' (p.247). In the space of a single paragraph, the sunlight, as it passes over furniture and photographs, illuminates their memories of childhood and, in one further paragraph, their thoughts of what their lives might have been (pp.247–8). Josephine is drawn to look outwards from the window at the sunlight. Constantia's memories are bathed in moonlight, but her usual vague dreaminess is replaced by a sharp recollection of the Bergsonian moments at which she had 'really felt herself' apart from 'this other life' of daily errands and subjection. However, her attempt to tell Josephine 'something frightfully important, about the future and what ...' trails off in formless ellipsis and, as at the door of their father's room, the sisters have one of their pathetically funny exchanges about who 'goes first', until neither can remember what she wanted to say. The sunlight has nurtured but a brief and incomplete epiphany. The story ends with a simple and saddening movement away from this symbol of a possible future to its obscuration in mental cloudiness. The sun is twice called 'thieving'; the time since the photographs on the piano began to fade has been time lost and the future will not change (pp.247, 248). We know that the sisters will never live the 'real' life that Constantia – and probably Josephine too – has glimpsed from time to time, but whose importance they cannot articulate. Mansfield was upset at accusations that her story was cruel and 'sneering'. 'It's almost terrifying to be so misunderstood', she wrote to William Gerhardi:

> There was a moment when I first had 'the idea' when I saw the
> two sisters as *amusing*; but the moment I looked deeper ... I
> bowed down to the beauty that was hidden in their lives ... All

was meant, of course, to lead up to that last paragraph, when my two flowerless ones turned with that timid gesture, to the sun. 'Perhaps *now*.' And after that, it seemed to me, they died as truly as Father was dead.

(Mansfield, 1984–96, vol.4, p.249)

The year 1921 was extremely productive for Mansfield despite her worsening health. Among the other stories on which she worked that year were three more of what Bowen calls her 'august, peaceful New Zealand stories' (1957, p.22): 'At the Bay', 'The Garden Party' and 'The Doll's House'. These, together with 'Prelude', have consistently been among the most popular of Mansfield's works. 'They would be miracles of memory', Bowen comments, 'if one considered them memories at all – more, they are what she foresaw them as: a re-living' (*ibid.*, p.22). I shall have space to discuss only 'At the Bay' in the rest of this chapter, but you should certainly read the remaining New Zealand stories for yourselves.

Myth and modernism: 'At the Bay'

Mansfield left an account of the process of writing 'At the Bay' in a letter of 1921 to the painter Dorothy Brett, in which she described the story as 'a continuation of "Prelude"'. 'It is so strange to bring the dead to life again', she wrote:

> I have tried to make it as familiar to 'you' as it is to me. You know the marigolds? You know those pools in the rocks? You know the mousetrap on the wash house window sill? And, too, one tried to go deep – to speak to the secret self we all have – to acknowledge that.

(Mansfield, 1984–96, vol.4, p.278)

Bringing the dead to life may suggest a straightforwardly mimetic view of fiction, yet we remember that Mansfield defined memory as a selective and creative faculty. Here, she also seems to see the reader's response as crucial to the process of 're-living' that her fiction performs. Kaplan describes this story as the 'most sophisticated development' of 'Mansfield's Modernism' (1991, p.217). You will notice when you read the story that it extends all the main characteristics that have been evident in the earlier stories, communicating mood and atmosphere through free indirect discourse, narrative discontinuity and the rich symbolic patterning of imagery whose psychological associations speak to the 'secret self' of her characters and readers. The story also shows Mansfield's continued interest in the workings of family, gender and sexuality.

Read 'At the Bay' now. What is distinctive about the timescale of this story?

Like 'Prelude' and 'The Daughters of the Late Colonel', the story was originally written in twelve sections (the last paragraph was divided off as a thirteenth section for the American edition of her stories; the Oxford World's Classics edition follows this pattern). However, the entire action of this story takes place in the space of a single day. The story begins before sunrise and ends when night has fallen. The story's opening, with its description of plants so drenched with dew that the landscape seems just to have emerged from the sea, echoes Mansfield's earlier vision of how 'this little island has dipped back into the dark blue sea during the night only to rise again at beam of day, all hung with bright spangles and glittering drops' (Mansfield, 1984–96, vol.1, p.331). The beginning of this particular day also invokes the creation of the world in the book of Genesis. Sea and land are indistinguishable, 'hidden under a white sea-mist', waiting for the first light to call them out of a formless void. The mist at the beginning of 'At the Bay' is emblematic of Mansfield's own creative method as she described it when writing about 'Prelude', where 'white milky mists rise and uncover some beauty, then smother it again and then again disclose it' (*ibid.*).

The sense that Mansfield's account of a single day is also a Creation myth is continued by the innocent pastoral scene of the shepherd and his flock described by the opening section. Later in the day, at sunset, there are echoes of the Day of Judgement (as described in the Book of Revelation) (p.309). As the story evolves, Mansfield uses the day as a parallel for the individual human life. This is made explicit in Jonathan Trout's exclamation on ' "The shortness of life! The shortness of life!" I've only one night or one day, and there's this vast dangerous garden, waiting out there, undiscovered, unexplored' (p.308).

In Mansfield's use of one day as the framework for her story 'two characteristically Modernist assumptions are conflated: man's life is no more than a single day ... but, conversely, the whole of a man's life can be revealed during a single day, even in an epiphanic moment' (Hanson and Gurr, 1981, p.99). The story ranges from the universal timescale of Creation itself, through the individual lifespan, to the representation of revelationary moments that parallel those depicted in 'Prelude'. As in 'Prelude', Kezia fleetingly confronts the certainty of death – this time the horrifying possibility that her grandmother could leave her (p.299). Beryl's encounters with the Kembers give her an insight into a predatory sexualized world. For Linda, there is a moment of epiphany that in some sense reverses the recognition of her hatred in the earlier story as she is overwhelmed with helpless love for her baby son (p.296). For her, the day ends in 'joyful beauty'; the evening sky, although reminiscent of a Judgement scene, looks 'infinitely joyful and loving' (p.309).

Mansfield's representation of gender in this story is also linked to its panoply of different timescales. Stanley's irritable clock-watching contrasts with the different, less mechanical sense of time associated with the female characters of the story. They are implicitly more closely connected with the cyclical motion of time associated with the sea and the movement of the day. Once Stanley has departed for town, time expands for the women left behind: 'the whole perfect day was theirs' (p.287). There is a rare sense of communion: 'Their very voices were changed as they called to one another; they sounded warm and loving and as if they shared a secret' (*ibid.*). Mansfield continues the rhythm evoked in this image of the women calling to each other, moving from Beryl's 'Have another cup of tea, mother' to Mrs Fairfax tossing the baby upwards and the girls running 'into the paddock like chickens let out of a coop' (*ibid.*). The sequence extends to the servant girl Alice plunging the teapot under the water 'as if it too was a man and drowning was too good for them' (p.288). The moment passes, however, and we see the individual women of the household mostly as solitary individuals, confronting the different but related implications of their gender. Linda's 'grudge against life' is that it is assumed to be 'the common lot of women to bear children', but that childbearing has left her 'broken' and unable to love her children (pp.295, 296). Meanwhile, Beryl feels threatened by the lack of the husband and family that cause Linda's suffering, and Alice is harshly unsettled by the widowed Mrs Stubbs's 'freedom's best!' (p.303). Relations between the sexes are generally even more distant than in 'Prelude', but there is one genuine moment of connection, in Section X of the story, between Linda and Jonathan Trout, whose communicativeness and lack of ambition are feminine traits that exasperate Stanley. Linda's encounter with Stanley on his return home in the next section of the story is in marked and comic contrast to her sympathetic exchange with her brother-in-law.

Mansfield's representation of life as a day in 'At the Bay' is one of the many aspects of this story that probably influenced Virginia Woolf's innovative modernist novel *The Waves* (1931). Other features that are echoed in the later novel include the extraordinary way in which Mansfield manages to give a simultaneous account of the psychology of a whole group of characters – including of her circle of card-playing children, predecessors of the group of child characters in Woolf's novel. Mansfield's use of the sea looks forward to the way in which Woolf structured her novel around episodes that describe the movement of the waves at different points in the day. In Mansfield's story, descriptions of the sea and waves at dawn, noon and night punctuate the story's beginning, middle and end, reinforcing parallels between the day and the human lifespan. 'At the Bay' begins by picturing that 'the sea had beaten up softly in the darkness, as though one immense wave had come rippling, rippling – how far?' (p.280). Section VII begins at midday, when 'The tide was out; the beach was deserted; lazily flopped the warm sea' (p.297). In the final paragraph, the 'deep, troubled' sound of the darkened sea fades into a 'vague murmur' before the final cadence 'All was still' (p.314). Noting the affinities between this story and Woolf's novel is one way of demonstrating that Mansfield, like Woolf, deserves the place within accounts of literary modernism that critics such as Kaplan have claimed for her.

Although moments of insight and connection are rare for Mansfield's characters, the text itself acquires a telepathic unity. The sophisticated orchestration of people, dialogue and imagery in 'At the Bay' achieves a movement between the minds of different characters that is more constant and fluid than in 'Prelude'. This is illustrated by the scene between the women of the household already discussed, and by the perfect comic timing of the children's card-playing scene, a virtuoso performance, in which snippets of dialogue and description suggest the slapping sound of cards on the table during a game of animal snap. The text moves between characters at a frenetic pace, communicating with the minimum of means a great deal about the psychology of each child and building a crescendo that terminates in the horrified silence at the moment when they hear something in the darkness outside (p.306). Sections such as this suggest analogies with musical movements, as well as with the textures and rhythms of music. This card-playing *scherzo* (a bustling and humorous symphonic movement, sometimes, as in Beethoven, with a macabre edge) is a vigorous contrast to the lyrical closing coda of the story and to the opening 'aubade' (a musical movement depicting dawn), in which land, sea, the sound and movements of a flock of sheep are woven together into a sinuous overture. Mansfield's clear, unmannered prose comes as near as that of any modernist writer to enacting Pater's influential dictum that '*All art constantly aspires to the condition of music*' (Pater, [1877] 1888, p.140).

Conclusion

My reading of 'At the Bay' has moved increasingly towards an account of the aesthetic qualities of Mansfield's writing. The fact that a concern with lived human experience, with gender and class relations, and with injustices of many kinds, is conspicuous in all her writing undermines any easy distinction between the categories of aesthetic and instrumental art that are debated in the different chapters of Part 1 of this book. In this respect there are also parallels with Woolf. Current studies of Woolf are likely to emphasize how strongly her work engages with issues such as gender, class and war. Mansfield's 'poetic' prose can likewise be shown to have relevance beyond its formal or biographical contexts. Interpretation of her stories is enriched by attention to their engagement with contemporary gender, class and race relations – aspects that I have been able to discuss briefly in this chapter. At the same time, I have been concerned, notwithstanding recent criticism of 'apolitical' readings of Mansfield, to pay due attention to the formal qualities that are fundamental to the experience of reading her work; the formal innovations of her writing play an integral part in its engagement with the world. The oblique nature of Mansfield's writing also means that, while her stories imply a critique of colonialism, they do not demand a detailed knowledge of European or colonial history; nor do they provide ready answers to readers who probe them for specific political comments or affiliations. Mansfield's work continues to lend itself to conscious appreciation of the methods through which it engages with these concerns: her symbolic use of imagery, the seductive, rhythmical qualities of her language and her extraordinarily subtle narrative technique.

Works cited

Alpers, A. (1980) *The Life of Katherine Mansfield*, New York: Viking.

Berkman, S. (1952) *Katherine Mansfield: A Critical Study*, London: Geoffrey Cumberlege; Oxford: Oxford University Press.

Bowen, E. (1957) 'Introduction', K. Mansfield, *34 Short Stories*, London: Collins.

Caffin, E. (1982) *Introducing Katherine Mansfield*, Auckland: Longman Paul.

Cather, W. (1936) *Not Under Forty*, London: Cassell.

Coroneos, C. (1997) 'Flies and Violets in Katherine Mansfield', in S. Raitt and T. Tait (eds), *Women's Fiction and the Great War*, Oxford: Clarendon Press, pp.197–218.

Cuddon, J.A. (1992) 'Satire' entry, in *The Penguin Dictionary of Literary Terms and Literary Theory*, Harmondsworth: Penguin.

Dunbar, P. (1997) *Radical Mansfield: Double Discourse in Katherine Mansfield's Short Stories*, Basingstoke: Macmillan.

Eliot, T.S. (1934) *After Strange Gods: A Primer of Modern Heresy*, The Page-Barbour lectures at the University of Virginia, 1933, London: Faber.

Essays in Criticism, 12 (1962) For the debate on Mansfield's 'The Fly', see pp.39–53, 335–51, 448–52.

Fullbrook, K. (1986) *Katherine Mansfield*, Key Women Writers, Brighton: Harvester.

Garver, L. (2001) 'The Political Katherine Mansfield', *MODERNISM/modernity*, 8, pp.225–43.

Gordon, I.A. (1954) *Katherine Mansfield*, British Council Writers and their Work, London: Longmans.

Hanson, C. and Gurr, A. (1981) *Katherine Mansfield*, London: Macmillan.

Ihimaera, W. (1989) *Dear Miss Mansfield: A Tribute to Katherine Mansfield Beauchamp*, Auckland: Viking.

Joyce, J. ([1922] 1993), *Ulysses*, ed. and intro. by J. Johnson, The World's Classics, Oxford: Oxford University Press.

Kaplan, S.J. (1991) *Katherine Mansfield and the Origins of Modernist Fiction*, Ithaca: Cornell University Press.

Mansfield, K. (1928) *The Letters of Katherine Mansfield*, ed. by J. Middleton Murry, 2 vols, London: Constable.

Mansfield, K. (1983) *The Aloe with Prelude*, ed. by V. O'Sullivan, Manchester: Carcanet.

Mansfield, K. (1984–96) *The Collected Letters of Katherine Mansfield*, ed. by V. O'Sullivan and M. Scott, 4 vols, Oxford: Clarendon Press.

Mansfield, K. (1987) *The Critical Writings of Katherine Mansfield*, ed. by C. Hanson, London: Macmillan.

Mansfield, K. (1997) *The Katherine Mansfield Notebooks*, ed. by M. Scott, 2 vols, Canterbury, NZ: Lincoln University Press; Wellington, NZ: Daphne Brasell Associates.

Mansfield, K. (2002) *Selected Stories*, ed. and intro. by A. Smith, Oxford World's Classics, Oxford: Oxford University Press.

Meisel, P. (1994) 'What the Reader Knows, or The French One', in R. Robinson (ed.), *Katherine Mansfield: In From the Margin*, Baton Rouge: Louisiana State University Press, pp.112–18.

O'Sullivan, V. (1997) 'Introduction', K. Mansfield, *New Zealand Stories*, Auckland: Oxford University Press, pp.1–14.

Pater, W. (1873) 'Conclusion', *Studies in the History of the Renaissance*, London: Macmillan.

Pater, W. ([1877] 1888) 'The School of Giorgione', in *The Renaissance: Studies in Art and Poetry*, 4th thousand, revised and enlarged, London: Macmillan.

Pilditch, J. (ed.) (1996) *The Critical Response to Katherine Mansfield*, Westport, CT: Greenwood.

Smith, A. (1999) *Katherine Mansfield and Virginia Woolf: A Public of Two*, Oxford: Clarendon Press.

Smith, A. (2000) *Katherine Mansfield: A Literary Life*, Basingstoke: Palgrave Macmillan.

Smith, A. (2002) 'Introduction', K. Mansfield, *Selected Stories*, Oxford World's Classics, Oxford: Oxford University Press, pp.ix–xxxii.

Stead, C.K. (1977) 'Introduction', *The Letters and Journals of Katherine Mansfield: A Selection*, London: Allen Lane, pp.9–20.

Tate, T. (ed.) (1995) *Women, Men and the Great War: An Anthology of Stories*, Manchester: Manchester University Press.

Tate, T. and Raitt, S. (1997) 'Introduction', in S. Raitt and T. Tate (eds), *Women's Fiction and the Great War*, Oxford: Clarendon Press, pp.1–17.

Williams, M. (2000) 'Mansfield in Maoriland: Biculturalism, Agency and Misreading', in H.J. Booth and N. Rigby (eds), *Modernism and Empire*, Manchester: Manchester University Press, pp.249–74.

Woolf, V. (1977a) *The Diaries of Virginia Woolf*, ed. by A.O. Bell, vols 2 and 3, London: Hogarth Press.

Woolf, V. (1977b) *The Letters of Virginia Woolf*, ed. by N. Nicholson, vol.3, London: Hogarth Press.

Further reading

Boddy, G. (1988) *Katherine Mansfield: The Woman and the Writer*, Harmondsworth: Penguin. An additional feminist account of Mansfield's life and work.

Gurr, A. (1981) *Writers in Exile: The Identity of Home in Modern Literature*, Brighton: Harvester. Mansfield is considered alongside other twentieth-century writers who wrote in 'exile' from their birthplace.

Hankin, C.A. (1983) *Katherine Mansfield and her Confessional Stories*, London: Macmillan. A psychoanalytic reading of Mansfield's life and work.

Mansfield, K. (1997) *New Zealand Stories*, ed. and intro. by V. O'Sullivan, Auckland: Oxford University Press. As well as her better-known New Zealand stories, the collection includes early work by Mansfield, such as 'In the Botanical Gardens' (1907), which helps to illustrate the relevance of the 'broad frame of Empire' to much of her writing (p.4).

Tomalin, C. (1987) *Katherine Mansfield: A Secret Life*, London: Viking. A major biography, along with that by Alpers. Tomalin gives a detailed account of Mansfield's medical history and investigates the context for the publication and subsequent repression of the story derived from Chekhov's 'Sleepy'.

CHAPTER 3

Lewis Grassic Gibbon, *Sunset Song*

DAVID JOHNSON

Overview

This chapter sets out by locating debates about what literature is for in the context of Scotland in the 1930s. There follows a part-by-part textual analysis of *Sunset Song* in the light of these concerns. Finally, I consider debates over *Sunset Song* from the 1930s to the present, looking at the reviews of the first edition, the disagreements over its nationalist or socialist credentials, and its place in contemporary Scottish education and culture.

Contexts

In 1934, the first issue of the British journal *Left Review* published a position statement by the Writers' International, a group of radical writers. The statement included the following thoughts on what role writers should play in British society:

> The decadence of the past twenty years of English literature and the theatre cannot be understood apart from all that separates 1913 and 1934. It is the collapse of a culture, accompanying the collapse of an economic system.
>
> There are already a number of writers who realize this; they desire and are working for the ending of the capitalist order of society. They aim at a new order based not on property and profit, but on co-operative effort. They realize that the working class will be the builders of this new order, and see that the change will be revolutionary in effect. Even those to whom politics are secondary desire to align themselves more closely with the class that will build socialism.
>
> It is time for these, together with the working-class journalists and writers who are trying to express the feelings of their class, to organize an association of revolutionary writers.
>
> (in Margolies, 1998, pp.23–4)

In this provocative statement, Britain's economy and culture alike are declared to be in a state of terminal decay. Literature, or rather a particular form of literature produced by writers opposed to capitalism and committed to a new co-operative order, is proposed as an appropriate antidote. In other words, literature is anything but elevated, self-contained or sacrosanct, as the aesthetes had claimed; rather, for the Writers' International, literature has the potential, even an obligation, to criticize society and to contribute to the building of a socialist future.

The *Left Review*'s editors invited responses to the Writers' International statement; succeeding issues published a wide range of views on the nature of literature, the relation between literature and society, and the political responsibilities of writers. One of the first contributions published was that of Alec Brown, who proposed an extreme instrumental view of literature, declaring that 'all our writing has one end in view, the revolutionary end of establishing a socialist republic, that is a working class democracy' (in Margolies, 1998, p.27). Lewis Grassic Gibbon joined the controversy, with his response published in the February 1935 issue of *Left Review*. **Read Gibbon's response to the Writers' International statement (Reader, Item 12.1) and note down his thoughts on what literature is for.**

In common with the Writers' International, and like Brown, Gibbon expressed an unequivocal hostility to capitalism and a commitment to revolutionary writing: 'I hate capitalism; all my books are explicit or implicit propaganda.' However, Gibbon's position differed in at least two important respects. First, he rejected the diagnosis of capitalist culture as decadent, arguing, on the contrary, that the 1930s was a period of cultural dynamism: 'Capitalist literature, whether we like it or not, is not in decay; capitalist economics have reached the verge of collapse, which is quite a different matter. Towards the end of a civilisation the arts, so far from decaying, always reach their greatest efflorescence.'

Second, Gibbon insisted that more than rhetorical commitment to socialism was needed for writers to serve the end of socialist revolution; in addition, writers must produce 'work of definite and recognised literary value'. He is scathing about revolutionary writers who produce (in his opinion) inferior work: 'From their own second-rateness [those 'revolutionary' writers] hate and despise good work as they look upon any measure of success accruing to a book (not written by one of their own intimate circle) with a moronic envy.'

Gibbon wrote this piece only two years after the publication, in September 1932, of *Sunset Song* – shortly before his early death in February 1935. In setting out his own concerns and ambitions as a writer, it is the closest Gibbon comes to providing a theory of his own literary practice. Gibbon's concerns as a writer expressed here overlap with our own exploration of the question 'What is literature for?' Two related questions can be extrapolated from Gibbon's contribution to the *Left Review* writers' controversy:

- Does *Sunset Song* succeed as 'explicit or implicit anti-capitalist propaganda'? In other words, does it qualify as literature that serves an instrumental function, which for Gibbon was to provide a critique of capitalism?

- Is *Sunset Song* a work of 'definite and recognised literary value'? In other words, can its value as a work of literature be separated from its propagandistic ambitions?

These difficult questions, implicit in Gibbon's own critical self-reflection, provide the framework for the discussion of *Sunset Song* in the pages that follow.

Figure 3.1 Lewis Grassic Gibbon, *c.*1930. (By permission of The Grassic Gibbon Centre.)

James Leslie Mitchell to Lewis Grassic Gibbon

Gibbon was born James Leslie Mitchell in 1901 in the Aberdeenshire farming parish of Auchterless. His father was a tenant farmer. Both his parents were of peasant ancestry: his family had worked in the region for 300 years. When Gibbon was aged eight, the family moved south from Auchterless to a small farm in the Howe of the Mearns. Gibbon attended school in Arbuthnott, and at the age of fifteen he moved to Mackie Academy in Stonehaven, where he remained for a year before leaving school. Determined to escape work on the land, he found employment as a junior reporter in Aberdeen. In 1919, he moved to Glasgow to continue working as a journalist, but he was dismissed from his job within months and joined the Royal Army Service Corps in August 1919. From 1919 to 1923, he served in the Middle East, India and Persia. When he failed to find alternative employment on his discharge in 1923, he joined the Royal Air Force as a clerk. He remained in the RAF for six years, during which time he married Rebecca Middleton in 1925 and published his first book, *Hanno: Or the Future of Exploration*, in 1928. In 1929, Gibbon left the RAF to support himself by full-time writing. Living first in Hammersmith, then from December 1931 in Welwyn Garden City, he produced an extraordinary quantity of literary and critical work before his death in 1935. There were seven novels published under his own name, from *Stained Radiance* (1930) to *Gay Hunter* (1934), a collaboration with Hugh MacDiarmid for the book *Scottish Scene* and, under the pseudonym Lewis Grassic Gibbon (adapted from his mother's name), the trilogy *A Scots Quair* (*Sunset Song*, *Cloud Howe* and *Grey Granite*).

Gibbon's lifetime – from 1901 to 1935 – was one of fundamental political, economic and cultural transition in Scotland, with the decade leading up to the publication of *Sunset Song* in particular marked by hardship and social upheaval. The critic Angus Calder summarizes the major economic and political events as follows:

> After the First World War the country's characteristic heavy industries – coal, iron, shipbuilding – had lost export markets, but although new consumer-goods industries maintained prosperity for many in southern England, Scotland neither created nor attracted such industries. Mass unemployment led to mass emigration. In the ten years leading up to 1931, nearly 400,000 Scots (say about one person in twelve), left Scotland, and despite high natural increase population actually declined. Politically, Scotland had swung precociously to the left. In 1922 Labour had returned the largest bloc of Scottish MPs and the eccentric constituency of Motherwell had actually elected a Communist. But the abortion of the General Strike was followed by further

disillusionment when in 1931 a Scottish premier, Ramsay MacDonald, defected from the Labour Party to head the 'National' government, and his former party, which had held over half Scotland's seats, was reduced from 37 to a mere 7.

In 1932, when *Sunset Song* was published, over a quarter of all Scottish workers were unemployed; in the worst hit areas well over half; in Greenock, three-quarters even two years later when the slump had abated somewhat.

(Calder, 1982, pp.104–5)

Historians of the period emphasize that economic suffering in Scotland during the Depression was substantially worse than in England, and that this contributed to the rise of a vigorous Scottish nationalism. David Craig, for example, suggests that 'in an autonomous culture like Scotland's there was also a precipitation of nationalism – the wounded morale of a Distressed Area that happened to have a national past ... So a heightened, and painful, sense of a separate entity was reborn' (1964, p.154).

Scottish writers responded energetically to this world described by Calder as one of 'social disaster' and 'horrific crisis' (1982, p.105): in the 1920s and 1930s there emerged what came to be known as a 'Scottish Renaissance' in literature and the arts. The central figure in this movement was the poet C.M. Grieve, better known by his pseudonym Hugh MacDiarmid, whose creative example and critical initiatives acted as a controversial focal point for the writers of the generation. MacDiarmid and Gibbon used their collaborative volume *Scottish Scene* to set out their own highly partial views on Scottish literature and politics, and although the two writers differed fundamentally on several key matters, they were united in their hostility towards the Scottish establishment. MacDiarmid's attack on this establishment in 'Postlude', published in *Scottish Scene*, captures the combative temper of their writing:

> Away, away, to the mune and the devil
> Wi' these muddlers, ditherers, ancient disputants,
> Auld Lichts, wee Frees, Burnsians, London Scots!
> Let them awa' like shadows at noon to their haunts!
> ...
> Away, wi' the old superstitions. Let the sun up at last
> And hurl a' sic spooks into their proper abysm.

(in Bold, 2001, p.169)

These robust words did not go unanswered, as MacDiarmid and Gibbon made many enemies. Despite such acrimony, Scottish literature flourished: works by writers such as Edwin Muir, Willa Muir, Neil M. Gunn, George Blake, James Bridie, Naomi Mitchison and James Barke contributed to the vitality of the Scottish Renaissance. New Scottish books, as well as contemporary writing from further afield, were reviewed in the numerous small Scottish literary and cultural journals – *Modern Scot, Scottish Bookman, Outlook, The Scots Magazine, Library Review, The Free Man*. These journals also published interventions in the literary, cultural and political debates of the day, notably the place of Scots dialect in writing in English, and the competing claims of class and nation in literary creativity and production. (I will return to these debates in the final section of the chapter.) Underlying the polemic of all these debates was the sense that literature *mattered* enormously, and that the potential contribution of literature to Scotland's regeneration was immense. This general optimism is captured in William Power's 1935 survey of 'The Literary Movement in Scotland', where he concludes: 'To regard the modern literary movement in Scotland as merely ancillary to the process of nation-building would be a profound mistake. Her writers are helping to create the kind of nation in which literature can flourish' (1935, p.183).

A kailyard, a bonnie brier bush and a house with green shutters

To appreciate the distinctiveness of *Sunset Song*, I want to begin by looking first at the kind of Scottish novel that Gibbon was self-consciously reacting *against*. He provides a strong hint to the identity of his immediate literary antecedents in the concluding paragraph of the Prelude in *Sunset Song*:

> So that was Kinraddie that bleak winter of nineteen eleven and the new minister, him they chose early next year, he was to say it was the Scots countryside itself, fathered between a kailyard and a bonny brier bush in the lee of a house with green shutters.
>
> (Gibbon, [1932] 1988, p.24; all subsequent page references are to this edition)

Readers familiar with Scottish literature may recognize that in this sentence Gibbon is locating the setting of *Sunset Song* between two competing literary versions of rural Scotland: between the quaint rustic community depicted in the nineteenth-century kailyard novels exemplified by Ian Maclaren's *Beside the Bonnie Brier Bush* (1894), and the fractious and malicious villagers described in George Douglas Brown's *The House with the Green Shutters* (1901).

Read the following two extracts – the first from *Beside the Bonnie Brier Bush* and the second from *The House with the Green Shutters* – and the brief introductions to their authors. For each passage in turn, consider what is distinctive about the language and in particular the use of standard English and Scots dialect. How are rural Scotland and its communities represented?

Beside the Bonnie Brier Bush

Ian Maclaren was the pseudonym of the Reverend John Watson, a Free Kirk minister in a Perthshire village who progressed to more prestigious parishes first in Glasgow and then Liverpool. Together with the Reverend Samuel Rutherford Crockett and James Matthew Barrie, Maclaren made up what came to be known as the 'Kailyard school'. *Kailyard* means literally 'cabbage patch', the humble vegetable garden of the small Scottish farmyard. Maclaren's stories of the Scots village Drumtochty were based on his memories of life in Perthshire. They were first published in 1893 in the *British Weekly*, then collected a year later in *Beside the Bonnie Brier Bush*. It was an astonishing commercial success, quickly selling 250,000 copies in Britain, and half a million in the USA. The extract below is from the fifth sketch in the collection, 'The Cunning Speech of Drumtochty'.

> Speech in Drumtochty distilled slowly, drop by drop, and the faces of our men were carved in stone. Visitors without discernment used to pity our dullness, and lay themselves out for missionary work. Before their month was over they spoke bitterly of us, as if we had deceived them, and departed with a grudge in their hearts. When Hillocks scandalised the Glen by letting his house and living in the bothie – through sheer greed of money – it was taken by a fussy little man from the South, whose control over the letter 'h' was uncertain, but whose self-confidence bordered on the miraculous.
>
> ...
>
> 'Whatna like man is that English veesitor ye've got, Hillocks? a' hear he's fleein' ower the glen, yammerin' and haverin' like a starlin'.'
>
> 'He's a gabby (talkative) body, Drumsheugh, there's nae doot o' that, but terrible ignorant.'
>
> 'Says he tae me nae later than yesterday, "That's a fine field o' barley ye've there, Maister Harris," an' sure as deith a' didna ken whaur tae luik, for it was a puckle aits.'
>
> 'Keep's a',' said Whinnie; 'he's been awfu' negleckit when he was a bairn, or maybe there's a want in the puir cratur.'
>
> Next Sabbath Mr Urijah Hopps appeared in person among the fathers – who looked at each other over his head – and enlightened them on supply and demand, the Game Laws, the production of cabbages for towns, the iniquity of an Established Church, and the bad metre of the Psalms of David.
>
> 'You must 'ave henterprise, or it's hall hup with you farmers.'

'Ay, ay,' responded Drumsheugh, after a long pause, and then every man concentrated his attention on the belfry of the kirk.

'Is there onything ava' in the body, think ye, Domsie,' as Mr Hopps bustled into kirk, 'or is't a' wind?'

'Three wechtfu's o' naething, Drumsheugh; a' peety the puir man if Jamie Soutar gets a haud o' him.'

Jamie was the cynic of the Glen – who had pricked many a wind bag – and there was a general feeling that his meeting with Mr Hopps would not be devoid of interest.

...

Mr Hopps explained to me, before leaving, that he had been much pleased with the scenery of our Glen, but disappointed in the people.

'They may not be hignorant,' said the little man doubtfully, 'but no man could call them haffable.'

It flashed on me for the first time that perhaps there may have been the faintest want of geniality in the Drumtochty manner, but it was simply the reticence of a subtle and conscientious people.

(Maclaren, [1894] 1896, pp.175–9)

In this extract, the most striking feature of the language is the division between the standard English used by the narrator, and the attempt to render Scots dialect, vocabulary and accent in the direct speech of the characters. The opening sentence establishes the identity of the narrator as a sophisticated native informant, an educated member of the Drumtochty community, who recounts and explains the idiosyncrasies of the community to a sympathetic outsider. The collective first-person pronouns – 'our', 'we', 'us' – regularly punctuate the passage, reminding the reader that the narrator has the authority of one who knows the community from within. In the direct speech of the characters, Maclaren tries to capture the distinctive features of spoken Scots, while at the same time taking care to ensure that non-Scots readers can still understand everything. When in doubt, Maclaren adds a translation in parenthesis, as in Hillocks's observation about Hopps, the outsider from the South: ' "He's a gabby (talkative) body, Drumsheugh, there's nae doot o' that, but terrible ignorant." ' The imagined reader or addressee (principally in England and the USA) is thus eased gently from the reliable narrator's standard English to a version of Scots speech modified to guarantee comprehensibility for non-Scots readers.

The rural Scots community in *Beside the Bonnie Brier Bush* is presented in a generous light. 'Visitors without discernment' might, like Mr Hopps, perceive the villagers as dull, in need of enlightening on matters of economics and religion, and unwelcoming to strangers. None of these prejudices, however, is supported in the story: Jamie Soutar, the cynic of the Glen, outwits the over-confident Hopps, dispelling any suspicion of rural backwardness; the time-honoured agricultural and religious practices of the village prove much superior to Hopps's attempts at innovation. The accusation that the community had been unwelcoming is dismissed by the narrator, who briefly doubts that 'perhaps there may have been the faintest want of geniality in the Drumtochty manner', but concludes reassuringly that this 'was simply the reticence of a subtle and conscientious people'. The physical beauty of the landscape is emphasized; the members of the community are depicted as intelligent, good-humoured, conscious of – and happy in – their allocated social places, and hospitable to outsiders who do not make the mistake of patronizing them.

The House with the Green Shutters

George Douglas Brown was brought up in straitened circumstances by his mother in an Ayrshire village. Through scholarships, he went to the universities of Glasgow and Oxford, where he was influenced by European realist and naturalist writers, such as Émile Zola. While trying to sustain an existence as a freelance journalist in London, Brown wrote *The House with the Green Shutters*, setting his novel in the imagined village of Barbie. Both controversy and critical acclaim greeted Brown's novel, and his premature death a year after its publication was mourned as a loss to Scottish literature. The extract below is from Chapter 5 of *The House with the Green Shutters*. **Once again, note the distinctive features of the language, considering in particular how Brown uses standard English and Scots dialect. Note, too, how he represents rural Scotland.**

> In every little Scotch community there is a distinct type known as 'the bodie'. 'What does he do, that man?' you may ask, and the answer will be, 'Really, I could hardly tell ye what he does – he's juist a bodie!' The 'bodie' may be a gentleman of independent means (a hundred a year from the Funds) fussing about in spats and light check breeches; or he may be a jobbing gardener; but he is equally a 'bodie'. The chief occupation of his idle hours (and his hours are chiefly idle) is the discussion of his neighbour's affairs. He is generally an 'auld residenter'; great, therefore, at the redding up of pedigrees. He can tell you exactly, for instance, how it is that young Pin-oe's taking geyly to the dram: for his grandfather, it seems, was a terrible man for the drink – ou, just terrible – why, he went to bed with a full jar of whisky once, and when he left it, he was dead, and it was empty. So ye see, that's the reason o't.

The genus 'bodie' is divided into two species: the 'harmless bodies' and the 'nesty bodies'. The bodies of Barbie mostly belonged to the second variety. Johnny Coe, and Tam Wylie, the baker, were decent enough fellows in their way, but the others were the sons of scandal. Gourlay spoke of them as a 'wheen damned auld wives'. – But Gourlay, to be sure, was not an impartial witness.

...

Tam was a wealthy old hunks, but it suited his humour to refer to himself constantly as 'a poor farming bodie'. And he dressed in accordance with his humour. His clean old crab-apple face was always grinning at you from over a white-sleeved moleskin waistcoat, as if he had been no better than a breaker of road metal.

'Faith aye!' said the Provost, cunning and quick – 'fodder should be cheap' – and he shot a covetous glimmer of a bargain-making eye at Mr Wylie.

Tam drew himself up. He saw what was coming.

'We're needing some hay for the burgh horse,' said the Provost. 'Ye'll be willing to sell at fifty shillings the ton, since it's like to be so plentiful.'

'Oh,' said Tam mournfully, 'that's on-possible! Gourlay's seeking the three pound! And where he leads we maun a' gang. Gourlay sets the tune and Barbie dances till't.'

(Brown, [1901] 1996, pp.26–7)

In this extract, there is also a division between standard English used by the narrator and a version of Scots used to represent the dialogue, but there are at least two important differences from Maclaren's *Bonnie Brier Bush*. First, the narrator in *The House with the Green Shutters* is detached from the community and functions as an omniscient narrator for much of the time. Occasionally the narrator addresses the reader directly, as in the second sentence in the extract (' "What does he do, that man?" you may ask'), but such moments are exceptional, and the narrative voice for most of the novel remains in the third person. A second difference is that on occasions the third-person narrator shifts from standard English to a version of Scots idiom, as in the final sentences of the first paragraph: 'He is generally an "auld residenter"; great, therefore, at the redding up of pedigrees. He can tell you exactly, for instance, how it is that young Pin-oe's taking geyly to the dram.' And so on. The Scots phrase 'auld residenter' is in quotation marks to register that it deviates from standard English, but in the next sentence no quotation marks accompany the Scots terms 'geyly' and 'dram'. The implication is that the narrator is making less of a concession to the non-

Scots reader, who accordingly has to follow the Scots. The dialogue attempts to reproduce the vocabulary and syntax of Scots speech as realistically as possible, with no explicit concession to the non-Scots reader in the form of parenthetical translations.

The village community of Barbie in *The House with the Green Shutters* is presented in a thoroughly negative light. The very name of the town – Barbie – suggests barbed comments or barbed wire, and the residents' most distinguishing feature would appear to be their capacity for malicious gossip. The narrator makes it clear that folk prejudice in Barbie is unforgiving, and survives for generations. Of the two kinds of 'bodies' in Barbie, only two people, Johnny Coe and Tam Wylie, are classed as 'harmless bodies' or 'decent enough fellows in their way'; all the rest are 'nesty bodies' or 'the sons of scandal'. In the dialogue between Tam Wylie and the Provost that follows immediately, even the 'harmless bodie' Wylie is revealed as shrewd and disingenuous in protecting his own material interests. The community is represented here as self-interested, petulant, devious and governed by a competitive individualism that delights in the humiliation of neighbours, town-folk and family members alike. Whereas for Maclaren the people of Drumtochty are a 'subtle and conscientious people', for Brown, Barbie is dominated by 'nesty bodies' and 'the sons of scandal'.

Text

Now read the Prelude of Gibbon's *Sunset Song*, 'The Unfurrowed Field' (pp.1–24), bearing in mind the same two questions.

- **What are the distinctive features of the language? (Focus in particular on the use of Scots, and on the relation between direct and reported speech.)**

- **How are the rural communities of Scotland represented?**

The language of the Prelude of *Sunset Song* is in the idiom of north-east rural Scotland. *Both* the main narrative voice *and* the dialogue of the characters are in Scots idiom, and dialogue is distinguished from the narrator's voice by being in italic print. The frequent use of Scots words and the elongated sentences that echo the rhythms of spoken speech contribute to the sense of authenticity. For readers unfamiliar with the Scots words, this 'authentic' Scots language might well slow reading speed, and even produce incomprehension. However, as many of the words can be guessed from their context, and the Glossary in the Canongate edition (pp.265–72) provides translations, slow initial progress should soon give way to easier reading. Gibbon explained that his ambition in *A Scots Quair* was 'to mould the English language into the rhythms and cadences of Scots spoken speech, and to inject into the English vocabulary such minimum number of words from Braid Scots as that remodelling requires' (in Bold, 2001, p.135).

The narrator in the Prelude is a member of the Kinraddie community, a venerable folk voice recounting first the myths and history of the region, then repeating gossip about the various members of the community in 1911. The history is uncertain, and there is little pretence that an objective record of the past is being provided:

> And [Cospatric's] son took the name Kinraddie, and looked out one day from the castle wall and saw the Earl Marischal come marching up from the south to join the Highlandmen in the battle that was fought at Mondynes, where now the meal-mill stands; and he took out his men and fought there, but on which side they do not say, but maybe it was the winning one, they were aye gey and canny folk, the Kinraddies. And the great-grandson of Cospatric, he joined the English against the cateran Wallace.
>
> (p.2)

The first sentence blurs the shift from myth (the tale of Cospatric the gryphon-killer) to history (the historical battle fought in 1094 at Mondynes between rival claimants to the Scottish throne). The narrator's hazy sense of the past is conveyed further by the confession that no-one quite remembers the Kinraddies' allegiances – 'he took out his men and fought there, but on which side they do not say, but maybe it was the winning one'. The suspicion that the narrator might not be altogether reliable is reinforced in the next sentence with the observation that the Kinraddies – 'gey and canny folk' – had fought with the English against the great Scottish hero William Wallace. At this very early stage of the novel, the narrator's confident judgements of people and events are thus thrown into some doubt. The reader is indirectly warned to proceed cautiously, and to resist the temptation of simply colluding with the prejudices – sometimes acute, sometimes vindictive – of the narrator.

The identity of the implied reader or addressee is also established in the opening pages of the Prelude. The absence of standard English in the main narrative suggests an implied reader familiar with the Scots idiom. This impression is reinforced by the frequent use of second-person address ('you'), which includes the implied reader into the process of storytelling. This process of inclusion is complicated, however, by the dual sense in which 'you' is used in the Prelude. The first use of 'you' is when the narrator addresses the reader directly. The clearest examples are in the explanations of where the different farms in Kinraddie are located:

> But if you went out of the kirk by the main door and took the
> road east a bit, and that was the road that served kirk and Manse
> and Mains, you were on to the turnpike then.
>
> (p.9)

> But if you turned east that winter along the Auchinblae road first
> on your right was Cuddiestoun, a small bit holding the size of
> Peesie's Knapp, and old as it, a croft from the far-off times.
>
> (p.13)

This direct-address use of 'you' gives the sense of the narrator interrupting
the flow of the narrative in order to inform the reader about a particularly
significant detail in the story.

The second and more frequent use of 'you' is the generic 'you', where
'you' might be substituted with 'one'. Note the following example:

> An Irish creature, Erbert Ellison was the name, ran the place for
> the trustees, he said, but if you might believe all the stories you
> heard he ran a hantle more silver into his own pouch than he ran
> into theirs. Well you might expect it, for once he'd been no more
> than a Dublin waiter, they said.
>
> (p.5)

What this suggests is a symmetry between the narrator and addressee, with
the result that the addressee is assumed to share the jaundiced views of the
narrator: that Ellison stole from the trustees, and that being an Irish waiter
predisposed him to theft. The final 'they said' in the last passage invokes the
vague but powerful authority of the community. This assumed symmetry is
especially evident when political views are expressed, as in the observation
that 'you worked from the blink of the day you were breeked to the flicker of
the night they shrouded you, and the dirt of gentry sat and ate up your rents
but you were as good as they were' (p.4). The use of this generic 'you' in the
Prelude is often also accompanied by the use of Scots words, as in the
comment that the proximity of Peesie's Knapp to the road 'was fair handy if
it didn't scunner you that you couldn't so much as change your sark without
some ill-fashioned brute gowking in at you' (p.9). The effect created is of
eavesdropping on the narrator (an old inhabitant of Kinraddie) regaling the
implied reader/addressee (a sympathetic inhabitant from a neighbouring
village) with the events of the novel.

The representation of rural Scotland in the Prelude of *Sunset Song* is
assembled by the narrator describing the different farms and tenants in
Kinraddie. (As you read the Prelude, you may find it useful to refer to the
map provided in the Canongate edition in order to clarify their respective
locations.) The diversity of the characters described, combined with the
unreliability of the narrator, makes it difficult to provide a definitive

summary of how Gibbon represents rural Scotland at this stage, but we can make certain preliminary generalizations. The description of the courtship and marriage of Ellison discloses several important aspects of the Kinraddie community:

> Some would have nothing to do with him, a poor creature of an Irishman who couldn't speak right and didn't belong to the Kirk, but Ella White she was not so particular and was fell long in the tooth herself. So when Ellison came to her at the harvest ball in Auchinblae and cried *Can I see you home to-night, me dear?* she said *Och, Ay.* And on the road home they lay among the stooks and maybe Ellison did this and that to make sure of getting her, he was fair desperate for any woman by then. They were married next New Year's Day, and Ellison had begun to think himself a gey man in Kinraddie, and maybe one of the gentry. But the bothy billies, the ploughmen and the orra men of the Mains, they'd never a care for gentry except to mock at them and on the eve of Ellison's wedding they took him as he was going into his house and took off his breeks and tarred his dowp and the soles of his feet and stuck feathers on them and then they threw him into the water-trough, as was the custom. And he called them *Bloody Scotch savages*, and was in an awful rage and at the term-time he had them sacked, the whole jing-bang of them, so sore affronted he had been.
>
> (p.6)

The community is characterized here as divided along several lines, most notably between locals and outsiders, and between 'the gentry' and the farm labourers. Ellison's outsider status is emphasized by drawing attention to his different accent (he 'couldn't speak right') and lack of the right Christian faith (he 'didn't belong to the Kirk'). More important in earning Ellison the hostility of the locals, however, is his identification with the landowners – Ellison 'had begun to think himself ... maybe one of the gentry', and the farm workers 'never [have] a care for gentry except to mock at them'. The collective hostility of the farm workers is expressed in the tarring-and-feathering of the landlord, but the latter ultimately wins this compressed moment of class war by firing them all. In addition to emphasizing the endemic conflict between the wealthy and the poor members of the community, the passage also suggests in the description of Ellison and Ella White coming together that sex and marriage is managed in Kinraddie less by romance and Christian modesty than by a combination of pragmatism, desperation and guilt.

In terms of language and the representation of rural Scotland, compare *Sunset Song* with its literary predecessors, *Beside the Bonnie Brier Bush* and *The House with the Green Shutters*.

As regards language, *Sunset Song* is unoriginal in using Scots words and speech rhythms; both Maclaren and Brown in depicting direct speech had done the same (as had many other Scots writers before them). What is distinctive about *Sunset Song*, however, is that the use of Scots is not confined to direct speech. Gibbon's unreliable narrator uses Scots, and direct speech is represented by italic print. Scots narrators had been used by earlier writers, but Gibbon's sustained novel-length use of Scots was still innovative at the time.

As a representation of rural Scottish communities, *Sunset Song* differs fundamentally from the kailyard tradition. Whereas Maclaren's Drumtochty is a cosy village world at peace with itself, Gibbon's Kinraddie is divided along uncompromising class lines (recall Ellison's encounter with the 'bothy billies'). Neither sex nor violence intrudes on the tales of Drumtochty, whereas Gibbon's Kinraddie is much preoccupied with sex, and violence – domestic, economic and political – is seldom far from the surface. The contrast between Kinraddie in *Sunset Song* and Barbie in *The House with the Green Shutters* is more complicated, as both Gibbon and Brown portray unflinchingly the less attractive aspects of rural Scotland and its communities. Where they differ is that Brown's Barbie has little positive to counter the self-interested and destructive individualism of the protagonist Gourlay. Gibbon's Kinraddie, for all its endemic tensions and cruelties, remains a community that sustains Gibbon's protagonist Chris Guthrie through a formidable sequence of crises, deaths and disasters.

A final difference we might note between Gibbon, Maclaren and Brown is in their respective motivations for writing. This is perhaps more difficult to deduce from these three short passages of their work, and Maclaren and Brown did not leave literary manifestos like Gibbon's *Left Review* contribution to help us understand their literary ambitions. However, from their respective literary and miscellaneous writings, we can conclude tentatively that Maclaren wrote literature principally to *entertain*, whereas Brown wrote to *reflect social reality*. Gibbon's conviction that his own literary output constituted 'explicit or implicit propaganda' against capitalism therefore contrasts with both Maclaren's and Brown's views of literature.

Following the Prelude, there are four parts – 'Ploughing', 'Drilling', 'Seed-time' and 'Harvest' – and a concluding 'Epilude' to *Sunset Song*. **As you read each part, continue thinking about the same questions: what are the distinctive features of Gibbon's literary language? How does he represent the communities of rural Scotland? Also, keep in mind Gibbon's dual ambitions to write 'explicit or implicit [anti-capitalist] propaganda' and 'work of definite and recognised literary value'. In the sections that follow, I highlight key passages in each of the four parts and the Epilude that shed light on these questions.**

Figure 3.2 Bloomfield (Blawearie). (By permission of The Grassic Gibbon Centre.)

'Ploughing'

Gibbon uses the narrative device of flashforward, or prolepsis, at the start of each of the four main parts of the novel. 'Ploughing' starts in June 1912 with Chris on the hillside next to the loch and Standing Stones that overlook Kinraddie; the succeeding pages describe in detail the events from 1911 onwards that have led to her being on the hillside. This narrative time sequence is repeated in the subsequent four parts, with Chris's temporal and spatial location in each instance situated looking down on Kinraddie from above, and from a future point in the chronology of the narrative.

Having introduced the cast of the novel in the Prelude, Gibbon focuses in 'Ploughing' on the Guthrie family in general, from their origins in Echt to their arrival at Blawearie, and on Chris Guthrie in particular. You will recall in the Prelude Gibbon's use of a direct-address 'you' and, more frequently, of a generic 'you'. One of the key devices he employs to convey Chris's consciousness is the use of 'you' in yet a third way. **Read the following paragraph carefully and identify who this third 'you' refers to.**

> So that was Chris and her reading and schooling, two Chrisses there were that fought for her heart and tormented her. You hated the land and the coarse speak of the folk and learning was brave and fine one day; and the next you'd waken with the peewits

crying across the hills, deep and deep, crying in the heart of you and the smell of the earth in your face, almost you'd cry for that, the beauty of it and the sweetness of the Scottish land and skies. You saw their faces in firelight, father's and mother's and the neighbours', before the lamps lit up, tired and kind, faces dear and close to you, you wanted the words they'd known and used, forgotten in the far-off youngness of their lives, Scots words to tell to your heart how they wrung it and held it, the toil of their days and unendingly their fight. And the next minute that passed from you, you were English, back to the English words so sharp and clean and true – for a while, for a while, till they slid so smooth from your throat you knew they could never say anything that was worth the saying at all.

(p.32)

In the second sentence, the 'you' who 'hated the land and the coarse speak of the folk' is clearly no longer the generic 'you' who concurs with the folk narrator; rather, this 'you' directs attention to the individual consciousness of the character Chris Guthrie. The implied reader becomes the single trusted confidant of Chris, who is privy to her most intimate thoughts, conflicts and aspirations. To reveal more effectively the consciousness of the character Chris, Gibbon therefore temporarily suspends the folk voice addressing a generic 'you', and assumes the voice of the character Chris addressing a confidant 'you'. One critic describes this 'you' as 'clearly self-referring and may appear to be self-addressing' (Trengove, 1975, p.51), as it refers back directly to the consciousness of the character.

The internal conflict between the English Chris and the Scots Chris is tilted in favour of the latter. Although the adjectives associated with the English Chris are positive ('learning was brave and fine', 'the English words so sharp and clean and true'), the descriptions of the Scots landscape, community and language are far more compelling. The accumulation of detail – from the peewits, or lapwings, and the smell of the earth, to the tired faces of family and neighbours in the firelight, to the Scots language so finely attuned to the landscape – registers the deep attachment of the Scots Chris to her inherited world. Of particular significance is Chris's sense that 'you knew [the English words] could never say anything that was worth the saying'. This line – expressing the character Chris's own faltering efforts to find a language adequate to the task of articulating her life, community and history – might indeed stand as a summary of why Gibbon wrote *Sunset Song* in Scots rather than English: only Scots is capable of expressing accurately the intimate details of the rural north-eastern Scotland of his youth.

Gibbon's description of Kinraddie in the Prelude refers matter-of-factly to sex – recall the 'courtship' of Ellison and Ella White. In 'Ploughing' sex acquires both a more central and a more complicated place. **Look at 'Ploughing' again and make a note of all the references to sex. What do you think is their significance?**

For the sake of clarity, I have numbered the references.

1   The early romance and courtship of Jean Murdoch and John Guthrie is recounted by Jean reminiscing to Chris (pp.27–8).

2   John Guthrie's desire for Jean is cast as extreme and destructive: 'his face would go black with rage at her because of that sweetness that tempted his soul to hell' (p.28).

3   Will's anger at his father's sexual appetite is expressed: 'Will said the old man was a fair beast and mother shouldn't be having a baby' (p.34).

4   Marget Strachan acts as the catalyst for Chris's emerging sexual consciousness: 'But Marget threw her arms around her when she said that, and kissed her with red, kind lips' (p.46).

5   The 'daftie' Andy sexually threatens and assaults Mistress Ellison, Maggie Jean Gordon and Chris (pp.48–52).

6   The sexual appetite of the new minister Gibbon is noted: 'and into their bedroom [Gibbon and his wife] went and closed the door and didn't come down for hours' (p.55).

7   John Guthrie's incestuous desire for Chris is hinted at: 'it had been as though [Chris] saw a caged beast peep from her father's eyes as he saw her stand in the tub' (p.60).

8   As a consequence of sex rather than a reference to sex itself, you might include the agonizing birth of the twins, which is vividly described: 'it was as though mother were being torn and torn in the teeth of beasts and couldn't thole it longer' (p.34).

The most basic point is that these many references register the centrality of sex in the lives and consciousnesses of Gibbon's characters. For Gibbon, to remain silent about sex – as his literary predecessors had done – would be to provide a limited picture of the Kinraddie community. Accordingly, he describes sexual desire and its consequences in their complex variety. The unreliability of the folk narrator makes it risky to try to deduce Gibbon's own morality from the pages of *Sunset Song*, but a couple of tentative observations might be ventured. Male desire is represented as frequently destructive: in the cases of John Guthrie, the daftie Andy and the Reverend Gibbon (although in his case, this unfolds later in the novel), their sexual desires threaten women, and by extension the community. In particular, John

Guthrie's lust produces Jean Guthrie's terrible sufferings in childbirth, then subsequently mutates into an incestuous desire for Chris. Female desire, by contrast, is sympathetically portrayed: both Jean Murdoch's initial attraction to John Guthrie and Chris's own coming to sexual consciousness are described as 'natural'. I will return to discuss this further in the section on 'Seed-time'.

One of the central institutions in Kinraddie is the church. Towards the end of this first part of the novel the community selects a new minister. The first candidate is dismissed peremptorily, but the sermons of the second two are described in some detail. **Read the descriptions of the sermons of Reverend Colquohoun and Reverend Gibbon (pp.53–5). How does Gibbon represent the church and its ministers?**

As a preliminary, we can simply note what each of the ministers preached, and the impression each of them made on the Kinraddie community. Colquohoun preached a version of history that emphasized pre-Christian civilizations in Scotland, then presented the birth of Christ in Palestine as Kinraddie's distant hope for redemption and light. His prayers were short, and did not acknowledge the king and royal family. Almost no-one in Kinraddie was impressed by Colquohoun's sermon, with Ellison and Mutch especially rankled by his failure to mention the royal family. The only ones sympathetic to Colquohoun were Chris and her father; Long Rob did not express an opinion on Colquohoun explicitly, but his dislike for Ellison and Mutch's love of royalty might be interpreted as a faint predisposition in Colquohoun's favour. Reverend Gibbon preached from the Song of Solomon, favouring the most erotic passages, and suggesting that they had a religious meaning directly relevant to his congregation, that they described the beauty of the Church of Scotland, and in particular provided a Christian guide for virtuous Scottish women. The Kinraddie community listened avidly to Reverend Gibbon, taking a prurient pleasure in the Song of Solomon, with his sanction, while also retaining their sense of piety. Only Long Rob criticized Gibbon's combination of religion and sex from the pulpit, suggesting that he was exploiting the hypocrisy of his congregation.

The picture of the church established in 'Ploughing' and reinforced in the subsequent parts of the novel is an overwhelmingly negative one. The responses of the congregations to the two ministers is significant. Reverend Colquohoun preaches a sermon with some intellectual substance and shows no deference to secular authorities, and is spurned by the congregation; Reverend Gibbon strategically tailors his sermon to popular tastes, and is embraced. An important technique Gibbon uses in assembling a picture of the church in Kinraddie is his characterization of contradictory attitudes to it. In general, the less sympathetic characters, such as Ellison and Mutch, happily go along with Gibbon's opportunism and hypocrisy, and are enthusiastic churchgoers, whereas more attractive characters, such as Chris and Long Rob, favour the spurned Colquohoun, and, in Long Rob's case, question the church, its teachings and its representatives. Nonetheless, it is made clear that Long Rob's hostile view is a minority one, and that for most of Kinraddie the church fulfils a necessary and valued social function. The complexity of Gibbon's representation of the church can be explained in relation to his desire to write novels that do not reproduce simplistic revolutionary propaganda, but aim instead to have 'definite literary value'. For Gibbon, 'definite literary value' demanded a realistic representation of society and, in particular, sensitivity to social contradictions. In the context of religion, Gibbon tries to capture those contradictions in *Sunset Song* in a number of ways: most of the Kinraddie community embrace the dubious Gibbon and reject the principled Colquohoun; the critical voice of Long Rob is isolated and largely irrelevant; the church exerts a strong hold on both unattractive characters (Ellison and Mutch) *and* more sympathetic ones (Chris and Chae Strachan).

'Drilling'

At the start of 'Drilling', in June 1913, Chris is on the hill with the Standing Stones and the loch; she is looking down on Kinraddie and pondering events of the previous year. The death of her mother and twin brothers the year before is registered in the second paragraph: 'The June of last year it had been, the day when mother had poisoned herself and the twins' (p.63). The second part of the novel first recounts the events immediately following the deaths of Jean Guthrie and the twins in June 1912, then describes events up to June 1913. The year's events include: the adoption of Chris's brothers Dod and Alec by Janet, John Guthrie's sister in Auchterless; the abundant harvest of the summer of 1912; Will's courtship of Mollie in Drumlithie; the burning-down of Chae Strachan's farm, Peesie's Knapp; and the local by-elections for government. The final pages move the chronology into the next agricultural cycle, describing the harvest of the summer of 1913, Will's emigration to Argentina in August 1913 and John Guthrie's ultimately fatal accident.

The narrative voice and mode of address continue to shift swiftly and often unexpectedly, demanding agile reading: the thoughts and points of view of the folk voice and of the different characters jostle and frequently contradict each other in succeeding sentences. A good example is provided in the conversation at the supper following the threshing of Chae Strachan's crops. **Read from 'Then more trampling ...' (p.85) to '... the poorest folk in Kinraddie!' (p.86) and list the shifts in point of view.**

Careful attention to the shifts in points of view reveals a sophisticated mode of narration that obliges readers to orientate themselves in relation to a variety of conflicting voices. For clarity, I have numbered the shifts in point of view.

1   The narrating folk voice sets the scene, describing people settling themselves for a meal after helping with the threshing of Chae's crop.

2   Cuddiestoun's point of view, that girls should work in the kitchen and not be educated, is presented in the first person by direct speech.

3   The perspective of the assembled community, that Cuddiestoun is right about girls' vocations, is presented by the third-person folk voice.

4   Chris's point of view, or more precisely the English Chris's perspective, that those around the table are ignorant yokels, is presented in the second half of the same sentence. Although still narrated in the third person, the thoughts of Chris are presented by the technique of internal focalization (the third-person narrator articulating a character's unspoken thoughts).

5   Alec Mutch's perspective, that Cuddiestoun is correct, follows.

6   The folk perspective ('Most said'), concurring with Cuddiestoun and Mutch, is presented by the use of the second-person generic 'you': 'teaching your children a lot of damned nonsense'; 'they'd turn round and give you their lip as soon as listen to you'.

7   Chae's contrary perspective, that girls should be educated, is presented first by the narrating folk voice describing his reaction ('he wouldn't have that'), then by direct speech: '*Damn't man, you're clean wrong to think that.*'

8   Long Rob's point of view, a variant of Chae's, is presented by a combination of third-person narrative and direct speech: '*the more education the more of sense and the less of kirks and ministers*'.

9   Cuddiestoun's perspective, that Long Rob's irreligious views are unacceptable, is presented by a combination of third-person narrative and direct speech.

10 Long Rob's point of view, that Cuddiestoun's views on anything did not deserve to be taken seriously, is again presented by a combination of third-person narrative and first-person direct speech.

11 The community perspective, that Long Rob had defeated Cuddiestoun in this battle of opinions, is presented in the third-person folk voice.

12 Chris's perspective, this time the point of view of the Scots Chris, that she had been wrong in passing such harsh judgement on Kinraddie's people, is presented by third-person internal focalization.

In this short passage, six points of view therefore compete: the community, Cuddiestoun, Chris, Mutch, Chae and Long Rob. Cuddiestoun and Mutch line up against Chae and Rob; the community and Chris are positioned as informal adjudicators. From the community perspective, the view of

Cuddiestoun and Mutch that girls should not be educated initially holds sway, but Chae and Long Rob's more progressive arguments finally prevail. From Chris's perspective, Cuddiestoun and Mutch's prejudices initially make her loathe the Kinradddie community, but Chae and Rob's interventions on her behalf make her reverse her judgement. For the Russian critic Mikhail Bakhtin, this kind of diversity of voices – termed 'heteroglossia' – is the defining quality of the novel as a genre. Bakhtin defines the novel as 'a diversity of social speech types (sometimes, even diversity of languages) and a diversity of individual voices, artistically organized' (1981, p.262). In his terms, *Sunset Song*, with its variety of speech types and individual voices, exploits fully the possibilities of the genre.

The supper following the threshing of Chae's harvest is one of many passages in 'Drilling' that describe the working lives of Kinraddie's peasant farmers. There are acutely observed details of the harvest of 1911 (pp.67–72), the burning of the chaff (pp.78–9), the threshing of the corn (pp.85–6) and the harvest of 1912 (p.101). Scots words describing specific aspects of the farming process – 'ley', 'yavil', 'coulter', 'stook' and 'sow' – are particularly prominent in these passages. Even at this relatively early stage of the novel, however, Gibbon introduces a melancholy note in reflecting on the future for this way of life and its farming practices.

Figure 3.3   Lewis Grassic Gibbon pulling a hay rake. (By permission of The Grassic Gibbon Centre.)

Read the following three passages: the first, from *Sunset Song*; the second, from Gibbon's 1934 essay 'The Land'; and the third, from the social historian Ian Carter's essay 'Lewis Grassic Gibbon, *A Scots Quair*, and the Peasantry'. Compare these three views of Scots small-farming communities at the dawn of the twentieth century.

from Gibbon's *Sunset Song*

It seemed like enough to John Guthrie ... the world was rolling fast to a hell of riches and the old slave days come back again, ministers went with it and whored with the rest. For the bitterness had grown and eaten into the heart of him in his year at Blawearie. So coarse the land proved in the turn of the seasons he'd fair been staggered, the crops had fared none so bad this once, but he saw in a normal year the corn would come hardly at all on the long, stiff slopes of the dour red clay. Now also it grew plain to him here as never in Echt that the day of the crofter was fell near finished, put by, the day of folk like himself and Chae and Cuddiestoun, Pooty and Long Rob of the Mill, the last of the farming folk that wrung their living from the land with their own bare hands.

(p.75)

from Gibbon's 'The Land'

But when I read or hear our new leaders and their plans for making of Scotland a great peasant nation, a land of little farms and farming communities, I am moved to a bored disgust ... They are promising the new Scotland a purgatory that would decimate it. They are promising it narrowness and bitterness and heart-breaking toil in one of the most unkindly agricultural lands in the world. They are promising to make of a young, ricketic man, with the phthisis of Glasgow in his throat, a bewildered labourer in pelting rains and the flares of head-aching suns, they are promising him years of a murderous monotony, poverty and struggle and loss of happy human relationships. They promise that of which they know nothing, except through sipping of the scum of kailyard romance.

For this life is for no modern man or woman – even the finest of these. It belongs to a different, an alien generation.

(in Bold, 2001, pp.84–5)

from Carter's 'Lewis Grassic Gibbon, *A Scots Quair*, and the Peasantry'

By the early 1930s ... [t]he northeast peasantry was dead as a class; though individual peasants, like Munro, Cuddiestoun, might trauchle on until their holdings were engrossed when they retired or died. The Great War was, for Gibbon, the final blow: but the commodity price boom of the war years merely formed the gale that blew away the empty husk of simple commodity production. The Mearns peasantry died because peasant children like Will Guthrie no longer were willing to suffer the costs and deprivations of labour on the family holding in expectation of future independence as a middle peasant. The peasant's mode of production always had held a contradiction deep within itself; the farmer's vaunted independence was bought at the cost of servitude for other household members. Emigration and education provided alternative futures for peasant children: as increasing numbers took these escape hatches so the contradiction between independence and discipline slowly dissolved, eviscerating the middle peasantry.

(Carter, 1978, p.180)

For both Gibbon and Carter, by the First World War the peasantry of north-east Scotland was in terminal decline: for Gibbon's character John Guthrie 'the day of the crofter was fell near finished'; for Gibbon-the-journalist, 'this [peasant] life is for no modern man or woman'; for Carter-the-historian, 'By the early 1930s ... [t]he northeast peasantry was dead as a class.' As regards the reasons for the decline, John Guthrie gropes for explanations in religious terms ('the world was rolling fast to a hell of riches'), whereas in 'The Land', Gibbon insists that the unrelenting harshness of peasant farming dictates that it simply cannot survive into modernity. For Carter, the peasantry declined principally because education and emigration offered its younger generations more attractive alternatives. As to when the peasantry ceased to be viable as a class, Gibbon in both *Sunset Song* and 'The Land' sees the peasantry surviving successfully up until the First World War, whereas the historian Carter, with the benefit of a longer perspective, dates the moment of decline earlier. More interesting are Gibbon's contrasting attitudes towards the decline of the peasantry in *Sunset Song* and 'The Land'. In the former, this decline is represented as the deeply mourned loss of a cherished way of life, whereas in the latter, the end of peasant farming is represented as liberation from servitude. Elsewhere in 'The Land', Gibbon professes a deep attachment to Scots peasant life, but his own conflicted feelings, both here and in *Sunset Song*, are not so much resolved as dramatized in his writings.

What does come through in *Sunset Song* is Gibbon's antipathy towards the increasingly dominant capitalist agriculture that replaces the small-scale peasant farming of the Mearns. All Gibbon's sympathetic characters – the Guthries, Chae Strachan, Long Rob and, more ambivalently, Ewan Tavendale – are associated with the traditional peasant way of life. In contrast, the characters who embrace small-scale capitalist production – Ellison, Mutch, Munro and Cuddiestoun – are represented as thoroughly unattractive. The disagreements at Chae Strachan's threshing meal between Chae and Long Rob, on the one hand, and Cuddiestoun and Mutch, on the other, are therefore more than simply Gibbon's attempt at a realistic representation of peasant society. Rather, they are carefully constructed to engage sympathy for one class (the declining peasantry) and to expose the flaws of another (the emergent capitalist farmers). Indeed, we might plausibly read Gibbon's characterization of these conflicts as yet another literary expression of his professed desire to write anti-capitalist propaganda, though in this case the complexity of the narrative would certainly suggest 'implicit' rather than 'explicit' propaganda. The same might be said of Gibbon's version of peasant history in *Sunset Song*: his political sympathies lie with the crofters and he represents the rise of capitalist farming in north-east Scotland as the triumph of the values of individual self-interest over those of community.

'Seed-time'

The longest of the four main parts of *Sunset Song*, 'Seed-time' commences with Chris in April 1914 once again on the hillside with the Standing Stones and the loch, reflecting on the events that have occurred since she had stood there the previous September. 'Seed-time' represents in detail two major communal rituals of Kinraddie – the funeral of John Guthrie, and the wedding of Ewan and Chris. In both cases, Gibbon sustains a fine tension between the generous and the malicious elements of Chris's community. At the funeral, 'folk at the gate were stopping to shake her hand, Long Rob and Chae to say they'd aye help her' (p.117), but soon after the reading of the will, the self-interested ambition of Auntie Janet and Uncle Tam to benefit from John Guthrie's death is exposed: 'Uncle Tam drew a long, deep breath, as though fair near choked he'd been *Not a word of his two poor, motherless boys!* It seemed he'd expected Alec and Dod would be left their share, maybe that was why he'd been so eager to adopt them the year before' (pp.118–19). At her wedding, Chris receives in quick succession depressing advice from Mistress Mutch and well-intentioned reassurances from Long Rob: Mistress Mutch warns, '*Don't let Ewan saddle you with a birn of bairns, Chris, it kills you and eats your heart away, forbye the unease and dirt of it*'; Rob then tells her, '*don't let any of those dammed women fear you, Chris; it's been the curse of the human race, listening to advice*' (p.162).

Gibbon develops the tension between Scots and English in 'Seed-time', both in describing the evolving identity of the character Chris, and in dramatizing the economic and cultural resonances of the respective languages. **Read the following two passages. Think about the narrative techniques used and how they reveal the development of the character Chris.**

> And then a queer thought came to her there in the drookèd fields, that nothing endured at all, nothing but the land she passed across, tossed and turned and perpetually changed below the hands of the crofter folk since the oldest of them had set the Standing Stones by the loch of Blawearie and climbed there on their holy days and saw their terraced crops ride brave in the wind and sun. Sea and sky and the folk who wrote and fought and were learnèd, teaching and saying and praying, they lasted but as a breath, a mist of fog in the hills, but the land was forever, it moved and changed below you, but was forever, you were close to it and it to you, not at a bleak remove it held you and hurted you. And she had thought to leave it all!
>
> (p.119)

> No night would she ever be her own again, in her body the seed of that pleasure she had sown with Ewan burgeoning and growing, dark, in the warmth below her heart. And Chris Guthrie crept out from the place below the beech trees where Chris Tavendale lay and went wandering off into the waiting quiet of the afternoon, Chris Tavendale heard her go, and she came back to Blawearie never again.
>
> (p.176)

Gibbon again uses the dual techniques of internal focalization and of the second-person confidant addressee in order to express Chris's mental turmoil after her father's funeral. The first passage begins in the third person ('a queer thought came to her'), shifts to the confidant 'you' ('it moved and changed below you'), then returns to the third person ('she had thought to leave it all'). Central to Chris's decision to remain at Blawearie is her reawakened sense of the past, as she defines her identity in relation both to the many generations of crofters of Kinraddie and to the land itself. Her identification with the land and the peasants past and present of Kinraddie is represented as irresistible, even painful ('you were close to it and it to you, not at a bleak remove it held you and hurted you'). The claims of the English Chris simply cannot compete: 'She could no more teach a school than fly' (p.120). Recall, too, that in her choice of the land, Chris is following her dead mother's injunction – '*Oh, Chris, my lass, there are better things than your books or studies or loving or bedding, there's the countryside your own*' (p.27). The second passage is recounted in the third person and describes Chris's pregnancy, an event that causes Chris Guthrie to mutate discreetly into Chris Tavendale. Gibbon's decision to write this major transition in Chris's identity in the third person rather than in the confidant second-person form of address has the effect of representing the change as objective fact, rather than as the subjective experience of Chris.

The conflict between the English and Scots Chrisses, temporarily resolved in favour of the latter with her marriage to Ewan, is echoed in the argument at her wedding celebration between Long Rob and Gordon. **Read the passage from 'Up at Rob's table ...' (p.156) to '... who could you blame?' (*ibid*.) and summarize the contrasting views on Scots and English.**

The disagreement in this passage is between Long Rob, who insists on the precision and appropriateness of Scots words and bemoans their gradual disappearance, and Mr Gordon, who argues that English is indispensable '*if folk are to get on in the world*' and progress beyond the fields of Kinraddie. Recall that in the argument at Chae Strachan's threshing supper, Rob and Chae lined up on the same side in favour of women's education. In this instance, however, Chae opposes Rob and sides with Gordon, leaving Rob even more isolated than usual in his views. The disagreement here between two sympathetic characters attests to Gibbon's own ambivalence about the conflict between, on the one hand, the language and culture of traditional community and, on the other, the imperatives of modernization.

The conflict between tradition and modernity in Kinraddie is also registered subtly at the level of popular culture. Songs enjoy substantial prominence in *Sunset Song*, especially at Chris's wedding. **Using the Notes to the Canongate edition of *Sunset Song* (p.263), identify the songs that are sung at Chris's wedding (pp.163–6) and their origins. Check through the Notes for references to songs elsewhere in the novel too. What significance do you attach to the mix of songs Gibbon includes in *Sunset Song*?**

The songs sung at Chris and Ewan's wedding in sequence were (the singer is given in parenthesis):

1 'Ladies of Spain', an English naval sea shanty dating from the early nineteenth century (Long Rob);

2 'The Lass that made the Bed to Me' by Robert Burns (1759–1796) (Long Rob);

3 'Roses and lilies her cheeks disclose', from Thomas D'Urfey's *Pills to Purge Melancholy* (*c.*1720) (Ellison);

4 'Villikins and his Dinah', a Victorian music-hall song (Ellison);

5 'Up in the Morning' by Burns (Chae);

6   'The Bonnie House of Airlie', a traditional ballad (Mistress Mutch);

7   'Auld Robin Gray' by Lady Anne Barnard (1750–1825) (Mistress Mutch);

8   'To a Mouse' by Burns (attempted recitation by Old Pooty);

9   'The Flowers of the Forest' by Jean Eliot (1727–1805) (Chris);

10 'Auld Lang Syne' by Burns (everyone present).

In the rest of the novel, there are at least five other references to songs that are of interest. The first two are to Burns songs: the daftie Andy releases Maggie Jean when he hears someone singing Burns's 'Bonny wee thing' (p.50); Will whistles Burns's 'Up in the Morning' as he walks off from Blawearie for the final time (p.102). The third reference to a song is after John Guthrie's death, when Auntie Janet hears the Reverend Gibbon singing and 'she could have sworn it was a song they sang in the bothies about the bedding of a lad and a lass' (p.111). The fourth reference is towards the end of 'Harvest', when the folk narrator observes that by the end of the war '[Kinraddie] was full of other tunes from the bothy windows now, *Tipperary* and squawling English things, like the squeak of a rat that is bedded in syrup, the *Long, Long Trail* and the like' (p.231). The final reference is in the Epilude, where the folk narrator observes: 'You heard feint the meikle of those old songs now, they were daft and old-fashioned, there were fine new ones in their places, right from America' (p.246).

The variety of different sources of the songs is striking: traditional bothy ballads (the crude song Reverend Gibbon is overheard singing); sentimental eighteenth-century Scottish ballads ('Auld Robin Gray' and 'The Flowers of the Forest'); five songs by Burns; English ballads ('Ladies of Spain'); Victorian music-hall standards (Ellison's songs); and, finally, popular tunes of the early twentieth century ('Tipperary' and 'Long, Long Trail'). There is no neat match between singer and choice of song. For example, it is not the bothy foreman Ewan who sings the bothy ballad, but the educated minister Gibbon; Long Rob, the most native of Kinraddie locals, has the English sea shanty 'Ladies of Spain' as his signature tune. The implication is that the characters choose the songs simply because they like them, not because of their origins. Discussing the importance of song in the literature of the 1930s, the critic Valentine Cunningham notes that 'Song defies the boundaries of ideology. Music's fluidity, its adaptability, its transgressive resistance to the corrals and boundaries of any particular politics, is what makes it useful to all and sundry' (1997, p.19). Singers therefore redefine the meanings of the songs by singing them in new contexts – in the case of Gibbon's *Sunset Song*, in the context of Kinraddie in the years 1911–20. (I return to this point in more detail below when I discuss Chris's affection for 'The Flowers of the Forest'.) Viewed collectively, the variety of songs suggests a society in transition, with the momentum of the transition away from the bothy ballads of traditional pre-capitalist agriculture and towards the commercial songs from England and America. The folk narrator's disdain for the new songs in 'Harvest' corresponds to Long Rob's dismay at the increasing dominance of English over Scots. In both cases, their attachment to the traditional is presented as worthy but futile. The ambivalence towards modernity is nicely captured in the flat contradiction between the folk narrator's dislike of the new songs as expressed in 'Harvest' ('like the squeak of a rat that is bedded in syrup') and the much more admiring attitude expressed in the Epilude ('those old songs ... were daft and old-fashioned, there were fine new ones in their place, right from America').

The second point to note about Gibbon's choice of songs in *Sunset Song* is the predominance of Burns. Burns songs are mentioned twice before the wedding; at the wedding, three of the nine songs are by Burns. Gibbon felt very strongly that Burns was the poet of Scotland's working people, and that his songs and poems had become woven into the texture of their lives. The strength of Gibbon's feelings about Burns is captured in this angry letter he wrote to the *Mearns Leader and Kincardineshire Mail* in February 1934 in response to a report of the speech by Alexander Mutch at the Mearns Burns Club annual supper in Stonehaven. **What do Gibbon's comments on Burns suggest about his own understanding of what literature is for?**

> This gentleman [Mutch] is reported to have said that: 'The realism of "Sunset Song" is in the direct tradition of ancient Scottish literature, but it is very interesting to note that Robert Burns set his face deliberately and resolutely against such ribaldry.' Mr Mutch, as an Aberdeen Literary Songster, should really read his Burns before talking about him – read 'Anna' or 'The Rigs of Barley' or 'The Lass that made the Bed to Me' or a section or so of 'Tam o' Shanter.' He will find in the Burns of those moods neither realism or ribaldry – he will find something much worse. The pornographic sniggerings of a drunken gauger.
>
> True that those moods do not represent the entire Burns: he was great enough to scale the heights and to plumb the depths. But to represent him in the likeness of a genteel Stonehaven spinster engaged in 'cleaning up Scottish song' is canting humbug.
>
> Burns lived a tormented life in a land which treats poets and genuinely creative writers as criminal lunatics – until they are safely dead. And, when it had safely killed him, Scotland proceeded to mummify Burns's corpse and set it up in a heathen shrine for the worship of the dull, the base and the flabbily loquacious. In life he hated and despised such people; in death they hold him a captive and cover away his angry pity for the common man under the blether of an annual alcoholic emotionalism. The horror that would fall on a Mearns Burns

> Club engaged in singing that a man was a man for a' that if the
> waiters sat down and claimed a practical equalitarianism! Or if a
> ploughman came dandering into the room, rough and common as
> Burns himself, and quite without a dress jacket!
>
> (Gibbon, 1934, p.1)

Gibbon's passionate attack on the appropriation of Burns by the Scottish
establishment reveals further clues to his own sense of what literature is for.
What Gibbon particularly likes about Burns is his realistic treatment of sex,
'his angry pity for the common man' and his 'practical equalitarianism'. All
these qualities shine through in Burns's poetry, according to Gibbon, but
they are either censored or misrepresented by Mutch and his ilk, who portray
Burns as 'a genteel Stonehaven spinster engaged in "cleaning up Scottish
song"' and cover him 'under the blether of an annual alcoholic
emotionalism'. Gibbon's intense identification with Burns suggests that he
sought to emulate the latter's work by producing literature that achieved the
same ends. For Burns (or at least, for Gibbon's version of Burns), literature
should record, even celebrate, the lives and loves of 'the common man'; it
should promote the values of 'practical equalitarianism', and it should be
directed against the snobbery and privilege of Scotland's ruling class. Many
Burns lovers would of course reject Gibbon's version of Scotland's national
poet; for our purposes, however, what is important is that Gibbon discovered
in Burns's poetry a kind of model answer to the question 'What is literature
for?' and aspired in his own writing to a comparable achievement.

'Harvest'

Whereas the time covered in each of the first three parts is roughly one year
(winter of 1911 to June 1912 in 'Ploughing'; June 1912 to August 1913 in
'Drilling'; September 1913 to April 1914 in 'Seed-time'), 'Harvest' spans the
years of the First World War. As in the first three parts, the opening
paragraph of 'Harvest' has Chris at the Standing Stones, on this occasion in
the late spring of 1920. She is accompanied by her son Ewan, and once again
recalls a recent death, this time that of her husband Ewan, 'whose hand lay
far from hers' (p.181). 'Harvest' goes on to record the events of the six years
from spring 1914 to spring 1920, from the birth of their son Ewan in
September 1914, through the war-dominated events in Kinraddie, to the
news of her husband's death.

The challenge Gibbon faces in this part of the novel is to convey the
impact of the war on the Kinraddie community. **Read the following four
passages: Reverend Gibbon's sermons (pp.192–7); Chae's reaction to
the destruction of the wood (pp.202–4); Ewan's return to Blawearie
after his military training (pp.222–9); and Chae recounting the news
of Ewan's death to Chris (pp.237–40). In these passages, what**

techniques does Gibbon use to convey the impact of the war on Kinraddie?

Reverend Gibbon's sermons during the war continue in the pattern of his opportunistic sermon on the Song of Solomon that won him the posting to Kinraddie in the first place. Gibbon's sermons are reported in the third-person voice of the folk narrator, who explains how the minister initially misjudged the mood of the times and preached that 'God was sending the Germans for a curse and a plague on the world because of its sins' (p.193), but immediately reversed his line when the congregation expressed its dismay. The next Sabbath, the congregation 'got all the patriotism they could wish, the minister said that the Kaiser was the Antichrist' (p.194). A week later, Gibbon preached an even more patriotic sermon, concluding that 'right here in our midst were traitors that sided with the Antichrist' (p.195), effectively inciting an attack by gullible members of the community on the anti-war Long Rob. Rob repulses this attack, but he becomes increasingly isolated by an overwhelming pro-war majority, which includes his friend Chae Strachan. Rob's views on the war are also reported in the gossipy voice of the folk narrator, which subtly slides into the idiom of Long Rob himself: 'He said it was a lot of damned nonsense, those that wanted to fight, the M.P.s and bankers and editors and muckers, should all be locked up in a pleiter of a park and made to gut each other with graips: there'd be no great loss to the world and a fine bit sight it would make for decent folk to look on at' (pp.194–5). At this stage of the novel, the characters are clearly delineated, and the allegiances of the implied reader are strongly inclined against the self-interested politicking of the Reverend Gibbon and in favour of the cynical Long Rob.

In 'Harvest', Gibbon describes how the precarious peasant economy of the prewar years is transformed by profiteering interests from both within and beyond Kinraddie. In the second passage, the changes in Kinraddie's economy are viewed principally from the perspective of Chae, who has returned from the front on leave. However, once again differing points of view in the community are reflected, particularly in relation to the destruction of the woods: for Mistress Strachan, 'it was only the long bit wood [and its destruction] made a gey difference to the look-out faith! but fine for Kinraddie the woodmen had been, they'd lodged at the Knapp and paid high for their board' (p.202); for Chae, 'he'd often minded of them out there in France, the woods, so bonny they were, and thick and brave, fine shelter and lithe for the cattle' (*ibid.*); and for Old Pooty, 'Folk had told him the trustees had sold it well, they got awful high prices, the trustees did, it was wanted for aeroplanes and such-like things' (p.203). For Mistress Strachan and Old Pooty, only the short-term economic benefits are apparent, but for Chae the felling of the woods symbolizes the destruction of the crofters' way of life, as he registers that with the woods gone, family-based peasant farming must inevitably give way to large-scale forms of capitalist agriculture. Chae's despondency, reinforced by the myopic self-interestedness of his neighbours, percolates these passages, and is expressed by the technique of third-person internal focalization: 'So Chae wandered his round of Kinraddie, a strange place and desolate with its crash of trees and its missing faces. And not that alone, for the folk seemed different, into the bones the War had eaten, they were money-mad or mad with grief for somebody killed or somebody wounded' (p.204). Chae is one of the very few characters other than Chris whose thoughts are conveyed by this technique, and his position as a local returning from the front (as opposed to Chris, who never leaves Kinraddie) gives his thoughts on the changes in the community particular authority.

In the third passage, Ewan's return to Blawearie after his military training is described from Chris's point of view by the internal focalization of her thoughts and fears. On the eve of Ewan's return, she looks at herself in the mirror and happily reflects 'she'd be fine to sleep with yet, she supposed – oh, Ewan!' (p.222). The Ewan who returns to her, however, is quite different from the husband who had left for the war: 'But it wasn't Ewan, her Ewan, someone coarse and strange ... had come back in his body to torment her' (p.224). His brutal behaviour and sexual cruelty rapidly transform Chris's feelings for him, and the image of a mirror is repeated as she grasps the sudden change in Ewan and its effect on her: 'The horror of his eyes upon her she would never forget, they burned and danced on that mirror that wheeled and wheeled in her brain' (p.225). The contrast between Chris and Ewan's union on their wedding night – 'he took her close to him, and they were one flesh' (p.168) – and the sexual violence of Ewan's return attests to the devastating impact of the war on the lives of these characters. Chris's response is to harden her feelings towards Ewan: 'He had gone away Ewan Tavendale, he came back a man so coarse and cruel that in place of love hate came singing in the heart of Chris' (p.225). Once Ewan leaves again, Chris weeps for her prewar husband, for 'that Ewan who had never come back, for the shamed, tormented boy with the swagger airs she had let go' (p.228).

The fact of Ewan's death is suggested in the first paragraph of 'Harvest' (p.181), so the arrival of the telegram informing Chris of his death in France (p.233) is no surprise. Chris's own initial shock is registered by third-person internal focalization of her grieving thoughts: 'Kinraddie was his land, Blawearie his, he was never dead for those things of no concern, he'd the crops to put in and the loch to drain and her to come back to' (p.235). John Grigson and Chris's son Ewan comfort her, and she is then subjected to the unhelpful platitudes of Kirsty Strachan and Mistress Munro, who tell Chris 'he'd died fine, for his country and King he'd died' (*ibid.*). Chris's angry response is represented in direct speech: '*Country and King? You're havering, havering! What have they to do with my Ewan, what was the King to him, what their damned country? Blawearie's his land, it's not his wight that others fight wars!'* (p.236). The circumstances of Ewan's death are finally conveyed to Chris by Chae when he is on leave from the front. The narration of Ewan's story starts in Chae's direct and reported words, but soon shifts to Ewan's point of view. Ewan's words, too, are recorded in a combination of reported speech – 'He had deserted in a blink of fine weather' (p.237) – and direct speech. The most important parts of the story, including Ewan's reasons for deserting and his last words for Chris, are recorded in direct speech: '*It was that wind that came with the sun, I minded Blawearie, I seemed to waken up smelling that smell*' (*ibid.*); and '*Oh man, mind me when next you hear the peewits over Blawearie – look at my lass for me when you see her again, close and close, for that kiss I'll never give her*' (p.240). By mediating events in France through the perspective of Chae, and by recounting Ewan's story in his own words, Gibbon is thus able to convey events in France without shifting the narrative frame beyond Kinraddie.

Epilude

The Epilude – also subtitled 'The Unfurrowed Field' – returns to the gossipy folk voice of the Prelude and describes how the Kinraddie community fared in the final years of the war and its immediate aftermath. The fates of the different characters vary, but the pattern of change is unequivocal: the peasantry (Ewan, Chae, Old Pooty and Long Rob) die off and their places are taken by capitalist farmers (Ellison, Gordon and Munro), who in a short time acquire all the land in Kinraddie.

The only substantial part of the Epilude *not* in the folk voice is the dedication of the war memorial delivered by the new minister, Robert Colquohoun. At its conclusion, the folk narrator passes damning judgement: 'folk stood dumbfounded, this was just sheer politics, plain what he meant' (p.257). **Read Colquohoun's memorial dedication (pp.255–6). What do you think is the message of its 'sheer politics'.**

Colquohoun identifies the four Kinraddie war dead – Chae, Long Rob, Ewan and James Leslie (who had replaced Ewan as foreman at the Upperhill bothy, and takes his name from James Leslie Mitchell) – with the traditional way of life of the crofter: '*these were the Last of the Peasants, the last of the Old Scots folk*'. He recognizes the inevitability of their passing ('*Nothing, it has been said, is true but change, nothing abides*'), but praises warmly the values that had guided their lives: '*the kindness of friends and the warmth of toil and the peace of rest – they asked no more from God or man*'. These sentiments are relatively uncontroversial, and indeed appropriate at a valediction service. The 'sheer politics' that affront the congregation lies, rather, in Colquohoun's scathing words about the class that has replaced the peasant farmers. This class – represented by characters like Ellison and Munro – is described obliquely, but nonetheless in terms that all the congregation recognize: '*those little prides and those little fortunes on the ruins of the little farms*'; '*greed of place and possession and great estate*'; '*the new oppressions and foolish greeds*'. What gives this political critique its particular edge, however, is that Colquohoun suggests that this new class's own days of ascendancy are numbered, and that they will themselves be superseded: the '*new oppressions*' are '*no more than mists that pass*', beyond their temporary reign '*shines a greater hope and newer world, undreamt when these four died*'. Colquohoun's concluding tribute for the four war dead is that they would have sided with those struggling to achieve this 'newer world'. Colquohoun's sentiments mirror those of Long Rob and Chae: a hatred of the rich and a stout defence of communalist peasant life. But they also have a forward-looking, utopian dimension. Through the character of Colquohoun, Gibbon adds another vivid dimension to the implicit anti-capitalist propaganda embedded in *Sunset Song*.

An important motivation at the core of Gibbon's writing, closely connected to his political commitment, is his desire to rescue the forgotten, unrecorded histories of Scotland's poor. **Read the extracts from Gibbon's letter to Helen Cruickshank and his essay 'The Antique Scene' (Reader, Items 12.2 and 12.3). What is the gist of Gibbon's arguments? Try to recall instances in *Sunset Song* where he rewrites what he sees as the lies of 'official' Scots history.**

In the Cruickshank letter, Gibbon insists that the great cultural achievements of the past must never be privileged in ways that silence the suffering that accompanied their creation. Quite the opposite: the torture of Athenian slaves is more important than the Parthenon, and the bloodletting at Goshen more important than the Pyramids. Extending this principle to Scottish history, Gibbon argues that the serfs in the mines of Fifeshire, no less than the poor in Glasgow's slums, should always be recalled when Mary Queen of Scots or the glories of National Art of the Scottish Renaissance are celebrated. Gibbon expresses here the same sentiment as his German contemporaries Bertolt Brecht, whose poem 'Questions from a worker who reads' asks 'Who built Thebes of the seven gates?' (1976, p.252), and Walter Benjamin, who asserts that 'There is no document of civilization which is not at the same time a document of barbarism' (1973, p.248). Whereas both Benjamin and Brecht write about the interconnectedness of violence and civilization in relation to European history, Gibbon's anger is focused principally on Scotland.

In 'The Antique Scene', Gibbon sets out his idiosyncratic blend of Scottish history-from-below and diffusionist anthropology (based on a view of a happy communal past corrupted by destructive 'civilization'), and moves swiftly from prehistoric communities to industrialized Glasgow. The central argument is that behind 'the fictitious faces of heroic Highlanders, hardy Norsemen, lovely Stewart queens, and dashing Jacobite rebels ... are the lives of millions of the lowly who wiped the sweats of toil from browned faces'. The inequalities and lies continue to the present, as the Industrial Revolution heralded a 'hundred and fifty years of unloveliness and pridelessness, of growing wealth and growing impoverishment' (in Bold, 2001, p.22).

In *Sunset Song*, Gibbon gives fictional expression to this view of Scottish history in several passages. The opening pages of the Prelude (pp.1–5) narrate in compressed fictional form a local variation of Scottish history that is elaborated, on the national scale, in 'The Antique Scene'. The folk narrator that Gibbon deploys in the novel is deliberately less reliable than Gibbon-the-popular-historian in 'The Antique Scene', but substantial details recur in both these versions of Scots history: the heroics of William Wallace, the brave resistance of the Covenanters and the centuries-long endurance of the peasants. The elder Colquhoun's sermon is a second instance of such blurring of history and fiction (pp.53–4). In both *Sunset Song* and 'The Antique Scene', Gibbon represents the church's role in Scottish history and society as reactionary and oppressive, though in the fictional character Colquhoun and in the historical figures of the missionary Saint Columba, who introduced Christianity to Scotland, and the sixteenth-century Protestant reformer John Knox he identifies certain honourable exceptions to this compromised record. Gibbon's journalistic views on Christianity in Scotland are close to those of his character Long Rob: the church was driven by political and material ambition; its agents were posturing, self-interested, ignorant and superstitious. Further, the church did nothing to improve the lives of the peasantry, who switched spiritual allegiance from druids to priests without any alleviation of the hardships in their lives. Gibbon's journalistic and literary accounts of Christianity in Scotland differ, however, in that the former expresses a singular anger towards the church, whereas a far greater variety of attitudes towards the church is conveyed in *Sunset Song*. A third moment where Gibbon's historical sensibility intrudes directly is in the passages describing Chris and Ewan's visit to Dunnottar Castle (pp.125–9). In 'The Antique Scene', Gibbon recounts the coming of 'the Covenanting Times, the call of the Church of Knox to be defended as the Church of the Commons, of the People, bitterly assailed by noble and King', and then describes the persecution of the Covenanters as 'such political Terror as has few parallels in history' (in Bold, 2001, pp.18, 19). At Dunnottar Castle, Chris's thoughts, expressed by internal focalization, convey the same passionate sympathy:

> [In the dungeons of Dunnottar Castle] the Covenanting folk had screamed and died while the gentry dined and danced in their lithe, warm halls, Chris stared at the places, sick and angry and sad for those folk she could never help now, that hatred of rulers and gentry a flame in her heart, John Guthrie's hate.
>
> (p.125)

Gibbon's final engagement with Scottish history in *Sunset Song* is expressed in the conclusion of the novel with the piper McIvor playing 'The Flowers of the Forest'. I want to end this section by thinking about Gibbon's treatment of this song in the novel, as it represents perhaps his most complex fictional treatment of Scottish history. Written in the eighteenth century by a member of the minor nobility, Jean Eliot, the song commemorates the defeat of the armies of James IV by Henry VIII's English troops at the Battle of Flodden in 1513. The battle is remembered principally – not least because of the song – for the deaths of many Scottish nobles. As one popular guide to Scottish history summarizes, 'King James and the flower of Scottish chivalry were slaughtered: 13 earls, 14 lords, an archbishop, a bishop, two abbots and numerous knights perished that day, and there was hardly a noble family that had not suffered loss' (Mackay, 1999, p.163). **Read the following three passages that show Chris's attitude to 'The Flowers of the Forest': the first, describing Chris's schooling (p.33); the second, her wedding (pp.165–6); and the third, the dedication of the war memorial that concludes the novel (p.257). What are the different connotations of the song in each passage?**

As an interpretation of Scottish history, 'The Flowers of the Forest' epitomizes in many respects the sentimental misrepresentation of Scotland's past that Gibbon savagely mocks in his essay 'The Antique Scene'. The distinction made in the Notes to the Canongate edition of *Sunset Song* that 'The Flowers of the Forest' is a ' "national", not a "folk" song' (p.263) is worth stressing, as the song constructs an elite eighteenth-century notion of Scottish national identity. The song is *not* the collective product of a communal/folk Scots culture (like the bothy ballads): its sympathies are directed in the first instance to the deaths of Scottish nobles (as opposed to the far more numerous deaths-in-war of Scotland's poor). However, this simplistic version of history and implicit class bias are no bar to Chris identifying with the sentiments expressed in 'The Flowers of the Forest', although the nature of her attachment shifts in the three passages.

In the first passage, Chris's attachment to the song is cast as the whim of a schoolgirl misled by her woefully inadequate school history lessons. Chris's thoughts, conveyed by internal focalization, merge with the song's narrative, as she identifies with the sadness of the war widows in the song. In the second passage, the song assumes a more symbolic dimension, as the content of the song becomes secondary to the maudlin atmosphere it evokes. For Chris, the sadness of Scottish songs – irrespective of their actual words – is consonant with the sadness of Scotland itself, from the unforgiving landscape to the lives of the people ('men and women of the land who had seen their lives and loves sink away'; pp.165–6). The song also functions as an ill-omen: its themes of war, Scottish deaths and English betrayals anticipate events in Kinraddie during the First World War. In the third passage, the song assumes a final sgnificance, as the community of Kinraddie mourning their four dead in the First World War is marked in the music of 'The Flowers of the Forest'. An eighteenth-century song mourning the deaths of sixteenth-century Scottish nobles at Flodden is redefined to express the sorrow of a community (or at least part of it) at the deaths of four peasant farmers in the Great War of the twentieth century. The folk narrator describes the diverse impact of the song on different members of the community: 'it lifted your hair and was eerie and uncanny'; the song itself was 'crying for the men that fell in battle', and Kirsty Strachan was 'weeping quietly and others with her'; but for the young ploughmen, the precise meaning of the song was inaccessible, since 'it belonged to times they had no knowing of'. In the first two passages, the song's meaning is therefore conveyed through Chris's thoughts, but in the third passage, the folk narrator expresses how the meaning of the song is understood by different members of the community to suit the sombre occasion.

Debates

Both Gibbon's manifesto in the *Left Review* and the text of *Sunset Song* give us a strong sense of how he might answer the question 'What is literature for?' This does not constitute the full picture, however, and in this final section I would like to consider how critics have interpreted Gibbon's critical and creative work. Of course, Gibbon had no control over how critics have chosen to read him, or indeed over how they might have understood the value and function of literature, but the reception of his work provides further answers to the questions raised by the chapters in Part 1 of this book. I start by looking at the first reviews of *Sunset Song*; then I consider two contrasting views of the novel's relationship to nationalism and socialism; finally, I assess how *Sunset Song* has been used in Scotland's education system, and explore its (potential) use as a film script.

Reviews of the first edition

Read the five short reviews of the first edition of *Sunset Song* (and Gibbon's response to one of them) (Reader, Items 13.1–13.5) and answer the following questions.

- **What were the major criticisms of *Sunset Song*?**

- **What aspects of *Sunset Song* were singled out for praise?**

- **For these reviewers, does Gibbon succeed (1) in writing 'explicit or implicit [anti-capitalist] propaganda'; or (2) in writing 'work of definite and recognised literary value'?**

Criticisms

The most severe criticisms of *Sunset Song* by some distance were in the anonymous reviews of the Scottish provincial newspapers like the *Fife Herald and Journal*, which complained bitterly about the excessive gratuitous sex: 'How some of it passed the publishers' censor we cannot fathom.' Objections about the sexual content of *Sunset Song* were not confined to provincial reviews; certain libraries of Scotland even restricted access to Gibbon's novel, as Helen Cruickshank recalls:

> In 1935 Aberdeen Public Library 'withdrew "Sunset Song" from the lending department as "unsuitable for general circulation" ... "Sunset Song" had not been banned, as one copy was available to anyone in the reference department. In all quarters of Scotland eager moralists seized their pens to tell the world through the local press how filthy and untrue to life Gibbon was'.
>
> (Cruickshank, 1939, p.354)

Second, the *Fife Herald and Journal* reviewer alleges a lack of realism in *Sunset Song*, comparing it unfavourably with Brown's *The House with the Green Shutters*, which 'was certainly realistic'. According to this reviewer, Gibbon in *Sunset Song* falls down in matters of detail: in contrast, Brown 'was a man who knew many phases of Scotland. He did not write of "inquests" in Scotland or a "B.A." of Aberdeen University as Lewis Grassic Gibbon does.' In addition, the reviewer finds Gibbon's attempts to render the language of the Mearns unconvincing and inconsistent: 'feint', 'futret' and 'meikle', as well as 'some vulgar words, these are about all the Scotch words in this "Scotch" novel'. A third criticism is that Gibbon fails to modulate his own experiences, feelings and prejudices, and to translate them into appropriate literary form in the writing of the novel. The *Modern Scot* review of *Sunset Song* expresses the criticism in more pretentious terms:

> For all its entertainment value, and its moving account of life on a croft, the reader feels that Mr Gibbon is making his novel, especially the first part, as Mr [George Bernard] Shaw says Mr [J.M.] Barrie makes his plays – as a milliner makes his bonnet, by matching and sewing together his materials – not by transmuting his impressions into an art-form. Mr Gibbon's story of Kinraddie is like the map drawn on the boards of the novel: it has not, in Mr Lubbock's words, 'shed its irrelevancy', has not 'passed through an imagination'.

The requirements that writers should 'transmute impressions into an art form' and that the experience of life should 'pass through an imagination' to become art are standard demands of the critical sensibility of the aesthete. According to the *Modern Scot*, Gibbon fails in terms of these requirements because his politics and religion are too transparent in *Sunset Song*; they have not been 'transmuted into art form by an imagination', and his achievement in purely artistic or literary terms has therefore been fatally compromised.

Praise

Gibbon is in fact substantially correct in his blistering 'response' to the *Fife Herald and Journal* when he declares that *Sunset Song* received 'much acclaim ... from the entire Press in Scotland and England'. The hostile reviews that did appear were venomous, but they were in a minority, and *Sunset Song* was widely applauded. The aspect of the novel most frequently singled out for praise was Gibbon's skill in rendering the language of the Mearns. The most influential reviewer, Compton Mackenzie in the London *Daily Mail*, was unstintingly generous on this point: 'Mr Gibbon is the first of our contemporary Scottish writers to use the dialect with such effect that the most fanatical admirer of B.B.C. English and accent will have to admit the impoverishment that English prose has suffered from its failure to absorb and use "braid Scots".' In the same vein, the *Modern Scot* notes that 'The dialogue of *Sunset Song* recaptures admirably the clipped, racy speech of the Mearns.' Peter Monro Jack in the *New York Times Book Review* provides the most extended discussion of Gibbon's language in *Sunset Song*. He praises both the 'cunning interplay' of English and Scotch words, and the way Gibbon 'has soaked his English in the Scottish rhythm and turn of phrase so that one seems to be listening to the village itself speaking'. The effect for Jack is successful to the extent that 'The Scottish farmer lives so completely in this novel that you can hear the tone of his voice.'

The second aspect of *Sunset Song* singled out for praise by the reviewers was its realistic depiction of the Scottish peasantry of the north-east. The *Aberdeen Bon Accord and Northern Chronicle* review argued that ' "Sunset Song" is the most realistic story of North-Eastern peasant-farmer life ever written ... [and] incidents of domestic life such as the wedding and the barn dance will be admired for their Dutch-like fidelity'; the *Modern Scot* acknowledged that *Sunset Song's* 'anecdotes of bed and bothy have the stamp of truth'; and for Jack in the *New York Times Book Review*, the descriptions of Kinraddie's village history and environment are precisely evoked. The sexual content in the novel, so offensive to certain reviewers, is defended in the *Aberdeen Bon Accord* as being realistic, and therefore quite appropriate:

> Many otherwise complaisant readers may think that sex is unduly obtruded, and that some, if not all the characters, are suffering from sex-obsession. Mr Gibbon may reply that the Scottish peasants rightly regard sex as the most important of the essential forces in their nature, and therefore as proper a topic of discussion as their religion or their victuals. The peasants own defence is that 'nothing which is natural can be nasty.' Let us leave it at that.

Figure 3.4   Stacks at Montgoldrum Cottage: a characteristic scene of Mearns farming life. (By permission of The Grassic Gibbon Centre.)

It is worth adding that enthusiastic responses acclaiming the accuracy and realism of *Sunset Song* were not limited to professional reviewers: Gibbon received many fan letters from fellow-writers and members of the reading public. J.W. Rust, a Scottish reader long resident in London, wrote to Gibbon in January 1933 to tell him 'I felt that having been born near "Kinraddie" you might like to know how much I liked your book and the forcible style of it which seems to convey better than any other the rhythms and cadences of the Mearns' (quoted in Munro, 1966, p.96).

Following on from the praise for the realism of *Sunset Song* was the frequent acclaim for the characterization in the novel. The *Aberdeen Bon Accord* commended Gibbon for being so 'successful in his character sketches ... [John Guthrie is] a perfectly realised specimen of the type of peasant nurtured on Calvinism [and Chris] retains the sympathy and affection of every sound-hearted reader throughout'; the *Modern Scot* found that 'the characters are lifelike'.

Reading both the positive first reviews of *Sunset Song* and the letters to Gibbon from sympathetic readers, the general impression is of women readers identifying passionately with the character of Chris, and of men readers falling in love with her. A letter written to Gibbon in 1938 (three years after his death) by Lisa Briden, a young Edinburgh woman, captures the vivid impact *Sunset Song* and its characters had on readers beyond the literary journals:

> You probably get lots of letters like this but I wanted to write and
> tell you of the pleasure your books have given me, especially
> *Sunset Song* and *Cloud Howe*. One character I especially like is
> Long Rob. I often think it would be nice to marry someone like
> this. (I am not a frustrated spinster because I'm still nineteen.) I
> think your view of life the sanest and clearest I have ever
> discovered.
>
> (quoted in Munro, 1966, p.94)

The enthusiasm of the first generation of *Sunset Song*'s readership for the
novel's characters has continued, and has been articulated in more detail in
the more detached language of literary criticism. Deirdre Burton, for
example, writing in the 1980s, has argued that 'What is surprising, and
impressive, here is Gibbon's sympathetic sense of the massive centrality of
the dilemma of contradictory subject positions in female experience. It is
seldom far from Chris's consciousness – or ours' (1984, pp.38–9). For
Burton, the characterization in *Sunset Song* is exemplary because 'it
foregrounds the female point of view, and in that way contributes to an
understanding of history beyond the limitations of patriarchy' (*ibid.*, p.46).

These competing assessments of *Sunset Song* bring different criteria to
bear in judging the novel. Is it realistic? Is its use of literary language skilful?
Is its characterization convincing? And so on. We now turn, however, to the
two criteria Gibbon proclaimed as central for his *own* writing, and consider
the reviews with an eye to whether Gibbon succeeded in his own terms.

Anti-capitalist propaganda or work of literary value

It is clear that none of these reviewers, even the most sympathetic of them,
shared Gibbon's commitment to writing that conveys 'explicit or implicit
[anti-capitalist] propaganda'. For them, the qualities that make a 'good
novel' are exclusively literary; political considerations are at best incidental to
the success of a novel, at worst a disabling distraction. In other words, they
judged the novel in terms that Gibbon would only partially accept and were
indifferent to one of his most important aims as a writer. This makes
answering the question rather difficult, but we might venture one tentative
conclusion. To measure whether *Sunset Song* achieves Gibbon's
instrumental/political ambition, we might ask whether reviewers were
persuaded by Gibbon's diagnosis of Scotland's social ills. On this question,
the critics are divided. Gibbon's political analysis fails to convince Mackenzie
in the *Daily Mail*, who actually disagrees with Gibbon about the fate of
Scottish peasant farming, whereas the *Aberdeen Bon Accord* reviewer accepts
Gibbon's view of the Scots peasantry as 'a class that is bound to disappear as
a result of the changed conditions caused by the war', and would also appear
to endorse Gibbon's characters as accurately typifying the different classes of
people of Scotland's north-east.

As to whether Gibbon succeeds with *Sunset Song* in writing 'work of definite and recognised literary value', the reviewers are again divided. For many of them, Gibbon has failed: for the *Fife Herald*, *Sunset Song* is but 'a bad copy of "The House with the Green Shutters" '; for *The Modern Scot*, it 'is readable, and probably the best recent Scottish story of its kind, but it leaves the novel where it was thirty years ago'. However, for the majority of reviewers, Gibbon has succeeded: for the *Aberdeen Bon Accord*, he has 'written a classic of Scottish peasant life'; for Mackenzie, he has produced 'the richest novel about Scottish life written for many years'; and for Jack, *Sunset Song* 'may be read with delight the world over'.

This kind of acclaim for Gibbon is repeated a couple of years later by the German critic F. Wolcken, who argues that for the Continental onlooker:

> Whereas [Brown's *The House with the Green Shutters* and Neil Gunn's *The Lost Glen*] seem to him to be the best Scottish books of our time, this trilogy [*A Scots Quair*], he ventures to think, has some qualities beyond this limitation. It seems to him to be no longer a novel, but the true saga of our times, grim and heroic in the face of despair, and the standards which have to be applied to it are the standards of great literature.
>
> (Wolcken, 1934, p.8)

This was not an isolated judgement: praise on this scale was also forthcoming from MacDiarmid, who declared with characteristic confidence that Gibbon's three Scots novels which made up *A Scots Quair* 'were in their different way as great a departure from the run of Scottish novels as James Joyce's *Ulysses* from the run of Irish novels' (1969, p.190). These reviewers, however, are unanimous in applauding the *literary* qualities of *Sunset Song*, and pay only subsidiary attention to its 'political message'. Indeed, judging from their reviews, it is doubtful whether certain of them were even aware that Gibbon had any such message.

On the basis of our close reading of these five newspaper reviews, we have a clear if contested sense of how *Sunset Song* was ranked in its day as a work of 'definite and recognised literary value' – of how Gibbon's novel might be judged in aesthetic terms. However, no clear sense emerges of how *Sunset Song* was judged in the 1930s as a work of explicit or implicit anti-capitalist propaganda. We must therefore read beyond these first reviews in order to understand the reception of Gibbon's work in political terms.

Sunset Song: nationalist or socialist novel?

There were in fact several critics of *Sunset Song* in the 1930s who gave extended consideration to the novel's potential to serve an instrumental social/political function; it is to two of these that we now turn. **Read the extracts from 'Nationalism in Writing: Tradition and Magic in the**

Work of Lewis Grassic Gibbon' (1938) by Neil M. Gunn, and 'Lewis Grassic Gibbon' (1936) by James Barke (Reader, Items 14.1 and 14.2). How does each critic answer the following questions?

- **What is literature for?**

- **Does Gibbon's *Sunset Song* represent a satisfactory solution to the question?**

Begin by reading the following paragraph on Gunn and his beliefs.

Gunn was a fellow-Scot, a contemporary of Gibbon, and an acclaimed author and critic in his own right. In 1936, he had debated the question 'Literature: Class or National?' in the Scottish journal *Outlook* with Lennox Kerr and Edward Scouller. Kerr had opened the debate by arguing that 'There is actually a greater gap in understanding, in culture, and in every practical ideal or problem between men of the same nation, but of different classes, than there is of men of different nations, but of the same social and economic class' (Kerr, 1936, p.75). Accordingly, for Kerr, class allegiance should take priority over nationalism as a political motivation for creative writing: 'new art will have nothing to do with a Scottish or any other national renaissance ... Its real body will be its inspiration in the working class' (*ibid.*, p.80). In his response, Gunn flatly rejected Kerr's working-class internationalism, both as a political and as a literary project. He argued that the national scale of the Russian Revolution proved the political inadequacies of internationalism – 'Lenin did not approach the crofters of Wester Ross before collaring the land of Russia for the Soviet Republics' (Gunn, 1936, p.56), and as regards literature, 'it would seem that a man creates most potently within his own national environment. Outside it he is not so sure of himself, not so fertile, not so profound' (*ibid.*, p.58).

In his 1938 essay 'Nationalism in Writing' in the *Scots Magazine*, Gunn developed these ideas and related them specifically to the work of Gibbon. Gunn recognizes at the outset Gibbon's dual ambitions to write 'work of literary value' and 'propaganda', identifying these preoccupations as 'on the one hand, the concern of the creative artist; on the other, the concern of the man for the iniquitous conditions of the poor'. He proceeds to try to paraphrase the details of Gibbon's political commitment, identifying two defining strains. The first is a conviction that world history was moving inexorably towards what Gibbon calls a 'Cosmopolis' (a utopian collective society), 'not because of any need for it *in itself*, but because it was for humanity's final good *on the material or economic plane*. When we attain Cosmopolis, economic slavery and physical want will have vanished.' The second is a 'genuine, profoundly sensitive concern for the downtrodden'. Gunn then quotes a polemical flourish from Gibbon's essay 'Glasgow' that conveys the nature of the latter's commitments. Gibbon writes:

> [I] would welcome the end of Braid Scots and Gaelic, our culture,
> our history, our nationhood under the heels of a Chinese army of
> occupation if it would cleanse the Glasgow slums, give a surety of
> food and play – the elementary right of every human being – to
> those people of the abyss.

Gunn only quotes this one passage from Gibbon's 'Glasgow' essay, but it is
worth pausing to emphasize quite *how* scathing Gibbon is about nationalism
here: 'What a curse to the earth are small nations! ... there is an appalling
number of disgusting little stretches of the globe claimed, occupied and
infected by groupings of babbling little morons – babbling militant on the
subjects (unendingly) of their *exclusive* cultures, their *exclusive* languages,
their *national* souls, their *national* genius' (in Bold, 2001, p.106). Gibbon's
solution? 'Glasgow's salvation, Scotland's salvation, the world's salvation lies
in neither nationalism nor internationalism, those twin halves of an idiot
whole. It lies in ultimate cosmopolitanism' (in *ibid.*, p.108). Rankled by
Gibbon's provocative anti-nationalism, Gunn claims finally that 'the Scots
people, reforming and running their own social system, could cleanse the
Glasgow slums without help either from the Chinese or from Cosmopolis'.
Gunn therefore regards Gibbon's anti-nationalism as woefully misconceived
and his cosmopolitanism as pie-in-the-sky fantasy, defending his own
nationalist position vis-à-vis Gibbon by reference to *Sunset Song*.
According to Gunn, Gibbon's finest work, *A Scots Quair*, is written not in
English (the language of Cosmopolis), but in a dying regional language of
Scotland, and this proves for Gunn that Gibbon's literary choices should be
accorded more authority than his political criticism.

In answer to the two questions posed, the simple answer for Gunn is that
literature has an instrumental function, that it is written for the nation that
produced it; internationalist or cosmopolitan aspirations can only be
considered once the national imperative is met. As to whether *Sunset Song*
satisfies this critical requirement, Gunn's answer would be in the affirmative,
but with the important qualification that Gibbon must remain true to his
instinct and write in the speech of the Scots peasant, as he does in *Sunset
Song*. When Gibbon thinks beyond his regional and national location, and
writes of cosmopolitanism and universal oppression, he flouts, indeed
sabotages, his authentic vocation as a Scottish writer.

Like Gunn, Barke was also a Scottish contemporary of Gibbon and the
author of several novels. In the opening paragraphs of his 1936 *Left Review*
article, Barke identifies Gunn and Gibbon as Scotland's two most significant
novelists. He categorizes Gunn (disapprovingly) as an idealist and nationalist,
and Gibbon (approvingly) as a materialist and internationalist. Barke argues
that Gibbon correctly subscribes to Marx's dictum that '"the mode of
production in material life determines the general character of the social,
political and spiritual processes of life"', and that Gibbon's idiosyncratic

socialism (the 'Cosmopolis') accorded with internationalist Marxism. Not only Gibbon's political philosophy and commitments win Barke's praise; Barke also acclaims Gibbon as the author of fine literature. Barke then sets out his own standards of judgement:

> To the reader unsympathetic or unconcerned with the struggle of the working class, to the critic who does not recognise the class war (far less the class nature of society) and who concerns himself with 'art' and 'literature' (deprecating, scorning 'propaganda') this insistence of the essential class content of *A Scots Quair* may appear irrelevant or even distorted. But there is no irrelevance or distortion. Even a superficial understanding of the content of *A Scots Quair* should reveal its true purpose, nature and significance. All art is propaganda. Gibbon had no illusions about this elementary truth.

In conclusion, Barke reflects on the appropriate critical frame for assessing Gibbon. He considers first the frame of Scottish literature, arguing that although Gibbon was never 'a perverted, illogical, reactionary Nationalist', *A Scots Quair* should be classed as 'probably the greatest Scots novel in Scottish literature'. Second, he considers Gibbon's work in the context of 'modern bourgeois art' and concludes that 'many of the bourgeois critics ... have been forced to recognize Gibbon as a literary artist of the highest standing'. Both these critical frames, however, are secondary for Barke to the emergent critical demands of revolutionary literature: 'For *A Scots Quair* is a worthy forerunner of the novel that will dominate the coming literary scene: the novel that will be written by workers for workers, expressing the hopes, ideals, aspirations of workers.'

Barke's answer to the question 'What is literature for?' is therefore that literature should express in literary form the class struggle and the materialist view of history. Literature is emphatically *not* for promoting or nurturing nationalism (Gunn's position), or for disinterested, apolitical contemplation (the position of the aestheticist critics of 'modern bourgeois art'). For Barke, Gibbon's *A Scots Quair* is exemplary in serving the instrumental function he prescribes – to express 'the hopes, ideals and aspirations of workers' – and will accordingly be remembered as 'a magnificent and heroic pioneer achievement'.

Sunset Song in schools and on film

These differences of opinion between Gunn, Barke and Gibbon, expressed in the most polemical and intemperate of terms, were never resolved in the 1930s. Certainly no critical consensus was ever reached as to what literature was for; partisans of competing nationalist, international-socialist and aestheticist answers to the question have continued to disagree in the decades that have followed. Similarly, Gibbon's work has continued on occasions to provide a focus for these debates. In the 1970s, Ian Carter followed Gunn, and located Gibbon as principally a Scottish writer who 'saw the fight for political nationalism and socialism to be a single struggle' (1978, p.181). In contrast, David Smith, a critic writing at the same time as Carter, followed Barke, and emphasized Gibbon-the-socialist, who in *A Scots Quair* 'has with a large degree of artistic success moulded his experience and his peasant consciousness to his revolutionary purpose' (1978, p.127). Such disagreements over Gibbon, and over what literature is for, continue into the twenty-first century. **To conclude this chapter, read 'The Gospels According to Saint Bakunin' by the critic Keith Dixon, and 'Earth Mother' by film director Terence Davies (Reader, Items 14.3 and 14.4). What do you think their arguments are? Try to draw your own conclusions as to what *you* think *Sunset Song* – and indeed literature in general – is for.**

Dixon argues that since the 1970s 'within Scottish academia, and subsequently within the secondary school curriculum in Scotland, [there] has been a substantial rewriting of [Gibbon's] politics, or the erasure of his politics altogether from academic discussion and educational presentation'. This rewriting, or erasure, of Gibbon's radical politics accompanied a general resurgence in Scottish nationalism in the 1970s; the 'respectabilisation' of Gibbon produced 'nationalist or nationalist/ruralist readings of Lewis Grassic Gibbon' that were 'innocuous', and congruent with the conservative ideals of the Scottish Education Department. Dixon summarizes the Notes to the widely used 1971 J.T. Low edition of *Sunset Song* and concludes: 'conveniently shorn of his subversive potentialities, hung, drawn and quartered by academic bad faith, transformed miraculously into the nationalist he had never been, Lewis Grassic Gibbon was, by the mid-1970s seen fit to enter the pantheon of ScotLit'. For Dixon, by a process of 'understatement and polite suppression, not to mention straightforward misrepresentation', *Sunset Song* has in fact been *abused* by Scotland's educational establishment. As a counter, Dixon therefore seeks to restore Gibbon's libertarian revolutionary commitments to all discussion of *Sunset Song*.

Terence Davies is the director of acclaimed feature films (*Distant Voices, Still Lives* (1988), *The Long Day Closes* (1992), *The House of Mirth* (2000)). He explains in this short extract how he understands *Sunset Song* and why he wants to make a film of it. Davies's opening paragraph recalls the powerful impression made on him not by the novel *Sunset Song*, but by the 1970s BBC television adaptation of it. For Davies, *Sunset Song* is 'about the power and cruelty of both family and nature, about the enduring presence of the land and the courage of the human spirit in the face of hardship'. The central story is of Chris Guthrie, who evolves 'from schoolgirl to wife to mother then finally becoming a symbol for Scotland itself'. For Davies, *Sunset Song* is 'both symbolic and rhapsodic', and it has universal relevance: 'The song is yours and mine, of all who feel and have suffered or been happy'; 'Chris sings the song of the earth for humanity, a rhapsody for us all as she charts the eternal cycle of birth, marriage and death, as the song explores the timeless mysteries of land, home, and family.'

The differences between Dixon and Davies over *Sunset Song* are stark. On the one hand, Dixon identifies the key to the novel in Gibbon's radical politics, which are premised on a hatred of capitalism, a hostility towards Scottish nationalism and a faith in the collective resources of the poor. On the other hand, Davies locates *Sunset Song* as a timeless tale of land, home and family; he identifies the key to the novel in Gibbon's faith in the human spirit, understood as a sensitivity to the cruelties of nature and the land, a symbolic identification of Chris Guthrie and Scotland, and a compassion for all locked in the eternal cycle of birth, marriage and death. These widely differing interpretations suggest equally divergent uses for the novel. For Dixon, *Sunset Song* is indeed 'explicit or implicit anti-capitalist propaganda': *in addition to* appreciating its literary or aesthetic qualities, he is convinced that the novel should be discussed and debated in political terms. For Davies, *Sunset Song* is exclusively a work of 'definite and recognised literary value' (his piece makes no mention of politics or economics) – the novel is for aesthetic pleasure, and for the contemplation of timeless truths about the human spirit confronting hardship.

Summing up

Thus far I have provided provisional answers to all the questions posed, but I am going to abandon this format and leave you to decide which of the two views of *Sunset Song* you find more convincing and to reflect on the question 'What is literature for?' I will also leave you to decide which of the two views you think is the more likely to prevail, both in the education system and more generally. Can you imagine a third position that reconciles these viewpoints, with elements of each selected and integrated in a happy compromise?

With these questions in mind, we turn now from Gibbon's attempts to negotiate these debates in novel form to consider how poets in the 1930s grappled with similar concerns.

Works cited

Bakhtin, M.M. (1981) *The Dialogic Imagination: Four Essays*, ed. by M. Holquist, trans. by C. Emerson and M. Holquist, Austin: University of Texas Press.

Benjamin, W. (1973) *Illuminations*, ed. and intro. by H. Arendt, London: Fontana.

Bold, V. (ed.) (2001) *Smeddum: A Lewis Grassic Gibbon Anthology*, Edinburgh: Canongate.

Brecht, B. (1976) *Poems*, ed. and trans. by J. Willett and R. Manheim, London: Eyre Methuen.

Brown, G.D. ([1901] 1996) *The House with the Green Shutters*, Edinburgh: Canongate.

Burton, D. (1984) 'A Feminist Reading of Lewis Grassic Gibbon's *A Scots Quair*', in J. Hawthorn (ed.), *The British Working-Class Novel in the Twentieth Century*, London: Edward Arnold, pp.34–46.

Calder, A. (1982) 'A Mania for Self-Reliance: Grassic Gibbon's *Scots Quair*', in D. Jefferson and G. Martin (eds), *The Uses of Fiction*, Milton Keynes: Open University Press, pp.99–113.

Carter, I. (1978) 'Lewis Grassic Gibbon, *A Scots Quair*, and the Peasantry', *History Workshop*, 6, pp.169–85.

Craig, D. (1964) 'A National Literature? Recent Scottish Writing', *Studies in Scottish Literature*, 1.3, pp.151–69.

Cruickshank, H. (1939) 'Mearns Memory: A Fellow-Countrywoman's View of Lewis Grassic Gibbon', *Scots Magazine*, 30.5, February, pp.350–4.

Cunningham, V. (1997) 'The Age of Anxiety and Influence; or Tradition and the Thirties Talents', in K. Williams and S. Matthews (eds), *Rewriting the Thirties: Modernism and After*, London: Longman, pp.5–22.

Gibbon, L.G. (1934) 'Canting Humbug! Mearns Author Reply to Burns Orator', *Mearns Leader and Kincardineshire Mail*, 8 February, p.1.

Gibbon, L.G. ([1932] 1971) *Sunset Song*, with notes by J.T. Low, Heritage of Literature, London: Longman.

Gibbon, L.G. ([1932] 1988) *Sunset Song*, Canongate Classics, Edinburgh: Canongate.

Gunn, N.M. (1936) 'Literature: Class or National?', *Outlook*, 1.4, July, pp.54–8.

Kerr, L. (1936) 'Literature: Class or National?', *Outlook*, 1.3, June, pp.74–80.

MacDiarmid, H. (1969) *Selected Essays of Hugh MacDiarmid*, ed. by D. Glen, London: Jonathan Cape.

Mackay, J. (1999) *Scottish History*, Bath: Parragon.

Maclaren, I. ([1894] 1896) *Beside the Bonnie Brier Bush*, London: Hodder & Stoughton.

Margolies, D. (ed.) (1998) *Writing the Revolution: Cultural Criticism from 'Left Review'*, London: Pluto.

Munro, I.S. (1966) *Leslie Mitchell: Lewis Grassic Gibbon*, Edinburgh: Oliver & Boyd.

Power, W. (1935) 'The Literary Movement in Scotland', *London Mercury*, 33.194, December, pp.179–83.

Smith, D. (1978) *Socialist Propaganda in the Twentieth-Century British Novel*, London: Macmillan.

Trengove, G. (1975) 'Who Is You? Grammar and Grassic Gibbon', *Scottish Literary Journal*, 2.2, pp.47–62.

Wolcken, F. (1934) 'Scottish Literature – Seen through Foreign Eyes', *Scots Observer*, 20 June, p.8.

Further reading

I would strongly encourage you to read the rest of *A Scots Quair* (*Cloud Howe* and *Grey Granite*), as well as other novels by Mitchell/Gibbon. *Spartacus* (1933) and *The Thirteenth Disciple* (1931) are the other two to have attracted critical attention, but the earlier novels are also of interest.

Bold, V. (ed.) (2001) *Smeddum: A Lewis Grassic Gibbon Anthology*, Edinburgh: Canongate. A comprehensive collection of Gibbon's critical writings (including his essays for *Scottish Scene*) that is indispensable for any further study.

McCullough, M.P. and Dunnigan, S.M. (eds) (2003) *A Flame in the Mearns. Lewis Grassic Gibbon: A Centenary Celebration*, Glasgow: Association for Scottish Literary Studies. A wide range of views on Gibbon are presented in this collection, with particularly useful essays (in the context of this chapter) by A. Lumsden, W.K. Malcolm, G. Carruthers and K. Dixon.

Malcolm, W.K. (1984) *A Blasphemer and Reformer: A Study of James Leslie Mitchell/Lewis Grassic Gibbon*, Aberdeen: Aberdeen University Press. The most scholarly single-volume study of Gibbon's work, with excellent chapters on Gibbon's intellectual background and *A Scots Quair*.

Malcolm, W.K. (2002) 'A Retrospective View of James Leslie Mitchell', *Edinburgh Review*, 110, pp.55–73. A useful survey and update of Gibbon criticism.

CHAPTER 4

The poetry of the 1930s

RICHARD DANSON BROWN

Overview

This chapter has five linked sections. The first considers how the poetry of the 1930s negotiates the question of the purpose of literature through a comparison of two poems that, in turn, reflect debates about poetry and difficulty. This section also introduces W.H. Auden as one of the central figures of the decade. The second explores debates about the function of poetry by contrasting the views of Auden and Virginia Woolf. The third considers the reaction of the poets of the period to the Spanish Civil War and the extent to which their work can be viewed as propagandist. The fourth looks at the very different aesthetics of those poets influenced by Surrealism, particularly David Gascoyne and Dylan Thomas. Finally, I explore a number of poems by Louis MacNeice as another way of framing the question 'What is literature for?' Though you will sometimes be asked directly to read a poem in order to answer specific questions on it, generally you should read poems as soon as they are mentioned. The main poems discussed are: Auden's 'Sir, no man's enemy', 'Ballad' and 'Spain'; John Betjeman's 'Slough'; John Cornford's 'A Letter from Aragon'; Gascoyne's 'And the Seventh Dream is the Dream of Isis' and 'The Very Image'; MacNeice's 'Autumn Journal III', 'An Eclogue for Christmas', 'Christina' and 'Bagpipe Music'; Stephen Spender's 'The Pylons' and 'Port Bou'; Thomas's 'And Death Shall Have No Dominion'; and Rex Warner's 'Hymn' (unless otherwise stated, all poetry is quoted from Skelton ([1964] 2000)).

Introduction

Looking back in time from a New York 'dive' immediately before the outbreak of the Second World War in Europe, the most celebrated English poet of the period characterized the 1930s as 'a low dishonest decade'. On 'September 1, 1939' – the date gives the poem its title – W.H. Auden's pessimism was unsurprising. In Europe, the 1930s had seen: the rise to power of Hitler's National Socialists in Germany, resulting in the brutal suppression of political opponents, the persecution of Jews and other minorities alongside the annexation of Austria, Czechoslovakia and, most recently, Poland into a 'Greater Germany'; the collapse of Spain's communist experiment in a bloody civil war, which led to General

Franco's right-wing dictatorship; the consolidation of Mussolini's grip on power in Italy. In Britain, though the fascist leader Oswald Mosley remained a peripheral and somewhat ludicrous figure, the decade witnessed what was for Auden and his contemporaries the ignominious collapse of the first Labour government in 1931. This was replaced by the so-called 'National government', a broad coalition of conservative forces, including the former Labour premier Ramsey McDonald, which showed little awareness of the dangers of fascism or appetite for challenging Hitler's territorial ambitions until late in the decade. Meanwhile, Britain's economy was chronically depressed, resulting in mass unemployment in major industrial cities. The poetry of this period is inevitably marked by its political turbulence. Yet the work of writers like Auden is not simply a verse documentary of the 1930s. This chapter will explore writers and texts from Skelton's *Poetry of the Thirties* anthology not only to observe the influence of the political zeitgeist on poetry, but to ask broader questions: should poetry be difficult or accessible? What was the social purpose of poetry in Britain in the first part of the twentieth century?

Functions of poetry I: does it have to be difficult?

Poetry is widely assumed to be the most demanding of literary forms. During the twentieth century, leading poets cultivated styles in which difficulty and obscurity were prized as virtues. One authoritative answer to the question 'What is literature for?' has been, 'To challenge the intellect'. T.S. Eliot's essay 'The Metaphysical Poets' (1921) stated that 'it appears likely that poets in our civilization ... must be *difficult* ... The poet must become more and more comprehensive, more allusive, more indirect, in order to force, to dislocate if necessary, language into his meaning' ([1932] 1951, p.289). According to this view, the complexity of the modern world necessitated a poetry that would itself be correspondingly involved. Eliot's poet is, perhaps unsurprisingly, reminiscent of Eliot himself: a highbrow, 'a refined sensibility' (*ibid.*), who produces an allusive, intellectually demanding poetry for an elite audience. It is worth stressing that 'difficult' poets were not necessarily elitist or reactionary. David Gascoyne argued in 1936 that the 'revolutionary poet' should avoid 'writ[ing] down to the masses ... in order to reach a wider public' because this would fatally compromise 'poetry's inherent complexity of subject-matter'; the attempts of writers like Auden to 'write down' were for Gascoyne 'symptom[s] of the disease called capitalism' (1998, p.29). Eliot's view helped to shape ideas of the demands and discipline of poetry as it was taught in British and American universities. William Empson's classic study *Seven Types of Ambiguity* (1930) insisted that ambiguity of meaning and uncertainty of interpretation, far from being blemishes, were integral components of the intellectual challenge of poetry as an art form.

But Eliot's was not the only theory of poetry available during the early part of the century. Louis MacNeice remarked fourteen years after 'The Metaphysical Poets' that Eliot's imitators tended to produce 'frigid intellectual exercises' (1987, p.23). This chapter will be concerned with poets who, like MacNeice, wanted to write poetry that was both experimental and approachable. As we shall see, these are ambitions that it is not always easy to reconcile, yet they do usefully indicate the contradictions the poets of the 1930s wrestled with between instrumental theories (in which poetry functions as an agent for social or political action) and aestheticist theories (in which poetry is an end in itself).

As you will see in Part 2 of this book, Eliot's own poetry is frequently as allusive and semantically 'dislocated' as his own theories demanded. Not all twentieth-century verse follows this recipe; John Betjeman's 'Slough' is a straightforward satire of town planning:

> Come, friendly bombs, and fall on Slough
> It isn't fit for humans now,
> There isn't grass to graze a cow
>   Swarm over, Death!

(p.74)

The poem's tone is immediate: it urges the destruction of Slough through an address to the 'friendly bombs'. Slough's ugliness, its 'air-conditioned' vulgarity, makes it the ideal target for a purgative blitzkrieg; as the third stanza puts it, 'Mess up the mess they call a town'. Such fantasies may strike you as tasteless rather than comic, but at the time of the poem's publication in 1937 the British public had had no direct experience of such air strikes, though the Spanish town Guernica had been destroyed in April 1937 by German bombing in support of Franco's forces (Figure 4.1). The realities of aerial warfare do not substantially impinge on 'Slough'. Nonetheless, the poem's tone and comic purpose should be immediately apparent: Slough is so ugly that it should be destroyed.

Betjeman's poem also shows that elitism was not the sole preserve of avant-garde writers like Eliot. The comic apocalypse he imagines conveys profound architectural and social snobbery. Though his poetic practice is very different from Eliot's, his conservative social criticism is close to the prejudices of the older writer. The 'bald young clerks' and 'Their wives' with 'peroxide hair' excite Betjeman's disdain for the emergent middle classes who lived in newly developing towns like Slough. Note the contemptuous irony that shapes the poem: Betjeman apostrophizes the inanimate bombs directly, as though they could respond to his request, but describes the inhabitants of the new towns as helplessly ignorant, as though they could have no conception of the horror of their lives: 'It's not their fault they often go / To Maidenhead' (p.75).

Figure 4.1   Guernica in flames.

So, twentieth-century poetry is not invariably difficult. Of course, there is no such thing as a 'typical' twentieth-century poem, and there are good reasons for Betjeman's clarity of address. An obscure satirical poem runs the risk that its readers will not get the joke. Wyndham Lewis's modernist verse satire *One-Way Song* is a good example of this. Though Lewis writes in energetic imitation of the heroic couplet ('You must know who your enemy is my god / By this time, or you're a very brainless sod!'; 1933, p.50), his targets are frequently so recondite that the uninformed reader can have little idea of what he was getting at. As Auden remarked of Lewis's novels in 1932, 'what promises to be really important degenerates into a private squabble between rival literary pushes' (1996, p.11). By virtue of its clarity, 'Slough' avoids any such hazards.

Auden is an interesting witness in these debates, since his first two volumes of poetry – *Poems* (1930) and *The Orators* (1932) – were notorious for their obscurity. **Now read 'Sir, no man's enemy' (p.201), which was the final text in *Poems*. This is by no means an easy poem, so you will need to read it through at least a couple of times. Try reading it aloud: the sound of the poem should help you to follow its structure. Choose a phrase that you think is particularly important to the poem's meaning, then write a short paragraph explaining your choice.**

Like most demanding poems, 'Sir, no man's enemy' has very little padding – you can find a way into it from virtually any phrase: do not worry if you have chosen a different phrase from me. I would choose the last four words, 'a change of heart', because they encapsulate the poem's focus on renewal. In terms of the poem as a whole, 'Harrow the house of the dead; look shining at / New styles of architecture, a change of heart' is a relatively direct statement. I will try to unpack it further. You may have noticed that Auden employs the imperative mode throughout the poem (you might indeed have chosen one of these phrases). Here the addressee – the 'Sir' of the first line – must 'Harrow' and 'look' where earlier he has had to 'be prodigal', 'send', 'Prohibit', 'correct', 'Cover' and 'Publish'. Auden requests this 'Sir' to 'Harrow', or plough, 'the house of the dead' while looking positively at 'New styles of architecture'. I take these lines to mean that he is to plough the dead back into the land – which suggests that they should be ignored – while welcoming a newer, and presumably better, world. Monroe K. Spears has suggested that 'Harrow' is further complicated by its allusion to the myth of the Harrowing of Hell, in which Christ rescues a select number of souls (notably Adam, Abraham and other biblical patriarchs) from Hell. Spears argues that Auden fuses this with criticism of modern civilization as a 'house of the dead' which must be abandoned (1963, pp.44–5).

That 'change of heart' encompasses in miniature the prescriptions of the rest of the poem. As has often been observed, Auden's early manner tends towards the diagnostic; in this respect, he recalls Chekhov, who as Sara Haslam suggested in Chapter 1, employed a 'diagnostic style' in his plays. Reading poems like this can feel like a consultation with an impressive but rather flashy medical expert who is keen to enlighten you as to the severity of your condition with a suitably intimidating technical vocabulary. This poem is effectively a list of chronic symptoms: the subject suffers from such dire-sounding ailments as 'intolerable neural itch' and 'ingrown virginity'. Auden diagnoses a state of moral and psychological illness, which will be cured by the advent of change.

Yet even when we have decoded some of the poem's meaning, its detail remains enigmatic; as Anthony Hecht notes, 'What [t]his poem does is to allow us to entertain ... many irreconcilable readings one after another, without the hope of clear resolution' (1993, p.27). Auden later dropped the poem from his collected works, and wrote in a friend's copy of *Poems* 'I bitterly regret the day I was snobbish enough to use an archaic genitive (= will's). I've been asked what this line means ever since' (quoted in Fuller, 1998, p.76). Your first response to this may well be, 'No wonder!' Indeed, though this helps a little with the opening couplet, allowing us to see that 'negative inversion' belongs to 'will', it does not satisfactorily explain Auden's compacted sentence structure. Such elisions are characteristic of Auden's earlier poetry, in which articles, pronouns and conjunctions that we typically expect of written English are swallowed into surrounding words and phrases. The tangled syntax of the opening couplet is clarified once we understand that the 'Sir' is, in John Fuller's words, a secular version of 'the God you can argue with' of religious poets like George Herbert or Gerard Manley Hopkins (1998, p.76). This allows us to make a speculative expansion of these lines: 'Sir, [you are] no man's enemy, [you] forgiv[e] all [except the human] will [which is your] negative inversion, [but inspite of this, please] be prodigal'. Though this makes the lines slightly clearer, we must register the cost: where Auden delivers a memorably odd poetic couplet, I have come up with a prose paraphrase, full of padding, which makes no pretension to poetry.

The point is that the density of Auden's syntax is an essential part of what makes the poem distinctive. The effort we must expend to make sense of 'Sir, no man's enemy, forgiving all / But will his negative inversion, be prodigal' forces us to read and reread the text with increased attentiveness. This is the kind of poetry Eliot anticipated in 'The Metaphysical Poets': difficult, allusive and indirect, it cannot be absorbed passively. Before we try to get some more purchase on Auden's meaning, we should note that the text is poetically pleasing as well as puzzling. Lines like 'Prohibit sharply the rehearsed response' and 'Publish each healer that in city lives' (note again [the] elision of [the] definite article) bristle with Auden's militant attitude to poetic language. The poem is written in the same metre that Shakespeare used, the iambic pentameter, which makes these phrases rhythmically familiar even though their sense may be alien. Compare 'Or **coun**try **hou**ses **at** the **end** of **drives**' with a line from Shakespeare's eighteenth sonnet, 'Rough **winds** do **shake** the **dar**ling **buds** of **May**' (Shakespeare, 1997, p.1929; I have emboldened the stressed syllables). Though it avoids the stanzaic structure of a Shakespearean sonnet (four quatrains followed by a couplet), this poem is a version of the sonnet form in that it is composed of fourteen lines of couplets. Auden, in other words, forces the most traditional of English lines to accommodate his innovative agenda.

To develop our understanding of that agenda, I would like to compare Auden's poem directly with Betjeman's 'Slough'. **Reread 'Slough' (pp.74–5) and 'Sir, no man's enemy' (p.201), then list three images, ideas or techniques that both poems have in common. What do you think are the major differences between the attitudes to society exhibited in these texts?**

Here are four points of comparison that occurred to me.

Mode of address

As we have seen, Betjeman uses the rhetorical device of apostrophe, inviting the bombs to 'fall on Slough'. Auden uses the related but subtly different trope of request or supplication, praying to the 'Sir' for moral renewal. (When he last reprinted the poem, in his *Collected Poems* of 1945, he entitled it 'Petition'.)

Use of rhyme

The humour of 'Slough' depends on Betjeman's inventive and obtrusive rhyming. He piles strong rhymes in the heavily endstopped longer lines of each stanza to create an effect of claustrophobic ugliness and ignorance: 'And talk of sports and makes of cars / In various bogus Tudor bars / And daren't look up and see the stars'. The timeless beauty of 'the stars' is coupled with the ephemeral vulgarity of contemporary 'cars' and 'bars'. 'Sir, no man's enemy' also rhymes, but to different effect. Auden employs half or slanted rhymes, which muffle the full rhyme sound, as in 'Prohibit sharply the rehearsed response / And gradually correct the coward's stance'. Though 'response' and 'stance' have similar sounds, the impact of the half rhyme is to defuse the reader's expectation of a satisfying aural closure.

Though this may seem a purely mechanical point, it marks the different literary commitments of the two writers. Half rhyme is a device that is chiefly associated with modernist or modernist-inspired writing. Betjeman, a conservative in poetics as much as in politics, eschewed it as he did free verse. The other five Betjeman poems in Skelton's *Poetry of the Thirties* all use full rhymes and traditional metres. Half rhyme had been used by both W.B. Yeats and Wilfred Owen, often for the kind of deflationary effect Auden aspires to here and Owen achieves in the opening of 'Insensibility': 'Happy are men who yet before they are killed / Can let their veins run cold' (1963, p.37).

The image of ploughing

Both poems climax with the image of something being ploughed back into the earth. In 'Slough', it is the town itself that will be ploughed after it has been bombed; as Betjeman gleefully exclaims, 'The cabbages are coming now'. For Auden, 'the house of the dead' will be harrowed. As we have seen, this is a complex image that encapsulates Auden's attitude towards the past. We might say that where Betjeman wants to return to an agricultural past, Auden wants to bury that same past.

Attitudes to architecture

Again, the poems exhibit diametrically opposed views. 'Slough' is prompted by Betjeman's abhorrence of the new town: like the 'Tudor bars', it is irredeemably bogus. Auden closes his poem with an invitation to 'look shining at / New styles of architecture'. It was a phrase he came to regret. In 1969, he confessed 'I once expressed a desire for "New styles of architecture"; but I have never liked modern architecture. I prefer *old* styles and one must be honest even about one's prejudices' (quoted in Fuller, 1998, pp.76–7). As Fuller observes, this is misleading since 'architecture' is clearly a metaphor for 'a change of heart' rather than a comment about modernist architecture per se. Irrespective of Auden's curmudgeonly second thoughts, the difference in emphasis is telling. Where Betjeman repudiates the modern, Auden welcomes it optimistically.

Such comparisons can provide answers to my earlier question: in terms of both form and content, the poems express different attitudes to society. Yet although Auden and Betjeman exhibit opposed social, political and aesthetic prejudices, their poems operate in similar ways, in that they manipulate poetic language to persuade their readers of particular opinions or ideas. They are both didactic poems. 'Slough' ascribes responsibility for modern vulgarity to the caricature capitalist of stanzas 4 and 5. By employing 'bald young clerks' to 'add [his] profits', this 'stinking cad' apparently establishes the market conditions that lead to new towns, mass-produced consumer goods, and even contemporary hairstyles. Betjeman does not object to the capitalist because he exploits his employees, as a socialist poet might have done, but because he is insensitive to the ugliness of the developments he sanctions. 'Slough' is nostalgic for a vanished – and varnished – rural idyll in which cows graze in grassy meadows and young men can recognize constellations and birdsong.

Where Betjeman focuses exclusively on the external details of contemporary Britain, Auden turns his attention inwards. In common with much of Auden's writing of the early 1930s, his programme for psychological renewal depends on the intervention of a 'healer'. This enigmatic figure derives from his reading of the German philosopher Friedrich Nietzsche and the writer D.H. Lawrence, as well as his immersion in the psychoanalytic theories of Sigmund Freud. In *Also Sprach Zarathustra* ('Thus Spoke Zarathustra'), Nietzsche asserted both that 'God is dead' and that humans should submit to the 'Übermensch', or 'Superman' ([1883–5] 1969, p.41). Lawrence followed Nietzsche in arguing that modern humans were corrupt and could only be salvaged by the 'fathomless submission to the heroic soul in a greater man' ([1922] 1995, p.299). Freud argued that the conscious mind represses unconscious desires, which then resurface in other forms, especially in dreams; Freudian thinking suggests there is a dichotomy between the conscious, repressing mind and the unconscious mind, which is more fully in touch with hidden desires. According to Auden's peculiar amalgam of these ideas, human beings would be liberated from their emotional shackles once they surrendered to their desires, and to the benign guidance of the healer or leader. This prospect is well captured in section 32 of C. Day Lewis's *The Magnetic Mountain* (1933), which lyrically imagines the psychic regeneration of England: 'We can tell you a secret, offer a tonic; only / Submit to the visiting angel, the strange new healer' (p.50). Like Auden, Day Lewis should have known that submitting to 'the strange new healer' was a dangerous business in the early 1930s, when Hitler and Mussolini seemed to embody the fantasy that 'strange' forms of political authority could magically revivify ailing societies. At this stage in his career, Auden's programme is, if anything, apolitical, or naive about the implications of his cult of the leader. As he was to comment much later of *The Orators* (a work that is centrally concerned with the myth of the leader), it seemed to have been written by someone 'who might well [have] ... become a Nazi' (quoted in Fuller, 1998, p.88). Though Auden endorsed socialism in the mid-1930s, in this poem his political ideas are less subtle than his psychological vocabulary is impressive.

I have spent some time on this poem, both because it repays careful reading, and because it is indicative of the fashions and attitudes that were characteristic of the poetry of the 1930s. When reading Auden, it is impossible to disentangle his work from the impact it had on his contemporaries, especially those with literary aspirations. This point is worth underlining: Auden's *Poems* were published in 1930 (when he was in his early twenties); by 1933, Charles Madge claimed that reading Auden had cured him of his adolescent alienation:

> there waited for me in the summer morning,
> Auden, fiercely. I read, shuddered and knew
> And all the world's stationary things
> In silence moved to take up new positions.

(quoted in Hynes, [1976] 1992, p.111)

Though we should be cautious of what Peter McDonald calls 'the Auden-centred image' of 'the so-called "1930s myth"' (1991, p.2), nonetheless Auden remains a pivotal and influential figure. Like Bob Dylan or John Lennon for later generations, he was viewed as a significant artist assumed to be 'in the know', mysteriously plugged into the zeitgeist. In a sense, Auden became for his fellow-poets the healer-cum-leader he had himself described. You can get a sense of this impact in the two parodies of Auden that Skelton reprints: William Empson's 'Just a Smack at Auden' (p.64), which pokes fun at the apocalyptic mode favoured by Auden and his friends, and Gavin Ewart's 'Audenesque for the Initiation' (pp.67–9), which sends up Auden's fascination with public schools and his stock imagery of water wheels, reservoirs and railways. But the deeper roots of Auden's influence are shown by poems like the Day Lewis text previously quoted. Auden's admirers followed not only his characteristic poetic practice, but also some of his more questionable ideas. Day Lewis saw nothing absurd in the fusion of Auden's Nietzschean leader with his broader socialist commitment. Where one stanza ends with the instruction to 'Submit to the visiting angel', the next proclaims 'You shall be leaders when zero hour is signalled, / Wielders of power and welders of a new world' (p.50). It looks as though, once the Auden style had been mastered, writers like Day Lewis (but we could also point to Madge, Warner and Geoffrey Parsons among others) employed it without much critical independence.

Yet the folly of Auden's imitators is easy to mock; it is more important that we should be able to see why he had this impact on his contemporaries. MacNeice's review of *Poems* is illuminating: he suggests that 'Auden's attempt is to put the soul across in telegrams' (1987, p.1). In other words, Auden's challenging, coded style belies the fact that the subject of his poetry is a traditional one: the human 'soul'. It is interesting that MacNeice does not use secular synonyms like 'spirit' or 'mind': 'soul' underlies Auden's quasi-religious agenda and anticipates his return to the Church of England by roughly ten years. The notion that Auden's poems 'put the soul across in telegrams' also conveys something of the power of poems like 'Sir, no man's enemy'. For all its opacity, the poem addresses significant emotional experiences. The lines 'Prohibit sharply the rehearsed response / And gradually correct the coward's stance' (p.201) deftly couple the inability to act spontaneously with cowardice as complementary forms of posture that impede 'a change of heart'. It is easy to see why a poetic telegram of this kind should have impressed Auden's first readers. The poem implies that its writer knows and sympathizes with all of his (young) readers' social and emotional hesitancies, and that such disorders will shortly be put right.

This comparison has given us a detailed sense of two important poems, an awareness of Auden's profile in the literary history of the decade, as well as a contrast between poems that pose different kinds of stimulus to their readers. For the rest of this chapter, most of the poems discussed will neither be as obscure as 'Sir, no man's enemy' nor as unambiguous as 'Slough'. The comparison also gives us a way into one of the most important debates of the period: what should the social function of poetry be? How should it aim to affect its readers?

Functions of poetry II: communication versus private pleasure

To gain a preliminary sense of the debates that surrounded the poetry of the 1930s, read through Skelton's Introduction (pp.13–37) and consider the following questions.

1   **Which historical forces does Skelton highlight as shaping the poetry of the 1930s?**

2   **How do you react to Skelton's criteria for including poems in the anthology?**

3   **What criticisms does Skelton make of propagandist poetry?**

1   Skelton suggests that the 'Thirties generation' was shaped by a number of related cultural forces: the aftermath of the First World War and the threat of another war; the possibility of a left-wing revolution; the ideas of Marx and Freud; and, more parochially, the influence of the English public school. His account stresses the impact of socialist ideology on

theories of poetry. For Day Lewis and Spender, both of whom joined the Communist Party during the 1930s, the attempt to harmonize the highbrow 'bourgeois' art of poetry with the revolutionary imperative to propagandize was an urgent intellectual obligation.

2   Skelton's criteria are implicit in the claim that there was a ' "Thirties generation" ' as a well as a ' "Thirties period" ' (p.14). With the exception of Michael Roberts, no poet born outside of the period 1904–16 is included. You may have noticed that Skelton himself was alive to some of the problems his structure presents: 'I must admit that 1904 is a more arbitrary date [than 1916]' (p.14); 'it looks as if these poets *ought* to find themselves with similar attitudes of mind' (p.15). As he realizes at the outset, 'the act of selection ... is also an act of judgement' (p.13). The anthologist privileges some writers at the expense of others; his or her judgements define – and limit – what the reader understands as 'the poetry of the Thirties'. Yet Skelton's judgements can be questioned on a number of levels. By excluding poets who were not born between 1904 and 1916, he implies that all the significant poetry of the period was written by people born between these dates. Skelton's generation, however, is a socially homogenous one of upper-middle-class young men, most of whom were educated at public schools and Oxbridge. The anthology almost completely excludes women (the exception is Anne Ridler with three poems), though major poets – such as Marianne Moore, Edith Sitwell and, further afield, Anna Akhmatova and Marina Tsevtayeva – were active during the decade. It is symptomatic of the datedness of Skelton's perspectives that his discussion of Geoffrey Grigson's mockery of Sitwell ignores the palpably gendered quality of the attack (pp.28–30). Though Grigson clearly wanted readers to think his objection to the Sitwells was a high-minded repugnance at their aristocratic amateurism, it is hard to read his vilification of 'the old Jane' as devoid of sexual antagonism. Another limitation of Skelton's work is its focus on English writers. We will be looking at two exceptions later. Though both MacNeice and Dylan Thomas lived in London, their respectively Northern Irish and Welsh origins differentiate them from their English contemporaries.

3   Skelton's main criticism of propagandist poetry is that there is a tension between political allegiance and the writing of successful poetry. You might note that Skelton assumes that propaganda is writing on behalf of a particular *political* position: Day Lewis was 'the most assiduous propagandist for poetry in the service of socialism' (p.22). But there are other forms of propaganda – religious propaganda, or indeed propaganda on behalf of the arts. These distinctions are worth bearing in mind especially as we read the work of Woolf and MacNeice. Day Lewis

is taxed for his 'tendency to place his trust in Marx first and the Muse second' (p.23); in discussing the self-consciousness of the poets of the 1930s, the suggestion is made that posture often impeded performance: 'Frequently the image of the poet gets in the way of the poetry' (p.30). Skelton makes the traditional distinction between literature and politics: in this view, you cannot be a loyal servant of both poetry and the revolution.

Before we have a closer look at contemporaneous critical debates, it is worth asking if this criticism is borne out by the poetry in Skelton's anthology. The first poem in the book is a good place to ask this question: it is an extract from MacNeice's *Autumn Journal* (1939), a text that aims to capture in diary form the political and personal anxieties of the autumn of 1938, the time of the Munich crisis and the German annexation of Czechoslovakia. What is MacNeice's attitude towards revolutionary politics in this particular entry in his journal? The text oscillates nimbly between opposing positions. The depiction of the end of the summer holidays veers between an imaginative sympathy with 'The workman' who must return to 'the eight-hour day' and mild contempt for ordinary people as conformists: 'Most are accepters, born and bred to harness, / And take things as they come' (p.45). The next couplet suggests a completely different political sensibility: 'But some refusing harness and more who are refused by it / Would pray that another and a better Kingdom come'. Even here, MacNeice hedges his bets: revolutionary feeling is 'travestied in slogans', though significantly the status quo is then attacked as 'an utterly lost and daft / System that gives a few at fancy prices / Their fancy lives'. I would suggest that the brilliance of this passage lies in its dramatization of MacNeice's hesitations and evasions. On the one hand, he largely endorses a socialist critique of capitalism; on the other, he is repelled by both the working classes and revolutionary politics. What makes this poem convincing as a testament to its writer's political engagement is that MacNeice concedes that he has 'the slave-owner's mind' himself.

In contrast, Rex Warner's 'Hymn' offers a much more straightforward commitment to revolutionary politics:

> Come away then,
> you fat man!
> You don't want your watch-chain.
> But don't interfere with us, because we know you too well.
> If you do that you will lose your top hat
> and be knocked on the head until you are dead.
> Come with us, if you can, and, if not, go to hell
> with your comfy chairs, your talk about the police,

> your doll wife, your cowardly life, your newspaper, your interests
>   in the East,
> You, there, who are so patriotic, you liar, you beast!

(pp.59–60)

After the balance and complexity of *Autumn Journal*, it would be easy to write 'Hymn' off as versified sloganeering. But there is an exuberance to Warner's poem that captures the enthusiasm of Oxbridge-educated young men for communism in the early 1930s. 'Hymn' quickly became a fashionable battle-cry: Day Lewis used its refrain as the epigraph to the first part of *The Magnetic Mountain* (1992, p.135). Note the nursery-rhyme quality of the poem's internal rhymes: 'If you do that you will lose your top hat'. While this is hardly a sophisticated poetic technique, it aptly registers Warner's exhilarated contempt for the bourgeoisie. The 'fat man' becomes a sort of Humpty Dumpty figure, who is bluntly presented with the Marxist alternative of joining with the workers' revolutionary struggle or going 'to hell'. Warner seems unconcerned about what he does; the refrain suggests the revolution is inevitable: 'Come, then, companions. This is the spring of blood, / heart's hey-day, movement of masses, beginning of good'.

So there is evidence for querying Skelton's sense that political engagement and poetic excellence are inevitably incompatible. While 'Hymn' is poetically crude, I would suggest that this is by design rather than accident: Warner exploits sing-song rhythms and cartoon-like description to put across his sense that 'This is the spring of blood'. This wide-eyed naivety and revolutionary enthusiasm, though hard to take seriously, are as typical of 1930s idealism as The Beatles' 'All You Need Is Love' is of the late 1960s. Equally, MacNeice's excavation of his social and political sympathies in *Autumn Journal* makes the point that at the time of pre-eminent crisis in Europe, political disengagement is irresponsible: 'the worst of all / Deceits is to murmur "Lord, I am not worthy" / And, lying easy, turn your face to the wall' (p.47). Like his contemporaries, MacNeice refuses to be politically indifferent; unlike Warner, he concedes serious doubts about the revolution.

Texts like *Autumn Journal* and 'Hymn' reveal the extent to which poets of the 1930s were troubled by questions of how to square poetic ambition with political commitment. Any reading of the critical debates about poetry written during the decade confirms this impression: poets and critics were endlessly preoccupied with the ethics of engagement and the tensions that arose between the art of poetry and the claims of the contemporary world. To illustrate these debates, we are going to read two contrasting pieces on the social function of poetry: Auden's Introduction to his *Oxford Book of Light Verse* and Virginia Woolf's attack on the poets of the 1930s, 'The Leaning Tower'.

Auden's interest in light verse typifies his poetic project in the later 1930s. The texts collected in *Poems* (1930) tended to be syntactically compacted and semantically abstruse in the manner of 'Sir, no man's enemy'. But as he matured as a writer, Auden became much less certain of the value of such modernist-style experiments, and suspicious of the obscurity of works like *The Orators*. He began to show an interest in the more immediate impact of lighter poetry. You can see this interest at work in one of his most celebrated poems of the decade: the 'Ballad' of 1934, later retitled 'O What Is That Sound' (pp.259–60). 'Ballad' is a useful title because it indicates Auden's ambition to write a poem in the idiom of folk-song. This extraordinary poem uses the rhythm and stanza of a traditional ballad to stage a miniature drama in which the first speaker is betrayed by his or her lover to 'the scarlet soldiers':

> O what is that light I see flashing so clear
>   Over the distance brightly, brightly?
> Only the sun on their weapons, dear,
>   As they step lightly.
>
> ...
>
> O where are you going? stay with me here.
>   Were the vows you swore me deceiving, deceiving?
> No, I promised to love you, dear,
>   But I must be leaving.
>
>   (pp.259–60)

The poem turns on Auden's accommodation of the speakers' conversational tones and characteristic repetitions to the tight space of the ballad stanza. The first speaker's anxieties are betrayed by a series of urgent repetitions ('brightly, brightly'; 'deceiving, deceiving'), while the second speaker's duplicity is shown by the increasingly hollow sound of reiterated false assurances ('Only the sun on their weapons'; 'I promised to love you, dear'). Though I hope you appreciate the subtlety of 'Sir, no man's enemy', 'Ballad' has a much more immediate impact. It dramatizes a situation that it is easy to empathize with and enter into imaginatively.

So light verse became for Auden an important and neglected kind of poetry. He used *The Oxford Book of Light Verse* (1938) to insist on its centrality to poetry in English; the Introduction is concerned with the history of all English poetry, not just 'light verse'. **With this in mind, now read the first section of the Introduction (Reader, Item 15). What does Auden suggest about 'the work of any creative artist'?**

Auden begins by asserting that all creative artists, including poets, have 'three principal wishes': 'to make something ... to perceive something ... to communicate these perceptions to others'. This account moves directly from the individual artist's creative impulse to the social contexts in which art is consumed. Note the insistence that because literature is made up of words – 'the medium of ordinary social intercourse' – it is not only created by individual geniuses. Auden underlines the social factors that contribute to the writing of poetry. This argument is largely a reaction against the Romantic idealization of poets as inspired seers, who, in Percy Bysshe Shelley's famous phrase (which Auden misquotes later in the Introduction), 'are the unacknowledged legislators of the World' (1977, p.508). More prosaically, but with much more of a sense of the impact of historical events and ideas on writing, Auden suggests that poetry cannot only be explained by reference 'to the idiosyncrasies of the individual poets themselves'. His approach stresses the importance of historical context: we have to read poetry with an awareness of both 'the state of society as a whole' and 'the kind of life which [the poet] ... leads'.

Now read the rest of the Introduction. What would you say it tells us about Auden's political views?

Auden's politics emerge at the end of the essay. Looking to the future, he anticipates an egalitarian non-elitist 'democracy', in which an 'adult' form of poetry will flourish. He suggests that such a development in literature will only be made possible by a comparable development in politics: 'poetry which is at the same time light and adult can only be written in a society which is both integrated and free'. Though Auden never joined the Communist Party, this is as close as he would get to revolutionary commitment.

The Introduction deploys what is essentially a Marxist perspective on literary history. Auden was influenced by Christopher Caudwell's theoretical study *Illusion and Reality* (1937). Caudwell was a committed communist and a hero of the literary Left, who died fighting for the International Brigade in Spain just before the publication of *Illusion and Reality*. Auden's laudatory review notes that Caudwell 'trace[s] the history of English poetry ... and show[s] the relation between its changes in technique and subject matter and the changes in economic production' (1996, p.386). Similarly, Auden's Introduction to *The Oxford Book of Light Verse* connects the Industrial Revolution and Romanticism as key moments in the history of poetry that ultimately divorce poets from their readers: 'As the old social community broke up, artists were driven to the examination of their own feelings and to the company of other artists. They became introspective, obscure, and highbrow.' We can compare this with T.S. Eliot's view in 'The Metaphysical Poets'. Where Eliot presents obscurity as a necessary aesthetic reaction to modernity, which will recover poetry's cultural prestige, Auden sees Romantic obscurantism as a retreat, in which poets 'turned away from the life of their time to the contemplation of their own emotions and the creation of imaginary worlds'. Though Auden tries to palliate this judgement somewhat, it remains a sharp attack. Where the pre-industrial artist 'was still sufficiently rooted in the life of his age to feel in common with his audience', the post-Romantic poet has become socially isolated and self-absorbed to the extent that he seldom connects with his audience. Auden is thinking especially of writers such as the nineteenth-century French poet Charles Baudelaire, who was the archetypical poetic dandy. He quotes from Baudelaire's 'J'aime le souvenir de ces époques nues' (1968, p.46). These lines can be translated as 'I love the memory of those naked epochs, when Apollo took pleasure in gilding statues'; Auden had already borrowed this phrase for his 1936 poem 'The Creatures': 'a vision of nude and fabulous epochs' (1977, p.158). Auden's evident relish of Baudelaire's poem is slightly at odds with his critical attitude towards 'decadent' poets.

What is Auden's conception of the role of poetry in this essay? As I hope you have seen already, he is concerned to break down the usual division between the poet and ordinary people: he does not overstate the influence of the 'major genius', and tends rather to mock the intense introspection of the great Romantics like William Wordsworth and Shelley. Any theory of poetry that so emphatically stresses the primacy of communication is likely to see the poet as a representative rather than an exceptional individual. This view underlies Auden's account of the predicament of modern poets: 'The problem for the modern poet, as for every one else to-day, is how to find or form a genuine community, in which each has his valued place and can feel at home.' In this formulation, egalitarian idealism is efficacious for poets *and* their readers: both need to live in a more equal society to flourish. Though Auden would lose this confidence in such idealism, the notion of moral equality between poets and their readers was one to which he would return. 'Heavy Date', a love poem of 1939, climaxes with a witty variant on this idea:

> When two lovers meet, then
> There's an end of writing
> Thought and Analytics:
>   Lovers, like the dead,
> In their loves are equal;
> Sophomores and peasants,
> Poets and their critics
>   Are the same in bed.

> (Auden, 1995, p.74)

As in *The Oxford Book of Light Verse*, Auden resists traditional claims for the exceptional nature of poets, though in this case equality is translated from a social aspiration to an erotic fundamental.

Though the Introduction does not directly address the question of whether poetry should propagandize, Auden's literary history and theory of poetry as communication suggest the desirability of revolutionary change. For Auden in 1938, light poetry becomes a means of imagining a kind of writing that might flourish in a better world: 'In such a society, and in such alone, will it be possible for the poet without sacrificing any of his subtleties of sensibility or his integrity, to write poetry which is simple, clear and gay.' Implicitly, bourgeois society as currently configured restricts human and poetic potential, which will be transformed by a new society. You might compare this passage with Auden's earlier poem 'A Communist to Others' (pp.54–9). It is worth noting at this point that *The Oxford Book of Light Verse* represents a relatively mild version of a socialist approach to literature. Alec Brown, whose ideas you encountered at the beginning of Chapter 3, writing in the *Left Review* of 1934, advocated a 'proletarianisation' of literary culture, backed up with a series of capitalized slogans: 'LITERARY ENGLISH FROM CAXTON TO US IS AN ARTIFICIAL JARGON OF THE RULING CLASS; WRITTEN ENGLISH BEGINS WITH US' (in Margolies, 1998, p.28). In contrast to this approach (which in fairness garnered little uncritical support even among communist readers), Auden's poetics are aspirational rather than revolutionary, though interestingly his anthology accommodates precisely the kinds of voice – of folk-singers and balladeers – that Brown claims 'LITERARY ENGLISH' had excluded.

Though Virginia Woolf's 'The Leaning Tower' concludes with the aspiration to 'a world without classes or towers' (1966, p.178), her sense of the role of the poet is radically different from Auden's. Woolf's essay, which was delivered as a lecture to the Workers' Educational Association in May 1940, attempts to place the work of Auden and his contemporaries through a brief literary history and an account of the material conditions that foster imaginative literature. You will be considering Woolf as a novelist in Part 2, but for now it is worth remembering that she belongs to the literary generation immediately before that of Auden and his contemporaries. As a member of the Bloomsbury Group of writers, artists and intellectuals, Woolf's literary politics were, as we shall see, very different from Auden's. **Now read the extract from 'The Leaning Tower' (Reader, Item 16). How would you compare Woolf's view of the writer with Auden's?**

The difference in emphasis is clear from the outset. In contrast to Auden's sense that poets ought to be more like their readers, Woolf stresses the radical strangeness of supremely gifted writers and the near impossibility of explaining their creative processes: 'Until we have more facts ... we cannot know much about ordinary people, let alone about extraordinary people.' She goes on to develop an account of literary history which argues that material wealth and social privilege are crucial for the development of good writers; as she puts it, 'To breed the kind of butterfly a writer is you must let him sun himself for three or four years at Oxford or Cambridge.' In direct contrast to Auden, who sees the social isolation of the poet as a function of the economic advances of capitalism, Woolf suggests the material prosperity of nineteenth-century England provided the ideal conditions for the writing of good books. Woolf's position, at least in the first half of the essay, is unashamedly elitist: good writers 'have all been raised above the mass of the people upon a tower of stucco – that is their middle-class birth; and of gold – that is their expensive education'.

This last quotation comes from the passage in which Woolf develops the complementary images of the chair and the tower. The chair – a metaphor for the writer's education – 'decides what he sees of human life'. The middle-class writer moves from this particular seat to 'a tower raised above the rest of us' at Oxford or Cambridge: again, this tower 'decides his angle of vision; it affects his power of communication'. For Woolf, accidents of birth and education are crucial to the development of the writer: 'Take away all that the working class has given to English literature and that literature would scarcely suffer.' These arguments are somewhat undermined by her inclusion of D.H. Lawrence – who, as she later concedes, was a miner's son from Eastwood in Nottinghamshire – in her list of the best writers of the early part of the twentieth century. And though Woolf positions herself here as one of the workers she was addressing, her social origins were every bit as bourgeois as those of Auden – as the daughter of Sir Leslie Stephen, the first editor of *The Dictionary of National Biography*, she is as guilty of social posturing as the writers she attacks. But the real purpose behind this schematic account is revealed when Woolf turns her attention to the 1930s generation. According to Woolf, these writers take a completely different attitude to their privileges of birth from their literary antecedents: instead of capitalizing on their good fortune, they 'bleat' and 'whimper' against the social system of which they are the supreme products.

Reread the extract from 'These tendencies are better illustrated by quotation …' to '… the poet in the thirties was forced to be a politician'. What is Woolf's major criticism of the 1930s generation? How justified do you feel her attack is?

Woolf's main criticism comes through her reading of *Autumn Journal*. She argues, using MacNeice as an exemplar, that these poets 'feel compelled to preach … the creation of a society in which everyone is equal … It explains the pedagogic, the didactic, the loud-speaker strain that dominates their poetry.' Woolf offers what is essentially a late Victorian poetic, in which preaching and pedagogy are inimical to poetry: she was, in other words, an aesthete, for whom art should always be first and foremost beautifully constructed. A similar kind of thinking underlies Skelton's suggestion that Day Lewis tended to prefer Marx to the Muse (p.33). Woolf quotes from MacNeice and Spender to argue that their work constitutes 'politician's poetry'; in contrast, an excerpt from Wordsworth is approvingly defined as 'poet's poetry'.

The question of how justified this attack is will depend on your own reading both of these poets and of Woolf's reaction to them. I would say that Woolf makes a number of telling observations about the social dilemmas and often parochial concerns of the 1930s poets. As we have seen in the case of Warner, there is a tendency for poems to become a series of rhythmical slogans. Further, Woolf's analysis of the social positioning of the 1930s poets is often acute. Writers like Auden and Spender were certainly conscious that they were 'trapped by their education, pinned down by their capital' and that they 'remained on top of their leaning tower'. However, beyond these generalizations, Woolf's readings of MacNeice and Spender are harder to endorse. For example, she asserts that MacNeice felt that 'the tower began to lean' while he was at Oxford, then quotes lines from entry III (pp.45–6). (You might note that Woolf's attitude to MacNeice's text is shown by her mislineation of the quotation: 'Their fancy lives' is a separate line. Similarly, she misquotes Auden's 'To a Writer on his Birthday': Auden wrote 'behind us only / The stuccoed suburb and expensive school' (p.167) and not 'Behind us we have stucco suburbs and expensive educations'. Though trivial in itself, such misquotation de-poeticizes the rich textures of both Auden and MacNeice.) Though *Autumn Journal* covers MacNeice's time at Oxford in entry XIII (not included in Skelton), by connecting two quite separate entries Woolf falsifies the full complexity of MacNeice's self-portrait. As we have seen, MacNeice scrupulously makes a case against himself in this section of *Autumn Journal*, which advertises his bourgeois allegiances: ' "What you want is not a world of the free in function / But a niche at the top, the skimmings of the cream" ' (p.46).

Even more problematic, I would suggest, is Woolf's juxtaposition of Spender and Wordsworth. Though Skelton does not reprint Spender's 'After they have tired of the brilliance of cities' (see Appendix), the weakness of Woolf's argument can be appreciated by reading one of the decade's most infamous poems, 'The Pylons' (pp.99–100). Like 'After they have tired ...', this is taken from Spender's first major volume, *Poems* (1933), and it exemplifies the exhilarating novelty of his content and idiom. Spender takes a pastoral landscape and inserts into it that peculiarly modern property, the pylon:

> The secret of these hills was stone, and cottages
> Of that stone made,
> And crumbling roads
> That turned on sudden hidden villages.
>
> Now over these small hills they have built the concrete
> That trails black wire:
> Pylons, those pillars
> Bare like nude, giant girls that have no secret.
>
> (p.99)

Far from being symbols of modern ugliness, the pylons embody an emergent and exciting future. In Spender's view – and this is a poem that is concerned to coerce its readers to look at pylons afresh – the pylons are startling intruders on a traditional landscape. The first stanza emphasizes that the beauty of the pastoral depends on secrecy and seclusion: 'The secret of these hills' is the fact that they and the cottages there are made of the same stone; 'crumbling roads' turn onto 'sudden hidden villages'. In shocking contrast, the pylons appear as 'nude, giant girls that have no secret'. The pylons have no hidden dimensions: they are 'Bare' 'concrete' structures that make the speaker conscious of the smallness of the hills on which they stand. The last two stanzas clarify the symbolic function of the pylons as prophetic metaphors:

> But far above and far as sight endures
> Like whips of anger
> With lightning's danger
> There runs the quick perspective of the future.
>
> This dwarfs our emerald country by its trek
> So tall with prophecy:
> Dreaming of cities
> Where often clouds shall lean their swan-white neck.

(p.100)

Spender confers a traditional lyricism on the kind of subject that does not usually receive such treatment. He aligns the pylons with 'the quick perspective of the future' while suggesting that this future with its enormous cities reaching into the clouds 'dwarfs' – and implicitly supersedes – the pastoral landscape. As Valentine Cunningham argues, 'The Pylons' is part of a group of texts that welcome the machine age as a herald of Soviet-style social and cultural advance: 'the British Grid's pylonic clutter could, with a pinch or two of optimism, be assimilated into the more obviously politically revolutionary Russian version' (1988, p.403).

Spender's poem hardly embodies a twenty-first-century reaction to the 'pylonic clutter' of twentieth-century Britain. But this is not the point. Woolf suggests that Spender is an inferior poet to Wordsworth because he is too didactic. Yet though Spender's enthusiasm about pylons has proved an easy target for mockery, it is hard to read the text as no more than a versified sermon in favour of communism or even progress. I would say that the strength of the poem lies in its taut juxtaposition of the new with the old. Though the balance of Spender's sympathy is with the pylons rather than with 'The valley with its gilt and evening look', the poem does not unambiguously celebrate novelty over tradition. Note the precise terms in which Spender couches 'the quick perspective of the future': it is something seen 'far above ... Like whips of anger / With lightning's danger'. This future

Figure 4.2   Tristram Hillier, *La Route des Alpes*, 1937, tempera on canvas, 60 ×
81 cm. (Presented by Contemporary Art Society, 1944. © Tate, London 2004.)
Hillier was an early exponent of Surrealist styles in English painting. Like Spender,
he was interested in using industrial landscapes as a distinctive feature of his work.

is hazardous and violent; though its beautiful cities may be inevitable, the
poem does not pretend that the new world will be achieved without risk or
conflict. In the final stanza, the sense of the new overpowering the old is
made poetically resonant as the future '*dwarfs* our emerald country' (my
emphasis). The coupling of this aggressive verb with a phrase pregnant with
the pathos of the traditional pastoral encapsulates the ambiguities of the
poem. Like the changing landscape it describes, 'The Pylons' itself is caught
between two antithetical ideals of beauty. This tension is evident even on a
formal level, as the poem shifts from the prosaic radicalism of half rhymes
like 'made' and 'roads' through to the more traditional full rhymes of 'trek'
and 'neck'.

In sum, the success of 'The Pylons' lies in the fact that it is not 'loud-
speaker' poetry, but rather that it offers a complex meditation on a changing
environment through the traditional tools of pastoral poetry. MacNeice's
rebuttal of Woolf's attack, 'The Tower that Once' (1941), singles out the
'inept comparison' of Spender with Wordsworth for particular attention:
Woolf 'ignores the fact that the great bulk of Wordsworth is pamphleteering
and that Spender's poetry is pre-eminently the kind – to use her own words –

"that people remember when they are alone" ' (MacNeice, 1987, p.121). In this view, Woolf overstates the extent to which poets like Spender, Auden and MacNeice were given to the pulpit manner, and misrepresents Wordsworth as a 'poet's poet', when he – like Spender and MacNeice – was also politically involved.

The comparison of Auden and Woolf demonstrates that there were very different conceptions both of the role of poetry in the present and its development in the past. These pieces offer diametrically opposing views of literary history. Where, for Auden, industrialization marks the retreat of poetry from direct engagement with its readers, for Woolf, the same period sets the material conditions in place that nurture writers like Jane Austen, Charles Dickens and Alfred Lord Tennyson. We might suggest that debates about the purpose of literature are conducted precisely through such arguments over the past. As MacNeice demonstrates, one way to undermine Woolf's authority is to question her literary history: 'Mrs Woolf's literary history is over-simplified ... even with the great Victorians, "All's well with the world" was not their most typical slogan; is *In Memoriam* a poem of placid or unconscious acceptance?' (1987, p.120). Analogous queries could be made of Auden: is the bond between poet and audience only ruptured by the economic changes of the eighteenth and nineteenth centuries, or had poetry already begun to lose readers to the competing form of the novel? During the 1930s, theories of literature are often based on such reinterpretations of history; the reading of history in turn betokens different political and aesthetic allegiances.

But as we have seen, the central contrast between Auden and Woolf is between a theory that is fundamentally communicative ('poetry is an art of communication that flourishes best in communities with shared values') and one that is fundamentally aestheticist ('poetry is something beautiful the reader remembers and enjoys in solitude'). Such competing theories necessarily privilege different kinds of poetry: Auden implicitly advocates what MacNeice calls an '*impure*' poetry (MacNeice, 1938, p.v), which is capable of taking political positions, while Woolf advocates a pure poetry, in which opinions and art are mutually incompatible. With these differing conceptions in mind, we now turn our attention to the response of these poets to the Spanish Civil War.

War poetry and propaganda

The Spanish Civil War began with a right-wing military rising during July 1936 in Spanish Morocco, which quickly spread to mainland Spain. The insurgents, most notably General Franco, aimed to replace the left-wing Popular Front government that had been democratically elected in February 1936. Franco and his cohorts expected that they would be able to gain power without much difficulty, but this did not happen: in Martin Blinkhorn's words, 'the result was a war among Spaniards of a bitterness and duration such as no-one, rebel or loyalist, could have imagined' (1986, p.3). Germany armed Franco's forces; the Soviet Union provided some military assistance to the government (though in fact Stalin did not want a communist revolution in Spain); the major western democracies of Britain, France and the USA remained neutral through the war.

The importance of these events to British writers of the 1930s cannot be overstated. As Julian Symons argues in his Introduction to George Orwell's account of his experience of the war, *Homage to Catalonia* (1938),

> To a generation of young people throughout Europe the crucial event of the 1930s was the Spanish Civil War ... When the attempt by General Franco to overthrow an elected government was supported by the Fascist powers, the lines seemed clearly drawn. Good was opposed to evil, democracy to dictatorship, and even though Britain and other European powers, with the exception of the Soviet Union, pursued a policy of 'non-intervention' with regard to the Republican government, it was possible for individuals to intervene, and to fight for democracy.
>
> (Symons, 1989, p.v)

Samuel Hynes elaborates on this sense of the Spanish Civil War as a dualistic conflict:

> it was the first battle in the apocalyptic struggle of Left and Right that the 'thirties generation had been predicting for years. There is a sense of relief in the first writings about the Spanish war, a sense that at last what had been a rhetorical and prophetic conflict had become actual, that in the morality play of 'thirties politics Good was striking back at Evil.
>
> (Hynes, 1992, p.242)

This initial sense of the war as a morality play in which the moral identity of the different protagonists is easy to read has profound implications for the literary responses to the conflict.

The most immediate issue that the Spanish Civil War throws up is how writers and poets should respond to these events. In 1935, Day Lewis had worried that 'With two million unemployed in the country and war growing daily more imminent, surely we are wasting our time singing away to ourselves in a corner' (in Margolies, 1998, p.51). The war seemed to offer the conditions in which this anxiety about the social value of poetry could be silenced: poets could either write propaganda pieces on behalf of the Republican government, or could fight on the side of the government themselves in the International Brigades. That the Spanish conflict was felt to be forcing writers and intellectuals to make a political stand is apparent in a letter of June 1937 'To the Writers and Poets of England, Scotland, Ireland and Wales', which was organized by the socialist poet Nancy Cunard, and signed by Auden and Spender alongside international literary figures such as Louis Aragon and Pablo Neruda:

> It is clear to many of us throughout the whole world that now, as certainly never before, we are determined or compelled, to take sides. The equivocal attitude, the Ivory Tower, the paradoxical, the ironic detachment, will no longer do ...
>
> To-day, the struggle is in Spain. To-morrow it may be in other countries – our own. But there are some who, despite the murder of Durango and Guernica, the enduring agony of Madrid, of Bilbao, and Germany's shelling of Almeria, are still in doubt, or who aver that it is possible that Fascism may still be what it proclaims it is: 'the saviour of civilization'.
>
> This is the question we are asking you:
>
> *Are you for, or against, the legal Government and the people of Republican Spain?*
>
> *Are you for, or against, Franco and Fascism?*
>
> For it is impossible any longer to take no side.
>
> Writers and Poets, we wish to print your answers. We wish the world to know what you, writers and poets, who are among the most sensitive instruments of a nation, feel.
>
> (in Cunningham, 1980, pp.49–50)

It was of course possible to resist both the analysis and the rhetoric of this plea. Writers with right-wing sympathies, such as Evelyn Waugh, Ezra Pound, T.S. Eliot and Roy Campbell, were in varying degrees hostile to the letter – indeed, Campbell fought and wrote in support of the Nationalists because of his Catholicism and his fears that a Communist Spain would eradicate the Catholic Church (Cunningham, 1980, pp.50–4). Even the unpredictably left-wing Orwell wrote of 'that damned rubbish of signing manifestos to say how wicked it all is' (1970, p.346). But of the poets represented in Skelton, the vast majority broadly agreed with the views expressed in the letter. John Cornford, Christopher Caudwell and Julian Bell fought in the International Brigades and died in Spain; Laurie Lee fought and survived; Spender and Gascoyne went to broadcast on behalf of the government; Auden went very briefly; and MacNeice made two visits (Cunningham, 1980, pp.30–2). Though Cunningham is clearly right to caution against the myth that it was a 'poet's war', the point remains that the Spanish Civil War was a major event in the literary politics of the 1930s. You can get a sense of the way in which Spain permeated diverse agendas by reading Ruthven Todd's beautiful poem of nostalgia for the island of Mull,

'In September', where the news from Spain actuates Todd's longing for home: 'In September, I saw the drab newsposters / Telling of wars, in Spain and in the East, / And I wished I'd stayed on Mull' (pp.97–8).

In terms of the debates that we have been looking at so far in this chapter, the crucial question which we need to ask when we read this poetry is not so much what its political orientation was – we know that already – but rather how it negotiates this sense that neutrality is no longer an option. Does poetry become all-out propaganda on behalf of the Spanish government, or are there still ambiguities and resistances in the work of these writers? **With these questions in mind, read through Skelton's section 'And I Remember Spain' (pp.133–63). Choose two or three texts that you think display contrasting attitudes to the war.**

Reading this section, I am struck by the variety of responses that the war provoked. It includes poems from the front line ('Full Moon at Tierz', 'Two Armies', 'A Moment of War', 'A Letter from Aragon', 'Port Bou'); political satires ('Prize for Good Conduct', 'A Thousand Killed', 'The Non-Interveners'); discursive historical poems ('Spain', 'Elegy on Spain', *Autumn Journal* VI); and even a love poem ('To Margot Heinemann'). The war did not produce a monochrome or univocal response from contemporary poets.

But it is worth underlining that Skelton's selection is very much that: it is far from a full account of the poetry of the Spanish Civil War. He finds no room for Jack Lindsay's extraordinary 'On Guard for Spain!', subtitled 'A Poem for Mass Recitation', a text that was publicly performed by a group of actors in Trafalgar Square in 1937, before going on tour around the country (Caesar, 1991, p.220). A brief quotation will give a flavour of Lindsay's work:

> Workers,
> drive off the fascist vultures gathering
> to pick the bones of Spanish cities,
> to leave the Spanish fields
> dunged with peasant dead
> that greed may reap the fattened crops ...
>
> On guard for the human future!
> On guard for the people of Spain!
>
> (in Cunningham, 1980, p.263)

Even Cornford's ideologically conscious 'Full Moon at Tierz' is less unambiguously instrumental than Lindsay's poem: Cornford's allegiance to 'The dialectic's point of change' is movingly offset by his candid account of his fears before battle: 'Then let my private battle with my nerves ... Fuse in the welded front our fight preserves' (pp.137–8). Skelton reprints that war poetry which fits his conception of the poetry of the 1930s as work that articulates 'movement of the passionate conscience' (p.36). Yet as I have said, there is variety even within Skelton's narrow selection. I am going to examine the different views of the war provided by three poems – 'Spain', 'A Letter from Aragon' and 'Port Bou' – to try to assess the extent to which the poets of the 1930s used poetry for propaganda purposes.

From its initial publication as a pamphlet in 1937, 'Spain' has been one of Auden's most controversial poems. As you can see from Skelton's 'A Note on the Texts Used', it is one of a group of poems which Auden only allowed to be reprinted with the proviso that ' "Mr W.H. Auden considers these five poems to be trash which he is ashamed to have written" ' (p.41). By 1963, Auden had long since turned his back on the political certainties that he thought poems like 'Spain' represented. 'Trash' is a strange word to use for a poem as formally elaborate and intellectually demanding as 'Spain'; even Orwell, whose critique of the poem we will turn to in a moment, prefaced his attack with a parenthesis of praise: 'incidentally this poem is one of the few decent things that have been written about the Spanish war' (1970, p.565). **Now reread the poem. What position do you think Auden outlines towards the war?**

Like 'Sir, no man's enemy', 'Spain' is not an easy poem: it does not disclose its purpose with anything like the directness of 'On Guard for Spain!' or 'Full Moon at Tierz'. Nonetheless, Auden's broad message is hard to avoid: precisely replicating the terms of the Cunard letter, 'to-day' there is a historic 'struggle' in Spain that engages crucial questions for human civilization. As the infamous last stanza insists, the stakes in this struggle are high: 'History to the defeated / May say alas but cannot help or pardon'. There are no prizes for coming second – it is vital that this struggle is won.

But this is not the whole story: Auden does not commit himself to the kind of direct statement of commitment that Cornford employs: 'Raise the red flag triumphantly / For Communism and for liberty' (p.139). By concentrating on the ways in which 'Spain' is structured, we can clarify its argument. John Fuller (1998, pp.284–5) identifies six sections: a summary of the past (stanzas 1–6); an invocation of 'the life' (stanzas 7–12); life's reply (stanzas 13–14); a call to arms (stanzas 15–19); a prophecy of the future (stanzas 20–5); and a conclusion (stanza 26). Anthony Hecht refines this structure by noting that the poem is 'built rhetorically around the historical trinity of past, present, and future, which recur as rhythmic refrains throughout the poem under the names of "Yesterday," "Today," and "Tomorrow" ' (1993, p.122). 'Spain' presents a condensed history of human civilization from the distant past of 'cromlech[s]' (stone circles), through a present tense characterized by 'the struggle' that is taking place in Spain, to a distant but tangible future. As a creative, left-leaning reinterpretation of history it bears comparison with the Introduction to

The Oxford Book of Light Verse: in each text, Auden uses rapid, authoritative-sounding snapshots of the past to advance his own reading of the present. His view of the current crisis is articulated most clearly in stanzas 17 and 18:

> On that arid square, that fragment nipped off from hot
> Africa, soldered so crudely to inventive Europe;
>   On that tableland scored by rivers,
> Our thoughts have bodies; the menacing shapes of our fever
>
> Are precise and alive. For the fears which made us respond
> To the medicine ad, and the brochure of winter cruises
>   Have become invading battalions

(p.135)

Note the ways in which Auden manipulates perspective to mobilize his argument: by reducing the Iberian peninsula to a hot 'fragment' of Africa that has been 'soldered' onto Europe, he rescales the country to the human dimensions of 'inventive' metalworking. It becomes poetically plausible to see that 'Our thoughts have bodies' in the Spanish landscape. Moreover, by his use of the first-person plural, Auden insists that the Spanish conflict necessarily engages the sympathies of his readers: 'our faces, the institute-face, the chain store, the ruin // Are projecting their greed as the firing squad and the bomb' (p.135). Though Hecht sees these lines as a facile and repellent assertion that 'what happens in Spain is our own fault' (1993, p.127), I suspect that Auden's argument is more complex. By suggesting that 'our' physical and emotional attributes are intimately engaged with the 'struggle' in Spain, Auden works to combat his readers' potential indifference to the Civil War. He is saying in effect 'this should matter to you – this engages you in ways that are directly relevant to your survival'. MacNeice makes the same point more directly at the close of *Autumn Journal* VI as he contrasts his visit to Spain in the Easter of 1936 with subsequent events: 'Not knowing that ... our spirit / Would find its frontier on the Spanish front, / Its body in a rag-tag army' (p.163).

'Spain' seems to be the kind of 'loud-speaker' poetry attacked by Woolf: Auden manipulates the rhetorical resources of poetry to persuade his readers that a particular course of action and a particular side in the conflict are objectively correct. Yet the critical attacks on 'Spain' have typically accused it of bad faith rather than bad poetics: Cunningham has described it as 'a poem seeking to be enthusiastic about a cause its author cannot work up much except despondency about' (1980, p.70). More substantially, Orwell's attack from 'Inside the Whale' (1940) presents the poem as a symptomatic case of the infatuation of the literary Left with a 'cult of Russia' (1970, p.565). Orwell homes in on the stanzas beginning 'To-morrow for the young poets' and 'To-day the deliberate increase' (p.136). The passage is worth quoting in full because it is such an exhilarating example of critical abuse:

> The second stanza is intended as a sort of thumbnail sketch of a day in the life of a 'good party man'. In the morning a couple of political murders, a ten-minutes' interlude to stifle 'bourgeois' remorse, and then a hurried luncheon and a busy afternoon and evening chalking walls and distributing leaflets. All very edifying. But notice the phrase 'necessary murder'. It could only be written by a person to whom murder is at most a *word*. Personally I would not speak so lightly of murder. It so happens that I have seen the bodies of numbers of murdered men – I don't mean killed in battle, I mean murdered. Therefore I have some conception of what murder means – the terror, the hatred, the howling relatives, the post-mortems, the blood, the smells. To me, murder is something to be avoided. So it is to any ordinary person. The Hitlers and Stalins find murder necessary, but they don't advertise their callousness, and they don't speak of it as murder; it is 'liquidation', 'elimination' or some other soothing phrase. Mr Auden's brand of amoralism is only possible if you are the kind of person who is always somewhere else when the trigger is pulled. So much of left-wing thought is a kind of playing with fire by people who don't even know that fire is hot.
>
> (Orwell, 1970, p.566)

Devastating though Orwell's critique is, it is important that we recognize its limitations as close reading. Orwell juxtaposes Auden's abstract account of 'the necessary murder' with his own particular experiences of murder. Set against 'the terror, the hatred, the howling relatives, the post-mortems, the blood, the smells', there does seem to be something rather glib about the phrase 'the necessary murder'. Yet the poem is more exact than Orwell allows for. 'To-day the deliberate increase in the chances of death, / The conscious acceptance of guilt in the necessary murder' hardly reads as the blasé pre-lunch musings of a Stalinist functionary. Auden's choice of the word 'guilt' recalls Christian theology rather than Marxist ideology. Arguably, these stanzas attempt to offset the gains that supporters of the Spanish government hope to win through the war with the painful realities of 'the struggle': combatants consciously accept that murder is necessary, they are therefore complicit in killing. Orwell's criticism implies that first-hand reportage of the kind he provided in *Homage to Catalonia* is always superior to such abstract thinking and indeed to poetry. Yet 'Spain' insists that there are occasions when poetry needs to generalize; its reception indicates the costs that can attend such generalization.

Auden was troubled enough by an earlier version of Orwell's critique to change the lines to 'To-day the inevitable increase in the chances of death; / The conscious acceptance of guilt in the fact of murder' when he collected the poem for his *Another Time* volume of 1940 (1977, p.212). Later, he lost faith in the poem and dropped it from his collected works. Yet he was clearly still irritated by Orwell's reading as late as 1963, when he wrote a letter to Monroe K. Spears to explain what he had meant:

> I was *not* excusing totalitarian crimes but only trying to say what, surely, every decent person thinks if he finds himself unable to adopt the absolute pacifist position. (1) To kill another human being is always murder and should never be called anything else. (2) In a war, the members of two rival groups try to murder their opponents. (3) *If* there is such a thing as a just war, then murder can be necessary for the sake of justice.
>
> (quoted in Spears, 1963, p.157, n.10)

Though we should be sceptical about poets' explanations of their own work (in that they are never neutral), I find this a more plausible reading than Orwell's. War is a form of legalized murder; if wars can be morally and politically legitimate – as non-pacifists argue – then there will be times when murder is necessary. What remains impressive about Auden's first version of 'Spain' is the fact that he was so prepared to face up to the moral implications of this idea. 'The conscious acceptance of guilt in the necessary murder' is not a comfortable formulation, but that is precisely the poem's point: 'we' are engaged in a struggle from which there is no easy escape. Whether 'we' win or lose the war, 'we' will remain guilty of murder. In this sense, I would say that 'Spain' is a more anguished and honest poem than Orwell or Cunningham allow for: Auden was not gung-ho about the Spanish Civil War, which is what makes his poem an impressive testament to the struggle it seeks to evoke.

Why then did Auden turn against the poem? Chiefly because of its last two lines: 'History to the defeated / May say alas but cannot help or pardon'. In 1966, he wrote that 'To say this is to equate goodness with success. It would have been bad enough if I had ever held this wicked doctrine, but that I should have stated it simply because it sounded to me rhetorically effective is quite inexcusable' (quoted in Fuller, 1998, pp.286–7). This is a good example of a poet's perverse reading of his own text: Auden misconstrues 'Spain' by his insistence that the lines are making a moral judgement about history. Certainly, the vision of the final stanza is harsh and unidealized: 'The stars are dead' (so there will be no help from the heavens); 'The animals will not look' (so nature is uninvolved in human conflicts); 'We are left alone with our day, and the time is short' (so we are isolated in an urgent crisis where action is imperative). As Fuller suggests, history is characterized here as a 'directionless accumulation of random events' rather than as a purposive force (1998, p.287). The final lines register the fact that there are no historical compensations for failure: 'History … May say alas', but it cannot change the course of events. In other words, rather than presenting history as an amoral force that colludes with the wickedly successful, 'Spain' presents a terrain in which human conflicts are not ultimately rectified by the stars, nature or history. The final stanza is reiterating the poem's central point that conscious engagement in 'the struggle' of today is the only way to deliver a better tomorrow.

As I hope you can see, the discussion of 'Spain' as propaganda is intensely problematic. Though Auden castigated himself for choosing a phrase 'because it sounded ... rhetorically effective' rather than because it was true, it is virtually impossible to resolve the poem into a convincing, or readily comprehensible, slogan. But is the situation any different when we turn to the work of a convinced communist, John Cornford? **Reread 'A Letter from Aragon' (pp.151–2). What are the main differences you notice between this poem and 'Spain'?**

'A Letter from Aragon' is strikingly different from 'Spain' in terms of both content and form. Where 'Spain' addresses the large questions of individual responsibility and historical change, 'A Letter from Aragon' is a particularized account of conditions on 'a quiet sector of a quiet front'. The poem overflows with detail: 'We buried Ruiz in a new pine coffin'; 'Clutched under one arm the naked rump of an infant'; 'A wounded militiaman moaning on a stretcher'. These details are impressive because of the form of Cornford's poem: while Auden writes in an elaborately rhetorical unrhymed stanza, Cornford uses free verse, where the shape of the poem seems dictated by the order and impression of events. To evoke Ruiz's 'ragged' burial, Cornford constructs an appropriately 'ragged' verse form:

> We buried Ruiz in a new pine coffin,
> But the shroud was too small and his washed feet stuck out.
> The stink of his corpse came through the clean pine boards
> And some of the bearers wrapped handkerchiefs round their faces.
> Death was not dignified.
> We hacked a ragged grave in the unfriendly earth
> And fired a ragged volley over the grave.

> (p.151)

Though in comparison with 'Spain' this may seem inelegant and unliterary, the very crudeness of Cornford's verse mirrors the lack of dignity in the events he describes. Note the way in which line length is dictated by syntax: the lines break as Cornford's material ends; they are not 'shaped' into predetermined lengths. Again, this is particularly effective since the poem describes a botched burial: as Ruiz's corpse does not quite fit in the 'new pine coffin', so Cornford's verse refuses to conform to a traditional shape – its feet stick out, much like Ruiz's. By presenting the burial so unsentimentally, Cornford convinces his readers of his reliability as a reporter, especially as in the next line he concedes 'no one much missed him'. Instead of the long historical perspectives of 'Spain', Cornford presents the war as it was actually happening. Though the two poems are so dissimilar, it is worth noting that both exploit the device of the refrain. Where Auden performs variations on 'Yesterday', 'to-day' and 'to-morrow', Cornford ironically juxtaposes the matter-of-fact statement 'This is a quiet sector of a quiet front' with the horrors he describes, as in the description of the militiaman 'still crying for water / Strong against death, but unprepared for such pain. // This on a quiet front.' Though 'A Letter from Aragon' seems to dispense with the formal structures of poetry, it remains a highly wrought piece of poetic description.

The major difference between the two poems comes with the last section of 'A Letter from Aragon', which articulates in the voice of 'an Anarchist worker' a much more convincing revolutionary slogan than anything in 'Spain': ' "Tell the workers of England ... if ever the Fascists again rule Barcelona / It will be as a heap of ruins with us workers beneath it." ' As Hynes observes, up until this, Cornford's poem is 'an example of anti-heroic realism in the tradition of [Wilfred] Owen' but 'These last lines are lines Owen couldn't have written because they assert ... that this war, for all its ugliness and fear, is a just and necessary one, in which the enemy *is* the enemy, and heroism *is* possible' (1992, pp.246–7). In other words, the close of 'A Letter from Aragon' reinterprets the horrific events of the rest of the poem and makes them historically purposive. Where Owen would have reported Ruiz's death as an illustration of the folly of all war, Cornford suggests that, despite its lack of dignity, individual death cumulatively has a meaning in terms of the conflict between workers and fascists.

Cornford's poem raises much more explicitly than Auden's the problem of how we react to propagandist poetry. Hynes comments that 'the dissonance between reality and rhetoric sounds ironic, and the brave words of the Anarchist have a hollow ring, after Ruiz and the women' (1992, p.247). This is, of course, a subjective comment disguised as dispassionate observation: Hynes means that he finds the words of the Anarchist less convincing than the rest of the poem. Yet there is a poetic difference between the final section of the poem and the rest in terms of the ideological design that the lines have on the reader: they are an attempt to extrapolate the events Cornford describes into a call for solidarity between the workers of England and the workers of Spain. Arguably, Cornford's rhetoric is plausible because he does not disguise the realities of war: the truthfulness of his account of the war is intended to verify the political truthfulness of the Anarchist's speech. Yet it remains the case that Cornford is using poetry as a vehicle for politics; in this sense, he emphatically avoids Woolf's aestheticist conception of the form and purpose of poetry.

In reviewing a posthumous memoir of Cornford in 1938, Stephen Spender claimed 'The spirit of Cornford and some of his comrades rises like a phoenix from the ashes of Spain, which are the ashes of Europe' (in

Cunningham, 1980, p.266). Spender's own war poems, however, are much less optimistic. When he collected these poems, including 'Port Bou', in *The Still Centre* (1939) he felt the need to explain his avoidance of 'a more heroic note':

> My reason is that a poet can only write about what is true to his own experience, not about what he would like to be true to his experience ... One day a poet will write truthfully about the heroism as well as the fears and anxieties of today; but such a poetry will be very different from the utilitarian heroics of the moment. I think that there is a certain pressure of external events on poets today, making them tend to write about what is outside their own limited experience. The violence of the times we are living in, the necessity of sweeping and general and immediate action, tend to dwarf the experience of the individual, and to make his immediate environment and occupations perhaps something that he is even ashamed of.
>
> (Spender, 1939, pp.10–11)

Spender's prose mirrors the hesitations of his thinking. On the one hand, he recognizes 'the necessity of sweeping ... action', but, on the other, he refuses to use his poetry in any way which is not 'true to his experience'. By 1939, Spender had become disillusioned with communism; he attempted in volumes like *The Still Centre* to reach an accommodation between his on-going commitment to broadly left-wing politics and his traditional, individualistic sense that poets must be true to 'their own limited experience'. **Now reread 'Port Bou'. How would you characterize Spender's attitude to the war?**

Spender – or rather the persona of the poet – is a key part of this poem. It begins with a description of his attempt to find an image to describe Port Bou: 'seeing an image I count out the coined words / To remember the childish headlands of the harbour' (p.147). The poem enacts this search with the comparison of the harbour with a child holding a pet: 'So the earth-and-rock flesh arms of this harbour / Embrace but do not enclose the sea' (p.146). Spender foregrounds poetic description as an end in itself: note the way in which the speaker's 'arms rest on a newspaper' that he does not actually read: he is too busy working on the image to be concerned with the news. He is interrupted by the appearance 'Of militiamen staring down at my French newspaper' (p.147), who introduce the political context in which this incident is happening. The focus now shifts from the description of the port to the war. Spender's attitude is shown firstly by his reaction to the militiaman:

'How do they speak of our struggle, over the frontier?'
I hold out the paper, but they refuse,
They did not ask for anything so precious
But only for friendly words and to offer me cigarettes.

(p.147)

These lines deftly suggest the same kind of atmosphere of trust between strangers with the same political views as Orwell outlines in the early pages of *Homage to Catalonia*. The militiamen are generous and curious; the poet mirrors their reactions. But 'Port Bou' does not rest with this image of camaraderie. As it develops into a description of the soldiers' weapons, the poem becomes more and more preoccupied with the physical effects of the war. The image of the 'terrible machine-gun' 'wrapped in a cloth' like an 'old mother in a shawl' anticipates the gruesome closing passage where the poet's body figuratively becomes 'a cloth which the machine-gun stitches / Like a sewing machine ... the carbines / Draw on long needles white threads through my navel' (p.148). Spender draws the description of war into the same imagistic framework that he had used earlier to describe the harbour. But in place of a purely poetic description, these lines graphically evoke the effects of the military technology on the human body. This image of the machine-gun as a kind of satanic sewing machine taps into a broader twentieth-century fascination with, and fear of, new technologies and machinery; indeed, Spender possibly alludes to Franz Kafka's horrific short story 'In the Penal Colony' (1919), in which condemned prisoners are executed on a sewing machine-like contraption that kills by embroidering the prisoners' sentences onto their backs (Kafka, 1993, pp.131–60). Spender conveys not the justice of the war, as Cornford and even Auden had done, but the frightening impact of bullets on skin. Cumulatively, his position develops from poetic detachment, through sympathetic involvement with the struggle, to an almost pacifist revulsion at military violence. 'Port Bou' embodies the qualms between commitment and individualism that Spender outlines in his Foreword to *The Still Centre*: he writes as a poet who wants to believe simultaneously in the moral and political authority of the struggle and in the independent authority of his own conscience.

This reading of 'Spain', 'A Letter from Aragon' and 'Port Bou' demonstrates that despite the initial sense in the literary Left that the Spanish Civil War presented a simple choice between Good and Evil, in practice poets found it difficult to write propaganda. This could be because, as Day Lewis had claimed in 1935, 'Poetry is of its nature more personal than "straight" propaganda' (in Margolies, 1998, p.54), although the work of Cornford and Lindsay shows that propagandist poetry was written during the period. I suspect that what the study of these poems really tells us is that, as Spender had admitted in 1933, 'The artist cannot renounce the bourgeois tradition because the proletariat has no alternative tradition which he could adopt' (1978, p.51). Middle-class poets like Spender and Auden necessarily write from 'the bourgeois tradition' that shaped them, as Woolf has reminded us, at public school and Oxford. Is it any wonder that, confronted with an actual war, their revolutionary enthusiasm ultimately resolved into the complex juxtapositions and ironic modifications characteristic of modern poetry?

Exploding geraniums in a squashy universe

We now approach the debate about the purpose of literature from a slightly different angle. So far, we have looked chiefly at the work of Auden and his colleagues. As the reaction to 'Spain' demonstrates, Auden did not command universal support even among the literary Left. There were other important poetic movements in Britain during the 1930s that are also represented in Skelton's anthology. This section focuses on those poets who were influenced by Surrealism. Like the styles associated with Auden, the Surrealists polarized critical responses: where to some they offered a liberating new way of being and creating, to Orwell they created only a 'squashy universe' (1970, p.543). As we study Surrealist and Surrealist-inspired poetry, we will be looking at the paradoxical quality of this work. Was Surrealism a radical departure from tradition, or did it repeat many traditional notions of poetry and the poetic?

Defining Surrealism is problematic. Though typically discussion focuses on the movement's inception in postwar France, Surrealism had a global influence, taking on different characteristics in different places (Remy, 1999, pp.15–16). Artists as diverse as the Spanish poet Federico García Lorca, the Mexican painter Frida Kahlo, the Spanish film-maker Luis Buñuel, as well as poets like Dylan Thomas and David Gascoyne, all in their different ways show the impact of Surrealism. Surrealist thought is revolutionary in character, and interdisciplinary in focus: as the subtitle of Jemima Montagu's 2002 book insists, the Surrealists were 'Revolutionaries in Art & Writing'. Surrealism aims to attack logical and rational thought processes in order to liberate the human imagination from the repressive hold of both the conscious mind and capitalism. The movement was influenced by both Marx and Freud; as Briony Fer puts it, 'The Surrealists saw the ideas of both men as a means to criticize the existing social order and the dominant culture' (1993, p.180). Yet as Montagu indicates, the relationship between Surrealism and communism was a troubled one throughout the 1920s and 1930s; during this time the liaisons between the two schools of thought were never fully clarified (2002, pp.17–20). Equally, though Freud's *Interpretation of Dreams* (1900) was a key text, which licensed interest in the unconscious and the use of dream imagery, as revolutionaries, Surrealists did not share Freud's therapeutic ambition of reconciling the unconscious with the conscious mind; indeed, Surrealist revolution is more often a gesture of rejection of bourgeois society rather than a coherent plan of action. We can get a sense of Surrealist writing from Gascoyne's poem 'And the Seventh Dream is the Dream of Isis' (pp.229–32). Described by Michel Remy as 'the first Surrealist poem published in English' (1999, p.44), Gascoyne's text gives the impression of being a bewildering sequence of unconnected yet vaguely threatening dream-like images:

> there is an explosion of geraniums in the ballroom of the hotel
> there is an extremely unpleasant odour of decaying meat
> arising from the depetalled flower growing out of her ear

(p.230)

Gascoyne's poem responds well to the definition of Surrealism made by its leading proponent, André Breton, in his *Surrealist Manifesto* of 1924:

> SURREALISM ... pure psychic automatism by which is intended to express ... the true function of thought. Thought dictated in the absence of all control exerted by reason, and outside all aesthetic or moral preoccupations ... Surrealism is based in the belief in the superior reality of certain forms of association heretofore neglected, in the omnipotence of dream, and in the disinterested play of thought.

(quoted in Remy, 1999, p.18)

Breton's definition almost describes the experience of reading Gascoyne's text, which seems to be a series of images constructed 'in the absence of all control exerted by reason', and which cumulatively demonstrates 'the omnipotence of dream'. Certainly, Gascoyne's deployment of what might be called a poetics of the disgusting in images like 'she was eating the excrement of dogs and horses' exemplifies a writing that is 'outside all aesthetic or moral preoccupations'. Gascoyne seems to have chosen such images not because they are pleasing or because they relate to some broader theme that the poem as a whole addresses, but rather because they exhibit 'the disinterested play of thought'.

The poem gives the impression of being an example of what Breton calls 'pure psychic automatism', or automatic writing. This is a form of literary experiment which – again in Breton's own words – 'represents *spoken thought*' (quoted in Montagu, 2002, p.9): the writer tries to access his or her unconscious by writing without conscious planning or any regard for structure, design or argument. Automatic texts typically result in the kinds of bizarre images we find in 'And the Seventh Dream is the Dream of Isis'. These techniques are linked to the Surrealists' broader agenda of demystifying the arts. As Gascoyne claimed in his *Short Survey of Surrealism* (1935), 'Surrealism represents the point at which poetry and painting merge into one another; and if poetry should be made by all, not one, then everyone should be able to make paintings also' (quoted in Batchelor, 1993, p.61). In some ways, this notion of art made by everyone mirrors Auden's theory in *The Oxford Book of Light Verse* of poetry as an art of communication. Yet where Auden envisages a community in which poets communicate freely with their peers, Gascoyne imagines a community in which everyone is an artist. Communication as such is not as important to Surrealists as the liberation of the self repressed by the conscious mind.

Such theories were, and remain, controversial. At the time of the International Surrealist Exhibition in June 1936 (Figure 4.3), Auden queried the extent to which Surrealist writing was 'always and absolutely automatic and never consciously worked over' (1996, p.136). Though Gascoyne's poem eschews sequential logic and rational design, it does not altogether dispense with conventional poetic structures. Note the way that the last four lines of the second section begin with similar phrases: 'she was standing at the window clothed only in a ribbon / she was burning the eyes of snails in a candle'. Disorientating though the poem may be, it remains a text in which the reader can see elements of traditional poetic structure. Conversely, a text like this raises the broader question of whether such poetry is aesthetically

Figure 4.3   Collage celebrating the International Surrealist Exhibition of 1936.

successful. As Adrian Caesar observes, 'At its worst Surrealist poetry tends towards a turgid stream of imagery graced with neither form nor thought' (1991, p.182). We can put the problem like this: while theoretically anyone can write a poem based on dream and using the techniques of automatic writing, will the resultant poem be interesting enough to justify anyone else reading it? This question connects with a broader problem that faced French Surrealists in the 1920s and English Surrealists in the 1930s: how can an artistic practice that stresses the primacy of the individual's unconscious mind and dream experience be squared with communist ideology? Breton left the French Communist Party because of his unwillingness to subscribe to Stalinist orthodoxy and his commitment to the ideas of Trotsky (Fer, 1993, p.204). It would be difficult to deduce any social or political message from a poem like 'And the Seventh Dream is the Dream of Isis' beyond a pervasive hostility to bourgeois morality implicit in lines like 'little girls stick photographs of genitals to the windows of their homes'.

Now read Gascoyne's 'The Very Image' (pp.234–5). Write a couple of sentences to summarize the poem. What does it communicate to you?

Gascoyne provides a series of prototypically Surreal images. In each of these vignettes, the ordinary is juxtaposed with the unusual, as in the opening lines, 'An image of my grandmother / her head appearing upside-down upon a cloud'. The poem offers no gloss to these images: they are only connected, apparently, by being assembled within this text.

But the poem's dedication, 'to René Magritte', explains Gascoyne's inspiration: each of these images recalls the paintings of the Belgian Surrealist. Magritte's work fuses meticulously accurate representations of familiar objects with bizarre and enigmatic situations. In *The Reckless Sleeper* (1928) (Figure 4.4), a figure sleeps in a wooden chest or coffin over what looks like a tombstone, in which a candle, a bow, a bowler hat, a hand mirror, an apple and a bird are displayed. As with most of his work, *The Reckless Sleeper* challenges the viewer to make sense of imagery that is realistically impossible. Magritte warned that 'People who look for symbolic meanings ... fail to grasp the inherent poetry and mystery of the image ... By asking "what does it mean?" they express a wish that everything be understandable' (quoted in Whitfield, 1992, cat. 40). I would suggest that 'The Very Image' is making a similar point: that there is no fixed or symbolic meaning to which these images refer. The reader – like the viewer of a Magritte painting – is not supposed to decode or interpret the text in terms of anything else, but must 'grasp the inherent poetry and mystery of the image'.

Gauging the artistic success of such works is not an easy matter. In the case of Magritte, the viewer is granted the traditional pleasures of painting that represents recognizable objects: in *The Reckless Sleeper*, the radicalism of the image derives not from its technique but from the abrupt juxtaposition of 'real' objects in an unreal, or fantastical, environment. Similarly, Paul Nash's *Landscape from a Dream* (1936–8) (Figure 4.5) is both an arresting image that suggests the strange textures of dreams and a traditionally executed oil painting of one of the most traditional subjects: a landscape. As with Magritte, the novelty of Nash's painting lies not so much in its form, but in the unsettling juxtapositions of its content: a falcon looking at itself in a mirror which presents to the viewer a landscape that overlies a further landscape behind. In the final stanza Gascoyne's poem exactly captures the effect of such juxtapositions: 'all these images ... are arranged like waxworks / in model bird-cages'. As such, it is effective as art criticism in verse: Gascoyne gives the reader an accurate sense of the visual impact of Surrealist paintings. Yet the question I asked you earlier remains: beyond Gascoyne's enthusiasm for Surrealist painting, what does this poem communicate?

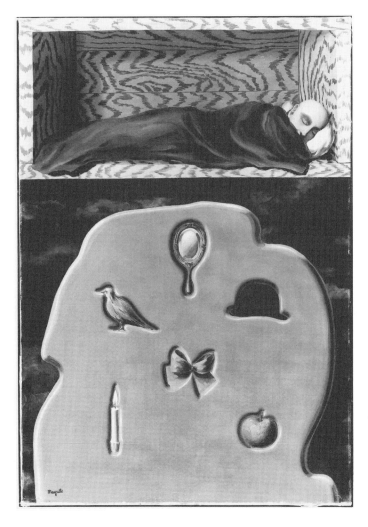

Figure 4.4 René Magritte, *The Reckless Sleeper*, 1928, oil on canvas, 116 × 810 × 2 cm. (© Tate, London 2004. © ADAGP, Paris and DACS, London 2004.)

Your answer to this question will depend on your own critical standpoint. As we have seen, Magritte and Gascoyne stress the 'inherent poetry' of imagery – its meaningfulness in terms of itself. Yet as communist critics argued during the 1930s, such positions are hard to square with Surrealism's commitment to revolutionary ideas. The Surrealists' emphasis on the liberation of the unconscious imagination can therefore be seen to recuperate a kind of aestheticism. This is precisely the criticism that A.L. Lloyd levelled at the movement in the *Left Review* in 1937: 'Surrealism is not revolutionary because its lyricism is socially irresponsible. It does not lead fantasy into any action of real social significance' (in Margolies, 1998, p.148). In other words, Surrealism is an aesthetic and political cul-de-sac, too concentrated on the articulation of the unconscious to achieve 'real social significance'. Though 'The Very Image' is clearly not a traditional poem (formally it is hinged only by the five-line stanza, eschewing both rhyme and a recurring metrical pattern), by concentrating on visual imagery alone, it resembles the aestheticist conception of poetry as an art form for the articulation of individual feeling. Such privatization of poetry may have been an inevitable reaction to the more politically engaged work of Auden and his followers. As we have seen, propagandist theories of poetry do not automatically lead to successful poems, or even to effective revolutionary slogans. And though the excesses of Surrealism are easy to parody (you might notice how often adjectives like 'leprous' recur in Skelton's section 'When Logics Die'), 'The

Figure 4.5   Paul Nash, *Landscape from a Dream*, 1936–8, oil on canvas, 68 × 102 cm. (Presented by Contemporary Art Society, 1946. © Tate, London 2004.)

Very Image' achieves the task it sets itself with some style. As a description of the artistic procedures of painters like Magritte and Nash, the poem encapsulates the visual in the verbal.

I close this section by examining a poem by Dylan Thomas to observe the impact of Surrealism on a powerfully individual poet. Though Skelton places Thomas alongside avowed Surrealists like Gascoyne and Hugh Sykes Davies, Thomas's relationship to Surrealism is complicated. As Walford Davies observes, 'much in the early Thomas smacks of Surrealism', but unlike Gascoyne, Thomas was far too much of a self-conscious craftsman to cede bardic control to the vagaries of automatic writing; Davies continues: 'whereas the Surrealists allowed no room for the selection, control, and development of images, Thomas ... seems busy with those very activities' (2001, pp.116–17). Thomas came from a different social milieu from writers like Auden and Spender. The son of a schoolteacher, he was born in Swansea and attended a grammar school rather than public school and Oxford. Even though he moved to London during the 1930s, Thomas remained independent of literary cliques. In a letter of 1938, he condemns most contemporary poets, referring contemptuously to Auden as the 'head-prefect' of the 'Brotherhood of Man' school and to Gascoyne's 'indigestible Dreams of Isis and peach melbas' (Thomas, 1985, pp.280–1).

Now read Thomas's 'And Death Shall Have No Dominion' (pp.216–17). Choose a line or image that you find striking. How would you describe Thomas's choice of words and phrases in this poem?

The line that I would choose is the poem's title and refrain, but you may have chosen almost any phrase. Every line of Thomas's poem is unusual, especially in comparison with the poems we have been looking at. The title phrase is a key facet of the poem's rhetorical grandeur: it is repeated six times and operates as a frame for each stanza. The grammar of the line contributes to its impact. By beginning with the simple connective 'And', Thomas freights his poem with the weight of familiar biblical cadences like 'And God said, Let there be light' (King James Bible, Genesis 1:3). In fact, Thomas paraphrases a verse from Paul's Epistle to the Romans: 'knowing that Christ being raised from the dead dieth no more; death hath no more dominion over him' (King James Bible, Romans 6:9). Like the Creation from Genesis, 'And death shall have no dominion' sounds like a command that is in the process of being carried out. This is why Thomas flouts the usual grammar rule that a sentence should not begin with a connective: 'And death shall have no dominion' implies precisely that death's magisterial tenure is at an end as we read the poem – Thomas gives the illusion that the Day of Judgement is literally at hand from the moment we start to read.

This line sets up a poetic and syntactic pattern that ripples through the rest of the text. Thomas structures the poem through pairs of cognate or antithetical terms: 'Though they go mad they shall be sane' juxtaposes the antithetical terms 'mad' and 'sane'; 'Under the windings of the sea / They lying long shall not die windily' punningly exploits the fact that the verb 'to wind' (here as the noun 'the windings') and the noun 'the wind' (here in its adverbial form 'windily') are the same word. In each case, Thomas works from the simple pairing of 'death' with 'dominion' in the refrain. The reader in turn begins to accept this movement and expects that each new term will be balanced by a similar or modifying paired word. This is, I think, what makes lines like 'Faith in their hands shall snap in two / And the unicorn evils run them through' so strangely effective. 'Faith' is answered by 'evils', but the complexity of the pairing is brilliantly enhanced by fabrication of the adjective 'unicorn'. Thomas has already evoked images of torture in the previous lines, which describe the dead 'Twisting on racks' and 'Strapped to a wheel'. In this case, the abstract quality of 'Faith' and 'evils' is made physically tangible by the image of the unicorn's flesh-puncturing horn.

Thomas's poetry is unlike anything we have encountered so far. Even Gascoyne's ultra-Surreal idiom in 'And the Seventh Dream is the Dream of Isis' accommodates the topical in details like 'pocket-cameras' and 'the wings of private airplanes' (pp.229, 231). Instead of the predominantly conversational diction deployed by most of the poets we have studied, Thomas adopts a style that is much more traditionally 'poetic'. As we have seen, 'And Death Shall Have No Dominion' evokes the rhythm and vocabulary of the King James Bible. In the first stanza alone, the nouns seem to have migrated from a Psalm: 'man', 'wind', 'moon', 'bones', 'stars', 'sea', 'love'. You might compare these deliberately timeless terms with the first verse of Auden's 'Song for the New Year', which reads almost as a command performance of sophisticated topicality, featuring such properties as 'the drawing-room's civilised cry', 'The frock-coated diplomat's social aplomb' and, perhaps inevitably, 'gas and ... bomb' (p.47).

So how does Thomas's work fit into the literary–political debates of the 1930s? As I stressed earlier, Thomas's own attitude to literary fashions was equivocal. His satirical 'Letter to my Aunt Discussing the Correct Approach to Modern Poetry' (1933) simultaneously sends up the pretensions of 'A genius like David G[ascoyne]', 'young Auden's coded chatter' and even his own fondness for half rhymes: 'Do not forget that "limpet" rhymes / With "strumpet" in these troubled times' (Thomas, 1982, pp.84–5). Though 'And Death Shall Have No Dominion' shows elements of Surrealism – especially in terms of its non-realist imagery and dream-like setting – it would be difficult to claim that such a conscious piece of literary craftsmanship had much in common with the automatism of 'And the Seventh Dream is the Dream of Isis'. Indeed, Thomas's cultivation of a consciously poetic register means that he is in many ways the most purist of all the poets we have studied. Shortly after the death of Thomas in 1953, MacNeice observed that Thomas's 'diction was as strictly controlled as his content; just as he would not and could not mention such a thing as a gasometer, so he eschewed the topical word and the slang word' (1987, p.185). The intense individuality of Thomas's work again shows the durability of an aestheticist model of poetry. Though 'And Death Shall Have No Dominion' evokes the Apocalypse, unlike Auden's 'Song for the New Year', Warner's 'Hymn', or even Betjeman's 'Slough', its evocation is an end in itself rather than a didactic warning: Thomas describes the end of the world purely for the challenge and pleasure of making that description.

Louis MacNeice: aesthete or preacher?

We conclude by looking at one of the decade's most individual poets, Louis MacNeice, because his work incarnates the tension between the instrumental and aesthetic ideas of poetry. Though MacNeice was commonly seen during the 1930s as just another member of the Auden gang (Roy Campbell amalgamated him with Spender, Auden and Day Lewis in the figure of the cowardly poetaster 'MacSpaunday'; Alexander, 1982, p.199), with the passage of time his achievement has been recognized as more complex than such caricatures suggest. In particular, he has been a formative influence on later Northern Irish poets; Seamus Heaney, Michael Longley, Derek Mahon and Paul Muldoon have all registered the effect of his work.

Though MacNeice was educated at public school and Oxford, his origins were different from those of his English contemporaries. He was the son of a Church of Ireland minister, born, as 'Carrickfergus' puts it, 'in Belfast between the mountain and the gantries / To the hooting of lost sirens and the clang of trams' (MacNeice, 1979, p.69; see Appendix). MacNeice's Irish identity reverberates – or hoots – like the sounds of those sirens throughout his work: hence 'Poem' juxtaposes an industrial city with an Irish landscape of 'turf-stacks' and 'The tawny mountain' (p.98). Yet MacNeice's identity is more problematic than such details might suggest. As 'Carrickfergus' explains, he 'was the rector's son, born to the Anglican order / Banned forever from the candles of the Irish poor'. His sense of Irishness was complicated by his family's Protestant allegiances and his cultural and economic exclusion from Catholic Ireland; as Edna Longley observes, 'the historical and social location of MacNeice's family epitomizes disunity' (1988, p.17). Though paradoxically his father supported Home Rule, because of his English education MacNeice was, in Terence Brown's formulation, 'spiritually hyphenated' between Ireland and England (1975, p.10).

Read through the thirteen MacNeice poems printed by Skelton (use the Index of Authors on p.292 to find them). What impression do these poems give you of MacNeice as a poet? What traces can you detect in them of 'spiritual hyphenation'?

These poems exhibit MacNeice's facility with a number of different forms: there are love poems ('Meeting Point', 'Sunlight in the Garden'), satires ('Bagpipe Music', 'London Rain'), cityscapes ('Birmingham') as well as longer, discursive poems ('An Eclogue for Christmas', *Autumn Journal*). MacNeice was a poet with wide interests and agendas.

Though Skelton does not reprint the poems in which MacNeice directly addresses his Irishness, spiritual hyphenation – or more accurately an acute sense of cultural dislocation – is apparent in many of these poems. In 'An Eclogue for Christmas' (pp.205–10) the idea of division underpins the poem's structure. In this modern pastoral, two anonymous speakers, the city dweller A and the country dweller B, reflect on the limitations of their environments. For A, city life has become 'a morose routine' (p.205), while for B 'things draw to an end, the soil is stale' (p.207); as McDonald comments, 'MacNeice offers hope for neither speaker's habitation' (1991, p.23). This sense of division and decay has become a part of the speakers' sense of their identities. A's review of modern art registers the shortfall between the formal advances of artists like Pablo Picasso and the spiritual implications of their work:

> I who was Harlequin in the childhood of the century
> Posed by Picasso beside an endless opaque sea
> Have seen myself sifted and splintered in broken facets
> Tentative pencillings, endless liabilities, no assets,
> Abstractions scalpelled with a palette-knife
> Without reference to this particular life.
>
> (p.206)

MacNeice extrapolates a sense of the self as being 'sifted and splintered' into a metaphor for modernity. The 'broken' appearance of the human subject in Picasso's paintings (Figure 4.6) symbolizes a deeper cultural shift in which the individual has become increasingly tenuous, or 'Tentative'. For MacNeice, individuality has become what B says it is: a pretence. This is why the speakers are given those cryptic, anonymizing tags: they are not individuals, they are figures who represent the erosion of individuality.

MacNeice does not always write with this level of abstraction. Even in the 'Eclogue' intellectual content is offset by what he called 'Lots of lovely particulars' (quoted in Stallworthy, 1995, p.140); the topical props of jazz and gramophones provide the soundtrack for A's decline: 'that is why I turn this jaded music on / To foreswear thought and become an automaton'. MacNeice is an interesting amalgam of a poet with serious intellectual ambitions and a sensuous consciousness of the world around him. At this

Figure 4.6   Pablo Picasso, *Family of Saltimbanques*, 1905, oil on canvas, 213 × 230 cm. (Chester Dale Collection, inv. no. 1963.10.190. © Board of Trustees, National Gallery of Art, Washington, DC. © Succession Picasso/DACS 2004.)

point, it is worth considering MacNeice's model of the poet in his manifesto, *Modern Poetry* (1938). As with Eliot's recipe in 'The Metaphysical Poets', the imagined poet resembles the actual writer. MacNeice assumes both the gender and sexual proclivities of his poet, although, as he well knew, Auden and Spender were homosexual:

> I consider that the poet is a blend of the entertainer and the critic or informer ... Poetic truth ... is distinct from scientific truth. The poet does not give you a full and accurate picture of the world nor a full and accurate picture of himself, but he gives you an amalgam which ... represents truthfully his own relation to the world ... My own prejudice ... is in favour of poets whose worlds are not too esoteric. I would have a poet able-bodied, fond of talking, a reader of the newspapers, capable of pity and laughter, informed in economics, appreciative of women, involved in personal relationships, actively interested in politics, susceptible to physical impressions.
>
> (MacNeice, 1938, pp.197–8)

MacNeice's poet as a man of the world necessarily recalls Auden's model of the poet as a communicator, though unlike Auden, MacNeice does not connect his social conception of poetry with a distinct political agenda. 'Poetic truth' is an independent, non-partisan value through which the poet 'represents truthfully his own relation to the world'. But what distinguishes this model from the work of the Surrealists is precisely MacNeice's sense that the world of things and ideas – of newspapers, economics, relationships and politics – can and should be at the centre of the poet's activities. This conception goes some way to answering speaker A's criticism of Picasso: in place of an art that is 'Without reference to this particular life', MacNeice stresses the overlapping liaisons between art and life.

This idea of a sociable, well-informed poet can be contrasted with the rather different account of MacNeice in Samuel Hynes's *The Auden Generation*. MacNeice is not the major focus of Hynes's study; one of its shortcomings is that it reads the literary politics of the 1930s wholly through the filter of Auden as the predominant poet of the period. Hynes assumes that MacNeice was a less important adjunct to Auden. In his accounts of *Modern Poetry* and *Autumn Journal*, he presents MacNeice as a chronic melancholic:

> the poetry that [MacNeice] wrote was autumnal and melancholy. Some of this quality was no doubt the tone of the professional lacrymose Irishman; but it was also the tone of the time, of living in the late 'thirties.
>
> (Hynes, 1992, p.334)

> clearly if the time allowed, he would have been content to go on as he was, a charming Irish classicist with upper-class tastes and a gift for making melancholy poems. But the time determined its exclusions, and the poet acknowledged them; they were all part of the loss.
>
> (*ibid.*, p.370)

> *Autumn Journal* is a passive poem, a record of a private life carried on the flood of history ... England has come to the end of *laissez faire*, but MacNeice has no alternatives to offer, beyond a vague solidarity of resistance against the common enemy.
>
> (*ibid.*, p.372)

Each of these extracts repeats the same idea: MacNeice was constitutionally suited to writing 'melancholy poems' (which Hynes spuriously connects with Irishness) but 'the time' did not allow him to do this and provoked him to write texts that express a passive (yet still melancholy) attitude to contemporary turmoils. Though I hope you can see this is rather muddled as criticism (it is highly problematic as an account of the relationship between nationality and writing), Hynes nevertheless raises a debate that has reverberated in the scholarly discussion of MacNeice since the late 1970s. How should we 'place' MacNeice? Is he the social poet he claims to be in *Modern Poetry*, or is he really a closet aesthete who would have preferred to be writing 'autumnal' love lyrics for his upper-class friends? Finally, how should MacNeice's ambivalent national affiliations shape the interpretation of his poetry?

To address these questions in detail, I would like to focus on two poems: 'Christina' (pp.256–7) and 'Bagpipe Music' (pp.72–3). Do these poems seem closer to the spirit of MacNeice's model of poetry and the poet in *Modern Poetry*, or to Hynes's characterization?

Of the two, 'Christina' is apparently the least concerned with contemporary issues. It juxtaposes, in a manner not wholly dissimilar from the procedures of the Surrealists, a nursery incident with an adult sexual encounter. It is a disturbed and disturbing poem, which suggests an overlap between the childhood world of the first three stanzas and the adult world of the final stanza. Note the sexualized description of the undressing of the doll: 'She smiled while you dressed her / And when you then undressed her / She kept a smiling face'. Dolls have but one expression – by stressing the otherwise unremarkable fact that Christina 'kept a smiling face' while being undressed, MacNeice animates the doll and associates her treatment with what happens in the final stanza: 'He went to bed with a lady ... And suddenly saw Christina / Dead on the nursery floor'. The poem is careful not to be too explicit: it does not explain the connection between the doll and the woman, but it implies that the breaking of Christina and the going 'to bed with a lady' are related. You might think about the effect of the line of dots between the third and fourth stanzas: they both mark the break between child and adult experience, and imply a connection between the two parts of the poem.

'Christina' is a devious and provocative poem, which aims to implicate the reader in its protagonist's complex transactions. Again, the poem's form tells us a lot about its meaning. MacNeice imitates the sing-song rhythms and repetitions of nursery rhyme. This has the effect of making the reader trust the poem because it sounds so familiar. 'Building motley houses / And knocking down your houses / And always building more' has the same kind of cadence and subject as 'London Bridge': 'London Bridge is broken down ... How shall we build it up again? ... Build it up with iron and steel' (in Auden, 1938, p.184). Like most nursery rhymes, 'Christina' is concerned with more than just entertainment: by suggesting that adult sexual neuroses are triggered by distant childhood memories, MacNeice sketches, in four short stanzas, an entire psychopathology. Arguably, 'Christina' shows the beneficial influence of Freud and psychology on poetry much more effectively than does the work of the Surrealists.

'Bagpipe Music' also uses lighter rhythms and comic rhymes, such as 'sofa' and 'poker'. But MacNeice's intention here is satirical. The poem was first published in the travel book *I Crossed the Minch* (1938). Readers of this text will discover that MacNeice did not enjoy his trips to the Hebrides; it was written as a potboiler as he tried to remain solvent after the collapse of his first marriage (Stallworthy, 1995, p.203). The poem, however, is more serious. MacNeice described it as 'a satirical elegy for the Gaelic districts of Scotland and indeed for all traditional culture' (quoted in *ibid.*, p.212). It fuses comic observation, such as the description of the Laird o'Phelps drunkenness, with a keen sense of the economic changes that were affecting Hebrideans: Willie Murray's brother catches 'three hundred cran [of herring] when the seas were lavish', but finds that he earns more by going 'upon the parish' than by selling what he has caught. Similarly, the penultimate stanza brilliantly evokes the political scepticism of the islanders: 'It's no go the Government grants, it's no go elections / Sit on your arse for fifty years and hang your hat on a pension'. MacNeice unsentimentally offsets the rich texture of island life with a perception of impending economic and political catastrophe. The acuteness of the poem lies in its deft accommodation of credible vernacular tones ('Sit on your arse', 'Threw the bleeders back') with an undeceived sense of political reality: 'Work your hands from day to day, the winds will blow the profit'. Put another way, Hebrideans have little chance of getting the things that they so energetically want in the poem's choruses.

On the basis of these two poems, I would say that it is difficult to endorse Hynes's portrait of MacNeice as a melancholy aesthete. MacNeice shows a searching concern with what poetry can accomplish: the dramatization of the relation between childhood and adulthood, or the breathless satire of a rapidly changing environment. Even such a limited acquaintance with MacNeice suggests that placing his work is a complex business: his poems are meticulously constructed (in this way they bear formal comparison with Thomas's) and profoundly involved in the concerns of 'this particular life'. Moreover, 'Bagpipe Music' shows that MacNeice's Irish identity was much more than an unfortunate detail he would have preferred to transfer eastwards. His imaginative interest in the plight of the Hebrideans shows a political consciousness of a kind that is distinct from anything in the work of Auden or Spender. In the brutal yet witty evocation of Mrs Carmichael's fifth pregnancy – ' "Take it away, I'm through with over-production" ' – MacNeice shows the ability to sympathize with a group of people quite unlike the London literary classes.

Conclusion: 'poetry makes nothing happen'?

In this chapter, we have looked at a wide range of poems, alongside sharply contrasting theories of poetry. It is worth asking which of these ideas had the deepest influence. You will have your own opinions about these theories and the kinds of poetry they produce; through the close reading of exemplary poems, we have gone some way to evaluating the merits of public and private poems. My point would not be that one theory is more important or valid than the other: the tension between poetry written for a purpose and poetry written for its own sake is as old as literature. Rather, I would alert you to the way in which Auden, Spender and MacNeice came increasingly to put their faith in the authority of 'poetic truth'. For MacNeice, this truth is a ballast against the siren voices of competing ideologies such as Marxism and Freudianism. Yet it is itself a belief system: the belief in the intrinsic merit and authority of poetry.

As a final snapshot, I will close by considering Auden's 'In Memory of W.B. Yeats' (see Appendix). In this elegy to the Irish poet, who died in January 1939, Auden both negotiates his own tense and tetchy relationship with Yeats's poetry (which he subsequently admitted became 'through no fault of [Yeats's] ... for me a symbol of my own devil of unauthenticity'; quoted in Smith, 1994, p.155), and articulates a much less optimistic poetic than he had a year earlier in *The Oxford Book of Light Verse*. 'In Memory of W.B. Yeats' is an act of literary homage that simultaneously rebukes Yeats for his 'silliness' and clarifies Auden's newly abrupt sense of the limitations of poetry:

> You were silly like us: your gift survived it all;
> The parish of rich women, physical decay,
> Yourself; mad Ireland hurt you into poetry.
> Now Ireland has her madness and her weather still,
> For poetry makes nothing happen: it survives
> In the valley of its saying where executives
> Would never want to tamper; it flows south
> From ranches of isolation and the busy griefs,
> Raw towns which we believe and die in; it survives,
> A way of happening, a mouth.

> (Auden, 1977, p.242)

Once again, Auden issues statements that are at once memorable, dogmatic and seemingly authoritative. Rapidly reviewing Yeats's career as a poet and Irish nationalist, Auden insists that Yeats's 'gift' had no real impact on 'mad Ireland' – 'Ireland has her madness and her weather still'. So Auden arrives at one of his most notorious formulations: 'poetry makes nothing happen'; it does not act as a force for social or political change. To an extent, the shift from texts like the Introduction to *The Oxford Book of Light Verse* and 'Spain' to 'In Memory of W.B. Yeats' reflects changes in Auden's life: by the time he wrote the Yeats elegy, he had emigrated to America and had become increasingly pessimistic about the future of Europe (Carpenter, 1992, p.255). Nonetheless, I think it is important that we register that there are ambiguities even in a passage which seems so unequivocally resistant to instrumental theories of poetry. The final lines – 'it survives, / A way of happening, a mouth' – counterpoise a sense of poetry's tenuous survival in a world dominated by executives and madness with the recognition that poetry can remain, through its articulacy, 'A way of happening'. Indeed, the figure of the 'mouth' connects this text with the theory of poetry as an art of communication outlined in the Introduction to *The Oxford Book of Light Verse*.

The conversation initiated by Auden is far from over. Paul Muldoon's long poem '7, Middagh Street', from *Meeting the British* (1987), presents the dramatic monologues of a series of famous characters who shared this address in New York during October 1940. Among such luminaries as Benjamin Britten, Salvador Dalí, Carson McCullers and Auden, Muldoon ventriloquizes MacNeice brooding both on 'In Memory of W.B. Yeats' and the murder of the poet Federico García Lorca by fascist troops in the Spanish Civil War:

> Lorca
> was riddled with bullets
>
> and lay mouth-down
> in the fickle shadow of his own blood.
> As the drunken soldiers of the *Gypsy Ballads*
> started back for town
>
> they heard him calling through the mist,
> 'When I die leave the balcony shutters open.'
> For poetry *can* make things happen –
> not only can, but *must* ...

(Muldoon, 2001, p.192)

This is both a bravura performance of poetic imitation (Muldoon imitates MacNeice who imitates García Lorca), in which the 'mouth' of the poet referred to by Auden continues to sound even after his execution, and a complex rebuke to Auden's pessimism. For Muldoon–MacNeice, poetry is inherently politically engaged, as in the bitter irony of García Lorca being killed by precisely the kind of people he had given voice to in his own works. In this sense, poetry does make things happen, but what those things are is ultimately beyond the control, if not the imagination, of the writer.

Works cited

Alexander, P. (1982) *Roy Campbell: A Critical Biography*, Oxford: Oxford University Press.

Auden, W.H. (ed.) (1938) *The Oxford Book of Light Verse*, Oxford: Clarendon Press.

Auden, W.H. (1977) *The English Auden: Poems, Essays and Dramatic Writings 1927–1939*, ed. by E. Mendelson, London: Faber & Faber.

Auden, W.H. (1995) *As I Walked Out One Evening: Songs, Ballads, Lullabies, Limericks and Other Light Verse by W.H. Auden*, ed. by E. Mendelson, London: Faber & Faber.

Auden, W.H. (1996) *W.H. Auden: Prose and Travel Books in Prose and Verse*, vol.1: *1926–1938*, ed. by E. Mendelson, London: Faber & Faber.

Batchelor, D. (1993) ' "This Liberty and this Order": Art in France after the First World War', in B. Fer, D. Batchelor and P. Wood (eds), *Realism, Rationalism, Surrealism: Art Between the Wars*, New Haven: Yale University Press in association with The Open University, pp.3–86.

Baudelaire, C. (1968) *Œuvres Complètes*, ed. by M.A. Ruff, Paris: Éditions du Seuil.

Blinkhorn, M. (ed.) (1986) *Spain in Conflict 1931–1939: Democracy and its Enemies*, London: Sage.

Brown, T. (1975) *Louis MacNeice: Sceptical Vision*, Dublin: Gill & Macmillan.

Caesar, A. (1991) *Dividing Lines: Poetry, Class and Ideology in the 1930s*, Manchester: Manchester University Press.

Carpenter, H. (1992) *W.H. Auden: A Biography*, Oxford: Oxford University Press.

Caudwell, C. (1937) *Illusion and Reality: A Study of the Sources of Poetry*, London: Lawrence & Wishart.

Cunningham, V. (ed.) (1980) *The Penguin Book of Spanish Civil War Verse*, Harmondsworth: Penguin.

Cunningham, V. (1988) *British Writers of the Thirties*, Oxford: Oxford University Press.

Davies, W. (2001) 'The Poetry of Dylan Thomas: Welsh Contexts, Narrative and the Language of Modernism', in J. Goodby and C. Wigginton (eds), *Dylan Thomas*, New Casebooks, Basingstoke: Palgrave.

Day Lewis, C. (1992) *The Complete Poems*, Stanford: Stanford University Press.

Eliot, T.S. ([1932] 1951) *Selected Essays*, London: Faber & Faber.

Empson, W. ([1930] 1984) *Seven Types of Ambiguity*, London: Hogarth Press.

Fer, B. (1993) 'Surrealism, Myth and Psychoanalysis', in B. Fer, D. Batchelor and P. Wood (eds), *Realism, Rationalism, Surrealism: Art Between the Wars*, New Haven: Yale University Press in association with The Open University, pp.171–249.

Fuller, J. (1998) *W.H. Auden: A Commentary*, London: Faber & Faber.

Gascoyne, D. (1998) *David Gascoyne: Selected Prose 1934–1996*, ed. by R. Scott, London: Enitharmon.

Hecht, A. (1993) *The Hidden Law: The Poetry of W.H. Auden*, Cambridge, MA: Harvard University Press.

Hynes, S. ([1976] 1992) *The Auden Generation: Literature and Politics in England in the 1930s*, London: Pimlico.

Kafka, F. (1993) *Collected Stories*, ed. and intro. by G. Josipovici, Everyman's Library, London: David Campell.

Lawrence, D.H. ([1922] 1995) *Aaron's Rod*, ed. by M. Kalnins, intro. and notes by S. Vine, Penguin Twentieth-Century Classics, London: Penguin.

Lewis, P. Wyndham (1933) *One-Way Song*, London: Faber & Faber.

Longley, E. (1988) *Louis MacNeice: A Critical Study*, London: Faber & Faber.

McDonald, P. (1991) *Louis MacNeice: The Poet in his Contexts*, Oxford: Clarendon Press.

MacNeice, L. (1938) *Modern Poetry: A Personal Essay*, Oxford: Oxford University Press.

MacNeice, L. (1979) *The Collected Poems of Louis MacNeice*, ed. by E.R. Dodds, London: Faber & Faber.

MacNeice, L. (1987) *Selected Literary Criticism of Louis MacNeice*, ed. by A. Heuser, Oxford: Clarendon Press.

Margolies, D. (ed.) (1998) *Writing the Revolution: Cultural Criticism from 'Left Review'*, London: Pluto.

Montagu, J. (2002) *The Surrealists: Revolutionaries in Art & Writing 1919–35*, London: Tate Publishing.

Muldoon, P. (2001) *Poems 1968–1998*, London: Faber & Faber.

Nietzsche, F. ([1883–5] 1969) *Thus Spoke Zarathustra*, trans. and intro. by R. Hollingdale, Penguin Classics, Harmondsworth: Penguin.

Orwell G. (1970) *The Collected Essays, Journalism and Letters of George Orwell*, vol.1: *An Age Like This 1920–1940*, ed. by S. Orwell and I. Angus, Harmondsworth: Penguin.

Owen, W. (1963) *The Collected Poems of Wilfred Owen*, ed. by C. Day Lewis, London: Chatto & Windus.

Remy, M. (1999) *Surrealism in Britain*, Aldershot: Ashgate.

Shakespeare, W. (1997) *The Norton Shakespeare*, ed. by S. Greenblatt, J.E. Howard, W. Cohen and K.E. Maus, New York: Norton.

Shelley, P.B. (1977) *Shelley's Poetry and Prose: Authoritative Texts and Criticism*, ed. by D.H. Reiman and S.B Powers, New York: Norton.

Skelton, R. (ed.) ([1964] 2000) *Poetry of the Thirties*, Penguin Classics, London: Penguin.

Smith, S. (1994) 'Persuasions to Rejoice: Auden's Oedipal Dialogues with W.B. Yeats', in K. Bucknell and N. Jenkins (eds), *W.H. Auden: 'The Language of Learning and the Language of Love': Uncollected Writing, New Interpretations*, Auden Studies 2, Oxford: Clarendon Press.

Spears, M.K. (1963) *The Poetry of W.H. Auden: The Disenchanted Island*, New York: Oxford University Press.

Spender, S. (1939) *The Still Centre*, London: Faber & Faber.

Spender, S. (1978) *The Thirties and After: Poetry, Politics, People (1933–75)*, London: Macmillan.

Stallworthy, J. (1995) *Louis MacNeice*, London: Faber & Faber.

Symons, J. (1989) 'Introduction', G. Orwell, *Homage to Catalonia*, London: Penguin, pp.v–xiii.

Thomas, D. (1982) *Dylan Thomas: The Poems*, ed. by D. Jones, London: Dent.

Thomas, D. (1985) *The Collected Letters of Dylan Thomas*, ed. by P. Ferris, London: Dent.

Whitfield, S. (1992) *Magritte*, London: South Bank Centre.

Woolf, V. (1966) *Collected Essays*, vol.2, London: Hogarth Press.

Further reading

Bozorth, R.R. (2001) *Auden's Games of Knowledge: Poetry and the Meanings of Homosexuality*, New York: Columbia University Press. A useful study that reads Auden's poetry in terms of his homosexuality.

Brown, R.D. (2002) ' "Your Thoughts Make Shape like Snow": Louis MacNeice on Stephen Spender', *Twentieth-Century Literature*, 48.3, pp.292–323. An exploration of MacNeice's reading of Spender, including close readings of 'Poem' and 'After they have tired of the brilliance of cities'.

MacNeice, L. (1965) *The Strings Are False: An Unfinished Autobiography*, London: Faber & Faber. An invaluable, very readable first-hand account of the literary scene during the 1930s.

Mendelson, E. (1981) *Early Auden*, London: Faber & Faber. A full-scale study of Auden's work in the 1930s.

O'Neill, M. and Reeves, G. (1992) *Auden, MacNeice, Spender: The Thirties Poetry*, Basingstoke: Macmillan. Close readings of the major works of the 1930s.

PART 2

Contending modernisms

Introduction to Part 2

SUMAN GUPTA

Approaching modernism/modernisms

In Part 2, you will study the work of four writers who can be regarded as modernist. Before doing so, however, it will be helpful to explore what is understood by the term 'modernism'. It is tempting to look for a broad definition, or at least a list of characteristics, especially when faced with such phrases as 'twentieth-century modernism', 'literary modernism', 'the modern age', 'the modern tradition', 'the modern temper', and so on. Some critics have tried to help by attempting to clarify (in a definitive spirit) some of the word's connotations or associations. Malcolm Bradbury and James McFarlane, for example, outline two linked sets of associations. The first set focuses on form:

> One of [modernism's] associations is with the coming of a new era of high aesthetic self-consciousness and non-representationalism, in which art turns from realism and humanistic representation towards style, technique, and spatial form in pursuit of a deeper penetration of life ... Indeed Modernism would seem to be the point at which the idea of the radical and innovating arts, the experimental, technical, aesthetic ideal that had been growing forward from Romanticism, reaches formal crisis – in which myth, structure and organization in a traditional sense collapse, and not only for formal reasons.
>
> (Bradbury and McFarlane, [1976] 1991, pp.25, 26)

The second set emphasizes context and themes:

> Modernism is our art [because] it is the one art that responds to the scenario of our chaos. It is the art consequent on Heisenberg's 'Uncertainty principle', of the destruction of civilization and reason in the First World War, of the world changed and reinterpreted by Marx, Freud and Darwin, of capitalism and constant industrial acceleration, of existential exposure to meaninglessness or absurdity. It is the literature of technology. It is the art consequent on the dis-establishing of communal reality and conventional notions of causality, on the destruction of traditional notions of the wholeness of individual character, on the linguistic chaos that ensues when public notions of language have been discredited and when all realities have become subjective fictions. Modernism is then the art of modernization.
>
> (Bradbury and McFarlane, 1991, p.27)

Conventionally, such characterizations of modernism are thought of as primarily relevant to the early twentieth century. Virginia Woolf dated the modern period with provocative precision as beginning with the Post-Impressionist Exhibition in London in 1910 (1966, p.321), and as late as 1977 we find Peter Faulkner's *Modernism* locating the 'era of modernism' squarely in two decades (1910–30). Others tend to stretch this to the Second World War, or simply allude approximately to the first half of the century.

Most recent introductions to modernism, however, refuse such definitive or schematic approaches, and maintain that any attempt to say something general about the term is to miss the point. Indeed, it is often averred that the very idea of a single modernist movement or tradition or period is mistaken, and that it is more accurate to speak of many different, and often contradictory, modernisms in a range of different contexts. As Peter Childs says, 'It is now ... perhaps both impossible and undesirable to speak of a single "Modernism", and the practice of referring to "Modernisms" dates back to the 1960s' (2000, p.12). Instead of dwelling on the definitive and the schematic, therefore, the rest of this Introduction attempts to sketch briefly a complex picture of modernism – still sticking with the singular, but only to lead up to an explanation of why the plural form, modernisms, is more apt. To do this it is necessary, first, to step further back than the period that is conventionally associated with modernism.

Up to the twentieth century

In the exploration of modernism in this book, the focus on twentieth-century literary studies provides us with a chronological starting point and a predetermined field of study. But this limited focus is not altogether satisfactory because twentieth-century literary figures who can be regarded as modernist were far from indifferent to modernist aspirations that preceded them, and they seldom confined their attention to literature alone. The period from the sixteenth to the twentieth century – which might be viewed as a long run-up to modernism – is full of people who strove self-consciously to change the world, materially or conceptually, roughly along the lines described by Bradbury and McFarlane (1991) and certainly with as far-reaching effects. In the nineteenth century, Europe in particular was thick with self-professed modernizers (who set about doing so) and modernists (who felt they were particularly in tune with such changes). And they in turn often seemed to echo intellectual ancestors such as the French philosopher René Descartes and the Italian polymath Giambattista Vico, who had before them erected all-encompassing systems of ideas after deliberately dispensing with older ones.

Society/politics

Friedrich Schlegel's announcement in 1800 that an idealist 'new mythology' was on its way, which would initiate a 'great revolution' that would 'seize all the arts and sciences' (Ellmann and Fiedelson, 1965, p.660), is merely one of many such pronouncements. In his lectures on the philosophy of history (presented in 1830–1), G.W.F. Hegel portrayed the Germany of what he referred to as 'the Modern Times' as a pinnacle of historical development. Within a couple of decades, Karl Marx, picking up where post-French Revolution utopian socialists (e.g. Charles Fourier, Claude St Simon) had left off, and with Hegel and his disciples still in sight, started an extraordinarily influential contribution to the effervescence of political ideas and activity that aimed to (in Marx's words) 'change the world'. From Marx's work there arose in the course of the nineteenth century at least two distinct ideas about how political transformation might come about: by revolution leading to an equal and just (egalitarian) society with common ownership of property, to be brought about by the proletariat (revolutionary socialism or communism); or by an incremental transformation to similar ends through legislative and democratic processes (democratic socialism). In the nineteenth century, however, these ideas competed for attention with a range of radical anarchist, nihilist and libertarian modernizing programmes.

These political debates arose in the context of changes in the capacity for mass industrial production and the consequent changes in financial and political organization that were materially changing human lives – for the better (particularly for industrialists, traders and bankers) and for the worse (for industrial workers). Those changes, in turn, fed into the social and political changes occurring in the course of the nineteenth century as the result of the consolidation and expansion of imperial domination outside Europe (across most of the globe), the administration of vastly different cultures and the growing evidence of anti-colonial stirrings. The division of Africa between European powers in the last three decades of the nineteenth century, the massive growth of an industry of knowledge that classified (archaeologically, physiognomically, anthropologically, philologically, etc.) 'Oriental' cultures and peoples, the sense of a shrinking world consequent on the movement of peoples and commodities across continents, and the shock of anti-colonial strife, from the Great Mutiny of 1857 in India to the Boer wars in South Africa (1880–1, 1899–1902) – all were seen as part of a modern phase of universal human history. Also in the nineteenth century, the political and social position of women in Europe was renegotiated – at least to the extent, for instance, of bringing the claims of the suffragettes in Britain closer to the only possible just outcome (women were allowed voting rights only in 1918, and these rights were not extended to all women).

Science

Scientific ideas come into the picture too, with perceivably transformative effects. The concept of time and space, and the place of human beings in the cosmos – and indeed the shape of the cosmos itself (all previously derived from classical Greek and Judaeo-Christian world views) – had been in the throes of change since the sixteenth century. However, change appeared to accelerate in the course of the nineteenth century, when a plethora of scientific explorations and discoveries seemed to announce a new age, and present a profound challenge to older, often theologically guided, ways of understanding the world. Some examples of these are: Charles Darwin's contribution to evolutionary theory (the convincing bringing together of extant ideas on organic mutation and the survival of the fittest) and the teasing out of its social and moral implications (by T.H. Huxley among others); the harnessing of steam and then electrical power on an industrial scale; formulations in mathematics that paved the way for the development of both macrocosmic (in particular the work of Albert Einstein) and microcosmic (atomic) physics in the early twentieth century; explorations of geology and earth science, which resulted in new understandings of the concept of time; delvings (often misguided) into human psychology by Richard Krafft-Ebbing, Havelock Ellis and others, which set the stage for the explosive impact of Sigmund Freud's ideas in the early twentieth century.

Literature

The cross-fertilization of explorations, ideas, activities and experiences across a wide range of fields in the nineteenth century also manifested itself in literature and the arts. As far as literary studies go (and this is true of any field that one may choose to focus on in this fashion), the range of influences and susceptibilities with a modernist turn are so wide and so varied that a comprehensive listing of them would be a voluminous affair. One way of approaching the topic is by way of the numerous self-conscious discussions about the function of literature that were current in the nineteenth century: these formed part of a many-pronged debate about the aesthetic function and the instrumentalist agenda of literature, undertaken with different nuances in different contexts. The manner in which this debate has been continued in some early twentieth-century texts was the connecting theme of Part 1.

As you have already seen, for some, literature was primarily about aesthetic expression without social/ethical/political responsibility – an approach often referred to as 'art for art's sake'. A cultivated aestheticism which (sometimes inconsistently) eschewed moral or political motives was also expressed in the critical writings of Oscar Wilde and Walter Pater. The French Symbolist poets (who are briefly discussed in Chapter 5) also (sometimes) systematically resisted an instrumental agenda for literature while at the same time exhibiting what was perceived as a kinship with the new sensibility of their times, and expressing their scepticism about traditional formal conventions.

The notion that literature should reflect and even intervene in modern social and political concerns is the substance of much nineteenth-century fiction. The vast canvases of society often presented in Victorian novels (by the Brontës, Charles Dickens, George Eliot, William Makepeace Thackeray, Thomas Hardy and others) had worked into them such ambitions, as did (more emphatically) the Norwegian plays of Henrik Ibsen. But possibly the most energetic aspirations to reflect and intervene in contemporary social and political realities arose in nineteenth-century Russia, against a background of Tsarist authoritarianism and repressive censorship. Such ideas resulted in the extraordinary novels of Fyodor Dostoevsky and Leo Tolstoy among others, and also in a strain of criticism that sought to understand literature in this context. Anton Chekhov's work, which you looked at in Part 1, came towards the end of such Russian debates and was deliberately awkwardly located in relation to them. It therefore provides a good starting point to begin thinking about the purpose of literature.

None of the writers cited here as espousing primarily aestheticist principles were indifferent to social and political realities, nor were those who adopted primarily instrumentalist agendas indifferent to aesthetic criteria. However, I think it is fair to say that, in their work, some writers made more of a conceptual investment in finding a balance between aesthetic and instrumentalist principles. The French Realists (particularly Gustave Flaubert) and Naturalists (particularly Émile Zola) were self-conscious modernizers and modernists, wielding their pens to give social realist and political ideas a particular formal coherence (ultimately with some notion of effacing the author from the text). In different ways, such syntheses were also sought at the beginning of the nineteenth century by the English Romantic poets, who aspired to write poetry either in the language of the 'common man' (at least William Wordsworth did) or with semi-mystical revolutionary zeal (Percy Bysshe Shelley mainly). Later in that century they could be seen in the moral–social and aesthetic prerogatives that bring together (uneasily) Matthew Arnold the poet and Matthew Arnold the critic.

Visual arts

To this rather breathless summary of (European) modernism in the nineteenth century should also be added movements in painting: notably, Impressionism (e.g. Paul Cézanne, Claude Monet, Édouard Manet) and Neo-Impressionism (e.g. Georges Seurat, Camille Pissarro, Paul Signac), the techniques of which were inspired to a significant degree by developments in optics and chemistry; and leading to the vivid psychic landscapes of Post-Impressionism (the wriggling worms that make up Vincent van Gogh's paintings, the exotic remoteness of Paul Gauguin's work). To come was a plethora of twentieth-century art movements, including Expressionism (Max Beckmann, Otto Dix, George Grosz), Vorticism (Wyndham Lewis), Futurism (Emilio Marinetti, Giacomo Balla), Cubism and Post-Cubism (Pablo Picasso, Georges Braque), Dada (Marcel Duchamp) and Surrealism (Salvador Dalí, Max Ernst).

Music

Developments in the visual arts rippled into music. Musical impressionism was tried out (Claude Debussy is the best-known exponent), in contrast to but influenced by the Romantic and indubitably grand reformulation of the operatic form by Richard Wagner. Wagner's patron, Franz Liszt, had used all twelve notes of the chromatic scale for the first time in 1854, in the first movement of his Faust Symphony. This development in compositional technique anticipated the compositions of Arnold Schoenberg in the twentieth century. These works, in which free chromaticism and atonality were harnessed by a twelve-note method of composition (a method perpetuated by his students Anton Webern and Alban Berg), were immensely influential, and widely regarded as revolutionary.

Into the twentieth century

The previous section's rather dense listing of self-consciously modern and transformative ideas, movements, efforts and their progenitors is meant to convey not a systematic picture but something of the complexity and sheer pace, scope and excitement of nineteenth-century modernism. If you find yourself a little disoriented as a result of that heady brew of names and references, you are probably getting a flavour of what many writers and thinkers felt at the beginning of the twentieth century.

Although the beginning of the twentieth century does not really mark a significant break in the fizzing and smoking of modernist change and making anew, it does appear to mark a pause – a moment of retrospection and stock-taking. To some extent the timing is of purely arbitrary significance, linked to the numerical quirks of the Gregorian calendar. Just as the recent beginning of the new millennium seemed imbued with symbolic significance, the change from the nineteenth to the twentieth century was also perceived as a neat symbolic ending and beginning.

In Britain and elsewhere, the first decade of the twentieth century was approached with both a sense of great changes having taken place, and some impatience at what was perceived as a post-*fin de siècle* slowing down. Virginia Woolf saw a great change occurring (admittedly over-schematically) 'On or about December 1910'. At this point 'All human relations shifted – those between masters and servants, husbands and wives, parents and children.

And when human relations change there is at the same time a change in religion, conduct, politics, and literature. Let us agree to place one of those changes about the year 1910' (1966, p.321). Woolf's one change was in literary production (let us call it the moment of twentieth-century literary modernism), for it seemed to her that there had been a dry period in literature between the late nineteenth century and 1910. In Britain, the late Victorian and Edwardian poets and novelists (e.g. Thomas Hardy, A.E. Housman, John Galsworthy, Arnold Bennett) seemed to be presenting a rather narrow British view of life and following stylistic conventions with which modernizers felt impatient. Ezra Pound, Wyndham Lewis, James Joyce, T.S. Eliot – all destined to become key figures of literary modernism – were seething with dissatisfaction, impatient to bring about change, to *modernize* literature in the English language.

And not just literature: in his poem 'September 1913' W.B. Yeats complained that, after the fall from grace of the charismatic Irish politician Charles Parnell (as a result of an adulterous affair), Ireland seemed to have gone into a political stupor. Other European colonies, after occasional bursts in the nineteenth century of nationalist and anti-colonial violence, were quietly simmering with dissatisfactions. In Russia, a period of hectic political dissidence which culminated in the assassination of Tsar Alexander II led to the uneasy and dissatisfied tranquillity which was so effectively depicted by Chekhov. V.I. Lenin was in exile for most of the first decade of the twentieth century, waiting to seize his moment. All Europe seemed to be caught in a momentary quietness that could not last.

This lull before the storm was followed by the First World War (1914–18), the Easter Rising in Ireland (1916), the Russian Revolution and formation of the Soviet Union (1918), the rise of fascism and the sharp polarization of politics between fascism and socialism which culminated in the Spanish Civil War (1936–9), the pursuit of a non-violent independence movement in India under the leadership of Mahatma Gandhi (marked by sporadic violent colonial repression), growing anti-colonial passions in a range of African and Caribbean countries (marked by ethnic rivalries), Stalinist purges (1934–8), the Second World War (1939–45) and Hitler's final solution, the 'liberation' of China under Mao Zedong after savage anti-Japanese and civil wars, the cold war thereafter and a spate of anti-colonial struggles and decolonizations (this is just a very small and select list). As you saw in Chapter 4, the poet W.H. Auden was bitter about the 'low dishonest decade' (in Skelton, [1964] 2000, p.280) that was the 1930s – all the changes and transformations that had accrued through the nineteenth century had burst into brutal bloodletting all over the world and more was to come in the remainder of the twentieth century.

Modernisms

The bid made by artists and writers to keep up with these changes, together with an awareness of the intellectual, political and social changes that had occurred in the preceding century, characterizes twentieth-century modernism. In a world that was (and continues to be) fiercely divided, such modernist expressions could not have developed uniform methods and directions. It is true that modernists in the twentieth century often aspired to an all-embracing characterization in the tradition of modernists from preceding centuries, and thought/wrote/painted and so on, with ambitions to apprehend the world in a singular fashion or transform it through the persuasiveness of a universal ideology. But there were numerous such aspiring ideologies and numerous such equally ambitious attempts at apprehension. In the latter part of the twentieth century, the feeling (and expressions thereof) that such holistic aspirations are destined to fail, and that multiple and even contradictory perspectives should be allowed to co-exist, is often dubbed 'postmodernism'. However, postmodernism is far from sounding the death-knell of the holistic ambitions of modernism, and even self-styled postmodernists may have ideological proclivities and convictions that are as holistic in application.

In literary terms, then, several contending – often sharply polarized – forms of modernism emerged, varying according to political/social/cultural location, ideological conviction and unresolved debates about the function of literature. These included the emphatically aestheticist and the determinedly instrumental, the apparently ideologically neutral and the overly ideologically determined, the religious fundamentalist and the fascist and the communist, the individualist and the collectivist, black and white, the patriarchal and the feminist, and so on – with numerous shades in between. It is easy to see why the singular term 'modernism' is no longer equal to so complex a picture; what we have (and, with hindsight, have always had) are numerous differently located and oriented modernisms.

The content of Part 2

In Part 2, you are invited to examine some of these contending modernisms by focusing on four texts.

In Chapter 5 you are taken back to the early twentieth century again (having already steamed forward in Part 1 to the 1930s), to examine the *Prufrock* poems of T.S. Eliot. Eliot is a key figure of what may be regarded as a 'mainstream' literary modernism – mainstream partly because those associated with it thought of themselves so defiantly and persistently as modernizers, and partly because of the institutional sanction they received and the influence they came to exercise.

The focus in Chapter 6 is on Virginia Woolf's *Orlando*. In this novel, Woolf blends a view of historical development with ambiguities of gender construction and determination, to present another perspective on modernism. This is informed by both her close association with the 'mainstream' modernists and her keen awareness and analysis of the position of women in her time.

Chapter 7 focuses on the work of Bertolt Brecht, through his play *Life of Galileo*. Unlike Eliot and Woolf (but like some of the poets and novelists of the 1930s that you have looked at already), Brecht was explicitly sympathetic to a Marxist ideology and enormously influential as such. As this chapter demonstrates, however, it is as much Brecht's formal innovations in the theatre as his engagement with on-going social and political happenings that give him a distinctive modernist position.

The final chapter of Part 2 discusses some of the remarkable poetry of the Nigerian author Christopher Okigbo, who brings together African mythology and social mores with a profound understanding of European tradition and modernity, to present a distinctive expression of postcolonial modernism.

Works cited

Bradbury, M. and McFarlane, J. (eds) ([1976] 1991) *Modernism: 1890–1930*, Harmondsworth: Penguin.

Childs, P. (2000) *Modernism*, New Critical Idiom, London: Routledge.

Ellmann, R. and Fiedelson, C. (eds) (1965) *The Modern Tradition*, New York: Oxford University Press.

Faulkner, P. (1977) *Modernism*, Critical Idiom, London: Methuen.

Skelton, R. (ed.) ([1964] 2000) *Poetry of the Thirties*, Penguin Classics, London: Penguin.

Woolf, V. (1966) *Collected Essays*, vol.1, London: Hogarth Press.

CHAPTER 5

T.S. Eliot, *Prufrock and Other Observations*

SUMAN GUPTA

Overview

This chapter begins with a reading of T.S. Eliot's 'The Love Song of J. Alfred Prufrock', in which I bring out certain characteristic features of the poems of *Prufrock and Other Observations* (1917). There follows an attempt to provide some of the material for a studied understanding of the *Prufrock* poems – primarily by focusing first on the effect of cultural dislocations and relocations on Eliot's poetry, second on the influence of the ideas of the philosopher Henri Bergson on these poems, and third on the impact of the work of the French Symbolist poet Jules Laforgue. I should say here that many critics would consider my focus on Bergson and Laforgue too selective; arguably, other poets (Dante, John Donne, Charles Baudelaire, for example) and other philosophers (F.H. Bradley is an obvious example, since, while Eliot was at Oxford, he wrote an unfinished dissertation on him) could have been discussed here as usefully. However, no particular selection is likely to be exhaustive, and a focus on Laforgue and Bergson is fruitful and has at least the merit of demonstrating how such influences may have worked on other poets and thinkers too. Bearing in mind the above-mentioned contexts, I return briefly to 'The Love Song' to reconsider the role of the allusions in the poem (and indeed in Eliot's poetry generally). In the final section, I look forward to the manner in which Eliot's poetry and reputation developed thereafter in concert with what is now understood as a mainstream literary modernist movement, and raise some debatable (and much debated) questions about the latter.

The main poems discussed in this chapter are: 'The Love Song of J. Alfred Prufrock', 'Portrait of a Lady', 'Rhapsody on a Windy Night', 'The Boston Evening Transcript' and 'Conversation Galante'. **Please make sure you have read all of these at least once before proceeding.**

The poet persona of 'The Love Song of J. Alfred Prufrock'

The poems of *Prufrock and Other Observations*, written between 1909 and 1914 but first published in 1917, stand not only at the threshold of Eliot's own career, but also at that of what is often regarded as mainstream literary modernism itself. Very few works in the English language can claim quite the same position (James Joyce's *Portrait of the Artist as a Young Man*, 1914–15, or possibly Ezra Pound's *Homage to Sextus Propertius*, 1919, or *Hugh Selwyn Mauberley*, 1920, come to mind). Pound, self-appointed mentor of and agent for Eliot in the early phase of his career, and grand impresario of a range of self-consciously modernist literary ventures, recognized in the *Prufrock* poems the birth of a distinctively modern and original poetic voice. They carried a flavour of new ideas from across the Channel; they were presented in a form that at the time was fresh and invigorating; they were erudite and unafraid to display an awareness of European (rather than just British) literary culture and tradition; yet they were squarely placed in a contemporary world that was urbane, cosmopolitan, and in the throes of ideological and intellectual uncertainties and transformations. Both formally and thematically they were quite different from late Victorian and Edwardian verse, such as that of Thomas Hardy or A.E. Housman, which seemed rather stiff and provincial by comparison. The popular poets of the first decade of the twentieth century who wrote in English depended largely on conservative verse forms and a more or less familiar poetic idiom, and addressed situations and sentiments that were embedded within narrower locations and literary traditions. This does not necessarily mean that their work was less complex or insightful, but it was the *perception* of a quaint and narrow stuffiness in contrast to the vigour and cosmopolitan character of modernist poetry such as Eliot's that made the difference.

However, more than any of the above-mentioned qualities it was the poetic consciousness manifest in the *Prufrock* poems, presented with immense self-awareness and deliberation, that gave them their distinctive modernist turn. Most of these poems appear to issue from a poet persona (the voice behind the verse) that unifies the thematic and formal qualities. This poet persona should not be identified with the biographical Eliot; it is *constructed* in the poems and emerges from them. The relationship between this poet persona and Eliot the person is matter for speculation based on biographical information. That is not the focus of this chapter. What concerns us here is the degree to which this poet persona, and the poems, are products of a particular intellectual context and of debates therein, and the degree to which the poet persona – especially as it developed through Eliot's later work – comes to embody mainstream literary modernism. Ultimately, the focus of this chapter is on the relationship between these poetic texts and the ideas and debates in terms of which they can be contextualized.

The clearest way to convey what I mean by a distinctive poet persona is to discern it within one of the *Prufrock* poems. The first, longest and best-known of these, 'The Love Song of J. Alfred Prufrock', provides an excellent introduction to this poet persona. **Read 'The Love Song of J. Alfred Prufrock' (Eliot, [1917] 2001, pp.3–7; all references are to this edition). Try to characterize the person – the 'I' in the poem – in** whose voice it issues. **What sort of person is this? What are the peculiarities of the manner in which his thoughts are presented in the poem? What difficulties do you face in reading it? (Eliot's poems have a reputation for being difficult.)**

What follows is a particular reading of the poem in answer to these questions. You need not agree with this reading at all, but it may help you put your own reading into perspective.

The whole is a monologue, by the first-person poet persona – perhaps he is called J. Alfred Prufrock, but there is nothing apart from the title to indicate that. The title is not to be trusted, for this is not in any obvious way a love song. Nor, for that matter, can we be entirely sure of the consistency of the poet persona, because it seems that he divides himself at the beginning into 'you and I' – both addressor and addressee of the monologue. It is, of course, possible that the 'you' is someone else: a lover would be the obvious inference given the title, or perhaps the reader, but then, just as the poem turns out not to be a love song, the 'you' turns out to be of little importance after the first stanza (except perhaps in the 'we' of the last three lines). Indeed, after the end of the first stanza, where 'you' are led to 'an overwhelming question', the only person concerned with 'overwhelming questions' (without any encouragement from the fashionable set among which he moves) is 'I' or the poet persona. Arguably then, 'you' merges into 'I', two aspects of the same poet persona, an initial and somewhat misleading schism to introduce the traits of hesitation and uncertainty that characterize the poet persona.

The perspective of the poet persona is thus introduced, and, at the same time (by the end of p.3), so is that of the urban environment. It is the modern city, unromantic, dirty, cheap, dull, but transformed by the poet persona who beholds it; not transformed in the sense of changing anything materially, but in giving even this unlovely subject matter an aesthetically pleasing expressive turn. From the supine image of 'the sky / Like a patient etherised upon a table' (p.3) to that of the playfully feline fog, unpromising fragmented images of a modern city are paradoxically united into poetry. The poetry brings together the poet persona and his environment into a continuum that encapsulates both within the dull repetitiveness of passing time (and the charm of the chanting 'There will be time, there will be time ...', or broadly the unfolding poem itself). With these in place the scene is set to expose both the poet persona and his environment to a harsh and interrogative, but not unsympathetic, light.

The poet persona is characterized by certain preoccupations. These preoccupations may be regarded as the emanations of his mind or the products of his environment, it is impossible to distinguish. These are outlined below.

World-weariness and a sense of the triviality of things around him. This comes across when he worries about the inconsequentiality of 'decisions and revisions which a minute will reverse' (p.4); when he ironically poses the anxiety of an ageing man about the bald patch in his hair against the enormity of the universe (*ibid.*); when he stresses repeatedly the banality of the tea ritual: 'Before the taking of a toast and tea' (*ibid.*); 'after tea and cakes and ices' (p.5); 'After the cups, the marmalade, the tea' (p.6); when he repeats his sense of 'having known them all already' (pp.4 and 5); when the sharp sense of his disgust at the 'butt-ends of my days and ways' (p.5) is expressed, and the despair of having 'measured out my life with coffee spoons' (p.4).

And yet, a certain absorption in trivial pursuits. The poet persona may know that these little 'decisions and revisions' are ultimately inconsequential and trivial, but he cannot escape them either. Whether he likes it or not, he does worry about the bald patch (and what 'they' will say about his appearance; p.5), and whether he would be understood by those who listen to him ('That is not what I meant at all. / That is not it, at all'; p.6), and whether he does not appear, 'At times, indeed, almost ridiculous – / Almost, at times, the Fool' (p.7), and whether ultimately, 'Shall I part my hair behind? Do I dare to eat a peach?' (*ibid.*). He cares very much about how he appears to other people and how other people look at him; he is intensely aware of 'The eyes that fix you in a formulated phrase' (p.4).

Nevertheless, he looks for, wishfully and yet hopelessly, something more than the trivialities that he abhors and yet cannot disregard – something inexpressibly all-comprehending and profound. Always at the horizon there lingers the 'overwhelming question' of the first stanza (p.3), the awareness of the greatness of the universe ('Do I dare / Disturb the universe?'; p.4), but he never quite comes to grips with it. So, he stops short of greatness and admits his fear of 'the eternal Footman' (p.5) – a personification of death; if he were to be misunderstood by the trivial people he despises and knows so well, he doubts whether it would

> have been worth while,
> To have bitten off the matter with a smile,
> To have squeezed the universe into a ball
> To roll it towards some overwhelming question,
> To say: 'I am Lazarus, come from the dead,
> Come back to tell you all, I shall tell you all'
>
> (p.6)

Finally, he gives up, with an exclamation and an image of nervous exhaustion: 'It is impossible to say just what I mean! / But as if a magic lantern threw the nerves in patterns on a screen' (p.6). Interestingly, in a 1955 recording of Eliot reading the poem, we find those last-quoted lines to be one of the few times when Eliot departs from a bored but well-modulated monotone to express a tiny throb of passion. Not surprisingly, whatever fantasy of hearing mermaids sing, of seeing mermaids (idyllic, otherworldly, beautiful), is entertained by the poet persona, it is finally drowned out by 'human voices' (p.7).

At the bottom of these somewhat contradictory perceptions and desires lies a certain self-obsession. Obviously, the whole monologue that is 'The Love Song' is the poet persona talking about himself, trying to understand himself. The self is the guiding motif. What do people see when they look at me? How should I behave? What pose should I assume? Should I allow myself to be swayed by trivialities? Should I try to express something extraordinary? Am I being formulated by trivial people? Am I not superior to them? The monologue represents the poet persona's response to such implicit questions. What makes the poet persona of 'The Love Song' interesting, though, is that he rises above any simple egotism or self-obsession towards presenting himself as a type – the representation of a modernist condition (environment/consciousness) – rather than a unique personality. When he pauses after the first burst of the monologue (after the break on p.5) and asks, meditatively:

> Shall I say, I have gone at dusk through narrow streets
> And watched the smoke that rises from the pipes
> Of lonely men in shirt-sleeves, leaning out of windows?

(p.5)

we might feel that those smoking 'lonely men in shirt-sleeves' could each be regarded as reflections of the poet persona, each with their own monologues, not unlike this one. When he evokes the most archetypal of literary figures to define himself *against* – 'No! I am not Prince Hamlet, nor was meant to be; / Am an attendant lord' (p.6) – he is moulding himself into an archetypal personality too, an anti-hero of sorts, like the Fool (a stock character in several Shakespeare plays, who is generally more wise than foolish, more often profound than ridiculous). The poet persona conflates the Fool here with the 'politic, cautious and meticulous' attendant lord, Polonius, in *Hamlet*, the anti-hero who is rather carelessly killed by the eponymous hero. In the modern environment/consciousness the Fool becomes a sort of Hamlet, it is suggested: 'No! I am not Prince Hamlet' has the air of being an emphatic denial to a question ('You are Prince Hamlet, aren't you?').

And along with the self-obsession, a tendency to blame women for everything. There are hints of this from the beginning of the poem; there is a streak of misogyny in most of the *Prufrock* poems. Between images of urban banality and boredom at the beginning of the poem appears that refrain: 'In the room the women come and go / Talking of Michelangelo' (pp.3 and 4), as some sort of culmination of tedium and triviality. What is the reader to infer from this: that Michelangelo is beyond discussion – particularly by women? perhaps even only by women? The answer to the 'overwhelming question' seems to be that women trivialize all attempts at being profound (such as Michelangelo's). The poet persona's attempts at making some earth-shattering statement are constantly thwarted by, it seems, women:

> Is it perfume from a dress
> That makes me so digress?
> Arms that lie along a table, or wrap about a shawl.
>   And should I then presume?
>   And how should I begin?

(p.5)

Soon after, momentarily, he sees himself as a sort of John the Baptist, at the crucial moment when his undoing by Salome is complete (Mark 6:17–29; Matthew 14:3–11): 'Though I have seen my head (grown slightly bald) brought in upon a platter, / I am no prophet – and here's no great matter'. No less than twice on one page the poet persona's grand ambitions are deflated by the scepticism or incomprehension of women:

> Would it have been worth while
> If one, settling a pillow or throwing off a shawl,
> And turning toward the window, should say:
>   'That is not it at all,
>   That is not what I meant, at all.'

(p.6)

The idea of women trivializing/thwarting the great pursuits of men reappears in other *Prufrock* poems that are discussed below, such as 'Conversation Galante', 'The Boston Evening Transcript' and 'Portrait of a Lady'. The tendency is clear: what you make of it is up to you. You might choose to see this misogynistic streak as simply a characteristic of the poet persona, a part of the deliberate and ironic construction of the self that lies at the centre of the whole *Prufrock* collection. You might see it as evidence of a deep gender prejudice in Eliot himself, a possibility that has received extensive critical attention. Or you might regard it as a prejudice at the heart of the self-consciously modernist enterprise of which Eliot was part (that environment/consciousness he was trying to express) – one that women writers associated with literary modernity (Gertrude Stein, Virginia Woolf, Katherine Mansfield, Djuna Barnes) would have to deal with and interrogate. (It should be noted here that Eliot had extended a most cordial invitation to Stein to contribute to *The Criterion*, a journal of which he was editor, which she accepted; that he enjoyed a warm friendship with Woolf particularly and also with Mansfield; and that he was Barnes's publisher, and admired her writing.)

This is a reading (one of many possible readings) of 'The Love Song' as a synthesis of a particular sort of poet persona and a particular apprehension of a modern environment that launched a modernist sensibility in English poetry. **Does my characterization agree with your own sense of the first-person persona?** In presenting this reading I have glossed over some of the obvious difficulties that a first-time reader of Eliot's poetry is likely to encounter. When I read *Prufrock* for the first time I was struck by two stylistic features that seemed to me to need unravelling: the fragmentary effect of the poem (more precisely, the somewhat disjunctive fashion in which the images of the poem and observations of the poet persona seem to come together, without following through an obvious chain of reasoning or a clear sequence of thoughts), and a subliminal awareness of allusions to other literary works (starting with the Italian epigram and continuing in obvious biblical and Shakespearean references, but also in the feeling that some lines and phrases had a familiar ring though I could not quite place them). These may raise certain readerly anxieties, as they did for me: have I missed out a coherent progression in the poem? Is there some sort of true understanding of the poem that has evaded me and that I should be looking for? Can I find it without being able to recognize all the allusions that are evidently in the poem? Am I sufficiently equipped to deal with this poem in a satisfactory manner? With hindsight I feel I can confidently assert that such anxieties were misplaced, despite being perfectly natural. Though I have tried to offer a particular interpretation, there is no single dominant or true reading (the structure of the poem defeats the idea of coherence); it is not necessary to identify and chart out the significance of all the obvious and not so obvious allusions (it is enough to register that they exist). A reasonably sound grasp of the poem and its intricacies is possible without those, and a more studied understanding involves no more than the exploration of some of the intellectual contexts that fed into the composition and reception of the *Prufrock* poems.

The passage from the USA to Europe

At this point, it is necessary to establish the sequence in which the *Prufrock* poems were written, and therefore the contextual influences that fed into them. The sequence in which, and the period over which, these poems were written is best given in Eliot's words – the following quotation is from a letter to Eudo C. Mason of 21 February 1936:

> *J. Alfred Prufrock* was written in 1911, but parts of it date from
> the preceding year. Most of it was written in the summer of 1911
> when I was in Munich. The text of 1917, which remains
> unchanged, does not differ from the original version in any way. I
> did at one time write a good bit more of it, but these additions I

destroyed without their ever being printed. It is by no means true that all of the other poems in the 1917 volume were written after *Prufrock*. *Conversation Galante*, for instance, was written in 1909, and all of the more important poems in the volume are earlier than *Prufrock*, except *La Figlia che Piange*, 1912, and two or three short pieces written in 1914 or '15.

(quoted in Ricks, 1996, p.xv)

Eliot kept a notebook in which most of the poems written between 1909 and 1917 were transcribed, including unpublished ones and an early draft of 'The Love Song of J. Alfred Prufrock' (with some sections that he had deleted from the final version). This notebook was entitled *Inventions of the March Hare*, and, in fact, Eliot did not destroy it but gave it to a friend and patron, John Quinn; the entire notebook was edited and published by Christopher Ricks in 1996. The earliest poems in this notebook are those written between November 1909 and early 1910, under the influence of French Symbolist poetry, especially that of Jules Laforgue. These included 'Conversation Galante' (1909), 'Prelude I' (1910), 'Prelude II' (1910) and 'Portrait of a Lady' (1910). In the summer of 1910, Eliot unexpectedly decided to spend a year in Paris, from where he returned to the USA in autumn 1911 via Munich (a brief stay there). In Paris he attended lectures given by the French philosopher Henri Bergson (Eliot might already have read or gleaned something of Bergson's *Matière et mémoire* (1896; trans. 1908 as *Matter and Memory*). Bergson's ideas also had an influence on the poems Eliot wrote in this period – 'Prelude III' (1910), 'Rhapsody on a Windy Night' (1911), 'The Love Song of J. Alfred Prufrock' (1911) and 'Prelude IV' (1911 or 1912). After returning to the USA Eliot enrolled as a graduate student in philosophy at Harvard University, and wrote very little poetry over the next couple of years – 'La Figlia Che Piange' (1912) and 'Mr. Apollinax' (1914) are from this time. Soon after, he left for Oxford to embark on a doctoral thesis on the English philosopher F.H. Bradley, which, however, he abandoned after moving to London in late 1914 and eventually settling there. It was at this time that the 'two or three short pieces written in 1914 or '15' came into being: 'The Boston Evening Transcript', 'Aunt Helen', 'Cousin Nancy'. In September 1914, he met Ezra Pound and showed him some of his poems. Pound was impressed by them and started trying to persuade various journals and publishers to take them on. It was at Pound's instance that two of them, 'Rhapsody on a Windy Night' and 'Preludes', appeared in the second and final issue of Wyndham Lewis's irreverent, experimental, avant-garde magazine *Blast* in 1915. Pound also managed to place poems in two other magazines: 'Portrait of a Lady' in *Others* (September 1915), edited by Alfred Kreymborg, and 'The Love Song' in *Poetry* (June 1915). *Prufrock and Other Observations* was finally published in 1917 by The Egoist Press.

The *Prufrock* poems, then, cover precisely the period of Eliot's migration from the USA to Europe (a physical migration via France to Britain, but more importantly an intellectual migration to Europe). Eliot was far from alone among US writers in undertaking this journey. Henry James was by then on his way to becoming a British subject, having settled in England; Gertrude Stein and Pound had also made the passage already; Ernest Hemingway, F. Scott Fitzgerald, Djuna Barnes, Robert McAlmon, Henry Miller, Anaïs Nin, Kay Boyle and others would soon be on their way. Eliot's migration appears to be symptomatic of a larger dissatisfaction among US writers at the turn of the century about their New World heritage, and a desire to belong to or draw upon a 'cultured' Europe. To a significant extent the shape of mainstream modernism in twentieth-century literature in English was moulded by the desires underlying such migration, and by such migrants (particularly Eliot). Eliot never quite overcame his sense of the limitations of US culture: scathing observations on US intellectuals and artists are scattered throughout his writings. And yet (a curious paradox) he did not fully leave the USA behind either. For Eliot, the European mind and European culture from the 1920s onwards (culminating in *Notes Toward a Definition of Culture*, 1949) was always understood in the context of the US environment; his Church of England religiosity in later life had been honed by his early experience of Unitarianism in Boston; and he was always eager for his writings to be made available in the USA.

Consideration of the sequence in which the *Prufrock* poems were written reveals an interesting pattern. Eliot's poetry in 1909–10, written as an undergraduate in the USA, consisted almost entirely of attempts at recreating in English certain French Symbolist techniques and themes. Presumably, it was this affinity with French literature that took him to Europe in 1910–11, where he managed to bring his early attempts to a finished state as self-contained products in the English language. With 'La Figlia Che Piange' the desire to emulate French Symbolists in English had been satiated. Thus far, it may be felt that Eliot was not writing *about* the USA, but actually expressing a kind of Europhile desire that was the product of his *being in* the USA. It was only after the summer of 1914 and in 1915, when he made the journey again to Europe (this time eventually to settle), that he looked back at what it was about the USA that disenchanted him, and actually wrote those 'two or three short pieces' that are squarely *about* the USA (at least as it appeared to him). In a curious way, therefore, it is possible to regard these chronologically later poems in *Prufrock* as expressing something of the feelings underlying the early burst of creativity between 1909 and 1912.

Arguably, the *Prufrock* poems can be placed in terms of an opposition or tension between the USA and Europe which some US and some European writers at the time (and for some time to come) pondered – indeed it became quite fashionable in certain circles to do so. The most influential example that Eliot would undoubtedly, like many others, have been interested in was Henry James's literary explorations on this theme. In fact, in 'Portrait of a Lady' Eliot pays a subtle homage to this precursor. The title alludes to James's novel of that name. In James's *Portrait of a Lady* (1880–1), a young American heiress makes the passage to Europe and finds herself torn between four men, two English – a fine passionate aristocrat and a charming invalid cousin – and two American – a super-sophisticated but ultimately shallow Europhile and an overbearing businessman. She finally chooses the American Europhile and is betrayed by him. Betrayal is also the theme of Eliot's poem, and arguably along similar lines. Consider the following quotation (p.11), which can be read as a play if I insert the name of the protagonists and some directions in italics at appropriate points:

Lady (speaking frankly, sentimentally, sincerely):

'But what have I, but what have I, my friend,
To give you, what can you receive from me?
Only the friendship and the sympathy
Of one about to reach her journey's end.

I shall sit here, serving tea to friends ...'

Poet persona (thinking guiltily, irately, defiantly – picking up his hat):

I take my hat: how can I make a cowardly amends
For what she has said to me?
You will see me any morning in the park
Reading the comics and the sporting page.
Particularly I remark
An English countess goes upon the stage.
A Greek was murdered at a Polish dance,
Another bank defaulter has confessed.
I keep my countenance,
I remain self-possessed

(Poet persona turns his back to the lady while she looks at him wistfully. A street-piano starts playing in the background, slightly off-tune and rather grating, one of those cloying melodies that linger irritatingly in the mind – summarizing fortuitously the impression this unfortunate lady has made.)

Except when a street-piano, mechanical and tired
Reiterates some worn-out common song
With the smell of hyacinths across the garden
Recalling things that other people have desired.

(Poet persona frowns thoughtfully as he walks away; lady hangs her head mournfully, resigned to her fate.)

Are these ideas right or wrong?

(End of Scene 2.)

In the 1955 recording of Eliot's reading of this poem he does the voices – the insinuating tones of the lady, the irate clipped accents of the poet persona, the whining quality of the street-piano – with pregnant pauses in between. The imposed dramatization here is more for entertainment than instruction, but it also serves to bring out the dramatic qualities that Eliot carefully moulded into his poetic form ('The Love Song' is a monologue, *The Waste Land* (1922) is famously a collection of voices juxtaposed against each other, and later in life Eliot wrote more drama in verse than poetry). And it draws our attention again to that important character who made an appearance in 'The Love Song': the poet persona. **Read in this (somewhat theatrical) fashion, does this stanza show evidence of a tension between the USA and Europe along the lines outlined above?**

Your answer to that question depends on how you interpret the stanza. On the one hand, you may feel that there is no evidence at all of a tension between the USA and Europe. Neither the poet persona nor the lady is clearly located in a specific geographical domain. The stanza is primarily (for instance) about the attitudes that different people strike (anywhere), the poses that they assume (anywhere), in certain circumstances: poses that hide and yet paradoxically reveal, often discordantly, different desires. The lady hides behind her 'serving tea to friends' and cannot give full vent to her longings; the poet persona hides behind his shallow self-possession and cannot either air his irritation or subdue his feelings of guilt. But in the midst of this farce – which I have exaggerated by putting in stage directions – there emerges the cruel reality of the lady's desire and the poet persona's indifference, which is compressed in the vivid image of the cloying street-piano tune. Indeed, the revelation and simultaneous repression of this cruel reality is expressed with increasing force through a series of images about the inability to express:

> And I must borrow every changing shape
> To find expression ... dance, dance
> Like a dancing bear,
> Cry like a parrot, chatter like an ape.
> Let us take the air, in a tobacco trance –

> (p.12)

On the other hand, with the James connection in mind, you may feel that there is indeed a USA–Europe tension to be discerned here. James's *Portrait of a Lady*, like some of his other novels, presents subtly constructed stereotypes: the straightforward and sincere and frank (and behind their matter-of-fact exteriors, sentimental) Americans, the splendidly urbane or naive but always refined (and ever so slightly remote) Europeans, and the cold and devious and self-conscious and yet insubstantial American Europhile characters (who are torn between two cultures, and fit neatly in neither). If we are aware of the Jamesian stereotypes while reading Eliot's poem, if they are brought to our minds by the Jamesian allusion in the title, then the USA–Europe tension seems unmistakable. The elderly lady serving tea is sincere, sentimental and frank, exactly as a Jamesian American would be. The poet persona is cold and devious and self-consciously insubstantial, much as Jamesian American Europhiles are. Note that the poet persona is self-conscious of his shallowness to the point of making shallowness itself seem pretty deep, a deliberate attitude: he knows that the image of a man reading the comics or the sports pages of a newspaper in a park is a recognizable type. Note also that when he comes to enumerate some of the details, they turn out to have nothing to do with either comics or sport. Instead, we are given a few snapshots of European stereotypes apparently going through an enormous continental melodrama (English countess on the stage, murdered Greek, Polish dance), given with all the deliberate knowingness and alienation of someone who is not European.

You may feel confirmed in your sense of the Jamesian echoes in Eliot's poem – the USA–Europe tensions – if I tell you that the lady of the poem is based on a real character in Harvard (one Madeleine), who did entertain students from the university (including Eliot and his friend Conrad Aiken, who later remembered her well) by serving them tea. It could all be plausibly set in the USA; the poet persona, whose perusal of the newspaper is so single-mindedly focused on what is happening in Europe, could be an in-between chap, reflecting on that condition of being between the USA and Europe. And then there is the epigram, taken from an exchange between Friar Barnardine (the first line) and Barabas (the rest) in Act 4, Scene 1, of Christopher Marlowe's *The Jew of Malta* (1588):

> *Thou hast committed –*
> *Fornication: but that was in another country,*
> *And besides, the wench is dead.*

(p.9)

This could be the poet persona at the moment of writing this poem on a betrayal in the past, hiding the guilt of that betrayal by reassuring himself that *it* had occurred in 'another country' – the USA. Apart from the Jamesian echoes, 'Portrait of a Lady' also has within it significant allusions to Laforgue's poetry, which gives the whole USA–Europe business a certain piquancy. I discuss the Laforguean touches later.

We can reconcile the two contrary ways in which the question above can be answered by recognizing that: (a) 'Portrait of a Lady' *may* have USA–Europe tensions worked into it, but (b) this is not done in an obvious fashion. The poem was written in 1910. At the time of writing it, Eliot was in the process of making the transition from the USA to Europe. Similar transitions were being undertaken and pondered by others, too, and had a significant effect on mainstream literary modernism, and ultimately on the twentieth century as a whole.

An Imagist connection

'The Boston Evening Transcript' (p.21) was written in 1914 or 1915, and has a sense of retrospection about the USA which suggests that Eliot felt he had made the passage to Europe and was drawing away from that moment of transition. The geographical domain is clear; it is unlikely that any significant quantity of *Boston Evening Transcript* readers can be found outside Boston. Since the geographical domain is clear, the counterpoints are easily understood. The *Boston Evening Transcript* readers, rooted most fixedly in their Boston environment (the reader may presume), are strikingly passive. They 'Sway in the wind like a field of ripe corn' – their passivity is not sterile, but satisfied, self-sufficient. The first three lines of the long stanza –

> When evening quickens faintly in the street,
> Wakening the appetites of life in some
> And to others bringing the *Boston Evening Transcript*,

> (p.21)

– make it clear that liveliness where that broadsheet is bought and sold is always muted (the evening 'quickens faintly' and 'appetites of life' are awakened only in 'some') and those who peruse it are excluded from even these muted possibilities (they are the 'others'). The final four lines place the poet persona ('I') as one of the 'some', who are oppressed (melancholy as one who bids farewell, weary) by the 'others' who surround him – *Boston Evening Transcript* readers, like Cousin Harriet. More interestingly, the counterpoint of the 'some' (lively) against the 'others' (dull), the poet persona against Cousin Harriet, is sharpened by the self-conscious craftedness of this poem: the US (Boston) environment is rendered through a deliberately (and avowedly) European poetic idiom. The beautifully concise opening image –

> The readers of the *Boston Evening Transcript*
> Sway in the wind like a field of ripe corn.

> (p.21)

– is given with a deliberation which is suggestive. It could be regarded as an attempt at doing what self-styled Imagists at the time were trying to do.

The poets most closely associated with Imagism were T.E. Hulme, Hilda Doolittle, Amy Lowell, J.G. Fletcher, F.S. Flint, D.H. Lawrence, Richard Aldington and that tireless champion of all things modern, Ezra Pound. Eliot could scarcely not have been aware of the Imagists when he wrote this poem in late 1914/15: Pound had already entered Eliot's life; *Poetry* for March 1913 had already carried Imagist statements of purpose (in the form of a brief essay by Flint entitled 'Imagisme', and another by Pound entitled 'A Few Don'ts by an Imagiste'); and the first Imagist anthology, *Des Imagistes* (March 1914), had already been published (three more were to follow by 1917). Pound's 'A Few Don'ts' usefully defined an image as follows:

> An 'Image' is that which presents an intellectual and emotional complex in an instant of time ...
>
> It is the presentation of such a 'complex' instantaneously which gives that sense of sudden liberation; that sense of freedom from time limits and space limits; that sense of sudden growth, which we experience in the presence of the greatest works of art.
>
> (in Jones, 1972, p.130)

Add to this the three points made by Flint in his essay and we have a sense of what the Imagists aspired to:

> 1 Direct treatment of the 'thing,' whether subjective or objective.
>
> 2 To use absolutely no word that did not contribute to the presentation.
>
> 3 As regarding rhythm: to compose in sequence of the musical phrase, not in sequence of a metronome.
>
> (in Jones, 1972, p.129)

The only further clarification of the Imagist agenda that I can suggest here is to recommend the contemplation of some complete Imagist poems with those statements in mind. The following are quoted entirely for your contemplative pleasure (I will not digress into discussing them): the first is by Pound and entitled 'In a Station of the Metro', the second – by Hulme – is entitled 'Above the Dock':

> The apparition of these faces in the crowd;
> Petals on a wet, black bough.
>
> (in Jones, 1972, p.95)

> Above the quiet dock in midnight,
> Tangled in the tall mast's corded height,
> Hangs the moon. What seemed so far away
> Is but a child's balloon, forgotten after play.
>
> (in Jones, 1972, p.48)

The first has something of the atmosphere of the city evoked by Eliot in 'The Love Song of J. Alfred Prufrock', as we have seen already. The parallel between the moon and a balloon in the second is something that Eliot uses too in 'Conversation Galante' – I discuss this later in the chapter.

By the time he wrote 'The Boston Evening Transcript', Eliot had recognized that the self-styled Imagists were doing something that he sympathized with. In his 1953 essay 'American Literature and the American Language' he said with some confidence that: 'The *point de repère* ['point of reference'] usually and conveniently taken as the starting-point of modern poetry is the group denominated 'imagists' in London about 1910' (in Eliot, 1965, p.58). **To what extent do these Imagist ideas apply to Eliot's 'The Boston Evening Transcript', and what bearing (if any) does Eliot's use of Imagist ideas have on his transition from the USA to Europe?**

The memorable opening image of 'The Boston Evening Transcript' (p.21) could legitimately be supposed to imitate something of Imagist directness and conciseness, and yet it does not actually fit in with Imagist ideas. For the Imagists, the clarity and the aptness of the image depend on the feeling (or object) to which the image is applied; the image and the feeling (or object) to which it is applied are expected to enhance each other. Eliot's image ('Sway in the wind …') and the object to which it is applied ('The readers of …') are not easily conjoined: there is a slight unease in their being brought together – the unease of those who, for instance, do not know much about Boston, or simply find it difficult to reconcile the image with any visualization of a group of people reading newspapers of any description. And yet the image is suggestive enough to do its work: it gives a sense (whether apt or not) of a particular view (the specific poet's) of an enclosed space (Boston – New England – the USA) from a distance (where such modes of expression are available). In the uneasiness of this image the unease of presenting things American through a European poetic idiom (Imagism) becomes almost opaque.

The European quality of the poetic idiom through which the US environment is presented is more laboriously brought out in the other striking image in this poem:

> I mount the steps and ring the bell, turning
> Wearily, as one would turn to nod good-bye to La Rochefoucauld,
> If the street were time and he at the end of the street,

(p.21)

The evocation of the French writer François La Rochefoucauld, best remembered for his *Réflexions ou sentences et maximes morales* ('Reflections or aphorisms and moral maxims') (1665), is carefully calculated. Turning away from La Rochefoucauld (and therefore towards Cousin Harriet, inveterate reader of the *Boston Evening Transcript*) is tantamount to turning away from a venerable European cultural milieu towards a dull American existence. The emphasis on the temporal distance ('if the street were time and he at the end of the street') actually leaves the unspoken geographical and perceived cultural distance foregrounded. But the image goes deeper: the image of the poet persona wearily nodding goodbye to La Rochefoucauld cannot help but take into account the particular associations of that name (and especially his renowned maxims). La Rochefoucauld's maxims are pithy, often obvious, not always consistent but invariably forthright statements of general moral observations, given with admirable concision. The moral credo behind them is less important than the art of presenting them; in their presentation moral attitudes are struck, often with a view to undercutting attitudinizing and hypocrisy rather than demonstrating a coherent ethical perspective. Wearily to nod goodbye to the author of these maxims is also to strike a self-conscious attitude (which is undercut by its self-consciousness), and is in addition a recognition of the nice balance between expression and conviction, which is beyond the ken of *Boston Evening Transcript* readers.

To summarize the main points of this section: *Prufrock and Other Observations* could be read as presenting a carefully charted transition from being located in a US environment and looking wistfully towards Europe (in which the negotiation between the two cultures is presented implicitly) to relocating in Europe and looking back at the USA (where the cultural negotiations are encountered more explicitly). This covers the period during which Eliot wrote the poems in this volume, from 1909/10 to 1914/15. This transition and the attendant cultural negotiations are, however, not presented simply as being between two polarized and opposed domains. They are complicated by the poetic voice of these poems – which issues from an almost painfully self-conscious poet persona, who undercuts all the poses that he assumes, and questions the very attitudes he professes even while declaring them. He is erudite, alludes to La Rochefoucauld or Henry James or Jules Laforgue in an offhand, matter-of-course fashion, and yet not without deliberation. His perceptions of the USA and Europe are naturally conditional on his poses and attitudes, which are laid bare in these poems.

Symbolism and the absolute: the influence of Jules Laforgue

> I remember getting hold of Laforgue years ago at Harvard, purely through reading Symons, and then sending to Paris for the texts. I puzzled it out as best I could, not finding half the words in my dictionary, and it was several years later before I came across anyone who had read him or could be persuaded to read him. I do feel more grateful to him than to anyone else, and I do not

think that I have come across any other writer since who meant so much to me as he did at that particular moment, or that particular year.

(Eliot to Robert Nichols, 8 August 1917; in Eliot, 1988, p.191)

This passage occurs in a letter responding to appreciative comments by Robert Nichols on *Prufrock and Other Observations*. Nichols was himself a poet, had – also in 1917 – published a volume of verse, *Ardours and Endurances*, and had in his letter no doubt commented on the influence of Laforgue on Eliot's poetry. Eliot's candid acknowledgement of the influence speaks for itself. Most of the *Prufrock* poems are variations on Laforguean themes: some are almost rewritings ('Conversation Galante'), in some there are telling echoes of Laforguean images ('Portrait of a Lady') and ideas (all the above, and particularly 'The Love Song of J. Alfred Prufrock'). For Eliot, the young Europhile American, Laforgue's French Symbolist poetry encapsulated a carefully constructed self-image, an aesthetic purity and a philosophical position, which were especially congenial to him and which he wished to emulate in English.

In this section I discuss the Laforguean aspects of 'Conversation Galante' and 'Portrait of a Lady'. The Laforguean elements in 'The Love Song' are discussed in a later section.

Eliot's approach to Laforgue was through an influential introduction to French Symbolist poetry for the English reader, Arthur Symons's *The Symbolist Movement in Literature* (1899). Some time in 1908, in Harvard, Eliot got hold of this book, which contained a useful introduction to the general ideals of French Symbolist poetry, discussions of Gérard de Nerval, Villiers de l'Isle Adam, Arthur Rimbaud, Paul Verlaine, Jules Laforgue and Stéphane Mallarmé. What Eliot read in the chapter on Laforgue had a profound influence on his poetry, particularly that of *Prufrock*. Before looking into that further, it will be helpful to obtain a sense of French Symbolism as it was understood then and has been understood since. After all, Eliot's approach to Laforgue was through the prism of the Symbolist movement, and arguably even after he had outgrown Laforgue he retained an affinity with the abstract aesthetic of French Symbolism.

An abstract aesthetic – difficult to define or pin down in words – characterizes French Symbolism. Those who are normally counted as French Symbolist poets (those named above, in fact) are actually stylistically quite different from each other. And yet there is a common denominator, a certain similarity of perspective, which is more easily experienced than expressed. Without having recourse to the experience of reading such poets here, it seems to me best to borrow the words of those who have studied them carefully and tried to express what Symbolism is. I have chosen three brief and relatively uncomplicated attempts of this sort and I simply quote them one after the other, in the hope that together they will convey something of the experience of reading Symbolist poetry. (Before reading the following it might be useful to remind yourself of a dictionary definition of 'symbol'.)

The first comes, naturally, from Arthur Symons's book, with rhetorical flourishes and metaphysical vagueness intact:

> [Symbolism] is all an attempt to spiritualise literature, to evade the old bondage of rhetoric, the old bondage of exteriority. Description is banished that beautiful things may be evoked, magically; the regular beat of verse is broken in order that words may fly, upon subtler wings. Mystery is no longer feared, as the great mystery in whose midst we are islanded was feared by those to whom that unknown sea was only a great void ...
>
> Here, then, in this revolt against exteriority, against rhetoric, against a materialistic tradition; in this endeavour to disengage the ultimate essence, the soul, of whatever exists and can be realised by the consciousness; in this dutiful waiting upon every symbol by which the soul of things can be made visible; literature, bowed down by so many burdens, may at last attain liberty, and its authentic speech. In attaining this liberty, it accepts a heavier burden; for in speaking to us so intimately, so solemnly, as only religion had hitherto spoken to us, it becomes itself a kind of religion, with all the duties and responsibilities of the sacred ritual.
>
> (Symons, 1899, pp.9–10)

The following is a particularly useful, and rather amazingly logical, exposition on Symbolism from Edmund Wilson's *Axel's Castle* (1931):

> The assumptions which underlay Symbolism lead us to formulate some such doctrine as the following. Every feeling or sensation we have, every moment of consciousness, is different from every other; and it is, in consequence, impossible to render our sensations as we actually experience them through the conventional and universal language of ordinary literature. Each poet has his unique personality; each of his moments has its special tone, its special combination of elements. And it is the poet's task to find, to invent, the special language which will alone be capable of expressing his personality and feelings. Such a language must make use of symbols: what is so special, so fleeting and so vague cannot be conveyed by direct statement or description, but only by a succession of words, of images, which will serve to suggest it to the reader. The Symbolists themselves, full of the idea of producing with poetry effects like those of music, tended to think of these images as possessing an abstract

value like musical notes and chords. But the words of our speech
are not musical notation, and what the symbols of Symbolism
really were, were metaphors detached from their subjects – for
one cannot, beyond a certain point, in poetry, merely enjoy colour
and sound for their own sake: one has to guess what the images
are being applied to. And Symbolism may be defined as an
attempt by carefully studied means – a complicated association of
ideas represented by a medley of metaphors – to communicate
unique personal feelings.

(Wilson, 1931, p.24)

And finally, A.G. Lehmann's attempt to convey something of Symbolism by
telling us what it is *not*, in *The Symbolist Aesthetic in France 1885–1895* (1950):

It is indeed a negative demarcation which most simply introduces
the limits of Symbolism ...

Negatively, Symbolism is

(a) a refusal to be attracted by social, propagandist, and other strictly
extra-artistic interests: which expressed in positive terms, puts us
under the obligation of saying what is meant by *l'art pour l'art* (no
easy problem) and noting a watery sort of literary mystique;

(b) a refusal to be bound by the conventions of writing which tended
to atrophy when attention was withdrawn from them to (strictly)
non-literary problems.

Both these negative definitions point towards the Symbolists'
main positive link with our own day: a critical preoccupation with
language as such, in the widest sense – the artist's peculiar field.

(Lehmann, 1950, p.14)

No attempt by me to summarize or synthesize these three statements would
produce anything more coherent. **It might, however, be useful for you –
and I suggest that you do this – to try to put in your own words what
you think are the principle features of Symbolism as understood by
the above three critics.** According to Wilson, it has something to do with
using language whereby metaphor-like phrases are deployed not so much to
illuminate an object or a situation as to convey a particular personality and
feeling. For Symons, it rises above poetic conventions and involves being able
to express precisely that which is difficult to express: something deeply
personal and/or entirely subjective and/or mystical and/or purely abstract
and/or pristinely aesthetic. Lehmann seems to me to bring Symons's and
Wilson's ideas together.

In his poetry as a whole, Eliot was generally attentive to Symbolist expression. In the *Prufrock* poems he was especially attentive to Laforgue's particular take on Symbolism. Laforgue's ideas and poetry offered the concrete experience of Symbolism that drew out the poet – the Anglophone Symbolist – in Eliot.

Now read Symons's brief chapter on Laforgue (Reader, Item 17). In this chapter Symons is not really trying to give a critical interpretation of Laforgue's work; he simply describes it, and gives samples or tasters to whet the reader's appetite. Symons's book offers a first-hand experience of Laforgue's writings, and that is exactly what Eliot found in it, at least enough experience for him to compose a few poems along Laforguean lines on its basis. Of course, he invested in more of Laforgue's poetry than Symons referred to as soon as he could and struggled, by his own admission, to master it (interview with Donald Hall in Clarke, 1990, pp.73–4); it is quite possible that Eliot had read more of Laforgue's prose writings than the *Moralités légendaires* ('Moral Tales') (1886), which Symons quoted (he must have delved into *Mélanges posthumes* ('Posthumous Miscellany') (1903), at least when he was in Paris). But the point is that Symons's quotations from Laforgue are definite and concrete instances of what Eliot's first experience of his work consisted in. They can therefore be used to obtain a reasonably clear sense of Eliot's indebtedness to Laforgue in *Prufrock*.

From Symons's chapter it is clear that there are two interrelated sides to Laforgue. He is a thinker and prose-writer, from whose *Moralités légendaires* a long quotation is given (and a particularly interesting one given our focus on the early Eliot), and he is a substantial poet, one of whose poems (and again an especially relevant one for Eliot), 'Autre Complainte de Lord Pierrot' ('Another Complaint from Lord Pierrot'), is quoted in full. Let us look at the impact on Eliot's *Prufrock* poems of these two sides of Laforgue, in so far as they appear in Symons's chapter.

The quotation from *Moralités légendaires* reveals Laforgue's penchant for grand or absolutist abstractions. Laforgue as thinker appears to think in terms of, and often personifies and addresses, these abstractions: 'O Totality', 'History', 'And thou, Silence', 'the great summing-up of consciousness before the Ideal'. Instead of paying attention to how material, tangible, down-to-earth happenings and phenomena work, Laforgue addresses a metaphysical realm of pure ideas and thoughts. In fact, Laforgue's metaphysical ideas derived from the German philosopher Eduard von Hartmann's *Philosophy of the Unconscious* (1869). (The continuity of ideas from Hartmann to Laforgue to Eliot is discussed succinctly by Piers Gray (1982) in *T.S. Eliot's Intellectual and Poetic Development 1909–1922*.) But it does not matter what Laforgue's metaphysical ideas really meant, or what Eliot understood of them and how firmly he believed them; what needs to be grasped is that Eliot found in Laforgue a certain kinship in idealistic metaphysical thinking, and that he used this in imitation of Laforgue for poetic purposes. It provided an intellectual portal that allowed his poetic art full flow. One cannot fail to notice the constant preoccupation in the *Prufrock* poems with grand abstractions, metaphysical ideals, inexpressible and inscrutable ideas. **How many such instances of idealistic and metaphysical moments come to your mind?**

In 'The Love Song of J. Alfred Prufrock' such an instance appears in the first stanza as 'an overwhelming question', which resurfaces (as we have already seen) occasionally in the rest of the poem, and culminates in the poet persona's frustrated realization that 'It is impossible to say just what I mean!' (p.6). There is a trace of it in the poet persona's somewhat manic expressions of his inability to express himself in 'Portrait of a Lady' (already quoted); a touch of it in: 'The notion of some infinitely gentle / Infinitely suffering thing' (p.14) of 'Preludes IV'; a crude misogynistic example of it in: 'You, madam, are the eternal humorist, / The eternal enemy of the absolute' (p.31) from 'Conversation Galante'. The misogynistic element, which I have commented on, is part of a pattern that is found in Laforgue's poetry too.

Clearly, Laforgue's idealistic tendency had an impact on Eliot's poetic world, but the influence goes deeper: Laforgue's poetic style itself was emulated in sophisticated ways by Eliot in *Prufrock*. Here, too, Symons's chapter is helpful: the 'Autre Complainte de Lord Pierrot', which is quoted there in full, gives us the opportunity to compare at a stylistic level a specific poem by Laforgue with specific poems by Eliot. **Do have a look at the French version in the Reader (Item 17), and use the following prose-translation by G.D. Martin if you need to:**

Autre Complainte de Lord Pierrot

She who's sure to give me the low-down on Woman! I'll say to her first, with my least cold air, 'The sum of the angles of a triangle, dear soul, is equal to two right angles.'

And if this cry issues from her: 'God of Gods! How I love you!' – 'God will recognize his own.' Or, if she's pricked to the quick: 'My keyboards have hearts, you'll be my only theme' – I: 'All is relative.'

All her eyes on me then, feeling herself too banal: 'Ah! You don't love me; so many others are jealous!' And I, with one eye intent on the Unconscious: 'Thank you, not bad; and you?'

'Let's play at "Who's the more faithful"!' – 'What's the point, O Nature?' – 'It's as good as playing "Loser takes all"!' – Next, another little set phrase: 'Ah, you'll tire of me first, I'm sure ...' – 'No, after you, please.'

> At last, if one evening she dies among my books, quietly;
> pretending not to believe my eyes, I'll react with a: 'Drat it, we
> had the Wherewithal to live on! Was it serious after all?'

(Laforgue, 1998, p.66)

The situation is, I think, immediately reminiscent of several poems in *Prufrock* – the exchange at cross-purposes between a man and a woman, the former a rather smug poet persona who pretentiously pursues a metaphysical realm but is distracted by the all too physical presence of the woman, the latter apparently condemned to be no more than a shallow and disregarded physical distraction (at least unless she dies, surrenders her physical presence). The very construction of Lord Pierrot, a stock mask for Laforgue, is in many respects similar to the deliberately posed and poised poet persona of most *Prufrock* poems (indeed, the names Pierrot and Prufrock have a similar ring). Most immediately, it is evident that 'Autre Complainte de Lord Pierrot' is very similar to Eliot's 'Conversation Galante' – the similarity is so striking that Eliot's poem is widely regarded as little more than an adaptation of Laforgue's.

This is the time to give 'Conversation Galante' (p.31) a leisurely and careful rereading, and to contemplate the following: **in what ways is Eliot's poem similar to Laforgue's and in what ways is it different? Does Eliot express anything different from Laforgue?** (Please note that in the edition used in this chapter, there are two typographical errors: 'How your digress' should read 'How you digress', and the opening quotation mark in 'Are we then so serious?' is missing.)

The similarities are too obvious to need much elaboration. The differences are subtle, and it is difficult to see in what way they are material. The obvious difference is that, in 'Conversation Galante', Eliot's poet persona takes the initiative and the woman undercuts his high-flown sentiments by her brief, shallow and self-centred rejoinders; in 'Autre Complainte de Lord Pierrot' it is the lady who takes the initiative throughout, and it is up to the poet persona to find brief, slightly off-the-point and cuttingly profound rejoinders. Eliot's poet persona is pretentious and garrulous while the woman, however petty, has the last word; Laforgue's poet persona is pretentious too but suave, and himself (to the bitter end) gets the last word. But that does not take Eliot's poet persona too far away from Laforgue's. Eliot is careful to retain the aura of Lord Pierrot around his poet persona, even down to the latter's moon-gaping first speech – which is actually reminiscent of the impressive opening of Lord Pierrot's preceding complaint, 'Complainte de Lord Pierrot':

> Au clair de la lune
> Mon ami Pierrot
> Filons, en costume,

Présider là-haut!
Ma carvelle est morte.
Que le Christ l'emporte!
Béons à la Lune,
La bouche en zero.

(By the light of the moon, Pierrot my friend, let's get dressed up to preside up above! My brain is dead. May Christ bear it away! Let's gape at the Moon, our mouths shaped like zeros.)

(Laforgue, 1998, p.61)

The comparison with Prester John's balloon, in 'Conversation Galante', has the same air of emptiness as mouths shaped like zeros. (Prester John was a mythical medieval Christian ruler in the East, rumoured to exist at the time of the Crusades.) The balloon image is also reminiscent of Hulme's 'Above the Dock', which I have quoted in full above in my discussion Imagism. The reversal observed between Laforgue's and Eliot's poet personae in these poems does not in my view serve to distinguish one from another particularly. Perhaps it is best regarded as a change that is necessitated by the English idiom, a cultural adjustment of sorts; perhaps the understated and dry discourse of love in English has to be played with somewhat differently than the far more vibrant and unabashed discourse of love in French. That might explain the subtle difference. But in the *attitudes* of the two poet personae and in the *characterization* of the ladies, and consequently the stylistic flow of the two poems in their respective languages, I see little to choose between them. A comparison seems to demonstrate convincingly the depth of Eliot's indebtedness to Laforgue. **Do you agree with me? Or do you discern more of a distinction between the two poems?**

It also occurs to me that the ending of 'Autre Complainte de Lord Pierrot' is markedly similar to the ending of 'Portrait of a Lady' – another point of comparison for you to consider:

Well! and what if she should die some afternoon,
Afternoon grey and smoky, evening yellow and rose;
Should die and leave me sitting pen in hand
With the smoke coming down above the housetops;
Doubtful, for a while
Not knowing what to feel or if I understand
Or whether wise or foolish, tardy or too soon ...
Would she not have the advantage, after all?

(p.12)

Again, there is little difference in tone or stylistic effect or attitude between Laforgue and Eliot where they are most recognizably close, where Eliot chooses to emulate Laforgue. The shifts that Eliot makes with Laforguean images and themes are shifts necessitated by a different linguistic idiom and ethos, but to similar ends. If there is a different nuance it is in this: the poet persona of Eliot appears to be curiously aware (that intense self-awareness and deliberation of the *Prufrock* poems) of being at a second remove from Laforgue, of being a careful emulation of Laforgue. The passage quoted above from the last stanza of 'Portrait of a Lady' gives some sense of this when compared with the final stanza of 'Autre Complainte de Lord Pierrot'. Eliot's passage sounds like a description of Laforgue's stanza. Laforgue's stanza is a compressed direct statement of an imagined situation. Eliot's passage is a descriptive interpretation, a kind of unravelling, of Laforgue's compressed statement. It almost has the air of being written *about* the last stanza of 'Autre Complainte de Lord Pierrot'.

What the above comparisons of Laforgue's ideas and poetry with those of Eliot have demonstrated, I hope, is the depth of the former's influence on the latter. But I have focused on only the closely comparable passages from both to make this point. Just as the transition from the USA to Europe and awareness of the Imagists' aspirations form linked threads in the *Prufrock* poems, so Eliot's awareness of the Symbolist movement and particularly his indebtedness to Laforgue forms another such thread. But there are others. There is, for instance, Eliot's poetic preoccupation with the ideas of Henri Bergson.

Time and the city: the ideas of Henri Bergson

Throughout Eliot's work there is a somewhat agonized consciousness of the passing of time, of clocks striking inexorably ('There will be time, there will be time', Prufrock thinks desperately in his 'Love Song'), of mortality and transience, of human (or rather *modern*) purposelessness and futility, and also of the limitations of seeing time in a purely linear fashion, of the past sediments that are to be found in the present and those of the present in the future. Indeed, a particular sensitivity to the nuances of time as a concept characterizes a large number of the works of so-called modernist writers and thinkers: so much so that the satirist and fellow-modernist Wyndham Lewis was to castigate most of his contemporaries for being subsumed by a 'time-mind' (Lewis, 1927). There was good reason for this sensitivity to the concept of time: the nineteenth century had seen a radical shake-up as a result of reconceptualizations of geological and evolutionary time, and reconsideration of scientific concepts of history; even while Eliot was engaged in writing the *Prufrock* poems, advances in theoretical physics were transforming the understanding of time as a physical measure (Einstein's formulation of the Special Theory of Relativity, using a non-Euclidean space–time geometry, was published in 1905). It is difficult to ascertain to what extent, and from what sources, Eliot might have absorbed his sensitivity to the concept of time. What is reasonably well established is that in so far as this was expressed in the *Prufrock* poems, it was couched in ideas that came from an immediate source – that of the philosophy of Henri Bergson. In 1910–11 in Paris, Eliot encountered and absorbed Bergson's ideas at first hand. Piers Gray cites a published letter by Eliot where he acknowledges a particular debt to *Matter and Memory* in some of his *Prufrock* poems (Gray, 1982, p.38). 'Eliot's biographer, Peter Ackroyd, gives a concise and succinct account of the influence Bergson had on Eliot:

> [In Paris Eliot] retained the habits of his undergraduate days; he studied French literature at the Sorbonne and French conversation with a private tutor, and in the first two months of 1911 he attended Bergson's Friday lectures at the Collège de France. He later recalled the packed lecture hall, and the atmosphere of excitement which the philosopher generated. Indeed he suffered a 'temporary conversion' to Bergsonism. Bergson was an effective teacher because ... he admitted no doubts, and it was his dogmatism which attracted Eliot's more diffident temperament. He affirmed the relativity of all conceptual knowledge, and his descriptions of the flux or chaos which lay beyond the reach of such knowledge would have appealed to the young poet of the 'Preludes'. Certainly his notion of 'real time', 'la durée', affected the poems which Eliot wrote in Paris ... but it is possible that he was drawn to the philosopher because he seemed to understand also the experience of poetic composition: 'intuition attains the absolute' was Bergson's phrase, affirming his belief that reality can only be grasped by an act of 'intellectual sympathy'.
>
> But the allegiance passed; it had disappeared by 1913, and a less credulous Eliot was to criticize Bergson for being fundamentally fatalistic. It could not have been otherwise. The notion of 'ideal duration', of immersion in time, of the flow of consciousness, is clearly an analogy for Eliot's own sense of experience and its claims. But he always withdrew from such experience, in the same manner that he withdrew from Bergson: he reverted to his need for order, for discipline, for tradition.
>
> (Ackroyd, 1985, pp.40–1)

That gives a reasonably clear account of the impact Bergson had on Eliot as a person and a poet (it is a biographer's account). Our concern here, however, is with the particular influence of Bergson on specific poems by Eliot. To assess this requires a juxtaposition of specific texts – Bergson's against Eliot's. **Read the beginning of Bergson's *L'Évolution créatrice* (1907; trans. 1911 as *Creative Evolution*), the best known of his philosophical writings, which summarizes the notion of *la durée* ('duration'), and** the brief extract from *Matter and Memory* on the meaning of 'the present' (Reader, Items 18.1 and 18.2). These are difficult passages, and you may not understand some of the arguments and phrases, but do not worry about that and do not spend much time trying to sort them out – just read through them. If you persist, together these will convey a *general* impression (Eliot was probably not interested in much more than that) of the kind of understanding of time Bergson is concerned with, and also, importantly, of Bergson's style (which a poet could scarcely not be attentive to). **Also read again, before proceeding further, the poem 'Rhapsody on a Windy Night', which is usually regarded as reworking some of Bergson's ideas. What connections do you find between Eliot's 'Rhapsody on a Windy Night' and the sections from Bergson's *Creative Evolution* and *Matter and Memory* that you have read?**

The following points cover some of my observations; some of these may match yours, and you may well have others.

Seeing and remembering

Most of the stanzas begin by announcing a specific hour of the night, from twelve to four o'clock. The regularity of time measured by the clock, of which the reader is reminded thus, is broken constantly in each passing stanza. This is done partly by dwelling on the inchoateness of memory – 'Dissolve the floors of memory / And all its clear relations, / Its divisions and precisions' (p.15), or again: 'The memory throws up high and dry / A crowd of twisted things' (*ibid.*) – and partly by the fragmentary effect of images that the memory throws up at every moment of the present, such as: 'A twisted branch upon the beach / ... / A broken spring in a factory yard' (*ibid.*); later: 'the hand of the child, automatic, / ... / I have seen eyes in the street / ... / And a crab one afternoon in a pool' (p.16); finally:

> The reminiscence comes
> Of sunless dry geraniums
> And dust in crevices,
> Smells of chestnuts in the streets,
> And female smells in shuttered rooms,
> And cigarettes in corridors
> And cocktail smells in bars.

> (pp.16–17)

The regularity of clock-time is also undermined by using the street-lamp as a poetic device to focus sharply on perception in the present: the poet persona's eye wanders and senses and absorbs images around him (highlighted as if by street-lamps), also in a fragmentary fashion – not unlike the images thrown up by memory. Thus, the poet persona's eye first lights on the slightly frayed woman of the second stanza, then takes in the flattened cat of the fourth stanza, and finally dwells on a thoroughly sordid anti-romantic moon in the fifth stanza. Each of these moments of immediate perception is given as if the street-lamp presents them (in its own voice) to the poet persona's gaze. These two ways of undermining the regularity of clock-time (inchoate memory images, and the fragmentary images of immediate perception) are constantly brought together and mixed up. So, the poem progresses by evoking alternately a fragmentary image that is immediately perceived (woman, cat, moon), which is described in the street-lamp's voice, and a series of consequent and equally fragmentary images thrown up by association from the memory (twisted branch, hand of child, geraniums, etc.). Together, these convey a powerful sense of an on-going and somewhat disorienting continuum (you might have noted my use of this word in my reading of 'The Love Song of J. Alfred Prufrock'. In the last stanza both regular clock-time and memory are absorbed into the present perception, into what the lamp says. The lamp announces the clock-time ('Four o'clock') and gives a little homily on the importance of memory ('Memory! / You have the key'; p.17), but ultimately both these are contained in the present, which also – fatalistically (predeterminedly, inescapably) – contains the future: appropriately, the last words of the lamp are 'prepare for life', an injunction that is like 'The last twist of the knife' (*ibid.*). In the poem, a continuous on-going many-faceted present draws into itself the associations of the past (memory) and the potentialities of the future.

This could be regarded as an accurate poetic exposition of Bergson's understanding of the 'present' in *Matter and Memory* (or, for that matter, of 'duration' in *Creative Evolution*). 'Rhapsody on a Windy Night', understood as outlined above, is a reasonably precise *performance* of the process that is described in the extract from *Matter and Memory*: it gives an impressionistic account of living through a continuous present while being aware of regular clock-time, of memories, of sensations and perceptions, and the determination of the future. As Bergson sees the matter in that extract: 'The psychical state ... that I call "my present," must be both a perception of the immediate past and a determination of the immediate future. Now the immediate past, in so far as it is perceived, is ... sensation ... and the immediate future, in so far as it is being determined, is action or movement'. In 'Rhapsody' this corresponds to the sequential description of the poet persona's perceptions/sensations (what the lamp says) and action (movement through the streets) in the course of one night – that is, in the course of a series of present moments (marked by clock-time). Bergson carries on in the extract to link this present to the advent of memories in the consciousness. A 'mass of accumulated memories' is constantly (indeed overwhelmingly) implicated in the physical awareness that is the present, and these memories are modified by the personality and intelligence of the mind in question. The last paragraph in the extract from *Matter and Memory* describes this cohesive process. In 'Rhapsody' this idea corresponds to the fragmentary images that surface after the 'what-the-lamp-said' sections. Their mode of surfacing gives a sense of the manner in which a 'mass of accumulated memories' is implicated in the continuous present. The quality of these memory-images and the style in which they are expressed conveys something about the personality of the poet persona.

Involuntariness

Much of 'Rhapsody' is pervaded by a sense of involuntariness, of the poet persona not being fully in control of himself. It is not just the perceptions/ sensations and memory-images that come in a fragmentary fashion; the poet persona himself is divided up and dissociated. His perceptions are, as observed already, given as observations from the street-lamps (as if outside himself); his memories appear with all the lack of volition that the remarkable image at the end of the first stanza conveys: 'Midnight shakes the memory / As a madman shakes a dead geranium' (p.15). Note that it is given as '*the* memory' rather than '*my* memory' – and soon afterwards again: '*The* memory throws up high and dry / A crowd of twisted things' (*ibid*.; my emphasis). And yet again: '*The* reminiscence comes / Of sunless dry geraniums' (p.16; my emphasis) – thus making those geraniums a leitmotiv for the involuntariness of the poet persona's memory. By and large, the poet persona is a passive presence, very seldom announcing himself as the first-person subject ('I') of the poem, though it is clear all through that he is the focal point of the poem. Where the first-person poet persona does announce himself most emphatically it is to present some striking images of involuntariness, of automata-like living beings and inanimate objects mixed up, blindly going through habitual motions:

> So the hand of the child, automatic,
> Slipped out and pocketed a toy that was running along the quay,
> I could see nothing behind that child's eye.
> I have seen eyes in the street
> Trying to peer through lighted shutters,
> And a crab one afternoon in a pool,
> An old crab with barnacles on his back,
> Gripped the end of a stick which I held him.

(p.16)

This aspect of the poem too, it appears to me, is linked to Bergson's *method* of philosophical analysis. What Bergson's analysis of the relationship between perceptions/sensations, actions, memories, personalities and, most importantly, time does is break down the integral cohesive human mind and body into distinct parts. The effect is of the human person who thinks and physically exists becoming a passive and automatic thing, which is acted upon in a more or less mechanistic fashion *by* time, instead of a creature that makes choices and exercises his or her will. The manner in which the following lines from *Matter and Memory* express the role of the body seems to make the body separate from its conscious existence and conditional to sensation, memory, time, etc. – the body seems to be regarded as an involuntary conduit that simply happens to be there: 'Situated between the matter which influences it and that on which it has influence, my body is a centre of action, the place where the impressions received choose intelligently the path they will follow to transform themselves into movements accomplished.'

Fragmentariness

The powerful sense of fragmentation and disorientation in 'Rhapsody' that I have mentioned above also draws on the ideas of Bergson. This sense of disorientation and fragmentation does not necessarily lead to incoherence – though that has been alleged of Eliot's poetry, especially of some of his later poems. In 'Rhapsody', at any rate, the fragments of perceptions/sensations and memory-images coalesce in certain ways: a coherent atmosphere is conveyed, an underlying rationale I have outlined already – a certain formal and aural quality – holds it all together. Some such level of coherence is arguably invariably found even in Eliot's least immediately coherent poems (*The Waste Land*, for example). The fragmentariness of perceptions/ sensations, memory-images, the continuity of time, that nevertheless coheres, is an easily identified element of Bergson's ideas. Consider the following passage from *Creative Evolution*:

> A thousand incidents arise, which seem to be cut off from those which precede them, and to be disconnected from those which follow. Discontinuous though they appear, however, in point of fact they stand out against the continuity of a background on which they are designed, and to which indeed they owe the intervals that separate them; they are the beats of the drum which break forth here and there in the symphony. Our attention fixes on them because they interest it more, but each of them is borne by the fluid mass of our whole psychical existence. Each is only the best illuminated point of a moving zone which comprises all that we feel or think or will – all, in short, that we are at any given moment. It is this entire zone which in reality makes up our state.

There it is, the fragmentariness that coheres. But that is not all that is interesting about this passage; it appears to employ images that Eliot specifically uses in 'Rhapsody'. '[T]he best illuminated point of a moving zone' could be regarded as an apt description of how the poem works, focusing on what came under the lamplight (what the lamp said) while drifting through the urban landscape of perception and memory. And, of course, there are those drum beats: 'Every street lamp that I pass / Beats like a fatalistic drum' (p.15).

Those are some of my observations on the connection between Bergson's ideas, as represented in the extracts you have read, and 'Rhapsody on a Windy Night' – as I said, you may well have different ideas. Although I have marked out the similarity between the expression of fragmentariness and underlying coherence in 'Rhapsody' and some of Bergson's statements, there is undoubtedly a significant difference between them. For Bergson the fragmentariness and underlying coherence of perceptions/sensations and memory-images is the *normal* experience of living. That, according to Bergson, simply *is* how we are and things are. Eliot's performative poetic rendering of these Bergsonian ideas, however, emphasizes the disorientation and the fragmentariness/underlying coherence as departures from the normal, as being somehow *amiss*. From the frenzied menace of the 'madman [who] shakes a dead geranium' (p.15), to the disturbing gaze of the woman ('the corner of her eye / Twists like a crooked pin'; *ibid.*) and the child ('I could see nothing behind that child's eye'; p.16), to the image of the diseased moon, to the claustrophobic smells, to the final melodramatic 'last twist of the knife', the overwhelming impression the poem makes is of a world that is out of joint.

The out-of-joint world of the poem is not, however, so much to do with the *general process* of perceiving/sensing, reminiscing, living through a continuity of presents (all Bergson's concerns) as with the *particular disposition* of the poet persona and his *environment* where that process takes place. The poem is therefore not simply a performance of Bergson's ideas, which is the view I have taken so far, but at the same time a commentary on the poet persona and his environment (a constant preoccupation of all the *Prufrock* poems). It is, I feel, an impression of the environment that conveys itself most powerfully in this poem: a desolate urban environment at night-time, in which a prostitute and a cat make fleeting appearances, seen through the eyes of a lonely and alienated city-dweller. The alienated citizen who is repulsed and yet bound by the city becomes part and parcel of the intensely self-conscious poet persona whom I have described in connection with other *Prufrock* poems already. The city was to reappear with enormous effect in Eliot's *The Waste Land*. The environment of the city became inextricably associated with Eliot's poetry, and has come to be regarded as a key element of Eliot's modernism. In assuming the unromantic tone vis-à-vis the city, Eliot followed, as in so many other matters, the example of Laforgue. 'Rhapsody' has in it numerous echoes of Laforgue, most obviously in the single French line of the poem: 'La lune ne garde aucune rancune' ('The moon harbours no ill feelings'), which is drawn from two lines of Laforgue's 'Complainte de cette bonne lune' ('The Lament of that Beautiful Moon'):

Là voyons mam'zell' la Lune,
Ne gardons pas ainsi rancune

(Look, there we can see that fine young lady the moon, let's not
harbour any ill feelings)

(in Southam, 1968, p.52)

The Laforguean turn of phrase and lunar motifs are merged in 'Rhapsody' –
as indeed they are in other *Prufrock* poems – with a Bergsonian sense of time
and fragmentation/coherence, and together these are used to make poetry of
the unbeautiful modern city. In this process are laid the foundations of
mainstream literary modernism in poetry.

Allusions and 'The Love Song' again

Back to the title poem once again, this time for a closer consideration of
allusions in Eliot's poetry in the light of the discussion above. 'The Love
Song of J. Alfred Prufrock' teems with allusions to Laforgue and Bergson,
with effects similar to those that have been discussed with reference to, for
example, 'Conversation Galante' or 'Rhapsody on a Windy Night'. But it is
not just allusions to Laforgue and Bergson that can be found here – there are
also biblical echoes, phrases and lines reminiscent of the so-called
metaphysical poets (John Donne and Andrew Marvell) and touches
(obviously including the epigram) of Dante and Shakespeare. Some of
these are usefully listed by B.C. Southam (1968) and mentioned by George
Williamson (1955), and more are to be found in the enormous quantity of
critical writing that the poem has attracted. It is very unlikely that any reader
would be able to identify all the allusions that Eliot deliberately or
inadvertently worked into the poem. But then what, you may wonder, is
the point of having those allusions? **If we sensibly assume that Eliot
probably did not put in all those allusions (some fairly obscure) in his
poetry with the expectation that they would all be recognized, then
why did he put them in?** Contemplate, in other words, the effects of the
allusions on your reading of the *Prufrock* poems, and particularly of 'The
Love Song', even if you do not recognize them all.

The following are some of the effects that I have come up with on
considering that question (and, as always, there are probably others).

Familiarity and complicity

Even if the Laforguean and Bergsonian allusions in 'The Love Song' are not
immediately recognized – actually they are only available to readers with a
keen interest in French poetry and philosophy – the Shakespearean and
biblical allusions can hardly be missed. 'I am Lazarus, come from the dead /
Come back to tell you all, I shall tell you all' (p.6) and 'No! I am not Prince
Hamlet, nor was meant to be' (*ibid.*), are two announcements that are fairly

sure to hit the mark. But it is not just obvious allusions of that sort that you would have picked up; consciously, or perhaps not wholly consciously, the biblical turn of phrases like 'But though I have wept and fasted, wept and prayed' (p.5) or 'There will be time, there will be time' (p.4) or 'Though I have seen my head (grown slightly bald) brought in upon a platter' (p.5), the quotations from Shakespeare in 'I know the voices dying with a dying fall' (p.4) or 'I grow old ... I grow old ...' (p.7), the Marvell-like irony of 'And indeed there will be time' (p.4), the Donne-like luminousness of 'Arms that are braceleted and white and bare / (But in the lamplight, downed with light brown hair!)' (p.5), and the Chaucer-like directness of 'Full of high sentence, but a bit obtuse' (p.7) – any or all of these are likely to come with an odd sense of familiarity if not outright recognition. In the density of its allusiveness Eliot's language seems at every moment to draw upon a whole history of literary themes and expressions. This quality of language usage would I think inevitably impress itself on a reasonably sensitive and experienced reader. 'Aha, I recognize that', you might have felt about some phrases and lines at first reading, or perhaps, 'there is something familiar about that, though I cannot put my finger on where I might have heard something similar before'. This feeling of recognition, near-recognition or just familiarity naturally establishes a certain complicity between the voice of the poet persona and the reader. Even if readers find themselves baffled as to the precise meaning of the poem (or parts of the poem), this complicity is likely, I think, to be established – and in this complicity lies some of the allure of the poem. Complicity between reader and poet persona, between speaker and addressee, is, of course, one of the obvious themes of the poem, established in the epigraph, which is taken from Dante's *Inferno*, stanza xxvii, lines 61–6. These are lines spoken by the spirit of Count Guido de Montefeltro – imprisoned for his sins in a flame in the underworld – to Dante, who is passing through hell under the guidance of the spirit of the Roman poet Virgil. Not realizing that Dante is alive (he has been given special dispensation to enter the underworld), Count Guido addresses these words to him:

> If I did think my answer were to one
> Who ever could return unto the world,
> This flame should rest unshaken. But since ne'er,
> If true be told me, any from this depth
> Has found his upward way, I answer thee,
> Nor fear lest infamy record the words.

(Dante, 1908, pp.114–15)

'Because you are a spirit like me I can speak to you', is in brief what Guido tells Dante. Similarly, it is implied, the poet persona's confession in 'The Love Song' is given on the (perhaps mistaken) assumption that the reader is much like him. If the reader recognizes some of the allusions, is drawn in by the allusive language, then indeed the reader has already established some common ground with the poet persona.

Organizing principles

Having considered the ways in which Laforgue and Bergson particularly influenced some of Eliot's *Prufrock* poems, we are in a position to understand the status of Eliot's allusions to their work. The identification of a specific reference to a Laforguean phrase, or being able to hit on a few particular words that are lifted from one of Bergson's books, though not helpful in itself, is easily done through some careful comparing. Eliot, for instance, observed that the Hamlet passage in 'The Love Song' was written under the influence of Laforgue's ideas – and, as it happens, Laforgue's thoughts on Hamlet are quoted in Symons's chapter (Reader, Item 17). The famous 'In the room the women come and go / Talking of Michelangelo' (pp.3 and 4) was adapted from Laforgue's 'Dans la pièce les femmes vont et viennent / En parlant des maitres de Sienne' ('In the room the women come and go / Talking of masters of the Sienese School'; see Southam, 1968, p.38). Numerous such adapted phrases and allusions to Laforgue are picked up and listed in Southam's *Guide* (1968). Also marked out there is a passage from Bergson's 'Introduction à la Métaphysique' (1903) (translated by T.E. Hulme in 1913; see Southam, 1968, p.36), from where Eliot may have adapted specific phrases that appear in 'The Love Song'. I do not wish to dwell on this micro-level of allusion here. Far more important than simply demonstrating a familiarity with Laforgue and Bergson is to recognize what these micro-allusions gesture towards – that is, a kind of macro-level of allusion whereby (as we have discussed already) some of Laforgue's and Bergson's ideas and stylistic tactics were used by Eliot as *organizing principles* for his own preoccupations. How this use of allusion operates I have already dwelt on at some length with regard to some of the other *Prufrock* poems – and that should make it easier to unravel how it works for 'The Love Song' too.

Here is one way of thinking about how Eliot uses Laforguean and Bergsonian allusions to gesture towards the organizing principles that govern the *Prufrock* poems, especially 'The Love Song'. There are two poles to Eliot's poetry in the *Prufrock* collection: observations on an external environment (in the USA or Europe; an unromantic urban landscape occupied by generally unheroic people – the modern world, say), and the introspections of an enormously self-conscious and erudite, and yet questioning and uncertain, poet persona who deliberately assumes certain poses and puts on certain attitudes (we may think of this as the modernist consciousness). The *mode* of presenting both these poles is inspired to a large extent by Laforgue: Laforgue-like smartness, deliberation, idioms, personae appear constantly in English in Eliot's *Prufrock* poems, with some adjustments necessary to Eliot's particular situation (as an American émigré, for instance). But the *Prufrock* poet needed something more: he needed a way of linking the two (often Laforguean) poles – described environment and poet persona. Some mechanism was needed to bring these together, to understand the relation between them, that was coherent with the stylistic devices (the fragmented images, the Symbolist intimacy) that had been employed. This is where Bergson's ideas came in handy for the *Prufrock* poet. Bergson presented concepts of time, memory and consciousness that established links between the outside world and the consciousness – modern environment and modernist poet persona – in precisely the way that the *Prufrock* poet was looking for. This splendid synthesis of observation, aesthetic expression and philosophical understanding is clearly evidenced in 'The Love Song'. To some extent this has been covered already in the introductory commentary on 'The Love Song' with which this chapter began.

Critical position

In the section 'Familiarity and complicity' above, I maintained that, 'In the density of its allusiveness Eliot's language seems at every moment to draw upon a whole history of literary themes and expressions.' This use of allusion is not simply (though that is an important aspect of it) a matter of establishing complicity between reader and poetic voice, but is also significant in the context of Eliot's critical ideas, being the result of a particular critical position and a particular understanding of literary modernity. Implicit in Eliot's use of allusions are ideas that he would only elaborate on later, especially in influential essays such as 'Tradition and the Individual Talent' (1919). These ideas are discussed in the next section.

Having thus put into perspective the use of allusions in the *Prufrock* poems (especially 'The Love Song') – often the main obstacle to reading them freely – it becomes easier to go through them with discernment and (perhaps) pleasure. Discernment in this instance is more a matter of finding interpretations so that all the fragments fit together, than of making a judgement. However, it is not in the influences and inspirations *behind* 'The Love Song' that its reputation lies for being a launch-pad of literary modernism; it is in its reception that such a reputation is acquired, retrospectively. It is in the life of this and other *Prufrock* poems *after* they were written and published that we must look for an understanding of their modernist status – that is where the debates and contexts of what is regarded as Eliot's mainstream literary modernity really lie.

The construction of a mainstream literary modernism

The process by which Eliot's early *Prufrock* poems gradually came to be regarded as one of the (if not *the*) starting points of mainstream, or 'high', literary modernism can be divided into three phases. In phase one, the poems were initially associated with especially Ezra Pound's, but also, indirectly, Wyndham Lewis's, assault on extant literary conventions. In phase two, as Eliot's critical writings came to prominence, the poems were read in the light of a set of critical ideas that he himself produced. In phase three, the poems were eventually accommodated as part of the canon of modern English literature, in which Eliot became the pre-eminent modernist establishment figure. I discuss each of these phases briefly in this section. My specific points about Eliot prompt larger questions, concerning the nature of mainstream or 'high' modernism. Such questions are placed at the end of my discussion of each phase. Although highlighted in bold, like other questions, they are slightly different, in that I do not expect you to be able to answer them from what you have read so far. In this section, the highlighted questions at the end of the subsections are those around which debates about the status and character of mainstream literary modernism are still on-going. As you study the work of the other modernist writers in this part of the book – Virginia Woolf, Bertolt Brecht and Christopher Okigbo – you will start to develop your own views in relation to these debates.

Phase one

Eliot met Pound on 22 September 1914 in London and showed him 'The Love Song of J. Alfred Prufrock'. Pound was enthusiastic about it, and set about trying to persuade various magazines and journals to publish it. He wrote to Harriet Monroe, the editor of *Poetry*:

> He has sent in the best poem I have yet had or seen from an American. *PRAY GOD IT BE NOT A SINGLE AND UNIQUE SUCCESS*. He has taken it back to get it ready for the press and you shall have it in a few days.
>
> He is the only American I know of who has made what I can call adequate preparation for writing. He has actually trained himself *and* modernized himself *on his own*. The rest of the *promising young* have done one or the other but never both (most of the swine have done neither). It is such a comfort to meet a man and not have to tell him to wash his face, wipe his feet, and remember the date (1914) on the calendar.
>
> (quoted in Goodwinn, 1966, p.106)

As it happened, Monroe was less impressed than Pound by 'The Love Song', but it was eventually published in the June 1915 issue of *Poetry* at Pound's insistence. As you may recall, he also managed to place 'Portrait of a Lady' in *Others* (September 1915), and 'Rhapsody on a Windy Night' and 'Preludes' in *Blast* (July 1915). Since 1913, Pound had been associated with a small magazine called *The Egoist* (a former suffragette magazine, *The New Freewoman*, which had been transformed into a literary magazine by its proprietors, Harriet Weaver and Dora Marsden, with Richard Aldington as assistant editor). He had published some of his prose in the magazine and – another instance of his literary patronage – had placed in it James Joyce's *Portrait of the Artist as a Young Man* (to appear in segments). In 1917, he persuaded Weaver to publish *Prufrock* as an Egoist Press title, and even secretly put up much of the cost of publication. It appeared in May 1917, to very little critical attention – a few dismissive reviews, and some energetic promotional reviews by Pound himself (see Clarke, 1990, vol.1 and Grant, 1982, vol.1).

Pound's extraordinary championing of Eliot's early work was not just a matter of literary enthusiasm and personal generosity; it was also because Eliot fitted in with Pound's own large ambition: nothing less than to transform and modernize British and US literary culture. This ambition was formed around Pound's creative and literary critical writings, as well as his activities as an editor (in some capacity) of a number of journals and magazines, and as a promoter of a range of modernist writers. It extended to all the fine arts, and culture generally, and eventually to economics and governance (a path that led eventually to Pound's embracing of fascism). The breadth of his ambition meant that Pound was never just a writer and critic; he always strove to set *movements* up. As I have noted already, Pound was behind the Imagist movement, and, during the period in which he was trying to sell Eliot's *Prufrock* poems, he was one of the key figures in Wyndham Lewis's Vorticist movement (fronted by the magazine *Blast*). In a larger sense, Pound could be regarded as the person who founded what is now regarded as a modernist movement in literature. He did this by bringing together in several ways – as a group of friends and acquaintances, as a group of writers who appeared in specific fora, as writers whose works can be critically assessed in a particular fashion – Eliot, Joyce, Aldington, Lewis, Woolf and others. To some extent, Eliot was to inherit from Pound the mantle of high priest of the modernist movement, and pursue in due course a similar range of activities but with a distinctly different style.

Pound's patronage, under the shadow of which the *Prufrock* poems initially appeared, inevitably affected their reception and categorization. Pound's great enthusiasm in 1914 and 1915 was Vorticism. Vorticism was seen as *the* movement of the time, to be incorporated into the great project of modernity. Its central idea had to do with painting, and it was proposed in contrast to other painting movements such as Futurism and Cubism. The theoretical underpinnings of Vorticism, both in painting and with relation to literature, are discussed enlighteningly in Dasenbrock (1985). However, you do not need a knowledge of Vorticist theory to study Eliot: unlike Pound, Eliot never subscribed to Vorticism, and was not regarded as a Vorticist. But his association with Pound, and, in particular, the fact that a couple of the *Prufrock* poems had appeared in *Blast*, meant that they were regarded as being aligned with the avant-garde, subversive, irreverent, and also humorous and optimistic, modernizing *temper* (not the *theory*) of Vorticism. This was observed in one of the few sympathetic reviews of *Prufrock* in 1917 that was not penned by Pound, that by the novelist May Sinclair in the *Literary Review* (December 1917, no.4), where she comments on the hostile reception of the book by some reviewers. This had to do, she argued, with the perception that Eliot kept bad company:

> But Mr. Eliot is dangerous. Mr. Eliot is associated with an unpopular movement and with unpopular people. His 'Preludes' and his 'Rhapsody' appeared in 'Blast'. They stood out from the experimental violences of 'Blast' with an air of tranquil and triumphant achievement; but, no matter; it was in 'Blast' that they appeared.
>
> (in Clarke, 1990, vol.1, p.14)

Read the extract from the Manifesto that was published in the first volume of *Blast* (Reader, Item 19). As you can see, the Manifesto does not present a particularly coherent set of principles or diktats (the theoretical underpinnings were always fluid), but it does give a flavour of the Vorticist/ *Blast* temper. Essentially, the Manifesto was a collection of suggestive provocations that expressed a particular attitude (this is self-evident and scarcely requires elaboration). It was primarily with this attitude that early critics assumed Eliot to be aligned at the time. This assumption appeared to be confirmed as *Poems 1920* was published, followed by *The Waste Land* in 1922, which was regarded as the pinnacle of modernist expression. (Pound notoriously edited this poem extensively and regarded it as the highest poetic achievement of modernism.) As much because of its association with Pound and like-minded contemporaries as because of its intrinsic qualities, the early work of Eliot – starting with the *Prufrock* poems and culminating with *The Waste Land* – came to be regarded as the high point of a coherent and thrilling revolutionary (with all the political connotations that implied) modernist movement. As the last statement of the *Blast* Manifesto says: 'The nearest thing in England to a great traditional French artist, is a great revolutionary English one.'

This initial understanding of Eliot's poetry, however, came to be regarded with unease as his ideological tendencies became clearer. It gradually emerged that, despite their aesthetic daring and provocativeness, the modernists – particularly Pound, Lewis and Eliot – were capable of holding ideological positions that were either deeply conservative or implicitly totalitarian. This I come to in phases two and three below.

This account of phase one leads me to one of the questions that continue to provoke debate. **To what extent was the so-called modernist movement in literature (and the arts): (a) the coherent product of** a specific period, or of the intellectual and political currents that characterize that period; (b) the deliberately constructed result of a particular group of talented writers and artists coming together in different ways and supporting each other's work; or (c) a retrospective construction put on texts and ideas that were distinct and not necessarily connected at the time?

As I explained above, this is not a question that you are expected to deal with immediately, but one towards which you can gradually build up a perspective as you read further in the subject.

Phase two

Eliot was writing literary book reviews for *The Little Review* and *The Egoist* by 1917, when he became assistant editor of the latter. Between 1917 and 1919 Eliot wrote a series of essays, primarily for *The Egoist*, which brought him a well-deserved reputation as a literary critic and an invitation from John Middleton Murry to become assistant editor of the prestigious journal the *Athenaeum*. Eliot felt that the position might be insecure and did not accept it, but wrote often for the journal and developed a close relationship with Murry. Eliot's first collection of critical essays, *The Sacred Wood*, was published in 1920 (in the same year as *Poems 1920*), and established what would continue for much of the twentieth century to be a powerful voice in literary criticism. Some of his best-known critical writings appeared in the period between 1917 and 1921, including the single most influential critical essay of the time, 'Tradition and the Individual Talent' (first published in 1919 in *The Egoist*). **Now read the extract from Eliot's essay (Reader, Item 20.1).** Other notable essays from this period are 'Reflections on *Vers Libre*' (*New Statesman*, 1917), 'Hamlet and his Problems' (*Athenaeum*, 1919), 'The Perfect Critic' (which became the opening essay of *The Sacred Wood*, 1920), and 'The Metaphysical Poets' (*Times Literary Supplement*, 1921). Eliot established his own journal, *The Criterion*, in 1922 and it became for the next seventeen years the principal channel for his critical and social/political views, though he continued to contribute critical articles to other magazines and journals in this period and thereafter.

The appearance in the same year of *Poems 1920* and *The Sacred Wood* naturally gave a particular tilt to assessments of Eliot's own poetry: it seemed logical to read his poetry in his own critical terms, and evaluate it according to the measures he had provided. In brief, Eliot's poetry and criticism have come to be regarded as part of a single enterprise, and it has been customary since the early 1920s to find a way into Eliot's poetry by using his critical ideas. I comment below on the manner in which this affects readings of the *Prufrock* poems in retrospect. Before that, however, a few general observations about Eliot's critical stance might be useful.

First, Eliot's critical thinking was ambitious in the sense that it seemed to be designed to change the critical theory and practice of his time. Many of his critical opinions, therefore, even when given in the context of discussions of specific themes, are presented as generalizations. A symptom of this is the manner in which certain critical phrases from Eliot's essays often become dislocated from their specific contexts and are used as critical ideas of general import: examples of this in 'Tradition and the Individual Talent' are the terms 'tradition' and 'contemporaneity', and the words 'the poet has, not a "personality" to express, but a particular medium'.

Second, at the broadest level, Eliot's literary critical presumptions appear to be consistent with those entertained by most of his modernist circle: these presumptions can be traced back to Hulme's essays (which had influenced the Imagists, especially Pound), and some had already been expressed with characteristic vivacity in the essays of Pound. There are two main thrusts in Eliot's 'Tradition and the Individual Talent', which, with occasional modifications, he stood by throughout his literary career. One was that, in attempting to write literary works in the present, the artist needs to maintain an awareness of (and therefore a conformity with) the whole 'tradition' of literary productions (such that the contemporary literary work is able to modify the past):

> The existing order is complete before the new work arrives; for order to persist after the supervention of novelty, the *whole* existing order must be, if ever so slightly, altered; and so the relations, proportions, values of each work of art toward the whole are readjusted; and this is conformity between the old and the new.

The second was the need for the artist to be strictly impersonal, and surrender personality to art:

> the poet has, not a 'personality' to express, but a particular medium, which is only a medium and not a personality, in which impressions and experiences combine in peculiar and unexpected ways. Impressions and experiences which are important for the man may take no place in the poetry, and those which become important in the poetry may play quite a negligible part in the man, the personality.

Eliot was soon to present this attitude to literary writing (tradition conscious and impersonal) as being 'classicist', and in *The Criterion* he later set up a debate on the merits and demerits of classicism as opposed to romanticism (see Margolis, 1972, pp.52–67). It was clear to all fellow-modernists that Eliot was championing the cause of modernist 'classicism', because this distinction had already been made influentially by Hulme in his essay 'Romanticism and Classicism' (1913–14), in which he had announced the 'exhaustion' of romanticism and an imminent 'classical revival'. **Read the extract from Hulme's essay (Reader, Item 20.2)**. Both the above arguments are also reminiscent of certain early essays by Pound. In 1913, Pound's 'The Serious Artist' (published in *The Egoist*), for instance, maintained the need to distinguish the artist from the person, roughly along the lines of Eliot's attempt to distinguish the artist from the personality:

> The desire to stand on the stage, the desire of plaudits has nothing to do with serious art. The serious artist may like to stand on the stage, he may, apart from his art, be any kind of imbecile you like, but the two things are not connected, at least they are not concentric.
>
> (Pound, 1954, p.47)

Much of Pound's critical writing consisted in prescriptions and compendiums of what would-be poets should read (culminating in his *ABC of Reading*, 1934), which had implicit within it an Eliot-like notion that an awareness of tradition is important.

Third, underlying most of the theoretical arguments (which are largely variations on, or extensions of, the arguments outlined above) in Eliot's essays is an understanding of the critic's function. Eliot did write several substantial essays about the principles that should govern criticism, which addressed ideas that were popular at the time (especially those of Matthew Arnold): examples are such early essays as 'The Perfect Critic' (1920) or 'The Function of Criticism' (1923), and such later essays as 'To Criticize the Critic' (1961). I do not need to go into the details of these for this section, but three observations in this regard can usefully be made. One, Eliot often wrote with the conviction that, as he says in 'The Perfect Critic', 'the critic and the creative artist should frequently be the same person' (in Eliot, [1920] 1960, p.16): that is, his criticism often seems to be directed to other writers and poets. Two, as a rhetorical strategy Eliot depended more on convinced authoritative statements than on arguments. Three, despite disagreements with Arnold, Eliot did believe that good poetry is self-evidently so and that it is not really necessary to dissect why it is so (an idea that owes something to Arnold's notion of 'touchstones'; 'The Study of Poetry', in Arnold, 1964, pp.241–3).

I hope the three previous paragraphs convey a general impression of Eliot's literary-critical interventions, and therefore of the manner in which they may have been brought to bear on his poetry. As far as the *Prufrock* poems go, we can now detect in them some obvious connections to Eliot's critical theories. The allusive character of Eliot's poetic language, which seems to embrace a whole literary tradition, becomes immediately significant in the light of Eliot's critical views. There appears to be a greater design in the allusiveness than might have been suspected otherwise – it is arguable that Eliot had deliberately followed his critical principles in his creative practice, and that his poems were meant to serve as exemplary demonstrations of awareness of tradition. Further, the carefully worked-in organizational principles drawn from Laforgue and Bergson can be regarded as modes of ensuring that artistic impersonality is maintained. The kind of self-consciousness that these necessitated, the careful positing of masks and juxtaposition of philosophical deliberation, ensured that the biographical poet would be effaced in favour of a constructed poet persona: that Eliot would disappear, as a hard-headed classicist should, behind newly erected modernist conventions (organizing principles).

If you were to try to establish connections between the ideas expressed in 'Tradition and the Individual Talent' and some of the *Prufrock* poems you would no doubt come up with more. The point, however, is that your effort to do so is an act of retrospective reconstruction once you become aware of Eliot's critical ideas. That has been the case for all attempts at understanding Eliot's early poetry in terms of critical ideas that he formulated later. And this question can be extended beyond Eliot to the work of other modernists – how self-consciously did Pound, or Lewis, or Aldington adhere to their (or such) modernist classicist critical principles?

Another question that is still the subject of much debate and research surfaces from these considerations. **To what extent are the critical principles that the modernist writers espoused consistent with their creative literary practice? How far were their creative efforts guided by such critical principles? Were these critical principles mainly a convenient method of expressing a new and unexpected position, or were they really central to what Pound, Eliot and others were attempting to do in their creative literary writing?**

Phase three

In 1922, Eliot founded his journal, *The Criterion*. This was established as a literary review and through the 1920s attracted several distinguished European and US contributors. Though its circulation remained small, it did acquire a certain prestige and as its editor Eliot established himself as a significant man of letters (not just a poet and critic, but a social commentator and publisher). He denied wishing to establish a coterie through this position but did admit a desire to draw together like-minded writers and intellectuals who would be inclined towards (but not exclusively) Tory values and classicist artistic principles (see Margolis, 1972, Chapter 2). Through *The Criterion* Eliot acquired such a group of acolytes (including Herbert Read and, at least at the beginning, Richard Aldington). Initially, he also found sympathy and support from Pound, but gradually Pound chose to distance himself from the journal. Lewis never quite got attached to it. In the 1930s,

Eliot diluted the journal's literary emphasis, and turned more to social and political matters (in an increasingly conservative and religious temper, but with interesting departures from that which allowed him to publish such socialist thinkers as the critic A.L. Rowse and poets like W.H. Auden and Hugh McDiarmid). Eliot stopped publication of *The Criterion* in 1939.

In 1922 also, in the first issue of *The Criterion*, Eliot published his long poem, *The Waste Land*. This quickly came to be regarded as the most adventurous and experimental work of modernist writing (worthy of a revolutionary spirit), which moreover expressed something of the postwar disenchantment that many felt at the time. A new generation of young poets emerged (the generation which would come into its own in the 1930s) who regarded Eliot as some sort of modernist patriarch and aesthetic radical, and who admired *The Waste Land*.

In 1925, Eliot left employment at Lloyd's Bank and joined the publishing concern Faber & Gwyer, later Faber & Faber, becoming one of the company's directors. Faber thereafter published all his major work and took over the publication of *The Criterion*, and Eliot became responsible for Faber's poetry list. Under Eliot's control this list became (and continues to be) one of the most prestigious in the English language. Along with the role of the publisher came the courtship of aspiring writers, and the opportunity to increase his circle of influence. Eliot continued his association with Faber & Faber until his death in 1965.

With these three developments Eliot became *the* establishment figure he is now firmly understood to be. His sphere of influence grew. Every kind of literary honour and distinction that was available was showered on him. An immense critical industry grew, and continues to grow, around his work. In later life (from the 1930s) he expanded his intellectual pursuits both within the literary sphere (he started writing plays) and outside it (he devoted himself to sociological, cultural and theological matters), and whatever he wrote or said was taken seriously and discussed widely. His poems and criticism came to be firmly placed in the English literary canon – in critical histories of literary modernism, and in university and school curricula. As he gradually became an establishment icon, his modernism also gradually became something of an establishment matter, with a few darker tones of rather unwholesome rigidity and narrowness mixed in. An ever more narrowly conceived religiosity led him to denounce most of his fellow-modernists as heretics in *After Strange Gods* (1934). This work was also notoriously controversial for a statement in it expressing doubts about the desirability 'of any large number of free thinking Jews'. A taint of anti-Semitism has been attributed to Eliot's writings and ideas at regular intervals since (see Julius, 1995). Eliot's later books on religious and social theory, such as *The Idea of a Christian Society* (1939) and *Notes Toward a Definition of Culture* (1949), express admiration for culturally and religiously homogeneous and hierarchical societies. As befits an establishment icon, after his death both his champions and his detractors have often been unreasonably partisan. On the one hand, there has been widespread speculation about his alleged fascist tendencies and possible sexual repressions, and the manner in which these may have influenced his writing. On the other hand, there have also been loud proclamations of the unquestionability of Eliot's literary achievements and moral qualities, and plenty of avowals of blind adulation. Interesting discussions of these issues are available in books by Christopher Ricks (1988), Anthony Julius (1995) and Kenneth Asher (1995).

There is a curious reversal in Eliot's progression from being seen as an experimental, avant-garde, subversive poet/critic to being regarded as a conservative, traditionalist and yet paradoxically modernist, establishment icon. This apparent change can be viewed in two ways – both of which have a profound impact on how his early poems (from the *Prufrock* poems to *The Waste Land*) are read.

One view is that there are two Eliots, a liberal younger one and a conservative older one. It is possible that Eliot's early work was indeed experimental, adventurous and anti-establishment in a manner that showed an open mind, reflecting an ideological position that was at least implicitly open and receptive. Somewhere in the late 1920s, his mind-set underwent a change. He converted to Anglo-Catholicism, and became more rigid in his speculations on classicism and conservatism. The creative and critical output of the later Eliot came to be ideologically differently oriented from that of the early Eliot, giving rise to the view that there are two Eliots. One was responsible for the writings from the *Prufrock* poems to *The Waste Land*, from the early philosophical writings to *The Sacred Wood* and to the early 1920s commentaries in *The Criterion*. The other was the poet of *Ash Wednesday* (1930) and *Four Quartets* (1944), the playwright who wrote *The Rock* (1934), *Murder in the Cathedral* (1935) and the other verse plays, the thinker who started writing about religious matters from *For Lancelot Andrewes* (1930) onwards. Both bodies of work can be regarded as having been produced by somewhat different people and should be understood on their own terms. It was the early Eliot who was truly modernist, while the later Eliot became the opposite – conservative and traditionalist. In different ways, this contradictoriness was also manifest in other modernists. Pound gravitated from a certain aesthetic nonconformism (reflexive of a liberal temper) to a particularly brutal anti-Semitism and fascism. Lewis too managed to bounce back and forth between a level-headed liberalism and some kind of fascism (not as drastic as Pound's, but unpleasant nevertheless).

An alternative view is that there are not two Eliots, but just one consistent Eliot. The different stances result from the fact that in matters of aesthetics and literary form he was a revolutionary, and in social, political and religious matters he was a conservative and a bigot. Aesthetic and poetic daring does not necessarily also represent daring in social, political and religious matters. Literary daring and political conservatism can be – and, for many modernist writers, was – part of the same mind-set. That for Eliot this combination operated in non-contradictory ways was clear from early on. It is no accident that his clarification of modernist principles comes with clarion calls for traditionalism and classicism. Even when writing of the most liberating formal assumptions of modern poetry, *vers libre* or free verse, Eliot could be straightforwardly politically conservative. There is little doubt that Eliot was one of the most influential practitioners of *vers libre* himself. But that was not because he regarded the form to be an open and liberal one. In his 1917 essay 'Reflections on *Vers Libre*', Eliot observed that *vers libre* could only be defined in a negative fashion as '(1) absence of pattern, (2) absence of rhyme, (3) absence of metre', and considering this an unsatisfactory situation, he came up with the following (obviously political) conclusion:

> As for *vers libre*, we conclude that it is not defined by absence of pattern or absence of rhyme, for other verse is without these; that it is not defined by the non-existence of metre, since even the *worst* verse can be scanned; and we conclude that the division between Conservative Verse and *vers libre* does not exist, for there is only good verse, bad verse, and chaos.
>
> (Eliot, 1953, p.86)

The *Prufrock* poems are inaugurations of a particular complex of ideas and attitudes, which could be simultaneously and coherently both unexpectedly nonconformist in some ways and yet quite conservative in others. That is the case, with different emphases, for the body of Eliot's work – and indeed of most works that are now thought of as modernist. The contradictoriness of Pound and Lewis, for instance, is not really contradictoriness but the coherent character of their creative and critical tendencies. Modernism was itself largely a complex of aesthetic nonconformism and political conservatism or absolutism. Emancipatory and liberal politics forms only a very small part of literary modernism, and has comparatively less to do with formal or aesthetic daring.

That is the long view of Eliot's career, and of the two ways in which the *Prufrock* poems particularly, and literary modernism generally, may be understood in that context. It too leads to a general question that continues to be debated and that you may wish to reflect on further before you eventually make up your own mind about the answer. **What is the relationship between modernist formal and stylistic innovations and the social and political convictions of modernist writers? What are the ways in which ideology and aesthetics are related to each other in the work of literary modernists like Eliot (and others)?**

The three phases together give a working outline of the construction of what is now regarded as mainstream literary modernism in the twentieth century, and the three questions raised in this section indicate areas where debates about mainstream establishment modernism have been concentrated and continue to be focused. A deeper engagement with these debates becomes possible only by going beyond the precincts of Eliot's kind of literary modernism, beyond this mainstream modernism, to other shades of modernism – in other streams and at the margins. Only then can this kind of modernism be contextualized and put into perspective adequately.

Works cited

Ackroyd, P. (1985) *T.S. Eliot*, London: Hamish Hamilton.

Arnold, M. (1964) *Essays in Criticism: First and Second Series*, intro. by G.K. Chesterton, Everyman's Library, London: Dent.

Asher, K. (1995) *T.S. Eliot and Ideology*, Cambridge: Cambridge University Press.

Bergson, H. (1908) *Matter and Memory*, trans. by N.M. Paul and W. Scott Palmer, London: Macmillan.

Bergson, H. (1911) *Creative Evolution*, trans. by A. Mitchell, London: Macmillan.

Clarke, G. (ed.) (1990) *T.S. Eliot: Critical Assessments*, 4 vols, London: Croom Helm.

Dante Alighieri (1908) *The Divine Comedy*, trans. by H. Cary, London: Dent.

Dasenbrock, R.W. (1985) *The Literary Vorticism of Ezra Pound and Wyndham Lewis*, Baltimore: Johns Hopkins University Press.

Eliot, T.S. (1953) *Selected Prose*, ed. by J. Hayward, Harmondsworth: Penguin (Peregrine).

Eliot, T.S. ([1920] 1960) *The Sacred Wood*, London: Methuen.

Eliot, T.S. (1965) *To Criticize the Critic*, London: Faber & Faber.

Eliot, T.S. (1988) *The Letters of T.S. Eliot*, vol.1: *1898–1922*, ed. by V. Eliot, London: Faber & Faber.

Eliot, T.S. (1996) *Inventions of the March Hare: Poems 1909–1917*, ed. by C. Ricks, London: Faber & Faber.

Eliot, T.S. ([1917] 2001) *Prufrock and Other Observations*, London: Faber & Faber.

Goodwinn, K.L. (1966) *The Influence of Ezra Pound*, London: Oxford University Press.

Grant, M. (ed.) (1982) *T.S. Eliot: The Critical Heritage*, 2 vols, London: Routledge & Kegan Paul.

Gray, P. (1982) *T.S. Eliot's Intellectual and Poetic Development 1909–1922*, Brighton: Harvester.

Jones, P. (1972) *Imagist Poetry*, Harmondsworth: Penguin.

Julius, A. (1995) *T.S. Eliot, Anti-Semitism and Literary Form*, Cambridge: Cambridge University Press.

Laforgue, J. (1998) *Selected Poems*, trans. by G.D. Martin, Harmondsworth: Penguin.

Lehmann, A.G. (1950) *The Symbolist Aesthetic in France 1885–1895*, Oxford: Basil Blackwell.

Lewis, W. (1927) *Time and the Western Man*, London: Chatto & Windus.

Margolis, J.D. (1972) *T.S. Eliot's Intellectual Development 1922–1939*, Chicago: University of Chicago Press.

Pound, E. ([1934] 1951) *ABC of Reading*, London: Faber & Faber.

Pound, E. (1954) *Literary Essays of Ezra Pound*, ed. by T.S. Eliot, London: Faber & Faber.

Ricks, C. (1988) *T.S. Eliot and Prejudice*, London: Faber & Faber.

Ricks, C. (1996) 'Preface', T.S. Eliot, *Inventions of the March Hare: Poems 1909–1917*, ed. by C. Ricks, London: Faber & Faber.

Southam, B.C. (1968) *A Student's Guide to the Selected Poems of T.S. Eliot*, London: Faber & Faber.

Symons, A. (1899) *The Symbolist Movement in Literature*, London: William Heinemann.

Williamson, G. (1955) *A Reader's Guide to T.S. Eliot: A Poem-By-Poem Analysis*, London: Thames & Hudson.

Wilson, E. (1931) *Axel's Castle: A Study in the Imaginative Literature of 1870–1930*, Glasgow: Collins.

Further reading

Ardis, A.L. (2002) *Modernism and Cultural Conflict 1880–1922*, Cambridge: Cambridge University Press. The author examines the ways in which modernists (the coterie around Pound, Eliot and Joyce) secured their cultural centrality, documents their support of mainstream attitudes towards science, and analyses the conservative cultural and sexual politics masked by their radical formalist poetics. Some instances of opposition to modernist self-fashioning in British socialism and feminism of the period are discussed. The book also considers how literary modernism's rise to aesthetic prominence paved the way for the institutionalization of English studies through the devaluation of other aesthetic practices.

Menand, L. (1988) *Discovering Modernism: T.S. Eliot and his Context*, Oxford: Oxford University Press. The book examines the crisis in literature that produced the entire modernist movement, and argues that the literary values of the nineteenth century became the problems of the twentieth century. This presents a useful analysis of the complex phenomenon of literary change, and tries to understand why Eliot's work was regarded as the voice of modernism.

Rainey, L. (1999) *Institutions of Modernism*, New Haven: Yale University Press. This account of modernism and its place in public culture looks at where modernism was produced and how it was transmitted to particular audiences. Using previously unexamined primary materials, the author considers five modernist figures – Joyce, Eliot, Pound, Hilda Doolittle and F.T. Marinetti – with a view to coming to grips with modernism itself.

CHAPTER 6

Virginia Woolf, *Orlando*

NICOLA J. WATSON

Overview

In this chapter I will be examining Virginia Woolf's experimental novel *Orlando*, considering it as characteristic of 'high' modernism in its bending of inherited conventions of genre and of character. The text is placed in the context of Woolf's own thinking about both the proper nature of modern fiction and the relationship between women and writing throughout history. Finally, I will be looking at how *Orlando* has been interpreted through adaptation, particularly in Sally Potter's film version of the 1990s.

Introduction

Whether viewed as an experimental modernist writer or as a revolutionary theorist and practitioner of women's writing (and although the two are bound up together, they are often written about as though they were separate people), Woolf has been perceived as a major literary figure within twentieth-century literature and culture by critics of all persuasions. A friend, lover or acquaintance of practically everyone who was anyone in London modernist circles, including Katherine Mansfield and T.S. Eliot, she was a prolific and important literary critic and essayist, in addition to producing some ten novels, each as experimental and original as the one that preceded it.

Orlando, a mature work published in 1928, is a sparkling example of the so-called 'high' modernism of the early twentieth century. Although you need to bear in mind the qualifications made in the Introduction to Part 2 with regard to the wide variety of modernisms, for the purposes of this chapter 'high' modernism means 'full-blown' or 'mature' modernism. (The adjective has sometimes tended, more or less accidentally, to carry connotations of quality, or elitism; it is not intended to do so here.) In conventional literary criticism, the term is usually taken to indicate experimental work – including writing – of the 1920s. English and English-speaking modernists circling around the metropolitan centre of interwar London had, despite their many differences, certain things in common. Many knew each other socially and professionally through loose coteries of lovers, family, undergraduate friendships and publishing ventures such as Woolf's own Hogarth Press. Much more importantly, they tended to have in common a certain intellectual milieu – which does not mean that all such writers had actually read all the thinkers by whom they were influenced. Rather, their ideas were 'in the air' of conversation and correspondence. The ideas of Henri Bergson on time and consciousness (which you looked at in Chapter 5), of Bertrand Russell on 'sense data' and of Sigmund Freud on subjectivity and sexuality, all find echoes and resonances in the writings of the Bloomsbury set (so-called because they were based in Bloomsbury, London) of which Woolf was a member. This circle, which included Lytton Strachey, Duncan Grant, Roger Fry, Vanessa Bell and E.M. Forster, shared with modernists more generally an urgent sense of 'modernity'. Broadly speaking, this produced a feeling that everything within the arts was to be radically remade, to match a radical change in aesthetic perception that Woolf had dated at around 1910. This sense of crisis and severance was much accentuated by the First World War, which subsequently slaughtered so many. Nothing now was to be taken for granted in the way of literary form, and unthinking reproduction of the familiar would be useless (in Chapter 5 you came across this view expressed by Eliot in 'Tradition and the Individual Talent').

Orlando self-consciously takes as its subject the coming and the nature of this modernity, concerns that were central to the project of inventing a modernist sensibility. Woolf flouted her readers' expectations by experimentally bending the realism that she and her contemporaries inherited from Victorian and Edwardian culture. She constructed an aesthetic of character, narrative and genre that is equivalent to the agenda of such works of the same decade as Eliot's *The Waste Land* (1922) or James Joyce's *Ulysses* (1922). *Orlando* allows us to examine how modernist speculations as to the nature of time and consciousness – which you have already encountered in relation to poetry in Chapter 5 – are realized in extended prose narrative. Moreover, it gives us a way to examine the opportunities that modernist aesthetics could offer to the woman writer in the 1920s, for one way of describing *Orlando* would be to regard it as a utopian fantasy of the coming-into-being of the fully enfranchized modern woman writer. (It is not incidental that 1928, the year of this novel's publication, was also the year in which universal suffrage was finally achieved by British women.) Drafted contemporaneously with Woolf's seminal essay *A Room of One's Own*, which we will be looking at towards the end of this chapter, *Orlando* shares something of that tract's delight in trespass, as well as many of its feminist preoccupations, including its interest in the problematic relation between the woman writer and her literary and national heritage. Since its first publication, as we shall see, *Orlando* continued to resonate behind much of twentieth-century literary endeavour, becoming in the 1990s a key text for so-called postmodernism and postfeminism.

If this sounds just a fraction dutifully intellectual, you will be glad to know that *Orlando* is anything but dutiful. In fact, Woolf herself conceived of it as a 'holiday' and a 'joke', and though we are going to take *Orlando* seriously, part of taking it seriously is to take pleasure in this euphoric concoction.

Questions of genre

Biography

Skip any of the trappings of modern scholarly editions for the moment – introduction, bibliography, chronology, explanatory notes. Instead, try to imagine this book as it would have presented itself to the reader in 1928, handsomely bound in hardback and published by Woolf's own consciously highbrow publishing concern, the Hogarth Press. And let us, moreover, with a perversity worthy of Woolf herself, start, not by reading the book, but by looking at the peripheries of the text – at the peculiar and resonant choice of title and subtitle, at the dedication, the Preface, the list of illustrations and the illustrations themselves, and, turning to the end, at the index.

What expectations does this title as a whole conjure up? What expectations do the Preface, index, footnotes and illustrations arouse in you?

At first glance, the book appears to be a mildly scholarly, non-fiction work, complete with meticulous acknowledgements and extensive name-dropping in the Preface, and an index that is entirely characteristic of a biography of the period, alphabetically atomizing the narrative into a litter of trivia chronologically listed: 'Orlando, appearance as a boy, 15; writes his first play, 16; visits Queen at Whitehall, 23; made Treasurer and Steward, 24', and so on (Woolf, [1928] 1998, p.316; all subsequent references are to this edition). This impression is reinforced by the illustrations (which in the first edition were spread throughout the text): reproductions of oil paintings, conscientiously captioned ('Orlando as a Boy'), supported by photographs, very much in the manner of biography – which, after all, is the claim made by the subtitle. Indeed, when the book first came out, booksellers insisted on marketing it as biography, to the comical dismay of Woolf herself, who wrote in her diary that this turn of events was a high price to pay for what she had regarded as a joke (1980, vol.3, pp.177, 198).

More careful examination reveals that we are indeed looking at a 'joke'. The Preface blandly spoofs the language and business of acknowledgement: 'I have had the advantage – how great I alone can estimate – of Mr Arthur Waley's knowledge of Chinese' (p.5). There is a world of irony embedded in that single sentence. Note how oddly the acknowledgements to people for their expertise on 'the law of property', or 'Chinese', or 'the understanding of the art of painting' strike the ear. In fact, they have the unmistakable air of being coterie in-jokes. If 'knowledge' gets a sardonic cold shoulder, research (note the 'arduous' but 'vain' researches of Miss M.K. Snowdon; p.5) and factual accuracy (note the rudeness at the expense of the 'gentleman in America'; p.7) are given equally short shrift. (This last crack turned out to be prophetic; *Orlando*, to Woolf's amused exasperation, immediately and ever after attracted solemn accusations of anachronism and inaccuracy.) The index, too, was evidently written with tongue well and truly in cheek. After all, what index entry on a biographee, even in our enlightened and surgically advanced days, usually starts with 'appearance as a boy' and blandly concludes with 'declared a woman'? And surely there is something fishy about a subject who can feature in what is clearly an Elizabethan painting *and* a modern photograph? By now, you should be suspecting that you have been led well and truly up the garden path, a suspicion that perhaps should already have insinuated itself from the title.

For there is, surely, something of a disjunction between title and subtitle. On the whole, biography is written about someone you have heard of, whether dead or alive – that is why there is a market for a biography of the person at all. But the name 'Orlando' hardly suggests a proper biographical subject – this subject is not locked into historical verifiability with a surname, a title or even the odd date. Rather, the name conjures up a set of references inimical to the sober facts and forensic documentation beloved of history and biography. 'Orlando' is a name that echoes from the caverns of romance, the lover and knight whose adventures are told variously in the anonymous *Chanson de Roland* (twelfth century), the late medieval poem by Matteomaria Boiardo, *Orlando Innamorato* (1487) and in Ludovico Ariosto's sequel to it, *Orlando Furioso* (1532), and who metamorphoses into the lover of the sexually ambiguous Rosalind in Shakespeare's romantic comedy *As You Like It* (1599–1600). Via these allusions, the name comes with a baggage of crusading adventure and exotic enchantment, metamorphosis and cross-dressing. The title, then, already signals that we might be drifting away from the high road of Victorian and Edwardian biography and about to foray into altogether more tricky and magical territory.

Any lingering expectations of a conventional biography vanish pretty soon as we read on. **Now read from the beginning of Chapter 1 through to '... and dipped an old stained goose quill in the ink' (1; p.16). How does this opening parody biographical conventions?**

The first sentence definitively explodes biographical convention, with its astonishing parenthetical interpolation, which sets even the sex of the subject momentarily in doubt: 'He – for there could be no doubt of his sex, though the fashion of the time did something to disguise it' (1; p.13). As Rachel Bowlby remarks in her Introduction to the Oxford World's Classics edition, 'Here the denial of the doubt is just what lets in the doubt, by saying what it says needs no saying' (1998, p.xxxvii). The ground of biography itself shifts, since on the whole one of the very few things that biographical narrative is not in any doubt over is the sex of its subject. The subsequent course of the narrative seems immediately uncertain, since, if you will forgive me a gross and partially inaccurate generalization, traditionally stories about women tend to be governed by the trajectory of heterosexual romance while those about men concentrate on descriptions of worldly achievement. The sentence also institutes a particular and unusual relationship between biographer and subject – one of imperfect knowledge, bafflement and 'doubt'. The biographer's voice is foregrounded – as it will be throughout – but it is confounded, and the biographical enterprise, at least as conceived of conventionally, is clearly already in danger of frustration. Woolf parodies Victorian phrenological analysis, which liked to see character and destiny in the shape of the head and face (if you know Charlotte Brontë's *Jane Eyre* (1847), you will recall that Mr Rochester, when disguised as a fortune-teller, conducts just such an analysis of Jane's physiognomy). Orlando is described as at first sight a biographer's dream subject:

> Happy the mother who bears, happier still the biographer who records the life of such a one! ... From deed to deed, from glory to glory, from office to office he must go, his scribe following after, till they reach whatever seat it may be that is the height of their desire. Orlando, to look at, was cut out precisely for some such career.

> (1; pp.14–15)

But a second glance divines from the forehead and eyes 'that riot and confusion of the passions and emotions which every good biographer detests' (1; p.16). Far from being a conventional biographical subject, Orlando is, this suggests, a spirit of 'confusion'.

This initial sense of Orlando as that which frustrates biographical convention will be confirmed in the following pages, as Woolf constantly shows up biographical truth as merely a matter of conventions of verisimilitude. Just a little further on, Woolf makes fun of the biographer's necessary habit of connecting up his or her subject's characteristics into a causal fiction of a motivated and consistent whole person:

> There is perhaps a kinship among qualities; one draws another along with it; and the biographer should here call attention to the fact that this clumsiness is often mated with a love of solitude. Having stumbled over a chest, Orlando naturally loved solitary places, vast views, and to feel himself for ever and ever and ever alone.

> (1; p.17)

To take another example from later in the text, here is the narrative voice fussing conscientiously and pedantically over 'documentation' – the essential grounding for biography:

> The biographer is now faced with a difficulty which it is better perhaps to confess than to gloss over. Up to this point in telling the story of Orlando's life, documents, both private and historical, have made it possible to fulfil the first duty of a biographer, which is to plod, without looking to right or left, in the indelible footprints of truth; unenticed by flowers; regardless of shade; on and on methodically till we fall plump into the grave and write *finis* on the tombstone above our heads. But now we come to an episode which lies right across our path, so that there is no ignoring it. Yet it is dark, mysterious, and undocumented.
>
> (2; p.63)

Indeed, the fate of documents in this book is often unhappy – the scorched and torn letters of Lieutenant Brigge and Miss Penelope Hartopp will bear witness to that (3; pp.122–3). As you read further, it will become plain that, anyway, this is not really a biography that believes that the 'verifiable' is necessarily the truth.

The reader, then, is confounded and wrong-footed, in a playful exuberance of experimentation. We are looking at a parody of the sorts of scholarly enterprise that might together feed into the making of a biography, a parody indeed of most of the conventions of biographical and historical writing. This is evident, for example, if we look carefully at the portraits and photographs. **Take a look at them now. In what ways do they fulfil or flout convention?**

As I have already remarked, despite the air of historical accuracy, it is clearly unusual – in fact, implausible – for the subject of a biography to appear in so many different historical periods. The portraits are not of the same person, though they are claimed to be so. On the other hand, it is clear that the 'Orlando' in the photographs is the same person, masquerading in different period costumes. Both sets of pictures, instead of functioning as you might expect in a biography, as hard documentary evidence, are fabrications. Both sets, in different ways, enact not historical reality but poses and performances of an imaginary self (Marcus, 1997, p.120).

The whole book thus has, even in these early pages, the air of an elaborate joke on us, a wild goose chase, as the very last paragraph of the whole will suggest. (Bowlby, entering into the wildly anarchic and anti-scholarly spirit of the thing, provides her own spurious footnote by way of addendum – I won't reference it, so that you can have the fun of looking out for it.) Yet Woolf herself regarded the piece as a mixture of seriousness and nonsense. So in what sense, if any, can we take seriously Woolf's claim that

Orlando is a 'biography'? **To get an idea of Woolf's own perception of the book as she was conceiving and writing it, take a look at the diary entries for 1927 and 1928 (Reader, Item 21). What sorts of 'biographical' writing does she have in mind to play with?**

The first extract, dated 20 September 1927, in addition to identifying 'Vita' as 'Orlando, a young nobleman', also notes that her friends – Lytton [Strachey], Roger [Fry], Duncan [Grant], Clive [Bell] and Adrian [Stephen] – should appear in 'truthful' 'but fantastic' guise. There is, therefore, a suggestion of a *roman-à-clef*. (A *roman-à-clef* – literally, a story with a key – is a novel whose characters are meant to be recognized as real people, though they are represented under fictional names, and whose action is usually based on a real-life scandal.) The entry also suggests an interest in a number of quasi-historical genres. The mention of a 'grand historical picture' including these friends conjures up imaginary scenes of contemporary or dead authors in company composed by both essayists and painters from around 1800. There is the suggestion of writing disguised 'memoirs of one's own times'. Finally, Woolf imagines a disparate collection of sketches, something, perhaps, along the lines of charades, tableaux, pageants or 'imaginary conversations'. (The genre of the 'imaginary conversation', pioneered by the early nineteenth-century essayist Walter Savage Landor and popular throughout the nineteenth century, offered readers the pleasure of eavesdropping on fabricated dialogues between historical celebrities.) By early October, however, she has settled on the notion of 'a biography beginning in the year 1500 & continuing to the present day'. Significantly, a language of pleasure begins to creep in; she describes the work as something to be dashed off, a 'treat', and by 22 October as 'a book ... which I write after tea', 'furtively but with all the more passion', and in 'rapture' and 'delight'.

As you may already have begun to realize, *Orlando* was genuinely first conceived as a biography – however fantastic – as a tribute and gift to Woolf's friend and sometime lover Vita Sackville-West. Nigel Nicolson, Sackville-West's son by her diplomat husband Harold Nicolson, described *Orlando* as 'the world's most charming love-letter' (Nicolson, 1973, p.201). Woolf first met Sackville-West in 1922, and their subsequent affair, which began in December 1925, lasted with the full knowledge of both their husbands until the early 1930s. Orlando's loves broadly fictionalize many of Sackville-West's real-life love affairs, in particular her lesbian affair with Violet Trefusis and her open marriage; above all, Orlando's house is modelled on Sackville-West's beloved family home, Knole, in Kent (Figure 6.1). Orlando's poetic ambitions parallel, sometimes unkindly, Sackville-West's own poetic career; Orlando's cherished poem 'The Oak Tree' is a pun on Knole's location in Sevenoaks; the lawsuit over Orlando's right to inherit is a parody of a real-life lawsuit, almost equally absurd (for which see Bowlby, 1998, pp.xxxix–xl); the text is littered with personal minutiae and private jokes (for which see Nigel

Nicolson's explanatory notes on the text, included at the back of the Oxford World's Classics edition). The published text is openly dedicated to Sackville-West, and the portraits and photographs are all, as you may already have worked out, of her or her ancestors and family members. This flavour of aristocratic insider gossip was something that certainly contributed to the book's instant popularity and excellent sales.

To this extent, then, *Orlando* really is a biography – even the biographical form is a sort of pun on the name Vita, which means 'life'. But it is a very particular sort of biography, inflected by Woolf's vision of Sackville-West's status as an aristocrat, the latest in the long line of Sackvilles. Modern biography and autobiography (by 'modern' I mean that written and published since the mid-eighteenth century) has had an escalating tendency to concentrate on endowing the public subject with the story of a private self – the story, in fact, of the development of that private self. This is perhaps especially the case for biographies and autobiographies of writers, from Jean-Jacques Rousseau's *Confessions* (1781–8) onwards. Writers achieve

Figure 6.1   Aerial view of house and park, Knole, Kent. (Reproduced with the permission of Simmons Aerofilms Ltd.) Now owned by the National Trust, Knole dates from the fifteenth century but has grown by accretion over the centuries, becoming the largest private house in England. It provides a compendium of architectural styles, and still contains many of the artefacts and portraits featured in *Orlando*. Until recently, the manuscript of *Orlando* was on display in the entrance hall.

triumph over personal mortality by entering into print, and then again by being written about by their biographers. As such, this sort of biography is fundamentally a middle-class form, because it founds the claim to importance of its subject not upon inherited title, landed wealth and power, but upon intellectual capital and individual self-transformation achieved in a single lifetime. The aristocracy as a class has not typically been imagined as subject to the same biological/biographical time-clock as the middle-class writer – its power *is* derived from genetic entitlement to power and land, from being in some way the same across generations. Its 'biography' has more to do with family lineage than with a single mortal body. In this sense, the fantasy qualities of Woolf's biography are no more than an aristocratic truth – the same long nose shows in all the Knole portraits and photographs, persisting across time, and the portraits stay together within Knole's space–time continuum.

In another sense, however, the biography is a fantasy, for Sackville-West was of the wrong sex to have an aristocratic 'biography'; as a woman, she could not inherit her beloved birthplace, Knole, and this was for her a personal tragedy. *Orlando*, in identifying its protagonist so closely with a fiction of Knole, endowed Sackville-West with Knole as imaginative property, the same trick that she herself had sought to bring off with her own book about her home and her pedigree, *Knole and the Sackvilles* (1922). This book is a biography of the great house itself – something that outlasts mere human generations, just as Orlando does – and from it Woolf drew some of her materials for the novel. *Orlando* redoes *Knole and the Sackvilles*, parodying its protocols, its photographs and its index, but also remaining true to its impulse – to turn the property itself into an imaginative inheritance. As Nigel Nicolson was to write: 'the novel identified her [Sackville-West] with Knole for ever. Virginia by her genius had provided Vita with a unique consolation for having been born a girl, for her exclusion from her inheritance' (1973, p.206). In place of the masculine privileges of primogeniture, Woolf offered her lover a fantasy of Knole through the centuries, with the figure of Vita/Orlando in the centre of the frame.

Finally, this biography can be seen as a fantasy of the continuity of the aristocracy. For Woolf, part of Sackville-West's attraction seems to have been the glamour of an aristocrat – with a different way of thinking, a different way of behaving, a different set of morals, expectations and opportunities. In some ways, *Orlando*'s love affair with Knole is a love affair with the idea of aristocracy, a love affair made possible, paradoxically, by the decline of the real power, influence and wealth of the aristocracy following the First World War (see Cannadine, 1990). That decline was completed by the Second World War: Knole was handed over to the National Trust in 1946. Woolf herself came from the well-heeled upper middle class, with family connections across the worlds of writing, publishing and high-level diplomacy; the very respectability of such a background made Sackville-West's loucheness all the more seductive. By contrast to Woolf's position as a member of the intelligentsia, characterized at the time by intermittently proclaimed socialism, anti-fascist sentiments, and a sense of especially refined sexualities and sensibilities, Sackville-West's aristocratic power licensed careless gender transgression and sexual experimentation. Alchemized by Woolf's imagination, Sackville-West's aristocratic privilege metamorphoses into something more alarmingly mobile and transgressive, dangerous enough even to seduce Vita into love with her own representation.

Yet clearly, however 'biographical' some of Woolf's material is, *Orlando* is much more in the nature of an exploration and explosion of the assumptions and conventions of biography – what we might call a mock-biography or a meta-biography. She wrote to Sackville-West that in writing the title *Orlando: A Biography* 'it sprung upon me how I could revolutionise biography in a night' (Woolf, 1977, vol.3, p.429). However unorthodox, *Orlando* grew out of a long-standing and serious interest in biography. Woolf was, after all, the daughter of Leslie Stephen, the founder of the *Dictionary of National Biography*, and the dedicatee of her friend Lytton Strachey's innovative and iconoclastic biographical studies *Eminent Victorians* (1918) and *Queen Victoria* (1921). She herself would write a joke biography of Elizabeth Barrett Browning's dog, *Flush* (1933), and a serious biography of her friend *Roger Fry* (1940). Her essays include a large number of studies of writers that are often vividly biographical, and she was notably interested in biographical and autobiographical writers, including, for example, the Romantic essayist Thomas De Quincey. Long before she began work on *Orlando*, Woolf had been experimenting in her early short stories with the genre: 'The Journal of Mistress Joan Martyn' (first published 1979) and 'Memoirs of a Novelist' (first published 1984) both explore the relationship between a woman biographer and her female subject, and, as a consequence, between private and public histories; biographical form is the backbone to her third novel, *Jacob's Room* (1922). Members of her circle were interested in biography as a form: in 1928, Strachey would publish the highly innovative *Elizabeth and Essex: A Tragic History*, and indeed, just before *Orlando*'s composition, Harold Nicolson was publishing a set of biographical essays. These were reviewed by Woolf in 1927, in an essay entitled 'The New Biography'.

In the brief history of biography with which she contextualizes her review, Woolf notes a problematic relation between factual accuracy and narrative. She broadly identifies a number of types of biography: early 'fact'-based biography that concentrates on action and exploits, and consequently is allied to memorial and obituary; Victorian biography, burdened with conscientiousness and embarrassed with 'countless documents' and factual minutiae; and twentieth-century biography by the likes of her friends Strachey and Nicolson, which foregrounds the biographer's voice in 'a method of writing about people and about himself as though they were at once real and imaginary' (Woolf, 1966, vol.4, p.475). Strikingly anecdotal, such modern biography abandons fact for the telling detail, and is ironical and self-conscious in its sense of its limitations. Woolf remarks especially on the problems of conflating 'the truth of real life' – factual 'granite-like' truth, the truth of the historian – with the truthful depiction of personality, which demands different techniques, drawn from fiction: 'For in order that the light of personality may shine through, facts must be manipulated; some must be brightened, some must be shaded' (*ibid.*, p.473). Fiction may be 'antagonistic' and yet be essential to the writing of biography. This gives rise to her formulation of biography: 'that queer amalgamation of dream and reality, that perpetual marriage of granite and rainbow', a phraseology that she will echo in *Orlando* (*ibid.*, p.478).

Woolf's essay points to some elements of her methodology in *Orlando* – even though it should already be clear that *Orlando* cannot be read (I almost said, dismissed) as mere/pure biography. The biographer will be visible and ironic. The focus will be on consciousness. The writer will claim 'the freedom, the artistry of fiction' and use 'the novelist's art of arrangement, suggestion, dramatic effect' (Woolf, 1966, vol.4, p.476). What is striking overall about this essay is Woolf's absolute conviction that biography without an admixture of 'rainbow' cannot convey the modern experience of the self. What concerns Woolf is not how to collate the external facts of a life led in history and in society (characteristically Edwardian realist ways of conceiving the self), but how to tell the story of a noticeably fluid consciousness, elongated, immaterial and migratory. *Orlando* at one point explicitly takes on her father's great life-work, the *Dictionary of National Biography*, to insist that not even lifespan is precise and verifiable in the way that it suggests:

> it cannot be denied that the most successful practitioners of the art of life … somehow contrive to synchronize the sixty or seventy different times which beat simultaneously in every normal human system … Of them we can justly say that they live precisely the sixty-eight or seventy-two years allotted them on the tombstone. Of the rest some we know to be dead though they walk among us; some are not yet born though they go through the forms of life; others are hundreds of years old though they call themselves thirty-six. The true length of a person's life, whatever the *Dictionary of National Biography* may say, is always a matter of dispute.

> (6; p.291)

The strategy of citing facts and dates, which was inherited from the Victorian biographers, does not capture the 'real'. As Woolf explains with mock modesty in her role as biographer at the opening of Chapter 3 of *Orlando*, she may be driven to fiction – to imagination – when fact has failed: 'often it has been necessary to speculate, to surmise, and even to use the imagination' (3; p.115). I will come back a little later to Woolf's thinking on the nature of fiction, but for now I will turn to the other documentary genre that she plays with – history.

At this point, you can choose to read straight on through *Orlando*, continuing with the material below afterwards, and rereading sections as appropriate. Alternatively, you may wish to read on now through the material below, in which case you will find that your reading of the novel will be organized into discrete stages.

History

History, with its investment in dates, locations, facts, documents and things, is the second major inherited genre with pretensions to realism that Woolf sets out to challenge. From very early on, *Orlando* complicates the notion of historical realism. **Read from 'So, after a long silence …' (1; p.17) to '… the deer, the fox, the badger, and the butterfly' (1; p.18). In what ways does this section complicate the idea of historical realism?**

Once Orlando reaches the (emblematically English) oak tree, history is rendered as an impossible panorama of the late sixteenth century. England is visible across 'thirty or forty' counties, bounded by the English Channel on one side and Wales on the other, with London in the middle, and is made up of vast mansions and land owned largely by Orlando's family, and fortifications otherwise. The vision is one of real and secure privilege, a view from the ruling class of the nation. This section alerts us to a non-realist strategy verging on allegory for representing 'history'. **Now read Chapters 1 and 2 right through. Try to identify some of the techniques Woolf uses to represent 'history' or 'period'. To what extent and in what ways do they challenge or parody conventional historical narrative?**

1 Woolf begins with the notion of 'family history' – embodied in the house and the possessions, trophies and heraldry that fill it, which speak of the power, deeds and lineage of Orlando's ancestors (1; pp.13–14). This is in part a history through 'things' that bespeak their owners.

2 History can also be conveyed by way of 'period detail'. The house is a specifically Elizabethan economy – 'stables, kennels, breweries, carpenters' shops, washhouses, places where they make tallow candles, kill oxen, forge horse-shoes, stitch jerkins – for the house was a town ringing with men at work at their various crafts' (1; p.17). In the same way, Orlando's clothes are used as an indicator of historical difference – 'shoes with rosettes on them as big as double dahlias' (1; p.20). Equally 'period' is the odd piece of archaic language, or the medicines and remedies applied to revive and cure Orlando at the beginning of

Chapter 2. This sort of history we might also call history through 'things', though here things inhabited – a language of costume-drama realism recognizably invented by Walter Scott.

3   Equally, history can be mocked up from contemporary print sources, another sort of 'thing'. These can be real – the account of the Great Frost, for example, derives from a Jacobean pamphlet by the playwright Thomas Dekker, as the explanatory notes in the Oxford World's Classics edition remark – or fictional, as in the case of the letters of Lieutenant Brigge and Miss Penelope Hartopp in Chapter 3. But it is worth remarking that the real sources quoted without a trace of disbelief are entirely unbelievable: the Frost turns a girl to powder, herds of swine are frozen in their tracks. The fictional documents, on the other hand, are entirely believable and very accomplished pastiche. Both types of source are unreliable – the account of the Great Frost because it does not conform to modern notions of historical realism, and the letters because they are not only fabricated but also supposedly damaged and incomplete. The one historical document that *is* reliable, the transcription of the Knole ledger (2; p.105), is also problematical because it does not bring history 'alive'.

4   Bringing history 'alive', making it believable and coherent, requires narrative to supplement and enliven the documentary record. The cameo appearance in the fictional text of a real historical figure – Queen Elizabeth – turns history into anecdote. Initially, Queen Elizabeth is seen from an 'odd' angle, a technique designed to defamiliarize her, hypothesizing the real physical body beneath the mask-like trappings of history. In her dealings with Orlando, the Queen reprises all the historical anecdotes of her old age and her last favourite that were in circulation in the 1920s (1; pp.22–6). (In many ways, this is a bravura condensation of Strachey's *Elizabeth and Essex*.) Throughout the text, by way of historical reference points, Woolf sprinkles high-profile characters on location – 'The King was walking in Whitehall. Nell Gwyn was on his arm. She was pelting him with hazel nuts' (2; pp.113–14). This element gives Woolf's historical panorama a cosy and charming air of kitsch and cliché, a whiff of the primary-coloured Ladybird history books for children, a hint of W.C. Sellar's and R.J. Yeatman's classic spoof *1066 and All That* (published only two years later, in 1930); it burlesques a familiar shorthand for English history born of Woolf's childhood reading in Charles Kingsley's *Westward Ho!* (1855) and Rudyard Kipling's *Puck of Pook's Hill* (1906), and still on display in Woolf's time in the form of the large and increasingly out-of-fashion history-paintings still being commissioned as civic murals. (See, for example, the series 'The

Builders of Britain', commissioned by Sir Henry Newbolt and unveiled in the Houses of Parliament at Westminster only a year before Woolf's novel appeared.)

5   A very different notion – but one equally typical of nineteenth-century historiography – is to see history as divided into 'ages', each of which is defined by some leading characteristic of thought or spirit. 'The spirit of the age' is an essence, an intellectual or emotional quality, and as such opposed to an idea of history as material things. As Woolf introduces this notion, she simultaneously affirms it and sends it up: 'The age was the Elizabethan; their morals were not ours; nor their poets; nor their climate; nor their vegetables even' (1; p.26). The joke is made by the juxtaposition of the fundamentally metaphorical and abstract idea of the 'age', as defined by thought (morals, poetry), with the literal and material, as represented by things (the different vegetables – and, as you may know, the Elizabethans did indeed have different vegetables). The 'climate' swings between the two – half metaphorical (as in 'the climate of opinion') and half actual (did they need different weather patterns to grow different vegetables?) (see Bowlby, 1988, pp.131–2).

6   The account of the Great Frost and the thaw counterposes two sorts of scenes of 'history' shown to a spectator. One shows history kinetically, as a tragic and incoherent jumble of bodies and things carried, in the throes of sex, procreation and birth, down the stream of time to inevitable death: 'a cat suckling its young; a table laid sumptuously for a supper of twenty; a couple in bed; together with an extraordinary number of cooking utensils' (1; p.61). The other shows history as the petrifaction of the living – a tableau preserved for the contemplation of spectators, like flies in amber or like the wrecked wherry boat and the dead bumboat woman preserved below the ice and wondered at by Orlando himself.

7   Finally, history is also something that passes through Orlando, becoming memory – imperfect, repressed, or even collective memory:

> though he was perfectly rational ... he appeared to have an imperfect recollection of his past life ... When the events of the last six months were discussed, he seemed not so much distressed as puzzled, as if he were troubled by confused memories of some time long gone or were trying to recall stories told him by another.

(2; pp.64–5)

At any rate, history is not merely a mass of facts and dates, as Woolf points out, forcing this idea of history to the point of the absurd: 'He had indeed just brought his feet together about six in the evening of the seventh of January

at the finish of some such quadrille or minuet when he beheld ... a figure'
(1; pp.35–6). And neither does Woolf's history move to the expected
rhythms and emphases. National 'history' is regularly forced into parenthesis
by domesticity: 'The towel horse in the King's bedroom ('and that was King
Jamie, my Lord,' [Mrs Grimsditch] said, hinting that it was many a day since
a King had slept under their roof; but the odious Parliament days were over
and there was now a Crown in England again) lacked a leg' (2; p.104).

By the end of the first two chapters, Woolf has by no means exhausted
her repertoire of ways of representing 'history'. As you read on through the
next three chapters, you should be able to recognize many of the techniques I
have been describing, along with a few more. Perhaps most startling is the
extraordinary vision of Victorian Britain, which takes two forms. One is a
virtuoso description of the new dampness of the climate, which brings on an
overpowering respectability of clothing. The other is the astonishing
description of the Albert Memorial piled high with things emblematic of
the age:

> a conglomeration ... of the most heterogeneous and ill-assorted
> objects, piled higgledy-piggledy in a vast mound ... Draped about
> a vast cross of fretted and floriated gold were widow's weeds and
> bridal veils; hooked on to other excrescences were crystal palaces,
> bassinettes, military helmets, memorial wreaths, trousers,
> whiskers, wedding cakes, cannon, Christmas trees, telescopes,
> extinct monsters, globes, maps, elephants, and mathematical
> instruments ... Orlando ... had never, in all her life, seen anything
> at once so indecent, so hideous, and so monumental.
>
> (5; pp.221–2)

It would not be helpful to try to identify a coherent vision of the proper
nature of historical narrative in *Orlando*. As perhaps you have already
noticed, Woolf's writing is highly hypothetical in its tendency, and the
narrator shifts ground bewilderingly and continuously. Clearly, some of
Woolf's techniques are 'realist' – one might cite her use of period detail or of
documentation. But equally, this 'realism', this simulacrum of the past, is
undercut by caricature and parody, as in the pastiche letters and the joke
about dates and times. Nonetheless, the balance wavers in favour of history
as enigmatic or incoherent, something requiring interpretation and
captioning. **Before you go any further, read on through Chapters 3,
4 and 5, if you have not already done so.**

One of the problems that Woolf sets up in *Orlando* by parading her hero/
heroine through four hundred years of history is the relationship between
subjectivity and period. This is a central problem for biography, for historical
fiction modelled after Walter Scott and for the sort of *Bildungsroman* (a novel
concerned with the education of a young person in the world) practised by

the nineteenth-century French novelist Stendhal. Is it the case that Orlando remains him/herself irrespective of 'the spirit of the age'? Or is it the case that s/he is formed by the 'spirit of the age'? As Bowlby puts it,

> Either individuals are wholly determined by their milieu, be this defined as material or spiritual, or they are spirits or souls – fully formed selves – who happen to live at the particular time and place ... Somewhere between these two poles ... is the 'life and times' model whose terms are posited as relatively independent of one another, but mutually influential ... By making Orlando's life a matter of several hundred years, Woolf gives herself a perfect opportunity to tease out the underlying assumptions of biographical conventions concerning the identity of the subject through time and in relation to his or her milieux.
>
> (Bowlby, 1988, pp.137–9)

Consider the following passage. What does it say about the relationship between Orlando and the age?

> Orlando had inclined herself naturally to the Elizabethan spirit, to the Restoration spirit, to the spirit of the eighteenth century, and had in consequence scarcely been aware of the change from one age to another. But the spirit of the nineteenth century was antipathetic to her in the extreme ... For it is probable that the human spirit has its place in time assigned to it; some are born of this age, some of that; and now that Orlando was grown a woman, a year or two past thirty indeed, the lines of her character were fixed, and to bend them the wrong way was intolerable.
>
> (5; p.233)

Actually, the passage seems to suggest two rather incompatible things: that, on the one hand, Orlando had easily and 'naturally' adapted without noticing to the average sensibility of the age, but that, on the other, her essence is fixed and happens to fit some periods better than others. This incompatibility is smoothed away under a fiction of 'growing-up'.

Orlando embodies the various spirits of the ages that s/he lives through as they were conceived in the 1920s, spirits largely extrapolated from the literature of the periods concerned. In highlighting the ways in which our concepts of an age are drawn from literary works, *Orlando* turns history and biography into a pageant of literary fashions. The various 'ages', from the Elizabethan through to the Victorian, are conceived as consonant with their typical literary forms and modes. The Elizabethan age is accorded special privilege as being closer in some respects to the spirit of modernity. As an Elizabethan, Orlando is dashing, enthusiastic, mildly androgynous in appearance, with strong sexual appetites, and a propensity for slumming it. All of these attributes were supposed by modernists to pertain to the

Shakespearean drama, and come under the sign of 'Shakespeare'. The Jacobean Orlando suffers from textbook melancholy derived from Robert Burton's *Anatomy of Melancholy* (1621) – the disorder that also afflicts Hamlet – and so takes to solitude, night-walking and musings on death that are strongly inflected by the plays of Shakespeare's contemporary and an especial modernist favourite, John Webster: 'how all pomp is built upon corruption; how the skeleton lies beneath the flesh ... how the crimson velvet turns to dust' (2; pp.68–9). With the restoration of Charles II, Woolf inserts the ambassador Orlando into a narrative of Constantinople that might have been written by that notable traveller (and cross-dresser) Lady Mary Wortley Montagu. Later in the text, Orlando will make his/her way through a series of narrative plots characteristic of each historical period. What these plots are will be determined by the current biological sex of Woolf's protagonist; the plots will then 'gender' the often resisting Orlando by assigning him/her certain preordained social/sexual roles. To see this gendering of plot, let us turn our attention to one of the most startling and original moments in the book, Orlando's adventures in Constantinople.

Questions of gender

As you will have discovered, it is during the Constantinople episode that Orlando the young diplomat is transformed into a young woman. Within Woolf's oeuvre 'Constantinople' has a history of being associated with ambiguous sexual identity and with a set of oblique sexual allusions that connect Constantinople's situation on the Golden Horn and Shelmerdine's voyages around Cape Horn (Horner, 1991, p.83). This episode is certainly Woolf's most audacious game with the reader's entrenched expectations of narrative realism. From bending genre she turns to bending gender, and as you read on I hope to persuade you that this episode and its aftermath suggest that the stability of genre is related in some interesting ways to the stability of gender categories, and indeed to the stability overall of the nation and its empire. **Now read from 'Here we must pause ...' (3; p.121) to '... which on her part were sincere' (3; p.146). What sparks Orlando's transformation? What literary genres govern the episode?**

Orlando is transformed into a woman at a moment of triumphant British imperialism, which is embodied in his personal power and sexual glamour. He seems to begin the transformation as he accepts the ducal circlet – this is the moment at which his inner nature turns out not to be quite masculine enough to support that double claim to aristocratic primogeniture and to empire. His assumption of the circlet is consequently associated with social disturbance expressed as the crossing of race and class boundaries – 'The natives pressed into the banqueting rooms' (3; p.126), the gipsy woman is hoisted up from the street into the balcony and so to the bedroom. The official order totters before insurrection and massacre; when the rioters break into Orlando's room they (surprisingly but tellingly) confine themselves to robbing him 'of his coronet and the robes of the Garter' (3; p.128). On becoming a woman, Orlando simply falls out of official history, and out of public view – in fact, he all but dies: 'Would that we might spare the reader what is to come and say to him in so many words, Orlando died and was buried' (3; p.129). The literary forms that govern the accounts of the party and subsequent disturbance in Constantinople – letters from both a man and a woman, the *Gazette* report, some sort of quasi-legal investigation – are all circulated as evidence within the public sphere. But Orlando's transformation escapes these realist documentary forms, and is described, appropriately enough, in an extended 'masque' of Purity, Chastity and Modesty, figures that endeavour to hide Orlando's female nakedness from the biographer's 'Truth, Candour, and Honesty'. (This section is a pastiche of Thomas De Quincey's baroquely overblown style in *Suspiria de Profundis*, 1845.) By becoming a woman, Orlando seems to discredit documentary history and with it British imperial power, atomizing it into a 'litter of waste-paper baskets, treaties, despatches, seals, sealing wax, etc.' (3; p.135). From this wreck of civilization she escapes into an ahistorical pastoral with the gipsies, which negates all previous claims to aristocratic status: 'the gipsy thought that there was no more vulgar ambition than to possess bedrooms by the hundred' (3; p.142).

Let us return to the moment of transformation, and see what Orlando makes of her change of sex. Her biographer insists that though she 'had become a woman',

> in every other respect, Orlando remained precisely as he had been. The change of sex, though it altered their future, did nothing whatever to alter their identity. Their faces remained, as their portraits prove, practically the same. His memory – but in future we must, for convention's sake, say 'her' for 'his', and 'she' for 'he' – her memory then, went back through all the events of her past life without encountering any obstacle. Some slight haziness there may have been, as if a few dark drops had fallen into the clear pool of memory; certain things had become a little dimmed; but that was all. The change seemed to have been accomplished painlessly and completely and in such a way that Orlando herself showed no surprise at it. Many people, taking this into account, and holding that such a change of sex is against nature, have been at great pains to prove (1) that Orlando had always been a woman, (2) that Orlando is at this moment a man. Let biologists and psychologists determine. It is enough for us to state the simple fact; Orlando was a man till the age of thirty; when he became a woman and has remained so ever since.
>
> (3; pp.133–4)

This remarkable passage starts by insisting that Orlando was just the same – by which is apparently meant that his 'identity' remains unchanged. That identity is read in the face (rather than in the sexed body), and within the memory. But if Orlando's 'identity' has not changed, his future, governed by the linguistic and social conventions that change his pronoun and change his clothes, will prove to have changed profoundly. So Orlando is and is not the same, and her trip back to England on the *Enamoured Lady* provides an opportunity for an extended meditation on the effects, not so much of the change of sex, as of the change of clothes. **Now read from 'Thus, there is much to support the view that it is clothes that wear us …' (4; p.180) to '… underneath the sex is the very opposite of what it is above' (4; p.181). Compare and contrast the two views presented in this passage concerning the relationship between clothes and body. What does this relationship suggest about the nature of femininity?**

Orlando's transformation introduces a set of instabilities within the novel – not just the sort of unbalancing of fictional, historical and biographical conventions I have been describing, but also a radical instability to do with gender itself. This instability is signalled in the very first line of the novel, yet nonetheless it seems to gather pace and momentum once Orlando becomes a woman, suggesting that the category of 'woman' is less stable and secure than that of 'man', and is, perhaps, more recognizably a 'modern' condition. Perhaps modernity is more 'feminine' because it is a new state, in which sexual difference is no longer a principal determinant of human fate. As in the first line of the novel, but more urgently, the proposition is that clothes may serve to signal or to 'disguise' the 'true' sex. In discussing the relationship between Orlando's change of clothes and her true sex, the narrator presents two alternative views. The first is that clothes, by supposedly indicating the sex of the wearer, in fact gradually create the wearer's sexual identity – the implication, then, is that sexual identity is not so much a biological fact as socially constructed. Orlando's female clothes hamper her (she must use her hands to 'keep the satins from slipping from her shoulders') and they betray her – they perpetually threaten to reveal more of shoulders and of ankles than they should. The second version is that 'Clothes are but a symbol of something hid deep beneath. It was a change in Orlando herself that dictated her choice of a woman's dress and of a woman's sex.' Here, Woolf seems to postulate something 'deeper' even than biological sex – a psychic sex, which triggers Orlando's physical transformation. The passage goes on to speculate that sexuality (as opposed to the biological sex) is subject to 'vacillation' and that clothes themselves, therefore, keep the social order in place by continuing to indicate maleness or femaleness, whether the sex below is male, female or a mixture at any given moment. Bowlby notes that this 'indeterminacy of sexual difference is only acknowledged, or even broached, from a feminine position. These narrative speculations are only engendered, after all, by Orlando's change of sex in the direction of femininity, and the narrator's subsequent attempt to come to terms with it' (Bowlby, 1988, p.55). Orlando's transformation to a woman seems to trigger a sexual mobility that is registered as convenience cross-dressing. This suggests either that femininity is an inherently unstable state or that its very condition is that of putting on and off the identities of one or the other sex. Woolf makes no attempt to resolve this dilemma, contenting herself with playfully asking quite serious questions about the significance or determinability of sexual difference (*ibid.*, p.59). If Orlando's transformation is read as central to the novel, then *Orlando* appears 'at once a demonstration of the groundlessness of existing differences, and a fantasy that they might simply be discounted' (*ibid.*, p.61). Woolf deploys – both seriously and satirically – many models of sexual difference in addition to this one. These models are often mutually exclusive and internally contradictory. **Before reading on, try to identify other models of sexual difference that are alluded to or discussed by Woolf, and test them against the discussion of contemporary debates surrounding gender and sexuality that follows.**

Orlando's problematic sexuality is very 'modern'. Despite its determined air of fantasy, Orlando's transformation is rooted in postwar debates concerning the nature of gender and sexuality, and both deploys and satirizes them, encoding and sending up current theories of androgyny, sexuality and homosexuality (Marcus, 1997, p.118). At the time, the culture was preoccupied with the problem of preserving gender difference, in the face of what was perceived as a closing of the gender gap. This could be and was construed as degeneracy: men becoming effeminate, women becoming masculine and the fabric of civilization tottering as a result. The theory and language of degeneration and consequent emasculation was readily to hand; it was not in itself new, having been a feature of turn-of-the-century cultural life. But its resurgence in the 1920s as a smoothing out of gender difference was probably a reaction to the enormous carnage of the First World War, which slaughtered and emasculated the young men and opened unprecedented opportunities to young women. At a popular level it manifested itself in the extreme fashions of the 1920s (Figure 6.2), which formed a stark contrast to pre-First World War fashions (Figure 6.3). The sudden transformation of the female figure into a perpetually youthful and athletic androgyne with flattened breasts also brought into fashion the figure of the willowy young man. (An example of this physical type is Jonathan Trout in Katherine Mansfield's short story 'At the Bay'.)

At their most theoretical, these debates over gender and sexuality can be located in the work of contemporary psychologists and sexologists, such as Sigmund Freud, Richard Krafft-Ebbing, Havelock Ellis and Edward Carpenter. In the passage quoted above, Woolf mentions 'biologists and

Figure 6.2 Fringed hem, 1924; fashion illustration from *Gazette du Bon Ton*, no.4, 1924–5, p.181. (Photo: Mary Evans Picture Library.) Note how these short dresses liberate the woman physically, while denying the existence of breasts, waist and hips. Note, too, the boyish 'shingle' haircut.

Figure 6.3 Longchamp races, 1910. (Photo: Roger Viollet/Rex Features.) By contrast, these clothes emphasize a mature waist and hips, and, in the case of the figure on the left, actually hobble the woman at the knees. The hats are heavy and immobilizing while again advertising femininity as fertility (the flowers) or as prey (the expensive and exotic feathers).

psychologists', an apparent reference to Freud's thinking, and perhaps especially to his contemporary essay 'Some Psychical Consequences of the Anatomical Distinction Between the Sexes' (1925), which concerns itself with the development of female sexuality. Freud had previously argued that boys had a primary sexual relationship with the mother until they entered what he called the 'Oedipal' stage. At this moment of development, the young boy discovers that his mother is already spoken for, by his father. He notices, moreover, that, unlike himself, girls are 'castrated'; considering this a threat, he prudently defers the desire he feels for his mother until he is grown up and can transfer it to another woman. In this essay, Freud notes that the mother is the young girl's first love, too, and that in the Oedipal stage, the young girl also discovers that her mother is spoken for by her father. More traumatically, she realizes that she will never possess her mother, even in the shape of a substitute, because she lacks a penis. Suffering from 'envy for the penis', she becomes 'female' (or rather, a heterosexual female) by transferring her affections away from her 'mutilated' mother to her father, and from him to some future male lover. Freud pointed out that such a transferral of desire from mother to father and then to future lover was elaborate, lengthy, tricky and often incomplete. Freud's essay was very modern in its closing acknowledgement 'that all human individuals, as a result of their bisexual disposition ... combine in themselves both masculine and feminine characteristics, so that pure masculinity and femininity remain theoretical constructions of uncertain content' (in Freud, 1977, p.342).

Freud's essay thus potentially unyoked the sexed body from the psychological sex, and set up a history of sexuality whereby girls start male and become female – just like Orlando. Orlando is first 'masculine', then 'feminine'; the continuity between these two stages is provided by his/her love of women, which, in turn, echoes Freud's account of both the male and the female child's pre-Oedipal identification with the mother. In the broader schema of a 'history of sexuality', Woolf seems to outline an increasing feminization of culture. Certainly, Orlando becomes more 'feminine' as the advance of the Victorian age outlaws sexual and gender freedoms and imposes a 'compulsory heterosexuality' on its members; sexual behaviours are not prior to culture, Woolf suggests, but substantially determined by it (Marcus, 1997, p.129). Freud's accompanying assumption – that women's sexual orientation was more fragilely heterosexual, given that they had to transfer their primary love from their mother to a man, rather than (in the case of the boy) simply from the forbidden mother to another, substitute, woman – is played out in Orlando's continued love for Sasha after Orlando has herself become a woman. Her transformation does not result in a change in her objects of desire:

> as all Orlando's loves had been women, now, through the culpable
> laggardry of the human frame to adapt itself to convention,
> though she herself was a woman, it was still a woman she loved;
> and if the consciousness of being of the same sex had any effect at
> all, it was to quicken and deepen those feelings which she had had
> as a man.

> (4; p.154)

However, Freud was not the only determinant for Woolf's discussion of
Orlando's sexuality; the book's alibi for Orlando's continuing love for Sasha
is something of a cover-story for its exploration of lesbian passion. It was a
necessary cover-story, for the reception of Radclyffe Hall's now celebrated
quasi-autobiographical and realist novel about lesbian passion, *The Well of
Loneliness*, published the same year, was altogether stormier. Its frank
treatment of lesbian passion occasioned a trial for obscenity, at which Woolf
had readied herself to be a defence witness; despite the support of many
writers, including E.M. Forster and Arnold Bennett, the book was banned,
sentenced to be destroyed and an appeal refused.

**Now read on to '… we may conclude that he or she is no better
than a corpse and so leave her' (6; p.257). What effect does Orlando's
change of gender have on her and on the portrayal of history and
literary history more generally?**

Most spectacularly, Orlando's change of gender changes her relationship
to social and ideological structures of power. From being the gazer out over
forty counties and holder of power over the lot, she becomes the looked-at,
the woman whose carelessly exposed ankle causes a sailor nearly to
overbalance at the masthead. From being proposer and seducer, she is
merely accorded a veto, and that not taken very seriously, as witness the
Archduke's persistence. As a woman, she loses not only her title, but also her
property:

> The chief charges against her were (1) that she was dead, and
> therefore could not hold any property whatsoever; (2) that she
> was a woman, which amounts to much the same thing … Thus it
> was in a highly ambiguous condition, uncertain whether she was
> alive or dead, man or woman, Duke or nonentity, that she posted
> down to her country seat.

> (4; p.161)

Re-sexed, she is at odds with the very spirit of the age, its ruling vision of
itself. This is made plain in the episode of her drive with Alexander Pope. As
Marcus remarks:

> Paradoxically, and at odds with the Enlightenment's valorization
> of the light of rationalism, Orlando experiences enlightenment
> during the stretches of darkness, praising Pope as 'the most
> august, most lucid of beams', and profound gloom, as well as
> disenchantment with the 'Great Man' during the brief moment of
> illumination ... [this] suggests that 'as a' woman, Orlando's 'state
> of mind' no longer mirrors 'the age' but enacts an exact reversal
> of its dominant tropes.
>
> (Marcus, 1997, p.122)

If history looks a little strange from the standpoint of one legally dead,
literary history looks different too. Orlando finds herself implicated in
different sorts of literary plots. She becomes a woman just in time to try her
hand at occupying some of the most important literary forms of the
succeeding centuries. She exchanges Shakespearean passion and exotic
adventures (reminiscent of Byron's 'Oriental' tales) for the feminocentric
novel – though she mostly finds it difficult, if not downright impossible, to
occupy any of these plots with any sense of conviction. She is unable
(because of her history) to obsess about her chastity, as do other heroines of
the eighteenth-century novel, such as Samuel Richardson's Clarissa in the
novel of that name (1747–8): 'chastity is their jewel, their centre-piece, which
they run mad to protect, and die when ravished of' (4; p.147). In the
nineteenth century, required to play both heroines of *Jane Eyre* and
Wuthering Heights at once, Orlando accommodates herself to this Gothic
romance of desire and marriage with considerable difficulty and virtuosity:
'She had just managed, by some dexterous deference to the spirit of the age,
by putting on a ring and finding a man on a moor, by loving nature and being
no satirist, cynic, or psychologist ... to pass its examination successfully' (6;
p.253). The twentieth century offers her the chance (which she refuses) to
play the sexually explicit fantasy of liaison between the earthy man and the
sex-starved aristocratic woman, of which D.H. Lawrence's *Lady Chatterley's
Lover*, published in the same year as *Orlando*, is such a shining example:

> Surely, since she is a woman, and a beautiful woman, and a
> woman in the prime of life, she will soon give over this pretence
> of writing and thinking and begin at least to think of a
> gamekeeper ... And then she will write him a little note ... and
> make an assignation for Sunday dusk and Sunday dusk will come;
> and the gamekeeper will whistle under the window – all of which
> is, of course, the very stuff of life and the only possible subject for
> fiction.
>
> (6; p.256)

That said, one of the striking things about the second half of *Orlando*, and one of the most consciously euphoric, is that it does not conform to the cadences of eighteenth- and nineteenth-century heterosexual romance, but instead takes a perfect delight in foiling them, escaping in a change of clothes into the more sexually disreputable plots associated with adventurer heroines such as those of Daniel Defoe's *Moll Flanders* (1722) and *Roxana* (1724) (4; p.209). One effect of this constant slithering through and out the other side of plots – or, more frankly, this knowing circumvention of them – is the decentring or deferral of the moral weight of each plot. A plot's social normativeness or force, which would have been considerable in its day, shifts and dissipates. In this, the novel is only repeating its treatment of 'history' which, as I have noted earlier, is frequently relegated to parenthesis and subordinate clause without being accorded the dignity of being the master-narrative: ' "Sale bosch!" she said (for there had been another war; this time against the Germans)' (6; p.288). Or, for that matter, redoubling its games with biographical narrative, with its expectations of a series of significant, climactic moments or events – here one thinks of the way in which the biographer takes the reader for a dignified turn around Kew Gardens instead of taking notes at the bedside while Orlando gives birth to her son. The expected rhythm of the narrative is disrupted, the accent falls differently. This, Woolf would have argued, was the condition of modern perception and modern subjectivity (which was especially 'feminine' in this sense), and, therefore, was necessarily also a condition of modern fiction.

Fiction and modernity

Woolf's view of the plight of fiction within modernity, as expressed in her critical essays, is strikingly similar to her view of biography. That is, if 'the real' escapes Victorian biography, so too does it escape Edwardian realist fiction. In 1924, Woolf published a major essay on the state of contemporary fiction, which is generally read as an account of the move from Edwardian realism to 'high' modernism. **Now read the extract from 'Mr Bennett and Mrs Brown' (1924) (Reader, Item 22). How does Woolf characterize established realist fiction, and what does she envisage in its place?**

In its entirety 'Mr Bennett and Mrs Brown' is a fictionalized account of a train journey from Richmond to Waterloo, in the company of an elderly 'Mrs Brown', who serves as a figure for the source of or stimulus to fiction: 'all novels begin with an old lady in the corner opposite' (Woolf, 1966, vol.1, p.324). Realism, in the persons of H.G. Wells, John Galsworthy and Arnold Bennett, is neatly and rather unfairly parodied as these authors tackle the problem of representing the enigmatic Mrs Brown: 'they said: "Begin by saying that her father kept a shop in Harrogate. Ascertain the rent. Ascertain the wages of shop assistants in the year 1878. Discover what her mother died of. Describe cancer. Describe calico. Describe —" But I cried: "Stop! Stop!"' Woolf insists that Mrs Brown escapes this 'ugly', 'clumsy', 'incongruous' representational tool because a shift in consciousness took place (parodically) 'in or about December, 1910'. Literary conventions are seen to be no longer adequate to represent reality and subjective experience, which now (after 1910) seem characterized by complexity, multiplicity, strangeness, collision, incongruity and disorder, verifiable by the reader him/ herself: 'In one day thousands of ideas have coursed through your brains; thousands of emotions have met, collided, and disappeared in astonishing disorder.' The result is 'a season of failures and fragments', writing characterized by 'the spasmodic, the obscure, the fragmentary, the failure', and the uncertain promise of a new future for fiction. The future, according to Woolf, is associated with Mrs Brown – a future of mobility, collision, disorder and incongruity. As a woman, 'Mrs Brown' challenges a realism that is gendered male and characterized as peculiarly aggressive and invasive. Fiction might profitably turn its attention to a new field, women's interior life, and take as its representational methodology something informed by a feminine, less autocratic or controlling, sensibility. Woolf's vision of the triumph of modernist aesthetics within the novel was to be realized only patchily; the legacy of these maligned Edwardians would live on within realist strands in the fiction of the later twentieth century.

A year later, Woolf published her essay 'Modern Fiction' (first drafted 1919/25), which covers some of the same ground but which turns its attention more thoroughly to what modern fiction might take as its subject matter and aesthetic. Like 'Mr Bennett and Mrs Brown', 'Modern Fiction' insists that received novelistic convention, by which Woolf means late realism, no longer captures 'life'. Instead she offers a manifesto for modernist narrative:

> Examine for a moment an ordinary mind on an ordinary day. The mind receives a myriad impressions – trivial, fantastic, evanescent, or engraved with the sharpness of steel. From all sides they come, an incessant shower of innumerable atoms; and as they fall, as they shape themselves into the life of Monday or Tuesday, the accent falls differently from of old; the moment of importance came not here but there; so that, if a writer were a free man and not a slave, if he could write what he chose, not what he must, if he could base his work upon his own feeling and not upon convention, there would be no plot, no comedy, no tragedy, no love interest or catastrophe in the accepted style ... Life is a luminous halo, a semi-transparent envelope surrounding us from the beginning of consciousness to the end. Is it not the task of the

novelist to convey this varying, this unknown and uncircumscribed spirit, whatever aberration or complexity it may display, with as little admixture of the alien and external as possible? ...

Let us record the atoms as they fall upon the mind in the order in which they fall, let us trace the pattern, however disconnected and incoherent in appearance, which each sight or incident scores upon the consciousness.

(Woolf, 1966, vol.2, p.106)

Note the insistence again on the 'myriadness' and incoherence – to the point of incipient nausea – of subjective experience. This incoherence breaks the inherited and enslaving cadence of experience – 'the accent falls differently from of old' – and, accordingly, of all inherited fictional shapes, plots and conventions. Henceforth, the subject matter of the novelist is to be not the 'external', but the nature of consciousness, examined with a quasi-scientific detachment.

This manifesto may well remind you of your earlier encounter with Walter Pater's formulation of life as a series of disconnected and intense moments (see Chapter 2 and Reader, Item 10), and indeed you may have noticed that he was acknowledged in the Preface to *Orlando*. Woolf goes on in her essay to consider some of the potential problems with such writing – its claustrophobic concentrement in one self, which militates against the 'jovial and magnanimous' (1966, vol.2, p.108). Nevertheless, in 1924 Woolf felt that 'we are trembling on the verge of one of the great ages of English literature', that writers were about to put into place a new literary language, a new range of representational techniques to depict the new reality.

Taken together, Woolf's critical writings on biography and on fiction suggest very strongly her central project as a mature writer – to invent a form of writing that superseded realism generally (including the realism of her own early work, such as *Night and Day*, 1919), concentrating on the subjective rather than the objective. Inevitably, then, her writing deliberately tries to break inherited genres, and especially the genre of realist fiction. Indeed, Woolf was to write in her *Diary* that 'I doubt I shall ever write another novel after *O.* I shall invent a new name for them' (1980, vol.3, p.176). This new freedom was opened up to Woolf by *Orlando*'s conscious irresponsibility as biography, history or fiction. One of the principal ways Woolf signals this is to make *Orlando* a historical fiction derived recognizably, if distantly, from the bestselling Waverley novels published a century before by Walter Scott. (You may recall that he too is acknowledged in the Preface.) For most of the twentieth century, historical fiction has hovered on the very edge of respectability. (Although Pat Barker won the Booker Prize for her historical novel *The Ghost Road* in 1995, most writers in this popular genre, such as Jean Plaidy, have never been shortlisted for a literary prize.) With its tendency to play fast and loose with both fictional and historical 'truths', the genre is viewed by the critics as not quite as serious as 'proper' fiction and definitely not as serious as history. However, with the abrupt arrival of the narrative in the present (in Chapter 6, somewhere around p.282), *Orlando* shifts gear. From having been a romp through history, an evocation of the national and imperial past, the novel turns towards describing recent history and eventually the present. Given that the nature of the modern was almost by definition one of the principal concerns of the modernists, let us take a careful look at Woolf's evocation of the present.

Before going any further, read Chapter 6 in its entirety, if you have not already done so. Then return to the passage that runs from 'There was something definite and distinct about the age …' (6; p.284) to '… Orlando was terribly late already' (6; p.285). How is modernity conveyed here, and by what is it characterized? How is it represented in relation to Orlando herself?

The modern is characterized as an age of 'distraction'. Orlando herself is represented as being ambushed by the violence of clock and calendar time:

> the clock ticked louder and louder until there was a terrific explosion right in her ear. Orlando leapt as if she had been violently struck on the head. Ten times she was struck. In fact it was ten o'clock in the morning. It was the eleventh of October. It was 1928. It was the present moment.
>
> (6; p.284)

The present is 'terrifying' and hard to survive; Orlando concentrates on balancing as she crosses 'the narrow plank of the present, lest she should fall into the raging torrent beneath' (6; p.285).

At this point *Orlando* becomes an altogether less comfortable read, as Woolf engages fully with the problem of conveying a sense of modernity. From now until the end of the novel, Woolf is principally interested in exploring how consciousness operates within the precarious present moment, within or despite the tyranny of Greenwich time. To do this she deploys a range of innovative representational techniques. Up to this point, *Orlando* has largely been a story of how a consciousness negotiates its contours with the spirit of the age – with its clothes, its customs, its characteristic sentiments and postures, and its governing narratives and genres. Although Orlando's consciousness has become ever more heterogeneous as she accumulates a longer past, composed of a collage of disparate and surprisingly juxtaposed memories of things – 'a piece of a policeman's trousers lying cheek by jowl with Queen Alexandra's wedding veil' (2; p.75) – until now, this heterogeneity has seemed by and large benignly cumulative. (You might disagree here and in regard to this very example; such deliberate incongruities in Woolf's text could be seen not as comfortable co-existence but as eating away at social and sexual hierarchies.)

But there has not been quite the sense of fracture that Woolf now evokes. For the modernists, the modern is more precarious and harder to inhabit than previous historical epochs – if for no other reason than that there are no established narratives. In the same way that the individual is fractured and layered by memory, so too the modern is fractured and layered by history. *Orlando* serves as a metaphor for both: 'Nothing is any longer one thing. I take up a handbag and I think of an old bumboat woman frozen in the ice. Someone lights a pink candle and I see a girl in Russian trousers' (6; pp.290–1). Neither personal time nor actual time corresponds with time measured by clock and calendar; 'the sixty or seventy different times which beat simultaneously in every normal human system' may 'chime in unison' or they may not (6; p.291).

In part, this fracture of consciousness is represented as an effect of modern urban living, and associated with modern technology. The imaginary geography of the modern is the urban department store. The department store is disorientating – the lift's magic movement deposits Orlando arbitrarily and confusingly at first one floor and then another. Within modernity there appears to be less necessary relation between things and bodies. Moreover, Orlando's body is much less central to the scene, less in control of it via its gaze. Once master of all he surveyed from his estate, Orlando has become all but mastered by the randomized things she surveys. This analysis of the effect of urban modernity on subjectivity is elaborated in the account of Orlando's drive out of London into the country.

Now reread from 'The Old Kent Road was very crowded ...' (6; p.292) to '... all precisely life-size' (6; p.293). As you read, ask yourself the following questions: how is the impression of speed given? What is the effect of starting with short sentences and then modulating into longer sentences? What is the relationship between London and the country?

Although the paragraph begins by locating Orlando very precisely in the Old Kent Road on Thursday, 11 October 1928, parodying the nineteenth-century realist novel, the prose is far more interested in conveying the sensory experience of driving along the road rather than describing it as an objectively existing place. The brilliance of the passage is this kinetic effect, which is closely related to the Vorticist/Futurist celebration of speed and the urban: the widening and narrowing of streets, the shrinking of vistas, the unmotivated and inassimilable juxtaposition of the incongruous – a market, a funeral, love and death. This kinesis is also achieved by the use of very short sentences, together with the dramatization of incomplete perception of things seen – there is no time to read the captions 'Ra–Un', 'Amor Vin', 'Undert–' let alone interpret them. The prose is shot through with anxiety about the failure of reading ('Nothing could be ... read from start to finish'), the failure of writing ('the body and mind were like scraps of torn paper'), and the failure of narrative closure, which it associates with the failure of love or relationship: 'What was seen begun – like two friends starting to meet each other across the street – was never seen ended.' The experience is death-like, it 'disassembles' Orlando. As the paragraph continues, and as Orlando drives into the country, the sentences become longer, mimicking the increased emptiness and coherence of the countryside after the crowded, unreadable metropolis. Her consciousness is ultimately reinstated by the countryside. Looked at carefully, though, this is not exactly a pastoral – it is true that the countryside sets things into proper syntactical relation (rather than chopping them up with full-stops) 'a cottage, a farmyard and four cows'. But Woolf insists this is an artificial pastoral, a saving painterly 'illusion' of order – two green screens enclosing an artfully composed vignette, 'all precisely life-size'. The vignette is 'life-like' not 'life' itself. Orlando, nearly 'disassembled', precariously held together in the moment and that by an 'illusion of holding things within' herself, is very much in the condition of modernity diagnosed by the modernists. The dialectic between London and the country, therefore, is not the traditional one. The impersonal, dehumanized, alienated London of Eliot's *The Waste Land*, counterposed to his fleeting visions of lost pastoral idylls, is here shadowed but not endorsed.

Overall, the narrative of *Orlando* could be read as suggesting that there has been a change in the forms of subjectivity over history – from the relatively unitary to the increasingly multiple. **Now reread from 'What then? Who then?' (6; p.296) to '… when communication is established they fall silent' (6; p.300). How does Woolf convey Orlando's rapidly oscillating selves? What brings this oscillation to a close?**

This is principally a drama of punctuation – of question by one self, answer by another; of slippage from perception to perception marked by semicolons, and slippage from self to self marked by parenthesis. It is the act of passing through the gates of Knole that fully reintegrates Orlando: 'The whole of her darkened and settled ... and bec[a]me what is called, rightly or wrongly, a single self, a real self' (6; p.299). Despite my caveat above, the suggestion here might seem to be that Knole is in some way an antidote to urban modernity – an antidote, at any rate, to fracture and dissociation. Knole (or the self that is associated with Knole) contains her multiplicity 'as water is contained by the sides of a well' (*ibid.*). That Knole serves as a temporary antidote to modern fluidity points us back to Woolf's undoubtedly conservative nostalgia for secure social hierarchy, represented here by the aristocratic great house, a nostalgia laced with (even generated by) a constant sense of that hierarchy's irreversible fading away.

Knole is much more than just an accidental part of *Orlando*; the dialectic between 'home' and away – mostly London – is arguably the defining structure of the book. Orlando's life and history is recorded, embodied and authenticated in Knole. The urban or cosmopolitan setting is typically shot through with Knole. Service at Elizabeth's court is rewarded by patents in Knole, the Turkish landscape is riven with a vision of Knole that prompts Orlando's return to England, legal trouble in London over her gender sends her back to Knole, where her staff notice no difference, the London department store is plundered for stores needed at Knole – sheets, bath-salts and boys' boots. **Reread now from 'Masterfully, swiftly, she drove up the curving drive …' (6; p.300) to the end of the book. To what extent is Knole conceived as an antidote to the modern, and to what extent has modernity changed it?**

On the one hand, Knole registers the 'real' – its parkland, its trees, its deer and its sheer weight of continuous history. It is home – familial, maternal – and Orlando's walk around the house 'was all in the day's routine. As soon would she come home and leave her own grandmother without a kiss as come back and leave the house unvisited' (6; p.301). It is organic (a bedroom shines 'like a shell'; 6; p.302) and animated, even anthropomorphic. Orlando fancies that 'the rooms ... stirred, opened their eyes as if they had been dozing in her absence' (6; p.301). The house is so alive that it knows all her secrets and history, and it will after her death be a repository for her soul, which 'would come and go forever with the reds on the panels and the greens on the sofa' (6; p.302). Its 'indomitable heart' still beats (6; p.303).

'Indomitable' that heart may be – but it is also 'frail' (6; p.303). This sense of physical integration and animation works in uneasy counterpoint with a sometimes anxious, sometimes vengeful, feeling of the modern. There is the ominous vision of the deer with its head twisted sideways by wire-netting, and that sense of something awry develops from a troubling solitude (her solitary arrival, the empty ambassador's bedroom, the empty chairs) into an uncomfortable set of figures that combine preservation with death or decay – the shell, the faded velvets, the withered pot-pourri, the lavender bags. Open to the public, the house is increasingly bound up in a living death. Orlando cannot reanimate it with her body (her sitting in the chairs, for example); she is forced now to depend on the eye of the imagination. The primary sense of Knole as 'organic' or 'real' is constantly put under strain by the precarious present moment – represented by the striking of the clock – which produces an extraordinary vividness of vision associated with the modern technological miracle of the microscope. The oldness of the house changes under the pressure of the present into something new, into something that looks like, but is not, the real thing: 'a scraped new photograph' (6; p.306). The dissociation between body and thing, and the peculiar fragmentation of bodily perception that arises, is underscored by 'the loud speaker condensing on the terrace a dance tune that people were listening to in the red velvet opera house at Vienna' (*ibid.*). The present is dangerous, fearful, painful, and threatens selfhood with fragmentation and mutilation. This is in part the point of Orlando's appalled faintness at the sight of the missing nail on Joe Stubbs's hand (6; p.307), though this episode is also, to return for a moment to the text's interest in Freud, a deferred scene of castration – the castration that took place so pleasantly, magically and unsurgically earlier in the text (Marcus, 1997, p.131), the castration that disinherits Orlando. The final vision of Knole is something between a simulacrum and the real thing – a 'phantom': 'There stood the great house with all its windows robed in silver. Of wall or substance there was none. All was phantom' (6; p.313).

Knole's phantom qualities should alert us to the ways in which Orlando's inheritance of house and land is a fleeting fantasy. In fact, divided like the photograph between representation and the real thing, between idea and body, between the present and the past, Knole had that year passed out of Sackville-West's immediate family on the death of her father. The vision of the arrival of the dead queen to the phantom house is therefore explicitly mendacious: 'Nothing has been changed. The dead Lord, my father, shall lead you in' (6; p.313). No wonder this passionately nostalgic act of denial is followed by 'the first stroke of midnight' and 'The cold breeze of the present' (*ibid.*). The ambiguous insistence on and denial of Knole's status as 'the real' in *Orlando* is registered in the fate of the manuscript; although Woolf published her novel in a much larger print-run (6,000) than any of her previous works, she gave the holograph manuscript itself to Sackville-West. It was a curiously lordly gesture, in that she gave Sackville-West back what she had lost – her centrality to Knole, even Knole itself, albeit a Knole of the imagination. The gift also recognized something unique and physical in the relationship between Sackville-West and Woolf and between Sackville-West and Knole. It is therefore appropriate that, until very recently, the manuscript of *Orlando* was displayed in the entrance hall of Knole – almost the first thing you might have seen as a tourist, the key or clue to the whole.

Embedded in this meditation on Orlando's relation to Knole as her (lost) inheritance is an episode that meditates on the fulfilment of Orlando's career as a poet, a coming into her literary inheritance. Orlando climbs up again into the implausibly panoramic landscape presided over by its symbolic oak tree, this time in order to bury, not the manuscript but the published book of 'The Oak Tree'. Perhaps, then, Orlando's real inheritance is the intellectual property associated with print culture. Perhaps the novel's plot is not so much the story of Sackville-West's aristocratic love affair with Knole but the story of the woman writer and her coming of age. In the next section I explore both the representation of Orlando's writing in relation to the tradition she inherits, and Woolf's own practice as a woman writer exemplified and even theorized in *Orlando*.

Women and writing

Orlando lives through all of English literature, from Shakespeare to Woolf's own most recently published novel *To the Lighthouse* (1927), and, constantly scribbling, recomposes it into a many-branching unity in her immense, organic, abundantly selling poem 'The Oak Tree'. At the same time as Woolf was drafting *Orlando*, she was also drafting a talk – provisionally entitled 'Women and Fiction' – to be given to the women undergraduates at Girton College, Cambridge, at the beginning of the new autumn term. She would later expand and develop this lecture into a short book entitled *A Room of One's Own* (1929), which is arguably one of the most influential texts of early twentieth-century feminism and feminist literary theory.

A Room of One's Own is essentially an essay about the social conditions under which it might be possible for women to write – and in many ways it shadows and is the obverse of *Orlando*, which is a mock-biography of a woman writer. It is Eliot's 'Tradition and the Individual Talent' thought through specifically in terms of the history of women's writing. Eliot's essay finds an echo in Woolf's in their shared interest in the relationship between the writer and his/her 'tradition'. Both Eliot and Woolf insist on the element of apprenticeship to literary heritage, and the necessity for a writer to have the whole of European literature simultaneously present to him/her as a resource and as something from which to diverge creatively. Orlando undergoes just such an apprenticeship to the tradition, with difficulty but successfully. *A Room of One's Own*, however, notes that should women succeed in overcoming the material difficulties that stand in the way of their becoming writers, they would still be faced with the problem of whether to adopt a masculine tradition or whether to 'think back through [their] mothers'. Woolf notes that this has made it especially difficult for women to write in the 'impersonal' way – irrespective of sex, for one thing – that both she and Eliot seem to favour. Nevertheless, *A Room of One's Own* makes clear the opportunities that developing a modernist, consciously revolutionary and 'new' aesthetic – an aesthetic at a slant to mainstream literary tradition – offered to Woolf as a woman writer. In many ways *A Room of One's Own* turns modernist literary aesthetics into feminist literary strategies. Or, to put it another way, in *A Room of One's Own*, as in *Orlando*, literary aesthetics and gender politics are inseparably intertwined. **Now read the passages reprinted from *A Room of One's Own* (Reader, Item 23). What connections can you make between Woolf's analysis of the problems and opportunities the woman writer might have in relation to literary tradition and Orlando's own writing career, both as a man and as a woman?**

Both *A Room of One's Own* and *Orlando* take Shakespeare as their presiding genius. Orlando's writing career is undertaken – having glimpsed Shakespeare sitting in the servants' quarters – under and within the sign of

Shakespeare's name. This surely is the point of the citation of the Bard late in the book when Orlando is haunted by the vision of 'Sh–p–re (for when we speak names we deeply reverence to ourselves we never speak them whole)' (6; p.298). Although there is clearly a biblical resonance in this refusal to speak the name that connects Shakespeare with the Creator, it may also be that Orlando does not speak the name whole so as to leave room for the insertion of her own writing within the tradition. Shakespeare's work as described in *A Room of One's Own* similarly makes him benignly incomplete. If in *A Room of One's Own* 'Shakespeare is the ground against which Woolf figures the woman writer as she has been and as she might become', 'Woolf's creation of the fantastic Orlando as Shakespeare's androgynous yet ultimately female counterpart articulates the ideal of the woman writer' (Froula, 1990, p.134). *Orlando* is utopian, *A Room of One's Own* realist (*ibid.*). The fictional biography of the ill-fated Judith Shakespeare is cast in the same genre as that of Orlando, but comes to a very different end. In Orlando, Woolf creates an imaginary female writer to whom is given all that male culture denies Judith Shakespeare, including a tradition: 'writing and rewriting "The Oak Tree" over four centuries, Orlando is her own tradition' (*ibid.*, p.135). The fantasy of *Orlando* is echoed in the concluding fantasy of *A Room of One's Own*:

> if we live another century or so – I am talking of the common life which is the real life and not of the little separate lives which we live as individuals ... then ... the dead poet who was Shakespeare's sister will put on the body which she has so often laid down.
>
> (Woolf, n.d., p.117)

Woolf's insistence that, on the whole, the life of women is invisible before the eighteenth century, and that becoming a middle-class woman writer would have been downright impossible – socially, financially and psychologically – before then, is surely one reason why Orlando starts off as a man. In the seventeenth and eighteenth centuries a woman might write if she were a lady of title and wealth, such as Lady Winchelsea – or Orlando. But, like Orlando with the manuscript of 'The Oak Tree', she will find herself writing in the margins and blank spaces. Changed into a woman, Orlando finds herself outside literary history, peeping into the coffee-room from outside, unable to hear a word spoken by the 'Great Men'. She finds herself instead acting principally as muse or patron. Even as late as the nineteenth century, she has been discouraged as a writer – and you will remember that *Orlando* contains a long passage about the way that compulsory heterosexuality both enables and enfeebles her writing. Putting on a wedding ring, she finds that 'Her page was written in the neatest sloping Italian hand with the most insipid verse she had ever read in her life' (5; p.227). The passage in *A Room of One's Own* about how women do not have a literary tradition – how they 'think back through [their] mothers' – finds an echo in some striking details in

Orlando that associate his/her writing with the dead mother: the manuscript is kept behind the dead mother's bed, his writing book is stitched together with silk from the mother's workbox (2; p.108).

A Room of One's Own identifies fiction as a peculiarly pliable mode and therefore amenable to the woman writer and to the women writer's syntax and body. Woolf's reading of her composite new author Mary Carmichael takes note of a new and unexpected rhythm, altered emphasis and new material. Both books take note of censorship – both from the outside and internalized. *A Room of One's Own* provides Sir Chartres Biron as a possible male censor, and even dramatizes Woolf's own self-censoring tendencies: 'I turned the page and read ... I am sorry to break off so abruptly. Are there no men present? Do you promise me that behind that red curtain over there the figure of Sir Chartres Biron is not concealed?' In the same way, a critic, Nick Greene, presides over much of Orlando's writing until she resolves to shake him off, but persists in the voice that comments on a quotation taken from Sackville-West's poem *The Land*:

> As she wrote she felt some power ... reading over her shoulder, and when she had written 'Egyptian girls', the power told her to stop. Grass, the power seemed to say, going back with a ruler such as governesses use to the beginning, is all right; the hanging cups of fritillaries – admirable; the snaky flower – a thought, strong from a lady's pen, perhaps, but Wordsworth, no doubt, sanctions it; but – girls? Are girls necessary? You have a husband at the Cape, you say? Ah, well, that'll do.
>
> (6; p.253)

Such censorship is very much associated in both texts with compulsory heterosexuality, against which are posited Woolf's controversial notions of androgyny and multiple sexuality. Woolf's games with her androgynous hero/ heroine in *Orlando* find an echo in *A Room of One's Own*, in the figure of the couple meeting in the taxi-cab. Taken together, these texts dramatize the ungendered, androgynous body – or the multiply gendered/sexed body. The two are by no means the same, and one formation may undo the other. Orlando's multiple and uncertain gender, after all, may be thought of as undoing androgyny rather than enforcing androgynous sameness.

Overall, *Orlando* can be read as a companion narrative to that of *A Room of One's Own*, both of them efforts to write first as a female writer, and then as an 'androgynous' writer. Read in conjunction with *A Room of One's Own*, *Orlando* appears to explore what would happen if we extended the idea of androgyny from the mind of the artist to the body's sexuality, if we took seriously the speculation put forward in *A Room of One's Own* that we could do with more than two sexes (see Silver, 1999, pp.222–3). Both texts are markedly hypothetical and provisional in spirit and methodology – the many models of writing and of sexual difference that they generate are not necessarily coherent or congruent with one another.

That said, *Orlando* is in some way less hypothetical about the woman writer than *A Room of One's Own*. It does, after all, take as its subject a real-life woman writer – Sackville-West. When Woolf published *Orlando* on 11 October 1928, Sackville-West herself may have been hugely flattered, but three days after publication her mother wrote to Woolf, bitterly complaining that she had published a very cruel book, and seeing it as a betrayal of a friend and sometime lover. This remark has frequently been written off as the fulminations of outraged respectability, and feminist, especially lesbian, readings of the novel have preferred to take up the son's dewy-eyed verdict of 'the longest ... love-letter in literature' (Bowlby, 1998, p.xviii). **Cast your mind back across the novel and consider how you might flesh out both of these claims.**

Clearly, the novel is physically affectionate about Vita/Orlando, dwelling on features such as her beautiful legs. Equally, the most prominent love affair of the novel, that between Sasha and Orlando, appears very thinly disguised as heterosexuality, given that the affair is remembered so passionately by Orlando as a woman. Orlando is endowed with deathless glamour, and in this sense, yes, the novel is a 'tribute'.

On the other hand, the novel is perhaps cruel about Sackville-West's pretensions as a writer. With hindsight, posterity has declared Woolf to be the greater writer, but Sackville-West had her own claims to fame. Winner of the Burdett-Coutts Prize for her poem *The Land* (note the way in which this title is jokingly incorporated into the name of Orlando), she had by 1928 enjoyed more success and acclaim than Woolf. Woolf represents her hero/heroine's writing as first of all clichéd, then as jejune or embarrassingly enthusiastic and naive, then as the butt of the critic and satirist Nicholas Greene. Although her struggle to write is represented as principled and dignified, it is also comic, and she regularly finds herself relegated to the role of patron or salonnière. If you look back at the passage I discussed in detail above (p.308), you will see that, although we have been led to expect that the narrative will climax with the publication and success of 'The Oak Tree', this climax is downgraded:

> Fame! (She laughed.) Fame! Seven editions. A prize. Photographs in the evening papers (here she alluded to the 'Oak Tree' and 'The Burdett Coutts' Memorial Prize which she had won; and we must snatch space to remark how discomposing it is for her biographer that this culmination to which the whole book moved, this peroration with which the book was to end, should be dashed from us on a laugh casually like this; but the truth is that when we write of a woman, everything is out of place – culminations

and perorations; the accent never falls where it does with a man).
Fame! she repeated. A poet – a charlatan; both every morning as
regularly as the post comes in.

(6; pp.297–8)

Musing on the hollowness of fame, Orlando thinks of her brief sight of
Shakespeare, and then, in prose of extraordinary beauty, she effectively
renounces her poetic claims: striving to catch the wild goose, her nets draw
'sometimes ... an inch of silver – six words – in the bottom of the net. But
never the great fish who lives in the coral groves' (6; p.299). Orlando's
relationship to her literary inheritance seems almost as precarious as her
relationship to the lost inheritance of the house. The two inheritances are
brought into tight juxtaposition in almost the last scene of the novel. **Reread
from 'The ferny path led ...' (6; p.308) to '... and housemaids
dusting?' (6; p.311). In what ways is poetry related to the land in this
passage?**

Orlando's poem is entitled 'The Oak Tree' and she brings it back to the
(emblematically British) oak as a sort of 'symbolical celebration'. She intends
to bury the book – autographed by author and artist – at the roots of the tree,
but she abandons the attempt. There is no room among the tree's roots, and
it would be silly. She leaves it 'unburied and dishevelled'. The aborted effort
to return 'to the land ... what the land has given me' (6; p.309) (and again it is
relevant here to remember that Sackville-West's prize-winning poem was
entitled *The Land*) results in her abandonment of the book, and her gaze
travels away from it across her equally forfeited lands. In some ways this
replays a central anxiety of the novel throughout – the relationship between
poetry (especially metaphor) and the real. It is possible, indeed, to read
Orlando as something of an extended meditation on the relationship between
language and the real. In what sense can language convey the real, or
language itself *be* real? Can metaphor make language more concrete? Such
preoccupations typically lurk within the poetic endeavour, less often within
prose fiction – but they certainly inhabit *Orlando*, and come to the fore in the
episodes that deal with Orlando's endeavours to write poetry. These episodes
reveal that *Orlando* has a peculiarly sceptical attitude towards metaphor and,
consequently, towards writing itself:

He was describing, as all young poets are for ever describing,
nature, and in order to match the shade of green precisely he
looked (and here he showed more audacity than most) at the
thing itself, which happened to be a laurel bush growing beneath
the window. After that, of course, he could write no more. Green
in nature is one thing, green in literature is another. Nature and
letters seem to have a natural antipathy; bring them together and
they tear each other to pieces.

(1; p.16)

Orlando's failure to bury the book points both to the inadequacy of writing compared with the real and to the inadequacy of any writerly entitlement to literary heritage to compensate for being disinherited from the land, here explicitly national. But the last word is still to come.

Woolf struggled ferociously with the problem of how to end *Orlando*. It is certainly true that at the end, perhaps more than anywhere else in the book, there is a sense of hypotheses being made and discarded. There was a real difficulty in finishing a biography of a living person, let alone a lover, and this is registered in the correspondence surrounding the event. In a letter to Sackville-West, Woolf recorded the exact moment that she drafted the three dots that mark the end of Orlando's speaking, and strikingly compared it to a public execution: 'Did you feel a sort of tug, as if your neck was being broken on Saturday last at 5 minutes to one? That was when he died – or rather stopped talking, with three little dots ...' (Woolf, 1977, vol.3, p.474). Sackville-West was equally anxious about the way in which she had been made into 'a waxwork'– very lifelike, but not alive (see Lee, 1997, p.512). What are we to make of this ending, with its montage of the clock striking midnight, the rushing aeroplane, the preposterously named Marmaduke Bonthrop Shelmerdine and the 'single wild bird'?

On the one hand, this is a fairy-tale ending. These are the midnight chimes that signal the end of Cinderella's fantasy, the vanishing of the fabric of illusion. But equally, there is a way in which the stroke of midnight does not just signal the end of a fantasy but the beginning of enormous transformative potential. The aeroplane has many potent meanings for Woolf, but here it is erotically and ecstatically associated with a vision of futurity – of technological innovation, of a new mode of being in modernity as land-bound beings take to the air. The vision represents a new post-national moment, in which the traditional dualism between land and sea – essential to the self-conception of an island-nation – is rendered meaningless by the transformation of Shelmerdine from sea-captain to aeronaut. Orlando will perhaps take off from the land, abandoning Knole – 'above all, an English house' 'with the tone of England' – and with it the whole constricting notion of national boundaries and national heritage (Sackville-West, [1922] 1949, p.2). But if that is too portentous a reading for you, in another sense this is simply the end of the wild goose chase – the wild goose that has, from the outset of the novel, been associated with writing, but that has, up to this point, always escaped, even if it has occasionally scattered its feathers for use as quills. It hovers, pentecostally, over the end of the book, and its final triumphant sighting in the flesh is on the date of publication of *Orlando* (Beer, 1996, p.165). Or, finally, you may feel it simply flies away with the whole seriousness of the enterprise, by way of an apology, or disclaimer.

Orlando's after-lives

Orlando was a major success, selling 8,104 copies in the first six months, eliciting a shower of enthusiastic letters and praise, and bringing Woolf into mainstream (progressive middle-class) fashion for the first time. As even the hostile Arnold Bennett, Woolf's target in 'Mr Bennett and Mrs Brown', wrote in his review, 'You cannot keep your end up at a London dinner-party in these weeks unless you have read Mrs Virginia Woolf's *Orlando*' (in Majumdar and McLaurin, 1975, p.232). Not everyone liked or admired the work; if you did not care for it, then perhaps Conrad Aiken's perceptive if hostile comments on Woolf's style will strike a chord:

> There is ... an important element of 'spoof' in *Orlando* ... Mrs Woolf ... is pulling legs, keeping her tongue in her cheek, and winking, now and then, a quite enormous and shameless wink ... It is a style which makes fun of a style: it is glibly rhetorical, glibly sentential, glibly poetic, glibly analytical, glibly austere, by turns – deliberately so; and while this might be, and is, extraordinarily diverting for a chapter or two ... one finds it a little fatiguing in a full-length book. Of course, Mrs Woolf's theme, with its smug annihilation of time, may be said to have demanded, if the whole question of credibility was to be begged, a tone quite frankly and deliberately artificial. Just the same, it is perhaps questionable whether she has not been *too* icily and wreathedly elaborate in this ... a little more of the direct and deep sincerity of the last pages, which are really beautiful and really moving, might have made *Orlando* a minor masterpiece.
>
> (in Majumdar and McLaurin, 1975, p.235)

Other critics also commented on the artificiality and conscious virtuosity of *Orlando* – Aiken's review suggests all sorts of interesting assumptions about what a novel is supposed to do to and for its readers. The dislike of Woolf's artificiality seems to carry just a little class animus, a suggestion that the artificiality is related to social and intellectual privilege and consequent social irresponsibility. This is in fact a succinct statement of the common charge that modernist literary experimentation was sterile, self-involved, politically conservative and locked up in an ivory tower of its own making. Other sorts of writing, it could be claimed, endeavoured with a proper political radicalism to intervene in the 'real' world – this is certainly one of the claims the poets of the 1930s would make for their work. The value placed on ingenuousness and sincerity here by Aiken, for example, may be said to underpin the critical sense of the earthy working-class 'authenticity' of a novel such as Lewis Grassic Gibbon's *Sunset Song* (1932), which might be thought to be politically more progressive.

Sympathetic critics, however, saw *Orlando* as an avant-garde exercise in the presentation of consciousness as compounded of memory and perception – an innovation in form: 'Mrs Woolf', wrote Cleveland B. Chase in the *New York Times* of 21 October 1928,

> has faced squarely one of the most puzzling technical and aesthetic problems that confront contemporary novelists. The mere fact that she has stated the problem as succinctly as she does in the course of this book is immensely stimulating, whether or not one feels that she has achieved a final solution of it.
>
> (in Majumdar and McLaurin, 1975, p.231)

Nevertheless, *Orlando* was perceived by many critics at the time and after as a 'pretender' within the 'dynasty' of Woolf's other novels (Raymond Mortimer's review, in Majumdar and McLaurin, 1975, p.241).

Over the course of the twentieth century, it has been the critical fate of *Orlando* to have been enjoyed but largely ignored in accounts of Woolf's career. This changed dramatically in the 1980s and 1990s, when *Orlando* began to receive an unprecedented amount of critical attention. For Bowlby (1988), for example, it became the 'key' text in writing about Woolf, displacing *To the Lighthouse*. At the same time, a series of adaptations of *Orlando* came to stage and screen. In 1980, Angela Carter began a never-to-be-finished opera libretto entitled *Orlando: or, the Enigma of the Sexes*; in 1981, Ulrike Ottinger's film *Freak Orlando* – a very free adaptation – was screened in art-house cinemas; Robert Wilson's one-woman show, *Orlando*, was premiered in Berlin in 1989 and starred Miranda Richardson at the Edinburgh Festival in 1996; in 1997, Robert North adapted the novel as a ballet, which was premiered at the Rome Opera House; and in 1992, Robin Brooks's adaptation, which treated the novel's action as a play within a play and featured Woolf and Sackville-West in the frame, was staged in Edinburgh and London. Most spectacularly, Sally Potter had a box-office hit in both Britain and the USA with her film *Orlando* (1992). Of course, this flurry of rereadings and reinterpretations of *Orlando* in the 1980s and 1990s says as much about late twentieth-century culture as it does about *Orlando*. And, it should perhaps be said, these rereadings and reinterpretations have conditioned many of the readings I have so far explored in this chapter. Examining Potter's adaptation of *Orlando* helps us to think about what it was that the late twentieth century – both inside and outside the academic context – found so congenial about *Orlando*.

Potter's film, like the original text to some degree, was ambivalently nostalgic about the past, which it conceived – again like its original – principally in terms of style and in terms of things. It is sumptuously detailed, crammed like a department store at Christmas with gorgeous things that have an air not of historical usefulness but of make-believe and frivolity.

Instead of trying to achieve an effect of historical realism, Potter went for an effect of conscious exaggeration. This exaggeration was too extensive to be called pastiche, too affectionate to be called parody, and perhaps is most akin to quotation. As such, it was appropriate to the spirit of the novel. Potter's aesthetic can be related to something of a cultural crisis in the 1990s over Englishness. This crisis took the form of, on the one hand, an appetite for the past turned into heritage consumables and, on the other, a definite anxiety about the relationship between a supposedly 'organic' and glorious past and a fractured, uncertain present. Potter's remarks about the film note that she was interested in

> the way the English place themselves in the world in relation to their past. There is an addiction in English culture to mythologies of the past ... and many of these mythologies are rooted in the reign of Elizabeth I, which provides the origin for a particular understanding of national identity. It is a familiar accusation that the English are unable to let go of the past.
>
> (quoted in an interview by Glaessner, 1992, p.14)

Though Potter went on to say that 'In the film, Orlando gradually [lets go of the past]: she loses everything, but gains herself in the process' (prefiguring the moment when New Labour cast off the past and the party's leader, Tony Blair, called for Britain to become a 'young' country once more), arguably it was the film's romancing of the past as style that really sold the tickets (quoted in an interview by Glaessner, 1992, p.14). Or perhaps the film provided both pleasures: the pleasures of the past, and the pleasurable fantasy of the possibility of the self – and by extension the nation – as surviving history, looking different, but essentially little changed from century to century.

The film was also seen as unusual in its depiction of gender and sexuality (Figures 6.4 and 6.5). Basing their thinking on a reading of Freud similar to the one outlined above, 'postfeminist' literary critics had been arguing that the sexed body does not necessarily predetermine gender. Just because one is born a woman does not guarantee that one 'becomes' a woman. Becoming a woman (and indeed a man) is a cultural process. Part of that process is learning how to 'perform' gender. In short, gender is not 'essential' (i.e. inbuilt and inalienable from the body) but performative (and possibly, therefore, though this is extremely contentious, elective). As Judith Butler influentially argued in her book *Gender Trouble* (1990), 'there is no original or foundational gender or sexuality, no original and copy but only copies ... gender/sex and the gendered/sexed subject are produced by repetitive acts of performance' (Silver, 1999, p.214, paraphrasing Butler). In this context, the film, full of cross-dressing, might seem especially to celebrate and to endorse the performativeness of gender and with it a mobility of gender identity

Figure 6.4   Tilda Swinton as Orlando, in the film *Orlando* (1992), directed by Sally Potter. (Photo by Liam Longman © Adventure Pictures.)

Figure 6.5   Quentin Crisp as Queen Elizabeth I, in the film *Orlando* (1992), directed by Sally Potter. (Photo by Liam Longman © Adventure Pictures.)

congenial to a culture that is wedded to ideas of individual freedom and self-expression, and in which (courtesy of chemical contraception and fertility technology) procreation has become decisively divorced from heterosexual sex.

Contextualizing Potter's film within the 'high theory' debates swirling in the academic conferences of the 1990s hardly explains its box-office success. In fact, its success suggests that the same anxieties informed both academic thinking and the culture at large – not very surprising, unless you believe that academic thinking somehow predates and initiates cultural change. Potter's achievement in adapting a 'high' modernist, elite text for a film audience suggests that the film intervened in an arena of cultural tension, in debates about feminism, gender, sexuality and androgyny. But exactly how and to what effect did it intervene? Did it reinforce normative ideas about gender and sexuality or did it undo them? Or, did it do both? **Now consider the task of adapting *Orlando* for the screen. What problems and opportunities does the novel present to a screenwriter?**

It has often been remarked that *Orlando* is 'filmic'; it is highly visual (a legacy from the influence upon the Bloomsbury group of the Post-Impressionists, notably Roger Fry), evoking history by way of panorama (think of the evocation of the Great Frost) and surreal montage (think of the monument to Victoriana). Perhaps less congenial to the tradition of classical film is Woolf's interest in portraying the experience of the visual from a subjective angle – that is, as kinetic and fragmentary: think of Orlando's vision of the old queen's hand or the car-journey down from London. But generally, visualizing *Orlando* should be easy. (As Potter wrote in her Introduction to the screenplay, 'the book worked primarily through imagery, and was therefore eminently cinematic'; 1994, p.ix.) What *Orlando* is notably short on is dialogue – there is hardly any, and where it exists, it is often reported. The film's dialogue, what there is to be of it, will have to be invented, and there may have to be a voice-over to cope with Orlando's intermittently chatty consciousness (think again of the car-drive through the country). The other problem for a director would be to decide how to cast Orlando – whether to cast a man, or a woman, or both sequentially. This decision will materially affect what the film says about the differences between the genders/sexes and the stability of gender itself.

Faced with these problems, and with a text composed largely of a series of pastiches of literary styles, Potter sets up elaborate panoramic scenes, which provide some sort of visual equivalent and which use the language of overstated clothes (appropriately enough) as an equivalent for literary style. The Elizabethan period, for example, is colour-coded red and gold, the Jacobean black and silver, and so on. Potter also constructs dialogue, and exteriorizes consciousness by means of voice-over. The centrality of Orlando's subjectivity is underscored by her pieces to camera – a non-realist, non-'classical' strategy. Potter deals with the casting problem by casting Tilda Swinton throughout as Orlando, but suggesting early in the film the provisionality of gender and its relation to masquerade. This is made clear both by Swinton's opening gesture of cross-dressing, backed by the explicit commentary in the voice-over, and by the cross-dressing of the Virgin Queen (punningly played by Quentin Crisp, author of *How to Become a Virgin*; 1981). If gender, according to Butler, is 'a stylized repetition of acts through time' (Silver, 1999, p.214), then the performance by these actors of cross-dressing is a performance of a body that is not quite 'male' *or* 'female'. Cross-dressing denaturalizes gender, and makes it appear (many critics would say reveals it as) a matter of convention.

In the rest of the film, Potter makes changes that are designed to pump up narrative motivation – Orlando's change of sex is triggered by a crisis in masculine identity that is brought on by her refusal to participate in the killing associated with war. She exaggerates what she sees as the feminist politics of the book, making Orlando abandon marriage and property both, and replacing Orlando's son with a daughter. She inserts the First and Second World Wars explicitly, and, in the spirit of the original, she brings the narrative up to date in the immediate present of the 1990s. Potter explained that, because the book was 'almost a running commentary on the history of literature as the vehicle of consciousness', she had found the equivalent of Woolf's post-First World War ending in the fracturing of a literary consciousness and 'the arrival of the electronic age' (Donohue, 2001, p.57). Orlando's writing gives way to her daughter's experimentation with the video camera.

Potter's film earned twenty awards but elicited mixed responses, especially in the USA: it was attacked for being gratuitously unfaithful to its source, for undoing gender difference, for not undoing gender difference, for eliminating lesbian sexuality or sexuality altogether, for being too camp or not camp enough, too feminist or not feminist enough, and for effacing the sexed/gendered body within a sort of comforting transcendent asexual deep self.

Conclusion

In the next chapter you will study another modernist meditation on ways of representing history and the self, Bertolt Brecht's *Life of Galileo*. But before you do so, it is worth revisiting the main features of Woolf's modernist experimentation in *Orlando*. **Test the general propositions about modernist narrative below against your reading of Woolf's novel; can you find examples to support or qualify each one?**

1   Because in modernity perceptions of reality had come to seem uncertain, provisional and momentary, the intense moment captured in a visionary image provided the truest sense of the nature of things.

2   Because, in parallel, character or personality now appeared split and precariously fragmentary, personal experience itself verged on incoherence. It was, therefore, best represented by a disassembled jumble of juxtaposed images or as fractured and fissured perceptions of other people and things, dissolving and reconstellating in a way reminiscent of one contemporary movement in the visual arts – Cubism.

3   Consequently, conventional realist ways of organizing narrative – through space and time – give way to other organizational logics. As David Lodge has put it:

> The structure of the traditional novel, with its rounded characters, logically articulated plot, and solidly specified setting, melts away ... climaxes of plot are progressively pushed to the margins of the discourse, mentioned in asides and parentheses ... the unity and coherence of the narratives comes increasingly to inhere in the repetition of motifs and symbols, while the local texture of the writing becomes more and more densely embroidered with metaphor and simile.
>
> (Lodge, 1977, p.177)

Works cited

Beer, G. (1996) *Virginia Woolf: The Common Ground*, Edinburgh: Edinburgh University Press.

Bowlby, R. (1988) *Virginia Woolf: Feminist Destinations*, Oxford: Basil Blackwell.

Bowlby, R. (1998) 'Introduction', V. Woolf, *Orlando*, Oxford World's Classics, Oxford: Oxford University Press, pp.xii–xlvii.

Cannadine, D. (1990) *The Decline and Fall of the English Aristocracy*, New Haven: Yale University Press.

Donohue, W. (2001) 'Immortal Longing: Walter Donohue Talks with Sally Potter', in G. Vincendeau (ed.), *Film/Literature/Heritage: A Sight and Sound Reader*, London: British Film Institute.

Freud, S. (1977) *On Sexuality: Three Essays on the Theory of Sexuality and other Works*, ed. by J. Strachey, Pelican Freud Library, vol.7, Harmondsworth: Penguin.

Froula, C. (1990) 'Virginia Woolf as Shakespeare's Sister: Chapters in a Woman Writer's Autobiography', in M. Novey (ed.), *Women's Re-Visions of Shakespeare: On the Responses of Dickinson, Woolf, Rich, H.D., George Eliot, and Others*, Urbana: University of Illinois Press, pp.123–42.

Glaessner, V. (1992) 'Fire and Ice', *Sight and Sound*, 2.4, August, pp.13–15.

Horner, A. (1991) 'Virginia Woolf, History, and the Metaphors of *Orlando*', *Essays and Studies*, 44, pp.70–87.

Lee, H. (1997) *Virginia Woolf: A Writer's Life*, London: Vintage.

Lodge, D. (1977) *The Modes of Modern Writing: Metaphor, Metonymy, and the Typology of Modern Literature*, Birkenhead: Edward Arnold.

Majumdar, R. and McLaurin, A. (eds) (1975) *Virginia Woolf: The Critical Heritage*, London: Routledge & Kegan Paul.

Marcus, L. (1997) *Virginia Woolf*, Plymouth: Northcote House in association with the British Council.

Nicolson, N. (1973) *Portrait of a Marriage*, London: Weidenfeld & Nicolson.

Potter, S. (1994) *Orlando*, London: Faber & Faber.

Sackville-West, V. ([1922] 1949) *Knole and the Sackvilles*, London: Lindsay Drummond.

Silver, B.R. (1999) *Virginia Woolf Icon*, Chicago: University of Chicago Press.

Woolf, V. (1966) *Collected Essays*, 4 vols, London: Hogarth Press.

Woolf, V. (1977) *The Letters of Virginia Woolf*, ed. by N. Nicolson, 6 vols, London: Hogarth Press.

Woolf, V. (1980) *The Diary of Virginia Woolf*, ed. by A.O. Bell, 5 vols, London: Hogarth Press.

Woolf, V. ([1928] 1998) *Orlando*, ed. and intro. by R. Bowlby, Oxford World's Classics, Oxford: Oxford University Press.

Woolf, V. ([1929] n.d.) *A Room of One's Own*, San Diego: Harvest/Harcourt Brace Jovanovich.

Further reading

Bowlby, R. (1988) *Virginia Woolf: Feminist Destinations*, Oxford: Basil Blackwell. Lively, accessible, and intelligently provocative readings of *A Room of One's Own*, 'Mr Bennett and Mrs Brown' and *Orlando*.

Lee, H. (1997) *Virginia Woolf: A Writer's Life*, London: Vintage. The essential modern biography interlaced with critical insights.

Woolf, V. ([1929] n.d.) *A Room of One's Own*, San Diego: Harvest/ Harcourt Brace Jovanovich. Essential reading for those interested in Woolf's position as the mother of modern feminist literary theory and history.

CHAPTER 7

Bertolt Brecht, *Life of Galileo*

DENNIS WALDER

Overview

> Brecht is the key figure of our time, and all theatre work today at
> some point starts from or returns to his statements and
> achievement.
>
> (Brook, 1972, p.80)

In this chapter I consider Brecht's play *Leben des Galileo* (*Life of Galileo*) as an
example of European modernist art aimed at provoking a radically new
understanding of social reality through a range of theatrical techniques
'alienating' the familiar or everyday. After describing the historical
background against which the play was written, I introduce Brecht's
practice as a playwright by means of a critical reading of the first scene. I
briefly discuss the influence of this practice on other writers and on
contemporary drama. Following an account of Brecht's life, I examine the
rest of the play in an attempt to consider the relation between Brecht's
context, his ideas and his practice. I discuss the contrasting views of a
number of contemporary and recent critics, raising the question of what kind
of play this is: 'popular realism', tragedy or comedy, or a new kind of
'dialectical' theatre.

Introduction

Bertolt Brecht's *Life of Galileo* is a play about one of the most important
scientists in history, the Italian astronomer and physicist Galileo Galilei
(1564–1642), who transformed our knowledge of the world and the way we
think about it. Yet, famously, Galileo submitted to the church's demand that
he withdraw his radical new beliefs about the structure of the universe. These
contradicted the system described by the ancient Greek Ptolemy, according
to which the earth was at the centre of the cosmos, with the other planets
circling around it. Galileo showed for the first time that the planets rotate
around their own axes, and orbit the sun rather than the earth. The earth was
thus just one of many planets, not the central object in the cosmos placed
there by God. The structure suggested by Galileo had already been proposed
in the fifteenth century by the Polish astronomer Copernicus. However, it
was Galileo's observations of the craters on the moon, sunspots, Jupiter's
moons and the phases of Venus, using a newly discovered instrument, the

telescope, that irrevocably challenged the old view of the cosmos. This led to a moment of historical crisis: faith in things as they were, or appeared to be, was being overtaken by experimentation and a resulting doubt.

Brecht lived at a time of crisis too, when new beliefs were displacing the old and when the whole conception of reality was being challenged by science once again, and not only by science but by events that undermined the familiar structures of society as well. These parallels touched a nerve in Brecht, and the resultant play engages with some of the major historical and cultural crises of our times. It is almost uncanny how far a play that is set in the seventeenth century seems to connect with some of the landmarks of recent history. Brecht wrote the play when the Danish physicist Niels Bohr's advances in atomic theory were first made public, which coincided with the Munich Agreement of 1938, when Hitler was poised on the brink of his attempt at world domination. The play was first revised after the dropping of the first nuclear bomb by the USA in 1945, which ended the Second World War. It was rewritten again at the height of the cold war after the death of Stalin in 1953. The history of its stage production is equally striking: first in neutral Switzerland in 1943, during the Second World War; then in postwar USA, to which so many German scientists and intellectuals had fled, contributing to the US's global ascendancy; and finally, in 1957, in two premieres within months of each other in what were then two cities – East and West Berlin – in a divided Germany, under the looming threat of nuclear catastrophe. Most plays change during the process from writing to performance, as well as between performances, but it is important to realize from the outset that *Life of Galileo* exists in three distinct versions.

Brecht, who had been forced to leave Germany when Hitler came to power, wrote the first version in three weeks in 1938 while in exile in Denmark. Initially, he called the play *Die Erde bewegt sich* ('The Earth Moves'), a remark supposedly made by Galileo, but he revised the title early in 1939 to *Life of Galileo*, which it remains. This so-called 'Danish' version was substantially unchanged for the Zurich premiere in 1943, by which time Brecht was living in the USA.

It was in the USA that Brecht met the well-known, left-wing British actor Charles Laughton, with whom he collaborated on an English-language version of the play. This was completed in 1945 but first performed (with Laughton in the title role and directed by the film-maker Joseph Losey) in 1947 in Beverly Hills. It became known as the 'American' or 'Californian' version, and is now available on video (with Topol, Michael Lonsdale, John Gielgud, Judy Parfitt and Edward Fox, 1974).

After the end of the war, in 1949, Brecht returned to Berlin. A few years later, he decided to make a new German version of the play, incorporating, while modifying, material from both the earlier versions. He was working on this version up to his death in August 1956. Shortly after this, the play was premiered in Cologne, followed a few months later by the Berliner Ensemble production in East Berlin. This *Berliner Fassung* ('Berlin version') became the basis for subsequent performance, publication and critical discussion.

It is this last version on which I will concentrate here. I will be referring to the Methuen Student Edition, translated by John Willett, with Commentary and Notes by Hugh Rorrison, re-issued in 1994. Although there is no need to read the Commentary in detail, you will find that it contains some useful quotations from Brecht's diary, a brief account of the play's history and its engagement with the present, as well as an outline (on pp.xxxiv–xxxviii) of Brecht's theory of 'epic theatre'. This is based on the table of his ideas set out in 'The Modern Theatre is the Epic Theatre' (Notes to the opera *Aufstieg und Fall der Stadt Mahagonny*; 1930, in Brecht, 1978, p.37). This table has often been taken as a convenient snapshot of Brecht's views on theatre, but it comes from one particular moment in his career and, as you will see, a much more complex picture of his ideas about the theatre emerges if the development of his career is considered. Moreover, a better source of Brecht's views post-1938 is provided by the lengthier and more considered essay *Kleines Organon für das Theater* (*A Short Organum for the Theatre*), first drafted in 1948. Extracts from this essay, which is reproduced in the Reader (Item 26), will be referred to in what follows.

As *A Short Organum for the Theatre* makes clear, Brecht was a hugely ambitious artist, who, like other modernists, set out to change forever the medium in which he worked. He saw himself as the Galileo of the theatre, experimenting with the form not merely for its own sake, but as a way of responding to, and influencing, the new scientific, technological and industrial world of the twentieth century. As Suman Gupta pointed out in the Introduction to Part 2, the idea that literature should reflect or even intervene in modern social and political concerns was challenged by many modernists, who emphasized the aesthetic dimension of their work. But, as Brecht's views indicate, an interest in relating quite consciously to the social, political and ideological currents of the time was also a powerful source of energy for certain twentieth-century modernists. *Life of Galileo* demonstrates Brecht's belief in a critical, scientific approach to life as a means of changing the world, not necessarily by using new artistic devices (although he does incorporate contemporary innovations such as the cinematic technique of cutting), but by the conscious use of all the familiar devices of the theatre in a way that delivers an experience of shock, or at least of unfamiliarity. This is designed to wake audiences up to the underlying realities of the times, transforming us from a 'general passive acceptance' of things to the required 'state of suspicious inquiry', for which we should develop 'that detached eye with which the great Galileo observed a swinging chandelier'. Galileo, Brecht says, 'was amazed by this pendulum motion, as if he had not expected it and could not understand its occurring, and this enabled him to come on the rules by which it was governed'. The theatre too must 'provoke' and 'amaze' us, 'and this can be achieved by a technique of alienating the familiar' (*A Short Organum for the Theatre*, paragraph 44).

Brecht's approach is in many ways comparable to the tactics of those avant-garde modernists who used artistic representation to alienate or upset people into changing the way they saw things. For a Marxist modernist such as Brecht, the aim was to use the means of representation to create an understanding of 'the rules' by which society was 'governed'. These rules had been explained by Karl Marx, but it was not necessary to be a Marxist to understand them; the point of the theatre was to bring the widest possible range of people into an awareness of how society really worked, in order to change it. As Louis Althusser has succinctly put it, Brecht 'wanted to make the spectator into an actor who would complete the unfinished play' (1971, p.204).

Reading the play: Scene 1

Brecht always insisted that his views were derived from practice, so let us begin by reading through Scene 1 of *Life of Galileo*, to get a preliminary idea of that practice. Brecht regarded his texts as indicative, not final versions, of the fuller reality of the performances, and you may well wish to revise what you think of the play as you work through the discussion below.

Consider the opening of the play (pp.5–6) in the light of the following questions.

1 **What do you think the spectator in the theatre first sees when this play opens? Think about setting, props, costume and any other details indicated in the text.**

2 **Look at the top illustration facing the title page, a photograph from the American production of the play, with Charles Laughton in the lead role. How would you describe the staging? What kind of play does it suggest?**

3 **What do you make of the language of the dialogue?**

4 **How are we encouraged to see Galileo at the start?**

1 There is an immediate problem that has to be resolved for each individual production: as the auditorium lights go down (assuming they do), the words 'Galileo Galilei, a teacher of mathematics at Padua, sets out to prove Copernicus's new cosmogony' (the bold headline at the top of p.5) must be highlighted, but how? It might perhaps be projected onto a screen, appear on a half curtain, or otherwise be visualized, for example by the unfurling of a banner. The headline is followed by the little ditty in the text beginning 'In the year sixteen hundred and nine'. For the

American production, three boy sopranos sang this to a score by Brecht's long-time collaborator Hans Eisler (and this was repeated in the 1974 film/video version). The heading and ditty precede, and therefore distance us at least momentarily from, the action. This really begins with the arrival of the housekeeper's son, Andrea, bearing a glass of milk and a roll for Galileo – who, we are told, is '*washing down to the waist, puffing and cheerful*'. It is morning, and this is his breakfast. The set suggests Galileo's '*rather wretched study in Padua*', and there is mention of star charts and a wooden model being brought out. From the emphasis on time and place, we might expect details of costume and set to be specific and realistic.

2   The photograph shows that for the American production the actors are isolated in lights against a stark background, with only a washstand, a chair, a table and the wooden model on the floor. Costumes appear to be simple, but in the style of an earlier period. These hints, plus the neutral staging, allow us the illusion of being present at a scene from the past; yet we have been made aware, from the opening title and song, that it is a *representation* of the past, a version of history. The scene seems to be offering to tell a story that we are broadly expected to know, but it is not obvious how far the narrative aspect is going to dominate. This could be the beginning of a period drama, or a chronicle play, despite the minimal amount of realistic detail, and the self-referring opening headline and song.

3   The language is trenchant and prosaic, although it contains technical or scientific terms. These, however, are explained to us in a direct, conversational manner, using a model. Galileo adopts a good-humoured, teacherly role towards his young assistant Andrea. There is some wordplay about 'making' and 'describing' a circle, which emphasizes the fact that this is a play about a mathematician who connects the real world and the world of geometry.

4   There is a strikingly visual, physically realized contrast between, on the one hand, Galileo the sensual, vigorous man and, on the other, Galileo the teacher, scientist or intellectual. This contrast is highlighted by Galileo being bare-chested, washing himself as he talks, and then having his back dried as he goes into an enthusiastic, lengthy explanation of why 'the old days are over and this is a new time'. Here, two aspects of Galileo – body and mind – seem to belong in comfortable co-existence, although there is a hint of things to come, and the pressures that will be exerted on him, in the reference to the milkman not being paid. Is it going to be possible to balance or reconcile this man's energetic yet easy-going

approach to life with the world-shattering discoveries he is announcing, we might wonder? Beyond his zest for life, and intellectual buoyancy, not much is revealed about Galileo's character.

The opening – starting a play at dawn, when that play is about the dawn of a 'new time' – is effective and dramatically appropriate. The American version of the opening omits the joke about the milk, which you might think an improvement. I did until I came across the original of the Berlin version, where it becomes clear that Brecht is appropriating the phrase 'einen Bogen um etwas machen', meaning to avoid something, literally 'to make a curve around something', and changing it to Andrea's 'einen Kreis um etwas machen' ('to make a circle around something'), so that Galileo can correct the boy with the proper mathematical term 'einen Kreis beschreiben' ('to describe a circle'). Translating jokes is always problematic, and explaining them robs them of their force, but this joke helps give the conversation between the two its relaxed, even intimate feel, while allowing the great man to enlighten the boy (and us) about his new view of the cosmos. It also reminds us of the important role of translation.

If you glance at the section on 'Staging', on pages xxxix–xl of the Commentary, you will find some more detailed information about how the opening was actually staged in the American and Berlin versions (photographs of the Berliner Ensemble production, including Scene 1, are reproduced at the end of the Notes).

Now read through the whole of Scene 1, and notice how quickly the play develops different aspects of Galileo in relation to those around him: that is to say, what his beliefs mean to different sections of society, and how this will affect his position. The focus of the scene appears to be rather more 'external' than 'internal', reinforcing its broadly historical emphasis, and insisting on the primacy of everyday life. This perspective is reinforced towards the end of Galileo's first speech, in which he expands on the wonderful possibilities of the new age of knowledge and discovery then coming into being.

Andrea's view that according to the old Ptolemaic system (which held that the stars and the planets were fixed to spheres encircling the earth) the world seemed 'so shut in' (p.6) prompts Galileo to elaborate on the implications of his new view of the universe and the earth's place in it. Galileo enthusiastically extols the wonders of the 'new time' of enquiry and doubt rather than faith – from workmen discarding ancient methods of shifting granite blocks to ships venturing forth to new continents. He suggests that minds have been 'cramped', but now things are changing:

GALILEO ... Each day something fresh is discovered ...

> And the earth is rolling cheerfully around the sun, and the fishwives, merchants, princes, cardinals and even the Pope are rolling with it.

> Suddenly there is a lot of room ...

> What does the poet say? O early morning of beginnings ...

ANDREA

> O early morning of beginnings
> O breath of wind that
> Cometh from new shores!

> And you'd better drink up your milk, because people are sure to start arriving soon.

(pp.7–8)

The poem quoted by Andrea comes from one of Brecht's main sources for the play, Emil Wohlwill's biography of Galileo, *Galilei und sein Kampf für die Copernicanische Lehre* ('Galileo and his Struggle for the Copernican Doctrine'; 1909).

Note the ironic contrast between Galileo's boyish enthusiasm for the discoveries that are going to challenge all authority and the boy Andrea's matter-of-fact intervention. The point made may be summed up by one of Brecht's favourite sayings: 'Erst kommt das Fressen; dann kommt die Moral' ('Food is the first thing. Morals follow on'; from *Die Dreigroschenoper* (*The Threepenny Opera*), Act 2, Scene 6, in Brecht, 1993, p.56). Brecht enjoyed both inventing and recording such sayings. You might notice that he gives one to Galileo shortly after this exchange: 'Gawping isn't seeing', Galileo exclaims, before demonstrating that we cannot trust the mere evidence of our eyes – or at least, not in the simple sense of assuming that everything we see is literally the truth. For example, when we see the sun go down in one place at sunset and rise again the next day in another, it looks as if the sun must move around the earth, rather than vice versa. Galileo's words are not only an aptly colloquial translation of 'Glotzen ist nicht sehen' in the original, but also a way of translating into everyday speech the central philosophical issue of the seventeenth century: whether or not immediate perception provides access to reality. How far can the relations between things be extrapolated from what we see before us? Are there deeper connections?

Although Brecht seems to have found an accessible, popular way of representing these issues, it is less the psychological or intellectual than the social implications of the new thinking that are most immediately dramatized in this scene. The first visitor arrives soon enough – it is Andrea's mother and Galileo's housekeeper, Mrs Sarti. **What do you make of her attitude towards her lodger?**

She talks to Galileo as if he were a kind of overgrown child, irresponsibly filling her son's head with 'blasphemies', instead of focusing on paying the bills. In later scenes she reveals a powerfully loyal streak, but her view of his ideas is unalterable. It suggests that this is how ordinary people will respond to Galileo's discoveries: the potential for a clash between Galileo and authority is hinted at, as is the fact that the authority of faith runs right through society.

The next of his visitors, by contrast, comes from the rich and powerful, land-owning aristocracy; Ludovico Marsili is sent by his mother to learn a little science, regard for which is apparently fashionable. Although Ludovico is presented as something of a buffoon, the practical result of his wealth – his freedom to travel – is that he informs Galileo about the invention of the telescope.

The comic elements in Scene 1 are developed further with the arrival of the pompous procurator of Padua University, from whom Galileo immediately begs a loan. But the procurator also brings the news that he cannot authorize the increase in salary that would release Galileo from the necessity of taking on pupils such as Ludovico and allow him to spend all his time on original research. What is revealed here is the financial implications behind the vaunted freedom of the progressive Republic of Venice:

> GALILEO Your protection of freedom of thought is pretty good business, isn't it? By showing how everywhere else the Inquisition prevails and burns people, you get good teachers cheap for this place. You make up for your attitude to the Inquisition by paying lower salaries than anyone.
>
> PROCURATOR That's most unfair. What use would it be to you to have limitless spare time for research if any ignorant monk in the Inquisition could just put a ban on your thoughts? Every rose has its thorn, Mr Galilei, and every ruler has his monks.

(p.15)

Freedom of thought was of great concern when Brecht was writing the play, and it is not long before this reference to the Inquisition takes on a more threatening aspect. But notice how the dialogue proceeds in terms of a debate about the issue introduced by the entrance of the procurator: the clash between immediately practical, commercial interests and the value of scientific ideas. It is a development of the earlier clash between Galileo's teaching and the necessity of paying the milk bill, resolved at the end of the scene, after the procurator has left, by Galileo's decision to offer the Republic the telescope he has constructed based on the information he has gleaned from Ludovico – 'That'll get us 500 scudi' (p.19). We are left with a sense of Galileo's willingness to sacrifice morality – presenting as his own somebody else's discovery – to survive. Yet how far is this really an immoral act? Is it not done in the cause of the greater freedom to continue his research on behalf of humanity?

The real difficulties of Galileo's situation have been staged as powerfully as his unwillingness to compromise. Throughout Scene 1 he is drawn away from his table, from his work: when Ludovico comes in, he exclaims 'This place is getting like a pigeon loft' (p.11); when the procurator arrives, he is busy '*jotting down figures on a piece of paper*' (p.13); and during the procurator's speech in defence of the Republic, '*Galileo glances longingly at his work table*' (p.16). The moment he is left alone '*for a moment or two*' he '*begins to work*' (p.18). Yet, paradoxically, as the scene also makes clear, were it not for these interruptions the important new technology of the telescope would not have become accessible to him for further research. Galileo resents the outside world but he is nonetheless dependent on it.

As Scene 1 demonstrates, Brecht's form of drama operates in terms of a progression of arguments, dramatized visually and through dialogue. We might note that the scene has a certain internal unity: it is carefully structured to bring us back to the questions raised at the beginning, as Galileo and Andrea are once again left alone on the stage in a visual echo of the start. The conflicts to come have been anticipated, as we realize if we already know the broad history of Galileo's silencing by the church. This is, of course, part of the point about using a familiar historical figure as the focus of the play: we are not expected to experience the usual elements of dramatic suspense here. Brecht's play is more interested in the issues that arise than in Galileo's inner thoughts.

The question of individual creativity and its relation to society that has been raised is not relevant merely to the seventeenth century of the play's setting. It is also pertinent to Brecht's personal situation when he first drafted this scene in exile in Denmark in 1938, and to the development of nuclear science during the 1930s and later, when the role of scientists in producing weapons of mass destruction was to become of even greater concern. You might also begin to think about the position of intellectuals or scientists more generally at the historical moments of the play's productions: having to decide whether or not to go into exile from fascism at one moment; at another, reconsidering their responsibilities towards societies, even 'free' ones, during or under threat of war.

The theatricality of the play – in terms of gesture, movement and tableau as well as speech and dialogic interaction, rather than characterization, large action or suspense – is intended to bring a fresh awareness of the social and political implications of the historical event around which it revolves. Does this meet our expectations of what a play by Brecht might offer? To answer this question, it will be helpful to leave the text aside for a moment and look at our own as well as Brecht's theatrical contexts; we will then return to the play.

What is 'Brechtian'?

Most people in English-speaking countries who know of Brecht probably do so through the common use of the adjective 'Brechtian' to describe a style of theatrical performance. There are at least two reasons for this: first, the German playwright was a particularly influential innovator in the theatre, creating a whole theatrical tradition that has pervaded European, and indeed world, theatre since the 1950s. Second, despite the fact of this influence, only a small group of Brecht's plays are generally produced, and even these not nearly as often as we might expect, given their 'classic' status. I am thinking of *The Threepenny Opera* (premiere 1928), *Mutter Courage und ihre Kinder* (*Mother Courage and her Children*; 1941), *Der Gute Mensch von Sezuan* (*The Good Person of Szechwan*) and *Life of Galileo* (both premiered 1943), and *Der Kaukasische Kreidekreis* (*The Caucasian Chalk Circle*; 1954). Although they have many differences in style, form and theme, these plays share a number of features that may be identified as Brechtian.

This is the first of many paradoxes about Brecht: the term implies that there was something unique about this playwright, a quality with which he managed to infuse his works as he created them. However, Brecht, anticipating later trends of literary-critical thought, argued against the Romantic individualist approach to the artist as sole creator of a unique artistic object, and in favour of a view of the artist as someone who produces art from the materials of history, in collaboration with others. This is also why there are different versions of his plays: Brecht saw every new production as an opportunity for revision, often using the insights of others. Moreover, the conditions of exile in which many of the plays were written meant that quick production was often impossible. In addition, variations were introduced by different translations.

But what are the features that have come to be called Brechtian, at least in the UK? To answer this fully requires some familiarity with post-1950s drama. I am thinking of plays such as John Arden's *Serjeant Musgrave's Dance* (premiere 1959), as well as a whole clutch of others that have earned the label 'Brechtian' – the work of authors such as David Edgar, Edward Bond, Caryl Churchill, David Hare, Trevor Griffiths and Howard Brenton. The writer/director John McGrath's 7:84 Company created *The Cheviot, the Stag and the Black, Black Oil* in Scotland in 1973, and this is a celebrated example that was also televised. McGrath, Edgar, Bond and the others mentioned were all quite happy to accept the label 'Brechtian', and, indeed, rejoiced in it; less likely to do so was John Osborne, although one at least of his plays – *The Entertainer* (premiere 1957) – may be called Brechtian. As one leading contemporary theatre critic, Laurence Kitchin, remarked in 1960, 'You scent [Brecht's] influence everywhere in the contemporary drama and some aspects of the new English work would be unaccountable without it' (1969, p.73)

What exactly makes the work of any of these playwrights or directors Brechtian? *The Entertainer*, for example, presented post-Suez Britain as a defunct music hall dominated by a seedy comedian, Archie Rice (first performed by Laurence Olivier), who, in the last act of the play, breaks the naturalistic illusion by directly addressing the members of the audience in the theatre, thereby distancing them from both character and action. This kind of thing is probably what most people think of as Brechtian: a character stepping outside his or her role to comment on the action, often in the form of a song or ballad. *The Entertainer* was also episodic in structure and anti-establishment in mood, energetically deploying popular theatrical elements, such as the comedian's patter, to enforce its political point about the historic decline of the country. In all these ways, *The Entertainer* confirmed the deep penetration of Brecht's influence, an influence that Osborne did not acknowledge. Arden openly proclaimed that the writer he 'most wished to resemble' was Brecht (Eddershaw, 1996, p.6). His *Serjeant Musgrave's Dance* was clearly Brechtian in its use of history, its episodic form and the exploitation of ballad-like popular music to articulate an anti-imperial message, while distancing the audience from its characters and plot. Similar features marked the work that emerged from the 7:84 Company, as well as that of the other playwrights mentioned. Many productions also used banners, songs and other forms of 'statement' to anticipate or comment on the action, as is done in *Life of Galileo*.

There is much more that can be said about the huge and complex legacy of Brecht in British theatre, as well as elsewhere in Europe and the wider world. The best recent study of at least the UK dimension of his work is Margaret Eddershaw's *Performing Brecht: Forty Years of British Performances* (1996). The scale of his legacy may be gauged from the director Peter Brook's remark in his book *The Empty Space* that 'Brecht is the key figure of our time, and all theatre work today at some point starts from or returns to his statements and achievement' (1972, p.80). Brecht's influence was probably at its peak when Brook was writing the book, yet it was during the mid-1950s that Brecht's work first made a discernible impact in Britain, with productions from the Berliner Ensemble identified by leading critics such as Kenneth Tynan as representing the future of the theatre. According to Richard Eyre and Nicholas Wright, throughout the 1960s and 1970s Brecht was 'revered by left-leaning theatricals as a sage whose slightest jottings could be relied on as a guide to morality, politics and life itself', although by the

1990s 'the collapse of Marxism put a stop to that'. This is simplistic, but it is true to say that Brecht's influence 'on the direction of plays – what they look like, how they're acted – is deep and lasting' (2000, p.212).

Brecht was unusual, if not unique, among modern dramatists in the extent to which he attempted to justify his theatre work, as well as consciously to influence other playwrights and directors. No account of any of his plays can afford to ignore what he claimed in various writings he was trying to do, with or through his theatrical practice. *Life of Galileo* is no exception; moreover, it is to *Life of Galileo* that Brecht most frequently refers in his major work of theory, *A Short Organum for the Theatre*. Every new production of a play in which he was involved (whether he had written it or not) provided an opportunity for Brecht to develop his thinking about the theatre, in collaboration with his colleagues.

Possibly the first words that spring to mind when thinking about what makes any theatre experience Brechtian are 'alienation' and 'distancing'. These are two of a handful of terms that have come to mark Brechtian theatre, along with 'epic' and 'gest'. 'Alienation' and 'distancing' refer to effects that prevent the audience from identifying easily with the characters on stage; 'epic' suggests an emphasis on narrative or history; 'gest' is the totality of spoken and physical manoeuvres conveying a viewpoint. I will be coming back to these terms, since none of them is really very straightforward in meaning or use; indeed, Brecht often changed his mind about what he meant by them, as can be seen from the large body of theoretical work he produced to explain what he was trying to do. There are no less than seven volumes in the current scholarly edition, of which *A Short Organum for the Theatre* is only a small part (see Brecht, 1978).

Brecht defined what he was doing against the Aristotelian form of drama, that is, the whole tradition of European drama up to his time, which was, he argued, based on the idea of getting members of the audience deeply involved emotionally with what they were seeing. As we can see from the opening of *Life of Galileo*, Brecht's vision was a form of theatre aimed, to some extent, at helping the audience to take a more detached and critical view, rather than immediately empathizing or identifying with individual characters on stage. This is a matter of degree, since if the audience feels *nothing* for the characters, it can hardly be interested in what happens to them.

Like so many modernist artists, Brecht was consciously 'making it new'. How far this was in fact the effect of what he did is another question. In contrast to writers such as Virginia Woolf, James Joyce and T.S. Eliot, Brecht believed that the focus of art should be on social and historical reality, rather than on the individual consciousness. He was interested in creating a kind of art engaged with what he perceived as the 'progressive' or socialist forces of history. To have held to such a view through the catastrophes of the rise of

Nazism, the Second World War, the atomic bomb and the communist dictatorship in the German Democratic Republic (GDR) suggests Brecht's tenacity and conviction, as well as his ability to survive – a quality that is also a key theme in *Life of Galileo*. But his views changed, too, becoming less dogmatic about how the theatre should work.

From dramaturg to playwright

To get to grips with Brecht's ideas and practice it is helpful to consider some of the shaping factors of his life and thought: not only because this makes it easier to understand how far and in what sense we may want to call *Life of Galileo* a modernist work, but also because, as one of his earliest major critics, Martin Esslin, observed: 'Brecht was more deeply involved in the conflicts of his age than most of his contemporaries' (1965, p.xii).

One of Brecht's early poems, 'Von armen B.B.' ('Of Poor B.B.'), begins:

> Ich, Bertolt Brecht, bin aus den schwarzen Wäldern.
> Meine Mutter trug mich in die Städte hinein
> Als ich in ihrem Leibe lag. Und die Kälte der Wälder
> Wird in mir bis zu meinem Absterben sein.

> (I, Bertolt Brecht, come from the black forests.
> My mother bore me to the cities while I lay
> Inside her. And the coldness of the forests
> Will be with me to my dying day.)

(Brecht, 1967, pp.246–7)

Brecht's mother did indeed come from the Black Forest, and Eugen Berthold Brecht was born on 10 February 1898 in Augsburg, an industrial town near Munich in Bavaria, southern Germany. He was the eldest son of relatively well-off bourgeois parents (his father became managing director of a paper factory). He preferred to be called by the more proletarian 'Bert' or 'Bertolt', the name usually attached to his works. He was at the centre of a circle of friends, including the future set designer and his long-time collaborator Casper Neher, and he wrote, played the guitar and went to the theatre. He may have discovered elements of his theory of theatre in the Augsburg fairground, where he could have seen a one-legged singer present bloodcurdling 'penny-dreadful' moralities (*Moralitaten*), using a flip-chart of garish illustrations, while accompanying himself with song, proverb and barrel-organ (Fuegi, 1987, pp.4–6).

By 1916, Brecht had moved to Munich, the art and beer capital of Germany, where he began medical studies, perhaps as a way of avoiding the call-up for the First World War. Before the end of the war he had become a medical orderly in a military hospital, where he witnessed scenes that provoked such bitter lyrics as the famous 'Legende vom Toten Soldaten'

('Legend of the Dead Soldier'), which was published in his first book of poems, a satiric collection entitled *Die Hauspostille* ('Devotions'; 1927). 'Legend of the Dead Soldier' was to earn him the displeasure of the Nazis; it is cast in the form of a ballad about a dead body, dug up and solemnly pronounced fit for military service in the fifth year of war:

> Und weil der Soldat nach Verwesung stinkt
> Drum hinkt ein Pfaffe voran
> Der über ihn ein Weihrauchfassschwingt
> Dass er nicht stinken kann.

> (And because the soldier smells of rot
> A priest with a limp does well
> To wave some incense over him
> So no one smells the smell.)

(Brecht, 1967, p.225)

After the war, Brecht became a freelance writer, critic, poet and songwriter based in Munich. His associates included Peter Suhrkamp, who was later to become the publisher of his works, and Karl Valentin, whose skits, monologues and interludes, performed in the local dialect with mime and gestural accompaniment, profoundly impressed him. So too did the work of the recently deceased actor–playwright Frank Wedekind, the author of *Frühlingserwachen* (*Spring Awakening*; 1891) and the so-called *Lulu* plays (*Erdgeist* (*Earth Spirit*; 1895) and *Die Büchse der Pandora* (*Pandora's Box*; 1904)). Wedekind was the scourge of the bourgeoisie and the indirect inspiration for Brecht's first play, *Baal* (1918–20). This was written during a turbulent time, with the bloody suppression of the short-lived Soviet Republic of Bavaria, and the murder by the paramilitary Freikorps of the communist leaders Rosa Luxemburg and Karl Liebknecht. In Brecht's play, the sensual Baal is locked in conflict with his opposite, death, and savagely rejects all ideals and beliefs – it is a vision articulated in a rapid succession of short scenes adapting the same bare set, which anticipates Brecht's later attempts to give shape to what was happening around him by means of a new kind of theatre.

It was some years before Brecht established himself as a playwright. His activities as critic and commentator brought an appointment as dramaturg (literary advisor and playreader) at the little Munich Kammerspiel (Chamber Theatre), and it was here that his play *Spartakus*, renamed *Trommeln in der Nacht* (*Drums in the Night*; 1919–22), became his first stage success. Set in postwar Berlin, the play described the difficulties encountered by a former soldier. Although it was in the traditional five-act form, it included explicit commentary displayed on streamers hung in the auditorium. Brecht's contract required him to produce plays as well as write them, and he began searching for an appropriate vehicle. He eventually decided on Christopher Marlowe's *Edward II* (1594), then in production in London, which his secretary and sometime lover, Elisabeth Hauptmann, had translated.

Edward II was a breakthrough: Brecht adapted the play to demonstrate how the author's intentions could be conveyed by a bare account of events, without excessive emotion or grand gesture; it also revealed that he was happy to use plots or stories already in existence, as long as these could be made to serve the needs of contemporary theatre. The set of *Edward II* (designed by Neher) recalled the Augsburg fairground, but included a ballad-monger and hurdy-gurdy to represent the street life of London. As Brecht later told the critic–philosopher Walter Benjamin, the production also brought the moment at which 'the idea of epic theatre first came into his head'. Here is Benjamin's revealing account of a conversation with Brecht about this moment:

> *29 June* [1938] ... It happened at a rehearsal for the Munich production of *Edward II*. The battle in the play is supposed to occupy the stage for three-quarters of an hour. Brecht couldn't stage-manage the soldiers, and neither could Asya [Lacis], his production assistant. Finally he turned in despair to Karl Valentin, at the time one of his closest friends, who was attending the rehearsal, and asked him: 'Well, what is it? What's the matter with these soldiers? What's wrong with them?' Valentin: 'They're pale, they're scared, that's what!' The remark settled the issue, Brecht adding: 'They're tired.' Whereupon the soldiers' faces were thickly made up with chalk. That was the day the style of the production was determined.
>
> (Benjamin, 1977, p.94)

'Epic' theatre was thus conceived not as 'acting' fear in the 'Method' style advocated by Konstantin Stanislavski, which was based on finding the inner emotions to represent a feeling realistically, but rather as demonstrating its existence externally and visually, in the way proposed by Valentin (see Figure 7.1).

Valentin not only contributed to Brecht's 'discovery': his stand-up music-hall routines were keeping the Kammerspiel afloat during the rehearsals of *Edward II*. A photograph of Brecht making a guest appearance at one of Valentin's performances, playing some sort of recorder, highlights his involvement in the popular cabaret scene of the time, while reminding us not to think of Brecht as a dramatist aloof from, or unaware of, the importance of appealing to the ordinary spectator (Figure 7.2). Brecht was seeking a theatre that emphasized ideas and control, while still engaging the onlooker. Yet during these early, chaotic days of the Weimar Republic, when various organizations of the extreme Left and Right were flourishing, and a

Figure 7.1 *Mann ist Mann (A Man's a Man)*, Berlin, 1931. (Ullstein Bild Berlin.) The grotesque appearance of the soldiers on stage, with their exaggerated make-up, costumes and stilts, using external features to represent the soldiers' inner condition, indicates the beginning of Brecht's 'epic' theatre.

Figure 7.2 Bertolt Brecht in Karl Valentin's Orchestra, 1921. (Bertolt-Brecht-Archiv, Foundation Academy of Arts, Berlin.)

young drifter called Adolf Hitler was beginning to make his mark in the German Workers' Party in Munich, Brecht had still to develop a sustained dramatic theory, or a firm political commitment.

By the end of 1926, Brecht had left Munich for Berlin, where he became deeply immersed in Marx's *Das Kapital* (1867) and began to develop the views that gave a focus, and were to remain central, to his life and work thereafter. He did not then (nor did he ever) join the Communist Party, but Marx's writings convinced him that a new society was coming into being, which it was his role to interpret and represent critically. That society was in some respects reaching its apogee in the most advanced capitalist nation, the USA, a country that both fascinated and appalled him. A 1926 entry in Hauptmann's diaries reveals Brecht reflecting on the need to change the theatre in order to make it relevant to the changing times:

> In the old kind of theatre we are as out of place with our plays as Jack Dempsey would be unable to show his skill in a tavern brawl, where someone could knock him out by hitting him over the head with a chair ... if it is realized that the present-day world does not fit the established dramatic form, then that dramatic form is no longer suitable for our world.
>
> (quoted in Esslin, 1965, pp.27, 31)

Brecht often preferred the companionship of sportsmen to intellectuals, and when the Dempsey–Tunney fight of 1926 was shown at a Berlin cinema, it was preceded by one of his poems. The new kind of theatre he sought was in fact already being practised in Berlin by the influential dramaturg Erwin Piscator. Piscator was the leading spirit of the Volksbühne (Workers' Theatre) in Berlin, which rejected the single-author play in favour of documents, newsreels, slides and songs, sometimes linked by one or more narrators, all designed to engage audiences with the import of what they were witnessing. The aim of 'objectively' exposing the workings of society to change the views of the audience was shared by Brecht and Piscator, although the latter never wrote any plays, placing little importance on literary values. For Piscator, the theatre was a weapon in the struggle of the working classes, whose sympathies he sought through productions in halls and factories (one of his performances concluded with a vote being taken among the audience). This anticipated later radical theatre workers such as Dario Fo and Augusto Boal. Many of Brecht's and Piscator's production methods coincided, and Brecht owed Piscator a good deal; where they differed was in Brecht's emphasis on detachment or distancing, rather than involvement, for gaining the desired effect.

Read the extract from Brecht's article 'Schwierigkeiten des epischen Theaters' ('The Epic Theatre and its Difficulties'), which was published in *Frankfurter Zeitung*, 27 November 1927 (Reader,

Item 24). There are a number of phrases in this contribution to contemporary debates about the theatre that reveal both Brecht's recent reading of Marx and his growing commitment to a new kind of theatre. Try to pinpoint the most relevant phrases.

You may have noticed the key phrase 'ideological superstructure' used as a way of describing 'theatre, art and literature' in relation to society, or to what Brecht calls 'our age's way of life'. Here, Brecht is evidently applying his recent reading of Marx, who held, in the Preface to *A Contribution to the Critique of Political Economy* (1859), that the material conditions of production formed the basis of the 'legal, political, religious, aesthetic or philosophic – in short, ideological forms' in which the conflicts of the age emerged (in Baxendall and Morawski, 1977, p.86). Even if you have not read Marx, you will notice how Brecht emphasizes this phrase as part of his argument in favour of the need for a '*radical transformation of the theatre*', in response to the 'really new' ideas of the changing times.

What characterizes the new theatre? Notice how Brecht distinguishes between individual plays and the theatre as a cultural institution, making the rather startling claim that 'It is not the play's effect on the audience but its effect on the theatre that is decisive at this moment.' This allows him to go on to argue for the kind of theatre he believes is the appropriate 'style of our time' – epic theatre, which he characterizes as a theatre that appeals to reason rather than emotion: 'Instead of sharing an experience the spectator must come to grips with things.' While not denying the appeal of emotion, he is nonetheless trying to shift the way that theatre is organized towards promoting a more detached, critical stance.

If, as this suggests, Brecht was moving towards the Left and greater political commitment during the later 1920s, it was not until after his first huge success with *The Threepenny Opera* in 1928 that there was a decisive shift in his work. This was most strikingly evident in the uniquely Brechtian form, the *Lehrstück* or didactic playlet, that he then created. Ironically, it was the financial success of *The Threepenny Opera* that gave Brecht the freedom henceforth to work only on projects that interested him, including the *Lehrstück*. The most popular and successful musical play of the time thus supported some of the most didactic – and least performed. But then, the aim was to change the theatre rather than the audience.

Brecht had already been working with the composer Kurt Weill for a year before the idea of adapting John Gay's eighteenth-century satirical comedy *The Beggar's Opera* emerged, in response to a plea from a wealthy actor friend to find a new production for the opening of a refurbished former theatre beside one of the canals in Berlin, the Schiffbauerdamm. This was eventually to become the home of the world-renowned Berliner Ensemble, the creation and building up of the repertory of which in postwar Berlin was to take up all Brecht's energies after his return from exile in 1949, until the time of his death in 1956. The Berliner Ensemble's visits to Paris and London in that year to perform Brecht's version of George Farquhar's *The Recruiting Officer* (1706), and his own *The Caucasian Chalk Circle* and *Mother Courage*, marked the beginning of his international reputation as a major theatrical innovator, as well as a playwright.

With *The Threepenny Opera*, Brecht had intended to satirize contemporary opera that he termed *kulinarisch* ('culinary', i.e. designed for easy consumption, not thought) by introducing such devices as exaggerated make-up, unrealistic sets and direct addresses to the audience. He drew on the medieval French poet François Villon and Rudyard Kipling for the ballads, and Weill drew on contemporary jazz for the score. The result was satisfyingly popular, if morally and politically ambivalent – encouraging enjoyment of the exploitation it so vividly captured. The musical was set in the London underworld and centred on the conflict between two types of men, represented by the scheming Peachum, godfather of a gang of fraudulent beggars, and the notorious sensualist Macheath. The latter falls for Peachum's daughter, although he is already involved with Jenny Diver (who was first performed by Weill's wife, Lotte Lenya). The work's cynical view of life was underlined by Weill's original score and such wonderfully mocking songs as *Die Moritat von Mackie Messer* ('Ballad of Mac the Knife'), a direct descendant of the *Moralitaten* of the Augsburg fairground and the Munich beer cellars where Valentin performed.

However, it was the *Lehrstücke* that demonstrated Brecht's growing interest in using the theatre as a more direct means of informing audiences, or rather, of educating all those participating in the process of performance itself – both actors and audience, breaking down the difference between them – to embody a theatre for producers in place of one for consumers. These pieces (they are all short) were wholly in the spirit of the time: experimental, 'utilitarian', 'objective', and based on contemporary events (such as Charles Lindbergh's flight across the Atlantic in 1927) and issues (such as the sacrifice of the individual for a 'higher' cause). They have not lasted well, but they were not intended to. They were a part of Brecht's overall project of changing the nature of the theatre to engage with the changing times. This was expressed at the same time in more commercial, large-scale ventures, such as his anti-opera *The Rise and Fall of the City of Mahagonny* (1931). This is set in the USA, but is evidently a parable for contemporary Germany, envisaged as a country hell-bent on its own destruction, in which anyone could be bought and sold. At the second Berlin performance in December 1931, the assembled Nazis 'created such an uproar that a hundred of them had to be ejected from the theatre', after which they gathered outside, shouting 'Deutschland erwache!' ('Germany awake!'; see Ewen, 1992, p.196). Brecht's days in Germany were clearly numbered.

He was not ready to leave just yet, but his difficulties were increasing. He was attacked as a communist, failed to find a theatre for a new play set in the Chicago slaughterhouses (*Die Heilige Johanna der Schlachthöfe* (*St Joan of the Stockyards*; written 1929–30)) and fell foul of the censors with a collaborative film project about the plight of a family trying to survive on the outskirts of Berlin, *Kuhle Wampe* (1932). His growing unease was apparent in both public and private utterances – for example, in poems directed at the blindness of the politicians to the danger of 'the housepainter' (Hitler). For Brecht, as for many on the Left, the failure of the working-class parties to present a united front against the Nazis was disastrous. At a time of economic depression, rapidly increasing unemployment and weak leadership, people of all classes were looking to new and more extreme ways of protecting their interests. The result was that, whereas in 1928 the Nazi Party had won less than a million votes, by 1930 it gained nearly six and a half million, becoming the second largest party in the Reichstag (Joll, 1983, p.330).

The lack of strong constitutional traditions in Germany and the ease with which ancient fears and hatreds could be played on opened the way for Hitler's rise from nationalist crank in the Munich underworld of the 1920s to chancellor and head of a coalition government by the end of January 1933. As he intended, the coalition immediately collapsed, new elections were called and a campaign marked by increasing violence followed. As a result of a single dramatic event – the burning down of the Reichstag on 27 February – the Nazis felt justified in clearing the streets of opposition. Stormtroopers immediately began rounding up communists and left-wing intellectuals. Among those who realized what was coming – and fled the next day – was Brecht. On 10 May 1933, his books were burned, along with those of many other writers. Within two years, Hitler's power had become total, as education, culture, local government, the unions and the churches were all brought under his control. Thereafter, only individual resistance was possible, at the risk of martyrdom. The parallels with Galileo's situation can easily be drawn.

At first, Brecht had seen the Nazis less as a threat and more as a pathetic, fascist support for capitalism, but after the Reichstag fire and the arrests that followed, he was quicker than most to grasp what was happening. With his new (second) wife, the actress Helene Weigel, and their son (their daughter was smuggled out later), he went in search of a place to live and work. They eventually ended up in a farmhouse on an island in the Danish province of Svendborg, a mere 56 kilometres from the German border. Here Brecht wrote some of his most powerful poetry, including 'Fragen eines lesenden Arbeiters' ('Questions from a Worker who Reads'; first published 1936) and *An die Nachgeborenen* ('To Those Born Later'; 1938), as well as a series of sketches of life under the Nazis, *Furcht und Elend des Dritten Reiches* (*Fear and*

Misery of the Third Reich; 1938), and also the first draft of *Mother Courage* and the first version of *Life of Galileo*. As war became inevitable, he moved again, first to Sweden, then to Finland. Finally, in 1941, just before the Nazis arrived, he moved to the USA, where he was to stay until 1947. He then returned to Europe, first to Zurich and, in 1949, to East Berlin.

Exile is difficult for anyone; for a practising dramatist who relied on collaboration, it was particularly hard. In 1935, the year his German citizenship was revoked by the Nazis, Brecht, with Neher and others, vainly tried to establish a Weimar-in-exile in the Soviet Union. But Moscow in the late 1930s was becoming less and less a refuge and more another place of terror. The denunciation of 'formalist' modernism (which was supposed to emphasize formal qualities at the expense of political or social ones) – as exemplified by the work of the composer Dmitri Shostakovitch and the film-maker Sergei Eisenstein – was merely another aspect of the increasingly totalitarian regime there. This impacted on exiled Germans as well as on native Russians, such as Brecht's friend, the playwright Sergei Tretiakov (later murdered by Stalin's police). The denunciation was unfortunately echoed by the Hungarian critic Georg Lukács, whose notion of 'socialist realism' differed from Brecht's, as we shall see. At the Soviet Writers' Congress of 1934 'socialist realism', which glorifies progress and the Communist Party, had been proclaimed the art form of the future, and artistic experimentation had been denounced. Nonetheless, Brecht's time in Moscow was a turning-point for the development of his thinking about the theatre, and his particular view of modernism.

Now read the extract from 'Verfremdungseffekte in der chinesischen Schauspielkunst' ('Alienation Effects in Chinese Acting') (Reader, Item 25). Can you identify the key theoretical term that Brecht uses here? What role was it supposed to play in the new kind of theatre Brecht was proposing?

The key term is *Verfremdungseffekt* ('alienation effect') or, as Brecht also puts it, the *V-Effekt* (translated as 'A-effect'). According to Willett, this is almost certainly the first mention in Brecht's writings of the word *Verfremdung*. Earlier he had used the more familiar word *Entfremdung*, which was employed by the German philosopher G.W.F. Hegel and by Marx to suggest the 'alienation' of the worker in the capitalist system. Brecht is clearly seeking something different from the philosophical usage; indeed, *Verfremdungseffekt* refers to a quite specific effect in the theatre.

Brecht concludes, 'Among other effects that a new theatre will need for its social criticism and its historical reporting of completed transformations is the A-effect.' The emphasis is on theatrical means, from the way the actor performs (including an awareness of being watched) to music and setting. The 'new', 'historical' way of thinking, of seeing character and event, is to be the aim of the new theatre, as opposed to that of the 'bourgeois' theatre, which emphasizes the timelessness and universality of its objects. Overall, the Chinese performance witnessed by Brecht appears to have provided him with the idea of how to make the everyday 'strange', to underline the historical aspect of the epoch, which in turn will assist in transforming it.

What is most striking about Brecht's 'discovery' is what prompted it: a specific performance by the leading Chinese actor Mei Lan-fang and his company, in Moscow in the winter of 1936. The artists and intellectuals (such as, again, Tretiakov) he met were familiar with the Russian critic Viktor Shklovsky's idea (introduced in 1917) of *ostranenie* or estrangement as a central feature of the new art the age required. But it took an example of actual – traditional Chinese – theatre to make the point for Brecht. Thereafter, Brecht was always interested in the perspective on western theatre created by the estranging or distancing effect of theatre from the East, especially China – an idea and a place he was later to use for his theatrical parable about the effects of capitalism, *The Good Person of Szechwan*.

Ironically, considering all his criticism of capitalism, it was in the USA that Brecht henceforth found the freedom to operate. However, like many other European artists and writers, despite gaining the support of influential people (such as the critic–translator Eric Bentley), he was never more than on the fringe of cultural activity. Further, he was often in disagreement with the communist Americans of Hollywood with whom he mixed (such as Joseph Losey), association with whom led to him having to testify before the House Committee on Un-American Activities in 1947. Here, however, he displayed his powers of canny evasion at their best, before leaving the country. At least in Switzerland there was a German-speaking theatre, which had not only premiered some of his most important plays during the war (including *Life of Galileo*), but was reviving one of them (*Mother Courage*) and preparing the premiere of another, *Herr Puntila und sein Knecht Matti* (*Mr Puntila and his Hired Man, Matti*; 1948).

While in Zurich in 1948 and 1949, Brecht was stimulated into composing a summary of his beliefs on the 'non-Aristotelian' drama, *A Short Organum for the Theatre*, and he began to write his last play, *Die Tage der Commune* (*The Days of the Commune*), before being invited back to Berlin to produce *Mother Courage*. There he became an honoured (although not uncritical) citizen of the GDR. The production of *Mother Courage* (with Helene Weigel in the lead) was a huge success for the new Berliner Ensemble in the rebuilt Theater am Schiffbauerdamm, which went on to feature both new productions and revisions of the plays of exile, including *Life of Galileo*. Brecht's attitude towards the East German regime may be gathered from a poem on the June 1953 uprising, in which he asked whether, since according to the Secretary of the Writer's Union the people had forfeited the government's confidence, it would not be simpler if the government dissolved the people and elected another ('Die Lösung' ('The Solution'), a poem circulated in pirated versions in the West before its appearance in the collected poems in 1964).

His views, on the theatre as on politics, were never as simple or straightforward as has often been assumed by those who dislike his Marxism. They emerged from his changing circumstances and became one of the central strands in modern world drama. A playwright as distant in time and place as the twentieth-century South African Athol Fugard, for example, makes repeated reference to Brecht's ideas. These Fugard introduced to the black township players with whom he collaborated on *Lehrstück*-style exercises before producing such great works as *Sizwe Bansi is Dead* (1972) and *The Island* (1973).

Theory and practice

Armed with a greater sense of what we might expect of Brechtian theatre, and of how that developed historically in terms of Brecht's involvement in the movements of his time, let us return to *Life of Galileo*. **If you have not already done so, you should read the whole play through, focusing closely on the effects aimed at, and the developing arguments and issues.** Some of these should already have become apparent, and they can be simply expressed in terms of conflicting effects and themes. For example: *effects* – distance versus sympathy, inner character versus story or narrative; *themes* – science versus belief, individual versus authority, truth versus compromise. I would like now to approach the play from a range of critical perspectives, including, to begin with, Brecht's own.

Brecht's ideas about the theatre were both radical and constantly changing, and his views about *Life of Galileo* were no exception. Early in 1939, not long after he had written the first draft of the play, he was already dissatisfied with it. 'Technically, *Life of Galileo* is a great step backwards, far too opportunistic, like *Señora Carrar's Rifles* [*Die Gewehre der Frau Carrar*, 1937, his Spanish Civil War drama]', Brecht noted in his diary at the time. Presumably he felt that it was connected all too closely with contemporary events, such as the Moscow show trials, or the fate of writers and intellectuals still working in Germany. The play should be 'completely rewritten', he continued, to convey the 'rosy dawn of science' while being 'more direct, without the interiors, the atmospherics, the empathy' (quoted in Brecht, 2001, p.164). But Brecht did not rewrite the first version until his collaboration with Laughton in Hollywood, and how far they managed to dispense with 'empathy' in favour of alienation or distancing remains questionable.

I want to consider how well the Berlin version of the play embodies the related ideas of alienation, epic and gest that Brecht developed, basing my discussion on the evidence of *A Short Organum for the Theatre*, as well as *Life of Galileo*. We have already noted how the latter's opening, with its headline and ditty, temporarily distances us from the action of Scene 1. It also supplies contextualization, while deliberately removing the element of plot suspense. Scene 1 provides a kind of mini-drama, reflecting the conflict between Galileo's view of the world and the views of those around him. Yet there is no Brechtian commentator to disturb the initial focus on the great man in a domestic setting, enjoying the everyday pleasures of a new morning and imparting to his young acolyte the Copernican idea of the universe.

The opening strikes a balance between the distancing effect of the staging, and the sympathetic impulse generated by the presentation of Galileo's character. Without reference to an actual performance, it is hard to be sure where this balance lies, as Brecht above all was always aware. This is made clear from Brecht's copious discussions with Laughton in Hollywood about how to handle the presentation of the central character – discussions that were later translated and published as 'Building Up a Part: Laughton's Galileo' (see Brecht, 2001, pp.163–8). Scene 2 confirms the sense of striving for a balance between opposite tendencies. While presenting the conflict apparent in Scene 1 from another angle, it advances our notion of the kind of man Galileo is. His willingness to deceive his paymasters is shown, as he hands over his pirated invention to the Venetian dignitaries whose mercenary attitude to science has encouraged this very tactic. Yet, at the same time, the new invention takes him further towards proving Copernicus right. Scene 3 shows Galileo's almost comical unconcern about the effect of his duplicity, when a shipload of telescopes arrives from Amsterdam. Crucially for the development of the plot, the scene also shows the impact on his friend Sagredo of the confirmation of Copernicus' theory that the earth is a planet like others, and not the centre of the universe: 'where is God in your cosmography?', asks Sagredo. He is 'Within ourselves' is Galileo's reply. 'Like the man they burned said', responds Sagredo (p.28), a reference to Giordano Bruno, Galileo's predecessor, who had been executed for questioning the Ptolemaic system. If, as we see, Galileo confidently believes not just in Copernicus' theory, but in reason and humanity, he is ahead of his time, when such beliefs merited the stake. In Hitler's Germany, they led to the concentration camp, in Stalin's Russia to the gulag and in the communist politician Walter Ulbricht's GDR to disgrace and imprisonment.

Galileo is blind to the potential threat to himself in expressing his beliefs and discoveries. Sagredo remarks on this when Galileo reveals he is about to approach a new patron, the Duke of Florence, to secure as he supposes greater freedom for his research (as well as an opportunity to savour 'the fleshpots'):

> How can you propose to leave the Republic with the truth in your
> pocket, risking the traps set by monks and princes and
> brandishing your tube. You may be a sceptic in science, but

you're childishly credulous as soon as anything seems likely to help you to pursue it. You don't believe in Aristotle, but you do believe in the Grand Duke of Florence.

(p.33)

How far do we continue to sympathize with Galileo at this point? Certainly, the discovery of the celestial phenomena that prove Copernicus' theory has just been strikingly staged – Jupiter and its accompanying stars are shown on the cyclorama while Galileo and Sagredo sit in darkness (p.27), thus infecting us with their excitement. But let us see what Brecht intended, and the terminology he used to try to ensure the play was performed the way he desired.

Read paragraphs 61–6 of *A Short Organum for the Theatre* **(Reader, Item 26), where Brecht runs through the opening scenes of this play, as an instance of the 'gestic content' of a 'fairly modern' drama. What is he getting at here, and how might it apply to our analysis of these scenes?**

Most of paragraph 63 seems to me to represent well enough the opening scene as we have found it, emphasizing the 'story' or narrative and Galileo's social context and the pressures on him, rather than providing much sense of his inner life. To begin with, Brecht sees him as 'a gallant child of the scientific age', but immediately reminds us that this will involve 'many horrible things' – as we will see much later in the play. The contradictions of Galileo's position are what interest Brecht most, and this is how Galileo should be presented: as a man caught between a number of alternative forces. At the same time, Brecht tells us, we are not to 'overlook the theatrical way' in which, for instance, Galileo excitedly outlines the discoveries he reveals to Sagredo in Scene 3. 'Perhaps, looked at in this way, his charlatanry does not mean much, but it still shows how determined this man is to take the easy course', he says – words that clearly anticipate Galileo's recantation when threatened by the Inquisition – 'and does not every capitulation bring the next one nearer?', he asks.

Charlatanry and capitulation are harsh words perhaps, implying a view of Galileo we have not yet considered, but they also provide an indication that Brecht came to see the early episodes of the play in terms of their anticipation of, and linkage with, the later scenes and Galileo's 'betrayal'. The vital importance of what links one part of this episodic yet dramatic narrative with another is confirmed by Brecht's remark in paragraph 65: 'Everything hangs on the "story"; it is the heart of the theatrical performance ... the theatre's great operation, the complete fitting together of all the gestic incidents.'

'Gestic' is the adjectival form of the obsolete word 'gest', which was chosen by Willett to translate Brecht's neologism *Gestus*. Willett uses 'gest' to signify a combination of 'gist' and 'gesture'. A 'gest' or 'social gest' is a theatrical move that encapsulates the smallest meaningful dramatic unit that will, in combination with others, make up the play. A drama company and its performers need to isolate and work on this in order to attain a result that encourages the more detached epic or 'alienated' effect Brecht is seeking. In paragraph 66, Brecht describes the 'basic gests' or defining incidents of Shakespeare's *Richard III* (1593), Marlowe's *Dr Faustus* (1594) and Georg Büchner's (unfinished) *Woyzeck* (1837), suggesting the antecedents for this kind of theatre, examples that also used pre-existing plots but with new twists to arrive at new understandings relevant for their times. Brecht insists that grouping together the characters on the stage in terms of their most important or defining movements brings the 'beauty' and 'elegance' which ensures that the specific 'gest' is 'set out and laid bare to the understanding of the audience'. For Brecht, aesthetic and political considerations come together if the theatrical 'gest' is properly understood and represented on stage.

For this to happen, the actors are expected not so much to lose themselves in their roles, as to make their characters available for inspection. This is a product of the estranging 'alienation effect' which Brecht said he had discovered in the Chinese style of acting and which, with his obstinate emphasis on the externals of the part he was playing (see Brecht, 2001, p.164), Laughton seemed to exemplify. However, as later sections in *A Short Organum for the Theatre* make clear, 'Not everything depends on the actor, even though nothing may be done without taking him into account. The "story" is set out, brought forward and shown by the theatre as a whole' (paragraph 70, in Brecht, 1978, p.202).

Episodes such as Scene 4 of *Life of Galileo* ensure that the 'story' is 'brought forward', rather than merely allowing continuing involvement in or identification with the character of Galileo. How is this done? Not only by the individual actor's 'alienated' performance, and the intervening headlines and ditties whose 'alienating' effect Brecht notes in paragraph 67, but by the structure of the scene: observe the length of the action that intervenes *before* Galileo enters. In the preceding scenes, his dominance is a function of his presence from the start or almost the start of each scene – as an active, speaking character, the centre of attention. Scene 4, by contrast, opens with Mrs Sarti preparing for Galileo to receive the court, and the scrap between Cosimo and Andrea. Mrs Sarti anticipates the worst, echoing the opening dialogue about paying the milkman, asserting she will 'never be able to meet the milkman's eye tomorrow' (p.34). Both she and her son imitate Galileo – down to the phrases he has used earlier, as in 'This place is getting like a pigeon loft' (p.35).

These little signs of Galileo's influence anticipate his engagement with the court and its scholars – the philosopher and the mathematician. We are encouraged to understand the underlying conflicts present in the situations defined by the scene and those that succeed it. Galileo's power over the members of his immediate domestic circle is a matter not just of his stature, but of their loyalty to him. This is tellingly demonstrated in Scene 5, when Mrs Sarti remains with him despite the plague, his daughter Virginia has to be forcibly taken away and Andrea returns to his master of his own accord, regardless of the danger to his life. Do we admire them for their loyalty? How far does Galileo appreciate what those around him do to support him, and does he deserve their commitment to him? At the least, we are invited to see him more and more critically, to become aware of his flaws, in particular his massive egocentricity, exaggerated even to the point of parody.

Parody and comic effects are more important for Brecht's kind of theatre than is often realized, even by theatre producers. They are part of his vision of the popular dimension of the theatre, the dimension of the Augsburg fairground and the Munich beer festival, themselves rooted in the people's entertainments of an earlier period. These effects require greater emphasis, according to Brecht, to renew the modern theatre. In this respect, he differed from his contemporary Lukács, whose idea of the popular was to be found in the great humanist and realist classics of the past (primarily the nineteenth-century novel). The debates between them continued for decades from the 1930s onwards as a major theme in Marxist criticism, forwarding different views of modernism. **Now read the following two extracts. The first is from Lukács's *The Meaning of Contemporary Realism* (1957) and the second from Brecht's 'The Popular and the Realistic' (1958). How do the positions they set out to define differ? Which do you find more convincing?**

Lukács, *The Meaning of Contemporary Realism*

It is the view of the world, the ideology or *weltanschauung* underlying a writer's work, that counts. And it is the writer's attempt to reproduce this view of the world which constitutes his 'intention' and is the formative principle underlying the style of a given piece of writing. Looked at in this way, style ceases to be a formalistic category. Rather, it is rooted in content; it is the specific form of a specific content.

Content determines form. But there is no content of which Man himself is not the focal point. However various the *données* [givens] of literature (a particular experience, a didactic purpose), the basic question is, and will remain: what is Man?

... Man is *zoon politikon*, a social animal. The Aristotelian dictum is applicable to all great realistic literature. Achilles and Werther, Oedipus and Tom Jones, Antigone and Anna Karenina: their individual existence – their *Sein an sich*, in the Hegelian terminology; their 'ontological being', as a more fashionable terminology has it – cannot be distinguished from their social and historical environment. Their human significance, their specific individuality, cannot be separated from the context in which they were created.

The ontological view governing the image of man in the work of leading modernist writers is the exact opposite of this. Man, for these writers, is by nature solitary, asocial, unable to enter into relationships with other human beings ...

The literature of realism, aiming at a truthful reflection of reality, must demonstrate both the concrete and abstract potentialities of human beings in extreme situations ... A character's concrete potentiality once revealed, his abstract potentialities will appear essentially inauthentic ...

Abstract potentiality belongs wholly to the realm of subjectivity; whereas concrete potentiality is concerned with the dialectic between the individual's subjectivity and objective reality. The literary presentation of the latter thus implies a description of actual persons inhabiting a palpable, identifiable world. Only in the interaction of character and environment can the concrete potentiality of a particular individual be singled out from the 'bad infinity' of purely abstract potentialities, and emerge as the determining potentiality of just this individual at just this phase of his development. This principle alone enables the artist to distinguish concrete potentiality from a myriad abstractions.

But the ontology on which the image of man in modernist literature is based invalidates this principle. If the 'human condition' – man as a solitary being, incapable of meaningful relationships – is identified with reality itself, the distinction between abstract and concrete potentiality becomes null and void. The categories tend to merge. Thus Cesare Pavese notes with John Dos Passos, and his German contemporary, Alfred Döblin, a sharp oscillation between 'superficial *verisme*' and 'abstract Expressionist schematism'. Criticizing Dos Passos, Pavese writes that fictional characters 'ought to be created by deliberate selection and description of individual features' – implying that Dos Passos' characterizations are transferable from one individual to another. He describes the artistic consequences: by exalting man's subjectivity, at the expense of the objective reality of his environment, man's subjectivity is itself impoverished.

The problem, once again, is ideological. This is not to say that the ideology underlying modernist writings is identical in all cases. On the contrary: the ideology exists in extremely various, even contradictory forms. The rejection of narrative objectivity, the surrender to subjectivity, may take the form of Joyce's stream of consciousness, or of Musil's 'active passivity', his 'existence without quality', or of Gide's '*action gratuite*', where abstract potentiality achieves pseudo-realization. As individual character manifests itself in life's moments of decision, so too in literature. If the distinction between abstract and concrete potentiality vanishes, if man's inwardness is identified with an abstract subjectivity, human personality must disintegrate.

[In the poem 'The Hollow Men',] T.S. Eliot described this phenomenon, this mode of portraying human personality, as

> Shape without form, shade without colour,
> Paralysed force, gesture without motion.

The disintegration of personality is matched by a disintegration of the outer world.

(Lukács, 1963, pp.19–20, 23–5)

Brecht, 'The Popular and the Realistic'

We now come to the concept of 'Realism'. It is an old concept which has been much used by many men and for many purposes, and before it can be applied we must spring-clean it too. This is necessary because when the people takes over its inheritance there has to be a process of expropriation. Literary works cannot be taken over like factories, or literary forms of expression like industrial methods. Realist writing, of which history offers many widely varying examples, is likewise conditioned by the question of how, when and for what class it is made use of: conditioned down to the last small detail. As we have in mind a fighting people that is changing the real world we must not cling to 'well-tried' rules for telling a story, worthy models set up by literary history, eternal aesthetic laws. We must not abstract the one and only realism from certain given works, but shall make a lively use of all means, old and new, tried and untried, deriving from art and deriving from other sources, in order to put living reality in the hands of living people in such a way that it can be mastered. We shall take care not to ascribe realism to a particular historical form of novel belonging to a particular period, Balzac's or Tolstoy's, for instance, so as to set up purely formal and literary criteria of realism ... Our conception of *realism* needs to be broad and political, free from aesthetic restrictions and independent of convention. *Realist* ... means: laying bare society's causal network / showing up the dominant viewpoint as the viewpoint of the dominators / writing from the standpoint of the class which has prepared the broadest solutions for the most pressing problems afflicting human society / emphasizing the dynamics of development / concrete and so as to encourage abstraction ...

We shall establish that so-called sensuous writing (in which everything can be smelt, tasted, felt) is not to be identified automatically with realist writing, for we shall see that there are sensuously written works which are not realist, and realist works which are not sensuously written. We shall have to go carefully into the question whether the story is best developed by aiming at an eventual psychological stripping-down of the characters. Our readers may quite well feel that they have not been given the key to what is happening if they are simply induced by a combination of arts to take part in the inner emotions of our books' heroes. By taking over the forms of Balzac and Tolstoy without a thorough inspection we might perhaps exhaust our readers, the people, just as these writers often do. Realism is not a pure question of form. Copying the methods of these realists, we should cease to be realists ourselves.

... Reality alters; to represent it the means of representation must alter too ...

Anybody who is not bound by formal prejudices knows that there are many ways of suppressing truth and many ways of stating it: that indignation at inhuman conditions can be stimulated in many ways, by direct description of a pathetic or matter-of-fact kind, by narrating stories and parables, by jokes, by over- and under-statement. In the theatre reality can be represented in a factual or a fantastic form. The actors can do without (or with the minimum of) makeup, appearing 'natural', and the whole thing can be a fake; they can wear grotesque masks and represent the truth. There is not much to argue about here: the means must be asked what the end is. The people knows how to ask this. Piscator's great experiments in the theatre (and my own), which repeatedly involved the exploding of conventional forms, found their chief support in the most progressive cadres of the working class ...

So the criteria for the popular and the realistic need to be chosen not only with great care but also with an open mind. They must not be deduced from existing realist works and existing popular works, as is often the case. Such an approach would lead to purely formalist criteria, and questions of popularity and realism would be decided by form.

(Brecht, 1978, pp.108–10, 112)

It may help Brecht's argument that his approach seems less abstract and more down to earth than Lukács, but surely both have a case? It should be clear that for Lukács the literary realism of earlier writers offered a reflection of the socio-historical whole, and the individual's place in it, whereas the fact that modernist writers place an emphasis on the 'subjective' aspect of individuals has led to a view of life that is fragmentary. Brecht insists that it is possible to create a realistic popular art of the present, using whatever techniques of the day might be appropriate, rather than having to rely on such surviving traditional forms as the classic novel. Both appear to be arguing for an idea of realism that connects with the truth of society, and against merely formalist approaches. However, they interpret the means of reaching that truth in different ways. Brecht, as the practising artist, seems more open to experiment in response to changed circumstances.

Both Lukács and Brecht wanted to undo the effect of capitalism, which, as they saw it, produced human beings fixed in relationships that denied their full humanity. For Lukács, drawing on Hegel through Marx (hence the abstract language), the writer could and should, by reflecting reality, show up the contradictions between the concrete, actual world and the abstract ideas with which it interacted. He believed that earlier realist novelists such as Honoré de Balzac and Leo Tolstoy were able to give their readers access to these contradictions through the completeness of their images of relationships in the historical reality of their times. For him, the fragmentation and 'attenuation' (a favourite term) of reality in modernist writings simply made individuals less aware of how they were being reduced to less than fully human beings. Brecht, on the other hand, saw the whole range of artistic devices, traditional and new, as a potent means of drawing spectators into a fresh awareness of the contradictions under which they lived. Ironically, while condemning Brecht's early work, Lukács went on to praise later plays such as *Life of Galileo* for returning to classic realist ways, arguing that they revealed the inner life and motivation of characters, who became 'living human beings, wrestling with conscience and with the world around them' (1963, p.88). Whether or not you agree with this view, it does not appear to be what Brecht desired would be the effect of his new kind of theatre work.

Look now at paragraph 71 in *A Short Organum for the Theatre* (Reader, Item 26), where Brecht continues to develop his view of the 'gest' as a theatrical manner that sums up what he is seeking to represent. Consider the 'carnival' scene (Scene 10) from *Life of Galileo*, which is used to further his argument. How successfully does it realize Brecht's views? Further, what does it tell us about the structuring of the play – the flow (or otherwise) of narrative?

What is most striking about Scene 10 is not only the absence of the physical Galileo from it, but the way in which the impact of his discoveries on the world is presented. This is done satirically, with a Brechtian presenter as a cabaret-style 'ballad-singer' (reminiscent of Valentin), extending the earlier parodic elements in the play into a whole scene, in which the central character is represented as a giant puppet. All of this would have had a considerable, indeed memorable, impact on stage, as can be seen from the illustration of the Berlin version on the penultimate pages of the Methuen Student Edition and in the video of the play.

This is Brecht's popular realism at work. The theatricality of his stagecraft is a function of its rootedness in 'popular' elements – telling gestures, exaggeration, tableau, carnival – used to appeal to 'the people' in an appropriate form. Scene 10 depicts the carnival of 1632. The traditional Fastnacht carnival of Germany (known as Carnevale in Italy, Mardi Gras in France and Shrove Tuesday in the UK) remains a time for processions, feasting and merrymaking. It was formerly also an opportunity for the medieval guilds to celebrate their strength in community, and – going even further back – for the appearance of a subversive devil-figure, or Fool, who scampered about entertaining everyone with lewd and blasphemous gestures, here embodied in Galileo. Clearly, the wider significance of Galileo's discoveries has permeated all levels of society, including artisans, itinerants and a watching crowd of the better-off, despite the establishment's attempts to suppress the truth.

The ballad-singer's song or *Moritat* has the subversive refrain, 'Who wouldn't like to say and do just as he pleases?' Comically, the ballad-singer changes his tune when his wife steps forward to say she told her husband she would also like to see 'If I could get some other fixed star / To do what he does for me' (pp.83–4). For the original version of this scene, Brecht appended a note for producers, pointing out that it could be developed into a ballet

> *in the style of Brueghel's* The Battle Between Carnival and Lent. *Following the first verse of the ballad a carnival procession can move across the square, including a man dressed as a BIBLE with a hole in it, and a cart with a monk stretching out, trying with both hands to hold back a collapsing ST. PETER'S THRONE. Then after the last verse, the MOON, SUN, EARTH and PLANETS can appear and demonstrate the new system of motion in a dance, to a severe musical setting.*
>
> (quoted in Brecht, 2001, p.182)

The Berlin version is less elaborate, yet more subversively humorous (rather than 'severe'): a woman holds an image of the sun as her child circles round her, a pumpkin over its head to represent the earth, before the carnival procession enters. The drumming ballad-singer is overtaken by louder drumming from the rear of the stage, as the figures of the Grand Duke, a puppet representing a cardinal, a dwarf with a sign saying 'The new age' and a beggar on crutches perform for the crowd. This is succeeded by the climax, Galileo as an '*over-lifesize puppet*' bowing to the audience, while a boy bearing an open Bible with crossed-out pages appears before him, and there is '*Huge laughter among the crowd*' (p.85).

Through exaggeration, mime and humour, the common people's view of the effect of Galileo's discoveries is presented in terms of social upheaval and the overturning of secular and religious authority. This anticipates the revolutions to come and indicates the reason for the Inquisition's attempt to silence Galileo. The ballad part of the scene and the concluding procession provide two representations of the impact of the new science on popular perception, neither of them unambiguously favourable: change may be necessary, but chaos may result.

The scene has a self-contained quality, making a 'knot' in the narrative that ties it to the rest of the play. The very next scene (Scene 11) gives us the moment of the Inquisition's summons to Galileo to appear before the court in Rome. Notice in paragraph 71 of *A Short Organum for the Theatre* Brecht's emphasis on the importance of ensuring that his collaborator Hans Eisler provided not mere 'expression' for the masked procession in the carnival scene, but 'a triumphant and threatening music', thereby commenting on it – the demand 'epic' theatre makes of all theatrical effects and devices.

Note 82 on page 124 of *Life of Galileo* indicates that Scene 10 was not included in the first version of the play, but was written into the American version. It was retained for the final, Berlin, version. Clearly, it emerged from discussions between Brecht and Laughton about their English-language version of the play. The note relates that Brecht commented:

> L[aughton] took the greatest interest in the tenth (carnival) scene, where the Italian people are shown relating Galileo's revolutionary doctrine to their own revolutionary demands ... It was so important to him to demonstrate that property relationships were being threatened by the doctrine of the earth's rotation that he declined a New York production where this scene was to be omitted.

Brecht found working with Laughton congenial: the latter's views about the relationship between the play's concerns and the Marxist interpretation of reality chimed with those of the playwright. It is not always so clear that Laughton's views about the role of the actor were precisely what Brecht had been aiming for, but what Laughton provided was what Brecht always sought in his chosen actors. This was a 'larger-than-life' quality that created a sense of the actor's own presence as distinct from the part he or she played, and a lively, intelligent interest in the significance of that part in the work. In this respect, Laughton set the standard for later performers, all of whom had to come to terms with Brecht's strong views and the traditions of Brechtian theatre embodied by the Berliner Ensemble.

Since, as a Marxist, Brecht might have been expected in *Life of Galileo* to represent the common people, it is striking how little they appear, apart from in Scene 10. This does not mean that their perspective is absent. Nor is the view that the Bible has a role in their lives left to comic subversion. This has already been suggested by the little monk's conversation with Galileo in Scene 8. The monk comes from the peasantry, on whose behalf he argues that the church gives meaning to their endurance: they should be kept ignorant of Galileo's new ideas, which, if true, will find their own way in any case. Galileo resists this assumption: 'unless they get moving and learn how to think, they will find even the finest irrigation systems won't help them ... I see your people's divine patience, but where is their divine anger?' (p.68). Galileo sees religion as a smokescreen for preserving the status quo. But what is *his* role, if any, in stirring the people up? The representation of Galileo as a puppet in the carnival scene suggests that he is always going to be subject to forces larger than himself; it also suggests that, in the long run, this does not matter. The little monk is apparently right: the truth will come out, as we know it did.

I would like to make one final point in relation to theory and practice. Brecht emphasizes the contribution of all the factors that create meaning in the theatre towards producing the desired effect, and this includes costume. The details of the carnival scene are not the only time in the play when costume is used for important dramatic effect. **Can you identify another scene or moment when costume may be said to provide perhaps the crucial element in creating the appropriate 'gest'?**

Costume or clothing is important all the way through from the opening scene, when Galileo strips to the waist to wash himself, his nakedness revealing the flesh that will prefer the fleshpots, the easy life, as he acknowledges. Costume also provides an indication of the period of the play, and, much more significantly, of the status of the players and the connection between wealth and power; there are certain scenes or moments when the significance of this familiar aspect of dramatic presentation is particularly highlighted. The first of these, I would suggest, is Scene 7, the masked ball at Cardinal Bellarmin's house in Rome, attended by Galileo and his daughter, Virginia, whose engagement to Ludovico Marsili is later callously broken off by her father (Scene 9). Galileo, we note, wears no mask, while Cardinals Bellarmin and Barberini, who inform him that the Copernican doctrine has been proscribed by Rome, bear the masks of a lamb and a dove. The scene includes an entertaining verbal duel between Galileo and Barberini (see the Notes, pp.121–2). This is simultaneously 'intellectual sport' and an opportunity for us to perceive – as Galileo begins to – the power of this suave, witty and intelligent churchman, who is no simpleton to be overawed by argument. Barberini is a mathematician and appears to be sympathetic towards Galileo, whose views he understands. This leads to Galileo's assumption that the arrival of Barberini as the new pope will ensure that 'Things are beginning to move' in the right direction (p.76).

The deep irony implicit in this remark (touching on the theme of movement, which – whether of the stars, people's views or behaviour – is central to the play) is forcefully clarified in Scene 12, when we see Barberini becoming Pope Urban VIII, as he is robed. The metamorphosis from cardinal to pope is elaborately visualized, and provides all the commentary necessary on the way in which the trappings of power turn the clever and responsive man of Scene 9 into an impersonal functionary of the church, like the Cardinal Inquisitor (who has no name other than his title). Scene 12 depicts the surrender of Barberini to the forces of reaction, as he realizes he must put the interests of the church before his personal interests, and so agree to the silencing of Galileo. The opening of the scene is intensely dramatic: 'No! No! No!', Barberini exclaims (p.90); by the end of the scene, fully robed as pope, he concedes that 'At the very most' Galileo can be shown the instruments of torture (p.94). The Inquisitor, who knows Galileo's propensity to weakness of the flesh, is as satisfied as he can be.

The scene is a feat of staging and is highly filmic too, as is magnificently confirmed by the Laughton–Losey film version. According to Eric Bentley, writing in 1969:

> Sometimes the setting, instead of creating the mood (which in Brecht it never is supposed to do), is in direct contrast with the mood. Not a new idea in itself, but not an exhausted one either, and most people felt they *had* seen something new when they witnessed the interaction between setting and actor in the Pope scene of Galileo. Here was the added piquancy that the setting is actually the costume. More precisely: what had been 'setting' – the Pope's robe on a dummy – becomes costume as it is transferred to the Pope's body; and when he is fully dressed, it becomes 'setting' again, because he is submerged under it.
>
> (Bentley, 1999, p.255)

As Bentley went on to remark, such innovations were not, for Brecht, in the first instance, 'aesthetic': 'In that respect, he was not an "avant-garde" writer at all: none of his idiosyncrasies claim any interest in themselves' (1999, p.260). They were fundamental to his vision of a modernist theatre that aims to make us see the realities of the present through developing a critical view of the past: 'The decorations should not be of a kind to suggest to the spectators that they are in a medieval Italian room or the Vatican. The audience should be conscious of being in a theatre', Brecht noted

(2001, p.136). If we are not conscious of being in the theatre as we observe the events of the play, we are less likely to be able to draw the necessary connections between what we see on stage and what we understand of the world in which we live. This is what Brechtian 'alienation' effects are all about.

What about the ending of *Life of Galileo*? How do we finally see the central character? Is he – as is often suggested – a tragic figure, and if so, how far is this contrary to Brecht's conception?

The closing scenes of the play

To answer these questions, we need to look at the closing scenes of the play. On 22 June 1633, when shown the instruments of torture (Figure 7.3), Galileo agreed to recant. Brecht's play situates this crucial action offstage (Scene 13). We see the effect of what is happening, as it happens, on Galileo's pupils, associates and family – the little monk, Federzoni the lens-grinder, Andrea and – by contrast – a silent, praying Virginia. Expecting the great bell of St Mark's to be rung on the hour to indicate his recantation, the pupils rejoice when at first nothing happens. Their jubilation and relief is abruptly cut short, to be followed by disbelief and anger, while Virginia's reaction is one of gratitude:

Figure 7.3   Charles Laughton in the title role of *Life of Galileo*, Beverly Hills production, 30 July 1947. (Bertolt-Brecht-Archiv, Foundation Academy of Arts, Berlin.) Over Laughton's left shoulder we see one of the instruments of torture that was shown to Galileo to help force him to recant.

> ANDREA ... Such a lot is won when even a single man gets to his feet and says No. *At this moment the bell of Saint Mark's begins to toll. All stand rigid.*
>
> VIRGINIA *gets up*: The bell of Saint Mark's. He is not damned!
> *From the street outside we hear the crier reading Galileo's recantation.*

(p.97)

Notice how light and sound reinforce the tension of the moment: the stage '*grows dark*' after the crier's announcement, during which Virginia departs in silence, and the bell continues tolling, but then it stops when the light returns. Andrea's anguished exclamation, 'Unhappy the land that has no heroes!', defines his despair at Galileo's betrayal and suggests a general truth; *at that moment* the broken Galileo enters, almost unrecognizable after his ordeal. He waits in vain to be greeted, his pupils backing away from him. It is a moment of great pathos. The scene ends after Galileo has ordered a glass of water for the furious Andrea, and, significantly, reworded his pupil's complaint to 'Unhappy the land where heroes are needed'. (The exchange is even more succinct, balanced and memorable in the original, as you might expect: 'Unglücklich das Land, das keine Helden hat' / 'Unglücklich das Land, das Helden nötig hat'.) A reading of an extract from the 'Discorsi' then cools things down, and presumably 'alienates' us to make us aware of the longer-term, historic perspective, in which Galileo's work survives.

The years pass (Scene 14) and we see Galileo surviving as the half-blind prisoner of the Inquisition, under the watchful but caring eyes of his daughter. He has continued to write his 'Discorsi', which are then locked away by the authorities, but at the expense of his sight he has made a transcript and hidden it (Figure 7.4). When his old pupil Andrea returns to visit him, still cold and resentful because of the recantation, and hears this, he is filled with remorse. He had assumed that Galileo's recantation was a pretext, enabling the scientist to carry on with his great work. But Galileo corrects Andrea: he recanted because he was afraid of physical pain, he says, and his recantation was a crime, a betrayal of both science and humanity, throwing away an opportunity to establish a code of conduct for the scientists of the future. He entrusts the 'Discorsi' to Andrea to carry across the border into Holland, before tucking into a meal of goose, which he received as a gift (see Note 109 on p.128: Brecht thought this a 'horrible' moment). In the final scene (Scene 15), among a group of children who argue about whether or not an old woman is a witch, noting the fact that no-one will let her have even a jug of milk (repeating the milk motif of the opening scene), Andrea asserts to a frontier guard that Galileo's manuscript is a work by Aristotle. After a cursory inspection Andrea is allowed to take the manuscript across the frontier.

Figure 7.4   Ernst Busch as the nearly blind Galileo works on the illegal copy of the 'Discorsi' in the 1956 Berlin production of *Life of Galileo*. (Bertolt-Brecht-Archiv, Foundation Academy of Arts, Berlin.)

In the first version of the play, Galileo's rephrasing of Andrea's bitter remark is the last thing we hear spoken in the recantation scene, the extract from the 'Discorsi' being then displayed on a curtain lowered before the audience. It is not important to enter into every detail of the differences between versions. Where there may well be a significant difference, however, is in the way Brecht developed the ending of the play. This was in response to the event that took place on 6 August 1945, when a US atomic bomb destroyed the Japanese city of Hiroshima, killing tens of thousands of people. As Brecht observed, Hiroshima was the 'debut' of the 'atomic age', and it took place in the middle of his work with Laughton on the American version of *Life of Galileo*. In his 'Preamble to the American Version' (1946), Brecht described how assistants of Niels Bohr – then engaged in research on the splitting of the atom – had helped him in reconstructing the Ptolemaic cosmology when he was first writing *Life of Galileo* in exile in Denmark. His 'intention' then was, among others, 'to give an unvarnished picture of a new age – a strenuous undertaking since all those around me were convinced that our own era lacked every attribute of a new age'. Nothing of 'this aspect' of the play's context had changed, he said, when he and Laughton began their collaboration – until, that is, Hiroshima:

> Overnight the biography of the founder of the new system of physics read differently. The infernal effect of the great bomb placed the conflict between Galileo and the authorities of his day in a new, sharper light. We had to make only a few alterations – not a single one to the structure of the play. Already in the original version the church was portrayed as a secular authority, its ideology as fundamentally interchangeable with many others. From the first, the keystone of the gigantic figure of Galileo was his conception of a science for the people. For hundreds of years and throughout the whole of Europe people had paid him the honour, in the Galileo legend, of not believing in his recantation.
>
> (quoted in Brecht, 2001, p.125)

Leaving aside for the moment the question of how far the Galileo of the play conceives of his science as 'for the people' (despite his sympathy, or even respect, for ordinary people, he seems unaware of the wider political implications of his actions until the end of the play), the later versions did involve significant alteration, specifically to do with the recantation and its effect.

In the 'Preamble to the American Version', Brecht summarized the change:

> The first version of the play ended differently. Galileo had written the *Discorsi* in the utmost secrecy. He uses the visit of his favourite pupil Andrea to get him to smuggle the book across the frontier. His recantation had given him the chance to create a seminal work. He had been wise.
>
> In the Californian version ... Galileo interrupts his pupil's hymns of praise to prove to him that his recantation had been a crime, and was not to be compensated by this work, important as it might be.
>
> In case anybody is interested, this is also the opinion of the playwright.
>
> (quoted in Brecht, 2001, p.131)

Was Galileo a wise man or a criminal? I am not sure that Brecht ultimately resolves the ambiguities of his central character's behaviour in the final version of the play – nor indeed that he should have. Clearly, the first version aimed to create a sympathetic figure, connecting audiences with all those who were struggling to survive and continue their intellectual work under Nazism or in exile. The later versions set up a character whose behaviour is altogether more questionable, who is oblivious to his duty to the rest of humanity. **But is this how you think of the Galileo in the play?**

We have seen how Galileo could be unscrupulous, in palming off as his own the Dutch invention of a telescope, in order to pay his bills and continue with his research. At the same time, we have seen how he is a great teacher and communicator of his ideas, aware of their immense importance in an age dominated by superstition and the authority of the church. We see him continue with his research when the plague sends others away from the city, and yet he sacrifices his daughter's marriage prospects to his work. From the point of view of the little monk, he has attacked oppression, but he has also followed the high and mighty in search of patronage, as well as to enjoy his pleasures. He is offhand to the ironfounder Vanni (representing the progressive middle classes), who wants him to escape. In the penultimate scene, he supports the authorities' suppression of the disaffected rope-makers, and can even laugh at the news that his lens-grinder Federzoni is back at his old job, because after all 'He doesn't know Latin' (p.103). Yet Galileo has ensured that his 'great book o'er the border went' (p.110), as the ballad has it, and in Andrea's concluding words a hint of guarded optimism may be detected: 'We're really just at the beginning' (p.113). Have we accepted Andrea's view of Galileo, against the great man's own self-analysis? The answer depends at least partly – some might say overwhelmingly – on the effect of Galileo's characterization: is he a hero or not?

One critic who has forcefully argued that the characterization of Galileo goes contrary to Brecht's intentions, and indeed his theory, is Ronald Speirs. **Now read the following extract from Speirs's detailed study of the play in *Bertolt Brecht* (1987), asking yourself if you are convinced by his argument. Is the play a tragedy in the Aristotelian sense, and hence more traditional in effect than Brecht's anti-Aristotelian ideas demanded?**

> Contrary to Brecht's express intentions, *The Life of Galileo* produces the effects of tragedy. It even conforms in a number of respects to Aristotle's account of the genre. As the story of a great man's fall its subject has the magnitude appropriate to the genre. Moreover, his fall is brought about by the same qualities that make him great (tragic irony), and these qualities are deeply rooted in his personal disposition (tragic necessity). In making him an unusually sensuous man who thinks productively because of the *pleasure* thinking affords him, nature simultaneously made him a man incapable of withstanding the *pain* of torture. Being gifted with a new way of seeing, Galileo is unable, in consequence, to perceive things that are very plain to others less gifted than himself but more attuned to the ways of existing society. The very faults which Brecht stressed in order to set this life at a critical distance from the audience make of him the type of 'mixed character' traditionally thought necessary for tragedy to

secure the belief and sympathy of the audience. Galileo's fateful choices are further constrained by the objective social conditions of his times: he only moved to aristocratic Florence because republican Venice did not offer him the working conditions he needed.

Not only does *Galileo* stand up to analysis in terms of Aristotelian *hamartia* (tragic error or flaw), the play also, even more surprisingly, has an obvious affinity with Nietzsche's Dionysian account of tragedy; that is, one which sees in the tragic hero the embodiment of an energy so great that it destroys its bearer. The parallel is suggested by Galileo's words: 'And the worst thing is that what I know I must tell people. Like a lover, like a drunkard, like a traitor.' [Scene 8, p.68] A laconic observation of Brecht's suggests the same connection: 'His productiveness destroys him.' ... As Brecht understood it (whether the audience would see it in the same way is another question), Galileo's *Forschungstrieb* or scientific impulse, the specific form of his productive energy, was a 'social phenomenon', as much motivated by the desire to communicate knowledge as to create it. Even allowing for this, however, the argument of the play remains tragic, a Marxist variation on a Nietzschean theme: Galileo's tragedy was to be born into an age that stimulated more productivity in him than the society of the time would or could accommodate.

(Speirs, 1987, pp.129–30)

To begin with, Speirs argues that the effect of the play is tragic; later, he says that it is the 'argument' of the play that is tragic. Perhaps this is what Brecht wanted after all? For Aristotle, tragedy was about the dramatic representation of a serious action involving a great figure, whose misfortune is brought about by an error of judgement that leads to misery; this inspires in the audience feelings of pity and fear that create the conditions for 'catharsis' or emotional discharge. The greater the person, in terms of power, status or prestige, the greater the distance he or she falls, and the more our feelings are relieved. From the Renaissance onwards, this formula has been revised and developed, most notably during the nineteenth century: Hegel suggested it could reconcile us to the most appalling loss, leading to a renewed sense of the complex nature of justice, while Nietzsche saw it as providing reassurance for the continuity of life despite the suffering and death of the individual. It is not easy to think of a twentieth-century play that conforms to this description, although, as the US playwright Arthur Miller famously observed in defending his *Death of a Salesman* (1949), the ordinary man can also be a tragic figure.

However, the point is not to force the play into a generic category or sub-category, but to see if generic considerations help us to understand the work and its impact better. Certainly, there seem to be elements in the characterization of Galileo that conform to what we might expect of tragedy – his exceptionality as a man, the remarkable trajectory of his life, the inextricability of his gifts and flaws, the strength of our (initial) sympathies for him. Yet how far are we led to identify with him, in order that the necessary emotional impact be gained? And is this contrary to what Brecht desired, as Speirs argues?

The answer is complicated by both the differences between different versions of the play and the fact that Brecht attempted to make Galileo less sympathetic towards the end of the play. The latter point amounts to an acknowledgement that Brecht saw that his character would seem sympathetic to begin with. The emphasis in the first nine scenes, up to the carnival scene, is generally positive; the carnival scene proposes that Galileo's discoveries have had an enormous, if not exactly revolutionary, effect on the people. However, thereafter Galileo's position becomes more complicated and less sympathetic, as his flaws become more evident, until the recantation and its aftermath, which Brecht certainly seems to have wanted to have led to condemnation by spectators. Yet I must say I find it hard to condemn a man who ruins his eyesight to document his research on what was to become the most important and influential scientific work for centuries, and ensures that one of his followers smuggles the text out of the country where his work is prohibited. This is not the same as saying that he is a tragic figure, of course, nor that the final effect on us is that of having our feelings purged. **What do you think?**

Brecht seems to have insisted that *Life of Galileo* is not a tragedy. In 1939, he wrote that 'the question will arise whether the *Life of Galileo* is to be presented as a tragedy or as an optimistic play'; the answer would be found in whether the emphasis was on the 'new age' speeches in Scene 1 or 'certain parts' of Scene 14. According to the 'prevailing rules', he continued, the end of the play would inevitably gain most emphasis, whereas he had not constructed it according to those rules: 'The play shows the dawn of a new age and tries to correct some of the prejudices about the dawn of a new age' (quoted in Brecht, 2001, pp.117–18). When rewriting the play in 1947 to connect it more closely with the 'new' atomic age, he observed that

> the 'hero' of this work is not Galileo but the people, as Walter Benjamin has said ... [it] shows how society extorts from its individuals what it needs from them ... In the end [Galileo] indulges his science like a vice, secretly, and probably with pangs of conscience. Confronted with such a situation, one can scarcely wish only to praise or only to condemn Galileo.
>
> (quoted in Brecht, 2001, pp.126–7)

Speirs goes on to suggest that the 'tragic interplay' of character and circumstance in *Life of Galileo* prompts the question of whether Brecht ultimately failed in creating a theatre that made us feel a sense of mastery over 'life's problems', rather than one that 'discouraged' us. But, he continues, the play shows not just the destructive consequences of Galileo's peculiar combination of talents and flaws, it also shows 'the urge to know and spread the truth asserting itself despite persecution' (pp.130–1). In that sense, the play may achieve what Brecht wanted of it: to create in audiences a sense of the need to resist the inequities of a society in which power is distributed unequally, making it almost impossible for even the most gifted individual to change things. Galileo's fate is shown to be exemplary: it is distanced from modern audiences by its historical placing and the various devices employed to reduce, but not eliminate, identification, yet it allows us to be both involved with and stimulated by the central character's rhetoric and his surrounding circumstances.

Bentley comments that

> it is not really heroism, but martyrdom, that is in question, and it is well known that only a thin line divides masochistic submission from true martyrdom. If Galileo were tortured, you wouldn't get a tragedy, but, from Brecht's viewpoint, a happy ending, with Galileo a martyr of science. In Brecht's view, Galileo should have been willing to die because the news of his refusal to recant could have been exploited by the right side.
>
> (Bentley, 1999, p.87)

This is to use the term 'martyr' in a modern, if debased, way. What Bentley does not consider here is the possibility that Brecht saw himself in Galileo, and hence to a degree resisted turning him into a martyr for the same reason that Brecht avoided martyrdom: because cunning, evasion and exile would allow him to continue with his work.

Nevertheless, *Life of Galileo* may be seen as a play of warning, in terms of a reinterpretation of the past through a reinterpretation of the historical figure at its centre. As Galileo says in his final long speech, he has no time for scientists who, intimidated by their self-interested rulers, limit themselves to 'piling up knowledge for knowledge's sake' and so turn science into a cripple and their inventions into fresh means for oppression:

> You may in due course discover all that there is to discover, and your progress will nonetheless be nothing but a progress away from mankind. The gap between you and it may one day become so wide that your cry of triumph at some new achievement will be echoed by a universal cry of horror.
>
> (pp.108–9)

For himself, he had a unique opportunity, since astronomy was already reaching the market-place; had he stood firm, scientists could have developed something like the Hippocratic oath, 'a vow to use their knowledge exclusively for mankind's benefit' (p.109). His words are echoed in the final ballad of the play, urging us to use science right, even as we kindle its light, 'Lest it be a flame to fall / Downward to consume us all' (p.110).

Life of Galileo as modernist comedy?

One of the most common views of Brecht as a playwright is that of a grim and serious figure, determined to impose his unworkable theories on us by means of a series of plays that – surprise, surprise – nonetheless work extremely well in the theatre. Thus, for example, the casting of Michael Gambon – then best known as a comic actor – in the role of Galileo in the 1980 National Theatre production of the play 'caused some initial surprise ... Few saw him as having the necessary "weight", in terms of seriousness, for this "heavy" Brechtian role' (Eddershaw, 1996, pp.107–8). Even the director, John Dexter, apparently not in awe of his task, seemed to the performers to emphasize technique rather than politics. But the result, according to one critic of the production, was that 'Dexter's great *Galileo* took the curse off Brecht in Britain' (quoted in *ibid.*, p.112). Gambon turned out to have precisely the right qualities, the mix of 'weight' and 'lightness' the part seems to require.

Brecht was something of a joker – as is confirmed by the mordant wit of his poetry, if not by his behaviour as well – but the comic and satiric elements in his works have often been obscured or ignored by well-meaning and 'committed' theatre workers. This is partly a matter of translation, of many in the English-speaking theatre world being unfamiliar with German, and in particular with the often demotic or colloquial German Brecht uses (you may recall my remarks about the opening wordplay in Scene 1). It is also a matter of which Brecht we focus on: the creator of *The Threepenny Opera*, the poet, the dramaturg or the writer of plays like *Mother Courage*, *The Good Person of Szechwan* and *Life of Galileo*. We have been considering the possibility of arguing for and against the character and fate of Galileo as tragic; what about the play as comic?

Several critics have come to see the play in this light, as more of a comedy than a tragedy. Walter H. Sokel argues this case in the following way:

> Brecht does not present the tragic individual and the tragic instance or particular fate with which the spectator identifies and which moves him to pity and fear. Instead he presents the tragic case, the tragic problem *per se*, which the spectator is to understand, to reflect on, to draw conclusions from. Brecht's

theoretical writings lead us to believe that there is a hard-and-fast distinction between his epic and intellectual (or 'cool') theater and the 'Aristotelian' emotional and plot-centered drama. Actually there are many fine shadings and transitions from this type of play to the classical drama. Mother Courage, Kattrin, Shen Te undoubtedly move us emotionally as characters in Aristotelian drama do, while Galileo and Puntila conform much more accurately to the Brechtian ideal of the intellectual, 'cool' theater. But in any event Brecht, in definite and sharp contrast to traditional Western tragedy, does not begin with the individual but with the problem ...

Since Brecht starts not with an individual fate but with a general problem acted out before us by his characters, his plays are akin to comedy as well as tragedy. Apart from the humor and wit of Brecht's plays their structure, and functionalism, and the typicality of their characters link them to comedy. With comedy, especially Molière's type of comedy, the Brecht play shares its appeal to the detached critical spirit and nonserious peripheral role of the plot which is too unimportant to involve the spectator emotionally. But unlike comedy and more like tragedy it shows the defeat of aspirations which represent the best in man. This intimate mixture of comedy and tragedy, the ironic subordination of plot, the preoccupation with problems rather than individuals unite Brecht with the spirit of the whole experimental theater of the twentieth century, with Pirandello, Schnitzler, Camus, Beckett, Ionesco, Genet.

(Sokel, 1962, pp.134–5)

This is helpful, in encouraging a more detached, informed perspective on the complex, modernist characterization of Galileo. However, Sokel perhaps exaggerates Brecht's links with playwrights whom we might identify as distinctly 'absurdist' in twentieth-century drama, even though some of Brecht's work – for instance his plays about Hitler, *Der aufhaltsame Aufstieg des Arturo Ui* ('The Resistable Rise of Arturo Ui'; 1941) and racism, *Die Rundköpfe and die Spitzköpfe* ('Roundheads and Pointed Heads'; first version 1932) – is undeniably comic, almost farcical, in both intention and effect. Surely there is a clear and important distinction to be made between, for example, the comic nihilism of Samuel Beckett's *Waiting for Godot* (1955) and the ironic outcome of *Life of Galileo*?

The question as to whether the play is tragedy or comedy, then, focuses on the final effect of *Life of Galileo*; this depends at least partially on specific performances. Are we left with a sense of acceptance, of the inevitability of Galileo's suffering for his beliefs? Or with a sense that, in the last analysis, change is necessary, things move on, so that we are encouraged to take up a less passive, more active role in life? A positive outcome suggests an understanding of the play ultimately as comedy.

Perhaps we should not worry over much about the generic, aesthetic categories within which we view Brecht's play, but focus more on the total vision of life it appears to convey. This would seem to be more appropriate for a playwright who insists that, while entertaining the audience is vital, the way we are engaged – or not – with the entertainment is more important, because more likely to encourage a change of view in us. If so, we should remember that, important as he is to the play, Galileo is far from being always at the centre of each scene. Moreover, it is his relationships with a whole range of other characters that have been significant from the opening onwards. This brings us back to the point I was stressing at the start of our discussion: the way in which *Life of Galileo* is structured as a series of almost self-contained scenes set up as part of a narrative. It also reminds us that how we see any single character on stage is always influenced by the presence of other, so-called minor, characters. Brecht clearly conceived this play in one sense as a series of images, or tableaux, in which the relations between different elements in the picture contribute to the impact of the whole. Roland Barthes went so far as to suggest that

> Brecht indicated clearly that in epic theatre (which proceeds by successive tableaux) all the burden of meaning and pleasure bears on each scene, not on the whole. At the level of the play itself, there is no development, no maturation; there is indeed an ideal meaning (given straight in every tableau) but there is no final meaning, nothing but a series of segmentations each of which possesses a sufficient demonstrative power. The same is true in Eisenstein: the film is a contiguity of episodes ... it is a question not of a dialectic ... but of a continuous jubilation made up of a summation of perfect instants.
>
> (Barthes, 1977, pp.72–3)

Barthes is sensitive here to the modernist, filmic quality of Brecht's method, but it would be difficult to see this as entirely the method of *Life of Galileo*. The play after all takes us through the life of its central character over twenty-six years and is at least to that extent concerned with linear development as well as static, dramatized moments. One might indeed describe that as a kind of 'dialectic'. Yet Barthes points us to a vital aspect of the play, which is the way in which the central figure is constantly realized in relation to others, sometimes, as in the carnival scene, to the extent that he disappears entirely.

One critic who has developed a useful way of highlighting this aspect of the play is Ernst Schumacher. **Read the extract from Schumacher's essay 'The Dialectics of *Galileo*' (Reader, Item 27) and consider how helpful this is in providing an account of the overall effect of the play.**

1   **Are there any characters you think have been less emphasized in the discussion so far that we might have taken into account? What aspects of their roles are brought out in Schumacher's discussion?**

2   **What is your view of Schumacher's claim that the form of characterization Brecht began to develop in the early 1950s is not so much 'epic' as 'dialectical'?**

1   We have already reflected on the part played by Andrea and his mother Mrs Sarti, as well as by the little monk and Cardinal Barberini, and, to a lesser extent, by Galileo's daughter Virginia. Schumacher not only shows how important the roles of these and other minor characters are in the play, but also draws attention to three aspects of the whole ensemble of characters: first, how far the known features of the historical figures from which they derive have been modified; second, how far they represent alternative or complementary viewpoints; and third, the extent to which each character's expression of the relation between the individual and the type represents or 'make[s] perceptible' a belief in the 'dialectic' processes of 'classical' Marxism. According to Schumacher, Brecht was moving away from 'epic' theatre, while retaining the narrative element, by developing a form of theatre in which the 'alienation' techniques were specifically aimed at revealing the contradictions inherent in social processes.

These aspects are shown in terms of the opposites or antitheses suggested by each character. For example, Virginia is based on the historical Galileo's daughter, yet is quite different from her. Her 'primary function' is said to be that of demonstrating that 'the conflict between a new science and an old faith, or – speaking more generally – between social progress and reaction, penetrates the personal and family sphere'. As Schumacher implies, to understand the play fully, we need to understand the role of characters such as Virginia. Certainly, even if her 'dialectic' function is not altogether as clear as he insists, there can be little doubt that her presence, and the changing relationship between herself and her father, is an important element in the complex tapestry of the play. The most striking example, perhaps, is the reversal of power that has occurred by the end of the play, when the daughter who was earlier nothing more than a means to an end for Galileo has now become the person on whom he most relies.

Such ironic reversals of fortune are apparent throughout, and do suggest the kind of patterning Schumacher discerns in the play, even if it seems – as it does to me – rather less schematic than he proposes. Nevertheless, as he points out, the contradictions abound, and may be felt in the very texture of the writing: in Sagredo's 'You don't believe in Aristotle but you do believe in the Grand Duke of Florence' (Scene 3, p.33); in Galileo's response to the little monk in Scene 8; most cogently in the famous exchange highlighted above: 'Unhappy the land that has no heroes!' / 'Unhappy the land where heroes are needed'.

2   According to Schumacher's persuasive conclusion, Brecht 'drew the truth from contradictions, through the play's murderous analysis'. I would prefer to emphasize the further contradiction, or 'dialectic', between the comic and the tragic elements in the play. This veers between satire and seriousness throughout, from the introductory ditty that comments on Scene 1 before the action begins, to the telling contrast between the children's superstitions and the joke against the authorities at the end. But Schumacher is probably right to suggest that, in terms of overall structure, the play evinces less of the theatrical techniques of Brecht's earlier 'epic' theatre (narrator commenting on the action, performers stepping out of their roles, numerous anti-illusionistic devices), and more of his flexible later method, as explained and developed in *A Short Organum for the Theatre*. As we know, Brecht was never finally satisfied with the play, and was revising it until his death. Arguably, what he managed in *Life of Galileo* was to internalize the interplay between sympathetic involvement and critical detachment, by means of a dialectical approach not only towards his characters, but to his audiences, thereby creating a satisfying sense of the real complexity of choice facing all of us in the modern world. Galileo remains simultaneously an image of greatness and weakness; the play remains simultaneously an image of the past and an image of the present.

Moving on

Most plays suffer from merely being read, and *Life of Galileo* is no exception. This is pre-eminently a play to be performed: its effects are visible, and visual, from banners to costume, from song to gesture and tableaux. This is most memorably relevant in the continuous display of scientific discovery through the models, telescopes and even written texts (as in the reading before the curtain of the 'Discorsi') that helped create the world of science and technology familiar to all of us today. Brecht was a man of the theatre, and we do him a disservice if we do not at least try to imagine how his work might appear in the medium for which it was developed.

One way of reading *Life of Galileo* in the absence of any production is to witness what other playwrights have made of it. Take, for example, the severely modified production of *Life of Galileo* written for performance by David Hare for the Almeida Theatre's 1994 season. This cut the plague scene, reduced the carnival sequence to a puppet interlude, dropped some minor characters and otherwise radically reduced the scope of the original. Why? Brecht provided too many alternative views, thought Hare, the full text was 'weighed down with qualifications', and what was needed was a 'clear line', to be 'affirmative about common action, common values' and create 'a contemporary political theatre out of the wreckage of Thatcherism' (Eddershaw, 1996, pp.154–5). For Hare and those who shared his views, the collapse of communism in Eastern Europe did not make Brecht's work redundant; on the contrary, it made him all the more relevant (see *ibid.*).

Some contemporary playwrights went further. Another Marxist playwright, Howard Brenton, rewrote *Life of Galileo* as a new play entitled *The Genius*, which was first performed at the Royal Court Theatre, London in 1983. In this play, which is also concerned with the responsibility of the scientist to society (its first title was *Galileo's Goose*), a brilliant US mathematician 'exiles' himself at a provincial UK university to avoid his new theories being used by the US military. Here, however, he finds that a female undergraduate has stumbled on the same discovery, and together they try to prevent their knowledge from becoming public. In a reversal of the main thrust of Brecht's play, they argue that the scientific quest has become essentially malign.

Although with Brecht the play leaves us with no clear answers about what to do, the important thing is that it has raised the questions, or at least renewed our sense of their importance. In other words, in modernist terminology, it has made the familiar strange. The energy and experimentation of modernism (whose effect we often lose through our familiarity with its canonical texts) may continue to work towards a culturally and political radical end. That, at any rate, was the aim of Brecht's play, which had an immense impact – on the modern theatre and how it handles politics, as well as on how we define both.

Works cited

Althusser, L. (1971) *Lenin and Philosophy and Other Essays*, trans. by B. Brewster, London: New Left Books.

Barthes, R. (1977) 'Diderot, Brecht, Eisenstein', in *Image–Music–Text*, selected and trans. by S. Heath, London: Fontana Original.

Baxendall, L. and Morawski, S. (eds) (1977) *Marx [and] Engels on Literature and Art: A Selection of Writings*, Documents on Marxist Aesthetics, New York: International General.

Benjamin, W. (1977) 'Conversations with Brecht', in *Aesthetics and Politics: Ernst Bloch, Georg Lukács, Walter Benjamin, Theodor Adorno*, afterword by F. Jameson, translation editor R. Taylor, London: New Left Books.

Bentley, E. (1999) *Bentley on Brecht*, New York: Applause.

Brecht, B. (1967) *Poems by Bertolt Brecht: Manual of Piety/Gedichte von Bertolt Brecht: Hauspostille*, bilingual edn, trans. by E. Bentley, New York: Grove.

Brecht, B. (1978) *Brecht on Theatre: The Development of an Aesthetic*, ed. and trans. by J. Willett, London: Methuen.

Brecht, B. (1993) *Collected Plays*, vol.2, part 2: *The Threepenny Opera*, ed. and trans. by J. Willett and R. Manheim, London: Methuen.

Brecht, B. (1994) *Life of Galileo*, trans. by J. Willett, with Commentary and Notes by H. Rorrison, Methuen Student Editions, London: Methuen.

Brecht, B. (2001) *Life of Galileo*, trans. by J. Willett, ed. by J. Willett and R. Manheim, London: Methuen.

Brenton, H. (1983) *The Genius*, London: Methuen in association with the Royal Court Theatre.

Brook, P. (1972) *The Empty Space*, Harmondsworth: Penguin.

Eddershaw, M. (1996) *Performing Brecht: Forty Years of British Performances*, London: Routledge.

Esslin, M. (1965) *Brecht: A Choice of Evils: A Critical Study of the Man, His Work, and His Opinions*, London: Mercury.

Ewen, F. (1992) *Bertolt Brecht: His Life, His Art, His Times*, New York: Carol.

Eyre, R. and Wright, N. (2000) *Changing Stages: A View of British Theatre in the Twentieth Century*, London: Bloomsbury.

Fuegi, J. (1987) *Bertolt Brecht: Chaos According to Plan*, Cambridge: Cambridge University Press.

Joll, J. (1983) *Europe Since 1870: An International History*, Harmondsworth: Penguin.

Kitchin, L. (1969) *Mid-Century Drama*, London: Faber.

Lukács, G. (1963) *The Meaning of Contemporary Realism*, London: Merlin.

Sokel, W.H. (1962) 'Brecht's Split Characters and his Sense of the Tragic', in P. Demetz (ed.), *Brecht: A Collection of Critical Essays*, Englewood Cliffs, NJ: Prentice Hall.

Speirs, R. (1987) *Bertolt Brecht*, Modern Dramatists, Basingstoke: Macmillan.

Wohlwill, E. (1909) *Galilei und sein Kampf für die Copernicanische Lehre*, Hamburg: Leopold Wofs.

Further reading

Brecht, B. (1970–) *Collected Plays*, vols 1–8 and *Poems 1913–1956*, annotated and ed. by J. Willett and R. Manheim, London: Methuen. The standard editions of Brecht's plays and poems, which should be consulted by anybody interested in Brecht's other work; all now available in paperback, too.

Brecht, B. (1978) *Brecht on Theatre: The Development of an Aesthetic*, ed. and trans. by J. Willett, 2nd edn, London: Methuen. A treasure-house of material: a wide selection of Brecht's critical writings over four decades, very well annotated, and including the complete *A Short Organum for the Theatre*.

Eddershaw, M. (1996) *Performing Brecht: Forty Years of British Performances*, London: Routledge. A lucid and informed survey of Brecht productions in Britain by a range of influential directors, including George Devine, Sam Wanamaker, William Gaskill and Howard Davies.

Fuegi, J. (1987) *Bertolt Brecht: Chaos According to Plan*, Cambridge: Cambridge University Press. Detailed, fully illustrated study of Brecht's day-to-day work as a theatre director, showing the evolution of his plays out of the confusions and contradictions of his life and professional practice.

Lunn, E. (1985) *Marxism and Modernism: An Historical Study of Lukács, Brecht, Benjamin, and Adorno*, London: Verso. An extremely useful, clearly written comparative analysis of how different modernist currents emerged in the outlooks of these four key European thinkers and cultural critics.

Thomson, P. and Sacks, G. (eds) (1994) *The Cambridge Companion to Brecht*, Cambridge: Cambridge University Press. This volume contains a wide range of critical and contextual material in the form of essays by leading scholars and theatre practitioners concerning almost every aspect of Brecht and his theatre.

CHAPTER 8

The poetry of Christopher Okigbo

DAVID RICHARDS

Overview

In this chapter I will try to assess the extraordinary, and to western readers unfamiliar, work of Christopher Okigbo. I begin by introducing the concept of an 'exchange' between twentieth-century African and European modern art movements with a consideration of Pablo Picasso's *Les Demoiselles d'Avignon*. I describe Okigbo's cultural and historical background and explore its influence on his work in a preliminary reading of some of his poems. I then go on to consider further works in relation to questions of post-colonial identity, poetic technique and international modernist art movements.

The chapter draws material from a number of different places and times: from Paris in the early twentieth century, from Spain in the 1930s, from West Africa in the nineteenth and twentieth centuries. It also touches upon a range of different disciplines: anthropology, history, music, religious studies, art history, as well as literary analysis.

The poems I will be discussing can be found in the selection of poems from *Labyrinths with Path of Thunder* reproduced in the Appendix at the end of this book. The selection follows the order of the original sequence, although it does not include all the poems. However, the selection does include a number of poems that are not studied in this chapter.

Africa and modernity

Christopher Okigbo was a Nigerian poet. He died young, and only one collection of poems (comprising only 72 pages), *Labyrinths with Path of Thunder*, was published after his death. Almost nothing else of his writings remains. I should say at the outset that Okigbo is a 'difficult' writer, and he will remain a 'difficult' writer when you have read this chapter and the accompanying materials. His poetic experiments, innovative image structures and complex sequences of poems have been a matter of debate since they were first published, provoking admiration, perplexity and condemnation of his use of 'modernist' themes and techniques in fairly equal measures. It is important to remember that modernism, in all its different guises, arose during a period of extensive European colonization of non-European peoples and cultures. Modernism was both exported from Europe to the colonies, and drew heavily on non-European art forms, during this period of imperial expansion. So, in the context of our overall theme of 'contending modernisms', I will try to give a sense of the wider impact European modernism had on colonial and postcolonial African cultures.

I want to begin, not in Africa, but in Paris in 1907, and to introduce the idea of an exchange between European and African artworks at a key moment in the development of European modernisms. Picasso had for some years prior to this date been collecting African sculpture, buying objects cheaply from traders and travellers returning from Africa to the Mediterranean seaports. These objects had very little value as works of art in Europe, where they were considered to be crude 'fetishes' indicative of the primitive level of African civilization. The major French anthropological expeditions to Africa returned with thousands of such objects, and these little-understood carvings were stored, gathering dust, in the cellars of the Palais de Chaillot, Place du Trocadéro, Paris. In 1907, Picasso spent a prolonged period viewing the Trocadéro collection of African masks, and

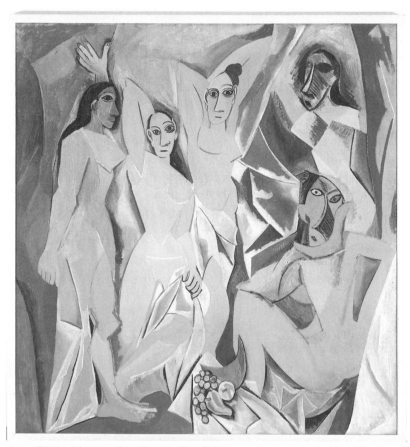

Figure 8.1 Pablo Picasso, *Les Demoiselles d'Avignon*, June–July 1907, oil on canvas, 244 × 234 cm, Museum of Modern Art, New York. (© 2003, digital image, The Museum of Modern Art, New York/SCALA, Florence. Acquired through the Lillie P. Bliss Bequest. 333.1939. © Succession Picasso/DACS 2004.)

many art historians identify this encounter as the moment when African art entered the consciousness of the modern European artist. Picasso seems to have combined his fascination for the African mask with his interests in archaic Iberian stone sculptures and contemporary artworks (principally those of Paul Cézanne) and the result appeared later that same year in the shape of his 'monumental' and 'unprecedented' canvas *Les Demoiselles d'Avignon* (Hughes, 1991, p.24). **Look at *Les Demoiselles d'Avignon* (Figure 8.1). Consider what you think is being represented in Picasso's painting. Compare the image of an African masquerader wearing a mask (Figure 8.2). Can you detect any African influences in the subject matter of *Les Demoiselles d'Avignon*?**

Figure 8.2   Oti Iri mask. (Photo: G.I. Jones Photographic Collection, courtesy of Cambridge University Museum od Archaeology and Anthropology, accession number N.13276.GIJ.) This photograph was taken in the late 1930s by G.I. Jones, a Cambridge anthropologist. It shows a masked figure, known as Oti Iri, from a masquerade performance (Okwanko) celebrated by an Igbo community in the village of Akanu Ohafia in south-eastern Nigeria.

The subject of *Les Demoiselles d'Avignon* is five naked prostitutes on display on the stage of a bordello. The painting depicts female sexuality as crude and aggressive, and to emphasize this Picasso has three of the women wearing African masks. The result is a vision of the savage compulsion of female desire, which is expressed as much by the primitive nature of the African masks the women wear as by their immodest poses. The painting has always been controversial, originally for its frank sexual content and dramatic use of line and colour, more recently for its problematic representation of debased female sexual aggression.

Look again at the image of an African masquerader wearing a mask (Figure 8.2). Do you feel that Figures 8.1 and 8.2 point to some significant differences in the purposes of art in these different contexts? Note in particular how the masked figure in Figure 8.2 is surrounded by people and appears to be engaged in a communal festival. Masquerade festivals of this kind are a common and very popular form of activity in sub-Saharan Africa and are often held to commemorate the ancestors and to celebrate a community's sense of identity.

In Africa, the mask's chief function is not only aesthetic; it also has an important role in the life of the community. In *Les Demoiselles d'Avignon*, the mask is emptied of any original cultural significance other than its usefulness as an emblem of savagery. The mask is of use to Picasso as a figurative and symbolic device, in which female sexuality converges with primitive fetishism.

Art historians argue about the meaning and importance of Picasso's use of African sculpture. A sense of these debates can be gained from the opposed points of view of Hal Foster (1985) and William Rubin (1985, following an exhibition in 1984). Foster argues that European artists have 'appropriated' African art, whereas Rubin sees a shared 'affinity' between African and European artists.

Picasso's encounter with African sculpture initiated a powerful 'primitivist' or anthropological strain in modernism, without which, as the anthropologist Steven Tyler writes,

> neither modern poetry nor modern art would be what it is today
> ... [it] has given modern artists the mood of distance and
> estrangement from their own familiar traditions, and, by enriching
> and relativizing the storehouse of knowledge, symbols, and odd
> and diverse facts out of which poets or artists fashion their work,
> has enabled their exploitation of the archaic, the exotic, the
> primitive, the primordial, the universality of myth and symbols,
> and the relativity of language and thought.

(Tyler, 1984, p.329)

The masks supply an archetypal reference point, a locus for western ideas of the 'primitive consciousness' and modernism's obsessions with the savage 'other'. But there is another equally important element in Picasso's use of the African masks. They are more than just convenient examples of primitive tendencies – look at the style of *Les Demoiselles d'Avignon*. Until this painting, the 'primitive' had been used by western figurative art as an allegorical or exotic subject; African and Oriental subjects in European painting had signified a glamorous or outlandish theme. Picasso's innovation was to rework African forms of representation into the practice of painting itself. African techniques of rendering spatial planes have become the stylistic medium for the painting: a new visual language of planes and facets arranged in a complex relationship of related viewpoints, which connect both an abstract and a mimetic style. The representation of the masks and bodies appears broken into simplified two-dimensional parts arranged in complex and angular relationships, juxtaposed in a composition that renders the scene uncompromisingly unfamiliar. The masks were used by Picasso to express his ideas about female sexuality and its closeness to dominant notions of the primitive, and also transformed the way in which he looked at form and painted space. The stylistic innovations the masks inspired in Picasso led directly to his collaborations with Georges Braque and the creation of the 'moment' of Cubism: in short, to the revolutionary impact of African form on European art, which, literally, reshaped modernist art during the years 1907–14. In this radical way, African art participated in modernity.

However this African influence is read, it was certainly powerfully felt in modernist art movements. The case for a similar African influence on literary modernism is more difficult to trace, not least because non-Islamic, sub-Saharan African cultures had strong and ancient oral traditions, but lacked any form of written expression. Nonetheless, the kinds of figurative and representational experimentation that African sculpture inspired in Picasso and Braque, and later in Emil Nolde, Amedeo Modigliani, Constantin Brancusi and many others, was carried over in the cross-fertilization of ideas between painting and sculpture and the literary arts. Just as Picasso translated an African visual language into his painting, so too literary modernists – Surrealists, Futurists, Vorticists – translated the techniques of fragmentation, juxtaposition and defamiliarization into the literary texts. In indirect, although nonetheless important, ways, Africa also participated in shaping the varieties of literary modernisms. I will try to explore through the poetry of Okigbo what happened when this version of traditional African art practices was returned to Africa, not as African, but as European modernism.

Understanding Okigbo: sequence and contexts

First, we must place Okigbo culturally and historically, and try to gain a sense of the kind of poet he was. Okigbo was born in 1932 in a small forest village in the province of Onitsha in eastern Nigeria. An Igbo by birth, he was, nonetheless, the product of the British colonial education system. (The Igbo are one of three main ethnic groupings in Nigeria, the others being the Yoruba in the south-west, and the Hausa in the north. There are also numerous other smaller but nonetheless distinct ethnicities.) He studied classics at the University of Ibadan, worked briefly with the Nigerian Tobacco and United Africa Companies, taught Latin at a grammar school, became a librarian at Nsukka University, and joined Cambridge University Press, again at Ibadan. He wrote the majority of his poems between 1956 and 1966, and the collected works published later as *Labyrinths with Path of Thunder* appeared originally through African presses as *Heavensgate* (1962), *Silences* (1963 and 1965), *Distances* (1964) and *Limits* (1964). During the mid-1960s, when Okigbo was assembling the final versions of his poems into the *Labyrinths* collection, a strong separatist movement was developing in the Eastern Region of the Nigerian Federation. When Biafra, as this region called itself, seceded from the Federation on 6 July 1967, civil war broke out. Okigbo joined the Biafran defence forces with the rank of major and was killed the following month in fighting near Nsukka. A separate sequence of poems, *Path of Thunder*, was published posthumously in 1968 and included alongside *Labyrinths* in 1971.

Figure 8.3 Photograph of Christopher Okigbo. (By permission of the Christopher Okigbo Foundation.)

Although they were published separately, Okigbo maintained that the poems were 'in fact, organically related' (see his 'Introduction' to *Labyrinths*; Reader, Item 29). The poems form a complex sequence, which unfolds as the collection progresses. It is important to acknowledge this 'organic relationship' but, like many poets influenced by modernism, Okigbo is an extremely eclectic writer, and his eclecticism often obscures the 'organic' qualities of his verse. His 'Introduction' cites writers and musicians, deities and ancestors, myths and legends, politicians and political events: Orpheus (ancient Greek lyric poet), the Western Nigeria Crisis of 1962, Patrice Lumumba (first Prime Minister of Congo, murdered in 1961), Obafemi Awolowo (leader of the opposition party in Nigeria, convicted of treason in 1962 and later released), Gerard Manley Hopkins (poet), Claude Debussy (composer), Herman Melville (novelist), Nathaniel Hawthorne (writer), Stephane Mallarmé (poet), Rabindranath Tagore (poet), Federico García Lorca (dramatist), Aeneas's helmsman Palinurus (character in Virgil's *Aeneid*), Ishthar (Babylonian goddess), Tammuz (Sumerian god), Minos (King of Crete), the Aro Ibos (south-eastern Nigerian state, now destroyed), the White Goddess (incarnation of Idoto), Gilgamesh (Babylonian hero) and T.S. Eliot (writer and poet). This list should be considered merely a selection of what actually appears in the poems, which often seem like a stream of partial, truncated quotations and allusions. Too quickly, the reader can become lost in this referential maze; better to begin with a sense of the kind of poet Okigbo was.

Read the first poem in 'I The Passage', the first section of the sequence from *Heavensgate*: 'Before you, mother Idoto' (Appendix). Consider for yourself what you think this poem is about. How does the poem situate you as a reader and determine your responses at this early stage in your reading?

The circumstances are recognizable enough, as the religious devotee makes his supplication at the holy spring of the goddess – you may have picked up the quotation from Psalm 130 in the last two lines. In many respects, this is also a very conventional, perhaps even hackneyed, invocation of the poet's muse, familiar in the works of the European canon from the ancient Greek poet Homer onwards. But here, this very European conventional invocation is rendered differently, as Okigbo begins his collection of poems with an invocation to the African – specifically Igbo – goddess Idoto. (As is common in traditional African belief, Okigbo was believed to be the reincarnation of his grandfather, who had been the priest of Idoto. Just before Okigbo died, he had contemplated assuming the familial role as priest.) The attendant image structure – the oilbean (an emblem sacred to the goddess), for example – disorientates the western reader, who is responsive to the convention but unaware of the meaning of the images it contains. This is, simultaneously, both a familiar and an unfamiliar, perhaps even uncomfortable, 'passage' into the poems.

Idoto (Figure 8.4) was a local incarnation of a much more widespread belief in female spirits in traditional Igbo religion, the most celebrated of which is Idemili, the daughter of the high god. Idoto is one of the many manifestations of Idemili, who was sent to earth in a pillar of water, and is associated with rivers, streams and lakes. An account of Idemili is available in the extract from the novel *Anthills of the Savannah* by Okigbo's friend Chinua Achebe, reproduced in the Appendix. As you will see from the extract, traditional Igbo society feared the rise of powerful individuals to the status of chief or king, and limited access to the most powerful titles by making them almost impossible to attain. In order to achieve the title that would allow a man to gain the powers of a tyrant, the supplicant must be introduced to Idemili's shrine by his daughter or the daughter of a kinsman and is required to sit on seven fingers of chalk without breaking any of them. If he is successful in this nearly impossible task, he must further await Idemili's approval, the only sign of which is that he is still alive three years later. We will shortly explore more fully the historical contexts for this need to restrain

Figure 8.4 Modern female figure. (Photo: G.I. Jones Photographic Collection, courtesy of Cambridge University Museum of Archaeology and Anthropology, accession number N.71917.GIJ.) This photograph, again taken by the Cambridge anthropologist G.I. Jones in the 1930s, shows a contemporary wood carving made by an Igbo artist from the town of Abiriba in the heart of Igboland. The figure displays all the characteristics of the Igbo water goddess, Idoto (Idemili).

the powerful in Igbo society, but first I want to consider why Okigbo chose religion as a major subject of his poetry and whether there was more than just religious belief at stake here.

One aspect of the wider role of religion can be seen in Okigbo's 'Introduction' to *Labyrinths* (Reader, Item 29), where he refers to the 'White Goddess'. Specifically, he had in mind the work of that name by the poet Robert Graves (1948), in which he saw a direct comparison with traditional Igbo belief in the creative power of female deities. Graves's rather esoteric argument, drawn from European classical sources, had been that poets derive their gifts from the 'female principle' in the image of a goddess in various forms. Like the numerous classical examples Graves had cited in *The White Goddess*, Idoto embodied the principles of order, balance and degree between genders and in society – principles that cluster around a complex system of beliefs and practices expressed, in Igbo, as *chi*. *Chi* is a difficult concept to describe briefly, but it is founded on the belief that each individual possesses another corresponding spirit, a personal god or guardian angel, with whom it is necessary to live in harmony. *Chi* is a belief in the essential doubleness of existence, which is expressed in the Igbo proverb, 'where one thing stands, another stands by it' (Achebe, 1975, p.160). When the balance of *chi* – the doubleness of the individual psyche and the wider social order – is disrupted, the culture falls apart. Through Idoto and *chi*, Okigbo defined Igbo cultural identity as possessing the imperatives of personal equilibrium and social harmony through the restraint of individual power.

Now read the second and third poems in 'I The Passage', the first section of the sequence from *Heavensgate*: 'Dark waters of the beginning' and 'Silent faces at crossroads' (Appendix).

1 **Try to identify the religious references in the poems and consider how Okigbo presents sets of 'opposed' images of light and dark, sunlight and shadow, animals and birds. What is being expressed through these oppositions?**

2 **What is the significance of the crossroads?**

1 You will notice that the poems contain numerous references to the biblical Genesis and Book of Revelation. There are also images of Africans attending church and organ music. These images are placed alongside references to traditional African religion: the boa constrictor and the sunbird. (The reference to Anna is both to the poet's mother and to St Anne, the mother of the Virgin Mary, a conjunction of the personal and the public spheres that is typical of Okigbo's writing; Fraser, 1986.) The poems refer to a specific historical moment – the coming of European missionaries and the establishment of Christianity in Africa. (You can obtain a vivid and moving account of this historical moment and its consequences from the novels of Chinua Achebe, particularly

Things Fall Apart; 1958.) These poems capture a moment when traditional Igbo belief and the new religion appear to co-exist, each reflecting and enriching the other – even the native wind listens to the 'loveliest fragment' of organ music. It would appear that the Igbo principle of *chi* is celebrated here as the two religions complement and enlighten each other ('Rays, violet and short, piercing the gloom'). But the poems also contain a foreboding of what is to come, 'the fire that is dreamed of' – an apocalyptic vision of struggle with the imperial forces that followed the missionaries and the consequent destruction of the balance of traditional Igbo society.

2 In many respects, Igbo history is itself at the crossroads alluded to in the poem as the conflicts and antagonisms of the European presences in Africa threaten to shatter and fragment Igbo culture.

The first interventions by European powers in what was to become the state of Nigeria began in the sixteenth century with a Portuguese slave trading post in Bonny. Slavery not only robbed Africa of her people, it also disrupted traditional societies by creating indigenous elites who benefited materially from selling their own people. But it was not until the mid-nineteenth century that Christian missions arrived, and throughout Africa the presence of missionaries was the precursor to further European trading and eventually imperial encroachment. After the Berlin Conference of 1884–5, when the European powers arbitrarily divided Africa among themselves, the British Oil Rivers Protectorate was established in the area of the Niger Delta in 1885. The Protectorate rapidly encroached on the interior, until in 1900 it dominated most of the north and south as well and effectively invented the modern geo-political entity of Nigeria.

In eastern Nigeria, the Igbo homeland proved to be a rather more intractable problem for the British in their newly created colonial state. The British colonial policy of indirect rule through traditional 'native' authorities made the Igbo a particularly difficult prospect for the British colonial authority. By tradition, the Igbo were 'acephalous', which means that they possessed neither chiefs nor kings. As we have seen, they resisted any attempts by individuals to assert their authority over their loose confederations, which were governed through Ndichie, elders and titleholders possessed by ancestral spirits. The Igbo's lack of 'properly' constituted authority, as the British saw it, or even minimal state apparatus, confirmed for them the Igbo's status as an exceptionally primitive society and therefore justified their pacification on the grounds of their lack of civilization. Indiscriminate slaughter and the destruction of villages took place and this was legalized by the Collective Punishment Ordinance of 1912. The last independent areas were absorbed in 1914 (Boahen, 1990).

Now read (in the Appendix):

the whole of 'II Initiations', the second section in the sequence from *Heavensgate*;

'Siren Limits II', in the sequence from *Limits*;

'Fragments out of the Deluge X', in the sequence from *Limits*.

What effect is Okigbo trying to create by juxtaposing so many 'fragments' from such diverse sources? 'Siren Limits II' refers to 'the selves', the 'voice and soul', the 'one self'. What is Okigbo saying here about identity and imperialism? (Try to summarize your response before reading the analysis that follows, which includes a considerable amount of contextual information that you would not be expected to provide.)

These poems recount the history of colonial intervention in Igbo culture and the destruction of the harmony glimpsed in 'Dark waters of the beginning'. Notice how each poem elaborates an increasingly complex and fragmentary image structure – of geometrical patterns in the poems in 'II Initiations', of forest growth in 'Siren Limits II' and of apocalyptic desecration in 'Fragments out of the Deluge X'. The poems create a complex set of allusions and connections with African history, European folklore, ancient myth and Igbo symbols.

The poems in 'II Initiations' fuse Christian imagery with the practice of branding slaves to signify ownership. The patterns burned into the flesh assume ever more elaborate configurations as 'man loses man, loses vision' in the new orders of the colonial state. A new world, without balance or harmony, ensues, populated by 'moron[s]', 'fanatics and priests', 'organizing secretaries and party managers' as the Igbo lose a sense of the 'pure line' of their culture. Even Keplanly, Okigbo's primary school teacher, makes an appearance, inducting the young poet into the Christian religion and the new colonial order.

The process intensifies in 'Siren Limits II', in which the 'shrub' of the imperial presence, nothing more than 'a low growth among the forest', is 'Thirsting for sunlight'. However, its insidious growth goes unchecked, extending its 'branches, / Into the moments of each living hour, / Feeling for audience', until triumphantly foreshadowing the 'Horsemen of the apocalypse' it becomes the dominant 'green cloud above the forest'. This is a reworking of a medieval parable of conflict between generations and the dangers of heresy (see the allegory of 'The oak and the briar' in Edmund Spenser's 'February', in *The Shepheardes Calendar*, 1579).

This phase of Igbo history reaches a climax in 'Fragments out of the Deluge X', which depicts the destruction of traditional Igbo shrines by colonial missionary and military interventions. This is 'the fire that is dreamed of' ('Dark waters of the beginning'). The allusions and traces this poem evokes are multiple and fragmentary. The 'sunbird' refers to Nwanza, described as 'the most powerful of Igbo religious symbols' (Anozie, 1972, p.93), and the 'twin-gods' are, according to Okigbo's own notes, the tortoise and the python, which, together with the oilbean, are symbols of the goddess Idoto. But these indigenous Igbo religious symbols are combined with other referents, such as Irkalla, the Sumerian queen of the underworld, and another incarnation of Idoto, the White Goddess. The fragmentary and italicized refrain, '*Malisons malisons, mair than ten*' is an ancient song taken from Sir James Frazer's *The Golden Bough* (1890), the great compendium of late nineteenth-century anthropological and folkloric knowledge. The quotation is a fragment of a fuller rhyme that was sung during the traditional 'hunting of the wren' ceremonies in Scotland, and is completed by the line 'That harry the Ladye of Heaven's hen!' (Frazer, 1890, vol.2, p.141). The fragment unites two of Okigbo's interests: the White Goddess (Idoto, 'the Ladye of Heaven') and the sunbird (Nwanza, the wren). Okigbo is dealing here with the destruction of the sacred emblems of Igbo culture – the goddess, the sunbird, the python and the tortoise. The alien divinity is revealed, at last, as an invading and colonizing power.

One last poem will complete this preliminary reading. 'Elegy for Slit-drum' comes from the group of poems entitled *Path of Thunder*, which were published posthumously and which Okigbo never intended to be included in the *Labyrinths* collection. The publication of this group in *Labyrinths with Path of Thunder* (1982) owes more to publishers' economies than to poetic intention. However, the inclusion makes sense for our purposes, because the *Path of Thunder* sequence, written on the eve of civil war and immediately before Okigbo's death, completes his meditation on the state of the Nigerian nation and the fate of Igbo culture. Before you embark on a reading of 'Elegy for Slit-drum', you will need some more contextual information.

The barbarous colonial regime described in *Labyrinths* engendered a number of social developments that eclipsed traditional Nigerian societies. Over the first half of the twentieth century, new elites in Nigeria grew to prosperity through farming and trade. These elites received western education and began to flex their political muscle in the colonial hierarchy. Having evolved outside the traditional structures of power, the elites co-operated initially with both 'native' political powers (essentially invented by the British) and the colonial authorities, and at first they mediated between traditional society and western culture. Those relationships began to fail, however, as the elites had wrongly hoped that Britain wanted to modernize Africa and would use their members as instruments in that modernization process. The British preferred the traditional rulers, especially those, as in the case of the Igbo, whose 'traditional' claims to power the British had invented. The new elites went into open opposition against the colonial authorities, while the 'traditional' rulers, who had come to depend on the British, could not accept the call for modernization without consigning themselves to an even more subsidiary role (Boahen, 1990, pp.208–16). Nigeria in the late 1950s and early 1960s, as it moved towards and into independence, was, therefore, fraught with tensions between competing and intertwined interest groups, classes, ethnicities and even generations, as the younger age groups became increasingly impatient with the previous generation's grip on the nation. All of this would lead, ultimately, to the Nigerian Civil War.

The underlying causes of the Nigerian Civil War are too numerous to enumerate here, but key factors were the rise of political parties and cultural associations that emerged from the new elites in the early twentieth century. These bodies claimed to represent, not a town or district as was the case with traditional authorities, nor an imperial 'ideal' as was the case with the British colonial authorities, but an emerging sense of the different ethnic identities within Nigeria – ethnic identities that were different from, and frequently at odds with, a Nigerian national identity. The elites found that they could oppose the British by appealing over the heads of the local traditional authorities to larger ethnically defined constituencies of Hausas, Yorubas and Igbos. In the newly independent nation state, these ethnic identities profoundly coloured federal politics in Nigeria, as strife between them increasingly took on a hostile aspect. Assassinations, coups and counter-coups followed until, in response to the massacre of some 10,000 to 30,000 Igbos by northern Hausa and Fulani peoples, who then dominated the government, the Republic of Biafra seceded from the Nigerian Federation in May 1967, and a terrible civil war ensued that raged until January 1970.

Now read 'Elegy for Slit-drum', trying to place the text within the context outlined. The poem was written during the period of political and ethnic strife described above (following a coup in 1966 after the assassination of the Prime Minister, Sir Abubakar Tafawa Balewa, and the rise to power of General Ironsi – the 'elephant' and 'General', respectively, of the poem; Fraser, 1986, p.135). Although still embedded in Okigbo's characteristic menagerie of totemic creatures, this is one of his most overtly political poems, depicting the death-throes of the postcolonial nation as 'Jungle tanks blast Britain's last stand'. The apocalyptic fire Okigbo had foretold in the poems of 1961 had not been extinguished by independence – on the contrary, the most destructive inferno was about to happen.

Reinventing a cultural identity

We began the previous section by looking at the ways in which a particular poem introduced some 'alien' and disruptive non-European elements from Igbo belief into a conventional poetic invocation. I wish now to develop these ideas a little further and to come to some conclusions about the poetic techniques Okigbo employed. In the previous section, I selected some poems from the sequence as it unfolds in *Labyrinths with Path of Thunder*, and tried to locate them in both their cultural and historical contexts. Necessarily, I have emphasized one particular strand in Okigbo's writing – the history of the collapse of traditional Igbo society under the pressure of British colonial intervention, and the subsequent turmoil of the independent postcolonial state of Nigeria. However, there are many strands in Okigbo's verse other than this rather bleak and pessimistic chronicle. This section will discuss Okigbo's writings in the contexts of debates about postcolonial cultural identities, poetic techniques and his relationship to modernist art movements.

Postcolonial cultural identities

In the context of the newly independent nation states, the forging of new African cultural identities was considered the vital task of a generation of writers and artists, and few of them would have disputed Achebe's famous defence of his reasons for writing: 'to help my society regain belief in itself and put away the complexes of the years of denigration and self-abasement' (1988, p.44). The subsequent cultural flowering of postcolonial Nigeria, to which Okigbo contributed, was truly remarkable. This was the period of the Mbari club and the Oshogbo artists (groupings of artists that developed in and around the city of Ibadan), of Hubert Ogunde and Duro Ladipo (hugely successful writers and performers of 'Yoruba opera'), of Wole Soyinka's *Africa Masks* (1960; the future Nobel laureate's first drama ensemble), of Flora Nwapa (novelist), of J.P. Clark's poetry, translations and criticism, and of the early extraordinary novels of Achebe. This burgeoning wealth of artistic productions changed the face of African culture.

In Nigeria, Okigbo, Achebe and Soyinka contributed energetically – often vociferously – to the debates on African cultural consciousness that preoccupied the postcolonial intelligentsia. These debates focused on issues of language and race: should African writers write only in African languages, eschewing the languages of the colonizers in favour of an 'authentic' African voice? Was there such a thing as an authentic African 'racial' identity anyway? These debates divided Africa along colonial lines. For Francophone Africa, 'negritude' dominated the debate. This was a poetic philosophy of resistance to European culture, which was strongly supported by the existentialist philosopher Jean-Paul Sartre and which proclaimed a distinct racial sensibility grounded in a black consciousness 'which emphasised Africans' emotive sensitivity'. Thus, it was possible for one of the movement's founders, the Senegalese poet Leopold Senghor, to proclaim that 'emotion is completely Negro as reason is Greek' (1964, p.24).

Against these appeals to a racial authenticity, Anglophone African writers and critics alleged that negritude merely reiterated racist dogma by changing negative colonial designations of the African into positive values:

'[Negritude] accepted one of the most commonplace blasphemies of racism, that the black man has nothing between his ears, and proceeded to subvert the power of poetry to glorify this fabricated justification of European cultural domination' (Soyinka, 1976, p.129).

On the matter of language, Achebe pleaded that English, whatever its origins, was the only means by which Africans could communicate with other Africans across the plethora of indigenous languages, and besides, Africans had so altered the English language over the generations that it was, to all intents and purposes, an African language (see Achebe, 1975).

Okigbo shared the disdain of Soyinka and many other Anglophone African writers for negritude. In a revealing letter of 1966 concerning an African arts festival held in Dakar in Senegal, he wrote:

> About Dakar. I did not go [...] I found the whole idea of a negro arts festival based on colour quite absurd. I did not enter any work either for the competition, and was most surprised when I heard a prize had been awarded to *Limits*. I have written to reject it.
>
> (quoted in Anozie, 1972, p.22)

Negritude was an 'absurd' project to Okigbo, because in its desire to define an African consciousness it reproduced a racial discourse that perpetuated the colonial ideologies that had brought Africa to its knees in the first place.

But Okigbo's poetry was itself the focus of controversy – a controversy that opens onto these wider issues of postcolonial African cultural identity. Critics tend to divide in their responses to Okigbo. For some, he was a pioneer of a new voice in Africa, combining knowledge of European and US literatures and forms with an African cultural content that transformed the literary landscape (see Fraser, 1986, for example). For others, he was a traitor to African traditions, betraying an ancient culture by writing in an elitist style that was inaccessible, incomprehensible and irrelevant to the majority of African people. The ferocity of the critical debate can be gauged from the responses described in Chinweizu, Madubuike and Jemie ([1980] 1985).

Now read an extract from *Towards the Decolonization of African Literature* (Reader, Item 28). Do you think Okigbo's critics are correct in rejecting his work? What are their grounds for doing so, and what are the implications of their approach?

The authors argued for a decolonization of African culture, by advocating both a return to the traditional oral poetry of pre-colonial Africa, and a more overtly expressed political agenda. For them, Okigbo was 'an obscurantist "poets' poet" whose main allegiances lay, not with traditional African culture, but with early twentieth century European and American artistic movements' (Chinweizu, Madubuike and Jemie, 1985, p.193). The debates raise several key issues for postcolonial African writers: should they attempt to 'return' to some kind of authentic African voice, purging all non-African influences? Or should they embrace the international modern movement and engage with the language and artistic forms of their erstwhile colonial masters?

Poetic techniques

Bearing issues of identity in mind, read the whole of 'IV Lustra', the fourth section in the sequence from *Heavensgate* (Appendix). Be alert to resonances from the writings of other poets, and pay attention to the verse form (particularly of the first poem, 'So would I to the hills again'). Consider how images evoking African cultural contexts relate to non-African themes.

The poems follow Okigbo's account of the growing threat to Igbo religion and traditional culture from Christian missionaries. You will notice that the tone of these poems is very different from the violent images and complex 'geometries' of 'II Initiations'. The tone – 'atmosphere' is perhaps a better term – is calmer and more celebratory than the previous poems in the collection. As readers, we seem to be in a different 'place' from the scene of brandings and mutilations of 'II Initiations'. This is a greener, more bucolic world of 'hills', 'springs', 'moonmist' and groves. Okigbo has introduced a pastoral interlude into the sequence (Fraser, 1986, p.111, describes this as a 'holiday' scene), and you may be familiar with similar interludes in other poetic sequences, particularly from the Elizabethan period. (Pastoral is a highly artificial, but very adaptable genre, where the poems are set in idealized rural surroundings and the poetic persona, often disguised as a shepherd, comments on larger social and religious issues of the day.) To reinforce the sense of a lost, harmonious world, Okigbo has also adopted a consciously archaic poetic voice in the first line, repeated later in the third verse, which is reminiscent perhaps of the shepherd/poet of Virgil's *Eclogues* or of 'the bucolic recollections of [A.E.] Housman and early [W.B.] Yeats' (Fraser, 1986, p.111). Similarly, the verse seems related to a conventional form: the first poem contains fourteen lines, recalling – but not quite being – a sonnet (it does not have a sonnet's rhyme scheme). The second poem ('The flower weeps, unbruised'), with its alternating voices (strophe and anti-strophe: call and answer) appears as a fragment from an ode. But, as with the invocation to Idoto, Okigbo introduces African images into these forms resonating with English references; the culmination of the first poem is an image of the offerings made to the goddess, and the song patterning of the second poem alternates traditional Igbo symbols with a reference to the Christian Messiah.

For Okigbo, contemporary African identity was a more complex manifestation of the past and present than either his critics with their evocation of an African oral culture, or negritude's 'emotive sensitivity', would allow. To Okigbo, pre-colonial and colonial cultures both co-existed and struggled with each other in the African postcolonial condition. In a poignant passage from *Silences*, he wrote:

> We carry in our worlds that flourish
> Our worlds that have failed ...

It is perhaps in relation to this that we should view Okigbo's poetics: the African poet exists between shifting points of identity, and the conjunctions of form and content from different cultural contexts evoke both 'flourishing' and 'failing' worlds. In form and subject matter, his poetics express this condition of being perpetually 'At confluence of planes' ('II Initiations'). In such a condition, the postcolonial African condition, all things are by their nature fragmentary, unfixed, allusions conjured out of traces, and poetry is the rehearsing of 'old lovely fragments':

> For we are listening in cornfields
>   among the windplayers,
> listening to the wind leaning over
>   its loveliest fragment ...

('Silent faces at crossroads')

As noted earlier, Okigbo's poetry is an eclectic assemblage of fragments citing writers and musicians, deities and ancestors, myths and legends, politicians and political events. There are also fragments of more personal memories and allusions: to his newborn niece in 'V Newcomer', the fifth section of the sequence from *Heavensgate*; to his mother, Anna; to a schoolteacher and other individuals from his childhood. The experience of a world broken into pieces may not, after all, be an unreasonable response to the history of colonial intervention in Igbo culture and Nigeria's collapse into civil war. But that is not the whole story, as these fragmentary references – 'globules of anguish strung together on memory' as he called them – do not mean that his poems are themselves 'fragmentary', but indicate a structure which Okigbo claimed was immanent in the poems and through which they are 'organically related'. The poems celebrate a 'spiritual and psychic ... homecoming' where the poetic persona achieves a state of 'aesthetic grace' (the quotations are from Okigbo's 'Introduction' to *Labyrinths*, Reader, Item 29). The linear structure of this psychological–religious–cultural quest embraces traditional Igbo belief, its disruption by colonial interventions and, eventually, a reinvention of the poet as the voice of a displaced culture. The juxtaposed fragmentary images in the poems do not indicate a falling apart into cultural dissolution and social chaos, but rather they represent a falling together into a different pattern of relationships between the different traces.

Okigbo's relationship to modernist art movements

The mention of a poetics of the fragment returns us immediately to the theme which was announced at the beginning of this chapter and which has been inherent in everything we have looked at so far – the relationship between Okigbo and modernism. A number of routes are open to us in trying to excavate Okigbo's relationship with western modernism and its connections with Igbo culture. One route would be to follow his interests in music, particularly that of Debussy, and Okigbo's accomplishments as a jazz musician. This has much to recommend it, since Okigbo was a fine jazz clarinetist, and his poetic form, which he himself described in musical terms, gives a jazz-like shape to his work. Okigbo's poetic language coincides with the musical language of jazz in the ways in which the fragmentary refrains nonetheless create a sense of progression and development of themes and rhythms. This is often through the use of strophes and anti-strophes, complex discords and free thematic improvizations that build upon each other and bind disparate elements together. There are also issues of postcolonial culture and identity involved in his use of jazz forms, if we consider the origins of jazz in the USA as a development of African musical forms transported through the slave trade. It would be interesting to pursue the question of how far Okigbo 'repatriates' African musical arrangements in his poetic forms. However, I do not have the space (or the expertise) to follow that line of enquiry further. I wish instead to consider Okigbo's engagement with European modernist art, since that was where I began, with my discussion of Picasso's (and modernism's) indebtedness to African sculpture. This may seem an odd choice, given that Okigbo does not deploy an extensive set of references to paintings. Indeed, only one painting is directly acknowledged in *Labyrinths with Path of Thunder*, compared with the dozens of allusions to music and poetry. Yet the single painting is central to the development of the sequence of poems, is a key to Okigbo's strategy and meaning, is fundamental to an understanding of Okigbo's visual imagination, and indicates his stance in the politics of contested identities in postcolonial Africa.

If, for a moment, we were to think of Okigbo as a modernist poet rather than an African poet, what kind of language would we use to describe his work? To help with this, look again at 'Fragments out of the Deluge X' with its multiple and fragmentary references to different contexts, and consider how far you think the term 'fragmentation' (based also, perhaps, on your reading of T.S. Eliot's *Prufrock* poems) provides an adequate description of Okigbo's work. Then, before you try to answer the question, read the following paragraph about collage.

In the field of visual art, collage was a key technique used by artists to explore the effects of fragmentation, juxtaposition and defamiliarization. 'Collage' comes from the French word *coller*, to glue. It is the practice of cutting, juxtaposing and gluing images from different contexts to make a new image. The technique was widely used by many of the major modernist artists: Braque, Picasso and Henri Matisse, for example. There are many accounts and theories of modernist collage, but one of the most interesting was that offered by Max Ernst, a committed collage artist for whom the principles of collage held deep significance: 'it is the chance meeting of two distant realities on an unfamiliar plane, the culture of displacement and its effects – and the spark of poetry that leaps across the gap as the two realities converge' (quoted in Spies, 1991, p.21). Collages employ fragments from different sources, invariably not made by the artist, placing them in new combinations, where they occupy strange hybrid landscapes. (See the discussion of Surrealism in Chapter 4.) Collage opens up a world of infinite possible combinations and recombinations of older, pre-existing materials, and creates new and unexpected meanings in these new contexts.

Okigbo's poetry bears the characteristic hallmarks of modernism: fragmentation, juxtaposition and defamiliarization. My contention is that if we were to think of Okigbo's use of the fragment, the quotation and the juxtaposition of images in modernist terms, with converging patterns and images breaking the lines into ellipses and discontinuities that splinter the poem into prismatic subdivisions, then we would begin to see his poetic technique as essentially that of the collage artist. The 'cutting' and 'gluing' of collaged fragments seems a particularly appropriate description of Okigbo's poetic technique, and offers a paradigm for a postcolonial 'culture of displacement' where meanings can associate, proliferate, collide, disintegrate and reform. The 'spark of poetry that leaps across the gap as the two realities converge' has a further poignancy in the African contexts we have been discussing, in that it catches precisely the different 'confluences' of Okigbo's analysis of the African postcolonial condition.

Let us take this connection between modernism and Okigbo's poetic technique a little further, by looking at how he employs a famous image from European modernism in his poetry. The single painting I referred to earlier (p.392) occurs in 'Fragments out of the Deluge X', in which Okigbo deals with the destruction of the traditional shrines and the culture they represent by missionaries and colonialists. The single painting is by Picasso, not *Les Demoiselles d'Avignon* but something infinitely darker:

> But at the window, outside, a shadow:
>
> The sunbird sings again
> From the LIMITS of the dream;
> The Sunbird sings again
> Where the caress does not reach,

> of *Guernica,*
> On whose canvas of blood,
> The slits of his tongue
> > cling to glue ...
>
> *& the cancelling out is complete.*

('Fragments out of the Deluge X')

This is a central crux in the complex argument of the 'organically related' poems. It is the moment when Okigbo's poetic voice changes from a detailing of the destruction of the traditional Igbo culture into a slow reconstruction of its fragments, and Picasso's *Guernica* (Figure 8.5) is the 'song' that Nwanza, the Igbo sunbird, sings to initiate that new order.

But, one could say, choosing a painting depicting the destruction of the ancient Basque city by Fascist forces in the Spanish Civil War on 26 April 1937 is not a very hopeful sign, particularly if one follows Michel Leiris's view. After seeing *Guernica* in 1937, he wrote that 'Picasso sends us our death notice: everything we love is going to die' (quoted in Conrad, 1998, p.168). Herbert Read too declared: 'Not only Guernica, but Spain; not only Spain, but Europe, are symbolised in this allegory. It is the modern Calvary,

Figure 8.5 *A Civil War is not very Relaxing,* poster produced by the South African anti-apartheid End Conscription Campaign (ECC), 1986, based on Pablo Picasso's *Guernica,* 1937. (© Succession Picasso/DACS 2004.) The version of *Guernica* reproduced here demonstrates an African adaptation of Picasso's famous image of the Spanish Civil War.

the agony in the bomb-shattered ruins of human tenderness and faith. It is a religious picture' (Read, 1945, p.319). In the context of Okigbo's use of the painting, Robert Fraser has written in a similar vein:

> Here allusion and prognosis fuse, for the reference to Picasso's canvas of 1937 brings us up against the perennial violence of every age at the very moment at which it highlights the plight of the Igbo, poised, as Okigbo wrote, a mere three years from the first bombing raids on Enugu.
>
> (Fraser, 1986, p.119)

Guernica, like traditional Igbo society before and Biafra to come, was one of those 'worlds that have failed' (*Silences*). How can I suggest, therefore, that Picasso's painting occupies a position of central importance in the poem, expressing symbolically a process by which postcolonial Igbo culture may discover its voice? This is hardly an auspicious omen of the future that is to follow, since surely the song the sunbird sings is one of annihilation not renewal?

The painting seems to have held a particular fascination for Okigbo personally. Sunday Anozie, who knew Okigbo well, reported that the poet carried in his wallet a slide of a newsprint image of *Guernica*, when he worked at Nsukka in 1961, six years before the onset of civil war, in the optimistic days of post-independence Nigeria and its artistic renaissance:

> If any single painting influenced Okigbo at the early stage of his poetic career it was undoubtedly Picasso's 'Guernica' ... What Okigbo particularly admired in Picasso was his genius for isolating particular aesthetic qualities with an unequalled ruthlessness and brilliance, and for doing it to an unequalled range and diversity of qualities. One of Okigbo's brilliant ideas about poetry – and an ambition he used in 1961 to vaunt to the present writer – was to do something analogous to Picasso in breaking down the human figure into fragments and building some of them up into a new construction within which the fragments retain their separate identities or, in other words, to break down art into its several elements and exhibit them separately.
>
> (Anozie, 1972, p.95)

Okigbo engaged not so much with *Guernica*'s subject matter as with its formal arrangement and innovation, in which he saw possibilities for a new African poetic. The last part of Anozie's text perfectly describes not only Picasso's artistic style but Okigbo's poetic practice. Okigbo's sunbird sings not so much of 'the tragedy' of Guernica, Igboland or Biafra, but of 'the art behind' (Anozie, 1972, p.96). It is the modernist techniques of representation, of 'breaking down ... fragments ... [and] ... building them up into a new construction ... [where] ... the fragments retain their separate identities', which rises, like the sunbird, from the ashes of failed worlds.

In my brief discussion of Picasso's borrowings from African sculpture, I argued that in significant ways, 'African art participates in modernity'. By this I meant that without the introduction of a host of African artistic innovations, European modernist techniques and styles – Cubism, collage, *Guernica* itself – would have been inconceivable. It is ironic perhaps, that Okigbo saw in *Guernica* what Picasso had seen in the African masks in the Trocadéro: not just subject matter, but also a formal innovation and 'a new construction'. In composing his poetry in accordance with what he observed as the 'art behind' *Guernica*, Okigbo had, in a sense, repatriated from European art an appropriated African visual and poetic language of open planes and facets, arranged in complex relative viewpoints, which were both abstract and figurative.

If we are to return to one of the stated aims of this chapter and to ask what was Okigbo's relationship with European modernism, the answer we get from his 'collage' of Nwanza and *Guernica* is a complex one. Okigbo was undoubtedly profoundly influenced by modernist techniques of fragmentation, juxtaposition and defamiliarization, possibly because they offered a new and appropriate way of addressing his own people's history of fragmentation, juxtaposition and defamiliarization. His chosen style was also indebted to the modernist technique of collage and the 'art behind' Picasso's *Guernica*, and his work draws together African subject matter and modernist technique. But it would be a mistake to believe that Picasso's modernism – his collage work, *Guernica* and *Les Demoiselles d'Avignon* – were 'pure' inventions; they were also 'hybrid' forms produced by blending European subject matter with African traditional (and other) forms of representation. In these exchanges, in which Picasso and Okigbo increasingly appear as each other's mirror image, it is not clear who is indebted to whom – Africa to Europe, or Europe to Africa – and for what.

Okigbo's African modernism?

Thus far, I have tried to examine the wider impact of twentieth-century European modernisms in the work of a leading African poet, to place Okigbo's poetry in its appropriate cultural and historical contexts, and to consider how Okigbo creatively deployed the tensions between his European and African inheritances. The issue of African postcolonial identity as it is presented in Okigbo's poetry has been broached and described in terms of a complex negotiation of competing demands, but we must now return to this matter of identity. For reasons to do with the global politics of inequality and the legacy of colonialism, readers – particularly academic readers – seem to demand that 'non-metropolitan', 'marginal', so-called 'minority' writers account for their existence through the discourses of identity politics. As a consequence, an African writer is 'required' or volunteers to write about his or her 'identity' in ways that a mainstream English writer is not. But Okigbo offers us the salutary lesson that 'identity politics' mean more than a fashionable theoretical discourse. People die because of who they are. I will try now to address these matters in the context of the political and ethnic strife that eventually claimed Okigbo's life.

Please now read Okigbo's 'Introduction' to *Labyrinths* (Reader, Item 29).

The 'Introduction' to *Labyrinths* is a testament to Okigbo's use of the technique of the eclectic collage. It is tortuously difficult to fathom out what is going on, as reference is piled upon reference, and name upon name. You would be forgiven for giving up on it, but you should view it as an extension of the poetry – like T.S. Eliot's notes to *The Waste Land* or the complex allusiveness of 'The Love Song of J. Alfred Prufrock' – rather than as a text that makes its intentions clear. I want to focus our attention on one small extract towards the end:

> Labyrinths is thus a fable of man's perennial quest for fulfilment. (The title may suggest Minos' legendary palace at Cnossus, but the double headed axe is as much a symbol of sovereignty in traditional Ibo society as in Crete. Besides, the long and tortuous passage to the shrine of the 'long-juju' of the Aro Ibos may perhaps, best be described as a labyrinth.)

This needs some unpicking. You are perhaps familiar with the references to Minos and Cnossus – the king and the palace complex of the ancient Mediterranean culture of Crete, where, in legend, the Minotaur was slain by Theseus. The Igbo references may be less familiar in this collage of cultural references. 'Ibo' is an older, alternative spelling for Igbo. 'Aro Ibos' refers to Arochukwu, a powerful state that predominated in south-eastern Nigeria from about 1690 until its destruction during the early period of British colonization. Arochukwu is still shrouded in enigma because its history did not fit with colonial historiography, and as a result it was largely ignored as an irrelevance by colonial historians (Nwauwa, 1995, p.353). Arochukwu was a confederation of three ethnic groups – the Igbo, Ibibio and Akpa – and was 'located astride two major trade routes which converged at the confluence of the Enyong and the Cross Rivers' (*ibid.*, p.358). Arochukwu controlled three essential resources: the main trade routes, the distribution of exotic goods and a justice system based on the 'long-juju' that Okigbo evokes in his 'Introduction'. The 'long-juju' was originally an insignificant oracle called Ibini-Ukpabi, which was controlled by the Ibibio and had been in existence before the foundation of the confederacy. It was developed by an itinerant priest–doctor into a place of pilgrimage and a powerful instrument of Arochukwu state control. The oracle combined religious and judicial functions. Its main purpose was to ensure peace between the different groups in Igboland and to mitigate and arbitrate inter-ethnic conflict. The delta peoples consulted it, the Ibibio venerated it, the Igbo regarded it as Chukwu, the high god, and the people of the confederacy became *umuchukwu*, the children of the high god (Manning, 1990, p.89; Nwauwa, 1995, p.359).

You have probably already guessed some of Arochukwu's significance for Okigbo. The Ibini-Ukpabi of Arochukwu was the archetypal sacred shrine of Igbo culture destroyed by the British and described in 'Fragments out of the Deluge X'. Arochukwu was also an earlier indigenous predecessor of the twentieth-century Nigerian confederacy. Whereas Arochukwu endured for more than two centuries as a successful synthesis of ethnicities welded into a sovereign entity, Nigeria was, as Okigbo recounts in *Path of Thunder*, convulsed by civil and ethnic strife in less than a decade of independence. Few Nigerian readers in 1965 could have missed the irony of Okigbo's historical allusion as he awakens the memory of another lost 'sovereignty', the Arochukwu confederacy, just as the Nigerian confederacy was on the verge of self-destruction. Yet Arochukwu also connects together a number of significant aesthetic and historical elements in Okigbo's work. Little is known for certain about how Arochukwu and the Ibini-Ukpabi actually functioned, but what is known suggests that together they represented a 'unique' state formation, as Apollos Nwauwa (1995) puts it, which held their multiple ethnic constituents together in supple, segmented and constantly changing ties of confederation. Arochukwu and the Ibini-Ukpabi thrived because they did not centralize authority, nor invest power in a single state entity, commanding individual or dominant ethnic group. Quite the reverse, as sovereignty was sustained by the dispersal of power, the refusal of chiefly titles to the powerful, and the right of all its peoples to regard themselves as the children of the high god. These ties of confederation were made from the joining together of different cultural identities, but they were so subtle and flexible that they were 'invisible' to the British, who assumed that they did not exist and consequently destroyed them. It is not too fanciful, I think, to see another reason why Okigbo held Arochukwu in such high regard; the kind of dispersed, inclusive culture that was the feature of Arochukwu society was not only a model of the state that Okigbo admired as an exemplar of Igbo cultural identity, but also the embodiment of his own eclectic and inclusive poetic practice. If it is possible to speak of the labyrinth of *Labyrinths* as having a centre, then it was probably the state of Arochukwu in both its historical and aesthetic manifestations. Okigbo's notions of historical Igbo sovereignty are at one with his poetics of fragmentation and collage, and in this image of Arochukwu the aesthetic and the political are merged.

Conclusion

I have tried to place Okigbo's poetry in the relevant contexts of Igbo history and culture and argued that his work reflects upon the changes wrought by his people's experiences of colonization. Most of his poetry is addressed to or concerns Igbo traditional religion and its encounter with missionary Christianity as a metaphor for wider cultural and political struggles. I have discussed the nature of traditional Igbo culture, as Okigbo and some of his contemporaries described it, as a complex network of restraints on would-be powerful individuals. It was this 'republican' state that the British failed to recognize, with disastrous consequences for traditional Igbo society. I have also looked at the remarkable cultural flowering of Nigerian arts during the early period of independence and the ways in which writers turned their attentions to the creation of unique ethnic identities within the Nigerian state. This productive period in African arts was not to last, and much that was precious was destroyed as Nigeria declined into civil war – a war that would bring about Okigbo's death.

I have argued that Okigbo's historical and cultural location cannot be separated from his poetic innovations and practices. His poetry brings together a vast range of referential fragments from ancient and modern African and European cultures, which he conveys through modernist techniques, particularly those associated with Picasso and collage. Okigbo's experimentation with modernist techniques provoked a debate among African critics that went to the heart of some essential questions of African identity and cultural representation. Whereas in Africa Okigbo was seen as influenced by European and US modernism (over-indebted, according to some critics), in the West his classification as an 'African writer' has obscured his credentials as a participant in international modernism. His borrowings from modernism do not represent the subjugation of Okigbo's African poetic to a European artistic agenda, since the foundations of modernism, in subject matter and style, can be discovered in traditional African artistic practices. I have tried to describe an intricate historical process of borrowings and re-borrowings, which has divided art critics and historians into those who believe that modernism shared an 'affinity' with African art, and those who believe that modernism 'appropriated' the cultural products of Europe's colonial possessions. Certainly, modernism's own history cannot be separated from the history of empire, and European art fed upon the remains of cultures damaged or destroyed by colonialism. I have suggested that, in the case of Okigbo's work, it is not simply a matter of either affinity or appropriation, but of something much more deeply intertwined with his vision as a postcolonial subject. He created neither the idyllic negritude nor 'nativist' version of a past African identity, nor was he a European cultural mimic, but his poetry deliberately plays these oppositions against each other. To paraphrase Ernst, Okigbo's 'culture of displacement' is realized in the 'spark of poetry that leaps across the gap' as 'realities converge'.

Works cited

Achebe, C. (1958) *Things Fall Apart*, London: Heinemann.

Achebe, C. (1975) *Morning Yet on Creation Day: Essays*, Studies in African Literature, London: Heinemann Educational.

Achebe, C. (1988) *Hopes and Impediments: Selected Essays 1965–87*, London: Heinemann.

Anozie, S.O. (1972) *Christopher Okigbo: Creative Rhetoric*, London: Evans.

Boahen, A.A. (1990) *General History of Africa London: J. Currey*, Berkeley, CA: University of California Press.

Chinweizu, Madubuike, I. and Jemie, O. (1985) *Towards the Decolonization of African Literature: African Fiction and Poetry and their Critics*, London: KPI.

Conrad, P. (1998) *Modern Times, Modern Places*, London: Thames & Hudson.

Foster, H. (1985) *Recodings: Art, Spectacle, Cultural Politics*, Port Townsend, WA: Bay Press.

Fraser, R. (1986) *West African Poetry: A Critical History*, Cambridge: Cambridge University Press.

Frazer, J.G. (1890) *The Golden Bough: A Study in Comparative Religion*, London: Macmillan.

Graves, R. (1948) *The White Goddess: A Historical Grammar of Poetic Myth*, London: Faber & Faber.

Hughes, R. (1991) *The Shock of the New: Art and the Century of Change*, London: BBC Books.

Manning, P. (1990) *Slavery and African Life: Occidental, Oriental and African Slave Trades*, Cambridge: Cambridge University Press.

Nwauwa, A. (1995) 'The Evolution of the Aro Confederacy in Southeastern Nigeria, 1690–1720: A Theoretical Synthesis of State Formation Process in Africa', *Anthropos*, 90.4–6, pp.353–64.

Okigbo, C. ([1971] 1982) *Labyrinths with Path of Thunder*, London: Heinemann in association with Ibadan: Mbari Publications.

Read, H.E. (1945) *A Coat of Many Colours: Occasional Essays*, London: G. Routledge.

Rubin, W. (ed.) (1985) *'Primitivism' in 20th Century Art: Affinity of the Tribal and the Modern*, exhibition catalogue, New York: Museum of Modern Art.

Senghor, L.S. (1964) *Negritude et humanisme*, Paris: Seuil.

Soyinka, W. (1976) *Myth, Literature and the African World*, Cambridge: Cambridge University Press.

Spies, W. (1991) *Max Ernst: A Retrospective*, Munich: Prestel.

Tyler, S.A. (1984) 'The Poetic Turn in Post-modern Anthropology: The Poetry of Paul Friedrich', *American Anthropologist*, 86.2, pp.328–36.

Further reading

Achebe, C. (1958) *Things Fall Apart*, London: Heinemann.

Senghor, L.S. (1976) *Prose and Poetry*, selected and trans. by J. Reed and C. Wake, London: Heinemann Educational.

Soyinka, W. (1975) *Death and the King's Horseman*, London: Eyre Methuen.

READER REFERENCES

Introduction to Part 1

Wilde, O., 'Preface', *The Picture of Dorian Gray*, ed. by I. Murray, Oxford World's Classics, Oxford: Oxford University Press, 1974, pp.xxii–xxiv (Reader, Item 1).

Orwell, G., Review of *The Novel Today* by Philip Henderson, in *The Collected Essays, Journalism and Letters of George Orwell*, vol.1: *An Age Like This*, ed. by S. Orwell and I. Angus, Harmondsworth: Penguin, 1970, pp.288–91 (Reader, Item 2).

Owen, W., 'Preface', *The Collected Poems of Wilfred Owen*, ed. by C. Day Lewis, London: Chatto & Windus, 1963, p.31 (Reader, Item 3).

Chapter 1 Anton Chekhov, *The Cherry Orchard*

Unsigned notice in *The Times*, in V. Emeljanow (ed.), *Chekhov: The Critical Heritage*, London: Routledge & Kegan Paul, 1981, p.92 (Reader, Item 4).

'A Note on Translations', in B. Hahn, *Chekhov: A Study of the Major Stories and Plays*, Cambridge: Cambridge University Press, 1977, pp.ix–xiii (Reader, Item 5).

Hingley, R., 'Peasant Benefactor and Chronicler', in *A New Life of Anton Chekhov*, Oxford: Oxford University Press, 1976, pp.167–8 (Reader, Item 6).

Smeliansky, A., 'Chekhov at the Moscow Art Theatre', in V. Gottlieb and P. Allain (eds), *The Cambridge Companion to Chekhov*, Cambridge: Cambridge University Press, 2000, pp.29–40 (Reader, Item 7).

Chapter 2 The stories of Katherine Mansfield

Kaplan, S.J., *Katherine Mansfield and the Origins of Modernist Fiction*, Ithaca: Cornell University Press, 1991, pp.114–17 (Reader, Item 8).

Hanson, C. and Gurr, A., 'The Short Story Form', in *Katherine Mansfield*, London: Macmillan, 1981, pp.17–19 (Reader, Item 9).

Pater, W., 'Conclusion', *Studies in the History of the Renaissance*, London: Macmillan, 1873, pp.207–13 (Reader, Item 10).

Bennett, A., and Royle, N., 'Pleasure', in *An Introduction to Literature, Criticism and Theory: Key Critical Concepts*, Hemel Hempstead: Prentice Hall, 1995, pp.187–96 (Reader, Item 11).

Chapter 3   Lewis Grassic Gibbon, *Sunset Song*

Gibbon, L.G., 'Contribution to The Writers' International Controversy', *Left Review*, 1.5, February 1935, pp.179–80 (Reader, Item 12.1).

Gibbon, L.G., Letter to Helen Cruickshank (1933), in W.K. Malcolm, 'Shouting Too Loudly: Leslie Mitchell, Humanism and the Art of Excess', in M.P. McCullough and S.M. Dunnigan (eds), *A Flame in the Mearns. Lewis Grassic Gibbon: A Centenary Celebration*, Glasgow: Association for Scottish Literary Studies, 2003, p.76 (Reader, Item 12.2).

Gibbon, L.G., 'The Antique Scene' (1934), in V. Bold (ed.), *Smeddum: A Lewis Grassic Gibbon Anthology*, Edinburgh: Canongate, 2001, pp.3–5 (Reader, Item 12.3).

J.F.G., '*Sunset Song*: Striking Story of Mearns Life', *Aberdeen Bon Accord and Northern Chronicle*, 9 September 1932, p.4 (Reader, Item 13.1).

MacKenzie, C., 'Four Good Novels', *Daily Mail*, 13 September 1932, p.4 (Reader, Item 13.2).

Anon., 'Review of *Sunset Song: A Novel*. By Lewis Grassic Gibbon', *Fife Herald and Journal*, 21 September 1932, p.2 (Reader, Item 13.3).

Gibbon, L.G., ' "Sunset Song." Author's Reply (To the Editor)', *Fife Herald and Journal*, 28 September 1932, p.2 (Reader, Item 13.3).

Anon., 'Two Scottish Novels: "Poor Tom." By Edwin Muir. "Sunset Song." By Lewis Grassic Gibbon', *Modern Scot*, 3.3, October 1932, pp.250–2 (Reader, Item 13.4).

Jack, P.M., 'A Scotch Novel that is Close to the Soil', *New York Times Book Review*, 2 April 1933, p.2 (Reader, Item 13.5).

Gunn, N.M., 'Nationalism in Writing: Tradition and Magic in the Work of Lewis Grassic Gibbon', *Scots Magazine*, 30.1, October 1938, pp.28–35 (Reader, Item 14.1).

Barke, J., 'Lewis Grassic Gibbon', *Left Review*, 2.5, February 1936, pp.220–5 (Reader, Item 14.2).

Dixon, K., 'The Gospels According to Saint Bakunin: Lewis Grassic Gibbon and Libertarian Communism', in M.P. McCullough and S.M. Dunnigan (eds), *A Flame in the Mearns. Lewis Grassic Gibbon: A Centenary Celebration*, Glasgow: Association for Scottish Literary Studies, 2003, pp.136–9 (Reader, Item 14.3).

Davies, T., 'Earth Mother', *Guardian*, Media Supplement, 18 August 2003, p.15 (Reader, Item 14.4).

Chapter 4   The poetry of the 1930s

Auden, W.H., 'Introduction to *The Oxford Book of Light Verse*', in *W.H. Auden: Prose and Travel Books in Prose and Verse*, vol.1: *1926–1938*, ed. by E. Mendelson, London: Faber & Faber, 1996, pp.430–6 (Reader, Item 15).

Woolf, V., 'The Leaning Tower', in *Collected Essays*, vol.2, London: Hogarth Press, 1966, pp.162–76 (Reader, Item 16).

Chapter 5   T.S. Eliot, *Prufrock and Other Observations*

Symons, A., 'Jules Laforgue', in *The Symbolist Movement in Literature*, London: William Heinemann, 1899, pp.105–14 (Reader, Item 17).

Bergson, H., *Creative Evolution*, trans. by A. Mitchell, London: Macmillan, 1911, pp.1–3 (Reader, Item 18.1).

Bergson, H., *Matter and Memory*, trans. by N.M. Paul and W. Scott Palmer, London: Macmillan, 1911, pp.176–8, 225–6 (Reader, Item 18.2).

Lewis, W. (ed.), *Blast*, vol.1, facsimile edn, Santa Barbara: Black Sparrow, 1981, pp.30–1, 40–3 (Reader, Item 19).

Eliot, T.S., 'Tradition and the Individual Talent', in *Selected Essays*, London: Faber & Faber, 1932, pp.13–22 (Reader, Item 20.1).

Hulme, T.E., 'Romanticism and Classicism', in *Speculations: Essays on Humanism and the Philosophy of Art*, ed. by H. Read, London: Routledge & Kegan Paul, 1924, pp.113–14; 116–22 (Reader, Item 20.2).

Chapter 6   Virginia Woolf, *Orlando*

Woolf., V., *The Diary of Virginia Woolf*, vol.3: *1925–1930*, ed. by A.O. Bell, London: Hogarth Press, pp.156–85 (Reader, Item 21).

Woolf, V., 'Mr Bennett and Mrs Brown', in *Collected Essays*, vol.1, London: Hogarth Press, 1966, pp.319–37 (Reader, Item 22).

Woolf, V., *A Room of One's Own*, San Diego: Harvest/Harcourt Brace Jovanovich, n.d., pp.48–52, 79–80, 83–6, 100–2, 108–9 (Reader, Item 23).

Chapter 7   Bertolt Brecht, *Life of Galileo*

Brecht, B., 'The Epic Theatre and its Difficulties', in J. Willet (ed. and trans.), *Brecht on Theatre: The Development of Aesthetic*: London: Methuen, 1974, pp.22–3 (Reader, Item 24).

Brecht, B., 'Alienation Effects in Chinese Acting', in J. Willet (ed. and trans.), *Brecht on Theatre: The Development of Aesthetic*, London: Methuen, 1974, pp.93–9 (Reader, Item 25).

Brecht, B., 'A Short Organum for the Theatre', in J. Willet (ed. and trans.), *Brecht on Theatre: The Development of Aesthetic*, London: Methuen, 1974, pp.192, 198–201, 203 (Reader, Item 26).

Schumacher, E., 'The Dialectics of *Galileo*', in C. Martin and H. Biol (eds), *Brecht Sourcebook*, London: Routledge, 2000, pp.113–23 (Reader, Item 27).

Chapter 8   The poetry of Christopher Okigbo

Chinweizu, Madubuike, I. and Jemie, O., *Towards the Decolonization of African Literature: African Fiction and Poetry and their Critics*, London: KPI, 1985, pp.188–92. (Reader, Item 28).

Okigbo, C., 'Introduction', *Labyrinths with Path of Thunder*, London: Heinemann, 1971, pp.xi–xiv (Reader, Item 29).

APPENDIX

Katherine Mansfield
The Aloe

There was not an inch of room for Lottie and Kezia in the buggy. When Pat swung them on top of the luggage they wobbled; the Grandmother's lap was full and ~~Mrs.~~ Linda Burnell could *not possibly* have held a lump of a child on hers for such a distance. Isabel, very superior perched beside Pat on the driver's seat. Hold-alls, bags and band boxes were piled upon the floor.

"These are *absolute* necessities that I will not let out of my sight for *one instant*," said ~~Mrs.~~ Linda Burnell, her voice trembling with fatigue and over excitement.

Lottie and Kezia stood on the patch of lawn just inside the gate all ready for the fray in their reefer coats with brass anchor buttons and little round caps with battle ship ribbons. Hand in hand. They stared with round inquiring eyes first at the "absolute necessities" and then at their Mother.

"We shall simply have to leave them. That is all. We shall simply have to cast them off" said ~~Mrs.~~ Linda Burnell. A strange little laugh flew from her lips; she leaned back upon the buttoned leather cushions and shut her eyes ... laughing silently.

Happily, at that moment, Mrs. Samuel Josephs, who lived next door and had been watching the scene from behind her drawing room blind, rustled down the garden path.

"Why nod leave the children with *be* for the afterdoon, Brs. Burnell. They could go on the dray with the storeban when he comes in the eveding. Those thigs on the path have to go. Dodn't they?"

"Yes, everything outside the house has to go," said ~~Mrs.~~ Linda Burnell, waving a white hand at the tables and chairs that stood, impudently, on their heads in front of the empty house.

"Well, dodn't you worry, Brs. Burnell. Loddie and Kezia can have tea with by children and I'll see them safely on the dray afterwards."

She leaned her fat, creaking body across the gate and smiled reassuringly. ~~Mrs.~~ Linda Burnell pretended to consider.

"Yes, it really is quite the best plan. I am *extremely* obliged to you, Mrs. Samuel Josephs, I'm *sure*. Children, say 'Thank you' to Mrs. Samuel Josephs." ...

(Two subdued chirrups: "Thank you, Mrs. Samuel Josephs.")

"And be good obedient little girls and – come closer – " – they advanced – "do not forget to tell Mrs. Samuel Josephs when you want to" ...

"Yes, Mother."

[...]

        ★   ★   ★   ★   ★

It was a familiar cry in the house "Linda's wedding ring has *gone again*" – Stanley Burnell could never hear that without horrible sense of discomfort. Good Lord! he wasn't superstitious – He left that kind of rot to people who had nothing better to think about – but all the same it was *devilishly* annoying. Especially as Linda made so light of the affair and mocked him and said "are they as expensive as all that" and laughed at him and cried, holding up her bare hand – "Look, Stanley, it has all been a dream." He was a fool to mind things like that, but they hurt him – they hurt like sin.

"Funny I should have dreamed about Papa last night" thought Linda, brushing her cropped hair that stood up all over her head in little bronzy rings. "What was it I dreamed?" No, she'd forgotten – "Something or other about a bird." But Papa was very plain – his lazy ambling walk. And she laid down the brush and went over to the marble mantelpiece and leaned her arms along it, her chin in her hands, and looked at his photograph. In his photograph he showed severe and imposing – a high brow, a piercing eye, clean shaven except for long "piccadilly weepers" draping his bosom. He was taken in the fashion of that time, standing, one arm on the back of a tapestry chair, the other clenched upon a parchment roll. "Papa!" said Linda. ~~Tenderly, wonderfully,~~ she smiled. "There you are my dear," she breathed, and then she shook her head quickly and frowned, and went on with her dressing.

Her Father had died the year that she married Burnell, the year of her sixteenth birthday [...]

Linda, his second youngest child, was his darling, his pet, his playfellow. ~~Ah,~~ She was a wild thing, always trembling on the verge of laughter, ready for anything and eager. When he put his arm round her and held her he felt her thrilling with life. He understood her so beautifully and gave her so much love that he became a kind of daily miracle to her and all her faith centred in him – People barely touched her; ~~and they called her~~ she was regarded as a cold, heartless little creature, but she seemed to have an unlimited passion for that violent sweet thing called life – just being alive and able to run and climb and swim in the sea and lie in the grass ~~and "bask"~~. In the evenings she and her Father would sit on the verandah – she on his knees – and "plan". "When I am grown up we shall travel everywhere – we shall see the whole world – won't we Papa?"

"We shall, my dear"

[...]

"And we shan't go as father and daughter," she tugged at his "piccadilly weepers" and began kissing him. "We'll just go as a couple of boys together – Papa."

[...]

★　★　★　★　★

Minnie was a wonderful servant. She did everything there was to be done in the house [...] – – So Mrs. Trout became a perfect martyr to headaches. [...] And as she lay there she used to wonder why it was that she was so certain that life held something terrible for her ~~she used to~~ and to try to imagine what that terrible thing could be – – – until by and by she made up perfect novels with herself for the heroine, all of them ending with some shocking catastrophe. "Dora" (for in these novels she always thought of herself in the third person: ~~it gave her greater freedom for touching [? the reader]~~ it was more "touching" somehow) "Dora felt strangely happy that morning. She lay on the verandah ~~listening to a~~ looking out on the peaceful garden and she felt how sheltered and how blest her life had been after all. Suddenly the gate opened: A ~~rough~~ working man, a perfect stranger to her pushed up the path and standing in front of her, he pulled off his cap, his rough face full of pity. 'I've bad news for you Mam' .... 'Dead?' cried Dora clasping her hands. 'Both dead?' "

    [...]

These dreams were so powerful that she would turn over buried her face in the ribbon work cushion and sobbed. But they were a profound secret – and Doady's melancholy was always put down to her dreadful headaches. [...] "I hope you will really like Tarana" she said, sitting back in her chair and sipping her tea. "Of course it is at its best now but I can't help feeling a little afraid that it will be very damp in the winter. Don't you feel that, Mother? [...] "I expect it will be flooded from the autumn to the spring" said Linda: "we shall have to set little frog traps Doady, little mouse traps in bowls of water baited with a spring of watercress instead of a piece of cheese – And Stanley will have to row to the office in an open boat. He'd love that. I can imagine the glow he would arrive in and the way he'd measure his chest twice a day to see how fast it was expanding." "Linda you are very silly – very" said Mrs. Fairfield. "What can you expect from Linda", said ~~Beryl~~ Dora "she laughs at everything. Everything. I often wonder if there will ever be anything that Linda will not laugh at." "Oh, I'm a heartless ~~little~~ creature!" said Linda. [...] "You mean you love to think you are" said Beryl, and she blew into her thimble, popped it on and drew the white satin dress towards her – and in the silence that followed she had a strange feeling – she felt her anger like a little serpent dart out of her bosom and strike at Linda. "Why do you always pretend to be so indifferent to everything," she said. "You pretend you don't care where you live, or if you see anybody or not, or what happens to the children or even what happens to you. You can't be sincere and yet you keep it up – you've kept it up for years – ~~ever since – and Beryl paused, shoved down a little pleat very carefully – ever since Father died. Oh she had such a sense of relief when she said that: she breathed freely again Linda's cheeks went white~~ – In fact" – and she gave a little laugh of joy and relief to be so rid of the serpent – she felt positively delighted – "I can't even remember when it started now – Whether it started *with* Stanley or before Stanley's time or after you'd had rheumatic fever or when Isabel was born –" "Beryl" said Mrs. Fairfield sharply. "That's quite enough, quite enough!" [...]

On the way home with her children Mrs. Trout began an entirely new "novel". It was night. Richard was out somewhere (He always was on these occasions.) She was sitting in the drawing room by candlelight playing over "Solveig's Song" when Stanley Burnell appeared – hatless – pale – at first he could not speak. "Stanley tell me what is it" .. and she put her hands on his shoulders. "Linda has gone!" he said hoarsely. [...] "She never cared," said Stanley – "God knows I did all I could – but she wasn't happy I knew she wasn't happy."

"Mum" said Rags "~~which does a calf belong to the cow or the bull, Mother~~ which would you rather be if you had to a duck or a fowl – I'd rather be a fowl, much rather."

The white duck did not look as if it had ever had a head when Alice placed it in front of Stanley Burnell that evening.

[...]

Stephen Spender

> After they have tired of the brilliance of cities
> And of striving for office where at last they may languish
> Hung round with easy chains until
> Death and Jerusalem glorify also the crossing-sweeper:
> Then those streets the rich built and their easy love
> Fade like old cloths, and it is death stalks through life
> Grinning white through all faces
> Clean and equal like the shine from snow.
>
> In this time when grief pours freezing over us,
> When the hard light of pain gleams at every street corner,
> When those who were pillars of that day's gold roof
> Shrink in their clothes; surely from hunger
> We may strike fire, like fire from flint?
> And our strength is now the strength of our bones
> Clean and equal like the shine from snow
> And the strength of famine and of our enforced idleness,
> And it is the strength of our love for each other.
>
> Readers of this strange language,
> We have come at last to a country
> Where light equal, like the shine from snow, strikes all faces,

Here you may wonder
How it was that works, money, interest, building, could ever hide
The palpable and obvious love of man for man.

Oh comrades, let not those who follow after
– The beautiful generation that shall spring from our sides –
Let not them wonder how after the failure of banks
The failure of cathedrals and the declared insanity of our rulers,
We lacked the Spring-like resources of the tiger
Or of plants who strike out new roots to gushing waters.
But through torn-down portions of old fabric let their eyes
Watch the admiring dawn explode like a shell
Around us, dazing us with its light like snow.

Louis MacNeice

Carrickfergus

I was born in Belfast between the mountain and the gantries
    To the hooting of lost sirens and the clang of trams:
Thence to Smoky Carrick in County Antrim
    Where the bottle-neck harbour collects the mud which jams

The little boats beneath the Norman castle,
    The pier shining with lumps of crystal salt;
The Scotch Quarter was a line of residential houses
    But the Irish Quarter was a slum for the blind and halt.

The brook ran yellow from the factory stinking of chlorine,
    The yarn-mill called its funeral cry at noon;
Our lights looked over the lough to the lights of Bangor
    Under the peacock aura of a drowning moon.

The Norman walled this town against the country
    To stop his ears to the yelping of his slave
And built a church in the form of a cross but denoting
    The list of Christ on the cross in the angle of the nave.

I was the rector's son, born to the anglican order,
    Banned for ever from the candles of the Irish poor;
The Chichesters knelt in marble at the end of a transept
    With ruffs about their necks, their portion sure.

The war came and a huge camp of soldiers
   Grew from the ground in sight of our house with long
Dummies hanging from gibbets for bayonet practice
   And the sentry's challenge echoing all day long;

A Yorkshire terrier ran in and out by the gate-lodge
   Barred to civilians, yapping as if taking affront:
Marching at ease and singing 'Who Killed Cock Robin?'
   The troops went out by the lodge and off to the Front.

The steamer was camouflaged that took me to England –
   Sweat and khaki in the Carlisle train;
I thought that the war would last for ever and sugar
   Be always rationed and that never again

Would the weekly papers not have photos of sandbags
   And my governess not make bandages from moss
And people not have maps above the fireplace
   With flags on pins moving across and across –

Across the hawthorn hedge the noise of bugles,
   Flares across the night,
Somewhere on the lough was a prison ship for Germans,
   A cage across their sight.

I went to school in Dorset, the world of parents
   Contracted into a puppet world of sons
Far from the mill girls, the smell of porter, the salt-mines
   And the soldiers with their guns.

W . H . A u d e n

In Memory of W.B. Yeats

(d. January 1939)

I

He disappeared in the dead of winter:
The brooks were frozen, the air-ports almost deserted,
And snow disfigured the public statues;
The mercury sank in the mouth of the dying day.
O all the instruments agree
The day of his death was a dark cold day.

Far from his illness
The wolves ran on through the evergreen forests,
The peasant river was untempted by the fashionable quays;
By mourning tongues
The death of the poet was kept from his poems.

But for him it was his last afternoon as himself,
An afternoon of nurses and rumours;
The provinces of his body revolted,
The squares of his mind were empty,
Silence invaded the suburbs,
The current of his feeling failed; he became his admirers.

Now he is scattered among a hundred cities
And wholly given over to unfamiliar affections;
To find his happiness in another kind of wood
And be punished under a foreign code of conscience.
The words of a dead man
Are modified in the guts of the living.

But in the importance and noise of to-morrow
When the brokers are roaring like beasts on the floor of the
    Bourse,
And the poor have the sufferings to which they are fairly
    accustomed,
And each in the cell of himself is almost convinced of his
    freedom;
A few thousand will think of this day
As one thinks of a day when one did something slightly unusual.

O all the instruments agree
The day of his death was a dark cold day.

II

You were silly like us: your gift survived it all;
The parish of rich women, physical decay,
Yourself; mad Ireland hurt you into poetry.
Now Ireland has her madness and her weather still,
For poetry makes nothing happen: it survives
In the valley of its saying where executives
Would never want to tamper; it flows south
From ranches of isolation and the busy griefs,
Raw towns that we believe and die in; it survives,
A way of happening, a mouth.

III

Earth, receive an honoured guest;
William Yeats is laid to rest:
Let the Irish vessel lie
Emptied of its poetry.

Time that is intolerant
Of the brave and innocent,
And indifferent in a week
To a beautiful physique,

Worships language and forgives
Everyone by whom it lives;
Pardons cowardice, conceit,
Lays its honours at their feet.

Time that with this strange excuse
Pardoned Kipling and his views,
And will pardon Paul Claudel,
Pardons him for writing well.

In the nightmare of the dark
All the dogs of Europe bark,
And the living nations wait,
Each sequestered in its hate;

Intellectual disgrace
Stares from every human face,
And the seas of pity lie
Locked and frozen in each eye.

Follow, poet, follow right
To the bottom of the night,
With your unconstraining voice
Still persuade us to rejoice;

With the farming of a verse
Make a vineyard of the curse,
Sing of human unsuccess
In a rapture of distress;

In the deserts of the heart
Let the healing fountain start,
In the prison of his days
Teach the free man how to praise.

Christopher Okigbo
Labyrinths with Path of Thunder

Heavensgate

I The Passage

BEFORE YOU, mother Idoto,[1]
    naked I stand;
before your watery presence,
    a prodigal

leaning on an oilbean,
lost in your legend.

Under your power wait I
    on barefoot,
watchman for the watchword
    at *Heavensgate*;

out of the depths my cry:
give ear and hearken ...

DARK WATERS of the beginning.

Rays, violet and short, piercing the gloom,
foreshadow the fire that is dreamed of.

Rainbow on far side, arched like boa bent to kill,
foreshadows the rain that is dreamed of.

Me to the orangery
solitude invites,
a wagtail, to tell
the tangled-wood-tale;
a sunbird, to mourn
a mother on a spray.

Rain and sun in single combat;
on one leg standing,
in silence at the passage,
the young bird at the passage.

---

[1] A village stream. The oilbean, the tortoise and the python are totems for her worship.

SILENT FACES at crossroads:
 festivity in black ...

Faces of black like long black
 column of ants,

behind the bell tower,
into the hot garden
where all roads meet:
festivity in black ...

O Anna at the knobs of the panel oblong,
hear us at crossroads at the great hinges

where the players of loft pipe organs
rehearse old lovely fragments, alone –

strains of pressed orange leaves on pages,
bleach of the light of years held in leather:

For we are listening in cornfields
 among the windplayers,
listening to the wind leaning over
 its loveliest fragment ...

II Initiations

SCAR OF the crucifix
over the breast,
by red blade inflicted
by red-hot blade,
on right breast witnesseth

mystery which I, initiate,
received newly naked
upon waters of the genesis
from Kepkanly.[2]

Elemental, united in vision
of present and future,
the pure line, whose innocence
denies inhibitions.

At confluence of planes, the angle:
man loses man, loses vision;

---

[2] A half-serious half-comical primary school teacher of the late thirties.

so comes John the Baptist
with bowl of salt water
preaching the gambit:
life without sin, without

life; which accepted,
way leads downward
down orthocenter
avoiding decisions.

Or forms fourth angle –
duty, obligation:

square yields the moron,
fanatics and priests and popes,
organizing secretaries and
party managers; better still,

the rhombus – brothers and deacons,
liberal politicians,
selfish selfseekers – all who are good
doing nothing at all;

the quadrangle, the rest, me and you ..

Mystery, which barring
the errors of the rendering
witnesseth
red-hot blade on right breast
the scar of the crucifix.

and the hand fell with Haragin,[3]
Kepkanly that wielded the blade;

with Haragin with God's light between them:

but the solitude within me remembers Kepkanly ...

---

[3] Kepkanly was reported to have died from excess of joy when he received arrears of salary awarded by the Haragin Commission of 1945.

AND THIS from Jadum,[4]

(Say if thou knowest
from smell of the incense
a village where liveth
in heart of the grassland
a minstrel who singeth)

to shepherds, with a lute on his lip:

Do not wander in speargrass,
After the lights,
Probing lairs in stockings,
To roast
The viper alive, with dog lying
Upsidedown in the crooked passage ...

Do not listen at keyholes,
After the lights,
To smell from other rooms,
After the lights –

Singeth Jadum from Rockland,
after the lights.

And there are here
the errors of the rendering ...

AND THIS from Upandru:[5]

Screen your bedchamber thoughts
with sun-glasses,
who could jump your eye,
your mind-window,

And I said:
The prophet only the poet.
And he said: Logistics.
(Which is what poetry is) ...

And he said to the ram: Disarm.
And I said:
Except by rooting,
who could pluck yam tubers from their base?

[4] A half-demented village minstrel.

[5] A village explainer.

And there are here
the errors of the rendering ...

III Watermaid

[...]

IV Lustra

SO WOULD I to the hills again
so would I
to where springs the fountain
there to draw from

And to hill top clamber
body and soul
whitewashed in the moondew
there to see from

So would I from my eye the mist
so would I
thro' moonmist to hilltop
there for the cleansing

Here is a new laid egg
here a white hen at midterm.

THE FLOWER weeps, unbruised,
for him who was silenced
whose advent dumb-bells celebrate
in dim light with wine song:

Messiah will come again
After the argument in heaven
Messiah will come again ...

Fingers of penitence bring
to a palm grove
vegetable offering with five
fingers of chalk ...

THUNDERING drums and cannons
in palm grove:
the spirit is in ascent.

I have visited;
on palm beam imprinted
my pentagon –

I have visited, the prodigal ...

In palm grove,
long-drums and cannons:
the spirit in the ascent.

V Newcomer

TIME for worship –

softly sing the bells of exile,
the angelus,
softly sings my guardian angel.

Mask over my face –

my own mask, not ancestral – I sign:
remembrance of calvary,
and of age of innocence, which is of ...

Time for worship:

Anna of the panel oblongs,
        protect me
from them fucking angels;
        protect me
my sandhouse and bones.

[...]

Limits

I–IV Siren Limits

[...]

II

FOR HE WAS a shrub among the poplars,
Needing more roots
More sap to grow to sunlight,
Thirsting for sunlight,

A low growth among the forest.

Into the soul
The selves extended their branches,
Into the moments of each living hour,
Feeling for audience

Straining thin among the echoes;

And out of the solitude
Voice and soul with selves unite,
Riding the echoes,

Horsemen of the apocalypse;

And crowned with one self
The name displays its foliage,
Hanging low

A green cloud above the forest.

[...]

V–XII Fragments out of the Deluge

[...]

X

AND TO US they came –
Malisons, malisons, mair than ten –
And climbed the bombax
And killed the Sunbird.

And they scanned the forest of oilbean,
Its approach; surveyed its high branches ...

And they entered into the forest,
and they passed through the forest of oilbean
And found them, the twin-gods[6] of the forest ...

And the beasts broke –
Malisons, malisons, mair than ten –
And dawn-gust grumbled,
Fanning the grove
Like a horse-tail-man,
Like handmaid of dancers,
Fanning their branches.

[6] The tortoise and the python.

Their talons they drew out of their scabbard,
Upon the tree trunks, as if on fire-clay,
Their beaks they sharpened;
And spread like eagles their felt-wings,
And descended upon the twin gods of Irkalla[7]

And the ornaments of him,
And the beads about his tail;
And the carapace of her,
And her shell, they divided.

[...]

XII

BUT AT THE WINDOW, outside, a shadow:

The sunbird sings again
From the LIMITS of the dream;
The Sunbird sings again
Where the caress does not reach,

 of Guernica,[8]
On whose canvas of blood,
The slits of his tongue
  cling to glue ...

& the cancelling out is complete.

Path of Thunder

[...]

Elegy for Slit-drum

With rattles accompaniment

CONDOLENCES ... from our swollen lips laden with condolences:

The mythmaker accompanies us
The rattles are here with us

condolences from our split-tongue of the slit drum condolences

one tongue full of fire
one tongue full of stone –

---

[7] In Sumerian myth, queen of the underworld.

[8] A work by Picasso.

condolences from the twin-lips of our drum parted in
    condolences:

the panther has delivered a hare
the hare is beginning to leap
the panther has delivered a hare
the panther is about to pounce –

condolences already in flight under the burden of this century:

parliament has gone on leave
the members are now on bail
parliament is now on sale
the voters are lying in wait –

condolences to caress the swollen eyelids of bleeding mourners.

the cabinet has gone to hell
the timbers are now on fire
the cabinet that sold itself
ministers are now in gaol –

condolences quivering before the iron throne of a new conqueror:

the mythmaker accompanies us (*the Egret had come and gone*)
Okigbo accompanies us the oracle enkindles us
the Hornbill is there again (*the Hornbill has had a bath*)
Okigbo accompanies us the rattles enlighten us –

condolences with the miracle of sunlight on our feathers:

The General is up ... the General is up ... commandments ...
the General is up the General is up the General is up –

condolences from our twin-beaks and feathers of condolences:

the General is near the throne
an iron mask covers his face
the General has carried the day
the mortars are far away –

condolences to appease the fever of a wake among tumbled tombs

the elephant has fallen
the mortars have won the day
the elephant has fallen
does he deserve his fate
the elephant has fallen
can we remember the date –

Jungle tanks blast Britain's last stand –

the elephant ravages the jungle
the jungle is peopled with snakes
the snake says to the squirrel
I will swallow you
the mongoose says to the snake
I will mangle you
the elephant says to the mongoose
I will strangle you

thunder fells the trees cut a path
thunder smashes them all – condolences ...

THUNDER that has struck the elephant
the same thunder should wear a plume – condolences

a roadmaker makes a road
the road becomes a throne
can we cane him for felling a tree – condolences ...

THUNDER that has struck the elephant
the same thunder can make a bruise – condolences

we should forget the names
we should bury the date
the dead should bury the dead – condolences

from our bruised lips of the drum empty of condolences:

trunk of the iron tree we cry *condolences* when we break,
shells of the open sea we cry *condolences* when we shake ...

[...]

Chinua Achebe

Anthills of the Savannah Chapter 8, 'Daughters'

Chinua Achebe was born in Ogidi, Eastern Nigeria, in 1930. His early life was similar to Christopher Okigbo's in many ways: an Igbo from a Christian family, he was educated at a Missionary Society school, at Government College and at University College, Ibadan. Also like Okigbo, he intended to study medicine, but changed to literature. After graduation he taught at a school for a short period before joining the Nigerian Broadcasting Company, where he was the director of external services. He worked as a diplomat during the Nigerian Civil War and after the defeat of

Biafra he took up a series of academic appointments in Nigeria and the USA. He was partially paralysed after a road traffic accident in 1990.

Chinua Achebe is Africa's greatest and most widely read novelist. His first novel, *Things Fall Apart*, was published in 1958 and has been translated into forty languages. Together with his subsequent novels, *No Longer at Ease* (1960) and *Arrow of God* (1964), the three works explore the history of the Igbo people through the pre-colonial, colonial and into the postcolonial periods. The novel *Anthills of the Savannah* (1987), from which this extract is taken, is set in a fictional state which bears a striking resemblance to Nigeria. Focusing on a small group of 'elite' intellectuals, the novel examines the precarious nature of postcolonial existence against a backdrop of political struggles. The extract relates contemporary political strife to an ancient Igbo mythological past, which is a hallmark of Achebe's narrative technique.

Idemili

That we are surrounded by deep mysteries is known to all but the incurably ignorant. But even they must concede the fact, indeed the inevitability, of the judiciously spaced, but nonetheless certain, interruptions in the flow of their high art to interject the word of their sponsor, the divinity that controls remotely but diligently the transactions of the market-place that is their world.

In the beginning Power rampaged through our world, naked. So the Almighty, looking at his creation through the round undying eye of the Sun, saw and pondered and finally decided to send his daughter, Idemili, to bear witness to the moral nature of authority by wrapping around Power's rude waist a loincloth of peace and modesty.

She came down in the resplendent Pillar of Water, remembered now in legend only, but stumbled upon, some say, by the most fortunate in rare conditions of sunlight rarer even than the eighteen-year cycle of Odunke festivals and their richly arrayed celebrants leading garlanded cattle in procession through village pathways to sacrifice. It rises majestically from the bowl of the dark lake pushing itself upward and erect like the bole of the father of iroko trees its head commanding not the forest below but the very firmament of heaven.

At first that holy lake was the sole shrine to Idemili. But as people multiplied and spread across the world they built little shrines farther and farther away from the lake wherever they found good land and water and settled. Still their numbers continued to increase and outstrip the provisions of every new settlement; and so the search for land and water also continued.

As it happened, good land was more plentiful than good water and before long some hamlets too far from streams and springs were relieving their burning thirst with the juice of banana stems in the worst years of dry weather. Idemili, travelling through the country disguised as a hunter, saw this and on her return sent a stream from her lake to snake through the parched settlements all the way to Orimili, the great river which in generations to come strange foreigners would search out and rename the Niger.

A deity who does as he says never lacks in worshippers. Idemili's devotees increased in all the country between Omambala and Iguedo. But how could they carry to the farthest limits of their dispersal adequate memories of the majesty of the Pillar of Water standing in the dark lake?

Man's best artifice to snare and hold the grandeur of divinity always crumbles in his hands, and the more ardently he strives the more paltry and incongruous the result. So it were better he did not try at all; far better to ritualize that incongruity and by invoking the mystery of metaphor to hint at the most unattainable glory by its very opposite, the most mundane starkness – a mere stream, a tree, a stone, a mound of earth, a little clay bowl containing fingers of chalk.

Thus it came about that the indescribable Pillar of Water fusing earth to heaven at the navel of the black lake became in numberless shrine-houses across the country, a dry stick rising erect from the bare, earth floor.

It is to this emblem that a man who has achieved wealth of crop and livestock and now wishes to pin an eagle's feather on his success by buying admission into the powerful hierarchy of *ozo* must go to present himself and offer sacrifices before he can begin the ceremonies, and again after he has concluded them. His first visit is no more than to inform the Daughter of the Almighty of his ambition. He is accompanied by his daughter or, if he has only sons, by the daughter of a kinsman; but a daughter it must be.

This young woman must stand between him and the Daughter of the Almighty before he can be granted a hearing. She holds his hand like a child in front of the holy stick and counts seven. Then she arranges carefully on the floor seven fingers of chalk, fragile symbols of peace, and then gets him to sit on them so lightly that not one single finger may be broken.

If all has gone well thus far he will then return to his compound and commence the elaborate and costly ceremonies of *ozo* with feasting and dancing to the entire satisfaction of his community and their ancient custom. Then he must go back to the Daughter of the Almighty to let her know that he has now taken the high and sacred title of his people.

Neither at the first audience nor at this second does Idemili deign to answer him directly. He must go away and await her sign and pleasure. If she finds him unworthy to carry the authority of *ozo* she simply sends death to smite him and save her sacred hierarchy from contamination and scandal. If,

however, she approves of him the only sign she condescends to give –
grudgingly and by indirection – is that he will still be about after three years.
Such is Idemili's contempt for man's unquenchable thirst to sit in authority
on his fellows.

The story goes that in the distant past a certain man handsome beyond
compare but in randiness as unbridled as the odorous he-goat from the
shrine of Udo planting his plenitude of seeds from a huge pod swinging
between hind legs into she-goats tethered for him in front of numerous
homesteads; this man, they said, finally desired also the *ozo* title and took the
word to Idemili. She said nothing. He went away, performed the rites, took
the eagle feather and the titular name Nwakibie, and returned to tell her
what he had done. Again she said nothing. Then as a final ritual he took
shelter according to custom for twenty-eight days in a bachelor's hut away
from his many wives. But though he lived there in the day for all to see he
would steal away at dead of night through circuitous moon-swept paths to
the hut of a certain widow he had fancied for some time; for as he was wont
to ask in his more waggish days: why will a man mounting a widow listen for
footsteps outside her hut when he knows how far her man has travelled?

On his way to resume his hard-lying pretence at cock-crow one morning
who should he behold stretched right across his path its head lost in the
shrubbery to the left and its tail likewise to the right? None other than Eke-
Idemili itself, royal python, messenger of the Daughter of God – the very one
who carries not a drop of venom in its mouth and yet is held in greater awe
than the deadliest of serpents!

His circuitous way to the bachelor's hut thus barred, his feet obeying a
power outside his will took him straight and true as an arrow to the
consternation of his compound and his funeral.

ACKNOWLEDGEMENTS

Grateful acknowledgement is made to the following source for permission to reproduce material within this book:

Extract from *The Collected Poems of Wilfred Owen* edited by C. Day Lewis published by Chatto & Windus. Used by permission of The Random House Group Limited.

'The Fish' from *The Complete Poems: 1927–1979* by Elizabeth Bishop. Copyright © 1979 and 1983 by Alice Helen Methfessel. Used by permission of Farrar, Straus and Giroux, LLC. All rights reserved.

Betjeman, J. (1937) 'Slough', *Collected Poems*, John Murray (Publishers) Ltd.

Warner, R. (1933) 'Hymn', © The Estate of Rex Warner.

Auden, W.H. (1934) 'Ballad', © The Estate of W.H. Auden. With permission from Faber & Faber, Curtis Brown, Ltd and Random House, Inc.

Auden, W.H. (1939) 'Heavy Date', *As I Walked Out One Evening*. © The Estate of W.H. Auden, with permission from Faber & Faber, Curtis Brown Ltd and Random House, Inc.

Spender, S. (1933) 'Pylons', *Poems*. Ed Victor Ltd.

Lindsay, J. (1937) 'On Guard for Spain', by kind permission of David Higham Associates. © The Estate of Jack Lindsay.

Auden, W.H. (1937) 'Spain', copyright © 1937 by W.H. Auden, renewed. Used by permission of Curtis Brown Ltd and Faber & Faber and Random House, Inc.

Cornford, J. (1936) 'A Letter from Aragon'. Random House Ltd.

Spender, S. (1939) 'Port Bou', *Poetry of the 1930s*, Faber & Faber Ltd.

MacNeice, L. (1934) 'An Eclogue for Christmas', *Collected Poems*, Faber & Faber Ltd. With kind permission from David Higham Associates Ltd.

'In Memory of W.B. Yeats', copyright 1940 and renewed 1968 by W.H. Auden, from *Collected Poems* by W.H. Auden. Used by permission of Random House, Inc., Curtis Brown, Ltd and Faber & Faber.

Muldoon, P. (2001) '7, Middagh Street', *Meeting the British*, Faber & Faber Ltd.

Eliot, T.S. 'Rhapsody on a Windy Night', 'The Love Song of J. Alfred Prufrock', 'Portrait of a Lady', 'The Boston Evening Transcript', 'Conversation Galante', *Prufrock and Other Observations*, Faber & Faber Ltd.

Hulme, T.E. 'Above the Dock', in *The Life and Opinions of T.E. Hulme*, by A.R. Jones (1960) Victor Gollancz Ltd.

Pound, E. 'In a Station of the Metro', *Collected Shorter Poems*, Faber & Faber Ltd.

Bowlby, R. (ed.) (1992) V. Woolf, *Orlando: A Biography*, Oxford University Press.

Brecht, B. (1967) 'Of Poor B.B.' and 'Legend of the Dead Soldier', *Manuel of Piety*, trans. by E. Bentley, Suhrkamp Verlag.

Eliot, T.S. (1963) 'The Hollow Men', *Collected Poems 1909–1962*, Faber & Faber Ltd.

Okigbo, C. (1971) 'Silences', 'Fragments out of the Deluge X' and 'The Passage', *Labyrinths with Path of Thunder*, reprinted by permission of Harcourt Education.

Spender, S. (1935) 'After they have tired ...', *Poems*, © Faber & Faber Ltd.

MacNeice, L. (1979) 'Carrickfergus', *The Collected Poems of Louis MacNeice*, published by Faber, with kind permission from David Higham Associates.

'In Memory of W.B. Yeats', copyright 1940 and renewed 1968 by W.H. Auden, from *Collected Poems* by W.H. Auden. Used by permission of Random House, Inc., Curtis Brown, Ltd and Faber & Faber.

Labyrinths with Path of Thunder, by Christopher Okigbo, 1971. Reprinted by permission of Harcourt Education.

Achebe, C. (1984) 'Daughters', *Anthills of the Savannah*, Pan Books Ltd.

Every effort has been made to contact copyright owners. If any have been inadvertently overlooked, the publishers will be pleased to make the necessary arrangements at the first opportunity.

INDEX